New Testament Verses Clarified by Old Testament Verses

New Testament Verses
Charted with Old Testament Verses

King James Version

Dr. Bruce A. Klein, Th.D.

Biblical Publishing Company

© 2012 Bruce Allen Klein

All rights reserved. Neither this work nor any part of it may be reproduced, distributed, or displayed in any medium, including electronic or digital, without permission in writing from the copyright owner.

ISBN 978-0-9827070-9-8

October 11, 2012

Bibleteach@hotmail.com

Introduction

The Old Testament verses stated per New Testament verse are not meant to be inclusive. Meaning many other verses possibly could have been added.

This book has the value of a commentary. A different kind of commentary; this commentary uses the Old Testament verses as commentary on a New Testament verse. This commentary is composed of Old Testament verses, only!

The context for the New Testament is the Old Testament

Old Testament verses are the schoolmaster.

The Old Testament verses should be used to interpret the New Testament verses.

This book can be used as a devotional by reading portions daily then meditating on those Scriptures.

This book is a great reference tool for writing sermons and Bible studies.

There are untold gems to be gleaned by comparing the Old Testament and the New Testament!

Introductory Verses

Romans 5:14 Nevertheless death reigned from Adam to Moses, even over them that had not sinned after the similitude of Adam's transgression, who is the figure of him that was to come.

1 Corinthians 10:6-11 Now these things were our examples, to the intent we should not lust after evil things, as they also lusted. 7 Neither be ye idolaters, as *were* some of them; as it is written, The people sat down to eat and drink, and rose up to play. 8 Neither let us commit fornication, as some of them committed, and fell in one day three and twenty thousand. 9 Neither let us tempt Christ, as some of them also tempted, and were destroyed of serpents. 10 Neither murmur ye, as some of them also murmured, and were destroyed of the destroyer. 11 Now all these things happened unto them for ensamples: and they are written for our admonition, upon whom the ends of the world are come.

1 Peter 3:20-21 Which sometime were disobedient, when once the longsuffering of God waited in the days of Noah, while the ark was a preparing, wherein few, that is, eight souls were saved by water. 21 The like figure whereunto *even* baptism doth also now save us (not the putting away of the filth of the flesh, but the answer of a good conscience toward God,) by the resurrection of Jesus Christ:

Hebrews 8:5-6 Who serve unto the example and shadow of heavenly things, as Moses was admonished of God when he was about to make the tabernacle: for, See, saith he, *that* thou make all things according to the pattern shewed to thee in the mount. 6 But now hath he obtained a more excellent ministry, by how much also he is the mediator of a better covenant, which was established upon better promises.

Hebrews 9:24 For Christ is not entered into the holy places made with hands, *which are* the figures of the true; but into heaven itself, now to appear in the presence of God for us:

1 Chronicles 23:30-32 And to stand every morning to thank and praise the LORD, and likewise at even; 31 And to offer all burnt sacrifices unto the LORD in the sabbaths, in the new moons, and on the set feasts, by number, according to the order commanded unto them, continually before the LORD: 32 And that they should keep the charge of the tabernacle of the congregation, and the charge of the holy *place*, and the charge of the sons of Aaron their brethren, in the service of the house of the LORD.

Nehemiah 8:4-7 And Ezra the scribe stood upon a pulpit of wood, which they had made for the purpose; and beside him stood Mattithiah, and Shema, and Anaiah, and Urijah, and Hilkiah, and Maaseiah, on his right hand; and on his left hand, Pedaiah, and Mishael, and Malchiah, and Hashum, and Hashbadana, Zechariah, *and* Meshullam. 5 And Ezra opened the book in the sight of all the people; (for he was above all the people;) and when he opened it, all the people stood up: 6 And Ezra blessed the LORD, the great God. And all the people answered, Amen, Amen, with lifting up their hands: and they bowed their heads, and worshipped the LORD with *their* faces to the ground. 7 Also Jeshua, and Bani, and Sherebiah, Jamin, Akkub, Shabbethai, Hodijah, Maaseiah, Kelita, Azariah, Jozabad, Hanan, Pelaiah, and the Levites, caused the people to understand the law: and the people *stood* in their place.

Jeremiah 6:16 Thus saith the LORD, Stand ye in the ways, and see, and ask for the old paths, where *is* the good way, and walk therein, and ye shall find rest for your souls. But they said, We will not walk *therein*.

Old Testament Quotes or Possible Allusions Found in the New Testament

New Testament	Old Testament
Matthew 1:1 The book of the generation of Jesus Christ, the son of David, the son of Abraham.	**Psalms 132:11** The LORD hath sworn *in* truth unto David; he will not turn from it; Of the fruit of thy body will I set upon thy throne. **Isaiah 11:1** And there shall come forth a rod out of the stem of Jesse, and a Branch shall grow out of his roots:
Matthew 1:2 Abraham begat Isaac; and Isaac begat Jacob; and Jacob begat Judas and his brethren;	**Genesis 21:2** For Sarah conceived, and bare Abraham a son in his old age, at the set time of which God had spoken to him. **Genesis 25:26** And after that came his brother out, and his hand took hold on Esau's heel; and his name was called Jacob: and Isaac *was* threescore years old when she bare them. **Genesis 29:35** And she conceived again, and bare a son: and she said, Now will I praise the LORD: therefore she called his name Judah; and left bearing.
Matthew 1:3 And Judas begat Phares and Zara of Thamar; and Phares begat Esrom; and Esrom begat Aram;	**1 Chronicles 2:4** And Tamar his daughter in law bare him Pharez and Zerah. All the sons of Judah *were* five. **Genesis 38:29** And it came to pass, as he drew back his hand, that, behold, his brother came out: and she said, How hast thou broken forth? *this* breach *be* upon thee: therefore his name was called Pharez. **Ruth 4:18** Now these *are* the generations of Pharez: Pharez begat Hezron, **1 Chronicles 2:5** The sons of Pharez; Hezron, and Hamul. **Ruth 4:19** And Hezron begat Ram, and Ram begat Amminadab, **1 Chronicles 2:9** The sons also of Hezron, that were born unto him; Jerahmeel, and Ram, and Chelubai.
Matthew 1:6 And Jesse begat David the king; and David the king begat Solomon of her *that had been the wife* of Urias;	**Ruth 4:22** And Obed begat Jesse, and Jesse begat David. **1 Samuel 16:1** And the LORD said unto Samuel, How long wilt thou mourn for Saul, seeing I have rejected him from reigning over Israel? fill thine horn with oil, and go, I will send thee to Jesse the Bethlehemite: for I have provided me a king among his sons. **1 Samuel 17:12** Now David *was* the son of that Ephrathite of Bethlehemjudah, whose name *was* Jesse; and he had eight sons: and the man went among men *for* an old man in the days of Saul. **1 Chronicles 2:15** Ozem the sixth, David the seventh: **1 Chronicles 12:18** Then the spirit came upon Amasai, *who was* chief of the captains, *and he said*, Thine *are we*, David, and on thy side, thou son of Jesse: peace, peace *be* unto thee, and peace *be* to thine helpers; for thy God helpeth thee. Then David received them, and made them captains of the band.

Matthew 1:7 And Solomon begat Roboam; and Roboam begat Abia; and Abia begat Asa;	**1 Kings 11:43** And Solomon slept with his fathers, and was buried in the city of David his father: and Rehoboam his son reigned in his stead. **1 Chronicles 3:10** And Solomon's son *was* Rehoboam, Abia his son, Asa his son, Jehoshaphat his son,
Matthew 1:12 And after they were brought to Babylon, Jechonias begat Salathiel; and Salathiel begat Zorobabel;	**1 Chronicles 3:17** And the sons of Jeconiah; Assir, Salathiel his son,
Matthew 1:21 And she shall bring forth a son, and thou shalt call his name JESUS: for he shall save his people from their sins.	**Psalms 2:7** I will declare the decree: the LORD hath said unto me, Thou *art* my **Son**; this day have I begotten thee. **Psalms 2:12** Kiss the **Son**, lest he be angry, and ye perish *from* the way, when his wrath is kindled but a little. Blessed *are* all they that put their trust in him. **Isaiah 7:14** Therefore the Lord himself shall give you a sign; Behold, a virgin shall conceive, and bear a **son**, and shall call his name Immanuel. **Isaiah 9:6** For unto us a child is born, unto us a son is given: and the government shall be upon his shoulder: and his name shall be called Wonderful, Counselor, The mighty God, The everlasting Father, The Prince of Peace. **Genesis 45:7** And God sent me before you to preserve you a posterity in the earth, and to save your lives by a great deliverance. **Isaiah 12:2** Behold, God *is* my salvation; I will trust, and not be afraid: for the LORD JEHOVAH *is* my strength and *my* song; he also is become my salvation.
Matthew 1:23 Behold, a virgin shall conceive and bear a son, and his name shall be called Emmanuel (which means, God with us).	**Deuteronomy 22:20-21** But if this thing is true, *that* tokens of **virginity** have not been found for the girl, then they shall bring out the girl to the door of her father's house. And the men of her city shall stone her with stones, and she shall die; because she has done fooly in Israel, to commit fornication in her father's house. And you shall cut off the evil from among you. **Deuteronomy 22:23-24** If a damsel *that is* a <u>**virgin be betrothed**</u> unto an husband, and a man find her in the city, and lie with her; 24 Then ye shall bring them both out unto the gate of that city, and ye shall stone them with stones that they die; the damsel, because she cried not, *being* in the city; and the man, because he hath **humbled his neighbour's <u>wife</u>**: so thou shalt put away evil from among you. **Psalms 35:23** Stir up thyself, and awake to my judgment, *even* unto my cause, my God and my Lord. **Isaiah 7:14** Therefore the Lord himself shall give you a sign; Behold, a virgin shall conceive, and bear a son, and shall call his name **Immanuel**. **Isaiah 8:8** And he shall pass through Judah; he shall overflow and go over, he shall reach *even* to the neck; and the stretching out of his wings shall fill the breadth of thy land, O **Immanuel**. **Isaiah 9:6** For unto us a child is born, unto us a son is given: and the government shall be upon his shoulder: and his name shall be called Wonderful, Counsellor, The mighty God, The everlasting Father, The Prince of Peace.

	Isaiah 25:9 And it shall be said in that day, Lo, this *is* our God; we have waited for him, and he will save us: this *is* the LORD; we have waited for him, we will be glad and rejoice in his salvation. **See 1 Timothy 2:5 "God"**
Matthew 2:2 Saying, Where is he that is born **King** of the Jews? for we have seen his star in the east, and are come to worship him.	**Psalms 97:7** Confounded be all they that serve graven images, that boast themselves of idols: worship him, all *ye* gods. **Psalms 47:7-8** For **God is the King** of all the earth: sing ye praises with understanding. 8 God reigneth over the heathen: God sitteth upon the throne of his holiness. **Isaiah 44:6** Thus saith the LORD the **King of Israel**, and his redeemer the LORD of hosts; I am the first, and I am the last; and beside me there is no God. **Jeremiah 10:10** But the LORD is the true God, he is the living God, and an everlasting **king**: at his wrath the earth shall tremble, and the nations shall not be able to abide his indignation. **Zechariah 9:9** Rejoice greatly, O daughter of Zion; shout, O daughter of Jerusalem: behold, thy **King** cometh unto thee: he *is* just, and having salvation; lowly, and riding upon an ass, and upon a colt the foal of an ass.
Matthew 2:6 And thou, Bethlehem, in the land of Juda, art not the least among the princes of Juda: for out of thee shall come a Governor, that shall rule my people Israel.	**Genesis 49:10** The sceptre shall not depart from Judah, nor a lawgiver from between his feet, until Shiloh come; and unto him *shall* the gathering of the people *be*. **Micah 5:2** But thou, Bethlehem Ephratah, though thou be little among the thousands of Judah, yet out of thee shall he come forth unto me that is to be ruler in Israel;
Matthew 2:10-11 When they saw the star, they rejoiced with exceeding great joy. 11 And when they were come into the house, they saw the young child with Mary his mother, and fell down, and worshipped him: and when they had opened their treasures, they presented unto him gifts; gold, and frankincense, and myrrh.	**Psalms 72:10** The kings of Tarshish and of the isles shall bring presents: the kings of Sheba and Seba shall offer gifts. **Psalms 97:7** Confounded be all they that serve graven images, that boast themselves of idols: worship him, all *ye* gods
Matthew 2:14 When he arose, he took the young child and his mother by night, and departed into Egypt:	**Genesis 37:36** And the Midianites sold him into Egypt unto Potiphar, an officer of Pharaoh's, *and* captain of the guard.
Matthew 2:15 Out of Egypt have I called my son.	**1 Kings 8:9-11** *There was* nothing in the ark save the two tables of stone, which Moses put there at Horeb, when the LORD made *a covenant* with the children of Israel, when they came out of the land of Egypt. 10 And it came to pass, when the priests were come out of the holy *place*, that the cloud filled the house of the LORD,11 So that the priests could not stand to minister because of the cloud: for the glory of the LORD had filled the house of the LORD. **Hosea 11:1** When Israel *was* a child, then I loved him, and called my son out of Egypt.
Matthew 2:17 Then was fulfilled that which was spoken by Jeremy the prophet, saying,	**Amos 3:7** Surely the Lord GOD will do nothing, but he revealeth his secret unto his servants the prophets.
Matthew 2:18 In Rama was there a	**Jeremiah 31:15** A voice was heard in Ramah, lamentation, and

voice heard, lamentation, and weeping, and great mourning, Rachel weeping for her children, and would not be comforted because they are not.	bitter weeping; Rahel weeping for her children refused to be comforted for her children, because they were not.
Matthew 2:19-20 But when Herod was dead, behold, an angel of the Lord appeareth in a dream to Joseph in Egypt, 20 Saying, Arise, and take the young child and his mother, and go into the land of Israel: for they are dead which sought the young child's life.	**Joshua 24:32** And the bones of Joseph, which the children of Israel brought up out of Egypt, buried they in Shechem, in a parcel of ground which Jacob bought of the sons of Hamor the father of Shechem for an hundred pieces of silver: and it became the inheritance of the children of Joseph.
Matthew 3:2 And saying, Repent ye: for the kingdom of heaven is at hand.	**Job 42:6** Wherefore I abhor myself, and repent in dust and ashes. **Ezekiel 14:6** Therefore say unto the house of Israel, Thus saith the Lord GOD; Repent, and turn yourselves from your idols; and turn away your faces from all your abominations. **Ezekiel 18:30** Therefore I will judge you, O house of Israel, every one according to his ways, saith the Lord GOD. Repent, and turn yourselves from all your transgressions; so iniquity shall not be your ruin.
Matthew 3:3 The voice of one crying in the wilderness, Prepare ye the way of the **Lord**, make his paths straight.	**Isaiah 9:6** For unto us a child is born, unto us a son is given: and the government shall be upon his shoulder: and his name shall be called Wonderful, Counsellor, The mighty God, The everlasting Father, The Prince of Peace. **Isaiah 40:3-5** The voice of him that crieth in the wilderness, Prepare ye the way of the Lord, make straight in the desert a highway for our God. 4 Every valley shall be exalted, and every mountain and hill shall be made low: and the crooked shall be made straight, and the rough places plain: 5 And the glory of the **LORD** shall be revealed, and all flesh shall see *it* together: for the mouth of the LORD hath spoken *it*.
Matthew 3:6 And were baptized of him in Jordan, confessing their sins.	See Acts 2:39 "Salvation"
Matthew 3:10 And now also the **axe is laid unto the root of the trees**: therefore every tree which bringeth not forth good fruit is hewn down, and cast into the fire.	**Psalms 52:5** God shall likewise destroy thee for ever, he shall take thee away, and pluck thee out of thy dwelling place, and **root thee out** of the land of the living. Selah. **Isaiah 5:24** Therefore as the fire devoureth the stubble, and the flame consumeth the chaff, so **their root shall be as rottenness**, and their blossom shall go up as dust: because they have cast away the law of the LORD of hosts, and despised the word of the Holy One of Israel.
Matthew 3:11 I indeed baptize you with water unto repentance: but he that cometh after me is mightier than I, whose shoes I am not worthy to bear: he shall baptize you with the Holy Ghost, and *with* fire: (Acts 2:3)	See Acts 2:38 "Salvation"
Matthew 3:16 And Jesus, when he was baptized, went up straightway out of the water: and, lo, the heavens were opened unto him, and he saw the Spirit of God descending like a dove, and lighting upon him:	**Genesis 41:38** And Pharaoh said unto his servants, Can we find *such a one* as this *is*, a man in whom the **Spirit of God** *is*? **Exodus 31:3** And I have filled him with the **spirit of God**, in wisdom, and in understanding, and in knowledge, and in all manner of workmanship, **1 Samuel 10:10** And when they came thither to the hill, behold, a

	company of prophets met him; and the **Spirit of God** came upon him, and he prophesied among them.
	Isaiah 9:6 For unto us a child is born, unto us a son is given: and the government shall be upon his shoulder: and his name shall be called Wonderful, Counseller, The mighty God, The everlasting Father, The Prince of Peace.
	Isaiah 11:2 And the spirit of the LORD shall rest upon him, the spirit of wisdom and understanding, the spirit of counsel and might, the spirit of knowledge and of the fear of the LORD;
	Isaiah 42:1 Behold my servant, whom I uphold; mine elect, *in whom* my soul delighteth; I have put my spirit upon him: he shall bring forth judgment to the Gentiles.
Matthew 3:17 And lo a voice from heaven, saying, This is my beloved Son, in whom I am well pleased.	**Genesis 22:2** And he said, Take now thy son, thine only *son* Isaac, whom thou lovest, and get thee into the land of Moriah; and offer him there for a burnt offering upon one of the mountains which I will tell thee of.
	Psalm 2:7 I will declare the decree: the LORD hath said unto me, Thou *art* my Son; this day have I begotten thee.
	Isaiah 42:1 Behold my servant, whom I uphold; mine elect, *in whom* my soul delighteth; I have put my spirit upon him: he shall bring forth judgment to the Gentiles.
Matthew 4:2 And when he had **fasted** forty days and forty nights, he was afterward hungry.	**See Matthew 17:21 "Fasting"**
Matthew 4:3 And when the tempter came to him, he said, If thou be the Son of God, command that these stones be made bread.	**Psalms 2:7** I will declare the decree: the LORD hath said unto me, Thou *art* my **Son**; this day have I begotten thee.
	Psalms 2:12 Kiss the **Son**, lest he be angry, and ye perish *from* the way, when his wrath is kindled but a little. Blessed *are* all they that put their trust in him.
	Isaiah 7:14 Therefore the Lord himself shall give you a sign; Behold, a virgin shall conceive, and bear a **son**, and shall call his name Immanuel.
	Isaiah 9:6 For unto us a child is born, unto us a son is given: and the government shall be upon his shoulder: and his name shall be called Wonderful, Counselor, The mighty God, The everlasting Father, The Prince of Peace.
Matthew 4:4 Man shall not live by bread alone, but by every word that proceedeth out of the mouth of God.	**Deuteronomy 8:3** And he humbled thee, and suffered thee to hunger, and fed thee with manna, which thou knewest not, neither did thy fathers know; that he might make thee know that **man doth not live by bread only, but by every *word* that proceedeth out of the mouth of the LORD** doth man live.
	Deuteronomy 30:1 But the word is very nigh unto thee, in thy mouth, and in thy heart, that thou mayest do it.
Matthew 4:6 He shall give His angels charge concerning thee and in their hands they shall bear thee up, lest at any time thou dash thy foot against a stone.	**Psalms 91:11-12** For he shall give his angels charge over thee, to keep thee in all thy ways. 12 They shall bear thee up in their hands, lest thou dash thy foot against a stone.
Matthew 4:7 Thou shall not tempt the Lord thy God.	**Genesis 39:10** And it came to pass, as she spake to Joseph day by day, that he hearkened not unto her, to lie by her, *or* to be with her.
	Deuteronomy 6:16 Ye shall not tempt the LORD your God,

Matthew 4:8 Again, the devil taketh him up into an exceeding high mountain, and sheweth him all the kingdoms of the world, and the glory of them;	**Genesis 3:6** And when the woman saw that the tree *was* good for food, and that it *was* pleasant to the eyes, and a tree to be desired to make *one* wise, she took of the fruit thereof, and did eat, and gave also unto her husband with her; and he did eat. **Joshua 7:21** When I saw among the spoils a goodly Babylonish garment, and two hundred shekels of silver, and a wedge of gold of fifty shekels weight, then **I coveted them**, and took them; and, behold, they *are* hid in the earth in the midst of my tent, and the silver under it. **2 Samuel 11:2** And it came to pass in an eveningtide, that David arose from off his bed, and walked upon the roof of the king's house: and from the roof **he saw** a woman washing herself; and the woman *was* very beautiful to look upon.
Matthew 4:10 Then saith Jesus unto him, Get thee hence, Satan: for it is written, … .	**Genesis 3:4** And the **serpent** said unto the woman, Ye shall not surely die: **Job 2:6** And the LORD said unto **Satan**, Behold, he *is* in thine hand; but save his life. **Isaiah 14:12-15** How art thou fallen from heaven, O **Lucifer**, son of the morning! how art thou cut down to the ground, which didst weaken the nations! 13 For thou hast said in thine heart, **I** will ascend into heaven, **I** will exalt my throne above the stars of God: **I** will sit also upon the mount of the congregation, in the sides of the north: 14 **I** will ascend above the heights of the clouds; **I** will be like the most High. 15 Yet thou shalt be brought down to hell, to the sides of the pit. **Ezekiel 28:15-19** Thou *wast* perfect in thy ways from the day that thou wast created, till iniquity was found in thee. 16 By the multitude of thy merchandise they have filled the midst of thee with violence, and thou hast sinned: therefore I will cast thee as profane out of the mountain of God: and I will destroy thee, O **covering cherub**, from the midst of the stones of fire. 17 Thine heart was lifted up because of thy beauty, thou hast corrupted thy wisdom by reason of thy brightness: I will cast thee to the ground, I will lay thee before kings, that they may behold thee. 18 Thou hast defiled thy sanctuaries by the multitude of thine iniquities, by the iniquity of thy traffick; therefore will I bring forth a fire from the midst of thee, it shall devour thee, and I will bring thee to ashes upon the earth in the sight of all them that behold thee. 19 All they that know thee among the people shall be astonished at thee: thou shalt be a terror, and never *shalt* thou *be* any more. **Zechariah 3:1-2** And he shewed me Joshua the high priest standing before the angel of the LORD, and **Satan** standing at his right hand to resist him. 2 And the LORD said unto Satan, The LORD rebuke thee, O Satan; even the LORD that hath chosen Jerusalem rebuke thee: *is* not this a brand plucked out of the fire?
Matthew 4:10 … Thou shalt worship the Lord thy God, and him only shalt thou serve.	**Exodus 34:14** For thou shalt worship no other god: for the LORD, whose name is Jealous, is a jealous God: **Deuteronomy 6:4** Hear, O Israel: **The LORD our God is one LORD:**" **Deuteronomy 6:13** Thou shalt fear the LORD thy God, and serve him, and shalt swear by his name. **Deuteronomy 10:20** Thou shalt fear the LORD thy God; him shalt thou serve, and to him shalt thou cleave, and swear by his name.

	Deuteronomy 32:43 Rejoice, O ye nations, *with* his people: for he will avenge the blood of his servants, and will render vengeance to his adversaries, and will be merciful unto his land, *and* to his people.
	Psalms 97:7 Confounded be all they that serve graven images, that boast themselves of idols: worship him, all *ye* gods.
Matthews 4:11 Then the devil leaveth him, and, behold, **angels** came and ministered unto him.	**See Hebrews 13:2 "Good and bad angels"**
Matthew 4:14-16 That it might be fulfilled which was spoken by Esaias the prophet, saying, 15 The land of Zabulon, and the land of Nephthalim, by the way of the sea, beyond Jordan, Galilee of the Gentiles; 16 The people which sat in darkness saw great light; and to them which sat in the region and shadow of death light is sprung up.	**Isaiah 9:1-2** Nevertheless the dimness *shall* not *be* such as *was* in her vexation, when at the first he lightly afflicted the land of Zebulun and the land of Naphtali, and afterward did more grievously afflict *her by* the way of the sea, beyond Jordan, in Galilee of the nations. 2 The people that walked in darkness have seen a great light: they that dwell in the land of the shadow of death, upon them hath the light shined. **Isaiah 42:7** To open the blind eyes, to bring out the prisoners from the prison, *and* them that sit in darkness out of the prison house.
Matthew 4:23 And Jesus went about all Galilee, **teaching in their synagogues**, and preaching the gospel of the kingdom, and healing all manner of sickness and all manner of disease among the people.	**See Ephesians 4:11 "Teach – Teachers"**
Matthew 5:2 And he opened his mouth, and **taught** them, saying,	**Ezra 7:10** For Ezra had prepared his heart to seek the law of the LORD, and to do *it*, and to **teach** in Israel statutes and judgments.
Matthew 5:5 Blessed *are* the **meek**: for they shall inherit the earth.	**Numbers 12:3** (Now the man Moses *was* very **meek**, above all the men which *were* upon the face of the earth.) **2 Chronicles 7:14** If my people, which are called by my name, shall **humble** themselves, and pray, and seek my face, and turn from their wicked ways; then will I hear from heaven, and will forgive their sin, and will heal their land. **Psalms 25:9** The **meek** will he guide in judgment: and the **meek** will he teach his way. **Psalms 37:11** But the **meek** shall inherit the earth; and shall delight themselves in the abundance of peace. **Proverbs 3:34** Surely he scorneth the scorners: but he giveth grace unto the **lowly**.
Matthew 5:6 Blessed *are* they which do hunger and thirst after righteousness: for they shall be **filled**.	**See Acts 2:38 "Holy Ghost baptism"**
Matthew 5:8 Blessed *are* the pure in heart: for they shall see God.	**Psalms 24:4** He that hath clean hands, and a pure heart; who hath not lifted up his soul unto vanity, nor sworn deceitfully. **Psalms 24:5** He shall receive the blessing from the LORD, and righteousness from the God of his salvation. **See Hebrews 12:14 "Holiness"**
Matthew 5:18 For verily I say unto you, Till heaven and earth pass, one jot or one tittle shall in no wise pass from the law, till all be fulfilled.	**Deuteronomy 8:3** And he humbled thee, and suffered thee to hunger, and fed thee with manna, which thou knewest not, neither did thy fathers know; that he might make thee know that **man doth not live by bread only, but by every *word* that proceedeth out**

of the mouth of the LORD doth man live.

Job 19:23-25 Oh that my words were now written! oh that they were printed in a book! 24 That they were graven with an iron pen and lead in the rock for ever! 25 For I know that my redeemer liveth, and *that* he shall stand at the latter *day* upon the earth:

Psalm 12:6-7 The Words of the LORD [are] pure Words: *as* silver tried in a furnace of earth, purified seven times. 7 Thou shalt keep them, O LORD, thou shalt **preserve** them from this generation forever.

Psalm 33:11 The counsel of the Lord standeth for ever, the **thoughts** of his heart to all generations

Isaiah 40:8 The grass withereth, the flower fadeth: but the **Word of our God shall stand for ever**.

Psalm 100:5 For the Lord is good; his mercy is everlasting; and **his truth** endureth to all generations."

Psalms 105:8 He hath remembered His covenant for ever, **the Word** *which* **He commanded to a thousand generations**.

Psalms 111:7-8 The works of his hands are verity and judgment; all his commandments are sure. **They stand fast for ever and ever**, and are done in truth and uprightness.

Psalms 117:2 ... the truth of the Lord **endureth for ever**. Praise ye the Lord.

Psalm 119:105 NUN. Thy word is a lamp unto my feet, and a light unto my path."

Psalms 119:89 LAMED. For ever, O LORD, thy word is settled in heaven.

Psalm 119:140 Thy word is very pure: therefore thy servant loveth it.

Psalms 119:152 Concerning thy testimonies, I have known of old that thou hast founded them for ever.

Psalm 119:160 Thy **Word** [is] true *from* the beginning: and every one of thy righteous judgments [endureth] **for ever**.

Proverbs 30:5 Every **word of God** *is* pure: he *is* a shield unto them that put their trust in him.

Isaiah 30:8 Now go, **write it before them in a table, and note it in a book,** that it may be **for the time to come for ever and ever**:

Isaiah 40:8 The grass withereth, the flower fadeth: but the **Word of our God shall stand for ever**.

Isaiah 55:11 So shall My **Word** be that goeth out **of My mouth**: it shall not return unto Me void, but it shall accomplish that which I please, and it shall prosper *in the thing* whereto I sent *it*.

Isaiah 59:21 As for me, this is my covenant with them, saith the Lord; My spirit that is upon thee, and **my words** which I have put in thy mouth, **shall not depart out of thy mouth**, nor out of the mouth of thy seed, nor out of the mouth of thy seed's seed, saith the Lord, from **henceforth and for ever**.

Jeremiah 1:12 Then said the LORD unto me, Thou hast well seen: for I will hasten my word to perform it.

Jeremiah 23:36 And the burden of the LORD shall ye mention no more: for every man's word shall be his burden; for ye have

	perverted the words of the living God, of the LORD of hosts our God.

Jeremiah 36:4 Then Jeremiah called Baruch the son of Neriah: and **Baruch wrote from the mouth of Jeremiah all the words of the LORD**, which he had spoken unto him, upon a roll of a book.

Jeremiah 36:23 And it came to pass, that when Jehudi had read three or four leaves, he cut it with the penknife, and cast it into the fire that was on the hearth, until all the roll was consumed in the fire that was on the hearth.

Jeremiah 36:27 Then the word of the LORD came to Jeremiah, **after that the king had burned the roll**, and the words which Baruch wrote at the mouth of Jeremiah, saying, 28 **Take thee again another roll, and write in it all the former words that were in the first roll**, which Jehoiakim the king of Judah hath burned.

Jeremiah 36:32 Then took Jeremiah another roll, and gave it to Baruch the scribe, the son of Neriah; **who wrote therein from the mouth of Jeremiah** <u>all</u> **the words of the book** which Jehoiakim king of Judah had burned in the fire: and there were **added besides unto them many like words**.

Jeremiah 51:63-64 And it shall be, when thou hast made an end of reading this book, that thou shalt bind a stone to it, and **cast it into the midst of Euphrates**: And thou shalt say, Thus shall Babylon sink, and shall not rise from the evil that I will bring upon her: and they shall be weary. Thus far are the words of Jeremiah. |
| **Matthew 5:21** Ye have heard that it was said by them of old time, Thou shalt not kill; and whosoever shall kill shall be in danger of the judgment: | **Exodus 20:13** Thou shalt not kill.

Deuteronomy 5:17 Thou shalt not kill. |
| **Matthew 5:22** But I say unto you, That whosoever is angry with his brother without a cause shall be in danger of the judgment: and whosoever shall say to his brother, Raca, shall be in danger of the council: but whosoever shall say, Thou fool, shall be in danger of **hell** fire. | **Psalms 14:1** To the chief Musician, A Psalm of David. The fool hath said in his heart, There is no God. They are corrupt, they have done abominable works, there is none that doeth good.

See Luke 16:23 "Hell" |
| **Matthew 5:27** Ye have heard that it was said by them of old time, **Thou shalt not commit adultery:** | **Genesis 38:24** And it came to pass about three months after, that it was told Judah, saying, Tamar thy daughter-in-law hath played the harlot; and also, behold, she *is* with child by whoredom. And Judah said, Bring her forth, and let her be burnt.

Exodus 20:14 Thou shalt not commit adultery.

Leviticus 18:20 Moreover thou shalt not lie carnally with thy neighbour's wife, to defile thyself with her.

Leviticus 20:10 And the man that committeth adultery with *another* man's wife, *even he* that committeth adultery with his neighbour's wife, the adulterer and the adulteress shall **surely be put to death**.

Leviticus 21:9 And the daughter of any priest, if she profane herself by playing the whore, she profaneth her father: she shall be burnt with fire.

Deuteronomy 5:18 Neither shalt thou commit adultery.

Deuteronomy 22:21-22 Then they shall bring out the damsel to |

the door of her father's house, and the men of her city shall stone her with stones that she die: because she hath wrought folly in Israel, to play the whore in her father's house: so shalt thou put evil away from among you. 22 If a man be found lying with a woman married to a husband, then they shall **both of them die**, *both* the man that lay with the woman, and the woman: so shalt thou put away evil from Israel.

Deuteronomy 24:1 When a man hath taken a wife, and married her, and it come to pass that she find no favour in his eyes, because he hath found some uncleanness in her: then let him write her a bill of divorcement, and give it in her hand, and send her out of his house. 2 And when she is departed out of his house, **she may go and be another man's wife.** 3 And if the latter husband hate her, and write her a bill of divorcement, and giveth it in her hand, and sendeth her out of his house; or if the latter husband die, which took her to be his wife; 4 **Her former husband, which sent her away, may not take her again to be his wife**, after that she is defiled; for that is abomination before the LORD: and thou shalt not cause the land to sin, which the LORD thy God giveth thee for an inheritance. 5 When a man hath taken a new wife, he shall not go out to war, neither shall he be charged with any business: but he shall be free at home one year, and shall cheer up his wife which he hath taken.

Job 24:15 The eye also of **the adulterer waiteth for the twilight, saying, No eye shall see me**: and disguiseth *his* face.

Proverbs 5:1-23 My son, attend unto my wisdom, *and* bow thine ear to my understanding: 2 That thou mayest regard discretion, and *that* thy lips may keep knowledge. 3 For **the lips of a strange woman drop *as* an honeycomb**, and **her mouth *is* smoother than oil**: 4 But her end is bitter as wormwood, sharp as a twoedged sword. 5 **Her feet go down to death; her steps take hold on hell.** 6 Lest thou shouldest ponder the path of life, her ways are moveable, *that* thou canst not know *them*. 7 Hear me now therefore, O ye children, and depart not from the words of my mouth. 8 **Remove thy way far from her**, and **come not nigh the door of her house**: 9 Lest thou give thine honour unto others, and thy years unto the cruel: 10 Lest strangers be filled with thy wealth; and thy labours *be* in the house of a stranger; 11 And thou mourn at the last, when thy flesh and thy body are consumed, 12 And say, How have I hated instruction, and my heart despised reproof; 13 And **have not obeyed the voice of my teachers, nor inclined mine ear to them that instructed me! 14 I was almost in all evil in the midst of the congregation and assembly.** 15 Drink waters out of thine own cistern, and running waters out of thine own well. 16 Let thy fountains be dispersed abroad, *and* rivers of waters in the streets. 17 Let them be only thine own, and not strangers' with thee. 18 Let thy fountain be blessed: and rejoice with the wife of thy youth. 19 *Let her be as* the loving hind and pleasant roe; let her breasts satisfy thee at all times; and be thou ravished always with her love. 20 And why wilt thou, my son, be ravished with a strange woman, and embrace the bosom of a stranger? 21 **For the ways of man *are* before the eyes of the LORD**, and he pondereth all his goings. 22 His own iniquities shall take the wicked himself, and **he shall be holden with the cords of his sins. 23 He shall die without instruction; and in the greatness of his folly he shall go astray.**

Proverbs 6:23-29 For the commandment is a lamp; and the law is

	light; and reproofs of instruction are the way of life: 24 To keep thee from the evil woman, from the flattery of the tongue of a strange woman. 25 Lust not after
	her beauty in thine heart; neither let her take thee with her eyelids. 26 For by means of a whorish woman a man is brought to a piece of bread: and the **adulteress will hunt for the precious life**. 27 For a whore *is* a deep ditch; and a strange woman *is* a narrow pit. 28 She also lieth in wait as *for* a prey, and increaseth the transgressors among men. 29 So **he that goeth in to his neighbour's wife; whosoever toucheth her shall not be innocent.**
	Proverbs 6:32 *But* **whoso committeth adultery with a woman lacketh understanding: he** *that* **doeth it destroyeth his own soul**.
	Jeremiah 3:9 And it came to pass through the lightness of her whoredom, that she defiled the land, and **committed adultery with stones and with stocks**.
	Jeremiah 23:14-15 I have seen also in **the prophets of Jerusalem an horrible thing: they** <u>commit adultery</u>, **and walk in lies: they strengthen also the hands of evildoers,** <u>that none doth return from his wickedness</u>**: they are all of them unto me as Sodom, and the inhabitants thereof as Gomorrah**.15 Therefore thus saith the LORD of hosts concerning the prophets; Behold, I will feed them with wormwood, and make them drink the water of gall: **for from the prophets of Jerusalem is profaneness gone forth into all the land**.
	Hosea 4:12 My people ask counsel at their stocks, and their staff declareth unto them: for the **spirit of whoredoms** hath caused *them* to err, and they have gone a whoring from under their God.
	Nahum 3:4 Because of the multitude of the whoredoms of the wellfavoured harlot, the mistress of witchcrafts, that selleth nations through her whoredoms, and families through her witchcrafts.
	Malachi 2:14 Yet ye say, Wherefore? Because the LORD hath been witness between thee and the wife of thy youth, against whom thou hast dealt treacherously: yet *is* she thy companion, and the wife of thy covenant.
	Malachi 3:5 And **I will come near to you to judgment**; and I will be a swift witness against the sorcerers, and **against adulterers**, ...
Matthew 5:28 But I say unto you, That whosoever looketh on a woman to lust after her hath committed **adultery** with her already in his heart.	**Job 31:1** I made a covenant with mine eyes; why then should I think upon a maid? **Psalms 119:37** Turn away mine eyes from beholding vanity; *and* quicken thou me in thy way. **See Matthew 5:27 "Adultery"** **See Hebrews 12:14 "Holiness"** **See 1 Timothy 2:9 "Adornment"**
Matthew 5:29-30 And if thy right eye offend thee, pluck it out, and cast *it* from thee: for it is profitable for thee that one of thy members should perish, and not *that* thy whole **body** should be cast into **hell**. 30 And if thy right hand offend thee, cut it off, and cast *it* from thee: for	**See Luke 16:23 "Hell"** **See 1 Thessalonians 5:23 "Body, soul, and spirit"**

it is profitable for thee that one of thy members should perish, and not *that* thy whole body should be cast into **hell**.	
Matthew 5:31 It hath been said, Whosoever shall put away his wife, let him give her a writing of divorcement:	**Deuteronomy 24:1** When a man hath taken a wife, and married her, and it come to pass that she find no favour in his eyes, because he hath found some uncleanness in her: then let him write her a bill of divorcement, and give *it* in her hand, and send her out of his house.
Matthew 5:32 But I say unto you, That whosoever shall put away his wife, saving for the cause of fornication, causeth her to commit adultery: and whosoever shall marry her that is divorced committeth **adultery**.	**See Matthew 5:27 "Adultery"**
Matthew 5:33 Again, ye have heard that it hath been said by them of old time, Thou shalt not forswear thyself, but shalt perform unto the Lord thine oaths:	**Exodus 20:7** Thou shalt not take the name of the LORD thy God in vain; for the LORD will not hold him guiltless that taketh his name in vain. **Leviticus 19:12** And ye shall not swear by my name falsely, neither shalt thou profane the name of thy God: I *am* the LORD. **Numbers 30:2** If a man vow a vow unto the LORD, or swear an oath to bind his soul with a bond; he shall not break his word, he shall do according to all that proceedeth out of his mouth. **Deuteronomy 23:21** When thou shalt vow a vow unto the LORD thy God, thou shalt not slack to pay it: for the LORD thy God will surely require it of thee; and it would be sin in thee.
Matthew 5:34-35 But I say unto you, Swear not at all; neither by heaven; for it is God's throne: 35 Nor by the earth; for it is his footstool: neither by Jerusalem; for it is the city of the great King.	**Isaiah 66:1** Thus saith the LORD, The heaven is my throne, and the earth is my footstool: where is the house that ye build unto me? and where is the place of my rest? **Psalms 48:2** Beautiful for situation, the joy of the whole earth, *is* mount Zion, *on* the sides of the north, the city of the great King.
Matthew 5:36 Neither shalt thou swear by thy head, because thou canst not make one hair white or black.	**Proverbs 16:31** The hoary head *is* a crown of glory, *if* it be found in the way of righteousness.
Matthew 5:38 Ye have heard that it hath been said, An eye for an eye, and a tooth for a tooth:	**Exodus 21:24** Eye for eye, tooth for tooth, hand for hand, foot for foot, **Leviticus 24:20** Breach for breach, eye for eye, tooth for tooth: as he hath caused a blemish in a man, so shall it be done to him *again*. **Deuteronomy 19:21** And thine eye shall not pity; but life shall go for life, eye for eye, tooth for tooth, hand for hand, foot for foot.
Matthew 5:39 But I say unto you, That ye resist not evil: but whosoever shall smite thee on thy right cheek, turn to him the other also.	**Leviticus 19:18** Thou shalt not avenge, nor bear any grudge against the children of thy people, but thou shalt love thy neighbour as thyself: I *am* the LORD. **Proverbs 20:22** Say not thou, I will recompense evil; *but* wait on the LORD, and he shall save thee. **Proverbs 24:29** Say not, I will do so to him as he hath done to me: I will render to the man according to his work.
Matthew 5:42 Give to him that asketh thee, and from him that would borrow of	**Deuteronomy 15:8** But thou shalt open thine hand wide unto him, and shalt surely lend him sufficient for his need, *in that* which he wanteth.

thee turn not thou away.	
Matthew 5:43 Ye have heard that it hath been said, **Thou shalt love thy neighbour**, and hate thine enemy.	**Leviticus 19:18** Thou shalt not avenge, nor bear any grudge against the children of thy people, but **thou shalt love thy neighbour** as thyself: I *am* the LORD.
Matthew 5:48 Be ye therefore perfect, even as your Father which is in heaven is perfect.	**Genesis 17:1** And when Abram was ninety years old and nine, the LORD appeared to Abram, and said unto him, I *am* the Almighty God; walk before me, and be thou perfect.
Matthew 6:1-4 Take heed that ye do not your alms before men, to be seen of them: otherwise ye have no reward of your Father which is in heaven. 2 Therefore when thou doest *thine* alms, do not sound a trumpet before thee, as the hypocrites do in the synagogues and in the streets, that they may have glory of men. Verily I say unto you, They have their reward. 3 But when thou doest alms, let not thy left hand know what thy right hand doeth: 4 That thine alms may be in secret: and thy Father which seeth in secret himself shall reward thee openly.	**See 1 John 3:17 "Poor"**
Matthew 6:6 But thou, when thou prayest, enter into thy closet, and when thou hast shut thy door, pray to thy Father which is in secret; and thy Father which seeth in secret shall reward thee openly.	**2 Kings 4:33** He went in therefore, and shut the door upon them twain, and prayed unto the LORD.
Matthew 6:7 But when ye pray, use not vain repetitions, as the heathen *do*: for they think that they shall be heard for their much speaking.	**1 Kings 18:28** And they cried aloud, and cut themselves after their manner with knives and lancets, till the blood gushed out upon them. **Proverbs 1:28** Then shall they call upon me, but I will not answer; they shall seek me early, but they shall not find me: **Isaiah 1:15** And when ye spread forth your hands, I will hide mine eyes from you: yea, when ye make many prayers, I will not hear: your hands are full of blood.
Matthew 6:14-15 For **if ye forgive** men their trespasses, **your heavenly Father will also forgive you**: 15 **But if ye forgive not** men their trespasses, **neither will your Father forgive your trespasses**.	**Psalms 66:18** If I regard iniquity in my heart, the Lord will not hear *me*:
Matthew 6:16 Moreover when ye **fast**, be not, as the hypocrites, of a sad countenance: for they disfigure their faces, that they may appear unto men to fast. Verily I say unto you, They have their reward.	**Isaiah 58:3** Wherefore have we fasted, *say they*, and thou seest not? *wherefore* have we afflicted our soul, and thou takest no knowledge? Behold, in the day of your fast ye find pleasure, and exact all your labours. **See Matthew 17:21 "Fasting"**
Matthew 6:18 That thou appear not unto men to **fast**, but unto thy Father which is in secret: and thy Father, which seeth in secret, shall reward thee openly.	**See Matthew 17:21 "Fasting"**
Matthew 6:19 Lay not up for	**Proverbs 23:4-5** Labour not to be rich: cease from thine own

yourselves treasures upon earth, where moth and rust doth corrupt, and where thieves break through and steal:	wisdom. 5 Wilt thou set thine eyes upon that which is not? for *riches* certainly make themselves wings; they fly away as an eagle toward heaven.
Matthew 6:22-23 The light of the body is the eye: if therefore thine eye be single, thy whole body shall be full of light. 23 But if thine eye be evil, thy whole body shall be full of darkness. If therefore the light that is in thee be darkness, how great *is* that darkness!	**Psalms 119:37** Turn away mine eyes from beholding vanity; *and* quicken thou me in thy way.
Matthew 6:24 No man can serve two masters: for either he will hate the one, and love the other; or else he will hold to the one, and despise the other. Ye cannot serve God and **mammon**.	**Deuteronomy 8: 16-17 Who fed thee in the wilderness with manna**, which thy fathers knew not, that he might humble thee, and that he might prove thee, to do thee good at thy latter end; 17 And thou say in thine heart, **My power and the might of *mine* hand hath gotten me this wealth**. 18 But thou shalt remember the LORD thy God: for *it is* **he that giveth thee power to get wealth**, that he may establish his covenant which he sware unto thy fathers, as *it is* this day. **Deuteronomy 17:16-17** But he shall not multiply horses to himself, nor cause the people to return to Egypt, to the end that he should multiply horses: forasmuch as the LORD hath said unto you, Ye shall henceforth return no more that way. 17 Neither shall he multiply wives to himself, that his heart turn not away: neither shall he greatly multiply to himself silver and gold. **Psalms 1:3** And he shall be like a tree planted by the rivers of water, that bringeth forth his fruit in his season; his leaf also shall not wither; and whatsoever he doeth shall prosper. **Proverbs 8:18-21** Riches and honour *are* with me; *yea*, durable riches and righteousness. 19 My fruit *is* better than gold, yea, than fine gold; and my revenue than choice silver. 20 I lead in the way of righteousness, in the midst of the paths of judgment: 21 That I may cause those that love me to inherit substance; and I will fill their treasures. **Proverbs 10:22** The blessing of the LORD, it maketh rich, and he addeth no sorrow with it. **Proverbs 11:4** Riches profit not in the day of wrath: but righteousness delivereth from death. **Proverbs 11:24-31** There is that scattereth, and yet increaseth; and *there is* that withholdeth more than is meet, but *it tendeth* to poverty. 25 The liberal soul shall be made fat: and he that watereth shall be watered also himself. 26 He that withholdeth corn, the people shall curse him: but blessing *shall be* upon the head of him that selleth *it*. 27 He that diligently seeketh good procureth favour: but he that seeketh mischief, it shall come unto him. 28 **He that trusteth in his riches shall fall**: but the righteous shall flourish as a branch. 29 He that troubleth his own house shall inherit the wind: and the fool *shall be* servant to the wise of heart. 30 The fruit of the righteous *is* a tree of life; and he that winneth souls *is* wise. 31 Behold, the righteous shall be recompensed in the earth: much more the wicked and the sinner. **Proverbs 18:11** The rich man's wealth *is* his strong city, and as an high wall in his own conceit. **Proverbs 23:3-5** Be not desirous of his dainties: for they *are* deceitful meat. 4 Labour not to be rich: cease from thine own

	wisdom. 5 Wilt thou set thine eyes upon that which is not? for *riches* certainly make themselves wings; they fly away as an eagle toward heaven.
	Ecclesiastes 5:10-17 He that loveth silver shall not be satisfied with silver; nor he that loveth abundance with increase: this *is* also vanity. 11 When goods increase, they are increased that eat them: and what good *is there* to the owners thereof, saving the beholding *of them* with their eyes? 12 The sleep of a labouring man *is* sweet, whether he eat little or much: but the abundance of the rich will not suffer him to sleep. 13 There is a sore evil *which* I have seen under the sun, *namely*, riches kept for the owners thereof to their hurt. 14 But those riches perish by evil travail: and he begetteth a son, and *there is* nothing in his hand. 15 As he came forth of his mother's womb, naked shall he return to go as he came, and shall take nothing of his labour, which he may carry away in his hand. 16 And this also *is* a sore evil, *that* in all points as he came, so shall he go: and what profit hath he that hath laboured for the wind? 17 All his days also he eateth in darkness, and *he hath* much sorrow and wrath with his sickness.
Matthew 6:25 Therefore I say unto you, Take no thought for your life, what ye shall eat, or what ye shall drink; nor yet for your body, what ye shall put on. Is not the life more than meat, and the body than raiment?	**Psalms 37:5-6** Commit thy way unto the LORD; trust also in him; and he shall bring *it* to pass. 6 And he shall bring forth thy righteousness as the light, and thy judgment as the noonday. **Psalms 37:25** I have been young, and *now* am old; yet have I not seen the righteous forsaken, nor his seed begging bread. **Psalms 55:22** Cast thy burden upon the LORD, and he shall sustain thee: he shall never suffer the righteous to be moved.
Matthew 6:26 Behold the fowls of the air: for they sow not, neither do they reap, nor gather into barns; yet your heavenly Father feedeth them. Are ye not much better than they?	**Job 38:41** Who provideth for the raven his food? when his young ones cry unto God, they wander for lack of meat. **Psalms 147:9** He giveth to the beast his food, *and* to the young ravens which cry.
Matthew 6:33 But seek ye first the kingdom of God, and his righteousness; and all these things shall be added unto you.	**1 Kings 3:13** And I have also given thee that which thou hast not asked, both riches, and honour: so that there shall not be any among the kings like unto thee all thy days. **1 Kings 3:14** And if thou wilt walk in my ways, to keep my statutes and my commandments, as thy father David did walk, then I will lengthen thy days.
Matthew 7:5 Thou hypocrite, first cast out the beam out of thine own eye; and then shalt thou see clearly to cast out the mote out of thy brother's eye.	**Proverbs 18:17** *He that is* first in his own cause *seemeth* just; but his neighbour cometh and searcheth him. **Proverbs 25:8** Go not forth hastily to strive, lest *thou know not* what to do in the end thereof, when thy neighbour hath put thee to shame.
Matthew 7:6 Give not that which is holy unto the dogs, neither cast ye your pearls before swine, lest they trample them under their feet, and turn again and rend you.	**Proverbs 9:7-8** He that reproveth a scorner getteth to himself shame: and he that rebuketh a wicked *man getteth* himself a blot. 8 Reprove not a scorner, lest he hate thee: rebuke a wise man, and he will love thee. **Proverbs 23:9** Speak not in the ears of a fool: for he will despise the wisdom of thy words.
Matthew 7:7 Ask, and it shall be given you; seek, and ye shall find; knock, and it shall be opened unto you:	**2 Chronicles 16:12-13** And Asa in the thirty and ninth year of his reign was diseased in his feet, until his disease [was] exceeding *great*: yet in his disease he sought not to the LORD, but to the

	physicians. 13 And Asa slept with his fathers, and died in the one and fortieth year of his reign.
Matthew 7:8 For every one that asketh receiveth; and he that seeketh findeth; and to him that knocketh it shall be opened.	**Proverbs 8:17** I love them that love me; and those that seek me early shall find me. **Jeremiah 29:12** Then shall ye call upon me, and ye shall go and pray unto me, and I will hearken unto you.
Matthew 7:11 If ye then, being evil, know how to give good gifts unto your children, how much more shall your Father which is in heaven give good things to them that ask him?	**Genesis 6:5** And GOD saw that the wickedness of man *was* great in the earth, and *that* every imagination of the thoughts of his heart *was* only evil continually. **Job 15:16** How much more abominable and filthy *is* man, which drinketh iniquity like water? **Jeremiah 17:9** The heart *is* deceitful above all *things*, and desperately wicked: who can know it?
Matthew 7:15 Beware of false prophets, which come to you in sheeps clothing, but inwardly they are ravening wolves.	**Deuteronomy 13:1-3** If there arise among you a prophet, or a dreamer of dreams, and giveth thee a sign or a wonder, 2 And the sign or the wonder come to pass, whereof he spake unto thee, saying, Let us go after other gods, which thou hast not known, and let us serve them; 3 Thou shalt not hearken unto the words of that prophet, or that dreamer of dreams: for the LORD your God proveth you, to know whether ye love the LORD your God with all your heart and with all your soul. **Jeremiah 14:14** Then the LORD said unto me, The prophets prophesy lies in my name: I sent them not, neither have I commanded them, neither spake unto them: they prophesy unto you a false vision and divination, and a thing of nought, and the deceit of their heart. **Jeremiah 23:21** I have not sent these prophets, yet they ran: I have not spoken to them, yet they prophesied. **Jeremiah 23:16** Thus saith the LORD of hosts, Hearken not unto the words of the prophets that prophesy unto you: they make you vain: they speak a vision of their own heart, *and* not out of the mouth of the LORD. **Jeremiah 27:14-15** Therefore hearken not unto the words of the prophets that speak unto you, saying, Ye shall not serve the king of Babylon: for they prophesy a lie unto you. 15 For I have not sent them, saith the LORD, yet they prophesy a lie in my name; that I might drive you out, and that ye might perish, ye, and the prophets that prophesy unto you. **Jeremiah 29:8-9** For thus saith the LORD of hosts, the God of Israel; Let not your prophets and your diviners, that *be* in the midst of you, deceive you, neither hearken to your dreams which ye cause to be dreamed. 9 For they prophesy falsely unto you in my name: I have not sent them, saith the LORD.
Matthew 7:17-20 Even so every good tree bringeth forth good fruit; but a corrupt tree bringeth forth evil fruit. 18 A good tree cannot bring forth evil fruit, neither *can* a corrupt tree bring forth good fruit. 19 Every tree that bringeth not forth good fruit is hewn down, and cast into the fire. 20 Wherefore by their fruits ye shall know them.	**See Hebrews 12:14 "Holiness"**

Matthew 7:22 Many will say to me in that day, Lord, Lord, have we not prophesied in thy name? and in thy name have cast out devils? and in thy name done many wonderful works?	See Matthew 7:15
Matthew 7:23 And then will I profess unto them, I never knew you: depart from me, ye that work iniquity.	**Psalm 6:8** Depart from me, all ye workers of iniquity; for the LORD hath heard the voice of my weeping.
Matthew 7:24 Therefore whosoever heareth these sayings of mine, and doeth them, I will liken him unto a wise man, which built his house upon a rock:	**Jerermiah 17:8** For he shall be as a tree planted by the waters, and *that* spreadeth out her roots by the river, and shall not see when heat cometh, but her leaf shall be green; and shall not be careful in the year of drought, neither shall cease from yielding fruit.
Matthew 7:26 And every one that heareth these sayings of mine, and doeth them not, shall be likened unto a foolish man, which built his house upon the sand:	**Ezekiel 13:11** Say unto them which daub *it* with untempered *morter*, that it shall fall: there shall be an overflowing shower; and ye, O great hailstones, shall fall; and a stormy wind shall rend *it*. **Ezekiel 13:12** Lo, when the wall is fallen, shall it not be said unto you, Where *is* the daubing wherewith ye have daubed *it*?
Matthew 7:28-29 And it came to pass, when Jesus had ended these sayings, the people were astonished at his doctrine: 29 For he taught them as *one* having authority, and not as the scribes."	**Psalms 25:8** Good and upright *is* the LORD: therefore will he teach sinners in the way.
Matthew 8:4 And Jesus saith unto him, See thou tell no man; but go thy way, shew thyself to the priest, and offer the gift that Moses commanded, for a testimony unto them.	**Leviticus 14:2-3** This shall be the law of the leper in the day of his cleansing: He shall be brought unto the priest: 3 And the priest shall go forth out of the camp; and the priest shall look, and, behold, if the plague of leprosy be healed in the leper;
Matthew 8:8 The centurion answered and said, Lord, I am not worthy that thou shouldest come under my roof: but speak the word only, and my servant shall be healed.	**Psalms 107:20** He sent his word, and healed them, and delivered *them* from their destructions.
Matthew 8:16 When the even was come, they brought unto him many that were possessed with **devils**: and he cast out the **spirits** with *his* word, and healed all that were sick:	See Hebrews 13:2 "Good and bad angels" See 1 Peter 2:24 "Healing"
Matthew 8:17 Himself took our infirmities, and bare our sicknesses	**Isaiah 53:4** Surely he hath borne our griefs, and carried our sorrows
Matthew 8:26 And he saith unto them, Why are ye fearful, O ye of little faith? Then he arose, and rebuked the winds and the sea; and there was a great calm.	**Job 26:12** He divideth the sea with his power, and by his understanding he smiteth through the proud. **Psalms 65:7** Which stilleth the noise of the seas, the noise of their waves, and the tumult of the people. **Psalms 107:29** He maketh the storm a calm, so that the waves thereof are still. **Isaiah 51:10** *Art* thou not it which hath dried the sea, the waters of the great deep; that hath made the depths of the sea a way for the ransomed to pass over? **Isaiah 51:15** But I *am* the LORD thy God, that divided the sea, whose waves roared: The LORD of hosts *is* his name.
Matthew 9:13 I will have mercy, and	**Hosea 6:6** For I desired mercy, and not sacrifice

not sacrifice	**Micah 6:8** He hath shewed thee, O man, what *is* good; and what doth the LORD require of thee, but to do justly, and to love mercy, and to walk humbly with thy God?
Matthew 9:15 And Jesus said unto them, Can the children of the bridechamber mourn, as long as the bridegroom is with them? but the days will come, when the bridegroom shall be taken from them, and **then shall they fast.**	**See Matthew 17:21 "fasting"**
Matthew 9:20 And, behold, a woman, which was diseased with an issue of blood twelve years, came behind *him*, and touched the hem of his **garment**:	**Leviticus 15:25** And if a woman have an issue of her blood many days out of the time of her separation, or if it run beyond the time of her separation; all the days of the issue of her uncleanness shall be as the days of her separation: she *shall be* unclean. **See Matthew 23:5 "Garments"**
Matthew 9:32-34 As they went out, behold, they brought to him a dumb man **possessed with a devil**. 33 And when the **devil** was cast out, the dumb spake: and the multitudes marvelled, saying, It was never so seen in Israel. 34 But the Pharisees said, He casteth out **devils** through the **prince of the devils**.	**See Hebrews 13:2 "Good and bad angels"**
Matthew 9:36 But when he saw the multitudes, he was moved with compassion on them, because they fainted, and were scattered abroad, as sheep having no shepherd.	**Jeremiah 23:1-4** Woe be unto the pastors that destroy and scatter the sheep of my pasture! saith the LORD. 2 Therefore thus saith the LORD God of Israel against the pastors that feed my people; Ye have scattered my flock, and driven them away, and have not visited them: behold, I will visit upon you the evil of your doings, saith the LORD. 3 And I will gather the remnant of my flock out of all countries whither I have driven them, and will bring them again to their folds; and they shall be fruitful and increase. 4 And I will set up shepherds over them which shall feed them: and they shall fear no more, nor be dismayed, neither shall they be lacking, saith the LORD. **Ezekiel 34:2-12** Son of man, prophesy against the shepherds of Israel, prophesy, and say unto them, Thus saith the Lord GOD unto the shepherds; Woe *be* to the shepherds of Israel that do feed themselves! should not the shepherds feed the flocks? 3 Ye eat the fat, and ye clothe you with the wool, ye kill them that are fed: *but* ye feed not the flock. 4 The diseased have ye not strengthened, neither have ye healed that which was sick, neither have ye bound up *that which was* broken, neither have ye brought again that which was driven away, neither have ye sought that which was lost; but with force and with cruelty have ye ruled them. 5 And they were scattered, because *there is* no shepherd: and they became meat to all the beasts of the field, when they were scattered. 6 My sheep wandered through all the mountains, and upon every high hill: yea, my flock was scattered upon all the face of the earth, and none did search or seek *after them*. 7 Therefore, ye shepherds, hear the word of the LORD; 8 *As* I live, saith the Lord GOD, surely because my flock became a prey, and my flock became meat to every beast of the field, because *there was* no shepherd, neither did my shepherds search for my flock, but the shepherds fed themselves, and fed not my flock; 9 Therefore, O ye shepherds, hear the word of the LORD; 10

	Thus saith the Lord GOD; Behold, I *am* against the shepherds; and I will require my flock at their hand, and cause them to cease from feeding the flock; neither shall the shepherds feed themselves any more; for I will deliver my flock from their mouth, that they may not be meat for them. 11 For thus saith the Lord GOD; Behold, I, *even* I, will both search my sheep, and seek them out. 12 As a shepherd seeketh out his flock in the day that he is among his sheep *that are* scattered; so will I seek out my sheep, and will deliver them out of all places where they have been scattered in the cloudy and dark day.
Matthew 10:1 And when he had called unto *him* his twelve disciples, he gave them power *against* unclean spirits, to cast them out, and **to heal all manner of sickness and all manner of disease.**	**2 Kings 20:7** And Isaiah said, Take a lump of figs. And they took and laid it on the boil, and he recovered. **Genesis 20:17** So Abraham prayed unto God: and God healed Abimelech, and his wife, and his maidservants; and they bare *children*. **Numbers 12:10** And the cloud departed from off the tabernacle; and, behold, Miriam *became* leprous, *white* as snow: and Aaron looked upon Miriam, and, behold, *she was* leprous. **Numbers 12:13** And Moses cried unto the LORD, saying, Heal her now, O God, I beseech thee. **1 Kings 13:6** And the king answered and said unto the man of God, Intreat now the face of the LORD thy God, and pray for me, that my hand may be restored me again. And the man of God besought the LORD, and the king's hand was restored him again, and became as *it was* before. **1Kings 17:21** And he stretched himself upon the child three times, and cried unto the LORD, and said, O LORD my God, I pray thee, let this child's soul come into him again. **1 Kings 17:22** And the LORD heard the voice of Elijah; and the soul of the child came into him again, and he revived. **2 Kings 4:16** And he said, About this season, according to the time of life, thou shalt embrace a son. And she said, Nay, my lord, *thou* man of God, do not lie unto thine handmaid. **2 Kings 4:17** And the woman conceived, and bare a son at that season that Elisha had said unto her, according to the time of life. **2 Kings 4:34** And he went up, and lay upon the child, and put his mouth upon his mouth, and his eyes upon his eyes, and his hands upon his hands: and he stretched himself upon the child; and the flesh of the child waxed warm. **2 Kings 5:13** And his servants came near, and spake unto him, and said, My father, *if* the prophet had bid thee *do some* great thing, wouldest thou not have done *it*? how much rather then, when he saith to thee, Wash, and be clean? **2 Kings 5:14** Then went he down, and dipped himself seven times in Jordan, according to the saying of the man of God: and his flesh came again like unto the flesh of a little child, and he was clean. **2 Kings 13:20** And Elisha died, and they buried him. And the bands of the Moabites invaded the land at the coming in of the year. **2 Kings 13:21** And it came to pass, as they were burying a man, that, behold, they spied a band *of men*; and they cast the man into

	the sepulchre of Elisha: and when the man was let down, and touched the bones of Elisha, he revived, and stood up on his feet. **Isaiah 38:9** The writing of Hezekiah king of Judah, when he had been sick, and was recovered of his sickness:
Matthew 10:10 Nor scrip for *your* journey, neither two coats, neither shoes, nor yet staves: for the workman is worthy of his meat.	**Leviticus 19:13** Thou shalt not defraud thy neighbour, neither rob *him*: the wages of him that is hired shall not abide with thee all night until the morning. **Deuteronomy 24:14** Thou shalt not oppress an hired servant *that is* poor and needy, *whether he be* of thy brethren, or of thy strangers that *are* in thy land within thy gates: **Deuteronomy 25:4** Thou shalt not muzzle the ox when he treadeth out *the corn*.
Matthew 10:15 Verily I say unto you, It shall be more tolerable for the land of **Sodom and Gomorrha** in the day of judgment, than for that city.	**See Romans 1:27 "Sexual sins"**
Matthew 10:21 And the brother shall deliver up the brother to death, and the father the child: and the children shall rise up against *their* parents, and cause them to be put to death.	**Micah 7:2** The good *man* is perished out of the earth: and *there is* none upright among men: they all lie in wait for blood; they hunt every man his brother with a net.
Matthew 10:26 Fear them not therefore: for there is nothing covered, that shall not be revealed; and hid, that shall not be known.	**Deuteronomy 31:6** Be strong and of a good courage, fear not, nor be afraid of them: for the LORD thy God, he *it is* that doth go with thee; he will not fail thee, nor forsake thee. **Deuteronomy 31:8** And the LORD, he *it is* that doth go before thee, he will be with thee, he will not fail thee, neither forsake thee: fear not, neither be dismayed. **Joshua 1:5** There shall not any man be able to stand before thee all the days of thy life: as I was with Moses, *so* I will be with thee: I will not fail thee, nor forsake thee. **Jeremiah 1:8** Be not afraid of their faces: for I *am* with thee to deliver thee, saith the LORD. **Ezekiel 2:6-7** And thou, son of man, be not afraid of them, neither be afraid of their words, though briers and thorns *be* with thee, and thou dost dwell among scorpions: be not afraid of their words, nor be dismayed at their looks, though they *be* a rebellious house. 7 And thou shalt speak my words unto them, whether they will hear, or whether they will forbear: for they *are* most rebellious. **Ezekiel 3:9** As an adamant harder than flint have I made thy forehead: fear them not, neither be dismayed at their looks, though they *be* a rebellious house.
Mathew 10:28 And fear not them which kill the body, but are not able to kill the **soul**: but rather fear him which is able to destroy both soul and body in **hell**.	**See Luke 16:23 "Hell"** **See 1 Thessalonians 5:23 "Body, soul, and spirit"**
Matthew 10:30 But the very hairs of your head are all numbered.	**1 Samuel 14:45** And the people said unto Saul, Shall Jonathan die, who hath wrought this great salvation in Israel? God forbid: *as* the LORD liveth, there shall not one hair of his head fall to the ground; for he hath wrought with God this day. So the people

	rescued Jonathan, that he died not.
Matthew 10:35-36 a man at variance against his father, and the daughter against her mother, and the daughter in law against her mother in law. And a man's foes shall be they of his own household.	**Micah 7:6** For the son dishonoureth the father, the daughter riseth up against her mother, the daughter in law against her mother in law; a man's enemies are the men of his own house. **Psalmx 41:9** Yea, mine own familiar friend, in whom I trusted, which did eat of my bread, hath lifted up *his* heel against me.
Matthew 10:41 He that receiveth a prophet in the name of a prophet shall receive a prophet's reward; and he that receiveth a righteous man in the name of a righteous man shall receive a righteous man's reward.	**1 Kings 17:10** So he arose and went to Zarephath. And when he came to the gate of the city, behold, the widow woman *was* there gathering of sticks: and he called to her, and said, Fetch me, I pray thee, a little water in a vessel, that I may drink. **1 Kings 17:11** And as she was going to fetch *it*, he called to her, and said, Bring me, I pray thee, a morsel of bread in thine hand. **1 Kings 17:15-16** And she went and did according to the saying of Elijah: and she, and he, and her house, did eat *many* days. 16 And the barrel of meal wasted not, neither did the cruse of oil fail, according to the word of the LORD, which he spake by Elijah. **1 Kings 17:21** And he stretched himself upon the child three times, and cried unto the LORD, and said, O LORD my God, I pray thee, let this child's soul come into him again. **2 Kings 4:8** And it fell on a day, that Elisha passed to Shunem, where *was* a great woman; and she constrained him to eat bread. And *so it was*, *that* as oft as he passed by, he turned in thither to eat bread. **2 Kings 4:17** And the woman conceived, and bare a son at that season that Elisha had said unto her, according to the time of life. **2 Kings 4:34** And he went up, and lay upon the child, and put his mouth upon his mouth, and his eyes upon his eyes, and his hands upon his hands: and he stretched himself upon the child; and the flesh of the child waxed warm.
Matthew 11:5 The blind receive their sight, and the lame walk, the lepers are cleansed, and the deaf hear, the dead are raised up, and the poor have the gospel preached to them.	**Exodus 4:11** And the LORD said unto him, Who hath made man's mouth? or who maketh the dumb, or **deaf**, or the seeing, or the blind? have not I the LORD? **Psalm 58:4** Their poison is like the poison of a serpent: they are like the **deaf adder** that stoppeth her ear; **Isaiah 29:18** And in that day shall the deaf hear the words of the book, and the eyes of the blind shall see out of obscurity, and out of darkness. **Isaiah 35:5-6** Then **the eyes of the blind shall be opened, and the ears of the deaf shall be unstopped.** 6 Then shall the lame man leap as an hart, and the tongue of the dumb sing: for in the wilderness shall waters break out, and streams in the desert. **Isaiah 42:18** Hear, ye deaf; and look, ye blind, that ye may see. **Isaiah 43:8** Bring forth the blind people that have eyes, and the deaf that have ears. **Isaiah 61:1** The Spirit of the Lord GOD *is* upon me; because the LORD hath anointed me to preach good tidings unto the meek; he hath sent me to bind up the brokenhearted, to proclaim liberty to the captives, and the opening of the prison to *them that are* bound;
Matthew 11:10 Behold, I send my messenger before thy face, which shall	**Exodus 23:20** Behold, I send an Angel before thee, to keep thee in

prepare thy way before thee.	the way, and to bring thee into the place which I have prepared. **Malachi 3:1** Behold, I will send my messenger, and he shall prepare the way before me: … .
Matthew 11:14 And if ye will receive *it*, this is Elias, which was for to come.	**Malachi 4:5** Behold, I will send you Elijah the prophet before the coming of the great and dreadful day of the LORD:
Matthew 11:19 The Son of man came eating and drinking, and they say, Behold a man **gluttonous**, and a winebibber, a friend of publicans and sinners. But wisdom is justified of her children.	**Numbers 11:32-34** And the people stood up all that day, and all *that* night, and all the next day, and they gathered the quails: he that gathered least gathered ten homers: and they spread *them* all abroad for themselves round about the camp. 33 And while the flesh *was* yet between their teeth, ere it was chewed, the wrath of the LORD was kindled against the people, and the LORD smote the people with a very great plague. 34 And he called the name of that place Kibroth-hattaavah: because there they buried the **people that lusted**. **Deuteronomy 21:20** And they shall say unto the elders of his city, This our son *is* stubborn and rebellious, he will not obey our voice; *he is* a **glutton**, and a drunkard. **Proverbs 23:2-3** And put a knife to thy throat, if thou *be* a man given to appetite. 3 Be not desirous of his dainties: for they *are* deceitful meat. **Proverbs 23:19-21** Hear thou, my son, and be wise, and guide thine heart in the way. 20 Be not among winebibbers; among riotous eaters of flesh: 21 For the drunkard and the **glutton** shall come to poverty: and drowsiness shall clothe *a man* with rags. **Proverbs 25:16** Hast thou found honey? eat so much as is sufficient for thee, lest thou be filled therewith, and vomit it.
Matthew 11:21 Woe unto thee, Chorazin! woe unto thee, Bethsaida! for if the mighty works, which were done in you, had been done in Tyre and Sidon, they would have repented long ago in sackcloth and ashes.	**2 Samuel 13:19** And Tamar put ashes on her head, and rent her garment of divers colours that *was* on her, and laid her hand on her head, and went on crying. **2 Kings 6:30** And it came to pass, when the king heard the words of the woman, that he rent his clothes; and he passed by upon the wall, and the people looked, and, behold, *he had* sackcloth within upon his flesh. **2 Kings 19:1** And it came to pass, when king Hezekiah heard *it*, that he rent his clothes, and covered himself with sackcloth, and went into the house of the LORD.
Matthew 11:23 And thou, Capernaum, which art exalted unto heaven, shalt be brought down to **hell**: for if the mighty works, which have been done in thee, had been done in **Sodom**, it would have remained until this day.	**Isaiah 14:13, 15** For thou hast said in thine heart, I will ascend into heaven, I will exalt my throne above the stars of God: I will sit also upon the mount of the congregation, in the sides of the north: 15 Yet thou shalt be brought down to hell, to the sides of the pit. **See Romans 1:27** "Sexual sins" **See Luke 16:23** "Hell"
Matthew 11:25 At that time Jesus answered and said, I thank thee, O Father, Lord of heaven and earth, because thou hast hid these things from the wise and prudent, and hast revealed them unto babes.	**Isaiah 29:14** Therefore, behold, I will proceed to do a marvellous work among this people, *even* a marvellous work and a wonder: for the wisdom of their wise *men* shall perish, and the understanding of their prudent *men* shall be hid. **Obadiah 1:8** Shall I not in that day, saith the LORD, even destroy the wise *men* out of Edom, and understanding out of the mount of Esau?
Matthew 11:28 Come unto me, all *ye* that labour and are heavy laden, and I	**Jeremiah 6:16** Thus saith the LORD, Stand ye in the ways, and see, and ask for the old paths, where *is* the good way, and walk

will give you rest.	therein, and ye shall find rest for your souls. But they said, We will not walk *therein*.
Matthew 11:29 Take my yoke upon you, and learn of me; for I am **meek** and lowly in heart: and **ye shall find rest unto your souls**.	**Numbers 12:3** (Now the man Moses *was* very **meek**, above all the men which *were* upon the face of the earth.) **Jeremiah 6:16** Thus saith the LORD, Stand ye in the ways, and see, and ask for the old paths, where *is* the good way, and walk therein, **and ye shall find rest for your souls**. But they said, We will not walk *therein*.
Matthew 12:1 At that time Jesus went on the sabbath day through the corn; and his disciples were an hungred, and began to pluck the ears of corn, and to eat.	**Leviticus 19:9-10** And when ye reap the harvest of your land, thou shalt not wholly reap the corners of thy field, neither shalt thou gather the gleanings of thy harvest. 10 And thou shalt not glean thy vineyard, neither shalt thou gather *every* grape of thy vineyard; thou shalt leave them for the poor and stranger: I *am* the LORD your God. **Leviticus 23:22** And when ye reap the harvest of your land, thou shalt not make clean riddance of the corners of thy field when thou reapest, neither shalt thou gather any gleaning of thy harvest: thou shalt leave them unto the poor, and to the stranger: I *am* the LORD your God. **Deuteronomy 23:25** When thou comest into the standing corn of thy neighbour, then thou mayest pluck the ears with thine hand; but thou shalt not move a sickle unto thy neighbour's standing corn.
Matthew 12:2 But when the Pharisees saw *it*, they said unto him, Behold, thy disciples do that which is not lawful to do upon the **sabbath** day.	**Exodus 20:10** But the seventh day *is* the sabbath of the LORD thy God: *in it* thou shalt not do any work, thou, nor thy son, nor thy daughter, thy manservant, nor thy maidservant, nor thy cattle, nor thy stranger that *is* within thy gates: **See Colossians 2:16 "Sabbath"**
Matthew 12:3 But he said unto them, Have ye not read what David did, when he was an hungred, and they that were with him;	**Exodus 29:33** And they shall eat those things wherewith the atonement was made, to consecrate *and* to sanctify them: but a stranger shall not eat *thereof*, because they *are* holy. **Leviticus 24:9** And it shall be Aaron's and his sons'; and they shall eat it in the holy place: for it *is* most holy unto him of the offerings of the LORD made by fire by a perpetual statute. **1 Samuel 21:6** So the priest gave him hallowed *bread:* for there was no bread there but the shewbread, that was taken from before the LORD, to put hot bread in the day when it was taken away.
Matthew 12:5 Or have ye not read in the law, how that on the sabbath days the priests in the temple profane the sabbath, and are blameless?	**Numbers 28:9-10** And on the sabbath day two lambs of the first year without spot, and two tenth deals of flour for a meat offering, mingled with oil, and the drink offering thereof: 10 This *is* the burnt offering of every sabbath, beside the continual burnt offering, and his drink offering.
Matthew 12:6 But I say unto you, That in this place is *one* greater than the temple.	**2 Chronicles 6:18** But will God in very deed dwell with men on the earth? behold, heaven and the heaven of heavens cannot contain thee; how much less this house which I have built!
Matthew 12:7 But if ye had known what *this* meaneth, I will have mercy, and not sacrifice, ye would not have condemned the guiltless.	**Hosea 6:6** For I desired mercy, and not sacrifice; and the knowledge of God more than burnt offerings.
Matthew 12:11 And he said unto them, What man shall there be among you, that shall have one sheep, and if it fall into a pit on the sabbath day, will he not lay	**Exodus 23:4** If thou meet thine enemy's ox or his ass going astray, thou shalt surely bring it back to him again. **Deuteronomy 22:1-4** Thou shalt not see thy brother's ox or his

hold on it, and lift *it* out?	sheep go astray, and hide thyself from them: thou shalt in any case bring them again unto thy brother. 2 And if thy brother *be* not nigh unto thee, or if thou know him not, then thou shalt bring it unto thine own house, and it shall be with thee until thy brother seek after it, and thou shalt restore it to him again. 3 In like manner shalt thou do with his ass; and so shalt thou do with his raiment; and with all lost thing of thy brother's, which he hath lost, and thou hast found, shalt thou do likewise: thou mayest not hide thyself. 4 Thou shalt not see thy brother's ass or his ox fall down by the way, and hide thyself from them: thou shalt surely help him to lift *them* up again.
Matthew 12:12 How much then is a man better than a sheep? Wherefore it is lawful to do well on the **sabbath days**.	**Genesis 1:27** So God created man in his *own* image, in the image of God created he him; male and female created he them. **See Colossians 2:16 "Sabbaths"**
Matthew 12:17 That it might be fulfilled which was spoken by Esaias the prophet, saying,	**Amos 3:7** Surely the Lord GOD will do nothing, but he revealeth his secret unto his servants the prophets.
Matthew 12:18-21 Behold my servant, whom I have chosen; my beloved, in whom my soul is well pleased: I will put my spirit upon him, and he shall shew judgment to the Gentiles. He shall not strive, nor cry; neither shall any man hear his voice in the streets. A bruised reed shall he not break, and smoking flax shall he not quench, till he send forth judgment unto victory. And **in his name shall the Gentiles trust**.	**Proverbs 18:10** The name of the LORD is a strong tower: the righteous runneth into it, and is safe. **Isaiah 42:1-4** Behold my servant, whom I uphold; mine elect, in whom my soul delighteth; I have put my spirit upon him: he shall bring forth judgment to the Gentiles. He shall not cry, nor lift up, nor cause his voice to be heard in the street. A bruised reed shall he not break, and the smoking flax shall he not quench: he shall bring forth judgment unto truth. He shall not fail nor be discouraged, till he have set judgment in the earth: and the isles shall wait for his law.
Matthew 12:22 Then was brought unto him one possessed with a **devil**, blind, and dumb: and he healed him, insomuch that the blind and dumb both spake and saw.	**See Hebrews 13:2 "Good and bad angels"**
Mathew 12:26 And if **Satan** cast out Satan, he is divided against himself; how shall then his kingdom stand?	**Genesis 3:4** And the **serpent** said unto the woman, Ye shall not surely die: **Zechariah 3:1-2** And he shewed me Joshua the high priest standing before the angel of the LORD, and **Satan** standing at his right hand to resist him. 2 And the LORD said unto Satan, The LORD rebuke thee, O Satan; even the LORD that hath chosen Jerusalem rebuke thee: *is* not this a brand plucked out of the fire? **See Matthew 4:10 "satan"**
Matthew 12:32 And whosoever speaketh a word against the Son of man, it shall be forgiven him: but whosoever speaketh against the Holy Ghost, it shall not be forgiven him, neither in this world, neither in the *world* to come.	**Leviticus 24:16** And he that blasphemeth the name of the LORD, he shall surely be put to death, *and* all the congregation shall certainly stone him: as well the stranger, as he that is born in the land, when he blasphemeth the name *of the LORD*, shall be put to death. **Numbers 15:30** But the soul that doeth *ought* presumptuously, *whether he be* born in the land, or a stranger, the same reproacheth the LORD; and that soul shall be cut off from among his people.
Matthew 12:34 O generation of vipers, how can ye, being evil, speak good things? for out of the abundance of the heart the mouth speaketh.	**Psalms 19:14** Let the words of my mouth, and the meditation of my heart, be acceptable in thy sight, O LORD, my strength, and my redeemer. **Psalms 40:10** I have not hid thy righteousness within my heart; I

	have declared thy faithfulness and thy salvation: I have not concealed thy lovingkindness and thy truth from the great congregation. **Isaiah 6:5** Then said I, Woe *is* me! for I am undone; because I *am* a man of unclean lips, and I dwell in the midst of a people of unclean lips: for mine eyes have seen the King, the LORD of hosts. **See James 3:8 "Tongue"**
Matthew 12:36 But I say unto you, That every idle word that men shall speak, they shall give account thereof in the day of judgment.	**Ecclesiastes 12:14** For God shall bring every work into judgment, with every secret thing, whether *it be* good, or whether *it be* evil.
Matthew 12:37 For by thy words thou shalt be justified, and by thy words thou shalt be condemned.	**2 Samuel 1:16** And David said unto him, Thy blood *be* upon thy head; for thy mouth hath testified against thee, saying, I have slain the LORD's anointed.
Matthew 12:39-40 Then certain of the scribes and of the Pharisees answered, saying, Master, we would see a sign from thee. 40 For as **Jonas was three days and three nights in the whale's belly**; so shall the Son of man be three days and three nights in the heart of the earth.	**Jonah 1:17** Now the LORD had prepared a great fish to swallow up Jonah. And Jonah was in the belly of the fish **three days and three nights**. **Jonah 2:1** Then Jonah prayed unto the LORD his God out of the fish's belly
Matthew 12:41 The men of Nineveh shall rise in judgment with this generation, and shall condemn it: because they repented at the preaching of Jonas; and, behold, a greater than Jonas *is* here.	**Jonah 3:4** And Jonah began to enter into the city a day's journey, and he cried, and said, Yet forty days, and Nineveh shall be overthrown. **Jonah 3:5** So the people of Nineveh believed God, and proclaimed a fast, and put on sackcloth, from the greatest of them even to the least of them.
Matthew 12:42 The queen of the south shall rise up in the judgment with this generation, and shall condemn it: for she came from the uttermost parts of the earth to hear the wisdom of Solomon; and, behold, a greater than Solomon *is* here.	**1 Kings 10:1, 3** And when the queen of Sheba heard of the fame of Solomon concerning the name of the LORD, she came to prove him with hard questions. 3 And Solomon told her all her questions: there was not any thing hid from the king, which he told her not. **2 Chronicles 9:1** And when the queen of Sheba heard of the fame of Solomon, she came to prove Solomon with hard questions at Jerusalem, with a very great company, and camels that bare spices, and gold in abundance, and precious stones: and when she was come to Solomon, she communed with him of all that was in her heart.
Matthew 13:14-15 By hearing ye shall hear, and shall not understand; and seeing ye shall see, and shall not perceive: For this people's heart is waxed gross, and their ears are dull of hearing, and their eyes they have closed; lest at any time they should see with their eyes, and hear with their ears, and should understand with their heart, and should be converted, and I should heal them.	**Isaiah 6:9-10** And he said, God, and tell this people, Hear ye indeed, but understand not; and see ye indeed, but perceive not. Make the heart of this people fat, and make their ears heavy, and shut their eyes; lest they see with their eyes, and hear with their ears, and understand with their heart, and convert, and be healed.
Matthew 13:18-23 But he that received seed into the good ground is he that heareth the word, and understandeth it; which also **bareth <u>fruit</u>**, and **bringeth**	**Genesis 26:12** Then Isaac sowed in that land, and received in the same year an <u>**hundredfold**</u>: and the Lord blessed him. **Isaiah 14:29** Rejoice not thou, whole Palestina, because the rod of him that smote thee is broken: for **out of the serpent's root shall**

forth, some an hundredfold, some sixty, some thirty.	**come forth a cockatrice, and his fruit shall be a fiery flying serpent.**
Matthew 13:35 I will open my mouth in parables; I will utter things which have been kept secret from the foundation of the world.	**Psalms 78:2** I will open my mouth in a parable: I will utter dark sayings of old
Matthew 13:39 The enemy that sowed them is the devil; the harvest is the end of the world; and the reapers are the **angels**.	**Joel 3:13** Put ye in the sickle, for the harvest is ripe: come, get you down; for the press is full, the fats overflow; for their wickedness *is* great. **See Hebrews 13:2 "Angels"**
Matthew 13:43 Then shall the righteous shine forth as the sun in the kingdom of their Father. Who hath ears to hear, let him hear.	**Daniel 12:3** And they that be wise shall shine as the brightness of the firmament; and they that turn many to righteousness as the stars for ever and ever.
Matthew 13:50 And shall cast them into the furnace of fire: there shall be wailing and gnashing of teeth.	**Psalms 140:10** Let burning coals fall upon them: let them be cast into the fire; into deep pits, that they rise not up again. **Daniel 3:6** And whoso falleth not down and worshippeth shall the same hour be cast into the midst of a burning fiery furnace.
Matthew 13:58 And he did not many mighty works there **because of their unbelief**.	**Psalm 78:41** ... limited the Holy One of Israel.
Matthew 14:4 For John said unto him, It is not lawful for thee to have her.	**Leviticus 18:16** Thou shalt not uncover the nakedness of thy brother's wife: it *is* thy brother's nakedness. **Leviicus 20:21** And if a man shall take his brother's wife, it *is* an unclean thing: he hath uncovered his brother's nakedness; they shall be childless.
Matthew 14:6 But when Herod's birthday was kept, the daughter of Herodias danced before them, and pleased Herod.	**Genesis 40:20** And it came to pass the third day, *which was* Pharaoh's birthday, that he made a feast unto all his servants: and he lifted up the head of the chief butler and of the chief baker among his servants.
Matthew 14:33 Then they that were in the ship came and worshipped him, saying, Of a truth thou art the Son of God.	**Exodus 34:14** For thou shalt worship no other god: for the LORD, whose name is Jealous, is a jealous God: **Deuteronomy 32:43** Rejoice, O ye nations, *with* his people: for he will avenge the blood of his servants, and will render vengeance to his adversaries, and will be merciful unto his land, *and* to his people. **Psalms 97:7** Confounded be all they that serve graven images, that boast themselves of idols: worship him, all *ye* gods.
Matthew 15:2 Why do thy disciples transgress the tradition of the **elders**? for they wash not their hands when they eat bread.	**See 1 Peter 5:1 "Elders"**
Matthew 15:4 For God commanded, saying, Honour thy father and mother: and, He that curseth father or mother, let him die the death.	**Exodus 20:12** Honour thy father and thy mother: that thy days may be long upon the land which the LORD thy God giveth thee. **Exodus 21:17** And he that curseth his father, or his mother, shall surely be put to death. **Leviticus 20:9** For every one that curseth his father or his mother shall be surely put to death: he hath cursed his father or his mother; his blood *shall be* upon him. **Deuteronomy 5:16** Honour thy father and thy mother, as the

	LORD thy God hath commanded thee; that thy days may be prolonged, and that it may go well with thee, in the land which the LORD thy God giveth thee. **Proverbs 20:20** Whoso curseth his father or his mother, his lamp shall be put out in obscure darkness.
Matthew 15:6 And honour not his father or his mother, *he shall be free*. Thus have ye made the commandment of God of none effect by your tradition.	**Isaiah 1:13-14** Bring no more vain oblations; incense is an abomination unto me; the new moons and sabbaths, the calling of assemblies, I cannot away with; *it is* iniquity, even the solemn meeting. 14 Your new moons and your appointed feasts my soul hateth: they are a trouble unto me; I am weary to bear *them*.
Matthew 15:8-9 This people draweth nigh unto me with their mouth, and honoureth me with their lips; but their heart is far from me. But in vain they do worship me, teaching for doctrines the commandments of men.	**Isaiah 29:13** Wherefore the Lord said, Forasmuch as this people draw near me with their mouth, and with their lips do honour me, but have removed their heart far from me, and their fear toward me is taught by the precept of men: **Ezekiel 33:31** And they come unto thee as the people cometh, and they sit before thee *as* my people, and they hear thy words, but they will not do them: for with their mouth they shew much love, *but* their heart goeth after their covetousness.
Mathew 15:18 But those things which proceed out of the mouth come forth from the heart; and they defile the man.	**Proverbs 23:16** Yea, my reins shall rejoice, when thy lips speak right things. **Psalms 19:14** Let the words of my mouth, and the meditation of my heart, be acceptable in thy sight, O LORD, my strength, and my redeemer. **Proverbs 16:24** Pleasant words *are as* a honeycomb, sweet to the soul, and health to the bones.
Matthew 15:19 For out of the heart proceed evil thoughts, murders, adulteries, fornications, thefts, false witness, blasphemies:	**Genesis 3:6** And when the woman saw that the tree *was* good for food, and that it *was* pleasant to the eyes, and a tree to be desired to make *one* wise, she took of the fruit thereof, and did eat, and gave also unto her husband with her; and he did eat. **Genesis 6:5** And GOD saw that the wickedness of man *was* great in the earth, and *that* every imagination of the thoughts of his heart *was* only evil continually. **Genesis 8:21** And the LORD smelled a sweet savour; and the LORD said in his heart, I will not again curse the ground any more for man's sake; for the imagination of man's heart *is* evil from his youth; neither will I again smite any more every thing living, as I have done. **Exodus 20:13-16** Thou shalt not kill. 14 Thou shalt not commit adultery. 15 Thou shalt not steal. 16 Thou shalt not bear false witness against thy neighbour. **Deuteronomy 31:29** For I know that after my death ye will utterly corrupt *yourselves*, and turn aside from the way which I have commanded you; and evil will befall you in the latter days; because ye will do evil in the sight of the LORD, to provoke him to anger through the work of your hands. **Joshua 7:21** When I saw among the spoils a goodly Babylonish garment, and two hundred shekels of silver, and a wedge of gold of fifty shekels weight, then **I coveted them**, and took them; and, behold, they *are* hid in the earth in the midst of my tent, and the silver under it. **2 Samuel 11:2** And it came to pass in an eveningtide, that David arose from off his bed, and walked upon the roof of the king's

	house: and from the roof **he saw** a woman washing herself; and the woman *was* very beautiful to look upon. **Proverbs 6:14** Frowardness *is* in his heart, he deviseth mischief continually; he soweth discord. **Jeremiah 17:9** The heart *is* deceitful above all *things*, and desperately wicked: who can know it?
Matthew 15:22 And, behold, a woman of Canaan came out of the same coasts, and cried unto him, saying, Have mercy on me, O Lord, *thou* Son of David; my daughter is grievously vexed with a **devil**.	**See Hebrews 13:2 "Good and bad angels"**
Matthew 15:25 Then came she and worshipped him, saying, Lord, help me.	**See 1 Timothy 2:5 "God"**
Matthew 15:30 And great multitudes came unto him, having with them *those that were* lame, blind, dumb, maimed, and many others, and cast them down at Jesus' feet; and he healed them:	**Isaiah 29:18** And in that day shall the deaf hear the words of the book, and the eyes of the blind shall see out of obscurity, and out of darkness. **Isaiah 35:5** Then the eyes of the blind shall be opened, and the ears of the deaf shall be unstopped.
Matthew 15:31 Insomuch that the multitude wondered, when they saw the dumb to speak, the maimed to be whole, the lame to walk, and the blind to see: and they glorified the God of Israel.	**Isaiah 35:4** Say to them that are of a fearful heart, Be strong, fear not: behold, your God will come with vengeance, even God with a recompence; he will come and save you. **Isaiah 61:1** The Spirit of the Lord GOD is upon me; because the LORD hath anointed me to preach good tidings unto the meek; he hath sent me to bind up the brokenhearted, to proclaim liberty to the captives, and the opening of the prison to them that are bound;
Matthew 15:36 And he took the seven loaves and the fishes, and gave thanks, and brake *them*, and gave to his disciples, and the disciples to the multitude.	**1 Samuel 9:13** As soon as ye be come into the city, ye shall straightway find him, before he go up to the high place to eat: for the people will not eat until he come, because he doth bless the sacrifice; *and* afterwards they eat that be bidden. Now therefore get you up; for about this time ye shall find him.
Matthew 16:4 A wicked and adulterous generation seeketh after a sign; and there shall no sign be given unto it, but the sign of the prophet Jonas. And he left them, and departed.	**Jonah 1:17** Now the LORD had prepared a great fish to swallow up Jonah. And Jonah was in the belly of the fish three days and three nights.
Matthew 16:14 And they said, Some *say that thou art* John the Baptist: some, Elias; and others, Jeremias, or one of the prophets.	**Ezekiel 1:10** As for the likeness of their faces, they four had the face of a man, and the face of a lion, on the right side: and they four had the face of an ox on the left side; they four also had the face of an eagle.
Matthew 16:18 And I say also unto thee, That thou art Peter, and upon this rock I will build my church; and the gates of **hell** shall not prevail against it.	**Psalms 118:22** The stone *which* the builders refused is become the head *stone* of the corner. **Isaiah 28:16** Therefore thus saith the Lord GOD, Behold, I lay in Zion for a foundation a stone, a tried stone, a precious corner *stone*, a sure foundation: he that believeth shall not make haste. **Isaiah 33:20** Look upon Zion, the city of our solemnities: thine eyes shall see Jerusalem a quiet habitation, a tabernacle *that* shall not be taken down; not one of the stakes thereof shall ever be removed, neither shall any of the cords thereof be broken. **See Luke 16:23 "Hell"**

Matthew 16:19 And I will give unto thee the keys of the kingdom of heaven: and whatsoever thou shalt bind on earth shall be bound in heaven: and whatsoever thou shalt loose on earth shall be loosed in heaven	**Psalms 102:20** To hear the groaning of the prisoner; to loose those that are appointed to death; **Proverbs 18:21** Death and life *are* in the power of the tongue: and they that love it shall eat the fruit thereof.
Matthew 16:21 From that time forth began Jesus to shew unto his disciples, how that he must go unto Jerusalem, and suffer many things of the **elders** and chief priests and scribes, and be killed, and be raised again the third day.	**Psalms 22:14** I am poured out like water, and all my bones are out of joint: my heart is like wax; it is melted in the midst of my bowels. **See 1 Peter 5:1 "Elders"**
Matthew 16:23 But he turned, and said unto Peter, Get thee behind me, Satan: thou art an offence unto me: for thou savourest not the things that be of God, but those that be of men.	**Genesis 3:4** And the **serpent** said unto the woman, Ye shall not surely die: **Zechariah 3:1-2** And he shewed me Joshua the high priest standing before the angel of the LORD, and **Satan** standing at his right hand to resist him. 2 And the LORD said unto Satan, The LORD rebuke thee, O Satan; even the LORD that hath chosen Jerusalem rebuke thee: *is* not this a brand plucked out of the fire? **See Matthew 4:10 "satan"**
Matthew 16:26 For what is a man profited, if he shall gain the whole world, and lose his own **soul**? or what shall a man give in exchange for his **soul**?	**See 1 Thessalonians 5:23 "Body, soul, and spirit"**
Matthew 16:27 For the Son of man shall come in the glory of his Father with his angels; and then he shall reward every man according to his works.	**Psalm 62:12** Also unto thee, O Lord, *belongeth* mercy: for thou renderest to every man according to his work. **Proverbs 24:12** If thou sayest, Behold, we knew it not; doth not he that pondereth the heart consider *it?* and he that keepeth thy soul, doth *not* he know *it?* and shall *not* he render to *every* man according to his works? **Jeremiah 17:10** I the LORD search the heart, *I* try the reins, even to give every man according to his ways, *and* according to the fruit of his doings. **Jeremiah 32:19** Great in counsel, and mighty in work: for thine eyes *are* open upon all the ways of the sons of men: to give every one according to his ways, and according to the fruit of his doings: **Ezekiel 7:27** The king shall mourn, and the prince shall be clothed with desolation, and the hands of the people of the land shall be troubled: I will do unto them after their way, and according to their deserts will I judge them; and they shall know that I *am* the LORD. **Ezekiel 33:20** Yet ye say, The way of the Lord is not equal. O ye house of Israel, I will judge you every one after his ways.
Matthew 17:5 While he yet spake, behold, a bright cloud overshadowed them: and behold a voice out of the cloud, which said, This is my beloved Son, in whom I am well pleased; hear ye him.	**Genesis 22:2** And he said, Take now thy son, thine only *son* Isaac, whom thou lovest, and get thee into the land of Moriah; and offer him there for a burnt offering upon one of the mountains which I will tell thee of. **Genesis 39:21** But the LORD was with Joseph, and shewed him mercy, and gave him favour in the sight of the keeper of the prison. **Deuteronomy 18:15** The LORD thy God will raise up unto thee a

	Prophet from the midst of thee, of thy brethren, like unto me; unto him ye shall hearken; **Deuteronomy 18:19** And it shall come to pass, *that* whosoever will not hearken unto my words which he shall speak in my name, I will require *it* of him. **Psalm 2:7** I will declare the decree: the LORD hath said unto me, Thou *art* my Son; this day have I begotten thee. **Isaiah 42:1** Behold my servant, whom I uphold; mine elect, in whom my soul delighteth; I have put my spirit upon him: he shall bring forth judgment to the Gentiles.
Matthew 17:10 And his disciples asked him, saying, Why then say the scribes that Elias must first come?	**Malachi 4:5** Behold, I will send you Elijah the prophet before the coming of the great and dreadful day of the LORD:
Matthew 17:18 And Jesus rebuked the **devil**; and he departed out of him: and the child was cured from that very hour.	**See Hebrews 13:2 "Good and bad angels"**
Matthew 17:20 And Jesus said unto them, Because of your unbelief: for verily I <u>say</u> unto you, **If ye have faith as a grain of mustard seed, ye shall say unto this mountain, Remove hence to yonder place; and it shall remove; and nothing shall be impossible unto you.**	**Exodus 14:15-16** And the LORD said unto Moses, Wherefore criest thou unto me? speak unto the children of Israel, that they go forward: 16 But lift thou up thy rod, and stretch out thine hand over the sea, and divide it: and the children of Israel shall go on dry ground through the midst of the sea. **Job 22:26-28** For then shalt thou have thy delight in the Almighty, and shalt lift up thy face unto God. 27 Thou shalt make thy prayer unto him, and he shall hear thee, and thou shalt pay thy vows. 28 <u>**Thou shalt also decree a thing, and it shall be established unto thee**</u>: and the light shall shine upon thy ways. **Jeremiah 1:12** Then said the LORD unto me, Thou hast well seen: for **I will hasten my word to perform it**. **Isaiah 55:11** So shall my word be that goeth forth **out of my mouth: it shall not return unto me void**, but it shall accomplish that which I please, and it shall prosper *in the thing* whereto I sent it.
Matthew 17:21 Howbeit this kind goeth not out but by **prayer** and **fasting**.	**1 Samuel 1:17** Then Eli answered and said, Go in peace: and the God of Israel grant *thee* thy **petition** that thou hast asked of him. **1 Kings 8:28** Yet have thou respect unto the prayer of thy servant, and to his supplication, O LORD my God, to hearken unto the cry and to the prayer, which thy servant **prayeth** before thee to day: **2 Chronicles 6:24** And if thy people Israel be put to the worse before the enemy, because they have sinned against thee; and shall return and confess thy name, and **pray** and make **supplication** before thee in this house; **2 Chronicles 16:12-13** And Asa in the thirty and ninth year of his reign was diseased in his feet, until his disease *was* exceeding *great*: yet in his disease <u>he sought not to the LORD, but to the physicians</u>. 13 And <u>Asa slept with his fathers</u>, and died in the one and fortieth year of his reign. **Psalms 142:1** I cried unto the LORD with my voice; with my voice unto the LORD did I make my **supplication** **Ezekiel 22:30** And I sought for a man among them, that should make up the hedge, and **stand in the gap** before me for the land, that I should not destroy it: but I found none.

Daniel 6:11 Then these men assembled, and found Daniel praying and making **supplication** before his God.

Malachi 1:9 And now, I pray you, **beseech** God that he will be gracious unto us: this hath been by your means: will he regard your persons? saith the LORD of hosts.

Exodus 34:28 And he was there with the LORD forty days and forty nights; he did **neither eat bread, nor drink water**. And he wrote upon the tables the words of the covenant, the ten commandments.

1 Samuel 31:13 And they took their bones, and buried them under a tree at Jabesh, and **fasted** seven days.

1 Kings 19:8 And he arose, and **did eat and drink, and went in the strength of that meat forty days and forty nights** unto Horeb the mount of God.

Ezra 8:21 Then I proclaimed a **fast** there, at the river of Ahava, that we might afflict (**humble**) ourselves before our God, to seek of him a right way for us, and for our little ones, and for all our substance.

Ezra 8:23 So we **fasted and besought** our God for this: and he was intreated of us.

Ezra 10:6 Then Ezra rose up from before the house of God, and went into the chamber of Johanan the son of Eliashib: and *when* he came thither, **he did eat no bread, nor drink water**: for he mourned because of the transgression of them that had been carried away.

Esther 4:16 Go, gather together all the Jews that are present in Shushan, and fast ye for me, and **neither eat nor drink three days, night or day**: I also and my maidens will fast likewise; and so will I go in unto the king, which is

not according to the law: and if I perish, I perish.

Psalms 35:13 But as for me, when they were sick, my clothing was sackcloth: I humbled my soul with **fasting**; and my prayer returned into mine own bosom.

Psalm 50:15 And **call upon me** in the day of trouble: I will deliver thee, and thou shalt glorify me.

Isaiah 58:1-8 Cry aloud, spare not, lift up thy voice like a trumpet, and shew my people their transgression, and the house of Jacob their sins. 2 Yet they seek me daily, and delight to know my ways, as a nation that did righteousness, and forsook not the ordinance of their God: they ask of me the ordinances of justice; they take delight in approaching to God. 3 Wherefore have we **fasted**, *say they*, and thou seest not? *wherefore* have we afflicted our soul, and thou takest no knowledge? Behold, in the day of your **fast** ye find pleasure, and exact all your labours. 4 Behold, ye **fast** for strife and debate, and to smite with the fist of wickedness: ye shall not **fast** as *ye do this* day, to make your voice to be heard on high. 5 Is it such a **fast** that I have chosen? a day for a man to afflict his soul? *is it* to bow down his head as a bulrush, and to spread sackcloth and ashes *under him*? wilt thou call this a **fast**, and an acceptable day to the LORD? 6 *Is* **not this the fast that I have chosen? to loose the bands of wickedness, to undo the heavy burdens, and to let the oppressed go free, and that ye break every yoke?** 7 *Is*

	it not to deal thy bread to the hungry, and that thou bring the poor that are cast out to thy house? when thou seest the naked, that thou cover him; and that thou hide not thyself from thine own flesh? 8 Then shall thy light break forth as the morning, and thine health shall spring forth speedily: and thy righteousness shall go before thee; the glory of the LORD shall be thy rereward. **Daniel 9:3** And I set my face unto the Lord God, to seek by prayer and supplications, with **fasting**, and sackcloth, and ashes: **Daniel 10:3** I ate no pleasant bread, neither came flesh nor wine in my mouth, neither did I anoint myself at all, till three whole weeks were fulfilled. **Jonah 3:5** So the people of Nineveh believed God, and proclaimed a **fast**, and put on sackcloth, from the greatest of them even to the least of them. **Joel 2:12** Therefore also now, saith the LORD, turn ye even to me with all your heart, and with **fasting**, and with weeping, and with mourning: **Zechariah 7:5** Speak unto all the people of the land, and to the priests, saying, When ye **fasted** and mourned in the fifth and seventh *month*, even those seventy years, did ye at all **fast** unto me, *even* to me?
Matthew 17:23 And they shall kill him, and the **third day** he shall be raised again. And they were exceeding sorry.	**Psalms 16:10** For thou wilt not leave my soul in hell; neither wilt thou suffer thine Holy One to see corruption. **Jonah 1:17** Now the LORD had prepared a great fish to swallow up Jonah. And Jonah was in the belly of the fish **three days and three nights**. **Jonah 2:1** Then Jonah prayed unto the LORD his God out of the fish's belly
Matthew 18:8 Wherefore if thy hand or thy foot offend thee, cut them off, and cast *them* from thee: it is better for thee to enter into life halt or maimed, rather than having two hands or two feet to be cast into everlasting fire.	**Deuteronomy 13:6-10** If thy brother, the son of thy mother, or thy son, or thy daughter, or the wife of thy bosom, or thy friend, which *is* as thine own soul, entice thee secretly, saying, Let us go and serve other gods, which thou hast not known, thou, nor thy fathers; 7 *Namely*, of the gods of the people which *are* round about you, nigh unto thee, or far off from thee, from the *one* end of the earth even unto the *other* end of the earth; 8 Thou shalt not consent unto him, nor hearken unto him; neither shall thine eye pity him, neither shalt thou spare, neither shalt thou conceal him: 9 But thou shalt surely kill him; thine hand shall be first upon him to put him to death, and afterwards the hand of all the people. 10 And thou shalt stone him with stones, that he die; because he hath sought to thrust thee away from the LORD thy God, which brought thee out of the land of Egypt, from the house of bondage.
Matthew 18:9 And if thine eye offend thee, pluck it out, and cast *it* from thee: it is better for thee to enter into life with one eye, rather than having two eyes to be cast into **hell** fire.	**See Luke 16:23 "Hell"**
Matthew 18:10 Take heed that ye despise not one of these little ones; for I say unto you, That in heaven their **angels** do always behold the face of my Father which is in heaven.	**Psalms 34:7** The angel of the LORD encampeth round about them that fear him, and delivereth them. **See Hebrews 13:2 "Good and bad angels"**

Matthew 18:15 Moreover if thy brother shall trespass against thee, go and tell him his fault between thee and him alone: if he shall hear thee, thou hast gained thy brother.	**Leviticus 19:17** Thou shalt not hate thy brother in thine heart: thou shalt in any wise rebuke thy neighbour, and not suffer sin upon him. **Proverbs 17:10** A reproof entereth more into a wise man than an hundred stripes into a fool.
Matthew 18:16 But if he will not hear [thee, then] take with thee one or two more, that in the mouth of two or three witnesses every word may be established.	**Leviticus 19:15** Ye shall do no unrighteousness in judgment: thou shalt not respect the person of the poor, nor honour the person of the mighty: *but* in righteousness shalt thou judge thy neighbour. **Numbers 35:30** Whoso killeth any person, the murderer shall be put to death by the mouth of witnesses: but one witness shall not testify against any person *to cause him* to die. **Deuteronomy 17:6** At the mouth of two witnesses, or three witnesses, shall he that is worthy of death be put to death; *but* at the mouth of one witness he shall not be put to death. **Deuteronomy 19:15** One witness shall not rise up against a man for any iniquity, or for any sin, in any sin that he sinneth: at the mouth of two witnesses, or at the mouth of three witnesses, shall the matter be established.
Matthew 18:18 Verily I say unto you, Whatsoever ye shall bind on earth shall be bound in heaven: and whatsoever ye shall loose on earth shall be loosed in heaven.	**Psalms 102:20** To hear the groaning of the prisoner; to loose those that are appointed to death; **Proverbs 18:21** Death and life *are* in the power of the tongue: and they that love it shall eat the fruit thereof.
Matthew 18:20 For where two or three are gathered together in my name, there am I in the midst of them.	**Psalms 139:7-8** Whither shall I go from thy spirit? or whither shall I flee from thy presence? ⁸ If I ascend up into heaven, **thou *art* there**: if I make my bed in hell, **behold, thou *art there***. **Proverbs 15:3** The eyes of the LORD *are* in **every place**, beholding the evil and the good. See 1 Timothy 2:5 "God"
Matthew 18:21-22 Then came Peter to him, and said, Lord, how oft shall my brother sin against me, and I forgive him? till seven times? 22 Jesus saith unto him, I say not unto thee, Until seven times: but, Until seventy times seven.	**Psalms 66:18** If I regard iniquity in my heart, the Lord will not hear *me*:
Matthew 18:35 So likewise shall my heavenly Father do also unto you, if ye from your hearts forgive not every one his brother their trespasses.	**Psalms 66:18** If I regard iniquity in my heart, the Lord will not hear *me*:
Matthew 19:4 And he answered and said unto them, Have ye not read, that he which made *them* at the beginning made them male and female,	**Genesis 1:27** So God created man in his *own* image, in the image of God created he him; male and female created he them. **Genesis 5:2** Male and female created he them; and blessed them, and called their name Adam, in the day when they were created.
Matthew 19:5-6 And said, For this cause shall a man leave father and mother, and shall cleave to his wife: and they twain shall be one flesh? 6 Wherefore they are no more twain, but one flesh. What therefore God hath joined together, let not man put asunder.	**Genesis 2:24** Therefore shall a man leave his father and his mother, and shall cleave unto his wife: and they shall be one flesh. **Malachi 2:15-16 And did not he make one?** Yet had he the residue of the spirit. And wherefore one? That he might seek a godly seed. Therefore take heed to your spirit, and **let none deal treacherously against the wife of his youth**. 16 For the LORD, the God of Israel, saith that **he hateth putting away**: for *one* covereth violence with his garment, saith the LORD of hosts:

	therefore take heed to your spirit, that ye deal not treacherously.
Matthew 19:7 They say unto him, Why did Moses then command to give a writing of divorcement, and to put her away?	**Deuteronomy 24:1** When a man hath taken a wife, and married her, and it come to pass that she find no favour in his eyes, because he hath found some uncleanness in her: then let him write her a bill of divorcement, and give *it* in her hand, and send her out of his house. **Jeremiah 3:1** They say, If a man put away his wife, and she go from him, and become another man's, shall he return unto her again? shall not that land be greatly polluted? but thou hast played the harlot with many lovers; yet return again to me, saith the LORD. **Exodus 7:2** Thou shalt speak **all that I command thee**: and Aaron thy brother shall speak unto Pharaoh, that he send the children of Israel out of his land. **Exodus 27:20** And thou shalt **command** the children of Israel, that they bring thee pure oil olive beaten for the light, to cause the lamp to burn always. **Joshua 11:15** As the LORD **commanded** Moses his servant, so did Moses **command** Joshua, and so did Joshua; he left nothing undone of all that the LORD **commanded** Moses. 16 So Joshua took all that land, the hills, and all the south country, and all the land of Goshen, and the valley, and the plain, and the mountain of Israel, and the valley of the same;
Matthew 19:9 And I say unto you, Whosoever shall put away his wife, **except** *it be* **for fornication**, and shall marry another, committeth **adultery**: and whoso marrieth her which is put away doth commit adultery.	**See Matthew 5:27 "Adultery"** **Deuteronomy 17:17** Neither shall he multiply wives to himself, that his heart turn not away: neither shall he greatly multiply to himself silver and gold. **Deuteronomy 22:22** If a man be found lying with a woman married to an husband, then **they shall both of them die**, *both* the man that lay with the woman, and the woman: so shalt thou put away evil from Israel.
Matthew 19:18 He saith unto him, Which? Jesus said, Thou shalt do no murder, Thou shalt not commit adultery, Thou shalt not steal, Thou shalt not bear false witness,	**Exodus 20:13-16** Thou shalt not kill. 14 Thou shalt not commit adultery. 15 Thou shalt not steal. 16 Thou shalt not bear false witness against thy neighbour. **Deuteronomy 5:18-20** Neither shalt thou commit adultery. 19 Neither shalt thou steal. 20 Neither shalt thou bear false witness against thy neighbour. **Deuteronomy 31:29** For I know that after my death ye will utterly corrupt *yourselves*, and turn aside from the way which I have commanded you; and evil will befall you in the latter days; because ye will do evil in the sight of the LORD, to provoke him to anger through the work of your hands. **See Matthew 5:27 "Adultery"**
Matthew 19:19 Honour thy father and *thy* mother: and, Thou shalt love thy neighbour as thyself.	**Exodus 20:12** Honour thy father and thy mother: that thy days may be long upon the land which the LORD thy God giveth thee. **Leviticus 19:17-18** Thou shalt not hate thy brother in thine heart: thou shalt in any wise rebuke thy neighbour, and not suffer sin upon him. 18 Thou shalt not avenge, nor bear any grudge against the children of thy people, but thou shalt love thy neighbour as thyself: I *am* the LORD.

	Deuteronomy 5:16 Honour thy father and thy mother, as the LORD thy God hath commanded thee; that thy days may be prolonged, and that it may go well with thee, in the land which the LORD thy God giveth thee.
Matthew 19:21 Jesus said unto him, If thou wilt be perfect, go *and* sell that thou hast, and give to the poor, and thou shalt have treasure in heaven: and come *and* follow me.	**Deuteronomy 15:11** For the poor shall never cease out of the land: therefore I command thee, saying, Thou shalt open thine hand wide unto thy brother, to thy poor, and to thy needy, in thy land. **Psalm 41:1** To the chief Musician, A Psalm of David. Blessed *is* he that considereth the poor: the LORD will deliver him in time of trouble. **Psalm 112:9** He hath dispersed, he hath given to the poor; his righteousness endureth for ever; his horn shall be exalted with honour. **See Hebrews 12:14 "Holiness"**
Matthew 19:23 Then said Jesus unto his disciples, Verily I say unto you, That a **rich** man shall hardly enter into the kingdom of heaven.	**Proverbs 11:28** He that trusteth in his riches shall fall: but the righteous shall flourish as a branch. **See Matthew 6:24 "Wealth"**
Matthew 19:26 But Jesus beheld *them,* and said unto them, With men this is impossible; but with God all things are possible.	**Job 42:2** I know that thou canst do every *thing*, and *that* no thought can be withholden from thee. **Jeremiah 32:17** Ah Lord GOD! behold, thou hast made the heaven and the earth by thy great power and stretched out arm, *and* there is nothing too hard for thee:
Matthew 19:28 And Jesus said unto them, Verily I say unto you, That ye which have followed me, in the regeneration when **the Son of man shall sit in the throne of his glory**, ye also shall sit upon twelve thrones, judging the twelve tribes of Israel.	**Psalms 103:19** The LORD hath prepared his throne in the heavens; and his kingdom ruleth over all. **Isaiah 14:13** For thou hast said in thine heart, I will ascend into heaven, I will exalt my throne above the stars of God: I will sit also upon the mount of the congregation, in the sides of the north: **Daniel 7:9** I beheld till the thrones were cast down, and the Ancient of days did sit, whose garment *was* white as snow, and the hair of his head like the pure wool: **his throne** *was like* the fiery flame, *and* his wheels *as* burning fire. **Zechariah 14:11** And *men* shall dwell in it, and there shall be no more utter destruction; but Jerusalem shall be safely inhabited.
Matthew 19:29 And every one that hath forsaken houses, or brethren, or sisters, or father, or mother, or wife, or children, or lands, for my name's sake, shall receive an **hundredfold**, and shall inherit everlasting life.	**Genesis 26:12** Then Isaac sowed in that land, and received in the same year an **hundredfold**: and the Lord blessed him. **Deuteronomy 33:9** Who said unto his father and to his mother, I have not seen him; neither did he acknowledge his brethren, nor knew his own children: for they have observed thy word, and kept thy covenant. **Job 42:12-13** So the LORD blessed the latter end of Job more than his beginning: for he had fourteen thousand sheep, and six thousand camels, and a thousand yoke of oxen, and a thousand she asses. 13 He had also seven sons and three daughters.
Matthew 20:18-19 Behold, we go up to Jerusalem: and the Son of man shall be betrayed unto the chief priests and unto the scribes, and they shall condemn him to death, 19 And shall deliver him to the Gentiles to mock, and to scourge, and to	**Jonah 1:17** Now the LORD had prepared a great fish to swallow up Jonah. And Jonah was in the belly of the fish **three days and three nights**. **Jonah 2:1** Then Jonah prayed unto the LORD his God out of the fish's belly

crucify *him*: and **the third day he shall rise again**.	
Matthew 20:21 And he said unto her, What wilt thou? She saith unto him, Grant that these my two sons may sit, the one on thy right hand, and the other on the left, in thy kingdom. **Matthew 20:23** And he saith unto them, Ye shall drink indeed of my cup, and be baptized with the baptism that I am baptized with: but to sit on my right hand, and on my left, is not mine to give, but it shall be given to them for whom it is prepared of my Father.	**Psalms 16:8** I have set the LORD always before me: because *he is* at my right hand, I shall not be moved. **Psalm 110:5** The Lord at thy right hand shall strike through kings in the day of his wrath. **Zechraiah 3:1** And he shewed me Joshua the high priest standing before the angel of the LORD, and Satan standing at his right hand to resist him.
Matthew 20:28 Even as the Son of man came not to be ministered unto, but to minister, and to give his life a ransom for many.	**Leviticus 6:7** And the priest shall make an atonement for him before the LORD: and it shall be forgiven him for any thing of all that he hath done in trespassing therein **Deuteronomy 16:5** Thou mayest not sacrifice the passover within any of thy gates, which the LORD thy God giveth thee: **2 Chronicles 29:24** And the priests killed them, and they made reconciliation with their blood upon the altar, to make an atonement for all Israel: for the king commanded *that* the burnt offering and the sin offering *should be made* for all Israel. **Nehemiah 10:33** For the shewbread, and for the continual meat offering, and for the continual burnt offering, of the sabbaths, of the new moons, for the set feasts, and for the holy *things,* and for the sin offerings to make an atonement for Israel, and *for* all the work of the house of our God. **Isaiah 53:6-12** All we like sheep have gone astray; we have turned every one to his own way; and the LORD hath laid on him the iniquity of us all. 7 He was oppressed, and he was afflicted, yet he opened not his mouth: he is brought as a lamb to the slaughter, and as a sheep before her shearers is dumb, so he openeth not his mouth. 8 He was taken from prison and from judgment: and who shall declare his generation? for he was cut off out of the land of the living: for the transgression of my people was he stricken. 9 And he made his grave with the wicked, and with the rich in his death; because he had done no violence, neither *was any* deceit in his mouth. 10 Yet it pleased the LORD to bruise him; he hath put *him* to grief: when thou shalt make his soul an offering for sin, he shall see *his* seed, he shall prolong *his* days, and the pleasure of the LORD shall prosper in his hand. 11 He shall see of the travail of his soul, *and* shall be satisfied: by his knowledge shall my righteous servant justify many; for he shall bear their iniquities. 12 Therefore will I divide him *a portion* with the great, and he shall divide the spoil with the strong; because he hath poured out his soul unto death: and he was numbered with the transgressors; and he bare the sin of many, and made intercession for the transgressors.
Matthew 21:5 Tell ye the daughter of Sion, Behold, thy King cometh unto thee, meek, and sitting upon an ass, and a colt the foal of an ass.	**Isaiah 62:11** Behold, the LORD hath proclaimed unto the end of the world, Say ye to the daughter of Zion, Behold, thy salvation cometh; behold, his reward *is* with him, and his work before him. **Zechariah 9:9** Rejoice greatly, O daughter of Zion; shout, O daughter of Jerusalem: behold, thy King cometh unto thee: he *is*

	just, and having salvation; lowly, and riding upon an ass, and upon a colt the foal of an ass.
Matthew 21:9 And the multitudes that went before, and that followed, cried, saying, Hosanna to the Son of David: Blessed *is* he that cometh in the name of the Lord; Hosanna in the highest.	**Psalms 118:26** Blessed *be* he that cometh in the name of the LORD: we have blessed you out of the house of the LORD.
Matthew 21:11 And the multitude said, This is Jesus the prophet of Nazareth of Galilee.	**Deuteronomy 18:18-19** I will raise them up a Prophet from among their brethren, like unto thee, and will put my words in his mouth; and he shall speak unto them all that I shall command him. 19 And it shall come to pass, *that* whosoever will not hearken unto my words which he shall speak in my name, I will require *it* of him.
Matthew 21:12 And Jesus went into the **temple** of God, and cast out all them that sold and bought in the **temple**, and overthrew the tables of the moneychangers, and the seats of them that sold doves,	**See Revelation 11:1 "temple"**
Matthew 21:13 And said unto them, It is written, My house shall be called the house of prayer; but ye have made it a den of thieves.	**Exodus 20:15** Thou shalt not steal. **Deuteronomy 31:29** For I know that after my death ye will utterly corrupt *yourselves*, and turn aside from the way which I have commanded you; and evil will befall you in the latter days; because ye will do evil in the sight of the LORD, to provoke him to anger through the work of your hands. **1 Kings 8:29** That thine eyes may be open toward this house night and day, *even* toward the place of which thou hast said, My name shall be there: that thou mayest hearken unto the prayer which thy servant shall make toward this place. **Isaiah 56:7** Even them will I bring to my holy mountain, and make them joyful in my house of prayer: their burnt offerings and their sacrifices *shall be* accepted upon mine altar; for mine house shall be called an house of prayer for all people. **Jeremiah 7:11** Is this house, which is called by my name, become a den of robbers in your eyes? Behold, even I have seen *it*, saith the LORD.
Matthew 21:16 And said unto him, Hearest thou what these say? And Jesus saith unto them, Yea; have ye never read, Out of the mouth of babes and sucklings thou hast perfected praise?	**Psalms 8:2** Out of the mouth of babes and sucklings hast thou ordained strength because of thine enemies, that thou mightest still the enemy and the avenger.
Matthew 21:22 And all things, whatsoever ye shall ask in **prayer**, believing, ye shall receive.	**See Matthew 17:21 "Prayer"**
Matthew 21:23 And when he was come into the temple, the chief priests and the **elders** of the people came unto him as he was teaching, and said, By what authority doest thou these things? and who gave thee this authority?	**See 1 Peter 5:1 "Elders"**
Matthew 21:30 And he came to the second, and said likewise. And he answered and said, I *go*, sir: and went	**Ezekiel 33:31** And they come unto thee as the people cometh, and they sit before thee *as* my people, and they hear thy words, but they will not do them: for with their mouth they shew much love,

43

not.	*but* their heart goeth after their covetousness.
Matthew 21:33 Hear another parable: There was a certain householder, which planted a vineyard, and hedged it round about, and digged a winepress in it, and built a tower, and let it out to husbandmen, and went into a far country:	**Psalms 80:8** Thou hast brought a vine out of Egypt: thou hast cast out the heathen, and planted it. **Isaiah 5:1-2** Now will I sing to my wellbeloved a song of my beloved touching his vineyard. My wellbeloved hath a vineyard in a very fruitful hill: 2 And he fenced it, and gathered out the stones thereof, and planted it with the choicest vine, and built a tower in the midst of it, and also made a winepress therein: and he looked that it should bring forth grapes, and it brought forth wild grapes. **Jeremiah 2:21** Yet I had planted thee a noble vine, wholly a right seed: how then art thou turned into the degenerate plant of a strange vine unto me? **Jeremiah 12:10** Many pastors have destroyed my vineyard, they have trodden my portion under foot, they have made my pleasant portion a desolate wilderness.
Matthew 21:38 But when the husbandmen saw the son, they said among themselves, This is the heir; come, let us kill him, and let us seize on his inheritance.	**Genesis 37:18** And when they saw him afar off, even before he came near unto them, they conspired against him to slay him. **Psalms 2:1** Why do the heathen rage, and the people imagine a vain thing?
Matthew 21:42 Jesus saith unto them, Did ye never read in the scriptures, The stone which the builders rejected, the same is become the head of the corner: this is the Lord's doing, and it is marvellous in our eyes?	**Psalms 118:22-23** The stone *which* the builders refused is become the head *stone* of the corner. 23 This is the LORD's doing; it *is* marvellous in our eyes. **Isaiah 8:14** And he shall be for a sanctuary; but for a stone of stumbling and for a rock of offence to both the houses of Israel, for a gin and for a snare to the inhabitants of Jerusalem. **Isaiah 28:16** Therefore thus saith the Lord GOD, Behold, I lay in Zion for a foundation a stone, a tried stone, a precious corner *stone*, a sure foundation: he that believeth shall not make haste. **Zechariah 4:7** Who *art* thou, O great mountain? before Zerubbabel *thou shalt become* a plain: and he shall bring forth the headstone *thereof with* shoutings, *crying,* Grace, grace unto it.
Matthew 21:43 Therefore say I unto you, The kingdom of God shall be taken from you, and given to a nation bringing forth the fruits thereof.	**Exodus 32:10** Now therefore let me alone, that my wrath may wax hot against them, and that I may consume them: and I will make of thee a great nation.
Matthew 21:44 And whosoever shall fall on this stone shall be broken: but on whomsoever it shall fall, it will grind him to powder.	**Isaiah 8:14** And he shall be for a sanctuary; but for a stone of stumbling and for a rock of offence to both the houses of Israel, for a gin and for a snare to the inhabitants of Jerusalem. **Zechariah 12:3** And in that day will I make Jerusalem a burdensome stone for all people: all that burden themselves with it shall be cut in pieces, though all the people of the earth be gathered together against it. **Daniel 2:34-35** Thou sawest till that a stone was cut out without hands, which smote the image upon his feet that were of iron and clay, and brake them to pieces. 35 Then was the iron, the clay, the brass, the silver, and the gold, broken to pieces together, and became like the chaff of the summer threshingfloors; and the wind carried them away, that no place was found for them: and the stone that smote the image became a great mountain, and filled the whole earth. **Daniel 2:44** And in the days of these kings shall the God of heaven

	set up a kingdom, which shall never be destroyed: and the kingdom shall not be left to other people, *but* it shall break in pieces and consume all these kingdoms, and it shall stand for ever.
Matthew 22:11-12 And when the king came in to see the guests, he saw there a man which had not on a wedding garment: 12 And he saith unto him, Friend, how camest thou in hither not having a wedding garment? And he was speechless.	**Ezekiel 44:9** Thus saith the Lord GOD; No stranger, uncircumcised in heart, nor uncircumcised in flesh, shall enter into my sanctuary, of any stranger that *is* among the children of Israel.
Matthew 22:13 Then said the king to the servants, Bind him hand and foot, and take him away, and cast him into **outer darkness**; there shall be weeping and gnashing of teeth	**See Luke 16:23 "Hell"**
Matthew 22:24 Saying, Master, Moses said, If a man die, having no children, his brother shall marry his wife, and raise up seed unto his brother.	**Genesis 38:8** And Judah said unto Onan, Go in unto thy brother's wife, and marry her, and raise up seed to thy brother. **Deuteronomy 25:5** If brethren dwell together, and one of them die, and have no child, the wife of the dead shall not marry without unto a stranger: her husband's brother shall go in unto her, and take her to him to wife, and perform the duty of an husband's brother unto her.
Mathew 22:29 Jesus answered and said unto them, Ye do err, not knowing the scriptures, nor the power of God.	**Amos 8:11** Behold, **the days come**, saith the Lord GOD, that **I will send a famine in the land**, not **a famine** of bread, nor a thirst for water, but **of hearing the words of the LORD**:
Matthew 22:32 I am the God of Abraham, and the God of Isaac, and the God of Jacob? God is not the God of the dead, but of the living.	**Exodus 3:6** Moreover he said, I *am* the God of thy father, the God of Abraham, the God of Isaac, and the God of Jacob. And Moses hid his face; for he was afraid to look upon God. **Exodus 3:15** And God said moreover unto Moses, Thus shalt thou say unto the children of Israel, The LORD God of your fathers, the God of Abraham, the God of Isaac, and the God of Jacob, hath sent me unto you: this *is* my name for ever, and this *is* my memorial unto all generations.
Matthew 22:37 Jesus said unto him, Thou shalt love the Lord thy God with all thy heart, and with all thy soul, and with all thy mind.	**Deuteronomy 6:5** And thou shalt love the LORD thy God with all thine heart, and with all thy soul, and with all thy might. **Deuteronomy 10:12** And now, Israel, what doth the LORD thy God require of thee, but to fear the LORD thy God, to walk in all his ways, and to love him, and to serve the LORD thy God with all thy heart and with all thy soul, **Deuteronomy 30:6** And the LORD thy God will circumcise thine heart, and the heart of thy seed, to love the LORD thy God with all thine heart, and with all thy soul, that thou mayest live.
Matthew 22:39 And the second *is* like unto it, Thou shalt love thy neighbour as thyself.	**Leviticus 19:18** Thou shalt not avenge, nor bear any grudge against the children of thy people, but thou shalt love thy neighbour as thyself: I *am* the LORD.
Matthew 22:39 And the second *is* like unto it, Thou shalt love thy neighbour as thyself.	**Leviticus 19:18** Thou shalt not avenge, nor bear any grudge against the children of thy people, but thou shalt love thy neighbour as thyself: I *am* the LORD.
Matthew 22:44 The LORD said unto my Lord, Sit thou on my right hand, till I make thine enemies thy footstool?	**Psalms 8:6** Thou madest him to have dominion over the works of thy hands; thou hast put all *things* under his feet: **Psalms 16:8** I have set the LORD always before me: because *he is* at my right hand, I shall not be moved.

	Psalms 110:1 The LORD said unto my Lord, Sit thou at my right hand, until I make thine enemies thy footstool.
	Psalm 110:5 The Lord at thy right hand shall strike through kings in the day of his wrath.
	Zechraiah 3:1 And he shewed me Joshua the high priest standing before the angel of the LORD, and Satan standing at his right hand to resist him.
Matthew 23:2 Saying, The scribes and the Pharisees sit in Moses' seat:	**Nehemiah 8:4-9** And Ezra the scribe stood upon a pulpit of wood, which they had made for the purpose; and beside him stood Mattithiah, and Shema, and Anaiah, and Urijah, and Hilkiah, and Maaseiah, on his right hand; and on his left hand, Pedaiah, and Mishael, and Malchiah, and Hashum, and Hashbadana, Zechariah, *and* Meshullam. 5 And Ezra opened the book in the sight of all the people; (for he was above all the people;) and when he opened it, all the people stood up: 6 And Ezra blessed the LORD, the great God. And all the people answered, Amen, Amen, with lifting up their hands: and they bowed their heads, and worshipped the LORD with *their* faces to the ground. 7 Also Jeshua, and Bani, and Sherebiah, Jamin, Akkub, Shabbethai, Hodijah, Maaseiah, Kelita, Azariah, Jozabad, Hanan, Pelaiah, and the Levites, caused the people to understand the law: and the people *stood* in their place.
	8 So they read in the book in the law of God distinctly, and gave the sense, and caused *them* to understand the reading. 9 And Nehemiah, which *is* the Tirshatha, and Ezra the priest the scribe, and the Levites that taught the people, said unto all the people, This day *is* holy unto the LORD your God; mourn not, nor weep. For all the people wept, when they heard the words of the law.
Matthew 23:3 All therefore whatsoever they bid you observe, *that* observe and do; but do not ye after their works: for they say, and do not.	**Deuteronomy 17:19** And it shall be with him, and he shall read therein all the days of his life: that he may learn to fear the LORD his God, to keep all the words of this law and these statutes, to do them:
Matthew 23:4 For they bind heavy burdens and grievous to be borne, and lay *them* on men's shoulders; but they *themselves* will not move them with one of their fingers.	**Isaiah 10:1** Woe unto them that decree unrighteous decrees, and that write grievousness *which* they have prescribed;
Matthew 23:5 But all their works they do for to be seen of men: they make broad their **phylacteries**, and enlarge the borders of their **garments**,	**Exodus 13:9-10** And it shall be for a sign unto thee upon thine hand, and for a **memorial** between thine eyes, that the LORD'S law may be in thy mouth: for with a strong hand hath the LORD brought thee out of Egypt. 10 Thou shalt therefore keep this ordinance in his season from year to year.
	Exodus 13:16 And it shall be for a token upon thine hand, and for **frontlets** between thine eyes: for by strength of hand the LORD brought us forth out of Egypt.
	Deuteronomy 6:8 And thou shalt bind them for a sign upon thine hand, and they shall be as **frontlets** between thine eyes.
	Deuteronomy 11:18 Therefore shall ye lay up these my words in your heart and in your soul, and bind them for a sign upon your hand, that they may be as **frontlets** between your eyes.
	Deuteronomy 22:12 Thou shalt make thee fringes upon the four

	quarters of thy vesture, wherewith thou coverest *thyself*.
	Numbers 15:38-39 Speak unto the children of Israel, and bid them that they make them **fringes in the borders of their garments** throughout their generations, and that they put upon the fringe of the borders a ribband of blue:
	39 And it shall be unto you for a fringe, that ye may look upon it, and remember all the commandments of the LORD, and do them; and that ye seek not after your own heart and your own eyes, after which ye use to go a whoring:
	Deuteronomy 22:12 Thou shalt make thee fringes upon the four quarters of thy **vesture**, wherewith thou coverest *thyself*.
	Zechariah 8:23 Thus saith the LORD of hosts; In those days *it shall come to pass*, that ten men shall take hold out of all languages of the nations, even shall take hold of the skirt of him that is a Jew, saying, We will go with you: for we have heard *that* God *is* with you.
Matthew 23:6 And love the uppermost rooms at feasts, and the chief seats in the synagogues,	**Deuteronomy 16:16** Three times in a year shall all thy males appear before the LORD thy God in the place which he shall choose; in the feast of unleavened bread, and in the feast of weeks, and in the feast of tabernacles: and they shall not appear before the LORD empty:
Matthew 23:9 And call no *man* your father upon the earth: for one is your Father, which is in heaven.	**Malachi 1:6** A son honoureth *his* father, and a servant his master: if then I *be* a father, where *is* mine honour? and if I *be* a master, where *is* my fear? saith the LORD of hosts unto you, O priests, that despise my name. And ye say, Wherein have we despised thy name?
Matthew 23:12 And whosoever shall exalt himself shall be abased; and he that shall humble himself shall be exalted.	**Job 22:29** When *men* are cast down, then thou shalt say, *There is* lifting up; and he shall save the humble person.
	Proverbs 29:23 A man's pride shall bring him low: but honour shall uphold the humble in spirit.
	Proverbs 15:33 The fear of the LORD *is* the instruction of wisdom; and before honour *is* humility.
Matthew 23:15 Woe unto you, scribes and Pharisees, hypocrites! for ye compass sea and land to make one proselyte, and when he is made, ye make him twofold more the child of **hell** than yourselves.	**See Luke 16:23 "Hell"**
Matthew 23:19 *Ye* fools and blind: for whether *is* greater, the gift, or the altar that sanctifieth the gift?	**Exodus 29:37** Seven days thou shalt make an atonement for the altar, and sanctify it; and it shall be an altar most holy: whatsoever toucheth the altar shall be holy.
	2 Chronicles 6:2 But I have built an house of habitation for thee, and a place for thy dwelling for ever.
Matthew 23:21 And whoso shall swear by the temple, sweareth by it, and by him that dwelleth therein.	**1 Kings 8:13** I have surely built thee an house to dwell in, a settled place for thee to abide in for ever.
Matthew 23:22 And he that shall swear by heaven, sweareth by the throne of God, and by him that sitteth thereon.	**Isaiah 66:1** Thus saith the LORD, The heaven *is* my throne, and the earth *is* my footstool: where *is* the house that ye build unto me? and where *is* the place of my rest?
Matthew 23:23 Woe unto you, scribes	**Genesis 14:20** And blessed be the most high God, which hath

and Pharisees, hypocrites! for ye pay **tithe** of mint and anise and cummin, and have omitted the weightier *matters* of the law, judgment, mercy, and faith: these ought ye to have done, and not to leave the other undone.	delivered thine enemies into thy hand. And he gave him tithes of all. **Genesis 28:22** And this stone, which I have set *for* a pillar, shall be God's house: and of all that thou shalt give me I will surely give the tenth unto thee. **Exodus 22:29** Thou shalt not delay *to offer* the first of thy ripe fruits, and of thy liquors: the firstborn of thy sons shalt thou give unto me. **Leviticus 27:30** And all the tithe of the land, *whether* of the seed of the land, *or* of the fruit of the tree, *is* the LORD'S: *it is* holy unto the LORD. **Numbers 18:21** And, behold, I have given the children of Levi all the tenth in Israel for an inheritance, for their service which they serve, *even* the service of the tabernacle of the congregation. **Deuteronomy 14:22** Thou shalt truly tithe all the increase of thy seed, that the field bringeth forth year by year. **1 Samuel 15:22** And Samuel said, Hath the LORD *as great* delight in burnt offerings and sacrifices, as in obeying the voice of the LORD? Behold, to obey *is* better than sacrifice, *and* to hearken than the fat of rams. **Nehemiah 10:38** And the priest the son of Aaron shall be with the Levites, when the Levites take tithes: and the Levites shall bring up the tithe of the tithes unto the house of our God, to the chambers, into the treasure house. Pro 3:9 Honour the LORD with thy substance, and with the firstfruits of all thine increase: **Hosea 6:6** For I desired mercy, and not sacrifice; and the knowledge of God more than burnt offerings. **Micah 6:8** He hath shewed thee, O man, what *is* good; and what doth the LORD require of thee, but to do justly, and to love mercy, and to walk humbly with thy God? **Malachi 3:8-10** Will a man rob God? Yet ye have robbed me. But ye say, Wherein have we robbed thee? In tithes and offerings. 9 Ye *are* cursed with a curse: for ye have robbed me, *even* this whole nation. 10 Bring ye all the tithes into the storehouse, that there may be meat in mine house, and prove me now herewith, saith the LORD of hosts, if I will not open you the windows of heaven, and pour you out a blessing, that *there shall* not *be room* enough *to receive it*.
Matthew 23:33 *Ye* serpents, *ye* generation of vipers, how can ye escape the damnation of **hell**?	**See Luke 16:23 "Hell"**
Matthew 23:35 That upon you may come all the righteous blood shed upon the earth, from the blood of righteous Abel unto the blood of Zacharias son of Barachias, whom ye slew between the temple and the altar.	**Genesis 4:8** And Cain talked with Abel his brother: and it came to pass, when they were in the field, that Cain rose up against Abel his brother, and slew him. **2 Chronicles 24:20-22** And the Spirit of God came upon Zechariah the son of Jehoiada the priest, which stood above the people, and said unto them, Thus saith God, Why transgress ye the commandments of the LORD, that ye cannot prosper? because ye have forsaken the LORD, he hath also forsaken you. 21 And they conspired against him, and stoned him with stones at the commandment of the king in the court of the house of the LORD.

	22 Thus Joash the king remembered not the kindness which Jehoiada his father had done to him, but slew his son. And when he died, he said, The LORD look upon *it*, and require *it*.
Matthew 23:37 O Jerusalem, Jerusalem, *thou* that killest the prophets, and stonest them which are sent unto thee, how often would I have gathered thy children together, even as a hen gather	**Ruth 2:12** The LORD recompense thy work, and a full reward be given thee of the LORD God of Israel, under whose wings thou art come to trust. **Psalms 17:8** Keep me as the apple of the eye, hide me under the shadow of thy wings, **Psalms 36:7** How excellent [is] thy lovingkindness, O God! therefore the children of men put their trust under the shadow of thy wings. **Psalms 57:1** ... Be merciful unto me: for my soul trusteth in thee: yea, in the shadow of thy wings will I make my refuge, until *these* calamities be overpast. **Psalms 61:4** I will abide in thy tabernacle for ever: I will trust in the covert of thy wings. Selah. **Psalms 63:7** Because thou hast been my help, therefore in the shadow of thy wings will I rejoice. **Psalms 91:4** He shall cover thee with his feathers, and under his wings shalt thou trust: his truth *shall be thy* shield and buckler.
Matthew 23:38 Behold, your house is left unto you desolate.	**Psalms 69:25** Let their habitation be desolate; *and* let none dwell in their tents. **Jeremiah 12:7** I have forsaken mine house, I have left mine heritage; I have given the dearly beloved of my soul into the hand of her enemies. **Jeremiah 22:5** But if ye will not hear these words, I swear by myself, saith the LORD, that this house shall become a desolation.
Matthew 23:39 For I say unto you, Ye shall not see me henceforth, till ye shall say, Blessed *is* he that cometh in the name of the Lord.	**Psalms 118:26** Blessed *be* he that cometh in the name of the LORD: we have blessed you out of the house of the LORD.
Matthew 24:2 And Jesus said unto them, See ye not all these things? verily I say unto you, There shall not be left here one stone upon another, that shall not be thrown down.	**1 Kings 9:7-8** Then will I cut off Israel out of the land which I have given them; and this house, which I have hallowed for my name, will I cast out of my sight; and Israel shall be a proverb and a byword among all people: 8 And at this house, *which* is high, every one that passeth by it shall be astonished, and shall hiss; and they shall say, Why hath the LORD done thus unto this land, and to this house? **Micah 3:12** Therefore shall Zion for your sake be plowed *as* a field, and Jerusalem shall become heaps, and the mountain of the house as the high places of the forest.
Matthew 24:4-5 And Jesus answered and said unto them, Take heed that no man deceive you. 5 For many shall come in my name, saying, I am Christ; and shall deceive many.	**Jeremiah 14:14** Then the LORD said unto me, The prophets prophesy lies in my name: I sent them not, neither have I commanded them, neither spake unto them: they prophesy unto you a false vision and divination, and a thing of nought, and the deceit of their heart. **Jeremiah 23:21** I have not sent these prophets, yet they ran: I have not spoken to them, yet they prophesied. **Jeremiah 23:25** I have heard what the prophets said, that prophesy lies in my name, saying, I have dreamed, I have dreamed.

	Jeremiah 27:14-15 Therefore hearken not unto the words of the prophets that speak unto you, saying, Ye shall not serve the king of Babylon: for they prophesy a lie unto you. 15 For I have not sent them, saith the LORD, yet they prophesy a lie in my name; that I might drive you out, and that ye might perish, ye, and the prophets that prophesy unto you. **Jeremiah 29:8-9** For thus saith the LORD of hosts, the God of Israel; Let not your prophets and your diviners, that *be* in the midst of you, deceive you, neither hearken to your dreams which ye cause to be dreamed. 9 For they prophesy falsely unto you in my name: I have not sent them, saith the LORD.
Matthew 24:7 For nation shall rise against nation, and kingdom against kingdom: and there shall be famines, and pestilences, and earthquakes, in divers places.	**Isaiah 19:2** And I will set the Egyptians against the Egyptians: and they shall fight every one against his brother, and every one against his neighbour; city against city, *and* kingdom against kingdom.
Matthew 24:8 All these are the **beginning of sorrows**.	**Jeremiah 30:7** Alas! for that day is great, so that none is like it: it is even the time of **Jacob's trouble**; but he shall be saved out of it. **Daniel 9:27** And he shall confirm the covenant with many for one week: and in the midst of the week he shall cause the sacrifice and the oblation to cease, and for the **overspreading of abominations** he shall make it desolate, even until the consummation, and that determined shall be poured upon the desolate. **Daniel 11:36** And the king shall do according to his will; and he shall exalt himself, and magnify himself above every god, and shall speak marvelous things against the God of gods, and shall prosper till the **indignation** be accomplished: for that that is determined shall be done. **Daniel 12:1-2** And at that time shall Michael stand up, the great prince which standeth for the children of thy people: and there shall be a time of **trouble**, such as never was since there was a nation *even* to that same time: and **at that time thy people shall be delivered**, every one that shall be found written in the book. 2 And many of them that sleep in the dust of the earth shall awake, some to everlasting life, and some to shame *and* everlasting contempt.
Matthew 24:14 And this gospel of the kingdom shall be preached in all the world for a witness unto all nations; and then shall the end come.	**Daniel 12:4** But thou, O Daniel, shut up the words, and seal the book, even to the time of the end: many shall run to and fro, and knowledge shall be increased.
Matthew 24:15 When ye therefore shall see the **abomination of desolation**, spoken of by Daniel the prophet, stand in the holy place, (whoso readeth, let him understand:)	**Daniel 8:13** Then I heard one saint speaking, and another saint said unto that certain *saint* which spake, How long *shall be* the vision *concerning* the daily *sacrifice,* and the transgression of **desolation**, to give both the sanctuary and the host to be trodden under foot? **Daniel 9:27** And he shall confirm the covenant with many for one week: and in the midst of the week he shall cause the sacrifice and the oblation to cease, and for the overspreading of **abominations** he shall make *it* desolate, even until the consummation, and that determined shall be poured upon the desolate. **Daniel 11:31** And arms shall stand on his part, and they shall pollute the sanctuary of strength, and shall take away the daily *sacrifice,* and they shall place the <u>**abomination** that maketh **desolate**</u>.

	Daniel 12:11 And from the time *that* the daily *sacrifice* shall be taken away, and the **abomination** that maketh **desolate** set up, *there shall be* a thousand two hundred and ninety days.
Matthew 24:20 and pray ye that your flight may not be in winter, nor on a **sabbath**;	**See Colossians 2:16 "Sabbath"**
Matthew 24:21 For then shall be **great tribulation**, such as was not since the beginning of the world to this time, no, nor ever shall be.	**Jeremiah 30:7** Alas! for that day *is* great, so that none *is* like it: it *is* even the time of Jacob's trouble; but he shall be saved out of it. **See Matthew 24:8 "Tribuation"**
Matthew 24:24 For there shall arise false Christs, and false prophets, and shall shew great signs and wonders; insomuch that, if *it were* possible, they shall deceive the very elect.	**Deuteronomy 13:1-3** If there arise among you a prophet, or a dreamer of dreams, and giveth thee a sign or a wonder, **2** And the sign or the wonder come to pass, whereof he spake unto thee, saying, Let us go after other gods, which thou hast not known, and let us serve them; **3** Thou shalt not hearken unto the words of that prophet, or that dreamer of dreams: for the LORD your God proveth you, to know whether ye love the LORD your God with all your heart and with all your soul.
Matthew 24:28 For wheresoever the carcase is, there will the eagles be gathered together.	**Job 39:30** Her young ones also suck up blood: and where the slain *are*, there *is* she.
Matthew 24:29 Immediately after the tribulation of those days shall the sun be darkened, and the moon shall not give her light, and the stars shall fall from heaven, and the powers of the heavens shall be shaken:	**Ezekiel 32:7** And when I shall put thee out, I will cover the heaven, and make the stars thereof dark; I will cover the sun with a cloud, and the moon shall not give her light. **Joel 2:10** The earth shall quake before them; the heavens shall tremble: the sun and the moon shall be dark, and the stars shall withdraw their shining: **Joel 2:31** The sun shall be turned into darkness, and the moon into blood, before the great and the terrible day of the LORD come. **Joel 3:15** The sun and the moon shall be darkened, and the stars shall withdraw their shining.
Matthew 24:30 And then shall appear the sign of the Son of man in heaven: and then shall all the tribes of the earth mourn, and **they shall see the Son of man coming** in the clouds of heaven with power and great glory.	**Psalm 50:3-5** Our God shall come, and shall not keep silence: a fire shall devour before him, and it shall be very tempestuous round about him. 4 He shall call to the heavens from above, and to the earth, that he may judge his people. 5 Gather my saints together unto me; those that have made a covenant with me by sacrifice. **Isaiah 13:9-10** Behold, the **day of the LORD cometh**, cruel both with wrath and fierce anger, to lay the land desolate: and he shall destroy the sinners thereof out of it. 10 For the stars of heaven and the constellations thereof shall not give their light: the sun shall be darkened in his going forth, and the moon shall not cause her light to shine. **See Acts 2:20 "Day of the Lord"** **Daniel 7:13** I saw in the night visions, and, behold, *one* like the Son of man came with the clouds of heaven, and came to the Ancient of days, and they brought him near before him.
	Exodus 19:19-20 And when the voice of the **trumpet** sounded long, and waxed louder and louder, Moses spake, and God answered him by a voice. 20 And the LORD came down upon mount Sinai, on the top of the mount: and the LORD called Moses *up* to the top of the mount; and **Moses went up**. **Leviticus 23:24-25** Speak unto the children of Israel, saying, In

Matthew 24:31 And he shall send his angels with a great sound of a trumpet, and they shall gather together his elect from the four winds, from one end of heaven to the other. .	the seventh month, in the first *day* of the month, shall ye have a sabbath, a memorial of blowing of trumpets, an holy convocation. 25 Ye shall do no servile work *therein*: but ye shall offer an offering made by fire unto the LORD. **Leviticus 23:24** Speak unto the children of Israel, saying, In the seventh month, in the first *day* of the month, shall ye have a sabbath, a memorial of blowing of trumpets, an holy convocation. **Numbers 10:9** And if ye go to war in your land against the enemy that oppresseth you, then ye shall blow an alarm with the trumpets; and ye shall be remembered before the LORD your God, and ye shall be saved from your enemies. **Numbers 29:1** And in the seventh month, on the first *day* of the month, ye shall have an holy convocation; ye shall do no servile work: it is a day of blowing the trumpets unto you. **2 Kings 2:11** And it came to pass, as they still went on, and talked, that, behold, there appeared a chariot of fire, and horses of fire, and parted them both asunder; and **Elijah went up** by a whirlwind into heaven. **Psalms 50:5** Gather my saints together unto me; those that have made a covenant with me by sacrifice. **Isaiah 11:12** And he shall set up an ensign for the nations, and shall assemble the outcasts of Israel, and gather together the dispersed of Judah from the four corners of the earth. **Isaiah 26:19** Thy dead *men* shall live, *together with* my dead body shall they arise. Awake and sing, ye that dwell in dust: for thy dew *is as* the dew of herbs, and the earth shall cast out the dead. **Isaiah 27:13** And it shall come to pass in that day, *that* the great trumpet shall be blown, and they shall come which were ready to perish in the land of Assyria, and the outcasts in the land of Egypt, and shall worship the LORD in the holy mount at Jerusalem. **Jerermiah 49:36** And upon Elam will I bring the four winds from the four quarters of heaven, and will scatter them toward all those winds; and there shall be no nation whither the outcasts of Elam shall not come. **Ezekiel 7:2** Also, thou son of man, thus saith the Lord GOD unto the land of Israel; An end, the end is come upon the four corners of the land. **Ezekiel 37:9** Then said he unto me, Prophesy unto the wind, prophesy, son of man, and say to the wind, Thus saith the Lord GOD; Come from the four winds, O breath, and breathe upon these slain, that they may live. **Daniel 7:2** Daniel spake and said, I saw in my vision by night, and, behold, the four winds of the heaven strove upon the great sea. **Daniel 8:8** Therefore the he goat waxed very great: and when he was strong, the great horn was broken; and for it came up four notable ones toward the four winds of heaven. **Daniel 11:4** And when he shall stand up, his kingdom shall be broken, and shall be divided toward the four winds of heaven; and not to his posterity, nor according to his dominion which he ruled: for his kingdom shall be plucked up, even for others beside those. **Daniel 12:1-2** And at that time shall Michael stand up, the great prince which standeth for the children of thy people: and there

	shall be a time of trouble, such as never was since there was a nation *even* to that same time: and at that time thy people shall be delivered, every one that shall be found written in the book. 2 And many of them that sleep in the dust of the earth shall awake, some to everlasting life, and some to shame *and* everlasting contempt. **Zechariah 2:6** Ho, ho, *come forth,* and flee from the land of the north, saith the LORD: for I have spread you abroad as the four winds of the heaven, saith the LORD.
Matthew 24:35 Heaven and earth shall pass away, but my words shall not pass away.	**Psalm 119:89** LAMED. For ever, O LORD, thy word is settled in heaven. **Isaiah 40:8** The grass withereth, the flower fadeth: but the word of our God shall stand for ever. **See Matt Isaiah 30:8** Now go, **write it before them in a table, and note it in a book,** that it may be **for the time to come for ever and ever**: **Isaiah 40:8** The grass withereth, the flower fadeth: but the **Word of our God shall stand for ever**. **Isaiah 59:21** As for me, this is my covenant with them, saith the Lord; My spirit that is upon thee, and **my words** which I have put in thy mouth, **shall not depart out of thy mouth**, nor out of the mouth of thy seed, nor out of the mouth of thy seed's seed, saith the Lord, from **henceforth and for ever**. **See Matthew 5:18 "Scripture"**
Matthew 24:37 But as the days of Noe *were,* so shall also the coming of the Son of man be.	**Genesis 6:5** And GOD saw that the wickedness of man *was* great in the earth, and *that* every imagination of the thoughts of his heart *was* only evil continually. **Genesis 6:9-12** These *are* the generations of Noah: Noah was a just man *and* **perfect in his generations**, *and* Noah walked with God. 10 And Noah begat three sons, Shem, Ham, and Japheth. 11 The earth also was corrupt before God, and the earth was filled with violence. 12 And God looked upon the earth, and, behold, it was corrupt; **for all flesh had corrupted his way upon the earth**.
Matthew 24:38 For as in the days that were before the flood they were eating and drinking, marrying and giving in marriage, until the day that Noe entered into the ark,	**Genesis 6:3** And the LORD said, My spirit shall not always strive with man, for that he also *is* flesh: yet his days shall be an hundred and twenty years. **Genesis 6:5** And GOD saw that the wickedness of man *was* great in the earth, and *that* every imagination of the thoughts of his heart *was* only evil continually. **Genesis 6:14-16** Make thee an ark of gopher wood; rooms shalt thou make in the ark, and shalt pitch it within and without with pitch. 15 And this *is the fashion* which thou shalt make it *of:* The length of the ark *shall be* three hundred cubits, the breadth of it fifty cubits, and the height of it thirty cubits. 16 A window shalt thou make to the ark, and in a cubit shalt thou finish it above; and the door of the ark shalt thou set in the side thereof; *with* lower, second, and third *stories* shalt thou make it. **Genesis 7:7** And Noah went in, and his sons, and his wife, and his sons' wives with him, into the ark, because of the waters of the flood. **Genesis 7:22** All in whose **nostrils** *was* the breath of life, of all that *was* in the dry *land,* died.
Matthew 24:39 And knew not until the	See verse above

flood came, and took them all away; so shall also the coming of the Son of man be.	
Matthew 25:21 His lord said unto him, Well done, *thou* good and faithful servant: thou hast been faithful over a few things, I will make thee ruler over many things: enter thou into the joy of thy lord.	**Genesis 2:15** And the LORD God took the man, and put him into the garden of Eden **to dress it and to keep it**. **Deuteronomy 8:18** But thou shalt remember the LORD thy God: for *it is* he that giveth thee power to get wealth, that he may establish his covenant which he sware unto thy fathers, as *it is* this day. **Haggai 2:8** The silver *is* mine, and the gold *is* mine, saith the LORD of hosts.
Matthew 25:27 Thou oughtest therefore to have put my money to the exchangers, and *then* at my coming I should have received mine own with usury.	**Deuteronomy 23:19-20** Thou shalt not lend upon usury to thy brother; usury of money, usury of victuals, usury of any thing that is lent upon usury: 20 **Unto a stranger thou mayest lend upon usury**; but unto thy brother thou shalt not lend upon usury: that the LORD thy God may bless thee in all that thou settest thine hand to in the land whither thou goest to possess it.
Matthew 25:30 And cast ye the unprofitable servant into **outer darkness**: there shall be weeping and gnashing of teeth	**See Luke 16:23 "Hell"**
Matthew 25:32 And before him shall be gathered all nations: and he shall separate them one from another, as a shepherd divideth *his* sheep from the goats:	**Ezekiel 34:17** And *as for* you, O my flock, thus saith the Lord GOD; Behold, I judge between cattle and cattle, between the rams and the he goats. **Ezekiel 34:20** Therefore thus saith the Lord GOD unto them; Behold, I, *even* I, will judge between the fat cattle and between the lean cattle.
Matthew 25:35 For I was an hungred, and ye gave me meat: I was thirsty, and ye gave me drink: I was a stranger, and ye took me in:	**Deuteronomy 15:7** If there be among you a poor man of one of thy brethren within any of thy gates in thy land which the LORD thy God giveth thee, thou shalt not harden thine heart, nor shut thine hand from thy poor brother: **Isaiah 58:7** *Is it* not to deal thy bread to the hungry, and that thou bring the poor that are cast out to thy house? when thou seest the naked, that thou cover him; and that thou hide not thyself from thine own flesh? **Ezekiel 18:7** And hath not oppressed any, *but* hath restored to the debtor his pledge, hath spoiled none by violence, hath given his bread to the hungry, and hath covered the naked with a garment; **Ezekiel 18:16** Neither hath oppressed any, hath not withholden the pledge, neither hath spoiled by violence, *but* hath given his bread to the hungry, and hath covered the naked with a garment,
Matthew 25:36 Naked, and ye clothed me: I was sick, and ye visited me: I was in prison, and ye came unto me.	**Isaiah 58:7** *Is it* not to deal thy bread to the hungry, and that thou bring the poor that are cast out to thy house? when thou seest the naked, that thou cover him; and that thou hide not thyself from thine own flesh?
Matthew 25:40 And the King shall answer and say unto them, Verily I say unto you, Inasmuch as ye have done *it* unto one of the least of these my brethren, ye have done *it* unto me.	**Proverbs 19:17** He that hath pity upon the poor lendeth unto the LORD; and that which he hath given will he pay him again.
Matthew 25:41 Then shall he say also	**Psalms 6:8** Depart from me, all ye workers of iniquity; for the

unto them on the left hand, Depart from me, ye cursed, into **everlasting fire**, prepared for the **devil** and his **angels**:	LORD hath heard the voice of my weeping. See Luke 16:23 "Hell" See Hebrews 13:2 "Good and bad angels" See Matthew 4:10 "satan"
Matthew 25:46 And these shall go away into everlasting punishment: but the righteous into life eternal.	**Isaiah 33:14** The sinners in Zion are afraid; fearfulness hath surprised the hypocrites. Who among us shall dwell with the devouring fire? who among us shall dwell with everlasting burnings? **Isaiah 38:18** For the grave cannot praise thee, death can *not* celebrate thee: they that go down into the pit cannot hope for thy truth. **Daniel 12:2** And many of them that sleep in the dust of the earth shall awake, some to everlasting life, and some to shame *and* everlasting contempt.
Matthew 26:3 Then assembled together the chief priests, and the scribes, and the **elders** of the people, unto the palace of the high priest, who was called Caiaphas,	**Psalms 2:2** The kings of the earth set themselves, and the rulers take counsel together, against the LORD, and against his anointed, *saying*, See 1 Peter 5:1 "Elders"
Matthew 26:11 For ye have the poor always with you; but me ye have not always.	**Deuteronomy 15:11** For the poor shall never cease out of the land: therefore I command thee, saying, Thou shalt open thine hand wide unto thy brother, to thy poor, and to thy needy, in thy land.
Matthew 26:15 And said *unto them,* What will ye give me, and I will deliver him unto you? And they covenanted with him for thirty pieces of silver.	**Genesis 37:28** Then there passed by Midianites merchantmen; and they drew and lifted up Joseph out of the pit, and sold Joseph to the Ishmeelites for twenty *pieces* of silver: and they brought Joseph into Egypt. **Zechariah 11:12-13** And I said unto them, If ye think good, give me my price; and if not, forbear. So they weighed for my price thirty *pieces* of silver. 13 And the LORD said unto me, Cast it unto the potter: a goodly price that I was prised at of them. And I took the thirty *pieces* of silver, and cast them to the potter in the house of the LORD.
Matthew 26:17 Now the first *day* of the *feast of* unleavened bread the disciples came to Jesus, saying unto him, Where wilt thou that we prepare for thee to eat the passover?	**Exodus 12:17** And ye shall observe *the feast of* unleavened bread; for in this selfsame day have I brought your armies out of the land of Egypt: therefore shall ye observe this day in your generations by an ordinance for ever.
Matthew 26:18 And he said, Go into the city to such a man, and say unto him, The Master saith, My time is at hand; I will keep the passover at thy house with my disciples.	**Leviticus 23:5-6** In the fourteenth *day* of the first month at even *is* the LORD's passover. 6 And on the fifteenth day of the same month *is* the feast of unleavened bread unto the LORD: seven days ye must eat unleavened bread.
Matthew 26:23 And he answered and said, He that dippeth *his* hand with me in the dish, the same shall betray me.	**Psalms 41:9** Yea, mine own familiar friend, in whom I trusted, which did eat of my bread, hath lifted up *his* heel against me.
Matthew 26:24 The Son of man goeth as it is written of him: but woe unto that man by whom the Son of man is betrayed! it had been good for that man if he had not been born.	**Psalms 109:6-19** Set thou a wicked man over him: and let Satan stand at his right hand. 7 When he shall be judged, let him be condemned: and let his prayer become sin. 8 Let his days be few; and let another take his office. 9 Let his children be fatherless, and his wife a widow. 10 Let his children be continually vagabonds, and beg: let them seek their bread also out of their desolate places.

	11 Let the extortioner catch all that he hath; and let the strangers spoil his labour. 12 Let there be none to extend mercy unto him: neither let there be any to favour his fatherless children. 13 Let his posterity be cut off; and in the generation following let their name be blotted out. 14 Let the iniquity of his fathers be remembered with the LORD; and let not the sin of his mother be blotted out. 15 Let them be before the LORD continually, that he may cut off the memory of them from the earth. 16 Because that he remembered not to shew mercy, but persecuted the poor and needy man, that he might even slay the broken in heart. 17 As he loved cursing, so let it come unto him: as he delighted not in blessing, so let it be far from him. 18 As he clothed himself with cursing like as with his garment, so let it come into his bowels like water, and like oil into his bones. 19 Let it be unto him as the garment which covereth him, and for a girdle wherewith he is girded continually.
Matthew 26:28 For this is my blood of the new testament, which is shed for many for the remission of sins.	**Exodus 12:7** And they shall take of the blood, and strike *it* on the two side posts and on the upper door post of the houses, wherein they shall eat it. **Exodus 12:13** And the blood shall be to you for a token upon the houses where ye *are:* and when I see the blood, I will pass over you, and the plague shall not be upon you to destroy *you,* when I smite the land of Egypt. **Exodus 12:22** And ye shall take a bunch of hyssop, and dip *it* in the blood that *is* in the bason, and strike the lintel and the two side posts with the blood that *is* in the bason; and none of you shall go out at the door of his house until the morning. **Exodus 24:6-8** And Moses took half of the blood, and put *it* in basons; and half of the blood he sprinkled on the altar. 7 And he took the book of the covenant, and read in the audience of the people: and they said, All that the LORD hath said will we do, and be obedient. 8 And Moses took the blood, and sprinkled *it* on the people, and said, Behold the blood of the covenant, which the LORD hath made with you concerning all these words. **Exodus 25:17** And thou shalt make a mercy seat *of* pure gold: two cubits and a half *shall be* the length thereof, and a cubit and a half the breadth thereof. **Exodus 30:10** And Aaron shall make an atonement upon the horns of it once in a year with the blood of the sin offering of atonements: once in the year shall he make atonement upon it throughout your generations: it *is* most holy unto the LORD. **Leviticus 5:9** And he shall sprinkle of the blood of the sin offering upon the side of the altar; and the rest of the blood shall be wrung out at the bottom of the altar: it *is* a sin offering. **Leviticus 17:11** For the life of the flesh is in the blood: and I have given it to you upon the altar to make an atonement for your souls: **for it is the blood that maketh an atonement for the soul**. **Leviticus 16:1-34** **Leviticus 17:11** For the life of the flesh is in the blood: and I have given it to you upon the altar to make an atonement for your souls: **for it is the blood that maketh an atonement for the soul**. **Leviticus 23:27-28** Also on the tenth *day* of this seventh month *there shall be* a **day of atonement**: it shall be an holy convocation unto you; and ye shall afflict your souls, and offer an offering made by fire unto the LORD. And ye shall do no work in that

	same day: for it *is* a **day of atonement**, to make an atonement for you before the LORD your God.

Leviticus 25:9 Then shalt thou cause the trumpet of the jubile to sound on the tenth [day] of the seventh month, in the **day of atonement** shall ye make the trumpet sound throughout all your land.

Psalms 14:7 Oh that the salvation of Israel *were come* out of Zion! when the LORD bringeth back the captivity of his people, Jacob shall rejoice, *and* Israel shall be glad.

Isaiah 27:9 By this therefore shall the iniquity of Jacob be purged; and this *is* all the fruit to take away his sin; when he maketh all the stones of the altar as chalkstones that are beaten in sunder, the groves and images shall not stand up.

Isaiah 53:4-5 Surely he hath borne our griefs, and carried our sorrows: yet we did esteem him stricken, smitten of God, and afflicted. 5 But he *was* wounded for our transgressions, *he was* bruised for our iniquities: the chastisement of our peace *was* upon him; and with his stripes we are healed.

Isaiah 59:20-21 And the Redeemer shall come to Zion, and unto them that turn from transgression in Jacob, saith the LORD. 21 As for me, this *is* my covenant with them, saith the LORD; My spirit that *is* upon thee, and my words which I have put in thy mouth, shall not depart out of thy mouth, nor out of the mouth of thy seed, nor out of the mouth of thy seed's seed, saith the LORD, from henceforth and for ever.

Jeremiah 31:31-33 Behold, the days come, saith the LORD, that **I will make a new covenant with the house of Israel**, and with the house of Judah: 32 Not according to the covenant that I made with their fathers in the day *that* I took them by the hand to bring them out of the land of Egypt; which my covenant they brake, although I was an husband unto them, saith the LORD: 33 But this *shall be* the covenant that I will make with the house of Israel; After those days, saith the LORD, I will put my law in their inward parts, and write it in their hearts; and will be their God, and they shall be my people. 34 And they shall teach no more every man his neighbour, and every man his brother, saying, Know the LORD: for they shall all know me, from the least of them unto the greatest of them, saith the LORD: for I will forgive their iniquity, and I will remember their sin no more.

Daniel 9:24 Seventy weeks are determined upon thy people and upon thy holy city, to finish the transgression, and to make an end of sins, and **to make reconciliation for iniquity**, and to bring in everlasting righteousness, and to seal up the vision and prophecy, and to anoint the most Holy.

Zechariah 9:11 As for thee also, **by the blood of thy covenant** I have sent forth thy prisoners out of the pit wherein *is* no water. |
| **Matthew 26:30** And when they had sung an hymn, they went out into the mount of Olives. | **See Colossians 3:16 "Music"** |
| **Matthew 26:31** Then saith Jesus unto them, All ye shall be offended because of me this night: for it is written, I will smite the shepherd, and the sheep of the flock shall be scattered abroad. | **Zechariah 13:7** Awake, O sword, against my shepherd, and against the man *that is* my fellow, saith the LORD of hosts: smite the shepherd, and the sheep shall be scattered: and I will turn mine hand upon the little ones. |

Matthew 26:38 Then saith he unto them, My **soul** is exceeding sorrowful, even unto death: tarry ye here, and watch with me.	**Psalms 69:20** Reproach hath broken my heart; and I am full of heaviness: and I looked *for some* to take pity, but *there was* none; and for comforters, but I found none. **See 1 Thessalonians 5:23 "Body, soul, and spirit"**
Matthew 26:47 And while he yet spake, lo, Judas, one of the twelve, came, and with him a great multitude with swords and staves, from the chief priests and **elders** of the people.	**See 1 Peter 5:1 "Elders"**
Matthew 26:52 Then said Jesus unto him, Put up again thy sword into his place: for all they that take the sword shall perish with the sword.	**Genesis 9:6** Whoso sheddeth man's blood, by man shall his blood be shed: for in the image of God made he man.
Matthew 26:57 And they that had laid hold on Jesus led *him* away to Caiaphas the high priest, where the scribes and the **elders** were assembled.	**See 1 Peter 5:1 "Elders"**
Matthew 26:59 Now the chief priests, and **elders**, and all the council, sought false witness against Jesus, to put him to death;	**Psalms 35:11** False witnesses did rise up; they laid to my charge *things* that I knew not. **See 1 Peter 5:1 "Elders"**
Matthew 26:56 But all this was done, that the scriptures of the prophets might be fulfilled. Then all the disciples forsook him, and fled.	**Zechariah 13:7** Awake, O sword, against my shepherd, and against the man *that is* my fellow, saith the LORD of hosts: smite the shepherd, and the sheep shall be scattered: and I will turn mine hand upon the little ones.
Matthew 26:60 But found none: yea, though many false witnesses came, *yet* found they none. At the last came two false witnesses,	**Exodus 20:16** Thou shalt not bear false witness against thy neighbour. **Leviticus 19:16** Thou shalt not go up and down *as* a talebearer among thy people: neither shalt thou stand against the blood of thy neighbour: I *am* the LORD. **Deutreonomy 5:20** Neither shalt thou bear false witness against thy neighbour. **Psalms 15:3** *He that* backbiteth not with his tongue, nor doeth evil to his neighbour, nor taketh up a reproach against his neighbour. **Psalms 35:11** False witnesses did rise up; they laid to my charge *things* that I knew not.
Matthew 26:63 But Jesus held his peace. And the high priest answered and said unto him, I adjure thee by the living God, that thou tell us whether thou be the Christ, the Son of God.	**Isaiah 53:7** He was oppressed, and he was afflicted, yet he opened not his mouth: he is brought as a lamb to the slaughter, and as a sheep before her shearers is dumb, so he openeth not his mouth.
Matthew 26:64 Jesus saith unto him, Thou hast said: nevertheless I say unto you, Hereafter shall ye see the Son of man sitting on the right hand of power, and coming in the clouds of heaven.	**Psalms 8:6** Thou madest him to have dominion over the works of thy hands; thou hast put all *things* under his feet: **Psalms 16:8** I have set the LORD always before me: because *he is* at my right hand, I shall not be moved. **Psalms 110:1** The LORD said unto my Lord, Sit thou at my right hand, until I make thine enemies thy footstool. **Psalm 110:5** The Lord at thy right hand shall strike through kings in the day of his wrath. **Daniel 7:13** I saw in the night visions, and, behold, *one* like the Son of man came with the clouds of heaven, and came to the

	Ancient of days, and they brought him near before him. **Zechraiah 3:1** And he shewed me Joshua the high priest standing before the angel of the LORD, and Satan standing at his right hand to resist him.
Matthew 26:66 What think ye? They answered and said, He is guilty of death.	**Leviticus 24:16** And he that blasphemeth the name of the LORD, he shall surely be put to death, *and* all the congregation shall certainly stone him: as well the stranger, as he that is born in the land, when he blasphemeth the name *of the LORD*, shall be put to death.
Matthew 26:67 Then did they spit in his face, and buffeted him; and others smote *him* with the palms of their hands,	**Job 16:10** They have gaped upon me with their mouth; they have smitten me upon the cheek reproachfully; they have gathered themselves together against me. **Isaiah 50:6** I gave my back to the smiters, and my cheeks to them that plucked off the hair: I hid not my face from shame and spitting.
Matthew 27:1 When the morning was come, all the chief priests and **elders** of the people took counsel against Jesus to put him to death:	**Psalms 2:2** The kings of the earth set themselves, and the rulers take counsel together, against the LORD, and against his anointed, *saying*, **See 1 Peter 5:1 "Elders"**
Matthew 27:3 Then Judas, which had betrayed him, when he saw that he was condemned, repented himself, and brought again the thirty pieces of silver to the chief priests and **elders**,	**See 1 Peter 5:1 "Elders"**
Matthew 27:9-10 Then was fulfilled that which was spoken by Jeremy the prophet, saying, And they took the thirty pieces of silver, the price of him that was valued, whom they of the children of Israel did value; And gave them for the potter's field, as the Lord appointed me. 10 And gave them for the potter's field, as the Lord appointed me.	**Zechariah 11:12-13** And I said unto them, If ye think good, give *me* my price; and if not, forbear. So they weighed for my price thirty *pieces* of silver. And the LORD said unto me, Cast it unto the potter: a goodly price that I was prised at of them. And I took the thirty *pieces* of silver, and cast them to the potter in the house of the LORD. 13 And the LORD said to me, Cast it to the potter: a goodly price that I was priced at of them. And I took the thirty pieces of silver, and cast them to the potter in the house of the LORD.
Matthew 27:12 And when he was accused of the chief priests and **elders**, he answered nothing.	**See 1 Peter 5:1 "Elders"**
Matthew 27:14 And he answered him to never a word; insomuch that the governor marvelled greatly.	**Isaiah 53:7** He was oppressed, and he was afflicted, yet he opened not his mouth: he is brought as a lamb to the slaughter, and as a sheep before her shearers is dumb, so he openeth not his mouth.
Mathew 27:20 But the chief priests and **elders** persuaded the multitude that they should ask Barabbas, and destroy Jesus.	**See 1 Peter 5:1 "Elders"**
Matthew 27:26 Then released he Barabbas unto them: and when he had scourged Jesus, he delivered *him* to be crucified.	**Psalms 129:3** The plowers plowed upon my back: they made long their furrows. **Isaiah 50:5-6** The Lord GOD hath opened mine ear, and I was not rebellious, neither turned away back. 6 I gave my back to the smiters, and my cheeks to them that plucked off the hair: I hid not my face from shame and spitting.
Matthew 27:30 And they spit upon him, and took the reed, and smote him on the head.	**Micah 5:1** Now gather thyself in troops, O daughter of troops: he hath laid siege against us: they shall smite the judge of Israel with a rod upon the cheek.

Matthew 27:34 They gave him vinegar to drink mingled with gall: and when he had tasted *thereof*, he would not drink.	**Psalms 69:21** They gave me also gall for my meat; and in my thirst they gave me vinegar to drink.
Matthew 27:35 And they crucified him, and parted his garments, casting lots: that it might be fulfilled which was spoken by the prophet, They parted my garments among them, and upon my vesture did they cast lots.	**Psalms 22:16-18** For dogs have compassed me: the assembly of the wicked have inclosed me: they pierced my hands and my feet. 17 I may tell all my bones: they look and stare upon me. 18 They part my garments among them, and cast lots upon my vesture. **Zechariah 12:10** And I will pour upon the house of David, and upon the inhabitants of Jerusalem, the spirit of grace and of supplications: and they shall look upon me whom they have pierced, and they shall mourn for him, as one mourneth for his only *son*, and shall be in bitterness for him, as one that is in bitterness for his firstborn.
Matthew 27:38 Then were there two thieves crucified with him, one on the right hand, and another on the left.	**Isaiah 53:12** Therefore will I divide him *a portion* with the great, and he shall divide the spoil with the strong; because he hath poured out his soul unto death: and he was numbered with the transgressors; and he bare the sin of many, and made intercession for the transgressors.
Matthew 27:39 And they that passed by reviled him, wagging their heads,	**Psalms 22:7-8** All they that see me laugh me to scorn: they shoot out the lip, they shake the head, *saying*, 8 He trusted on the LORD *that* he would deliver him: let him deliver him, seeing he delighted in him. **Psalms 69:20** Reproach hath broken my heart; and I am full of heaviness: and I looked *for some* to take pity, but *there was* none; and for comforters, but I found none. **Psalms 109:25** I became also a reproach unto them: *when* they looked upon me they shaked their heads.
Matthew 27:41 Likewise also the chief priests mocking *him*, with the scribes and **elders**, said,	**See 1 Peter 5:1 "Elders"**
Matthew 27:43 He trusted in God; let him deliver him now, if he will have him: for he said, I am the Son of God.	**Psalms 22:7-9** All they that see me laugh me to scorn: they shoot out the lip, they shake the head, saying, 8 He trusted on the LORD that he would deliver him: let him deliver him, seeing he delighted in him. 9 But thou art he that took me out of the womb: thou didst make me hope when I was upon my mother's breasts.
Matthew 27:45 Now from the sixth hour there was darkness over all the land unto the ninth hour.	**Amos 8:9** And it shall come to pass in that day, saith the Lord GOD, that I will cause the sun to go down at noon, and I will darken the earth in the clear day:
Matthew 27:46 And about the ninth hour Jesus cried with a loud voice, saying, Eli, Eli, lama sabachthani? that is to say, My God, my God, why hast thou forsaken me?	**Psalms 22:1** My God, my God, why hast thou forsaken me? *why art thou so* far from helping me, *and from* the words of my roaring?
Matthew 27:48 And straightway one of them ran, and took a spunge, and filled *it* with vinegar, and put *it* on a reed, and gave him to drink.	**Psalms 69:3** I am weary of my crying: my throat is dried: mine eyes fail while I wait for my God. **Psalms 69:21** They gave me also gall for my meat; and in my thirst they gave me vinegar to drink.
Matthew 27:51 And, behold, the veil of the temple was rent in twain from the top to the bottom; and the earth did quake, and the rocks rent;	**2 Chronicles 3:14** And he made the vail *of* blue, and purple, and crimson, and fine linen, and wrought cherubims thereon.
Matthew 27:55-56 And many women	**Psalms 38:10-11** My heart panteth, my strength faileth me: as for

were there beholding afar off, which followed Jesus from Galilee, ministering unto him: 56 Among which was Mary Magdalene, and Mary the mother of James and Joses, and the mother of Zebedee's children.	the light of mine eyes, it also is gone from me. 11 My lovers and my friends stand aloof from my sore; and my kinsmen stand afar off.
Matthew 27:57 When the even was come, there came a rich man of Arimathaea, named Joseph, who also himself was Jesus' disciple:	**Isaiah 53:9** And he made his grave with the wicked, and with the rich in his death; because he had done no violence, neither *was any* deceit in his mouth.
Matthew 27:58 He went to Pilate, and begged the body of Jesus. Then Pilate commanded the **body** to be delivered.	**See 1 Thessalonians 5:23 "Body, soul, and spirit"**
Matthew 27:63 Saying, Sir, we remember that that deceiver said, while he was yet alive, **After three days I will rise again**.	**Jonah 1:17** Now the LORD had prepared a great fish to swallow up Jonah. And Jonah was in the belly of the fish **three days and three nights**. **Jonah 2:1** Then Jonah prayed unto the LORD his God out of the fish's belly,
Matthew 28:1 And on the eve of the sabbaths, at the dawn, toward the first of the sabbaths, came Mary the Magdalene, and the other Mary, to see the sepulchre,	**See Colossians 2:16 "Sabbath"**
Matthew 28:3 His countenance was like lightning, and his raiment white as snow:	**Daniel 7:9** I beheld till the thrones were cast down, and the Ancient of days did sit, whose garment *was* white as snow, and the hair of his head like the pure wool: his throne *was like* the fiery flame, *and* his wheels *as* burning fire.
Matthew 28:6 He is not here: for he is risen, as he said. Come, see the place where the Lord lay.	**Psalms 16:10-11** For thou wilt not leave my soul in hell; neither wilt thou suffer thine Holy One to see corruption. 11 Thou wilt shew me the path of life: in thy presence is fulness of joy; at thy right hand *there* are pleasures for evermore. **Psalms 49:15** But God will redeem my soul from the power of the grave: for he shall receive me. Selah.
Matthew 28:9 And as they went to tell his disciples, behold, Jesus met them, saying, All hail. And they came and held him by the feet, and worshipped him.	**Psalms 97:7** Confounded be all they that serve graven images, that boast themselves of idols: worship him, all *ye* gods
Mathew 28:12 And when they were assembled with the **elders**, and had taken counsel, they gave large money unto the soldiers,	**See 1 Peter 5:1 "Elders"**
Matthew 28:18 And Jesus came and spake unto them, saying, All power is given unto me in heaven and in earth.	**Genesis 41:40** Thou shalt be over my house, and according unto thy word shall all my people be ruled: only in the throne will I be greater than thou. **Daniel 7:14** And there was given him dominion, and glory, and a kingdom, that all people, nations, and languages, should serve him: his dominion *is* an everlasting dominion, which shall not pass away, and his kingdom *that* which shall not be destroyed. **See 1 Timothy 2:5 "God"**
Matthew 28:20 Teaching them to observe all things whatsoever I have	**Psalms 139:7-8** Whither shall I go from thy spirit? or whither shall I flee from thy presence? 8 If I ascend up into heaven, **thou *art***

commanded you: and, lo, I am with you alway, *even* unto the end of the world. Amen.	**there**: if I make my bed in hell, **behold, thou *art there***. **Proverbs 15:3** The eyes of the LORD *are* in **every place**, beholding the evil and the good.
Mark 1:1 The beginning of the gospel of Jesus Christ, the Son of God;	**Psalms 2:7** I will declare the decree: the LORD hath said unto me, Thou *art* my **Son**; this day have I begotten thee. **Psalms 2:12** Kiss the **Son**, lest he be angry, and ye perish *from* the way, when his wrath is kindled but a little. Blessed *are* all they that put their trust in him. **Isaiah 7:14** Therefore the Lord himself shall give you a sign; Behold, a virgin shall conceive, and bear a **son**, and shall call his name Immanuel. **Isaiah 9:6** For unto us a child is born, unto us a son is given: and the government shall be upon his shoulder: and his name shall be called Wonderful, Counselor, The mighty God, The everlasting Father, The Prince of Peace. **Micah 5:2** But thou, Bethlehem Ephratah, though thou be little among the thousands of Judah, yet out of thee shall he come forth unto me that is to be ruler in Israel; whose goings forth have been from of old, from everlasting.
Mark 1:2 As it is written in the prophets, Behold, I send my messenger before thy face, which shall prepare thy way before thee.	**Exodus 23:20** Behold, I send an Angel before thee, to keep thee in the way, and to bring thee into the place which I have prepared. **Malachi 3:1** Behold, I will send my messenger, and he shall prepare the way before me:
Mark 1:3 The voice of one crying in the wilderness, Prepare ye the way of the Lord, make his paths straight.	**Isaiah 40:3-5** The voice of him that crieth in the wilderness, Prepare ye the way of the Lord, make straight in the desert a highway for our God. 4 Every valley shall be exalted, and every mountain and hill shall be made low: and the crooked shall be made straight, and the rough places plain: 5 And the glory of the LORD shall be revealed, and all flesh shall see [it] together: for the mouth of the LORD hath spoken *it*.
Mark 1:4 John did baptize in the wilderness, and preach the baptism of repentance for the remission of sins.	**See Acts 2:38 "Salvation"**
Mark 1:6 And John was clothed with camel's hair, and with a girdle of a skin about his loins; and he did eat locusts and wild honey;	**2 Kings 1:8** And they answered him, *He was* an hairy man, and girt with a girdle of leather about his loins. And he said, It *is* Elijah the Tishbite. **Leviticus 11:22** *Even* these of them ye may eat; the locust after his kind, and the bald locust after his kind, and the beetle after his kind, and the grasshopper after his kind.
Mark 1:8 I indeed have baptized you with water: but he shall baptize you with the Holy Ghost.	**Isaiah 44:3** For I will pour water upon him that is thirsty, and floods upon the dry ground: I will pour my spirit upon thy seed, and my blessing upon thine offspring: **Joel 2:28** And it shall come to pass afterward, *that* I will pour out my spirit upon all flesh; and your sons and your daughters shall prophesy, your old men shall dream dreams, your young men shall see visions:
Mark 1:11 And there came a voice from heaven, *saying,* Thou art my beloved Son, in whom I am well pleased.	**Genesis 22:2** And he said, Take now thy son, thine only *son* Isaac, whom thou lovest, and get thee into the land of Moriah; and offer him there for a burnt offering upon one of the mountains which I will tell thee of. **Psalm 2:7** I will declare the decree: the LORD hath said unto me,

	Thou *art* my Son; this day have I begotten thee. **Isaiah 42:1** Behold my servant, whom I uphold; mine elect, *in whom* my soul delighteth; I have put my spirit upon him: he shall bring forth judgment to the Gentiles.
Mark 1:13 And he was there in the wilderness forty days, tempted of **Satan**; and was with the wild beasts; and the angels ministered unto him.	**Genesis 3:4** And the **serpent** said unto the woman, Ye shall not surely die: **Zechariah 3:1-2** And he shewed me Joshua the high priest standing before the angel of the LORD, and **Satan** standing at his right hand to resist him. 2 And the LORD said unto **Satan,** The LORD rebuke thee, O **Satan**; even the LORD that hath chosen Jerusalem rebuke thee: *is* not this a brand plucked out of the fire? **See Matthew 4:10 "satan"**
Mark 1:15 And saying, The time is fulfilled, and the kingdom of God is at hand: repent ye, and believe the gospel.	**Isaiah 56:1** Thus saith the LORD, Keep ye judgment, and do justice: for my salvation *is* near to come, and my righteousness to be revealed. **Job 42:6** Wherefore I abhor myself, and repent in dust and ashes. **Ezekiel 14:6** Therefore say unto the house of Israel, Thus saith the Lord GOD; Repent, and turn yourselves from your idols; and turn away your faces from all your abominations. **Ezekiel 18:30** Therefore I will judge you, O house of Israel, every one according to his ways, saith the Lord GOD. Repent, and turn yourselves from all your transgressions; so iniquity shall not be your ruin.
Mark 1:21 And they go on to Capernaum, and immediately, on the **sabbaths**, having gone into the synagogue, he was teaching,	**See Colossians 2:16 "Sabbath"**
Mark 1:22 And they were astonished at his doctrine: **for he taught them as one that had authority**, and not as the scribes.	**See Ephesians 4:11 "Teach – Teachers"**
Mark 1:38 And he said unto them, Let us go into the next towns, that I may preach there also: for therefore came I forth.	**Isaiah 61:1** The Spirit of the Lord GOD *is* upon me; because the LORD hath anointed me to preach good tidings unto the meek; he hath sent me to bind up the brokenhearted, to proclaim liberty to the captives, and the opening of the prison to *them that are* bound;
Mark 1:44 And saith unto him, See thou say nothing to any man: but go thy way, shew thyself to the priest, and offer for thy cleansing those things which Moses commanded, for a testimony unto them.	**Leviticus 13** **Leviticus 14:1** And the LORD spake unto Moses, saying, **Leviticus 14:2** This shall be the law of the leper in the day of his cleansing: He shall be brought unto the priest: **Leviticus 14:3** And the priest shall go forth out of the camp; and the priest shall look, and, behold, *if* the plague of leprosy be healed in the leper;
Mark 2:5 When Jesus saw their faith, he said unto the sick of the palsy, Son, **thy sins be forgiven thee**.	**Exodus 34:6-7** And the LORD passed by before him, and proclaimed, The LORD, The LORD God, merciful and gracious, longsuffering, and abundant in goodness and truth, ⁷Keeping mercy for thousands, **forgiving iniquity and transgression and sin**, and that will by no means clear *the guilty*; visiting the iniquity of the fathers upon the children, and upon the children's children, unto the third and to the fourth *generation*. **Isaiah 43:25** I, even I, am he that blotteth out thy transgressions

	for mine own sake, and will not remember thy sins. **Psalms 32:5** I acknowledged my sin unto thee, and mine iniquity have I not hid. I said, I will confess my transgressions unto the LORD; and thou forgavest the iniquity of my sin. Selah. **See 1 Timothy 2:5 "God"**
Mark 2:7 Why doth this *man* thus speak blasphemies? who can forgive sins but God only?	**Psalms 32:5** I acknowledged my sin unto thee, and mine iniquity have I not hid. I said, I will confess my transgressions unto the LORD; and thou forgavest the iniquity of my sin. Selah. **Isaiah 43:25** I, *even* I, *am* he that blotteth out thy transgressions for mine own sake, and will not remember thy sins. **Psalms 51:1-5** { To the chief Musician, A Psalm of David, when Nathan the prophet came unto him, after he had gone in to Bathsheba. } Have mercy upon me, O God, according to thy lovingkindness: according unto the multitude of thy tender mercies blot out my transgressions. 2 Wash me throughly from mine iniquity, and cleanse me from my sin. 3 For I acknowledge my transgressions: and my sin *is* ever before me. 4 Against thee, thee only, have I sinned, and done *this* evil in thy sight: that thou mightest be justified when thou speakest, *and* be clear when thou judgest. 5 Behold, I was shapen in iniquity; and in sin did my mother conceive me. **Proverbs 28:13** He that covereth his sins shall not prosper: but whoso confesseth and forsaketh *them* shall have mercy.
Mark 2:8 And immediately when **Jesus perceived in his spirit** that they so reasoned within themselves, he said unto them, Why reason ye these things in your hearts?	**1 Kings 8:39** Then hear thou in heaven thy dwelling place, and forgive, and do, and give to every man according to his ways, **whose heart thou knowest**; (for thou, *even* thou only, knowest the hearts of all the children of men;) **See 1 Thessalonians 5:23 "Body, soul, and spirit"**
Mark 2:20 But the days will come, when the bridegroom shall be taken away from them, and then shall they **fast** in those days.	**See Matthew 17:21 "fasting"**
Mark 2:23 And it came to pass, that he went through the corn fields on the sabbath day; and his disciples began, as they went, to pluck the ears of corn.	**Deuteronomy 23:25** When thou comest into the standing corn of thy neighbour, then thou mayest pluck the ears with thine hand; but thou shalt not move a sickle unto thy neighbour's standing corn.
Mark 2:24 And the Pharisees said unto him, Behold, why do they on the sabbath day that which is not lawful?	**Exodus 20:10-11** But the seventh day *is* the sabbath of the LORD thy God: *in it* thou shalt not do any work, thou, nor thy son, nor thy daughter, thy manservant, nor thy maidservant, nor thy cattle, nor thy stranger that *is* within thy gates: 11 For *in* six days the LORD made heaven and earth, the sea, and all that in them *is*, and rested the seventh day: wherefore the LORD blessed the sabbath day, and hallowed it.
Mark 2:25 And he said unto them, Have ye never read what David did, when he had need, and was an hungred, he, and they that were with him?	**1 Samuel 21:6** So the priest gave him hallowed *bread*: for there was no bread there but the shewbread, that was taken from before the LORD, to put hot bread in the day when it was taken away.
Mark 2:26 How he went into the house of God in the days of Abiathar the high priest, and did eat the shewbread, which is not lawful to eat but for the priests,	**Leviticus 24:9** And it shall be Aaron's and his sons'; and they shall eat it in the holy place: for it *is* most holy unto him of the offerings of the LORD made by fire by a perpetual statute.

and gave also to them which were with him?	
Mark 2:27-28 And he said unto them, The **sabbath** was made for man, and not man for the **sabbath**: 28 Therefore the Son of man is Lord also of the **sabbath**.	See Colossians 2:16 "Sabbaths"
Mark 3:5 And when he had looked round about on them with anger, being grieved for the hardness of their hearts, he saith unto the man, Stretch forth thine hand. And he stretched *it* out: and his hand was restored whole as the other.	**1 Kings 13:6** And the king answered and said unto the man of God, Intreat now the face of the LORD thy God, and pray for me, that my hand may be restored me again. And the man of God besought the LORD, and the king's hand was restored him again, and became as *it was* before.
Mark 3:23 And he called them *unto him,* and said unto them in parables, How can **Satan** cast out **Satan**? **Mark 3:26** And if **Satan** rise up against himself, and be divided, he cannot stand, but hath an end.	**Genesis 3:4** And the **serpent** said unto the woman, Ye shall not surely die: **Zechariah 3:1-2** And he shewed me Joshua the high priest standing before the angel of the LORD, and **Satan** standing at his right hand to resist him. 2 And the LORD said unto **Satan,** The LORD rebuke thee, O **Satan**; even the LORD that hath chosen Jerusalem rebuke thee: *is* not this a brand plucked out of the fire? See Matthew 4:10 "satan"
Mark 4:2 And **he taught them many things by parables**, and said unto them in his doctrine,	See Ephesians 4:11 "Teach – Teachers"
Mark 4:8 And other fell on good ground, and did yield fruit that sprang up and increased; and brought forth, some thirty, and some sixty, and some an **hundred**.	**Genesis 26:12** Then Isaac sowed in that land, and received in the same year an <u>hundredfold</u>: and the Lord blessed him.
Mark 4:12 That seeing they may see, and not perceive; and hearing they may hear, and not understand; lest at any time they should be converted, and *their* sins should be forgiven them.	**Isaiah 6:9-10** And he said, God, and tell this people, Hear ye indeed, but understand not; and see ye indeed, but perceive not. Make the heart of this people fat, and make their ears heavy, and shut their eyes; lest they see with their eyes, and hear with their ears, and understand with their heart, and convert, and be healed.
Mark 4:15 And these are they by the way side, where the word is sown; but when they have heard, Satan cometh immediately, and taketh away the word that was sown in their hearts.	**Genesis 3:4** And the **serpent** said unto the woman, Ye shall not surely die: **Zechariah 3:1-2** And he shewed me Joshua the high priest standing before the angel of the LORD, and **Satan** standing at his right hand to resist him. 2 And the LORD said unto **Satan,** The LORD rebuke thee, O **Satan**; even the LORD that hath chosen Jerusalem rebuke thee: *is* not this a brand plucked out of the fire? See Matthew 4:10 "satan"
Mark 4:20 And these are they which are sown on good ground; such as hear the word, and receive it, and bring forth <u>fruit</u>, some thirtyfold, some sixty, and some an hundred.	**Isaiah 14:29** Rejoice not thou, whole Palestina, because the rod of him that smote thee is broken: for **out of the serpent's root shall come forth a cockatrice, and his <u>fruit</u> shall be a fiery flying serpent**.
Mark 4:22 For there is nothing hid, which shall not be manifested; neither was any thing kept secret, but that it should come abroad.	**Job 12:22** He discovereth deep things out of darkness, and bringeth out to light the shadow of death.

Mark 4:29 But when the fruit is brought forth, immediately he putteth in the sickle, because the harvest is come.	**Joel 3:13** Put ye in the sickle, for the harvest is ripe: come, get you down; for the press is full, the fats overflow; for their wickedness *is* great.
Mark 4:38-41 And he was in the hinder part of the ship, asleep on a pillow: and they awake him, and say unto him, Master, carest thou not that we perish? 39 And he arose, and rebuked the wind, and said unto the sea, Peace, be still. And the wind ceased, and there was a great calm. 40 And he said unto them, Why are ye so fearful? how is it that ye have no faith? 41 And they feared exceedingly, and said one to another, What manner of man is this, that even the wind and the sea obey him?	**Psalms 78:65** Then the Lord awaked as one out of sleep, *and* like a mighty man that shouteth by reason of wine. **Psalms 107:29** He maketh the storm a calm, so that the waves thereof are still.
Mark 5:2 And when he was come out of the ship, immediately there met him out of the tombs a man with an **unclean spirit**,	**See Hebrews 13:2** "Good and bad angels"
Mark 5:7 And cried with a loud voice, and said, What have I to do with thee, Jesus, *thou* Son of the **most high God**? I adjure thee by God, that thou torment me not.	**Genesis 14:18** And Melchizedek king of Salem brought forth bread and wine: and he *was* the priest of the **most high God**. **Psalms 78:56** Yet they tempted and provoked the **most high God**, and kept not his testimonies: **Daniel 3:26** Then Nebuchadnezzar came near to the mouth of the burning fiery furnace, *and* spake, and said, Shadrach, Meshach, and Abednego, ye servants of the **most high God**, come forth, and come *hither*. Then Shadrach, Meshach, and Abednego, came forth of the midst of the fire.
Mark 5:10 And he besought him much that he would not send **them away** out of the country.	**See Hebrews 13:2** "Angels"
Mark 5:25 And a certain woman, which had an issue of blood twelve years,	**Leviticus 15:25** And if a woman have an issue of her blood many days out of the time of her separation, or if it run beyond the time of her separation; all the days of the issue of her uncleanness shall be as the days of her separation: she *shall be* unclean.
Mark 5:26 And had <u>suffered many things of many physicians</u>, and had <u>spent all that she had</u>, and was nothing bettered, <u>but rather grew worse,</u>	**2 Chronicles 16:12-13** And Asa in the thirty and ninth year of his reign was diseased in his feet, until his disease [was] exceeding *great*: yet in his disease **he sought not to the LORD**, <u>but to the physicians</u>. 13 And <u>Asa slept with his fathers</u>, and died in the one and fortieth year of his reign.
Mark 5:29 And straightway the fountain of her blood was dried up; and she felt in *her* body that she was healed of that **plague**.	**Numbers 11:33** And while the flesh *was* yet between their teeth, ere it was chewed, the wrath of the LORD was kindled against the people, and the LORD smote the people with a very great **plague**. **2 Samuel 24:15** So the LORD sent a **pestilence** upon Israel from the morning even to the time appointed: and there died of the people from Dan even to Beersheba seventy thousand men. **2 Samuel 24:25** And David built there an altar unto the LORD, and offered burnt offerings and peace offerings. So the LORD was intreated for the land, and the **plague** was stayed from Israel.
Mark 6:11 And whosoever shall not receive you, nor hear you, when ye depart thence, shake off the dust under	**See Romans 1:27** "Sexual sins"

your feet for a testimony against them. Verily I say unto you, It shall be more tolerable for **Sodom and Gomorrha** in the day of judgment, than for that city.	
Mark 6:13 And they cast out many devils, and anointed with oil many that were sick, and **healed** them.	**See 1 Peter 2:24 "Healing"**
Mark 6:18 For John had said unto Herod, It is not lawful for thee to have thy brother's wife.	**Leviticus 18:16** Thou shalt not uncover the nakedness of thy brother's wife: it *is* thy brother's nakedness. **Leviticus 20:21** And if a man shall take his brother's wife, it *is* an unclean thing: he hath uncovered his brother's nakedness; they shall be childless.
Mark 6:21 And when a convenient day was come, that Herod on his birthday made a supper to his lords, high captains, and chief *estates* of Galilee;	**Genesis 40:20** And it came to pass the third day, *which was* Pharaoh's birthday, that he made a feast unto all his servants: and he lifted up the head of the chief butler and of the chief baker among his servants.
Mark 6:34 And Jesus, when he came out, saw much people, and was moved with compassion toward them, because they were as sheep not having a shepherd: and he began to teach them many things.	**Numbers 27:17** Which may go out before them, and which may go in before them, and which may lead them out, and which may bring them in; that the congregation of the LORD be not as sheep which have no shepherd. **1 Kings 22:17** And he said, I saw all Israel scattered upon the hills, as sheep that have not a shepherd: and the LORD said, These have no master: let them return every man to his house in peace. **Jeremiah 23:1-4** Woe be unto the pastors that destroy and scatter the sheep of my pasture! saith the LORD. :2 Therefore thus saith the LORD God of Israel against the pastors that feed my people; Ye have scattered my flock, and driven them away, and have not visited them: behold, I will visit upon you the evil of your doings, saith the LORD. 3 And I will gather the remnant of my flock out of all countries whither I have driven them, and will bring them again to their folds; and they shall be fruitful and increase. :4 And I will set up shepherds over them which shall feed them: and they shall fear no more, nor be dismayed, neither shall they be lacking, saith the LORD. **Ezekiel 34:5** And they were scattered, because *there is* no shepherd: and they became meat to all the beasts of the field, when they were scattered.
Mark 6:41 And when he had taken the five loaves and the two fishes, he looked up to heaven, and blessed, and brake the loaves, and gave *them* to his disciples to set before them; and the two fishes divided he among them all.	**1 Samuel 9:13** As soon as ye be come into the city, ye shall straightway find him, before he go up to the high place to eat: for the people will not eat until he come, because he doth bless the sacrifice; *and* afterwards they eat that be bidden. Now therefore get you up; for about this time ye shall find him.
Mark 6:56 And whithersoever he entered, into villages, or cities, or country, they laid the sick in the streets, and besought him that they might touch if it were but the border of his **garment**: and as many as touched him were made whole.	**See Matthew 23:5 "Garments"**
Mark 7:3 For the Pharisees, and all the Jews, except they wash *their* hands oft, eat not, holding the tradition of the	**See 1 Peter 5:1 "Elders"**

elders.	
Mark 7:5 Then the Pharisees and scribes asked him, Why walk not thy disciples according to the tradition of the **elders**, but eat bread with unwashen hands?	See 1 Peter 5:1 "Elders"
Mark 7:6-7 He answered and said unto them, Well hath Esaias prophesied of you hypocrites, as it is written, This people honoureth me with *their* lips, but their heart is far from me. Howbeit in vain do they worship me, teaching *for* doctrines the commandments of men.	**Isaiah 29:13** Wherefore the Lord said, Forasmuch as this people draw near me with their mouth, and with their lips do honour me, but have removed their heart far from me, and their fear toward me is taught by the precept of men: **Ezekiel 33:31** And they come unto thee as the people cometh, and they sit before thee *as* my people, and they hear thy words, but they will not do them: for with their mouth they shew much love, *but* their heart goeth after their covetousness.
Mark 7:8 For laying aside the commandment of God, ye hold the tradition of men, *as* the washing of pots and cups: and many other such like things ye do. 9 And he said unto them, Full well ye reject the commandment of God, that ye may keep your own tradition.	**Isaiah 1:13-14** Bring no more vain oblations; incense is an abomination unto me; the new moons and sabbaths, the calling of assemblies, I cannot away with; *it is* iniquity, even the solemn meeting. 14 Your new moons and your appointed feasts my soul hateth: they are a trouble unto me; I am weary to bear *them*.
Mark 7:10 For Moses said, Honour thy father and thy mother; and, Whoso curseth father or mother, let him die the death:	**Exodus 20:12** Honour thy father and thy mother: that thy days may be long upon the land which the LORD thy God giveth thee. **Exodus 21:17** And he that curseth his father, or his mother, shall surely be put to death. **Leviticus 20:9** For every one that curseth his father or his mother shall be surely put to death: he hath cursed his father or his mother; his blood *shall be* upon him. **Deuteronomy 5:16** Honour thy father and thy mother, as the LORD thy God hath commanded thee; that thy days may be prolonged, and that it may go well with thee, in the land which the LORD thy God giveth thee. **Deuteronomy 27:16** Cursed *be* he that setteth light by his father or his mother. And all the people shall say, Amen. **Proverbs 20:20** Whoso curseth his father or his mother, his lamp shall be put out in obscure darkness.
Mark 7:13 Making the word of God of none effect through your tradition, which ye have delivered: and many such like things do ye.	**Isaiah 1:13-14** Bring no more vain oblations; incense is an abomination unto me; the new moons and sabbaths, the calling of assemblies, I cannot away with; *it is* iniquity, even the solemn meeting. 14 Your new moons and your appointed feasts my soul hateth: they are a trouble unto me; I am weary to bear *them*.
Mark 7:21 For from within, out of the heart of men, proceed evil thoughts, adulteries, fornications, murders,	**Genesis 6:5** And GOD saw that the wickedness of man *was* great in the earth, and *that* every imagination of the thoughts of his heart *was* only evil continually. **Genesis 8:21** And the LORD smelled a sweet savour; and the LORD said in his heart, I will not again curse the ground any more for man's sake; for the imagination of man's heart *is* evil from his youth; neither will I again smite any more every thing living, as I have done. **Exodus 20:13** Thou shalt not kill.

	Proverbs 6:14 Frowardness *is* in his heart, he deviseth mischief continually; he soweth discord.
	Proverbs 22:15 Foolishness *is* bound in the heart of a child; *but* the rod of correction shall drive it far from him.
	Jeremiah 17:9 The heart *is* deceitful above all *things*, and desperately wicked: who can know it?
Mark 7:26 The woman was a Greek, a Syrophenician by nation; and she besought him that he would cast forth the **devil** out of her daughter.	**See Hebrews 13:2** "Good and bad angels"
Mark 7:32 And they bring unto him one that was deaf, and had an impediment in his speech; and they beseech him to put his hand upon him.	**See Matthew 11:5** "Deaf and Blind" **See 1 Peter 2:24** "Healing"
Mark 7:37 And were beyond measure astonished, saying, He hath done all things well: he maketh both the deaf to hear, and the dumb to speak.	**Genesis 1:31** And God saw every thing that he had made, and, behold, *it was* very good. And the evening and the morning were the sixth day. **Deuteronomy 32:4** He *is* the Rock, his work *is* perfect: for all his ways *are* judgment: a God of truth and without iniquity, just and right *is* he. **See Matthew 11:5** "Deaf and Blind" **See 1 Peter 2:24** "Healing"
Mark 8:12 And he sighed deeply in his **spirit**, and saith, Why doth this generation seek after a sign? verily I say unto you, There shall no sign be given unto this generation.	**See 1 Thessalonians 5:23** "Body, soul, and spirit"
Mark 8:18 Having eyes, see ye not? and having ears, hear ye not? and do ye not remember?	**Jeremiah 5:21** Whoso curseth his father or his mother, his lamp shall be put out in obscure darkness. **Ezekiel 12:2** Son of man, thou dwellest in the midst of a rebellious house, which have eyes to see, and see not; they have ears to hear, and hear not: for they *are* a rebellious house.
Mark 8:31 And he began to teach them, that the Son of man must suffer many things, and be rejected of the **elders**, and *of* the chief priests, and scribes, and be killed, and **after three days rise again**.	**See 1 Peter 5:1** "Elders" **Jonah 1:17** Now the LORD had prepared a great fish to swallow up Jonah. And Jonah was in the belly of the fish **three days and three nights**. **Jonah 2:1** Then Jonah prayed unto the LORD his God out of the fish's belly,
Mark 8:33 But when he had turned about and looked on his disciples, he rebuked Peter, saying, Get thee behind me, **Satan**: for thou savourest not the things that be of God, but the things that be of men.	**Genesis 3:4** And the **serpent** said unto the woman, Ye shall not surely die: **Zechariah 3:1-2** And he shewed me Joshua the high priest standing before the angel of the LORD, and **Satan** standing at his right hand to resist him. 2 And the LORD said unto **Satan**, The LORD rebuke thee, O **Satan**; even the LORD that hath chosen Jerusalem rebuke thee: *is* not this a brand plucked out of the fire? **See Matthew 4:10** "satan"
Mark 8:37 Or what shall a man give in exchange for his soul?	**Psalms 49:8** (For the redemption of their soul *is* precious, and it ceaseth for ever:)
Mark 9:7 And there was a cloud that	**Genesis 22:2** And he said, Take now thy son, thine only *son* Isaac,

overshadowed them: and a voice came out of the cloud, saying, This is my beloved Son: hear him.	whom thou lovest, and get thee into the land of Moriah; and offer him there for a burnt offering upon one of the mountains which I will tell thee of. **Deuteronomy 18:15** The LORD thy God will raise up unto thee a Prophet from the midst of thee, of thy brethren, like unto me; unto him ye shall hearken; **Psalms 2:7** I will declare the decree: the LORD hath said unto me, Thou *art* my Son; this day have I begotten thee. **Isaiah 42:1** Behold my servant, whom I uphold; mine elect, *in whom* my soul delighteth; I have put my spirit upon him: he shall bring forth judgment to the Gentiles.
Mark 9:11 And they asked him, saying, Why say the scribes that Elias must first come?	**Malachi 4:5** Behold, I will send you Elijah the prophet before the coming of the great and dreadful day of the LORD:
Mark 9:12 And he answered and told them, Elias verily cometh first, and restoreth all things; and how it is written of the Son of man, that he must suffer many things, and be set at nought.	**Psalms 22:6** But I *am* a worm, and no man; a reproach of men, and despised of the people. **Isaiah 53:4** Surely he hath borne our griefs, and carried our sorrows: yet we did esteem him stricken, smitten of God, and afflicted. **Daniel 9:26** And after threescore and two weeks shall Messiah be cut off, but not for himself: and the people of the prince that shall come shall destroy the city and the sanctuary; and the end thereof *shall be* with a flood, and unto the end of the war desolations are determined.
Mark 9:13 But I say unto you, That Elias is indeed come, and they have done unto him whatsoever they listed, as it is written of him.	**Malachi 4:5-6** Behold, I will send you Elijah the prophet before the coming of the great and dreadful day of the LORD: **6** And he shall turn the heart of the fathers to the children, and the heart of the children to their fathers, lest I come and smite the earth with a curse.
Mark 9:24 And straightway the father of the child cried out, and said with tears, Lord, I believe; **help thou mine unbelief**.	**Psalm 78:41** ... limited the Holy One of Israel.
Mark 9:25 When Jesus saw that the people came running together, he rebuked the foul spirit, saying unto him, Thou dumb and deaf spirit, I charge thee, come out of him, and enter no more into him.	**See Matthew 11:5 "Deaf and Blind"** **See 1 Peter 2:24 "Healing"**
Mark 9:29 And he said unto them, This kind can come forth by nothing, but by prayer and **fasting**.	**See Matthew 17:21 "Fasting"**
Mark 9:31 For he taught his disciples, and said unto them, The Son of man is delivered into the hands of men, and they shall kill him; and after that he is killed, **he shall rise the third day**.	**Jonah 1:17** Now the LORD had prepared a great fish to swallow up Jonah. And Jonah was in the belly of the fish **three days and three nights**. **Jonah 2:1** Then Jonah prayed unto the LORD his God out of the fish's belly
Mark 9:43 And if thy hand offend thee, cut it off: it is better for thee to enter into life maimed, than having two hands to go into hell, into the fire that never	**Deuteronomy 32:22** For a fire is kindled in mine anger, and shall burn unto the lowest hell, and shall consume the earth with her increase, and set on fire the foundations of the mountains.

shall be quenched:	**Isaiah 1:31** And the strong shall be as tow, and the maker of it as a spark, and they shall both burn together, and none shall quench *them*.
Mark 9:44 Where their worm dieth not, and the fire is not quenched. **Mark 9:46** Where their worm dieth not, and the fire is not quenched.	**Isaiah 66:24** And they shall go forth, and look upon the carcases of the men that have transgressed against me: for their worm shall not die, neither shall their fire be quenched; and they shall be an abhorring unto all flesh. **See Luke 16:23 "Hell"**
Mark 9:47 And if thine eye offend thee, pluck it out: it is better for thee to enter into the kingdom of God with one eye, than having two eyes to be cast into **hell** fire:	**See Luke 16:23 "Hell"**
Mark 9:48 Where their worm dieth not, and the fire is not quenched.	**Isaiah 66:24** And they shall go forth, and look upon the carcases of the men that have transgressed against me: for their worm shall not die, neither shall their fire be quenched; and they shall be an abhorring unto all flesh.
Mark 9:49 For every one shall be salted with fire, and every sacrifice shall be salted with salt.	**Leviticus 2:13** And every oblation of thy meat offering shalt thou season with salt; neither shalt thou suffer the salt of the covenant of thy God to be lacking from thy meat offering: with all thine offerings thou shalt offer salt. **Numbers 31:23** Every thing that may abide the fire, **ye shall make** *it* **go through the fire, and** **it shall be clean**: nevertheless it shall be purified with the water of separation: and all that abideth not the fire ye shall make go through the water. **See Acts 2:38 "Fire Baptism"**
Mark 10:4 And they said, Moses suffered to write a bill of divorcement, and to put *her* away.	**Deuteronomy 24:1** When a man hath taken a wife, and married her, and it come to pass that she find no favour in his eyes, because he hath found some uncleanness in her: then let him write her a bill of divorcement, and give *it* in her hand, and send her out of his house. **Jeremiah 3:1** They say, If a man put away his wife, and she go from him, and become another man's, shall he return unto her again? shall not that land be greatly polluted? but thou hast played the harlot with many lovers; yet return again to me, saith the LORD.
Mark 10:6 But from the beginning of the creation God made them male and female.	**Genesis 1:27** So God created man in his *own* image, in the image of God created he him; male and female created he them. **Genesis 5:2** Male and female created he them; and blessed them, and called their name Adam, in the day when they were created.
Mark 10:7-8 For this cause shall a man leave his father and mother, and cleave to his wife; 8 And they twain shall be one flesh: so then they are no more twain, but **one flesh**.	**Genesis 2:24** Therefore shall a man leave his father and his mother, and shall cleave unto his wife: and they shall be one flesh. **Malachi 2:15 And did not he make one?** Yet had he the residue of the spirit. And wherefore one? That he might seek a godly seed. Therefore take heed to your spirit, and let none deal treacherously against the wife of his youth.
Mark 10:11 And he saith unto them, Whosoever shall put away his wife, and marry another, committeth **adultery** against her.	**See Matthew 5:27 "Adultery"**
Mark 10:12 And if a woman shall put away her husband, and be married to	**Exodus 20:14** Thou shalt not commit adultery.

another, she committeth **adultery**.	**Leviticus 20:10** And the man that committeth adultery with *another* man's wife, *even he* that committeth adultery with his neighbour's wife, the adulterer and the adulteress shall surely be put to death. **Deuteronomy 5:18** Neither shalt thou commit adultery. **Proverbs 6:32** *But* whoso committeth adultery with a woman lacketh understanding: he *that* doeth it destroyeth his own soul. **See Matthew 5:27 "Adultery"**
Mark 10:18 And Jesus said unto him, Why callest thou me **good**? *there is* none good but one, *that is,* God.	**Isaiah 64:6** But we are all as an unclean *thing,* and all our **righteousnesses** *are* as filthy rags; and we all do fade as a leaf; and our iniquities, like the wind, have taken us away.
Mark 10:19 Thou knowest the commandments, Do not commit adultery, Do not kill, Do not steal, Do not bear false witness, Defraud not, Honour thy father and mother.	**Exodus 20:12-16** Honour thy father and thy mother: that thy days may be long upon the land which the LORD thy God giveth thee. 13 Thou shalt not kill. 14 Thou shalt not commit adultery. 15 Thou shalt not steal. 16 Thou shalt not bear false witness against thy neighbour. **Exodus 21:12** He that smiteth a man, so that he die, shall be surely put to death. **Exodus 21:15-17** And he that smiteth his father, or his mother, shall be surely put to death. 16 And he that stealeth a man, and selleth him, or if he be found in his hand, he shall surely be put to death. 17 And he that curseth his father, or his mother, shall surely be put to death. **Leviticus 19:13** Thou shalt not defraud thy neighbour, neither rob *him:* the wages of him that is hired shall not abide with thee all night until the morning. **Deuteronomy 5:16-20** Honour thy father and thy mother, as the LORD thy God hath commanded thee; that thy days may be prolonged, and that it may go well with thee, in the land which the LORD thy God giveth thee. 17 Thou shalt not kill. 18 Neither shalt thou commit adultery. 19 Neither shalt thou steal. 20 Neither shalt thou bear false witness against thy neighbour. **See Matthew 5:27 "Adultery"**
Mark 10:21 Then Jesus beholding him loved him, and said unto him, One thing thou lackest: go thy way, sell whatsoever thou hast, and give to the poor, and thou shalt have treasure in heaven: and come, take up the cross, and follow me.	**Deuteronomy 15:11** For the poor shall never cease out of the land: therefore I command thee, saying, Thou shalt open thine hand wide unto thy brother, to thy poor, and to thy needy, in thy land.
Mark 10:23 And Jesus looked round about, and saith unto his disciples, How hardly shall they that have riches enter into the kingdom of God!	**Proverbs 11:28** He that trusteth in his riches shall fall: but the righteous shall flourish as a branch.
Mark 10:27 And Jesus looking upon them saith, With men *it is* impossible, but not with God: for with God all things are possible.	**Job 42:2** I know that thou canst do every *thing,* and *that* no thought can be withholden from thee. **Jeremiah 32:17** Ah Lord GOD! behold, thou hast made the heaven and the earth by thy great power and stretched out arm, *and* there is nothing too hard for thee:
Mark 10:30 But he shall receive an **hundredfold** now in this time, houses, and brethren, and sisters, and mothers,	**Genesis 26:12** Then Isaac sowed in that land, and received in the same year an **hundredfold**: and the Lord blessed him.

and children, and lands, with persecutions; and in the world to come eternal life.	
Mark 10:33-34 *Saying,* Behold, we go up to Jerusalem; and the Son of man shall be delivered unto the chief priests, and unto the scribes; and they shall condemn him to death, and shall deliver him to the Gentiles: 34 And they shall mock him, and shall scourge him, and shall spit upon him, and shall kill him: and **the third day he shall rise again**.	**Jonah 1:17** Now the LORD had prepared a great fish to swallow up Jonah. And Jonah was in the belly of the fish **three days and three nights**. **Jonah 2:1** Then Jonah prayed unto the LORD his God out of the fish's belly
Mark 10:37 They said unto him, Grant unto us that we may sit, one on thy right hand, and the other on thy left hand, in thy glory. **Mark 10:40** But to sit on my right hand and on my left hand is not mine to give; but it shall be given to them for whom it is prepared.	**Psalms 8:6** Thou madest him to have dominion over the works of thy hands; thou hast put all *things* under his feet: **Psalms 16:8** I have set the LORD always before me: because *he is* at my right hand, I shall not be moved. **Psalms 110:1** The LORD said unto my Lord, Sit thou at my right hand, until I make thine enemies thy footstool. **Psalms 110:5** The Lord at thy right hand shall strike through kings in the day of his wrath. **Zechraiah 3:1** And he shewed me Joshua the high priest standing before the angel of the LORD, and Satan standing at his right hand to resist him.
Mark 11:9 And they that went before, and they that followed, cried, saying, Hosanna; Blessed *is* he that cometh in the name of the Lord:	**Psalms 118:26** Blessed *be* he that cometh in the name of the LORD: we have blessed you out of the house of the LORD.
Mark 11:10 Blessed *be* the kingdom of our father David, that cometh in the name of the Lord: Hosanna in the highest.	**Psalms 118:26** Blessed *be* he that cometh in the name of the LORD: we have blessed you out of the house of the LORD.
Mark 11:17 And he taught, saying unto them, Is it not written, My house shall be called of all nations the house of prayer? but ye have made it a den of thieves.	See Matthew 17:21 "Prayer" **1 Kings 8:29** That thine eyes may be open toward this house night and day, *even* toward the place of which thou hast said, My name shall be there: that thou mayest hearken unto the prayer which thy servant shall make toward this place. **Deuteronomy 12:11** Then there shall be a place which the LORD your God shall choose to cause his name to dwell there; thither shall ye bring all that I command you; your burnt offerings, and your sacrifices, your tithes, and the heave offering of your hand, and all your choice vows which ye vow unto the LORD: **Isaiah 56:7** Even them will I bring to my holy mountain, and make them joyful in my house of prayer: their burnt offerings and their sacrifices [shall be] accepted upon mine altar; for mine house shall be called an house of prayer for all people. **Jeremiah 7:11** Is this house, which is called by my name, become a den of robbers in your eyes? Behold, even I have seen [it], saith the LORD.
	Psalms 37:22 For *such as be* blessed of him shall inherit the earth; and *they that be* **cursed** of him shall be cut off. **Psalms 62:4** They only consult to cast *him* down from his

Mark 11:21 And Peter calling to remembrance saith unto him, Master, behold, the fig tree which thou **cursedst** is withered away.	excellency: they delight in lies: they bless with their mouth, but they **curse** inwardly. Selah. **Psalms 119:21** Thou hast rebuked the proud *that are* **cursed**, which do err from thy commandments. **Proverbs 3:33** The **curse** of the LORD *is* in the house of the wicked: but he blesseth the habitation of the just. **Proverbs 20:20** Whoso **curseth** his father or his mother, his lamp shall be put out in obscure darkness. **Proverbs 24:24** He that saith unto the wicked, Thou *art* righteous; him shall the people **curse**, nations shall abhor him: **Proverbs 26:2** As the bird by wandering, as the swallow by flying, so <u>the **curse** causeless shall not come</u>. **Proverbs 28:27** He that giveth unto the poor shall not lack: but he that hideth his eyes shall have many a **curse**.
Mark 11:22-23 And Jesus answering saith unto them, Have faith in God. 23 For verily I say unto you, That whosoever shall say unto this mountain, Be thou removed, and be thou cast into the sea; and shall not doubt in his heart, but shall believe that those things which he saith shall come to pass; he shall have whatsoever he saith.	**Exodus 14:15-16** And the LORD said unto Moses, **Wherefore criest thou unto me?** speak unto the children of Israel, that they go forward: 16 But lift thou up thy rod, and stretch out thine hand over the sea, and divide it: and the children of Israel shall go on dry ground through the midst of the sea. **Job 22:26-28** For then shalt thou have thy delight in the Almighty, and shalt lift up thy face unto God. 27 Thou shalt make thy prayer unto him, and he shall hear thee, and thou shalt pay thy vows. 28 **<u>Thou shalt also decree a thing, and it shall be established unto thee</u>**: and the light shall shine upon thy ways. **Jeremiah 1:12** Then said the LORD unto me, Thou hast well seen: for **I will hasten my word to perform it**. **Isaiah 55:11** So shall my word be that goeth forth **out of my mouth: it shall not return unto me void**, but it shall accomplish that which I please, and it shall prosper *in the thing* whereto I sent it.
Mark 11:24 Therefore I say unto you, What things soever ye desire, when ye pray, believe that ye receive *them*, and ye shall have *them*.	**Jeremiah 29:12** Then shall ye call upon me, and ye shall go and pray unto me, and I will hearken unto you. See 1 Peter 2:24 "Healing"
Mark 11:27 And they come again to Jerusalem: and as he was walking in the temple, there come to him the chief priests, and the scribes, and the **elders**,	See 1 Peter 5:1 "Elders"
Mark 11:28 And say unto him, By what authority doest thou these things? and who gave thee this authority to do these things?	**Exodus 2:14** And he said, Who made thee a prince and a judge over us? intendest thou to kill me, as thou killedst the Egyptian? And Moses feared, and said, Surely this thing is known.
Mark 12:1 And he began to speak unto them by parables. A *certain* man planted a vineyard, and set an hedge about *it*, and digged *a place for* the winefat, and built a tower, and let it out to husbandmen, and went into a far country.	**Isaiah 5:1-2** Now will I sing to my wellbeloved a song of my beloved touching his vineyard. My wellbeloved hath a vineyard in a very fruitful hill: 2 And he fenced it, and gathered out the stones thereof, and planted it with the choicest vine, and built a tower in the midst of it, and also made a winepress therein: and he looked that it should bring forth grapes, and it brought forth wild grapes. **Jeremiah 12:10** Many pastors have destroyed my vineyard, they have trodden my portion under foot, they have made my pleasant portion a desolate wilderness.

Mark 12:10-11 And have ye not read this scripture; The stone which the builders rejected is become the head of the corner: This was the Lord's doing, and it is marvellous in our eyes?	**Psalms 118:22** The stone *which* the builders refused is become the head *stone* of the corner. 23 This is the LORD'S doing; it *is* marvellous in our eyes. **Isaiah 28:16** Therefore thus saith the Lord GOD, Behold, I lay in Zion for a foundation a stone, a tried stone, a precious corner *stone*, a sure foundation: he that believeth shall not make haste. **Zechariah 4:7** Who *art* thou, O great mountain? before Zerubbabel *thou shalt become* a plain: and he shall bring forth the headstone *thereof with* shoutings, *crying,* Grace, grace unto it.
Mark 12:13 And they send unto him certain of the Pharisees and of the Herodians, to catch him in *his* words.	**Exodus 12:5** Your lamb shall be without blemish, a male of the first year: ye shall take *it* out from the sheep, or from the goats:
Mark 12:19 Master, Moses wrote unto us, If a man's brother die, and leave *his* wife *behind him,* and leave no children, that his brother should take his wife, and raise up seed unto his brother.	**Genesis 38:8** And Judah said unto Onan, Go in unto thy brother's wife, and marry her, and raise up seed to thy brother. **Deuteronomy 25:5** If brethren dwell together, and one of them die, and have no child, the wife of the dead shall not marry without unto a stranger: her husband's brother shall go in unto her, and take her to him to wife, and perform the duty of an husband's brother unto her.
Mark 12:24 And Jesus answering said unto them, **Do ye not therefore err, because ye know not the scriptures,** neither the power of God?	**Amos 8:11** Behold, **the days come,** saith the Lord GOD, that **I will send a famine in the land,** not **a famine** of bread, nor a thirst for water, but **of hearing the words of the LORD:** **See Matthew 5:18 "Scripture"**
Mark 12:26 And as touching the dead, that they rise: have ye not read in the book of Moses, how in the bush God spake unto him, saying, I *am* the God of Abraham, and the God of Isaac, and the God of Jacob?	**Exodus 3:6** Moreover he said, I *am* the God of thy father, the God of Abraham, the God of Isaac, and the God of Jacob. And Moses hid his face; for he was afraid to look upon God. **Exodus 3:15** And God said moreover unto Moses, Thus shalt thou say unto the children of Israel, The LORD God of your fathers, the God of Abraham, the God of Isaac, and the God of Jacob, hath sent me unto you: this *is* my name for ever, and this *is* my memorial unto all generations.
Mark 12:29 And Jesus answered him, The first of all the commandments *is,* Hear, O Israel; The Lord our God is one Lord:	**Deuteronomy 6:4** Hear, O Israel: The LORD our God *is* one LORD: Tell ye, and bring them near; yea, let them take counsel together: who hath declared this from ancient time? who hath told it from that time? **Isaiah 45:5-6** I am the LORD, and there is none else, **there is no God beside me**: I girded thee, though thou hast not known me: 6 That they may know from the rising of the sun, and from the west, that there is none beside me. I am the LORD, and there is none else. **Isaiah 45:21-22** have not I the LORD? and **there is no God else beside me**; a just God and a Saviour; there is none beside me. 22 Look unto me, and be ye saved, all the ends of the earth: for **I am God, and there is none else**. **Deuteronomy 32:39; 2 Samuel 7:22; 1 Chronicles 17:20; Psalm86:10; Isaiah 44:6, 8-10; Isaiah 45:21-23; Isaiah 46:9; Malachi 2:10**
Mark 12:30 And thou shalt love the Lord thy God with all thy heart, and with all thy soul, and with all thy mind, and with all thy strength: this *is* the first	**Deuteronomy 6:5** And th:ou shalt love the LORD thy God with all thine heart, and with all thy soul, and with all thy might. **Deuteronomy 10:12** And now, Israel, what doth the LORD thy

commandment.	God require of thee, but to fear the LORD thy God, to walk in all his ways, and to love him, and to serve the LORD thy God with all thy heart and with all thy soul, **Deuteronomy 30:6** And the LORD thy God will circumcise thine heart, and the heart of thy seed, to love the LORD thy God with all thine heart, and with all thy soul, that thou mayest live.
Mark 12:31 And the second *is* like, *namely* this, Thou shalt love thy neighbour as thyself. There is none other commandment greater than these.	**Leviticus 19:18** Thou shalt not avenge, nor bear any grudge against the children of thy people, but thou shalt love thy neighbour as thyself: I *am* the LORD.
Mark 12:32 And the scribe said unto him, Well, Master, thou hast said the truth: for there is one God; and there is none other but he:	**Deuteronomy 4:35** Unto thee it was shewed, that thou mightest know that the LORD he *is* God; *there is* none else beside him. **Deuteronomy 6:4** Hear, O Israel: The LORD our God *is* one LORD :
Mark 12:33 And to love him with all the heart, and with all the understanding, and with all the soul, and with all the strength, and to love *his* neighbour as himself, is more than all whole burnt offerings and sacrifices.	**Leviticus 19:18** Thou shalt not avenge, nor bear any grudge against the children of thy people, but thou shalt love thy neighbour as thyself: I *am* the LORD. **Deuteronomy 6:5** And thou shalt love the LORD thy God with all thine heart, and with all thy soul, and with all thy might.
Mark 12:36 For David himself said by the Holy Ghost, The LORD said to my Lord, Sit thou on my right hand, till I make thine enemies thy footstool.	**Psalms 8:6** Thou madest him to have dominion over the works of thy hands; thou hast put all *things* under his feet: **Psalms 16:8** I have set the LORD always before me: because *he is* at my right hand, I shall not be moved. **Psalms 110:1** The LORD said unto my Lord, Sit thou at my right hand, until I make thine enemies thy footstool. **Psalms 110:5** The Lord at thy right hand shall strike through kings in the day of his wrath. **Zechraiah 3:1** And he shewed me Joshua the high priest standing before the angel of the LORD, and Satan standing at his right hand to resist him.
Mark 12:39 And the chief seats in the synagogues, and the uppermost rooms at feasts:	**Deuteronomy 16:16** Three times in a year shall all thy males appear before the LORD thy God in the place which he shall choose; in the feast of unleavened bread, and in the feast of weeks, and in the feast of tabernacles: and they shall not appear before the LORD empty:
Mark 12:41 And Jesus sat over against the treasury, and beheld how the people cast money into the treasury: and many that were rich cast in much.	**2 Kings 12:9** But Jehoiada the priest took a chest, and bored a hole in the lid of it, and set it beside the altar, on the right side as one cometh into the house of the LORD: and the priests that kept the door put therein all the money *that was* brought into the house of the LORD.
Mark 13:2 And Jesus answering said unto him, Seest thou these great buildings? there shall not be left one stone upon another, that shall not be thrown down.	**1 Kings 9:7-8** Then will I cut off Israel out of the land which I have given them; and this house, which I have hallowed for my name, will I cast out of my sight; and Israel shall be a proverb and a byword among all people: 8 And at this house, *which* is high, every one that passeth by it shall be astonished, and shall hiss; and they shall say, Why hath the LORD done thus unto this land, and to this house? **Micah 3:12** Therefore shall Zion for your sake be plowed *as* a field, and Jerusalem shall become heaps, and the mountain of the house as the high places of the forest.

Mark 13:5 And Jesus answering them began to say, Take heed lest any *man* deceive you:	**Jeremiah 29:8** For thus saith the LORD of hosts, the God of Israel; Let not your prophets and your diviners, that *be* in the midst of you, deceive you, neither hearken to your dreams which ye cause to be dreamed.
Mark 13:6 For many shall come in my name, saying, I am *Christ*; and shall deceive many.	**Jeremiah 14:14** Then the LORD said unto me, The prophets prophesy lies in my name: I sent them not, neither have I commanded them, neither spake unto them: they prophesy unto you a false vision and divination, and a thing of nought, and the deceit of their heart. **Jeremiah 23:21** I have not sent these prophets, yet they ran: I have not spoken to them, yet they prophesied.
Mark 13:8 For nation shall rise against nation, and kingdom against kingdom: and there shall be earthquakes in divers places, and there shall be famines and **troubles**: these *are* the beginnings of sorrows.	**Isaiah 19:2** And I will set the Egyptians against the Egyptians: and they shall fight every one against his brother, and every one against his neighbour; city against city, *and* kingdom against kingdom. **Daniel 12:1-2** And at that time shall Michael stand up, the great prince which standeth for the children of thy people: and there shall be a time of **trouble**, such as never was since there was a nation *even* to that same time: and at that time thy people shall be delivered, every one that shall be found written in the book. 2 And many of them that sleep in the dust of the earth shall awake, some to everlasting life, and some to shame *and* everlasting contempt.
Mark 13:12 Now the brother shall betray the brother to death, and the father the son; and children shall rise up against *their* parents, and shall cause them to be put to death.	**Ezekiel 38:21** And I will call for a sword against him throughout all my mountains, saith the Lord GOD: every man's sword shall be against his brother. **Micah 7:6** For the son dishonoureth the father, the daughter riseth up against her mother, the daughter in law against her mother in law; a man's enemies *are* the men of his own house.
Mark 13:14 But when ye shall see the abomination of desolation, spoken of by Daniel the prophet, standing where it ought not, (let him that readeth understand,) then let them that be in Judaea flee to the mountains:	**Daniel 8:13** Then I heard one saint speaking, and another saint said unto that certain *saint* which spake, How long *shall be* the vision *concerning* the daily *sacrifice,* and the transgression of desolation, to give both the sanctuary and the host to be trodden under foot? **Daniel 9:27** And he shall confirm the covenant with many for one week: and in the midst of the week he shall cause the sacrifice and the oblation to cease, and for the overspreading of abominations he shall make *it* desolate, even until the consummation, and that determined shall be poured upon the desolate. **Daniel 11:31** And arms shall stand on his part, and they shall pollute the sanctuary of strength, and shall take away the daily *sacrifice,* and they shall place the abomination that maketh desolate. **Daniel 12:11** And from the time *that* the daily *sacrifice* shall be taken away, and the abomination that maketh desolate set up, *there shall be* a thousand two hundred and ninety days. **Amos 3:7** Surely the Lord GOD will do nothing, but he revealeth his secret unto his servants the prophets.
Mark 13:22 For false Christs and false prophets shall rise, and shall shew signs and wonders, to seduce, if *it were* possible, even the elect.	**Deuteronomy 13:1-3** If there arise among you a prophet, or a dreamer of dreams, and giveth thee a sign or a wonder, 2 And the sign or the wonder come to pass, whereof he spake unto thee, saying, Let us go after other gods, which thou hast not known, and let us serve them; 3 Thou shalt not hearken unto the words of that prophet, or that dreamer of dreams: for the LORD your God

	proveth you, to know whether ye love the LORD your God with all your heart and with all your soul.
Mark 13:24 But in those days, after that tribulation, the sun shall be darkened, and the moon shall not give her light,	**Isaiah 13:9-10** Behold, the day of the LORD cometh, cruel both with wrath and fierce anger, to lay the land desolate: and he shall destroy the sinners thereof out of it. 10 For the stars of heaven and the constellations thereof shall not give their light: the sun shall be darkened in his going forth, and the moon shall not cause her light to shine. **Ezekiel 32:7** And when I shall put thee out, I will cover the heaven, and make the stars thereof dark; I will cover the sun with a cloud, and the moon shall not give her light. **Joel 2:31** The sun shall be turned into darkness, and the moon into blood, before the great and the terrible day of the LORD come. **Joel 3:15** The sun and the moon shall be darkened, and the stars shall withdraw their shining.
Mark 13:26 And then shall they see the Son of man coming in the clouds with great power and glory.	**Daniel 7:13** I saw in the night visions, and, behold, *one* like the Son of man came with the clouds of heaven, and came to the Ancient of days, and they brought him near before him.
Mark 13:27 And then shall he send his angels, and shall gather together his elect from the four winds, from the uttermost part of the earth to the uttermost part of heaven.	**Isaiah 11:12** And he shall set up an ensign for the nations, and shall assemble the outcasts of Israel, and gather together the dispersed of Judah from the four corners of the earth. Jerermiah 49:36 And upon Elam will I bring the four winds from the four quarters of heaven, and will scatter them toward all those winds; and there shall be no nation whither the outcasts of Elam shall not come. **Ezekiel 7:2** Also, thou son of man, thus saith the Lord GOD unto the land of Israel; An end, the end is come upon the four corners of the land. **Ezekiel 37:9** Then said he unto me, Prophesy unto the wind, prophesy, son of man, and say to the wind, Thus saith the Lord GOD; Come from the four winds, O breath, and breathe upon these slain, that they may live. **Daniel 7:2** Daniel spake and said, I saw in my vision by night, and, behold, the four winds of the heaven strove upon the great sea. **Daniel 8:8** Therefore the he goat waxed very great: and when he was strong, the great horn was broken; and for it came up four notable ones toward the four winds of heaven. **Daniel 11:4** And when he shall stand up, his kingdom shall be broken, and shall be divided toward the four winds of heaven; and not to his posterity, nor according to his dominion which he ruled: for his kingdom shall be plucked up, even for others beside those. **Zechariah 2:6** Ho, ho, *come forth,* and flee from the land of the north, saith the LORD: for I have spread you abroad as the four winds of the heaven, saith the LORD.
Mark 13:31 Heaven and earth shall pass away: but my words shall not pass away.	**Isaiah 40:8** The grass withereth, the flower fadeth: but the word of our God shall stand for ever. **Isaiah 51:6** Lift up your eyes to the heavens, and look upon the earth beneath: for the heavens shall vanish away like smoke, and the earth shall wax old like a garment, and they that dwell therein shall die in like manner: but my salvation shall be for ever, and my righteousness shall not be abolished.

	See Matthew 5:18 "Words"
Mark 14:7 For ye have the poor with you always, and whensoever ye will ye may do them good: but me ye have not always.	**Deuteronomy 15:11** For the poor shall never cease out of the land: therefore I command thee, saying, Thou shalt open thine hand wide unto thy brother, to thy poor, and to thy needy, in thy land.
Mark 14:12 And the first day of unleavened bread, when they killed the passover, his disciples said unto him, Where wilt thou that we go and prepare that thou mayest eat the passover?	**Exodus 12:17** And ye shall observe *the feast of* unleavened bread; for in this selfsame day have I brought your armies out of the land of Egypt: therefore shall ye observe this day in your generations by an ordinance for ever.
Mark 14:18 And as they sat and did eat, Jesus said, Verily I say unto you, One of you which eateth with me shall betray me.	**Psalms 41:9** Yea, mine own familiar friend, in whom I trusted, which did eat of my bread, hath lifted up *his* heel against me.
Mark 14:24 And he said unto them, This is my blood of the new testament, which is shed for many.	**Jeremiah 31:31-33** Behold, the days come, saith the LORD, that **I will make a new covenant with the house of Israel**, and with the house of Judah: 32 Not according to the covenant that I made with their fathers in the day *that* I took them by the hand to bring them out of the land of Egypt; which my covenant they brake, although I was an husband unto them, saith the LORD: 33 But this *shall be* the covenant that I will make with the house of Israel; After those days, saith the LORD, I will put my law in their inward parts, and write it in their hearts; and will be their God, and they shall be my people. 34 And they shall teach no more every man his neighbour, and every man his brother, saying, Know the LORD: for they shall all know me, from the least of them unto the greatest of them, saith the LORD: for I will forgive their iniquity, and I will remember their sin no more. **See Matthew 26:28 "Atonement"**
Mark 14:27 And Jesus saith unto them, All ye shall be offended because of me this night: for it is written, I will smite the shepherd, and the sheep shall be scattered.	**Zechariah 13:7** Awake, O sword, against my shepherd, and against the man *that is* my fellow, saith the LORD of hosts: smite the shepherd, and the sheep shall be scattered: and I will turn mine hand upon the little ones.
Matthew 26:38 Then saith he unto them, My **soul** is exceeding sorrowful, even unto death: tarry ye here, and watch with me.	**See 1 Thessalonians 5:23 "Body, soul, and spirit"**
Mark 14:43 And immediately, while he yet spake, cometh Judas, one of the twelve, and with him a great multitude with swords and staves, from the chief priests and the scribes and the **elders**.	**See 1 Peter 5:1 "Elders"**
Mark 14:48 And Jesus answered and said unto them, Are ye come out, as against a thief, with swords and *with* staves to take me? **Mark 14:50** And they all forsook him, and fled.	**Job 19:13** He hath put my brethren far from me, and mine acquaintance are verily estranged from me. **Psalms 31:11** I was a reproach among all mine enemies, but especially among my neighbours, and a fear to mine acquaintance: they that did see me without fled from me. **Psalms 69:8** I am become a stranger unto my brethren, and an alien unto my mother's children.
Mark 14:53 And they led Jesus away to the high priest: and with him were assembled all the chief priests and the	**See 1 Peter 5:1 "Elders"**

elders and the scribes.	
Mark 14:56-57 For many bare false witness against him, but their witness agreed not together. 57 And there arose certain, and bare false witness against him, saying,	**Genesis 39:19** And it came to pass, when his master heard the words of his wife, which she spake unto him, saying, After this manner did thy servant to me; that his wrath was kindled. **Psalms 109:2-3** For the mouth of the wicked and the mouth of the deceitful are opened against me: they have spoken against me with a lying tongue. 3 They compassed me about also with words of hatred; and fought against me without a cause.
Mark 14:61 But he held his peace, and answered nothing. Again the high priest asked him, and said unto him, Art thou the Christ, the Son of the Blessed?	**Isaiah 53:7** He was oppressed, and he was afflicted, yet he opened not his mouth: he is brought as a lamb to the slaughter, and as a sheep before her shearers is dumb, so he openeth not his mouth.
Mark 14:62 And Jesus said, I am: and ye shall see the Son of man sitting on the right hand of power, and coming in the clouds of heaven.	**Psalms 8:6** Thou madest him to have dominion over the works of thy hands; thou hast put all *things* under his feet: **Psalms 16:8** I have set the LORD always before me: because *he is* at my right hand, I shall not be moved. **Psalms 110:1** The LORD said unto my Lord, Sit thou at my right hand, until I make thine enemies thy footstool. **Psalms 110:5** The Lord at thy right hand shall strike through kings in the day of his wrath. **Daniel 7:13** I saw in the night visions, and, behold, *one* like the Son of man came with the clouds of heaven, and came to the Ancient of days, and they brought him near before him. **Zechraiah 3:1** And he shewed me Joshua the high priest standing before the angel of the LORD, and Satan standing at his right hand to resist him.
Mark 14:65 And some began to spit on him, and to cover his face, and to buffet him, and to say unto him, Prophesy: and the servants did strike him with the palms of their hands.	**Job 16:10** They have gaped upon me with their mouth; they have smitten me upon the cheek reproachfully; they have gathered themselves together against me. **Isaiah 50:6** I gave my back to the smiters, and my cheeks to them that plucked off the hair: I hid not my face from shame and spitting.
Mark 15:1 And straightway in the morning the chief priests held a consultation with the **elders** and scribes and the whole council, and bound Jesus, and carried *him* away, and delivered *him* to Pilate.	**Psalms 2:2** The kings of the earth set themselves, and the rulers take counsel together, against the LORD, and against his anointed, *saying,* **See 1 Peter 5:1 "Elders"**
Mark 15:4-5 And Pilate asked him again, saying, Answerest thou nothing? behold how many things they witness against thee. 5 But Jesus yet answered nothing; so that Pilate marvelled.	**Psalms 38:13-14** But I, as a deaf *man*, heard not; and *I was* as a dumb man *that* openeth not his mouth. 14 Thus I was as a man that heareth not, and in whose mouth *are* no reproofs.
Mark 15:24 And when they had crucified him, they parted his garments, casting lots upon them, what every man should take.	**Psalms 22:16-18** For dogs have compassed me: the assembly of the wicked have inclosed me: they pierced my hands and my feet. 17 I may tell all my bones: they look and stare upon me. 18 They part my garments among them, and cast lots upon my vesture. **Zechariah 12:10** And I will pour upon the house of David, and upon the inhabitants of Jerusalem, the spirit of grace and of supplications: and they shall look upon me whom they have pierced, and they shall mourn for him, as one mourneth for his only

	son, and shall be in bitterness for him, as one that is in bitterness for his firstborn.
Mark 15:28 And the scripture was fulfilled, which saith, And he was numbered with the transgressors.	**Isaiah 53:12** Therefore will I divide him *a portion* with the great, and he shall divide the spoil with the strong; because he hath poured out his soul unto death: and he was numbered with the transgressors; and he bare the sin of many, and made intercession for the transgressors.
Mark 15:29 And they that passed by railed on him, wagging their heads, and saying, Ah, thou that destroyest the temple, and buildest *it* in three days,	**Psalms 22:7** All they that see me laugh me to scorn: they shoot out the lip, they shake the head, *saying,* **Psalms 69:20** Reproach hath broken my heart; and I am full of heaviness: and I looked *for some* to take pity, but *there was* none; and for comforters, but I found none. **Psalms 109:25** I became also a reproach unto them: *when* they looked upon me they shaked their heads.
Mark 15:34 And at the ninth hour Jesus cried with a loud voice, saying, Eloi, Eloi, lama sabachthani? which is, being interpreted, My God, my God, why hast thou forsaken me?	**Psalms 22:1** My God, my God, why hast thou forsaken me? *why art thou so* far from helping me, *and from* the words of my roaring?
Mark 15:36 And one ran and filled a spunge full of vinegar, and put *it* on a reed, and gave him to drink, saying, Let alone; let us see whether Elias will come to take him down.	**Psalms 69:21** They gave me also gall for my meat; and in my thirst they gave me vinegar to drink.
Mark 15:38 And the veil of the temple was rent in twain from the top to the bottom.	**2 Chronicles 3:14** And he made the vail *of* blue, and purple, and crimson, and fine linen, and wrought cherubims thereon.
Mark 15:40 There were also women looking on afar off: among whom was Mary Magdalene, and Mary the mother of James the less and of Joses, and Salome;	**Psalms 38:11** My lovers and my friends stand aloof from my sore; and my kinsmen stand afar off.
Mark 15:43 Joseph of Arimathaea, an honorable counselor, which also waited for the kingdom of God, came, and went in boldly unto Pilate, and craved the **body** of Jesus.	See 1 Thessalonians 5:23 "Body, soul, and spirit"
Mark 16:1-2 And the **sabbath** having past, Mary the Magdalene, and Mary of James, and Salome, bought spices, that having come, they may anoint him, 2 and early in the morning of the first of the **sabbaths**, they come unto the sepulchre, at the rising of the sun,	See Colossians 2:16 "Sabbath"
Mark 16:6 And he saith unto them, Be not affrighted: Ye seek Jesus of Nazareth, which was crucified: he is risen; he is not here: behold the place where they laid him.	**Psalms 16:10-11** For thou wilt not leave my soul in hell; neither wilt thou suffer thine Holy One to see corruption. 11 Thou wilt shew me the path of life: in thy presence is fulness of joy; at thy right hand *there* are pleasures for evermore. **Psalms 49:15** But God will redeem my soul from the power of the grave: for he shall receive me. Selah.
Mark 16:9 Now when *Jesus* was risen early the first *day* of the week, he	See Hebrews 13:2 "Good and bad angels"

appeared first to Mary Magdalene, out of whom he had cast seven **devils**.	
Mark 16:16 He that believeth and is baptized shall be saved; but he that believeth not shall be damned.	**Exodus 40:12** And thou shalt bring Aaron and his sons unto the door of the tabernacle of the congregation, and wash them with water. **Psalm 51:2** Wash me throughly from mine iniquity, and cleanse me from my sin. **Isaiah 1:16** Wash you, make you clean; put away the evil of your doings from before mine eyes; cease to do evil; **See Acts 2:38 "Salvation"**
Mark 16:17 And these **signs** shall follow them that believe; In my name shall they cast out **devils**; they shall **speak with new tongues**;	**Genesis 11:9** Therefore is the name of it called Babel; because the LORD did there **confound the language** of all the earth: and from thence did the LORD scatter them abroad upon the face of all the earth. **Exodus 4:28** And Moses told Aaron all the words of the LORD who had sent him, and **all the signs** which he had commanded him. **Exodus 4:30** And Aaron spake all the words which the LORD had spoken unto Moses, and **did the signs** in the sight of the people. **Exodus 10:1** And the LORD said unto Moses, Go in unto Pharaoh: for I have hardened his heart, and the heart of his servants, that I might shew these **my signs** before him: **Numbers 14:11** And the LORD said unto Moses, How long will this people provoke me? and how long will it be ere they believe me, for **all the signs** which I have shewed among them? **2 Kings 20:8-11** And Hezekiah said unto Isaiah, What shall be the **sign that the LORD will heal me**, and that I shall go up into the house of the LORD the third day? 9 And Isaiah said, This **sign** shalt thou have of the LORD, that the LORD will do the thing that he hath spoken: shall the shadow go forward ten degrees, or go back ten degrees? 10 And Hezekiah answered, It is a light thing for the shadow to go down ten degrees: nay, but let the shadow return backward ten degrees. 11 And Isaiah the prophet cried unto the LORD: and he brought the shadow ten degrees backward, by which it had gone down in the dial of Ahaz. **2 Chronicles 32:24** In those days Hezekiah was sick to the death, and prayed unto the LORD: and he spake unto him, and he gave him a **sign**. **Judges 6:36** And Gideon said unto God, If thou wilt save Israel by mine hand, as thou hast said, 37 Behold, I will put a **fleece** of wool in the floor; and if the dew be on the fleece only, and it be dry upon all the earth beside, then shall I know that thou wilt save Israel by mine hand, as thou hast said. 38 And it was so: for he rose up early on the morrow, and thrust the **fleece** together, and wringed the dew out of the **fleece**, a bowl full of water. 39 And Gideon said unto God, Let not thine anger be hot against me, and I will speak but this once: let me prove, I pray thee, but this once with the **fleece**; let it now be dry only upon the **fleece**, and upon all the ground let there be dew. 40 And God did so that night: for it was dry upon the fleece only, and there was dew on all the ground. **Psalms 50:15** And call upon me in the day of trouble: **I will deliver thee**, and thou shalt glorify me. **Isaiah 28:11** For with stammering lips and another tongue will he

	speak to this people.

Isaiah 33:19 Thou shalt not see a fierce people, a people of a deeper speech than thou canst perceive; of a **stammering tongue**, *that thou canst* not understand.

Ezekiel 13:17-23 Likewise, thou son of man, set thy face against the daughters of thy people, which prophesy out of their own heart; and prophesy thou against them, 18 And say, Thus saith the Lord GOD; **Woe to the *women* that sew pillows to all armholes, and make kerchiefs upon the head of every stature to <u>hunt souls</u>! Will ye <u>hunt the souls</u> of my people, and will ye <u>save the souls alive</u>** *that come* unto you? 19 And will ye pollute me among my people for handfuls of barley and for pieces of bread, **to slay the souls that should not die**, and **to save the souls alive that should not live, by your lying to my people that hear** *your* **lies**? 20 Wherefore thus saith the Lord GOD; Behold, I *am* against your pillows, wherewith ye there <u>**hunt the souls**</u> **to make** *them* **fly**, and I will tear them from your arms, and will let the souls go, *even* the <u>**souls that ye hunt**</u> to make *them* fly. 21 Your kerchiefs also will I tear, and **deliver my people out of your hand, and they shall be no more in your hand to be hunted**; and ye shall know that I *am* the LORD. 22 Because with lies ye have made the heart of the righteous sad, whom I have not made sad; and strengthened the hands of the wicked, that he should not return from his wicked way, by promising him life: 23 Therefore ye shall see no more vanity, nor divine divinations: for **I will deliver my people out of your hand**: and ye shall know that I *am* the LORD.

Daniel 6:27 He delivereth and rescueth, and he worketh **signs** and wonders in heaven and in earth, who hath delivered Daniel from the power of the lions.

See Hebrews 13:2 "Good and bad angels" |
| **Mark 16:18** They shall take up serpents; and if they drink any deadly thing, it shall not hurt them; they shall **lay hands on the sick, and they shall recover.** | **2 Kings 4:39-41** And one went out into the field to gather herbs, and found a wild vine, and gathered thereof wild gourds his lap full, and came and shred them into the pot of pottage: for they knew them not. 40 So they poured out for the men to eat. And it came to pass, as they were eating of the pottage, that they cried out, and said, O thou man of God, there is death in the pot. And they could not eat thereof. 41 But he said, Then bring meal. And he cast it into the pot; and he said, Pour out for the people, that they may eat. And there was no harm in the pot.

Psalm 23:6 Surely goodness and mercy shall follow me all the days of my life: and I will dwell in the house of the LORD for ever.

Psalms 59:11 ... O Lord our shield.

Psalms 84:9 ... O God our shield, ...

Psalms 91:4 He shall cover thee with his feathers, and under his wings shalt thou trust: his truth *shall be thy* shield and buckler.

Proverb 1:33 But whoso hearkeneth unto me shall dwell safely, and shall be quiet from fear of evil.

Proverbs 2:8 He keepeth the paths of judgment, and preserveth the way of his saints.

Proverbs 11:14 Where no counsel is, the people fall: but in the multitude of counsellors there is safety.

Proverb 30:5 Every word of God *is* pure: he *is* a shield unto them |

	that put their trust in him. **See 1 Peter 2:24 "Healing"**
Mark 16:19 So then after the Lord had spoken unto them, he was received up into heaven, and sat on the right hand of God.	**Psalms 8:6** Thou madest him to have dominion over the works of thy hands; thou hast put all *things* under his feet: **Psalms 16:8** I have set the LORD always before me: because *he is* at my right hand, I shall not be moved. **Psalms 68:18** Thou hast ascended on high, thou hast led captivity captive: thou hast received gifts for men; yea, *for* the rebellious also, that the LORD God might dwell *among them.* **Psalms 110:1** The LORD said unto my Lord, Sit thou at my right hand, until I make thine enemies thy footstool. **Psalms 110:5** The Lord at thy right hand shall strike through kings in the day of his wrath. **Isaiah 52:13** Behold, my servant shall deal prudently, he shall be exalted and extolled, and be very high. **Zechraiah 3:1** And he shewed me Joshua the high priest standing before the angel of the LORD, and Satan standing at his right hand to resist him.
Mark 16:20 And they went forth, and preached every where, **the Lord working with** *them*, and confirming the word with **signs** following. Amen.	**Psalms 139:7-10** Whither shall I go from thy spirit? or whither shall I flee from thy presence? 8 If I ascend up into heaven, thou art there: if I make my bed in hell, behold, thou art there. 9 If I take the wings of the morning, and dwell in the uttermost parts of the sea; 10 Even there shall thy hand lead me, and thy right hand shall hold me. **See Mark 16:17 "Signs"**
Luke 1:9 According to the custom of the priest's office, his lot was to burn incense when he went into the temple of the Lord.	**Exodus 30:7** And Aaron shall burn thereon sweet incense every morning: when he dresseth the lamps, he shall burn incense upon it.
Luke 1:10 And the whole multitude of the people were praying without at the time of incense.	**Deuteronomy 33:10** They shall teach Jacob thy judgments, and Israel thy law: they shall put incense before thee, and whole burnt sacrifice upon thine altar. **Malachi 1:11** For from the rising of the sun even unto the going down of the same my name *shall be* great among the Gentiles; and in every place incense *shall be* offered unto my name, and a pure offering: for my name *shall be* great among the heathen, saith the LORD of hosts.
Luke 1:15 For he shall be great in the sight of the Lord, and **shall drink neither wine nor strong drink**; and he shall be filled with the Holy Ghost, even from his mother's womb.	**Leviticus 10:9** Do not drink wine nor strong drink, thou, nor thy sons with thee, when ye go into the tabernacle of the congregation, lest ye die: *it shall be* a statute for ever throughout your generations: **Deuteronomy 14:26** And thou shalt bestow that money for whatsoever thy soul lusteth after, for oxen, or for sheep, or for wine, or for strong drink, or for whatsoever thy soul desireth: and thou shalt eat there before the LORD thy God, and thou shalt rejoice, thou, and thine household, **Judges 13:4** Now therefore beware, I pray thee, and drink not wine nor strong drink, and eat not any unclean *thing*: **Proverbs 20:1** Wine *is* a mocker, strong drink *is* raging: and whosoever is deceived thereby is not wise.

	Isaiah 5:11 Woe unto them that rise up early in the morning, *that* they may follow strong drink; that continue until night, *till* wine inflame them!
Luke 1:16 And many of the children of Israel shall he turn to the Lord their God.	**Malachi 4:6** And he shall turn the heart of the fathers to the children, and the heart of the children to their fathers, lest I come and smite the earth with a curse. { THE END OF THE PROPHETS. }
Luke 1:17 And he shall go before him in the spirit and power of Elias, to turn the hearts of the fathers to the children, and the disobedient to the wisdom of the just; to make ready a people prepared for the Lord.	**Malachi 4:5-6** And he shall turn the heart of the fathers to the children, and the heart of the children to their fathers, lest I come and smite the earth with a curse.
Luke 1:18 And Zacharias said unto the angel, Whereby shall I know this? for I am an old man, and my wife well stricken in years.	**Genesis 17:17** Then Abraham fell upon his face, and laughed, and said in his heart, Shall *a child* be born unto him that is an hundred years old? and shall Sarah, that is ninety years old, bear? **Genesis 18:12** Therefore Sarah laughed within herself, saying, After I am waxed old shall I have pleasure, my lord being old also?
Luke 1:25 Thus hath the Lord dealt with me in the days wherein he looked on *me*, to take away my reproach among men.	**Genesis 30:23** And she conceived, and bare a son; and said, God hath taken away my reproach: **Isaiah 4:1** And in that day seven women shall take hold of one man, saying, We will eat our own bread, and wear our own apparel: only let us be called by thy name, to take away our reproach.
Luke 1:31 And, behold, thou shalt conceive in thy womb, and bring forth a son, and shalt call his name JESUS.	**Isaiah 9:6** For unto us a child is born, unto us a son is given: and the government shall be upon his shoulder: and his name shall be called Wonderful, Counsellor, The mighty God, The everlasting Father, The Prince of Peace.
Luke 1:32 He shall be great, and shall be called the Son of the Highest: and the Lord God shall give unto him the throne of his father David:	**Psalms 89:3-4** I have made a covenant with my chosen, I have sworn unto David my servant, 4 Thy seed will I establish for ever, and build up thy throne to all generations. Selah. **Psalms 89:29** His seed also will I make *to endure* for ever, and his throne as the days of heaven. **Psalms 89:36-37** His seed shall endure for ever, and his throne as the sun before me. 37 It shall be established for ever as the moon, and *as* a faithful witness in heaven. Selah. **Psalms 132:11** The LORD hath sworn *in* truth unto David; he will not turn from it; Of the fruit of thy body will I set upon thy throne. **Isaiah 9:7** Of the increase of *his* government and peace *there shall be* no end, upon the throne of David, and upon his kingdom, to order it, and to establish it with judgment and with justice from henceforth even for ever. The zeal of the LORD of hosts will perform this. **Isaiah 11:1** And there shall come forth a rod out of the stem of Jesse, and a Branch shall grow out of his roots: **Isaiah 11:10** And in that day there shall be a root of Jesse, which shall stand for an ensign of the people; to it shall the Gentiles seek: and his rest shall be glorious.
Luke 1:33 And he shall reign over the house of Jacob for ever; and of his kingdom there shall be no end.	**1 Chronicles 22:10** He shall build an house for my name; and he shall be my son, and I *will be* his father; and I will establish the throne of his kingdom over Israel for ever.

	Psalms 45:6 Thy throne, O God, *is* for ever and ever: the sceptre of thy kingdom *is* a right sceptre.
	Psalms 89:36 His seed shall endure for ever, and his throne as the sun before me.
	Jeremiah 23:5 Behold, the days come, saith the LORD, that I will raise unto David a righteous Branch, and a King shall reign and prosper, and shall execute judgment and justice in the earth.
	Daniel 2:44 And in the days of these kings shall the God of heaven set up a kingdom, which shall never be destroyed: and the kingdom shall not be left to other people, *but* it shall break in pieces and consume all these kingdoms, and it shall stand for ever.
	Daniel 4:3 How great *are* his signs! and how mighty *are* his wonders! his kingdom *is* an everlasting kingdom, and his dominion *is* from generation to generation.
	Daniel 6:26 I make a decree, That in every dominion of my kingdom men tremble and fear before the God of Daniel: for he *is* the living God, and stedfast for ever, and his kingdom *that* which shall not be destroyed, and his dominion *shall be even* unto the end.
	Daniel 7:14 And there was given him dominion, and glory, and a kingdom, that all people, nations, and languages, should serve him: his dominion *is* an everlasting dominion, which shall not pass away, and his kingdom *that* which shall not be destroyed.
	Daniel 7:27 And the kingdom and dominion, and the greatness of the kingdom under the whole heaven, shall be given to the people of the saints of the most High, whose kingdom *is* an everlasting kingdom, and all dominions shall serve and obey him.
	Micah 4:7 And I will make her that halted a remnant, and her that was cast far off a strong nation: and the LORD shall reign over them in mount Zion from henceforth, even for ever.
	Exodus 40:34 Then a cloud covered the tent of the congregation, and the glory of the LORD filled the tabernacle.
	Psalms 2:7 I will declare the decree: the LORD hath said unto me, Thou *art* my **Son**; this day have I begotten thee.
Luke 1:35 And the angel answered and said unto her, The Holy Ghost shall come upon thee, and the power of the Highest shall overshadow thee: therefore also that holy thing which shall be born of thee shall be called the Son of God.	**Psalms 2:12** Kiss the **Son**, lest he be angry, and ye perish *from* the way, when his wrath is kindled but a little. Blessed *are* all they that put their trust in him.
	Isaiah 7:14 Therefore the Lord himself shall give you a sign; Behold, a virgin shall conceive, and bear a **son**, and shall call his name Immanuel.
	Isaiah 9:6 For unto us a child is born, unto us a son is given: and the government shall be upon his shoulder: and his name shall be called Wonderful, Counselor, The mighty God, The everlasting Father, The Prince of Peace.
Luke 1:37 For with God nothing shall be impossible.	**Jeremiah 32:17** Ah Lord GOD! behold, thou hast made the heaven and the earth by thy great power and stretched out arm, *and* there is nothing too hard for thee:
Luke 1:39 And Mary arose in those days, and went into the hill country with haste, into a city of Juda;	**2 Samuel 6:2** And David arose, and went with all the people that *were* with him from Baale of Judah, to bring up from thence **the ark** of God, whose name is called by the name of the LORD of

	hosts that dwelleth *between* the cherubims.
Luke 1:42 And she spake out with a loud voice, and said, Blessed *art* thou among women, and blessed *is* the fruit of thy womb.	**2 Samuel 6:11** And **the ark** of the LORD continued in the house of Obededom the Gittite three months: and the LORD **blessed** Obededom, and all his household. **2 Samuel 6:12** And it was told king David, saying, The LORD hath **blessed** the house of Obededom, and all that *pertaineth* unto him, because of **the ark** of God. So David went and brought up the ark of God from the house of Obededom into the city of David with gladness. **2 Samuel 6:15** So David and all the house of Israel brought up **the ark** of the LORD with shouting, and with the sound of the trumpet.
Luke 1:43 And whence *is* this to me, that the mother of my Lord should come to me?	**2 Samuel 6:9** And David was afraid of the LORD that day, and said, How shall **the ark** of the LORD come to me?
Luke 1:44 For, lo, as soon as the voice of thy salutation sounded in mine ears, the babe leaped in my womb for joy.	**2 Samuel 6:16** And as **the ark** of the LORD came into the city of David, Michal Saul's daughter looked through a window, and saw king David leaping and dancing before the LORD; and she despised him in her heart.
Luke 1:47 And my spirit hath rejoiced in God my Saviour.	**Job 19:25** For I know *that* my redeemer liveth, and *that* he shall stand at the latter *day* upon the earth: **Isaiah 60:16** Thou shalt also suck the milk of the Gentiles, and shalt suck the breast of kings: and thou shalt know that I the LORD *am* thy Saviour and thy Redeemer, the mighty One of Jacob.
Luke 1:48 For he hath regarded the low estate of his handmaiden: for, behold, from henceforth all generations shall call me blessed.	**1 Samuel 1:11** And she vowed a vow, and said, O LORD of hosts, if thou wilt indeed look on the affliction of thine handmaid, and remember me, and not forget thine handmaid, but wilt give unto thine handmaid a man child, then I will give him unto the LORD all the days of his life, and there shall no razor come upon his head.
Luke 1:50 And his mercy *is* on them that fear him from generation to generation.	**Exodus 20:6** And shewing mercy unto thousands of them that love me, and keep my commandments. **Psalms 103:17** But the mercy of the LORD *is* from everlasting to everlasting upon them that fear him, and his righteousness unto children's children;
Luke 1:51 He hath shewed strength with his arm; he hath scattered the proud in the imagination of their hearts.	**Isaiah 51:9** Awake, awake, put on strength, O arm of the LORD; awake, as in the ancient days, in the generations of old. *Art* thou not it that hath cut Rahab, *and* wounded the dragon? **Isaiah 52:10** The LORD hath made bare his holy arm in the eyes of all the nations; and all the ends of the earth shall see the salvation of our God. **Psalms 33:10** The LORD bringeth the counsel of the heathen to nought: he maketh the devices of the people of none effect.
Luke 1:52 He hath put down the mighty from *their* seats, and exalted them of low degree.	**1 Samuel 2:8** He raiseth up the poor out of the dust, *and* lifteth up the beggar from the dunghill, to set *them* among princes, and to make them inherit the throne of glory: for the pillars of the earth *are* the LORD'S, and he hath set the world upon them. **Psalms 107:41** Yet setteth he the poor on high from affliction, and maketh *him* families like a flock. **Psalms 113:7** He raiseth up the poor out of the dust, *and* lifteth the

	needy out of the dunghill;
Luke 1:54 He hath holpen his servant Israel, in remembrance of *his* mercy;	**Isaiah 30:18** And therefore will the LORD wait, that he may be gracious unto you, and therefore will he be exalted, that he may have mercy upon you: for the LORD *is* a God of judgment: blessed *are* all they that wait for him. **Isaiah 41:9** *Thou* whom I have taken from the ends of the earth, and called thee from the chief men thereof, and said unto thee, Thou *art* my servant; I have chosen thee, and not cast thee away.
Luke 1:55 As he spake to our fathers, to Abraham, and to his seed for ever.	**Genesis 17:19** And God said, Sarah thy wife shall bear thee a son indeed; and thou shalt call his name Isaac: and I will establish my covenant with him for an everlasting covenant, *and* with his seed after him. **Genesis 22:18** And in thy seed shall all the nations of the earth be blessed; because thou hast obeyed my voice.
Luke 1:56 And Mary abode with her about three months, and returned to her own house.	**2 Samuel 6:11-12** And the ark of the LORD continued in the house of Obededom the Gittite three months: and the LORD blessed Obededom, and all his household. 12 And it was told king David, saying, The LORD hath blessed the house of Obededom, and all that *pertaineth* unto him, because of the ark of God. So David went and brought up the ark of God from the house of Obededom into the city of David with gladness.
Luke 1:59 And it came to pass, that on the eighth day they came to circumcise the child; and they called him Zacharias, after the name of his father.	**Genesis 17:12** And he that is eight days old shall be circumcised among you, every man child in your generations, he that is born in the house, or bought with money of any stranger, which *is* not of thy seed. **Leviticus 12:3** And in the eighth day the flesh of his foreskin shall be circumcised.
Luke 1:66 And all they that heard *them* laid *them* up in their hearts, saying, What manner of child shall this be! And the hand of the Lord was with him.	**2 Kings 6:16-17** And he answered, Fear not: for they that *be* with us *are* more than they that *be* with them. 17 And Elisha prayed, and said, LORD, I pray thee, open his eyes, that he may see. And the LORD opened the eyes of the young man; and he saw: and, behold, the mountain *was* full of horses and chariots of fire round about Elisha.
Luke 1:69 And hath raised up an horn of salvation for us in the house of his servant David;	**Psalms 18:2** The LORD *is* my rock, and my fortress, and my deliverer; my God, my strength, in whom I will trust; my buckler, and the **horn of my salvation**, *and* my high tower. **Psalms 132:17** There will I make the horn of David to bud: I have ordained a lamp for mine anointed.
Luke 1:70 As he spake by the mouth of his holy prophets, which have been since the world began:	**Deuteronomy 13:1-3** IF there arise among you a prophet, or a dreamer of dreams, and giveth thee a sign or a wonder, 2 And the sign or the wonder come to pass, whereof he spake unto thee, saying, Let us go after other gods, which thou hast not known, and let us serve them; 3 Thou shalt not hearken unto the words of that prophet, or that dreamer of dreams: for the LORD your God proveth you, to know whether ye love the LORD your God with all your heart and with all your soul. **2 Samuel 23:2** The Spirit of the LORD spake by me, and his word *was* in my tongue. **See Hebrews 12:14 "Holiness"**
Luke 1:72-73 To perform the mercy *promised* to our fathers, and to	**Genesis 12:3** And I will bless them that bless thee, and curse him that curseth thee: and in thee shall all families of the earth be

remember his holy covenant; 73 The oath which he sware to our father Abraham,	blessed. **Genesis 15:17-18** And it came to pass, that, when the sun went down, and it was dark, behold a smoking furnace, and a burning lamp that passed **between** those pieces. [18] In the same day **the LORD made a <u>covenant</u> with Abram**, saying, Unto thy seed have I given this land, from the river of Egypt unto the great river, the river Euphrates: **Genesis 22:16** And said, By myself have I sworn, saith the LORD, for because thou hast done this thing, and hast not withheld thy son, thine only *son* **Exodus 6:4** And I have also established my covenant with them, to give them the land of Canaan, the land of their pilgrimage, wherein they were strangers. **Psalms 105:9** Which *covenant* he made with Abraham, and his oath unto Isaac;
Luke 1:76 And thou, child, shalt be called the prophet of the Highest: for thou shalt go before the face of the Lord to prepare his ways;	**Malachi 3:1** Behold, I will send my messenger, and he shall prepare the way before me: … .
Luke 1:77 To **give knowledge of salvation** unto his people by **the remission of their sins,**	See Acts 2:39 "Salvation"
Luke 1:78 Through the tender mercy of our God; whereby the dayspring from on high hath visited us,	**Numbers 24:17** I shall see him, but not now: I shall behold him, but not nigh: there shall come a Star out of Jacob, and a Sceptre shall rise out of Israel, and shall smite the corners of Moab, and destroy all the children of Sheth. **Malachi 4:2** But unto you that fear my name shall the Sun of righteousness arise with healing in his wings; and ye shall go forth, and grow up as calves of the stall.
Luke 1:79 To give light to them that sit in darkness and *in* the shadow of death, to guide our feet into the way of peace.	**Isaiah 9:2** The people that walked in darkness have seen a great light: they that dwell in the land of the shadow of death, upon them hath the light shined. **Isaiah 42:7** To open the blind eyes, to bring out the prisoners from the prison, *and* them that sit in darkness out of the prison house.
Luke 2:4 And Joseph also went up from Galilee, out of the city of Nazareth, into Judaea, unto the city of David, which is called Bethlehem; (because he was of the house and lineage of David:)	**1 Samuel 16:4-5** And Samuel did that which the LORD spake, and came to Bethlehem. And the elders of the town trembled at his coming, and said, Comest thou peaceably? 5 And he said, Peaceably: I am come to sacrifice unto the LORD: sanctify yourselves, and come with me to the sacrifice. And he sanctified Jesse and his sons, and called them to the sacrifice. **Micah 5:2** But thou, Bethlehem Ephratah, *though* thou be little among the thousands of Judah, *yet* out of thee shall he come forth unto me *that is* to be ruler in Israel; whose goings forth *have been* from of old, from everlasting.
Luke 2:11 For unto you is born this day in the city of David a Saviour, which is Christ the Lord.	**Job 19:25** For I know *that* my redeemer liveth, and *that* he shall stand at the latter *day* upon the earth: **Isaiah 9:6** For unto us a child is born, unto us a son is given: and the government shall be upon his shoulder: and his name shall be called Wonderful, Counsellor, The mighty God, The everlasting Father, The Prince of Peace. **Isaiah 45:21** Tell ye, and bring *them* near; yea, let them take counsel together: who hath declared this from ancient time? *who*

	hath told it from that time? *have* not I the LORD? and *there is* no God else beside me; a just God and a **Savior**; *there is* none beside me.
	Isaiah 60:16 Thou shalt also suck the milk of the Gentiles, and shalt suck the breast of kings: and thou shalt know that I the LORD *am* thy Saviour and thy Redeemer, the mighty One of Jacob.
	Jeremiah 10:10 But the LORD is the true God, he is the living God, and an everlasting king: at his wrath the earth shall tremble, and the nations shall not be able to abide his indignation.
	Daniel 9:24-25 Seventy weeks are determined upon thy people and upon thy holy city, to finish the transgression, and to make an end of sins, and to make reconciliation for iniquity, and to bring in everlasting righteousness, and to seal up the vision and prophecy, and to anoint the most Holy. 25 Know therefore and understand, *that* from the going forth of the commandment to restore and to build Jerusalem unto the Messiah the Prince *shall be* seven weeks, and threescore and two weeks: the street shall be built again, and the wall, even in troublous times.
Luke 2:21-22 And when eight days were accomplished for the circumcising of the child, his name was called JESUS, which was so named of the angel before he was conceived in the womb. 22 And when the days of her purification according to the law of Moses were accomplished, they brought him to Jerusalem, to present him to the Lord;	**Genesis 17:12** And he that is eight days old shall be circumcised among you, every man child in your generations, he that is born in the house, or bought with money of any stranger, which *is* not of thy seed. **Leviticus 12:3-4** And in the eighth day the flesh of his foreskin shall be circumcised. 4 And she shall then continue in the blood of her purifying three and thirty days; she shall touch no hallowed thing, nor come into the sanctuary, until the days of her purifying be fulfilled.
Luke 2:23 (As it is written in the law of the Lord, Every male that openeth the womb shall be called holy to the Lord;)	**Exodus 13:2** Sanctify unto me all the firstborn, whatsoever openeth the womb among the children of Israel, [both] of man and of beast: it [is] mine. **Numbers 3:13** Because all the firstborn *are* mine; *for* on the day that I smote all the firstborn in the land of Egypt I hallowed unto me all the firstborn in Israel, both man and beast: mine shall they be: I *am* the LORD. **Numbers 8:16-19** For they *are* wholly given unto me from among the children of Israel; instead of such as open every womb, *even instead of* the firstborn of all the children of Israel, have I taken them unto me. 17 For all the firstborn of the children of Israel *are* mine, *both* man and beast: on the day that I smote every firstborn in the land of Egypt I sanctified them for myself. 18 And I have taken the Levites for all the firstborn of the children of Israel. 19 And I have given the Levites *as* a gift to Aaron and to his sons from among the children of Israel, to do the service of the children of Israel in the tabernacle of the congregation, and to make an atonement for the children of Israel: that there be no plague among the children of Israel, when the children of Israel come nigh unto the sanctuary. **Numbers 18:15** Every thing that openeth the matrix in all flesh, which they bring unto the LORD , *whether it be* of men or beasts, shall be thine: nevertheless the firstborn of man shalt thou surely redeem, and the firstling of unclean beasts shalt thou redeem.
Luke 2:24 And to offer a sacrifice according to that which is said in the law	**Leviticus 12:8** And if she be not able to bring a lamb, then she shall bring two turtles, or two young pigeons; the one for the burnt

of the Lord, A pair of turtledoves, or two young pigeons.	offering, and the other for a sin offering: and the priest shall make an atonement for her, and she shall be clean.
Luke 2:30 For mine eyes have seen thy salvation,	**Psalms 98:2** The LORD hath made known his salvation: his righteousness hath he openly shewed in the sight of the heathen. **Isaiah 52:10** The LORD hath made bare his holy arm in the eyes of all the nations; and all the ends of the earth shall see the salvation of our God.
Luke 2:32 A light to lighten the Gentiles, and the glory of thy people Israel.	**Isaiah 42:6** I the LORD have called thee in righteousness, and will hold thine hand, and will keep thee, and give thee for a covenant of the people, for a light of the Gentiles; **Isaiah 49:6** And he said, It is a light thing that thou shouldest be my servant to raise up the tribes of Jacob, and to restore the preserved of Israel: I will also give thee for a light to the Gentiles, that thou mayest be my salvation unto the end of the earth. **Psalms 27:1** The **LORD** *is* **my light** and my salvation; whom shall I fear? the LORD is the strength of my life; of whom shall I be afraid? **Isaiah 42:16** And I will bring the blind by a way *that* they knew not; I will lead them in paths *that* they have not known: I will make darkness light before them, and crooked things straight. These things will I do unto them, and not forsake them. **Isaiah 60:1** Arise, shine; for thy light is come, and the glory of the LORD is risen upon thee. **Isaiah 60:19-20** The sun shall be no more thy light by day; neither for brightness shall the moon give light unto thee: but the LORD shall be unto thee an **everlasting light**, and thy God thy glory. 20 Thy sun shall no more go down; neither shall thy moon withdraw itself: for the **LORD shall be thine everlasting light**, and the days of thy mourning shall be ended.
Luke 2:34 And Simeon blessed them, and said unto Mary his mother, Behold, this *child* is set for the fall and rising again of many in Israel; and for a sign which shall be spoken against;	**Psalms 118:22** The stone *which* the builders refused is become the head *stone* of the corner. **Isaiah 8:14** And he shall be for a sanctuary; but for a stone of stumbling and for a rock of offence to both the houses of Israel, for a gin and for a snare to the inhabitants of Jerusalem. **Isaiah 28:16** Therefore thus saith the Lord GOD, Behold, I lay in Zion for a foundation a stone, a tried stone, a precious corner *stone*, a sure foundation: he that believeth shall not make haste.
Luke 2:36 And there was one **Anna, a prophetess**, the daughter of Phanuel, of the tribe of Aser: she was of a great age, and had lived with an husband seven years from her virginity;	**Exodus 15:20** And **Miriam the prophetess**, the sister of Aaron, took a timbrel in her hand; and all the women went out after her with timbrels and with dances. **2 Kings 22:14-15** So Hilkiah the priest, and Ahikam, and Achbor, and Shaphan, and Asahiah, went unto Huldah the prophetess, the wife of Shallum the son of Tikvah, the son of Harhas, keeper of the wardrobe; (now she dwelt in Jerusalem in the college;) and they communed with her. 15 And she said unto them, Thus saith the LORD God of Israel, Tell the man that sent you to me, **2 Chronicles 34:22** And Hilkiah, and they that the king had appointed, went to **Huldah the prophetess**, the wife of Shallum the son of Tikvath, the son of Hasrah, keeper of the wardrobe; (now she dwelt in Jerusalem in the college:) and they spake to her

	to that effect. **Judges 4:4** And **Deborah, a prophetess**, the wife of Lapidoth, she judged Israel at that time. **Micah 6:4** For I brought thee up out of the land of Egypt, and redeemed thee out of the house of servants; and I sent before thee Moses, Aaron, and **Miriam**.
Luke 2:37 And she was a widow of about fourscore and four years, which departed not from the temple, but served God with **fastings** and prayers night and day.	**See Matthew 17:21 "Fasting"**
Luke 2:40 And the child grew, and waxed strong in **spirit**, filled with wisdom: and the grace of God was upon him.	**See 1 Thessalonians 5:23 "Body, soul, and spirit"**
Luke 2:41 Now his parents went to Jerusalem every year at the feast of the **passover**.	**Leviticus 23:5** In the fourteenth *day* of the first month at even *is* the LORD's **passover**. **Deuteronomy 16:1-4** Observe the month of Abib, and keep the **passover** unto the LORD thy God: for in the month of Abib the LORD thy God brought thee forth out of Egypt by night. 2 Thou shalt therefore sacrifice the passover unto the LORD thy God, of the flock and the herd, in the place which the LORD shall choose to place his name there. 3 Thou shalt eat no leavened bread with it; seven days shalt thou eat unleavened bread therewith, *even* the bread of affliction; for thou camest forth out of the land of Egypt in haste: that thou mayest remember the day when thou camest forth out of the land of Egypt all the days of thy life. 4 And there shall be no leavened bread seen with thee in all thy coast seven days; neither shall there *any thing* of the flesh, which thou sacrificedst the first day at even, remain all night until the morning.
Luke 2:52 And Jesus increased in wisdom and stature, and in favour with God and man.	**1 Samuel 2:26** And the child Samuel grew on, and was in favour both with the LORD, and also with men.
Luke 3:3 And he came into all the country about Jordan, preaching the baptism of repentance for the remission of sins;	**See Acts 2:38 "Salvation"**
Luke 3:4-6 As it is written in the book of the words of Esaias the prophet, saying, The voice of one crying in the wilderness, Prepare ye the way of the Lord, make his paths straight. Every valley shall be filled, and every mountain and hill shall be brought low; and the crooked shall be made straight, and the rough ways *shall be* made smooth; And all flesh shall see the salvation of God.	**Psalms 98:2** The LORD hath made known his salvation: his righteousness hath he openly shewed in the sight of the heathen. **Isaiah 40:3-5** The voice of him that crieth in the wilderness, Prepare ye the way of the Lord, make straight in the desert a highway for our God. Every valley shall be exalted, and every mountain and hill shall be made low: and the crooked shall be made straight, and the rough places plain: And the glory of the LORD shall be revealed, and all flesh shall see *it* together: for the mouth of the LORD hath spoken *it*. **Isaiah 52:10** The LORD hath made bare his holy arm in the eyes of all the nations; and all the ends of the earth shall see the salvation of our God.
Luke 3:9 And now also **the axe is laid unto the root of the trees**: every tree	**Psalms 52:5** God shall likewise destroy thee for ever, he shall take thee away, and pluck thee out of thy dwelling place, and **root thee**

therefore which bringeth not forth good fruit is hewn down, and cast into the fire.	out of the land of the living. Selah. **Isaiah 5:24** Therefore as the fire devoureth the stubble, and the flame consumeth the chaff, so **their root shall be as rottenness**, and their blossom shall go up as dust: because they have cast away the law of the LORD of hosts, and despised the word of the Holy One of Israel.
Luke 3:10 And the people asked him, saying, What shall we do then?	**Malachi 3:7** Even from the days of your fathers ye are gone away from mine ordinances, and have not kept *them*. Return unto me, and I will return unto you, saith the LORD of hosts. But ye said, Wherein shall we return?
Luke 3:13 And he said unto them, Exact no more than that which is appointed you.	**Exodus 20:15** Thou shalt not steal.
Luke 3:14 And the soldiers likewise demanded of him, saying, And what shall we do? And he said unto them, Do violence to no man, neither accuse *any* falsely; and be content with your wages.	**Exodus 20:16** Thou shalt not bear false witness against thy neighbour. **Deuteronomy 31:29** For I know that after my death ye will utterly corrupt *yourselves*, and turn aside from the way which I have commanded you; and evil will befall you in the latter days; because ye will do evil in the sight of the LORD, to provoke him to anger through the work of your hands.
Luke 3:16-17 John answered, saying unto *them* all, I indeed baptize you with water; but one mightier than I cometh, the latchet of whose shoes I am not worthy to unloose: he shall **baptize you with** the Holy Ghost and **with fire**: 17 Whose fan is in his hand, and he will thoroughly purge his floor, and will gather the wheat into his garner; but **the chaff he will burn with fire unquenchable**.	**See Acts 2:38** "Fire baptism" **See Acts 2:38** "Holy Ghost baptism"
Luke 3:16 John answered, saying unto *them* all, I indeed baptize you with water; but one mightier than I cometh, the latchet of whose shoes I am not worthy to unloose: he shall baptize you with the Holy Ghost and with fire:	**Leviticus 14:31** *Even* such as he is able to get, the one *for* a sin offering, and the other *for* a burnt offering, with the meat offering: and the priest shall make an atonement for him that is to be cleansed before the LORD. **Isaiah 44:3** For I will pour water upon him that is thirsty, and floods upon the dry ground: I will pour my spirit upon thy seed, and my blessing upon thine offspring: **Ezekiel 39:29** Neither will I hide my face any more from them: for I have poured out my spirit upon the house of Israel, saith the Lord GOD. **Joel 2:28** And it shall come to pass afterward, *that* I will pour out my spirit upon all flesh; and your sons and your daughters shall prophesy, your old men shall dream dreams, your young men shall see visions:
Luke 3:17 Whose fan *is* in his hand, and he will throughly purge his floor, and will gather the wheat into his garner; but the **chaff he will burn with fire unquenchable**.	**See Luke 16:23** "Hell"
Luke 3:22 And the Holy Ghost descended in a bodily shape like a dove upon him, and a voice came from	**Genesis 22:2** And he said, Take now thy son, thine only *son* Isaac, whom thou lovest, and get thee into the land of Moriah; and offer him there for a burnt offering upon one of the mountains which I

heaven, which said, Thou art my beloved Son; in thee I am well pleased.	will tell thee of. **Psalms 2:7** I will declare the decree: the LORD hath said unto me, Thou *art* my Son; this day have I begotten thee. **Isaiah 42:1** Behold my servant, whom I uphold; mine elect, *in whom* my soul delighteth; I have put my spirit upon him: he shall bring forth judgment to the Gentiles.
Luke 3:33 Which was *the son* of Aminadab, which was *the son* of Aram, which was *the son* of Esrom, which was *the son* of Phares, which was *the son* of Juda,	**Genesis 49:10** The sceptre shall not depart from Judah, nor a lawgiver from between his feet, until Shiloh come; and unto him *shall* the gathering of the people *be*.
Luke 3:36 Which was *the son* of Cainan, which was *the son* of Arphaxad, which was *the son* of Sem, which was *the son* of Noe, which was *the son* of Lamech,	**Genesis 10:22** The children of Shem; Elam, and Asshur, and Arphaxad, and Lud, and Aram.
Luke 3:38 Which was *the son* of Enos, which was *the son* of Seth, which was *the son* of Adam, which was *the son* of God.	**Genesis 4:25** And Adam knew his wife again; and she bare a son, and called his name Seth: For God, *said she*, hath appointed me another seed instead of Abel, whom Cain slew. **Genesis 5:3** And Adam lived an hundred and thirty years, and begat *a son* in his own likeness, after his image; and called his name Seth:
Luke 4:2 Being forty days tempted of the devil. And in those days he did eat nothing: and when they were ended, he afterward hungered.	**Exodus 34:28** And he was there with the LORD forty days and forty nights; he did neither eat bread, nor drink water. And he wrote upon the tables the words of the covenant, the ten commandments. **Deuteronomy 9:9** When I was gone up into the mount to receive the tables of stone, *even* the tables of the covenant which the LORD made with you, then I abode in the mount forty days and forty nights, I neither did eat bread nor drink water: **1 Kings 19:8** And he arose, and did eat and drink, and went in the strength of that meat forty days and forty nights unto Horeb the mount of God. **See Matthew 17:21 "Fasting"**
Luke 4:4 And Jesus answered him, saying, It is written, That man shall not live by bread alone, but by every word of God.	**Deuteronomy 8:3** man doth not live by bread only, but by every word that proceedeth out of the mouth of the LORD doth man live.
Luke 4:8 And Jesus answered and said unto him, Get thee behind me, Satan: for it is written, Thou shalt worship the Lord thy God, and him only shalt thou serve.	**Deuteronomy 6:13** Thou shalt fear the LORD thy God, and serve him, and shalt swear by his name. **Deuteronomy 10:20** Thou shalt fear the LORD thy God; him shalt thou serve, and to him shalt thou cleave, and swear by his name. **1 Samuel 7:3** And Samuel spake unto all the house of Israel, saying, If ye do return unto the LORD with all your hearts, *then* put away the strange gods and Ashtaroth from among you, and prepare your hearts unto the LORD, and serve him only: and he will deliver you out of the hand of the Philistines. **Genesis 3:4** And the **serpent** said unto the woman, Ye shall not surely die: **Zechariah 3:1-2** And he shewed me Joshua the high priest

	standing before the angel of the LORD, and **Satan** standing at his right hand to resist him. 2 And the LORD said unto **Satan,** The LORD rebuke thee, O **Satan**; even the LORD that hath chosen Jerusalem rebuke thee: *is* not this a brand plucked out of the fire? **See Matthew 4:10 "satan"**
Luke 4:10-11 For it is written, He shall give his angels charge over thee, to keep thee: And in *their* hands they shall bear thee up, lest at any time thou dash thy foot against a stone.	**Psalms 91:11-12** For he shall give his angels charge over thee, to keep thee in all thy ways. They shall bear thee up in their hands, lest thou dash thy foot against a stone.
Luke 4:12 And Jesus answering said unto him, It is said, Thou shalt not tempt the Lord thy God.	**Deuteronomy 6:16** Ye shall not tempt the LORD your God,
Luke 4:16 And he came to Nazareth, where he had been brought up: and, as his custom was, he went into the synagogue on the sabbath day, and stood up for to read.	**Nehemiah 8:4-6** And Ezra the scribe stood upon a pulpit of wood, which they had made for the purpose; and beside him stood Mattithiah, and Shema, and Anaiah, and Urijah, and Hilkiah, and Maaseiah, on his right hand; and on his left hand, Pedaiah, and Mishael, and Malchiah, and Hashum, and Hashbadana, Zechariah, *and* Meshullam. 5 And Ezra opened the book in the sight of all the people; (for he was above all the people;) and when he opened it, all the people stood up: 6 And Ezra blessed the LORD, the great God. And all the people answered, Amen, Amen, with lifting up their hands: and they bowed their heads, and worshipped the LORD with *their* faces to the ground.
Luke 4:18-19 The Spirit of the Lord *is* upon me, because he hath **anointed** me to preach the gospel to the poor; he hath sent me to heal the brokenhearted, to preach deliverance to the captives, and recovering of sight to the blind, to set at liberty them that are bruised, To preach the acceptable year of the Lord.	**Leviticus 4:5** And the priest that is **anointed** shall ... **Leviticus 4:16** And the priest that is **anointed** shall bring of the bullock's blood to the tabernacle of the congregation: **1 Samuel 2:35** And I will raise me up a faithful priest, that shall do according to that which is in mine heart and in my mind: and I will build him a sure house; and he shall walk before mine **anointed** for ever. **1 Samuel 24:10** Behold, this day thine eyes have seen how that the LORD had delivered thee to day into mine hand in the cave: and some bade me kill thee: but mine eye spared thee; and I said, I will not put forth mine hand against my lord; for he is the LORD'S **anointed**. **2 Samuel 1:14** And David said unto him, How wast thou not afraid to stretch forth thine hand to destroy the LORD'S **anointed**? **2 Samuel 19:21** But Abishai the son of Zeruiah answered and said, Shall not Shimei be put to death for this, because he cursed the LORD'S **anointed**? **1 Chronicles 16:22** Saying, **Touch not mine anointed**, and do my prophets no harm. **Psalms 147:3** He healeth the broken in heart, and bindeth up their wounds. **Isaiah 10:27** And it shall come to pass in that day, *that* his burden shall be taken away from off thy shoulder, and his yoke from off thy neck, and **the yoke shall be destroyed because of the anointing**. **Isaiah 11:2** And the spirit of the LORD shall rest upon him, the spirit of wisdom and understanding, the spirit of counsel and might, the spirit of knowledge and of the fear of the LORD;

	Isaiah 35:4 Say to them that are of a fearful heart, Be strong, fear not: behold, your God will come with vengeance, even God with a recompence; he will come and save you.

Isaiah 42:7 To open the blind eyes, to bring out the prisoners from the prison, *and* them that sit in darkness out of the prison house.

Isaiah 58:6 *Is* not this the fast that I have chosen? to loose the bands of wickedness, to undo the heavy burdens, and to let the oppressed go free, and that ye break every yoke?

Isaiah 61:1-2 The Spirit of the Lord GOD *is* upon me; because the LORD hath **anointed** me to preach good tidings unto the meek; he hath sent me to bind up the brokenhearted, to proclaim liberty to the captives, and the opening of the prison to them *that are bound*; To proclaim the acceptable year of the LORD, <u>and the day of vengeance of our God; to comfort all that mourn;</u> |
| **Luke 4:22** And all bare him witness, and wondered at the gracious words which proceeded out of his mouth. And they said, Is not this Joseph's son? | **Psalms 45:2** Thou art fairer than the children of men: grace is poured into thy lips: therefore God hath blessed thee for ever. |
| **Luke 4:25-26** But I tell you of a truth, many widows were in Israel in the days of Elias, when the heaven was shut up three years and six months, when great famine was throughout all the land; | **1 Kings 17:1** And Elijah the Tishbite, *who was* of the inhabitants of Gilead, said unto Ahab, *As* the LORD God of Israel liveth, before whom I stand, there shall not be dew nor rain these years, but according to my word.

1 Kings 17:7 And it came to pass after a while, that the brook dried up, because there had been no rain in the land.

1 Kings 17:9 Arise, get thee to Zarephath, which *belongeth* to Zidon, and dwell there: behold, I have commanded a widow woman there to sustain thee.

1 Kings 18:1-2 And it came to pass *after* many days, that the word of the LORD came to Elijah in the third year, saying, Go, shew thyself unto Ahab; and I will send rain upon the earth. 2 And Elijah went to shew himself unto Ahab. And there was a sore famine in Samaria. |
| **Luke 4:27** And many lepers were in Israel in the time of Eliseus the prophet; and none of them was cleansed, saving Naaman the Syrian. | **2 Kings 5:14** Then went he down, and dipped himself seven times in Jordan, according to the saying of the man of God: and his flesh came again like unto the flesh of a little child, and he was clean. |
| **Luke 4:33** And in the synagogue there was a man, which had a spirit of an **unclean devil**, and cried out with a loud voice, | See Hebrews 13:2 "Good and bad angels" |
| **Luke 4:36** And they were all amazed, and spake among themselves, saying, **What a word *is* this!** for with authority and power he commandeth the unclean spirits, and they come out. | See Matthew 5:18 "Scripture"

See Hebrews 13:2 "Good and bad angels" |
| **Luke 5:14** And he charged him to tell no man: but go, and shew thyself to the priest, and offer for thy cleansing, according as Moses commanded, for a testimony unto them. | **Leviticus 13:2** When a man shall have in the skin of his flesh a rising, a scab, or bright spot, and it be in the skin of his flesh *like* the plague of leprosy; then he shall be brought unto Aaron the priest, or unto one of his sons the priests:

Leviticus 14:2 This shall be the law of the leper in the day of his cleansing: He shall be brought unto the priest: |
| **Luke 5:21** And the scribes and the | **Psalms 32:5** I acknowledged my sin unto thee, and mine iniquity |

Pharisees began to reason, saying, Who is this which speaketh blasphemies? Who can forgive sins, but God alone?	have I not hid. I said, I will confess my transgressions unto the LORD; and thou forgavest the iniquity of my sin. Selah. **Proverbs 28:13** He that covereth his sins shall not prosper: but whoso confesseth and forsaketh *them* shall have mercy. **Isaiah 43:25** I, *even* I, *am* he that blotteth out thy transgressions for mine own sake, and will not remember thy sins.
Luke 6:1 And it came to pass on the second sabbath after the first, that he went through the corn fields; and his disciples plucked the ears of corn, and did eat, rubbing *them* in *their* hands.	**Deuteronomy 23:25** When thou comest into the standing corn of thy neighbour, then thou mayest pluck the ears with thine hand; but thou shalt not move a sickle unto thy neighbour's standing corn.
Luke 6:2 And certain of the Pharisees said unto them, Why do ye that which is not lawful to do on the sabbath days?	**Exodus 20:10** But the seventh day *is* the sabbath of the LORD thy God: *in it* thou shalt not do any work, thou, nor thy son, nor thy daughter, thy manservant, nor thy maidservant, nor thy cattle, nor thy stranger that *is* within thy gates:
Luke 6:3-4 And Jesus answering them said, Have ye not read so much as this, what David did, when himself was an hungred, and they which were with him; 4 How he went into the house of God, and did take and eat the shewbread, and gave also to them that were with him; which it is not lawful to eat but for the priests alone?	**Leviticus 24:5-6** And thou shalt take fine flour, and bake twelve cakes thereof: two tenth deals shall be in one cake. 6 And thou shalt set them in two rows, six on a row, upon the pure table before the LORD. **Leviticus 24:9** And it shall be Aaron's and his sons'; and they shall eat it in the holy place: for it *is* most holy unto him of the offerings of the LORD made by fire by a perpetual statute. **1 Samuel 21:6** So the priest gave him hallowed *bread:* for there was no bread there but the shewbread, that was taken from before the LORD, to put hot bread in the day when it was taken away.
Luke 6:12 And it came to pass in those days, that he went out into a mountain to **pray**, and continued all night in **prayer** to God.	**See Matthew 17:21 "Prayer"**
Luke 6:21 Blessed *are ye* that hunger now: for ye shall be filled. Blessed *are ye* that weep now: for ye shall laugh.	**Isaiah 61:3** To appoint unto them that mourn in Zion, to give unto them beauty for ashes, the oil of joy for mourning, the garment of praise for the spirit of heaviness; that they might be called trees of righteousness, the planting of the LORD, that he might be glorified.
Luke 6:24 But woe unto you that are rich! for ye have received your consolation.	**Amos 6:1** Woe to them *that are* at ease in Zion, and trust in the mountain of Samaria, *which are* named chief of the nations, to whom the house of Israel came!
Luke 6:25 Woe unto you that are full! for ye shall hunger. Woe unto you that laugh now! for ye shall mourn and weep.	**Isaiah 65:13-14** Therefore thus saith the Lord GOD, Behold, my servants shall eat, but ye shall be hungry: behold, my servants shall drink, but ye shall be thirsty: behold, my servants shall rejoice, but ye shall be ashamed: 14 Behold, my servants shall sing for joy of heart, but ye shall cry for sorrow of heart, and shall howl for vexation of spirit.
Luke 6:27 But I say unto you which hear, Love your enemies, do good to them which hate you,	**Exodus 23:4** If thou meet thine enemy's ox or his ass going astray, thou shalt surely bring it back to him again. **Proverbs 25:21** If thine enemy be hungry, give him bread to eat; and if he be thirsty, give him water to drink:
Luke 6:30 Give to every man that asketh of thee; and of him that taketh away thy goods ask *them* not again.	**Deuteronomy 15:7** If there be among you a poor man of one of thy brethren within any of thy gates in thy land which the LORD thy God giveth thee, thou shalt not harden thine heart, nor shut thine hand from thy poor brother:

Luke 6:34 And if ye lend *to them* of whom ye hope to receive, what thank have ye? for sinners also lend to sinners, to receive as much again.	**Deuteronomy 15:8** But thou shalt open thine hand wide unto him, and shalt surely lend him sufficient for his need, *in that* which he wanteth.
Luke 6:38 Give, and it shall be given unto you; good measure, pressed down, and shaken together, and running over, shall men give into your bosom. For with the same measure that ye mete withal it shall be measured to you again.	**Genesis 24:40** And he said to me, Jehovah, before whom I walk, will send His Angel with you and prosper your way. And you shall take a wife for my son from my family, from my father's house. **Deuteronomy 28:29** And you shall grope at noonday as the blind grope in darkness. And you shall not prosper in your ways. and you shall be always oppressed and plundered all the days; and there will be no one to save. **2 Chronicles 31:10** And Azariah the chief priest of the house of Zadok answered him, and said, Since *the people* began to bring the offerings into the house of the LORD, we have had enough to eat, and have left plenty: for the LORD hath blessed his people; and that which is left *is* this great store. **Psalms 1:3** And he shall be planted like a tree by the rivulets of waters, which will give its fruit in its seasons; and its leaf will not wither; and all which he does will prosper. **Psalms 122:6** Pray for the peace of Jerusalem; those who love you shall prosper. **Proverbs 3:9-10** Honour the LORD with thy substance, and with the firstfruits of all thine increase: 10 So shall thy barns be filled with plenty, and thy presses shall burst out with new wine. **Proverbs 10:22** The blessing of the LORD, it maketh rich, and he addeth no sorrow with it. **Proverbs 11:24-25** There is that scattereth, and yet increaseth; and *there is* that withholdeth more than is meet, but *it tendeth* to poverty. 25 The liberal soul shall be made fat: and he that watereth shall be watered also himself. **Proverbs 19:17** He that hath pity upon the poor lendeth unto the LORD; and that which he hath given will he pay him again. **Proverbs 22:9** He that hath a bountiful eye shall be blessed; for he giveth of his bread to the poor. **Proverbs 28:13** He covering his sins never prospers; but he confessing and forsaking them shall have pity. **Proverbs 28:27** He that giveth unto the poor shall not lack: but he that hideth his eyes shall have many a curse. **Ecclesiastes 11:1** Cast thy bread upon the waters: for thou shalt find it after many days. **Isaiah 55:11** so shall My word be, which goes out of My mouth; it shall not return to Me void, but it shall accomplish that which I please, and it shall prosper in what I sent it to do! **Isaiah 58:10** And *if* thou draw out thy soul to the hungry, and satisfy the afflicted soul; then shall thy light rise in obscurity, and thy darkness *be* as the noonday:
Luke 6:48 He is like a man which built an house, and digged deep, and laid the foundation on a rock: and when the flood arose, the stream beat vehemently upon that house, and could not shake it:	**Psalms 118:22** The stone *which* the builders refused is become the head *stone* of the corner. **Isaiah 28:16** Therefore thus saith the Lord GOD, Behold, I lay in Zion for a foundation a stone, a tried stone, a precious corner

for it was founded upon a rock.	*stone*, a sure foundation: he that believeth shall not make haste. **Isaiah 33:20** Look upon Zion, the city of our solemnities: thine eyes shall see Jerusalem a quiet habitation, a tabernacle *that* shall not be taken down; not one of the stakes thereof shall ever be removed, neither shall any of the cords thereof be broken. **See 1 Timothy 2:5 "God"**
Luke 7:3 And when he heard of Jesus, he sent unto him the **elders** of the Jews, beseeching him that he would come and heal his servant.	**See 1 Peter 5:1 "Elders"**
Luke 7:22 Then Jesus answering said unto them, Go your way, and tell John what things ye have seen and heard; how that the blind see, the lame walk, the lepers are cleansed, the deaf hear, the dead are raised, to the poor the gospel is preached.	**Isaiah 29:18** And in that day shall the deaf hear the words of the book, and the eyes of the blind shall see out of obscurity, and out of darkness. **Isaiah 35:4-6** Say to them that are of a fearful heart, Be strong, fear not: behold, your God will come with vengeance, even God with a recompence; he will come and save you. 5 Then the eyes of the blind shall be opened, and the ears of the deaf shall be unstopped. 6 Then shall the lame *man* leap as an hart, and the tongue of the dumb sing: for in the wilderness shall waters break out, and streams in the desert. **Isaiah 61:1** The Spirit of the Lord GOD *is* upon me; because the LORD hath anointed me to preach good tidings unto the meek; he hath sent me to bind up the brokenhearted, to proclaim liberty to the captives, and the opening of the prison to *them that are* bound; **See Matthew 11:5 "Deaf and Blind"** **See 1 Peter 2:24 "Healing"**
Luke 7:27 This is *he*, of whom it is written, Behold, I send my messenger before thy face, which shall prepare thy way before thee.	**Exodus 23:20** Behold, I send an Angel before thee, to keep thee in the way, and to bring thee into the place which I have prepared. **Malachi 3:1** Behold, I will send my messenger, and he shall prepare the way before me:
Luke 7:29-30 And all the people that heard him, and the publicans, justified God, being baptized with the baptism of John. 30 But the Pharisees and lawyers rejected the counsel of God against themselves, being not baptized of him.	**See Acts 2:38 "Salvation"**
Luke 7:48 And he said unto her, **Thy sins are forgiven**.	**See 1 Timothy 2:5 "God"**
Luke 8:2 And certain women, which had been healed of **evil spirits** and infirmities, Mary called Magdalene, out of whom went seven **devils**,	**See Hebrews 13:2 "Good and bad angels"**
Luke 8:8 And other fell on good ground, and sprang up, and bare fruit an **hundredfold**. And when he had said these things, he cried, He that hath ears to hear, let him hear.	**Genesis 26:12** Then Isaac sowed in that land, and received in the same year an **hundredfold**: and the Lord blessed him.
Luke 8:10 And he said, Unto you it is given to know the mysteries of the kingdom of God: but to others in parables; that seeing they might not see,	**Isaiah 6:9-10** And he said, God, and tell this people, Hear ye indeed, but understand not; and see ye indeed, but perceive not. 10 Make the heart of this people fat, and make their ears heavy, and shut their eyes; lest they see with their eyes, and hear with their

and hearing they might not understand.	ears, and understand with their heart, and convert, and be healed. **Ezekiel 12:2** Son of man, thou dwellest in the midst of a rebellious house, which have eyes to see, and see not; they have ears to hear, and hear not: for they *are* a rebellious house. **Jeremiah 5:21** Hear now this, O foolish people, and without understanding; which have eyes, and see not; which have ears, and hear not:
Luke 8:13 They on the rock are they, which, when they hear, receive the word with joy; and **these have no root**, which for a while believe, and in time of temptation fall away.	**Psalms 52:5** God shall likewise destroy thee for ever, he shall take thee away, and pluck thee out of thy dwelling place, and <u>**root**</u> **thee out** of the land of the living. Selah. **Isaiah 5:24** Therefore as the fire devoureth the stubble, and the flame consumeth the chaff, so **their** <u>**root**</u> **shall be as rottenness**, and their blossom shall go up as dust: because they have cast away the law of the LORD of hosts, and despised the word of the Holy One of Israel.
Luke 8:15 But that on the good ground are they, which in an honest and good heart, having heard the word, keep it, and bring forth <u>**fruit**</u> with patience.	**Isaiah 14:29** Rejoice not thou, whole Palestina, because the rod of him that smote thee is broken: for **out of the serpent's root shall come forth a cockatrice, and his** <u>**fruit**</u> **shall be a fiery flying serpent**.
Luke 8:25 And he said unto them, Where is your faith? And they being afraid wondered, saying one to another, What manner of man is this! for he commandeth even the winds and water, and they obey him.	**Job 26:12** He divideth the sea with his power, and by his understanding he smiteth through the proud. **Psalms 107:25** For he commandeth, and raiseth the stormy wind, which lifteth up the waves thereof. **Isaiah 51:15** But I *am* the LORD thy God, that divided the sea, whose waves roared: The LORD of hosts *is* his name.
Luke 8:27 And when he went forth to land, there met him out of the city a certain man, which had **devils** long time, and **ware no clothes**, neither abode in *any* house, but in the tombs.	**See Hebrews 13:2 "Good and bad angels"** **See 1 Timothy 2:9 "Adornment"**
Luke 8:44 Came behind *him*, and touched the border of his **garment**: and immediately her issue of blood stanched.	**See Matthew 23:5 "Garments"**
Luke 8:52-55 And all wept, and bewailed her: but he said, Weep not; she is not dead, but sleepeth. 53 And they laughed him to scorn, knowing that she was dead. 54 And he put them all out, and took her by the hand, and called, saying, Maid, arise. 55 And her spirit came again, and she arose straightway: and he commanded to give her meat.	**1 Kings 17:21-22** And he stretched himself upon the child three times, and cried unto the LORD, and said, O LORD my God, I pray thee, let this child's soul come into him again. 22 And the LORD heard the voice of Elijah; and the soul of the child came into him again, and he revived. **2 Kings 4:34** And he went up, and lay upon the child, and put his mouth upon his mouth, and his eyes upon his eyes, and his hands upon his hands: and he stretched himself upon the child; and the flesh of the child waxed warm.
Luke 9:22 Saying, The Son of man must suffer many things, and be rejected of the **elders** and chief priests and scribes, and be slain, and **be raised the third day**.	**See 1 Peter 5:1 "Elders"** **Jonah 1:17** Now the LORD had prepared a great fish to swallow up Jonah. And Jonah was in the belly of the fish **three days and three nights**. **Jonah 2:1** Then Jonah prayed unto the LORD his God out of the fish's belly
Luke 9:35 And there came a voice out of the cloud, saying, This is my beloved	**Deuteronomy 18:15** The LORD thy God will raise up unto thee a Prophet from the midst of thee, of thy brethren, like unto me; unto

Son: hear him.	him ye shall hearken; **Deuteronomy 18:19** And it shall come to pass, *that* whosoever will not hearken unto my words which he shall speak in my name, I will require *it* of him. **Psalm 2:7** I will declare the decree: the LORD hath said unto me, Thou *art* my Son; this day have I begotten thee. **Isaiah 42:1** Behold my servant, whom I uphold; mine elect, *in whom* my soul delighteth; I have put my spirit upon him: he shall bring forth judgment to the Gentiles.
Luke 9:54 And when his disciples James and John saw *this,* they said, Lord, wilt thou that we command fire to come down from heaven, and consume them, even as Elias did?	**2 Kings 1:10** And Elijah answered and said to the captain of fifty, If I *be* a man of God, then let fire come down from heaven, and consume thee and thy fifty. And there came down fire from heaven, and consumed him and his fifty. **2 Kings 1:12** And Elijah answered and said unto them, If I *be* a man of God, let fire come down from heaven, and consume thee and thy fifty. And the fire of God came down from heaven, and consumed him and his fifty.
Luke 9:61 And another also said, Lord, I will follow thee; but let me first go bid them farewell, which are at home at my house.	**1 Kings 19:20-21** And he left the oxen, and ran after Elijah, and said, Let me, I pray thee, kiss my father and my mother, and *then* I will follow thee. And he said unto him, Go back again: for what have I done to thee? 21 And he returned back from him, and took a yoke of oxen, and slew them, and boiled their flesh with the instruments of the oxen, and gave unto the people, and they did eat. Then he arose, and went after Elijah, and ministered unto him.
Luke 9:62 And Jesus said unto him, No man, having put his hand to the plough, and looking back, is fit for the kingdom of God.	**Proverbs 26:11** As a dog returneth to his vomit, *so* a fool returneth to his folly.
Luke 10:4 Carry neither purse, nor scrip, nor shoes: and salute no man by the way.	**2 Kings 4:29** Then he said to Gehazi, Gird up thy loins, and take my staff in thine hand, and go thy way: if thou meet any man, salute him not; and if any salute thee, answer him not again: and lay my staff upon the face of the child.
Luke 10:7 And in the same house remain, eating and drinking such things as they give: for the labourer is worthy of his hire. Go not from house to house.	**Leviticus 19:13** Thou shalt not defraud thy neighbour, neither rob *him*: the wages of him that is hired shall not abide with thee all night until the morning. **Deuteronomy 24:14** Thou shalt not oppress an hired servant *that is* poor and needy, *whether he be* of thy brethren, or of thy strangers that *are* in thy land within thy gates: **Deuteronomy 25:4** Thou shalt not muzzle the ox when he treadeth out *the corn.*
Luke 10:12 But I say unto you, that it shall be more tolerable in that day for **Sodom**, than for that city.	**See Romans 1:26-27 "Sexual sins"**
Luke 10:15 And thou, Capernaum, which art exalted to heaven, shalt be thrust down to **hell**.	**Isaiah 14:13** For thou hast said in thine heart, I will ascend into heaven, I will exalt my throne above the stars of God: I will sit also upon the mount of the congregation, in the sides of the north: **Isaiah 14:15** Yet thou shalt be brought down to hell, to the sides of the pit. **See Luke 16:23 "Hell"**
Luke 10:18 And he said unto them, I beheld **Satan** as lightning fall from	**Genesis 3:4** And the **serpent** said unto the woman, Ye shall not

heaven.	surely die: **Zechariah 3:1-2** And he shewed me Joshua the high priest standing before the angel of the LORD, and **Satan** standing at his right hand to resist him. 2 And the LORD said unto **Satan,** The LORD rebuke thee, O **Satan**; even the LORD that hath chosen Jerusalem rebuke thee: *is* not this a brand plucked out of the fire? **See Matthew 4:10 "satan"**
Luke 10:19 Behold, I give unto you power to tread on serpents and scorpions, and over all the power of the enemy: and **nothing shall by any means hurt you**.	**Psalms 91:9-13** Because thou hast made the LORD, *which is* my refuge, *even* the most High, thy habitation; 10 There shall no evil befall thee, neither shall any plague come nigh thy dwelling. 11 For he shall give his angels charge over thee, to keep thee in all thy ways. 12 They shall bear thee up in *their* hands, lest thou dash thy foot against a stone. 13 Thou shalt tread upon the lion and adder: the young lion and the dragon shalt thou trample under feet. **Isaiah 54:17** No weapon that is formed against thee shall prosper; and every tongue *that* shall rise against thee in judgment thou shalt condemn. This *is* the heritage of the servants of the LORD, and their righteousness *is* of me, saith the LORD.
Luke 10:20 Notwithstanding in this **rejoice** not, that the **spirits** are subject unto you; but rather rejoice, because **your names are written in heaven**.	**Daniel 7:10** A fiery stream issued and came forth from before him: thousand thousands ministered unto him, and ten thousand times ten thousand stood before him: the judgment was set, and the books were opened. **Daniel 12:1** And at that time shall Michael stand up, the great prince which standeth for the children of thy people: and there shall be a time of trouble, such as never was since there was a nation *even* to that same time: and at that time thy people shall be delivered, every one that shall be found written in the book. **See Revelation 3:5 "Book of life"** **See Hebrews 13:2 "Good and bad angels"** **Habakkuk 3:17** Although the fig tree shall not blossom, neither *shall* fruit *be* in the vines; the labour of the olive shall fail, and the fields shall yield no meat; the flock shall be cut off from the fold, and *there shall be* no herd in the stalls: 18 Yet I will **rejoice** in the LORD, I will joy in the God of my salvation.
Luke 10:21 In that hour Jesus rejoiced in spirit, and said, I thank thee, O Father, Lord of heaven and earth, that thou hast hid these things from the wise and prudent, and hast revealed them unto babes: even so, Father; for so it seemed good in thy sight.	**Nehemiah 4:15** And it came to pass, when our enemies heard that it was known unto us, and God had brought their counsel to nought, that we returned all of us to the wall, every one unto his work. **Job 5:12** He disappointeth the devices of the crafty, so that their hands cannot perform *their* enterprise. **Psalms 33:10** The LORD bringeth the counsel of the heathen to nought: he maketh the devices of the people of none effect. **Isaiah 8:10** Take counsel together, and it shall come to nought; speak the word, and it shall not stand: for God *is* with us. **Isaiah 19:3** And the spirit of Egypt shall fail in the midst thereof; and I will destroy the counsel thereof: and they shall seek to the idols, and to the charmers, and to them that have familiar spirits, and to the wizards. **Isaiah 29:14** Therefore, behold, I will proceed to do a marvellous work among this people, *even* a marvellous work and a wonder: for the wisdom of their wise *men* shall perish, and the

	understanding of their prudent *men* shall be hid.
	Obad 1:8 Shall I not in that day, saith the LORD, even destroy the wise *men* out of Edom, and understanding out of the mount of Esau?
Luke 10:22 All things are delivered to me of my Father: and no man knoweth who the Son is, but the Father; and who the Father is, but the Son, and *he* to whom the Son will reveal *him*.	**Psalms 8:6** Thou madest him to have dominion over the works of thy hands; thou hast put all *things* under his feet:
Luke 10:27 And he answering said, Thou shalt love the Lord thy God with all thy heart, and with all thy soul, and with all thy strength, and with all thy mind; and thy neighbour as thyself.	**Leviticus 19:18** Thou shalt not avenge, nor bear any grudge against the children of thy people, but thou shalt love thy neighbour as thyself: I *am* the LORD. **Deuteronomy 6:5** And thou shalt love the LORD thy God with all thine heart, and with all thy soul, and with all thy might. **Deuteronomy 10:12** And now, Israel, what doth the LORD thy God require of thee, but to fear the LORD thy God, to walk in all his ways, and to love him, and to serve the LORD thy God with all thy heart and with all thy soul, **Deuteronomy 30:6** And the LORD thy God will circumcise thine heart, and the heart of thy seed, to love the LORD thy God with all thine heart, and with all thy soul, that thou mayest live.
Luke 10:28 And he said unto him, Thou hast answered right: this do, and thou shalt live.	**Leviticus 18:5** Ye shall therefore keep my statutes, and my judgments: which if a man do, he shall live in them: I *am* the LORD.
Luke 10:42 But one thing is needful: and Mary hath chosen that good part, which shall not be taken away from her.	**Psalms 27:4** One *thing* have I desired of the LORD, that will I seek after; that I may dwell in the house of the LORD all the days of my life, to behold the beauty of the LORD, and to inquire in his temple.
Luke 11:9-10 And I say unto you, Ask, and it shall be given you; **seek**, and ye shall find; knock, and it shall be opened unto you. 10 For every one that asketh receiveth; and he that seeketh findeth; and to him that knocketh it shall be opened.	**2 Chronicles 16:12-13** And Asa in the thirty and ninth year of his reign was diseased in his feet, until his disease *was* exceeding *great*: yet in his disease he sought not to the LORD, but to the physicians. 13 And Asa slept with his fathers, and died in the one and fortieth year of his reign. **Psalms 50:15** And call upon me in the day of trouble: I will deliver thee, and thou shalt glorify me. **Jeremiah 29:11-14** For I know the thoughts that I think toward you, saith the LORD, thoughts of peace, and not of evil, to give you an expected end. 12 Then shall ye call upon me, and ye shall go and pray unto me, and I will hearken unto you. 13 And **ye shall seek me**, and find *me*, when ye shall search for me with all your heart. 14 And I will be found of you, saith the LORD: and I will turn away your captivity, and I will gather you from all the nations, and from all the places whither I have driven you, saith the LORD; and I will bring you again into the place whence I caused you to be carried away captive. **See 1 Peter 2:24 "Healing"**
Luke 11:18 If **Satan** also be divided against himself, how shall his kingdom stand? because ye say that I cast out devils through Beelzebub.	**Genesis 3:4** And the **serpent** said unto the woman, Ye shall not surely die: **Zechariah 3:1-2** And he shewed me Joshua the high priest standing before the angel of the LORD, and **Satan** standing at his right hand to resist him. 2 And the LORD said unto **Satan**, The LORD rebuke thee, O **Satan**; even the LORD that hath chosen

	Jerusalem rebuke thee: *is* not this a brand plucked out of the fire? **See Matthew 4:10** "satan" **See Hebrews 13:2** "Good and bad angels"
Luke 11:26 Then goeth he, and taketh to him seven other **spirits** more wicked than himself; and they enter in, and dwell there: and the last state of that man is worse than the first.	**See Hebrews 13:2** "Good and bad angels"
Luke 11:29 And when the people were gathered thick together, he began to say, This is an evil generation: they seek a sign; and there shall no sign be given it, but the sign of Jonas the prophet.	**Jonah 1:17** Now the LORD had prepared a great fish to swallow up Jonah. And Jonah was in the belly of the fish three days and three nights.
Luke 11:30 For as Jonas was a sign unto the Ninevites, so shall also the Son of man be to this generation.	**Jonah 1:17** Now the LORD had prepared a great fish to swallow up Jonah. And Jonah was in the belly of the fish three days and three nights. **Jonah 3:1-10** **Jonah 4:1-11**
Luke 11:31 The queen of the south shall rise up in the judgment with the men of this generation, and condemn them: for she came from the utmost parts of the earth to hear the wisdom of Solomon; and, behold, a greater than Solomon *is* here.	**1 Kings 10:1-4** And when the queen of Sheba heard of the fame of Solomon concerning the name of the LORD, she came to prove him with hard questions. 2 And she came to Jerusalem with a very great train, with camels that bare spices, and very much gold, and precious stones: and when she was come to Solomon, she communed with him of all that was in her heart. 3 And Solomon told her all her questions: there was not any thing hid from the king, which he told her not. 4 And when the queen of Sheba had seen all Solomon's wisdom, and the house that he had built, **1 Kings 10:6** And she said to the king, It was a true report that I heard in mine own land of thy acts and of thy wisdom. **2 Chronicles 9:1-2** And when the queen of Sheba heard of the fame of Solomon, she came to prove Solomon with hard questions at Jerusalem, with a very great company, and camels that bare spices, and gold in abundance, and precious stones: and when she was come to Solomon, she communed with him of all that was in her heart. 2 And Solomon told her all her questions: and there was nothing hid from Solomon which he told her not.
Luke 11:32 The men of Nineve shall rise up in the judgment with this generation, and shall condemn it: for they repented at the preaching of Jonas; and, behold, a greater than Jonas *is* here.	**Jonah 3:5** So the people of Nineveh believed God, and proclaimed a fast, and put on sackcloth, from the greatest of them even to the least of them.
Luke 11:33-36 No man, when he hath lighted a candle, putteth *it* in a secret place, neither under a bushel, but on a candlestick, that they which come in may see the **light**. 34 The **light** of the body is the eye: therefore when thine eye is single, thy whole body also is full of **light**; but when *thine eye* is **evil**, thy body also *is* full of **darkness**. 35 Take heed therefore that the **light** which is in thee be not **darkness**. 36 If thy whole body therefore *be* full of **light**, having no	**Isaiah 5:20** Woe unto them that call **evil** good, and good evil; that put **darkness** for **light**, and **light** for **darkness**; that put bitter for sweet, and sweet for bitter!

part **dark**, the whole shall be full of **light**, as when the bright shining of a candle doth give thee **light**.	
Luke 11:41 But rather give alms of such things as ye have; and, behold, all things are clean unto you.	**See 1 John 3:17** "Poor"
Luke 11:42 But woe unto you, Pharisees! for ye **tithe** mint and rue and all manner of herbs, and pass over judgment and the love of God: these ought ye to have done, and not to leave the other undone.	**Deuteronomy 10:12** And now, Israel, what doth the LORD thy God require of thee, but to fear the LORD thy God, to walk in all his ways, and to love him, and to serve the LORD thy God with all thy heart and with all thy soul, **1 Samuel 15:22** And Samuel said, Hath the LORD *as great* delight in burnt offerings and sacrifices, as in obeying the voice of the LORD? Behold, to obey *is* better than sacrifice, *and* to hearken than the fat of rams. **Hosea 6:6** For I desired mercy, and not sacrifice; and the knowledge of God more than burnt offerings. **Micah 6:8** He hath shewed thee, O man, what *is* good; and what doth the LORD require of thee, but to do justly, and to love mercy, and to walk humbly with thy God? **See Matthew 23:23** "Tithing"
Luke 11:46 And he said, Woe unto you also, *ye* lawyers! for ye lade men with burdens grievous to be borne, and ye yourselves touch not the burdens with one of your fingers.	**Isaiah 10:1** Woe unto them that decree unrighteous decrees, and that write grievousness *which* they have prescribed;
Luke 11:51 From the blood of Abel unto the blood of Zacharias, which perished between the altar and the temple: verily I say unto you, It shall be required of this generation.	**Genesis 4:8** And Cain talked with Abel his brother: and it came to pass, when they were in the field, that Cain rose up against Abel his brother, and slew him. **2 Chronicles 24:20-21** And the Spirit of God came upon Zechariah the son of Jehoiada the priest, which stood above the people, and said unto them, Thus saith God, Why transgress ye the commandments of the LORD, that ye cannot prosper? because ye have forsaken the LORD, he hath also forsaken you. 21 And they conspired against him, and stoned him with stones at the commandment of the king in the court of the house of the LORD.
Luke 12:2 For there is nothing covered, that shall not be revealed; neither hid, that shall not be known.	**Job 12:22** He discovereth deep things out of darkness, and bringeth out to light the shadow of death.
Luke 12:4 And I say unto you my friends, Be not afraid of them that kill the body, and after that have no more that they can do.	**Isaiah 51:7** Hearken unto me, ye that know righteousness, the people in whose heart *is* my law; fear ye not the reproach of men, neither be ye afraid of their revilings. **Jeremiah 1:8** Be not afraid of their faces: for I *am* with thee to deliver thee, saith the LORD.
Luke 12:5 But I will forewarn you whom ye shall fear: Fear him, which after he hath killed hath power to cast into **hell**; yea, I say unto you, Fear him.	**See Luke 16:23** "Hell"
Luke 12:7 But even the very hairs of your head are all numbered. Fear not therefore: ye are of more value than	**1 Samuel 14:45** And the people said unto Saul, Shall Jonathan die, who hath wrought this great salvation in Israel? God forbid: *as* the LORD liveth, there shall not one hair of his head fall to the

many sparrows.	ground; for he hath wrought with God this day. So the people rescued Jonathan, that he died not. **2 Samuel 14:11** Then said she, I pray thee, let the king remember the LORD thy God, that thou wouldest not suffer the revengers of blood to destroy any more, lest they destroy my son. And he said, *As* the LORD liveth, there shall not one hair of thy son fall to the earth. **1 Kings 1:52** And Solomon said, If he will shew himself a worthy man, there shall not an hair of him fall to the earth: but if wickedness shall be found in him, he shall die.
Luke 12:19 And I will say to my soul, Soul, thou hast much goods laid up for many years; take thine ease, eat, drink, *and* be merry.	**Ecclesiastes 11:9** Rejoice, O young man, in thy youth; and let thy heart cheer thee in the days of thy youth, and walk in the ways of thine heart, and in the sight of thine eyes: but know thou, that for all these *things* God will bring thee into judgment.
Luke 12:20 But God said unto him, *Thou* fool, this night thy soul shall be required of thee: then whose shall those things be, which thou hast provided?	**Jeremiah 17:11** *As* the partridge sitteth *on eggs*, and hatcheth *them* not; *so* he that getteth riches, and not by right, shall leave them in the midst of his days, and at his end shall be a fool.
Luke 12:22 And he said unto his disciples, Therefore I say unto you, Take no thought for your life, what ye shall eat; neither for the body, what ye shall put on.	**Psalms 55:22** Cast thy burden upon the LORD, and he shall sustain thee: he shall never suffer the righteous to be moved.
Luke 12:24 Consider the ravens: for they neither sow nor reap; which neither have storehouse nor barn; and God feedeth them: how much more are ye better than the fowls?	**Job 38:41** Who provideth for the raven his food? when his young ones cry unto God, they wander for lack of meat. **Psalms 147:9** He giveth to the beast his food, *and* to the young ravens which cry.
Luke 12:31 But rather seek ye the kingdom of God; and all these things shall be added unto you.	**Psalms 37:25** I have been young, and *now* am old; yet have I not seen the righteous forsaken, nor his seed begging bread.
Luke 12:33 Sell that ye have, and **give alms**; provide yourselves bags which wax not old, a treasure in the heavens that faileth not, where no thief approacheth, neither moth corrupteth.	**See 1 John 3:17** "Poor" **See Luke 6:38** "Prosperity"
Luke 12:49-50 I am come to send **fire** on the earth; and what will I, if it be already kindled? 50 But I have a **baptism** to be **baptized with**; and how am I straitened till it be accomplished!	**Numbers 31:23** Every thing that may abide the fire, **ye shall make** *it* **go through the fire, and** **it shall be clean**: nevertheless it shall be purified with the water of separation: and all that abideth not the fire ye shall make go through the water.
Luke 12:53 The father shall be divided against the son, and the son against the father; the mother against the daughter, and the daughter against the mother; the mother in law against her daughter in law, and the daughter in law against her mother in law.	**Micah 7:6** For the son dishonoureth the father, the daughter riseth up against her mother, the daughter in law against her mother in law; a man's enemies *are* the men of his own house.
Luke 13:3 I tell you, Nay: but, except ye repent, ye shall all likewise perish.	**Job 42:6** Wherefore I abhor myself, and repent in dust and ashes. **Ezekiel 14:6** Therefore say unto the house of Israel, Thus saith the Lord GOD; Repent, and turn yourselves from your idols; and turn

	away your faces from all your abominations. **Ezekiel 18:30** Therefore I will judge you, O house of Israel, every one according to his ways, saith the Lord GOD. Repent, and turn yourselves from all your transgressions; so iniquity shall not be your ruin.
Luke 13:14 And the ruler of the synagogue answered with indignation, because that Jesus had healed on the sabbath day, and said unto the people, There are six days in which men ought to work: in them therefore come and be healed, and not on the sabbath day.	**Exodus 20:9-11** Six days shalt thou labour, and do all thy work: 10 But the seventh day *is* the sabbath of the LORD thy God: *in it* thou shalt not do any work, thou, nor thy son, nor thy daughter, thy manservant, nor thy maidservant, nor thy cattle, nor thy stranger that *is* within thy gates: 11 For *in* six days the LORD made heaven and earth, the sea, and all that in them *is*, and rested the seventh day: wherefore the LORD blessed the sabbath day, and hallowed it. **Deuteronomy 5:13-14** Six days thou shalt labour, and do all thy work: 14 But the seventh day *is* the sabbath of the LORD thy God: *in it* thou shalt not do any work, thou, nor thy son, nor thy daughter, nor thy manservant, nor thy maidservant, nor thine ox, nor thine ass, nor any of thy cattle, nor thy stranger that *is* within thy gates; that thy manservant and thy maidservant may rest as well as thou. **Ezekiel 20:12** Moreover also I gave them my sabbaths, to be a sign between me and them, that they might know that I *am* the LORD that sanctify them.
Luke 13:16 And ought not this woman, being a daughter of Abraham, whom **Satan** hath bound, lo, these eighteen years, be loosed from this bond on the sabbath day?	**Genesis 3:4** And the **serpent** said unto the woman, Ye shall not surely die: **Zechariah 3:1-2** And he shewed me Joshua the high priest standing before the angel of the LORD, and **Satan** standing at his right hand to resist him. 2 And the LORD said unto **Satan,** The LORD rebuke thee, O **Satan**; even the LORD that hath chosen Jerusalem rebuke thee: is not this a brand plucked out of the fire? **See Matthew 4:10 "satan"**
Luke 13:27 But he shall say, I tell you, I know you not whence ye are; depart from me, all *ye* workers of iniquity.	**Psalms 6:8** Depart from me, all ye workers of iniquity; for the LORD hath heard the voice of my weeping.
Luke 13:29 And they shall come from the east, and *from* the west, and from the north, and *from* the south, and shall sit down in the kingdom of God.	**Isaiah 2:2-3** And it shall come to pass in the last days, *that* the mountain of the LORD's house shall be established in the top of the mountains, and shall be exalted above the hills; and all nations shall flow unto it. 3 And many people shall go and say, Come ye, and let us go up to the mountain of the LORD, to the house of the God of Jacob; and he will teach us of his ways, and we will walk in his paths: for out of Zion shall go forth the law, and the word of the LORD from Jerusalem.
Luke 13:34 O Jerusalem, Jerusalem, which killest the prophets, and stonest them that are sent unto thee; how often would I have gathered thy children together, as a hen *doth gather* her brood under *her* wings, and ye would not!	**Psalms 91:4** He shall cover thee with his feathers, and under his wings shalt thou trust: his truth *shall be thy* shield and buckler. **See Matthew 23:37 "Wings of protection"**
Luke 13:35 Behold, your house is left unto you desolate: and verily I say unto you, Ye shall not see me, until *the time* come when ye shall say, Blessed *is* he that cometh in the name of the Lord.	**Psalms 118:26** Blessed *be* he that cometh in the name of the LORD: we have blessed you out of the house of the LORD. **Isaiah 1:7** Your country *is* desolate, your cities *are* burned with fire: your land, strangers devour it in your presence, and *it is*

	desolate, as overthrown by strangers. **Jeremiah 7:34** Then will I cause to cease from the cities of Judah, and from the streets of Jerusalem, the voice of mirth, and the voice of gladness, the voice of the bridegroom, and the voice of the bride: for the land shall be desolate. **Jeremiah 12:7** I have forsaken mine house, I have left mine heritage; I have given the dearly beloved of my soul into the hand of her enemies. **Jeremiah 22:5** But if ye will not hear these words, I swear by myself, saith the LORD, that this house shall become a desolation.
Luke 14:1 And it came to pass, on his going into the house of a certain one of the chiefs of the Pharisees, on a **sabbath**, to eat bread, that they were watching him, **Luke 14:3** and Jesus answering spake to the lawyers and Pharisees, saying, `Is it lawful on the **sabbath**-day to heal?'  **Luke 14:5** and answering them he said, `Of which of you shall an ass or ox fall into a pit, and he will not immediately draw it up on the **sabbath**-day?'	**See Colossians 2:16 "Sabbath"**
Luke 14:8 When thou art bidden of any *man* to a wedding, sit not down in the highest room; lest a more honourable man than thou be bidden of him;	**Proverbs 25:6** Put not forth thyself in the presence of the king, and stand not in the place of great *men*:
Luke 14:10 But when thou art bidden, go and sit down in the lowest room; that when he that bade thee cometh, he may say unto thee, Friend, go up higher: then shalt thou have worship in the presence of them that sit at meat with thee.	**Proverbs 25:6-7** Put not forth thyself in the presence of the king, and stand not in the place of great *men*: 7 For better *it is* that it be said unto thee, Come up hither; than that thou shouldest be put lower in the presence of the prince whom thine eyes have seen.
Luke 14:11 For whosoever exalteth himself shall be abased; and he that humbleth himself shall be exalted.	**Job 22:29** When *men* are cast down, then thou shalt say, *There is* lifting up; and he shall save the humble person. **Proverbs 11:2** *When* pride cometh, then cometh shame: but with the lowly *is* wisdom. **Proverbs 15:33** The fear of the LORD *is* the instruction of wisdom; and before honour *is* humility. **Proverbs 16:18** Pride *goeth* before destruction, and an haughty spirit before a fall. **Proverbs 18:12** Before destruction the heart of man is haughty, and before honour *is* humility. **Proverbs 29:23** A man's pride shall bring him low: but honour shall uphold the humble in spirit.
Luke 14:16 Then said he unto him, A certain man made a great supper, and bade many:	**Isaiah 25:6** And in this mountain shall the LORD of hosts make unto all people a feast of fat things, a feast of wines on the lees, of fat things full of marrow, of wines on the lees well refined.
Luke 15:7 I say unto you, that likewise joy shall be in heaven over one sinner that repenteth, more than over ninety	**Isaiah 55:7** Let the wicked forsake his way, and the unrighteous man his thoughts: and let him return unto the LORD, and he will have mercy upon him; and to our God, for he will abundantly

and nine just persons, which need no repentance.	pardon.
Luke 15:21 And the son said unto him, Father, I have sinned against heaven, and in thy sight, and am no more worthy to be called thy son.	**2 Samuel 12:13** And David said unto Nathan, I have sinned against the LORD. And Nathan said unto David, The LORD also hath put away thy sin; thou shalt not die. **Psalms 51** **Proverbs 28:13** He that covereth his sins shall not prosper: but whoso confesseth and forsaketh *them* shall have mercy.
Luke 16:15 And he said unto them, Ye are they which justify yourselves before men; but God knoweth your hearts: for that which is highly esteemed among men is abomination in the sight of God.	**1 Samuel 16:7** But the LORD said unto Samuel, Look not on his countenance, or on the height of his stature; because I have refused him: for *the LORD seeth* not as man seeth; for man looketh on the outward appearance, but the LORD looketh on the heart. **1 Chronicles 28:9** And thou, Solomon my son, know thou the God of thy father, and serve him with a perfect heart and with a willing mind: for the LORD searcheth all hearts, and understandeth all the imaginations of the thoughts: if thou seek him, he will be found of thee; but if thou forsake him, he will cast thee off for ever. **Psalms 7:9** Oh let the wickedness of the wicked come to an end; but establish the just: for the righteous God trieth the hearts and reins.
Luke 16:17 And it is easier for heaven and earth to pass, than one tittle of the law to fail.	**Isaiah 40:8** The grass withereth, the flower fadeth: but the word of our God shall stand for ever.
Luke 16:18 Whosoever putteth away his wife, and marrieth another, committeth adultery: and whosoever marrieth her that is put away from *her* husband committeth adultery.	**See Matthew 5:27 "Adultery"**
Luke 16:22-23 And it came to pass, that the beggar died, and was carried by the **angels** into **Abraham's bosom**: the rich man also died, and was buried; 23 And in **hell** he lift up his eyes, being in torments, and seeth Abraham afar off, and Lazarus in his bosom.	**Genesis 35:18** And it came to pass, **as her soul was in departing**, (for she died) that she called his name Benoni: but his father called him Benjamin. **Genesis 37:35** And all his sons and all his daughters rose up to comfort him; but he refused to be comforted; and he said, For **I will go <u>down</u> into the grave <u>unto my son</u>** mourning. Thus his father wept for him. **Numbers 16:32-33** And the earth opened her mouth, and swallowed them up, and their houses, and all the men that *appertained* unto Korah, and all *their* goods. 33 They, and all that *appertained* to them, went down alive into the pit, and the earth closed upon them: and they perished from among the congregation. **Deuteronomy 32:22** For a fire is kindled in mine anger, and shall burn unto the **lowest hell**, and shall consume the earth with her increase, and set on fire the foundations of the mountains. **1 Samuel 28:15** And Samuel said to Saul, **Why hast thou disquieted me, to bring me up?** And Saul answered, I am sore distressed; for the Philistines make war against me, and God is departed from me, and answereth me no more, neither by prophets, nor by dreams: therefore I have called thee, that thou mayest make known unto me what I shall do. **2 Samuel 22:6** The **sorrows of hell** compassed me about; the

	snares of death prevented me;
	Psalms 9:17 The wicked shall be turned into hell, *and* all the nations that forget God.
	Psalms 16:10 For thou wilt not leave my **soul** in hell; neither wilt thou suffer thine Holy One to see corruption.
	Psalms 86:13 For great *is* thy mercy toward me: and thou hast delivered my **soul** from the <u>lowest</u> **hell**.
	Psalms 116:3 The sorrows of death compassed me, and the pains of **hell** gat hold upon me: I found trouble and sorrow.
	Proverbs 5:5 Her feet go down to death; her steps take hold on **hell**.
	Proverbs 7:27 Her house *is* the way to **hell**, going down to the chambers of death.
	Proverbs 9:18 But he knoweth not that the dead *are* there; *and that* her guests *are* in the depths of **hell**.
	Proverbs 15:24 The way of life *is* above to the wise, that he may depart from hell beneath.
	Isaiah 14:9-10 Hell from beneath is moved for thee to meet *thee* at thy coming: it stirreth up the dead for thee, *even* all the chief ones of the earth; it hath raised up from their thrones all the kings of the nations. 10 All they shall speak and say unto thee, Art thou also become weak as we? art thou become like unto us?
	Isaiah 14:15 Yet thou shalt be brought down to hell, to the sides of the pit.
	Nahum 1:2-3 God *is* jealous, and the LORD revengeth; the LORD revengeth, and *is* furious; **the LORD will take vengeance on his adversaries**, and **he reserveth** *wrath* **for his enemies**. 3 The LORD *is* slow to anger, and great in power, and **will not at all acquit** *the wicked*: the LORD hath his way in the whirlwind and in the storm, and the clouds *are* the dust of his feet.
	See Hebrews 13:2 "Angels"
Luke 16:24 And he cried and said, Father Abraham, have mercy on me, and send Lazarus, that he may dip the tip of his finger in water, and cool my tongue; for I am tormented in this flame.	**Isaiah 66:24** And they shall go forth, and look upon the carcases of the men that have transgressed against me: for their worm shall not die, neither shall their fire be quenched; and they shall be an abhorring unto all flesh.
Luke 16:29 Abraham saith unto him, They have Moses and the prophets; let them hear them.	**Isaiah 8:20** To the law and to the testimony: if they speak not according to this word, *it is* because *there is* no light in them.
	Isaiah 34:16 Seek ye out of the book of the LORD, and read: no one of these shall fail, none shall want her mate: for my mouth it hath commanded, and his spirit it hath gathered them.
Luke 17:3 Take heed to yourselves: If thy brother trespass against thee, rebuke him; and if he repent, forgive him.	**Leviticus 19:17** Thou shalt not hate thy brother in thine heart: thou shalt in any wise rebuke thy neighbour, and not suffer sin upon him.
	Proverbs 17:10 A reproof entereth more into a wise man than an hundred stripes into a fool.
Luke 17:4 And if he trespass against thee seven times in a day, and seven times in a day turn again to thee, saying,	**Psalms 66:18** If I regard iniquity in my heart, the Lord will not hear *me*:

I repent; thou shalt forgive him.	
Luke 17:14 And when he saw *them*, he said unto them, Go shew yourselves unto the priests. And it came to pass, that, as they went, they were cleansed.	**Leviticus 13:2** When a man shall have in the skin of his flesh a rising, a scab, or bright spot, and it be in the skin of his flesh *like* the plague of leprosy; then he shall be brought unto Aaron the priest, or unto one of his sons the priests: **Leviticus 14:2** This shall be the law of the leper in the day of his cleansing: He shall be brought unto the priest:
Luke 17:26-27 And as it was in the days of Noe, so shall it be also in the days of the Son of man. 27 They did eat, they drank, they married wives, they were given in marriage, until the day that Noe entered into the ark, and the flood came, and destroyed them all.	**Genesis 6:5** And GOD saw that the wickedness of man *was* great in the earth, and *that* every imagination of the thoughts of his heart *was* only evil continually. **Genesis 6:9-12** These *are* the generations of Noah: Noah was a just man *and* **perfect in his generations**, *and* Noah walked with God. 10 And Noah begat three sons, Shem, Ham, and Japheth. 11 The earth also was corrupt before God, and the earth was filled with violence. 12 And God looked upon the earth, and, behold, it was corrupt; **for all flesh had corrupted his way upon the earth**. **Genesis 7:7** And Noah went in, and his sons, and his wife, and his sons' wives with him, into the ark, because of the waters of the flood. **See Matthew 24:38**
Luke 17:28-29 Likewise also as it was in the days of Lot; they did eat, they drank, they bought, they sold, they planted, they builded; 29 But the same day that Lot went out of **Sodom** it rained fire and brimstone from heaven, and destroyed *them* all.	**Genesis 19:24** Then the LORD rained upon Sodom and upon Gomorrah brimstone and fire from the LORD out of heaven; **Deuteronomy 29:23** *And that* the whole land thereof *is* brimstone, and salt, *and* burning, *that* it is not sown, nor beareth, nor any grass groweth therein, like the overthrow of Sodom, and Gomorrah, Admah, and Zeboim, which the LORD overthrew in his anger, and in his wrath: **Isaiah 1:9** Except the LORD of hosts had left unto us a very small remnant, we should have been as Sodom, *and* we should have been like unto Gomorrah. **Isaiah 13:19** And Babylon, the glory of kingdoms, the beauty of the Chaldees' excellency, shall be as when God overthrew Sodom and Gomorrah. **Jeremiah 50:40** As God overthrew Sodom and Gomorrah and the neighbour *cities* thereof, saith the LORD; *so* shall no man abide there, neither shall any son of man dwell therein. **Amos 4:11** I have overthrown *some* of you, as God overthrew Sodom and Gomorrah, and ye were as a firebrand plucked out of the burning: yet have ye not returned unto me, saith the LORD. **See Romans 1:27** "Sexual sins"
Luke 17:30 Even thus shall it be in the day when the Son of man is revealed.	**Genesis 19:24** Then the LORD rained upon Sodom and upon Gomorrah brimstone and fire from the LORD out of heaven; **Exodus 20:18** And all the people saw the thunderings, and the lightnings, and the noise of the trumpet, and the mountain smoking: and when the people saw *it*, they removed, and stood afar off.
Luke 17:32 Remember Lot's wife.	**Genesis 19:26** But his wife looked back from behind him, and she became a pillar of salt.
Luke 17:37 And they answered and said unto him, Where, Lord? And he said	**Job 39:30** Her young ones also suck up blood: and where the slain *are*, there *is* she.

unto them, Wheresoever the body *is*, thither will the eagles be gathered together.	
Luke 18:11 The Pharisee stood and prayed thus with himself, God, I thank thee, that I am not as other men *are*, extortioners, unjust, adulterers, or even as this publican.	**Proverbs 6:16-19** These six *things* doth the LORD hate: yea, seven *are* an abomination unto him: 17 A **proud look**, a lying tongue, and hands that shed innocent blood, 18 An heart that deviseth wicked imaginations, feet that be swift in running to mischief, 19 A false witness *that* speaketh lies, and he that soweth discord among brethren. **Proverbs 16:18** Pride *goeth* before destruction, and an haughty spirit before a fall. **Isaiah 1:15-16** And when ye spread forth your hands, I will hide mine eyes from you: yea, when ye make many prayers, I will not hear: your hands are full of blood. 16 Wash you, make you clean; put away the evil of your doings from before mine eyes; cease to do evil;
Luke 18:13 And the publican, standing afar off, would not lift up so much as *his* eyes unto heaven, but smote upon his breast, saying, God be merciful to me a sinner.	**Proverbs 28:13** He that covereth his sins shall not prosper: but whoso confesseth and forsaketh *them* shall have mercy. **Isaiah 55:7** Let the wicked forsake his way, and the unrighteous man his thoughts: and let him return unto the LORD, and he will have mercy upon him; and to our God, for he will abundantly pardon.
Luke 18:14 I tell you, this man went down to his house justified *rather* than the other: for every one that exalteth himself shall be abased; and he that humbleth himself shall be exalted.	**Job 22:29** When *men* are cast down, then thou shalt say, *There is* lifting up; and he shall save the humble person. **Proverbs 15:33** The fear of the LORD *is* the instruction of wisdom; and before honour *is* humility. **Proverbs 18:12** Before destruction the heart of man is haughty, and before honour *is* humility. **Proverbs 29:23** A man's pride shall bring him low: but honour shall uphold the humble in spirit.
Luke 18:20 Thou knowest the commandments, Do not commit adultery, Do not kill, Do not steal, Do not bear false witness, Honour thy father and thy mother.	**Exodus 20:12-16** Honour thy father and thy mother: that thy days may be long upon the land which the LORD thy God giveth thee. 13 Thou shalt not kill. 14 Thou shalt not commit adultery. 15 Thou shalt not steal. 16 Thou shalt not bear false witness against thy neighbour. **Deuteronomy 5:17-20** Thou shalt not kill. 18 Neither shalt thou commit adultery. 19 Neither shalt thou steal. 20 Neither shalt thou bear false witness against thy neighbour. **See Matthew 5:27 "Adultery"**
Luke 18:22 Now when Jesus heard these things, he said unto him, Yet lackest thou one thing: sell all that thou hast, and distribute unto the poor, and thou shalt have treasure in heaven: and come, follow me.	**Deuteronomy 15:11** For the poor shall never cease out of the land: therefore I command thee, saying, Thou shalt open thine hand wide unto thy brother, to thy poor, and to thy needy, in thy land.
Luke 18:24 And when Jesus saw that he was very sorrowful, he said, How hardly shall they that have riches enter into the kingdom of God!	**Proverbs 11:28** He that trusteth in his riches shall fall: but the righteous shall flourish as a branch.
Luke 18:27 And he said, The things which are impossible with men are	**Job 42:2** I know that thou canst do every *thing*, and *that* no thought can be withholden from thee.

possible with God.	**Jeremiah 32:17** Ah Lord GOD! behold, thou hast made the heaven and the earth by thy great power and stretched out arm, *and* there is nothing too hard for thee:
Luke 18:29 And he said unto them, Verily I say unto you, There is no man that hath left house, or parents, or brethren, or wife, or children, for the kingdom of God's sake,	**Deuteronomy 33:9** Who said unto his father and to his mother, I have not seen him; neither did he acknowledge his brethren, nor knew his own children: for they have observed thy word, and kept thy covenant.
Luke 18:30 Who shall not receive manifold more in this present time, and in the world to come life everlasting.	**Job 42:12** So the LORD blessed the latter end of Job more than his beginning: for he had fourteen thousand sheep, and six thousand camels, and a thousand yoke of oxen, and a thousand she asses.
Luke 18:31 Then he took *unto him* the twelve, and said unto them, Behold, we go up to Jerusalem, and all things that are **written by the prophets** concerning the Son of man shall be accomplished.	**Exodus 24:12** And the LORD said unto Moses, Come up to me into the mount, and be there: and I will give thee tables of stone, and **a law**, and **commandments which I have written**; that thou mayest teach them. **Exodus 31:18** And he gave unto Moses, when he had made an end of communing with him upon mount Sinai, two tables of testimony, tables of stone, **written with the finger of God**. **Exodus 34:27-28** And the LORD said unto Moses, **Write thou these words**: for after the tenor of these words I have made a covenant with thee and with Israel. And he was there with the LORD forty days and forty nights; he did neither eat bread, nor drink water. And **he wrote upon the tables the words of the covenant, the Ten Commandments**. **Joshua 24:26** And Joshua wrote these words in the book of the law of God, and took a great stone, and set it up there under an oak, that was by the sanctuary of the LORD. **1 Samuel 10:25** Then Samuel told the people the manner of the kingdom, and wrote it in a book, and laid it up before the LORD. And Samuel sent all the people away, every man to his house. **Isaiah 30:8** Now go, **write it before them in a table, and note it in a book, that it may be for the time to come for ever and ever**: **Jeremiah 36:2** Take thee a roll of a book, and **write therein all the words that I have spoken unto thee against Israel**, and against Judah, and against all the nations, from the day I spake unto thee, from the days of Josiah, even unto this day. **Jeremiah 36:4** Then Jeremiah called Baruch the son of Neriah: and **Baruch wrote from the mouth of Jeremiah all the words of the LORD**, which he had spoken unto him, upon a roll of a book. **Psalms 22:6** But I *am* a worm, and no man; a reproach of men, and despised of the people. **Isaiah 53:7** He was oppressed, and he was afflicted, yet he opened not his mouth: he is brought as a lamb to the slaughter, and as a sheep before her shearers is dumb, so he openeth not his mouth.
Luke 19:22 And he saith unto him, Out of thine own mouth will I judge thee, *thou* wicked servant. Thou knewest that I was an austere man, taking up that I laid not down, and reaping that I did not sow:	**2 Samuel 1:16** And David said unto him, Thy blood *be* upon thy head; for thy mouth hath testified against thee, saying, I have slain the LORD's anointed.

Luke 19:23 Wherefore then gavest not thou my money into the bank, that at my coming I might have required mine own with usury?	**Deuteronomy 23:19-20** Thou shalt not lend upon usury to thy brother; usury of money, usury of victuals, usury of any thing that is lent upon usury: 20 **Unto a stranger thou mayest lend upon usury**; but unto thy brother thou shalt not lend upon usury: that the LORD thy God may bless thee in all that thou settest thine hand to in the land whither thou goest to possess it.
Luke 19:30-31 Saying, Go ye into the village over against *you*; in the which at your entering ye shall find a colt tied, whereon yet never man sat: loose him, and bring *him hither*. 31 And if any man ask you, Why do ye loose *him*? thus shall ye say unto him, Because the Lord hath need of him.	See 1 Corinthians 12:8 "Word of Knowledge"
Luke 19:38 Saying, Blessed [be] the King that cometh in the name of the Lord: peace in heaven, and glory in the highest.	**Psalms 118:26** Blessed *be* he that cometh in the name of the LORD: we have blessed you out of the house of the LORD.
Luke 19:40 And he answered and said unto them, I tell you that, if these should hold their peace, the stones would immediately cry out.	**Habakkak 2:11** For the stone shall cry out of the wall, and the beam out of the timber shall answer it.
Luke 19:44 And shall lay thee even with the ground, and thy children within thee; and they shall not leave in thee one stone upon another; because thou knewest not the time of thy visitation.	**1 Kings 9:7-8** Then will I cut off Israel out of the land which I have given them; and this house, which I have hallowed for my name, will I cast out of my sight; and Israel shall be a proverb and a byword among all people: 8 And at this house, *which* is high, every one that passeth by it shall be astonished, and shall hiss; and they shall say, Why hath the LORD done thus unto this land, and to this house? **Micah 3:12** Therefore shall Zion for your sake be plowed *as* a field, and Jerusalem shall become heaps, and the mountain of the house as the high places of the forest.
Luke 19:46 Saying unto them, It is written, My house is the house of prayer: but ye have made it a den of thieves.	**Isaiah 56:7** Even them will I bring to my holy mountain, and make them joyful in my house of prayer: their burnt offerings and their sacrifices *shall be* accepted upon mine altar; for mine house shall be called an house of prayer for all people. **Jeremiah 7:11** Is this house, which is called by my name, become a den of robbers in your eyes? Behold, even I have seen *it*, saith the LORD.
Luke 20:1 And it came to pass, *that* on one of those days, as **he taught the people** in the temple, and preached the gospel, the chief priests and the scribes came upon *him* with the **elders**,	See Ephesians 4:11 "Teach – Teachers" See 1 Peter 5:1 "Elders"
Luke 20:9 Then began he to speak to the people this parable; A certain man planted a vineyard, and let it forth to husbandmen, and went into a far country for a long time.	**Isaiah 5:1** Now will I sing to my wellbeloved a song of my beloved touching his vineyard. My well beloved hath a vineyard in a very fruitful hill: **Isaiah 5:7** For the vineyard of the LORD of hosts *is* the house of Israel, and the men of Judah his pleasant plant: and he looked for judgment, but behold oppression; for righteousness, but behold a cry.
Luke 20:16 He shall come and destroy these husbandmen, and shall give the	**Isaiah 5:13-14** Therefore my people are gone into captivity, because they have no knowledge: and their honourable men are

vineyard to others. And when they heard it, they said, God forbid.	famished, and their multitude dried up with thirst. 14 Therefore hell hath enlarged herself, and opened her mouth without measure: and their glory, and their multitude, and their pomp, and he that rejoiceth, shall descend into it. **Jeremiah 12:10** Many pastors have destroyed my vineyard, they have trodden my portion under foot, they have made my pleasant portion a desolate wilderness.
Luke 20:17 And he beheld them, and said, What is this then that is written, The stone which the builders rejected, the same is become the head of the corner?	**Psalms 118:22** The stone *which* the builders refused is become the head *stone* of the corner. **Isaiah 8:14** And he shall be for a sanctuary; but for a stone of stumbling and for a rock of offence to both the houses of Israel, for a gin and for a snare to the inhabitants of Jerusalem. **Isaiah 28:16** Therefore thus saith the Lord GOD, Behold, I lay in Zion for a foundation a stone, a tried stone, a precious corner *stone,* a sure foundation: he that believeth shall not make haste. **Zechariah 4:7** Who *art* thou, O great mountain? before Zerubbabel *thou shalt become* a plain: and he shall bring forth the headstone *thereof with* shoutings, *crying,* Grace, grace unto it.
Luke 20:18 Whosoever shall fall upon that stone shall be broken; but on whomsoever it shall fall, it will grind him to powder.	**Isaiah 8:14** And he shall be for a sanctuary; but for a stone of stumbling and for a rock of offence to both the houses of Israel, for a gin and for a snare to the inhabitants of Jerusalem. **Daniel 2:34** Thou sawest till that a stone was cut out without hands, which smote the image upon his feet *that were* of iron and clay, and brake them to pieces. **Daniel 2:44** And in the days of these kings shall the God of heaven set up a kingdom, which shall never be destroyed: and the kingdom shall not be left to other people, *but* it shall break in pieces and consume all these kingdoms, and it shall stand for ever. **Zechariah 12:3** And in that day will I make Jerusalem a burdensome stone for all people: all that burden themselves with it shall be cut in pieces, though all the people of the earth be gathered together against it.
Luke 20:28 Saying, Master, Moses wrote unto us, If any man's brother die, having a wife, and he die without children, that his brother should take his wife, and raise up seed unto his brother.	**Genesis 38:8** And Judah said unto Onan, Go in unto thy brother's wife, and marry her, and raise up seed to thy brother. **Deuteronomy 25:5** If brethren dwell together, and one of them die, and have no child, the wife of the dead shall not marry without unto a stranger: her husband's brother shall go in unto her, and take her to him to wife, and perform the duty of an husband's brother unto her.
Luke 20:37 Now that the dead are raised, even Moses shewed at the bush, when he calleth the Lord the God of Abraham, and the God of Isaac, and the God of Jacob.	**Exodus 3:6** Moreover he said, I *am* the God of thy father, the God of Abraham, the God of Isaac, and the God of Jacob. And Moses hid his face; for he was afraid to look upon God. **Exodus 3:15** And God said moreover unto Moses, Thus shalt thou say unto the children of Israel, The LORD God of your fathers, the God of Abraham, the God of Isaac, and the God of Jacob, hath sent me unto you: this *is* my name for ever, and this *is* my memorial unto all generations.
Luke 20:42-43 And David himself saith in the book of Psalms, The LORD said unto my Lord, Sit thou on my right hand, Till I make thine enemies thy footstool.	**Psalms 8:6** Thou madest him to have dominion over the works of thy hands; thou hast put all *things* under his feet: **Psalms 16:8** I have set the LORD always before me: because *he is* at my right hand, I shall not be moved.

	Psalms 110:1 The LORD said unto my Lord, Sit thou at my right hand, until I make thine enemies thy footstool.
Psalms 110:5 The Lord at thy right hand shall strike through kings in the day of his wrath.
Zechraiah 3:1 And he shewed me Joshua the high priest standing before the angel of the LORD, and Satan standing at his right hand to resist him.
Luke 20:46 Beware of the scribes, which desire to walk in long robes, and love greetings in the markets, and the highest seats in the synagogues, and the chief rooms at feasts;	**Deuteronomy 16:16** Three times in a year shall all thy males appear before the LORD thy God in the place which he shall choose; in the feast of unleavened bread, and in the feast of weeks, and in the feast of tabernacles: and they shall not appear before the LORD empty:
Luke 21:1 And he looked up, and saw the rich men casting their gifts into the treasury.	**2 Kings 12:9-11** But Jehoiada the priest took a chest, and bored a hole in the lid of it, and set it beside the altar, on the right side as one cometh into the house of the LORD: and the priests that kept the door put therein all the money *that was* brought into the house of the LORD. 10 And it was *so*, when they saw that *there was* much money in the chest, that the king's scribe and the high priest came up, and they put up in bags, and told the money that was found in the house of the LORD. 11 And they gave the money, being told, into the hands of them that did the work, that had the oversight of the house of the LORD: and they laid it out to the carpenters and builders, that wrought upon the house of the LORD,
Luke 21:6 *As for* these things which ye behold, the days will come, in the which there shall not be left one stone upon another, that shall not be thrown down.	**Micah 3:12** Therefore shall Zion for your sake be plowed *as* a field, and Jerusalem shall become heaps, and the mountain of the house as the high places of the forest.
Luke 21:7 And they asked him, saying, Master, but when shall these things be? and what sign *will there be* when these things shall come to pass?	**Daniel 12:6-8** And *one* said to the man clothed in linen, which *was* upon the waters of the river, How long *shall it be to* the end of these wonders? 7 And I heard the man clothed in linen, which *was* upon the waters of the river, when he held up his right hand and his left hand unto heaven, and sware by him that liveth for ever that *it shall be* for a time, times, and an half; and when he shall have accomplished to scatter the power of the holy people, all these *things* shall be finished. 8 And I heard, but I understood not: then said I, O my Lord, what *shall be* the end of these *things?*
Luke 21:8 And he said, Take heed that ye be not deceived: for many shall come in my name, saying, I am *Christ*; and the time draweth near: go ye not therefore after them.	**Jeremiah 14:14** Then the LORD said unto me, The prophets prophesy lies in my name: I sent them not, neither have I commanded them, neither spake unto them: they prophesy unto you a false vision and divination, and a thing of nought, and the deceit of their heart.
Jeremiah 23:21 I have not sent these prophets, yet they ran: I have not spoken to them, yet they prophesied.
Jeremiah 29:8 For thus saith the LORD of hosts, the God of Israel; Let not your prophets and your diviners, that *be* in the midst of you, deceive you, neither hearken to your dreams which ye cause to be dreamed.
Luke 21:9 But when ye shall hear of wars and commotions, be not terrified: for these things must first come to pass; but the end *is* not by and by.	**Jeremiah 51:46** And lest your heart faint, and ye fear for the rumour that shall be heard in the land; a rumour shall both come *one* year, and after that in *another* year *shall come* a rumour, and violence in the land, ruler against ruler.
Luke 21:10 Then said he unto them,	**Isaiah 19:2** And I will set the Egyptians against the Egyptians:

Nation shall rise against nation, and kingdom against kingdom:	and they shall fight every one against his brother, and every one against his neighbour; city against city, *and* kingdom against kingdom.
Luke 21:11 And great earthquakes shall be in divers places, and famines, and pestilences; and fearful sights and great **signs** shall there be from heaven.	**Isaiah 29:6** Thou shalt be visited of the LORD of hosts with thunder, and with earthquake, and great noise, with storm and tempest, and the flame of devouring fire. **Jeremiah 29:17** Thus saith the LORD of hosts; Behold, I will send upon them the sword, the famine, and the pestilence, and will make them like vile figs, that cannot be eaten, they are so evil. 18 And I will persecute them with the sword, with the famine, and with the pestilence, and will deliver them to be removed to all the kingdoms of the earth, to be a curse, and an astonishment, and an hissing, and a reproach, among all the nations whither I have driven them: **See Mark 16:17 "Signs"**
Luke 21:12 But before all these, they shall lay their hands on you, and persecute *you,* delivering *you* up to the synagogues, and into prisons, being brought before kings and rulers for my name's sake.	**Daniel 3:13** Then Nebuchadnezzar in anger and wrath commanded to bring Shadrach, Meshach, and Abednego. Then they brought these men before the king. **Isaiah 43:2** When you pass through the waters, I will be with you; and through the rivers, they shall not overflow you. When you walk in the fire, you shall not be burned, nor shall the flame kindle on you.
Luke 21:15 For I will give you a mouth and wisdom, which all your adversaries shall not be able to gainsay nor resist.	**Exodus 4:12** Now therefore go, and I will be with thy mouth, and teach thee what thou shalt say. **Isaiah 54:17** No weapon that is formed against thee shall prosper; and every tongue *that* shall rise against thee in judgment thou shalt condemn. This *is* the heritage of the servants of the LORD, and their righteousness *is* of me, saith the LORD.
Luke 21:18 But there shall not an hair of your head perish.	**1 Samuel 14:45** And the people said unto Saul, Shall Jonathan die, who hath wrought this great salvation in Israel? God forbid: *as* the LORD liveth, there shall not one hair of his head fall to the ground; for he hath wrought with God this day. So the people rescued Jonathan, that he died not. **2 Samuel 14:11** Then said she, I pray thee, let the king remember the LORD thy God, that thou wouldest not suffer the revengers of blood to destroy any more, lest they destroy my son. And he said, *As* the LORD liveth, there shall not one hair of thy son fall to the earth. **1 Kings 1:52** And Solomon said, If he will shew himself a worthy man, there shall not an hair of him fall to the earth: but if wickedness shall be found in him, he shall die.
Luke 21:20 And when ye shall see Jerusalem compassed with armies, then know that the desolation thereof is nigh.	**Daniel 9:27** And he shall confirm the covenant with many for one week: and in the midst of the week he shall cause the sacrifice and the oblation to cease, and for the overspreading of abominations he shall make *it* desolate, even until the consummation, and that determined shall be poured upon the desolate.
Luke 21:22 For these be the days of vengeance, that all things which are written may be fulfilled.	**Daniel 9:26** And after threescore and two weeks shall Messiah be cut off, but not for himself: and the people of the prince that shall come shall destroy the city and the sanctuary; and the end thereof

	shall be with a flood, and unto the end of the war desolations are determined.
Luke 21:25 And there shall be signs in the sun, and in the moon, and in the stars; and upon the earth distress of nations, with perplexity; the sea and the waves roaring;	**Isaiah 13:10** For the stars of heaven and the constellations thereof shall not give their light: the sun shall be darkened in his going forth, and the moon shall not cause her light to shine. **Ezekiel 32:7** And when I shall put thee out, I will cover the heaven, and make the stars thereof dark; I will cover the sun with a cloud, and the moon shall not give her light. **Ezekiel 32:8** All the bright lights of heaven will I make dark over thee, and set darkness upon thy land, saith the Lord GOD. **Joel 2:10** The earth shall quake before them; the heavens shall tremble: the sun and the moon shall be dark, and the stars shall withdraw their shining: **Joel 2:31** The sun shall be turned into darkness, and the moon into blood, before the great and the terrible day of the LORD come. **Joel 3:15** The sun and the moon shall be darkened, and the stars shall withdraw their shining.
Luke 21:27 And then shall they see the Son of man coming in a cloud with power and great glory.	**Daniel 7:13** I saw in the night visions, and, behold, *one* like the Son of man came with the clouds of heaven, and came to the Ancient of days, and they brought him near before him.
Luke 21:33 Heaven and earth shall pass away: but my words shall not pass away.	**Psalms 102:26** They shall perish, but thou shalt endure: yea, all of them shall wax old like a garment; as a vesture shalt thou change them, and they shall be changed: **Isaiah 51:6** Lift up your eyes to the heavens, and look upon the earth beneath: for the heavens shall vanish away like smoke, and the earth shall wax old like a garment, and they that dwell therein shall die in like manner: but my salvation shall be for ever, and my righteousness shall not be abolished. **See Matthew 5:18 "Words"**
Luke 21:34 And take heed to yourselves, lest at any time your hearts be overcharged with **surfeiting**, and **drunkenness**, and cares of this life, and *so* that day come upon you unawares.	**Deuteronomy 21:20** And they shall say unto the elders of his city, This our son *is* stubborn and rebellious, he will not obey our voice; *he is* a **glutton**, and a drunkard. **Proverbs 23:21** For the drunkard and the **glutton** shall come to poverty: and drowsiness shall clothe *a man* with rags. **Proverbs 25:16** Hast thou found honey? eat so much as is sufficient for thee, lest thou be filled therewith, and vomit it. **See Ephesians 5:18 "Drunkards"**
Luke 21:35 For as a snare shall it come on all them that dwell on the face of the whole earth.	**Isaiah 24:17** Fear, and the pit, and the snare, *are* upon thee, O inhabitant of the earth.
Luke 22:1 Now the feast of unleavened bread drew nigh, which is called the Passover.	**Leviticus 23:6** And on the fifteenth day of the same month *is* the feast of unleavened bread unto the LORD: seven days ye must eat unleavened bread.
Luke 22:2 And the chief priests and scribes sought how they might kill him; for they feared the people.	**Psalms 2:2** The kings of the earth set themselves, and the rulers take counsel together, against the LORD, and against his anointed, *saying,*
Luke 22:3 Then entered **Satan** into Judas surnamed Iscariot, being of the number of the twelve.	**Genesis 3:4** And the **serpent** said unto the woman, Ye shall not surely die: **Zechariah 3:1-2** And he shewed me Joshua the high priest

	standing before the angel of the LORD, and **Satan** standing at his right hand to resist him. 2 And the LORD said unto **Satan,** The LORD rebuke thee, O **Satan**; even the LORD that hath chosen Jerusalem rebuke thee: *is* not this a brand plucked out of the fire? **See Matthew 4:10 "satan"**
Luke 22:14-15 And when the hour was come, he sat down, and the twelve apostles with him. 15 And he said unto them, With desire I have desired to eat this passover with you before I suffer:	**Leviticus 23:5-6** In the fourteenth *day* of the first month at even *is* the LORD's passover. 6 And on the fifteenth day of the same month *is* the feast of unleavened bread unto the LORD: seven days ye must eat unleavened bread.
Luke 22:20 Likewise also the cup after supper, saying, This cup *is* the new testament in my blood, which is shed for you.	**Jeremiah 31:31-33** Behold, the days come, saith the LORD, that **I will make a new covenant with the house of Israel**, and with the house of Judah: 32 Not according to the covenant that I made with their fathers in the day *that* I took them by the hand to bring them out of the land of Egypt; which my covenant they brake, although I was an husband unto them, saith the LORD: 33 But this *shall be* the covenant that I will make with the house of Israel; After those days, saith the LORD, I will put my law in their inward parts, and write it in their hearts; and will be their God, and they shall be my people. 34 And they shall teach no more every man his neighbour, and every man his brother, saying, Know the LORD: for they shall all know me, from the least of them unto the greatest of them, saith the LORD: for I will forgive their iniquity, and I will remember their sin no more. **See Matthew 26:28 "Atonement"**
Luke 22:22 And truly the Son of man goeth, as it was determined: but woe unto that man by whom he is betrayed!	**Psalms 41:9** Yea, mine own familiar friend, in whom I trusted, which did eat of my bread, hath lifted up *his* heel against me.
Luke 22:31 And the Lord said, Simon, Simon, behold, **Satan** hath desired *to have* you, that he may sift *you* as wheat:	**See Matthew 4:10 "satan"**
Luke 22:37 For I say unto you, that this that is written must yet be accomplished in me, And he was reckoned among the transgressors: for the things concerning me have an end.	**Isaiah 53:12** Therefore will I divide him *a portion* with the great, and he shall divide the spoil with the strong; because he hath poured out his soul unto death: and he was numbered with the transgressors; and he bare the sin of many, and made intercession for the transgressors.
Luke 22:44 And being in an agony he prayed more earnestly: and his sweat was as it were great **drops of blood** falling down to the ground.	**See Matthew 26:28 "Atonement"**
Luke 22:45 And when he rose up from **prayer**, and was come to his disciples, he found them sleeping for sorrow,	**See Matthew 17:21 "Prayer"**
Luke 22:63 And the men that held Jesus mocked him, and smote *him*.	**Job 16:10** They have gaped upon me with their mouth; they have smitten me upon the cheek reproachfully; they have gathered themselves together against me. **Isaiah 50:6** I gave my back to the smiters, and my cheeks to them that plucked off the hair: I hid not my face from shame and spitting.
Luke 22:66 And as soon as it was day, the **elders** of the people and the chief priests and the scribes came together, and led him into their council, saying,	**Psalms 2:2** The kings of the earth set themselves, and the rulers take counsel together, against the LORD, and against his anointed, *saying,*

	See 1 Peter 5:1
Luke 22:69 Hereafter shall the Son of man sit on the **right hand** of the power of God.	**Psalms 8:6** Thou madest him to have dominion over the works of thy **hands**; thou hast put all *things* under his feet: **Psalms 16:8** I have set the LORD always before me: because *he is* **at my right hand**, I shall not be moved. **Psalms 110:1** The LORD said unto my Lord, **Sit thou at my right hand**, until I make thine enemies thy footstool. **Psalms 110:5** The Lord **at thy right hand** shall strike through kings in the day of his wrath. **Daniel 7:9** I beheld till the thrones were cast down, and the **Ancient of days did sit**, whose garment *was* white as snow, and the hair of his head like the pure wool: his throne *was like* the fiery flame, *and* his wheels *as* burning fire. **Zechraiah 3:1** And he shewed me Joshua the high priest standing before the angel of the LORD, and **Satan standing at his right hand** to resist him.
Luke 23:3 And Pilate asked him, saying, Art thou the **King** of the Jews? And he answered him and said, Thou sayest it.	**Psalms 47:7-8** For **God is the King** of all the earth: sing ye praises with understanding. 8 God reigneth over the heathen: God sitteth upon the throne of his holiness. **Isaiah 44:6** Thus saith the LORD the **King of Israel**, and his redeemer the LORD of hosts; I am the first, and I am the last; and beside me there is no God. **Jeremiah 10:10** But the LORD is the true God, he is the living God, and an everlasting **king**: at his wrath the earth shall tremble, and the nations shall not be able to abide his indignation.
Luke 23:29 For, behold, the days are coming, in the which they shall say, Blessed *are* the barren, and the wombs that never bare, and the paps which never gave suck.	**Isaiah 54:1** Sing, O barren, thou *that* didst not bear; break forth into singing, and cry aloud, thou *that* didst not travail with child: for more *are* the children of the desolate than the children of the married wife, saith the LORD.
Luke 23:30 Then shall they begin to say to the mountains, Fall on us; and to the hills, Cover us.	**Isaiah 2:19** And they shall go into the holes of the rocks, and into the caves of the earth, for fear of the LORD, and for the glory of his majesty, when he ariseth to shake terribly the earth. **Hosea 10:8** The high places also of Aven, the sin of Israel, shall be destroyed: the thorn and the thistle shall come up on their altars; and they shall say to the mountains, Cover us; and to the hills, Fall on us.
Luke 23:31 For if they do these things in a green tree, what shall be done in the dry?	**Zechariah 13:6** And *one* shall say unto him, What *are* these wounds in thine hands? Then he shall answer, *Those* with which I was wounded *in* the house of my friends.
Luke 23:33 And when they were come to the place, which is called Calvary, there they crucified him, and the malefactors, one on the right hand, and the other on the left.	**Psalm 22:16** For dogs have compassed me: the assembly of the wicked have inclosed me: they pierced my hands and my feet. **Zechariah 12:10** And I will pour upon the house of David, and upon the inhabitants of Jerusalem, the spirit of grace and of supplications: and they shall look upon me whom they have pierced, and they shall mourn for him, as one mourneth for his only *son*, and shall be in bitterness for him, as one that is in bitterness for his firstborn.
Luke 23:34 Then said Jesus, Father, forgive them; for they know not what they do. And they parted his raiment,	**Psalm 22:18** They part my garments among them, and cast lots upon my vesture.

and cast lots.	**Isaiah 53:12** Therefore will I divide him *a portion* with the great, and he shall divide the spoil with the strong; because he hath poured out his soul unto death: and he was numbered with the transgressors; and he bare the sin of many, and made intercession for the transgressors.
Luke 23:45 And the sun was darkened, and the veil of the temple was rent in the midst.	**Amos 8:9** And it shall come to pass in that day, saith the Lord GOD, that I will cause the sun to go down at noon, and I will darken the earth in the clear day:
Luke 23:46 And when Jesus had cried with a loud voice, he said, Father, into thy hands I commend my spirit: and having said thus, he gave up the ghost.	**Psalms 31:5** Into thine hand I commit my spirit: thou hast redeemed me, O LORD God of truth.
Luke 23:48-49 And all the people that came together to that sight, beholding the things which were done, smote their breasts, and returned. 49 And all his acquaintance, and the women that followed him from Galilee, stood afar off, beholding these things.	**Psalms 38:10-11** My heart panteth, my strength faileth me: as for the light of mine eyes, it also is gone from me. 11 My lovers and my friends stand aloof from my sore; and my kinsmen stand afar off.
Luke 23:52 This *man* went unto Pilate, and begged the **body** of Jesus.	**See 1 Thessalonians 5:23 "Body, soul, and spirit"**
Luke 23:54 And the day was a preparation, and **sabbath** was approaching, **Luke 23:56** and having turned back, they made ready spices and ointments, and on the **sabbath**, indeed, they rested, according to the command.	**See Colossians 2:16 "Sabbath"**
Luke 24:26 Ought not Christ to have suffered these things, and to enter into his glory?	**Isaiah 50:6** I gave my back to the smiters, and my cheeks to them that plucked off the hair: I hid not my face from shame and spitting. **Isaiah 53:5** But he *was* wounded for our transgressions, *he was* bruised for our iniquities: the chastisement of our peace *was* upon him; and with his stripes we are healed.
Luke 24:27 And beginning at Moses and all the prophets, he expounded unto them in all the scriptures the things concerning himself.	**Genesis 3:15** And I will put enmity between thee and the woman, and between thy seed and her seed; it shall bruise thy head, and thou shalt bruise his heel. **Genesis 22:18** And in thy seed shall all the nations of the earth be blessed; because thou hast obeyed my voice. **Genesis 26:4** And I will make thy seed to multiply as the stars of heaven, and will give unto thy seed all these countries; and in thy seed shall all the nations of the earth be blessed; **Genesis 49:10** The sceptre shall not depart from Judah, nor a lawgiver from between his feet, until Shiloh come; and unto him *shall* the gathering of the people *be*. **Deuteronomy 18:15** The LORD thy God will raise up unto thee a Prophet from the midst of thee, of thy brethren, like unto me; unto him ye shall hearken; **Psalms 132:11** The LORD hath sworn *in* truth unto David; he will not turn from it; Of the fruit of thy body will I set upon thy throne. **Isaiah 7:14** Therefore the Lord himself shall give you a sign;

	Behold, a virgin shall conceive, and bear a son, and shall call his name Immanuel.
	Isaiah 40:10 Behold, the Lord GOD will come with strong *hand*, and his arm shall rule for him: behold, his reward *is* with him, and his work before him.
	Jeremiah 23:5 Behold, the days come, saith the LORD, that I will raise unto David a righteous Branch, and a King shall reign and prosper, and shall execute judgment and justice in the earth.
	Ezekiel 34:23 And I will set up one shepherd over them, and he shall feed them, *even* my servant David; he shall feed them, and he shall be their shepherd.
	Ezekiel 37:25 And they shall dwell in the land that I have given unto Jacob my servant, wherein your fathers have dwelt; and they shall dwell therein, *even* they, and their children, and their children's children for ever: and my servant David *shall be* their prince for ever.
	Daniel 9:24 Seventy weeks are determined upon thy people and upon thy holy city, to finish the transgression, and to make an end of sins, and to make reconciliation for iniquity, and to bring in everlasting righteousness, and to seal up the vision and prophecy, and to anoint the most Holy.
Luke 24:32 And they said one to another, Did not **our heart burn within us**, while he talked with us by the way, and while he opened to us the Scriptures?	**Numbers 31:23** Every thing that may abide the fire, **ye shall make** *it* **go through the fire, and** <u>**it shall be clean**</u>: nevertheless it shall be purified with the water of separation: and all that abideth not the fire ye shall make go through the water.
Luke 24:39 Behold my hands and my feet, that it is I myself: handle me, and see**; for a spirit hath not flesh and bones**, as ye see me have.	**Exodus 33:20** And he said, Thou canst not see my face: for there shall no man see me, and live. **See 1 Thessalonians 5:23 "Body, soul, and spirit"**
Luke 24:46 And said unto them, Thus it is written, and thus it behoved Christ to suffer, and to rise from the dead the third day:	**Psalms 16:8-11** I have set the LORD always before me: because he is at my right hand, I shall not be moved. 9 Therefore my heart is glad, and my glory rejoiceth: my flesh also shall rest in hope. 10 For thou wilt not leave my soul in hell; neither wilt thou suffer thine Holy One to see corruption. 11 Thou wilt shew me the path of life: in thy presence is fulness of joy; at thy right hand there are pleasures for evermore. **Isaiah 53:5** But he *was* wounded for our transgressions, *he was* bruised for our iniquities: the chastisement of our peace *was* upon him; and with his stripes we are healed. **Daniel 9:24-26** Seventy weeks are determined upon thy people and upon thy holy city, to finish the transgression, and to make an end of sins, and to make reconciliation for iniquity, and to bring in everlasting righteousness, and to seal up the vision and prophecy, and to anoint the most Holy. 25 Know therefore and understand, *that* from the going forth of the commandment to restore and to build Jerusalem unto the Messiah the Prince *shall be* seven weeks, and threescore and two weeks: the street shall be built again, and the wall, even in troublous times. 26 And after threescore and two weeks shall Messiah be cut off, but not for himself: and the people of the prince that shall come shall destroy the city and the sanctuary; and the end thereof *shall be* with a flood, and unto the end of the war desolations are determined.

	Hosea 6:2 After two days will he revive us: in the third day he will raise us up, and we shall live in his sight.
Luke 24:51 And it came to pass, while he blessed them, he was parted from them, and carried up into heaven.	**Psalms 68:18** Thou hast ascended on high, thou hast led captivity captive: thou hast received gifts for men; yea, *for* the rebellious also, that the LORD God might dwell *among them.*
John 1:1-2 In the beginning was the Word, and the Word was with God, and the Word was God. 2 The same was in the beginning with God.	**Job 36:26** Behold, God is great, and we know him not, **neither can the number of his years be searched out.** **Psalms 90:2** Before the mountains were brought forth, or ever thou hadst formed the earth and the world, even **from everlasting to everlasting, thou art God.** **Proverb 8:22-23** The LORD possessed me in the beginning of his way, before his works of old. 23 I was set up from everlasting, from the beginning, or ever the earth was. **Micah 5:2** But thou, Bethlehem Ephratah, *though* thou be little among the thousands of Judah, *yet* out of thee shall he come forth unto me *that is* to be ruler in Israel; whose goings forth *have been* from of old, **from everlasting**. **Isaiah 9:6** For unto us a child is born, unto us a son is given: and the government shall be upon his shoulder: and his name shall be called Wonderful, Counseller, The mighty God, The everlasting Father, The Prince of Peace. **Isaiah 40:3-5** The voice of him that crieth in the wilderness, Prepare ye the way of the Lord, make straight in the desert a highway for our God. 4 Every valley shall be exalted, and every mountain and hill shall be made low: and the crooked shall be made straight, and the rough places plain: 5 And the glory of the LORD shall be revealed, and all flesh shall see *it* together: for the mouth of the LORD hath spoken *it.* **Isaiah 43:10** Ye are my witnesses, saith the LORD, and my servant whom I have chosen: that ye may know and believe me, and understand that I am he: before me there was no God formed, neither shall there be after me.
John 1:3 All things were made by him; and without him was not any thing made that was made.	**Genesis 1:1** In the beginning God created the heaven and the earth. **Genesis 1:2** And the earth was without form, and void; and darkness was upon the face of the deep. And **the Spirit of God moved** upon the face of the waters. **Genesis 1:3** And God said, Let there be light: and there was light. **Genesis 1:6** And God said, Let there be a firmament in the midst of the waters, and let it divide the waters from the waters. **Genesis 1:7** And God made the firmament, and divided the waters which *were* under the firmament from the waters which *were* above the firmament: and it was so. **Genesis 1:26** And God said, Let us make man in our image, after our likeness: and let them have dominion over the fish of the sea, and over the fowl of the air, and over the cattle, and over all the earth, and over every creeping thing that creepeth upon the earth. **Exodus 20:11** For *in* six days the LORD made the heaven and the earth, the sea, and all that in them [is], and rested the seventh day; wherefore the LORD blessed the Sabbath day, and hallowed it.

	Nehemiah 9:6 Thou, *even* thou, *art* LORD alone; thou hast made heaven, the heaven of heavens, with all their host, the earth, and all *things* that *are* therein, the seas, and all that *is* therein, and thou preservest them all; and the host of heaven worshippeth thee.
	Job 26:13 By his Spirit he hath garnished the heavens; his hand hath formed the crooked serpent.
	Job 33:4 The Spirit of God hath made me, and the breath of the Almighty hath given me life.
	Psalms 33:6 By the word of the LORD were the heavens made; and all the host of them by the breath of his mouth.
	Psalms 102:25-27 Of old hast thou laid the foundation of the earth: and the heavens [are] the work of thy hands. They shall perish, but thou shalt endure: yea, all of them shall wax old like a garment; as a vesture shalt thou change them, and they shall be changed: But thou [art] the same, and thy years shall have no end.
	Psalms 104:30 Thou sendest forth thy Spirit, they are created: and thou renewest the face of the earth.
	Isaiah 37:16 O LORD of hosts, God of Israel, that dwellest *between* the cherubims, thou *art* the God, *even* thou alone, of all the kingdoms of the earth: thou hast made heaven and earth.
	Isaiah 40:28 Hast thou not known? hast thou not heard, *that* the everlasting God, the LORD, the **Creator** of the ends of the earth, fainteth not, neither is weary? *there is* no searching of his understanding.
	Isaiah 44:24 Thus saith the LORD, thy redeemer, and he that formed thee from the womb, I *am* the LORD that maketh all *things*; that stretcheth forth the heavens alone; that spreadeth abroad the earth by myself;
	Isaiah 45:12 I have made the earth, and created man upon it: I, *even* my hands, have stretched out the heavens, and all their host have I commanded.
John 1:6 There was a man sent from God, whose name *was* John.	**Malachi 3:1** Behold, I will send my messenger, and he shall prepare the way before me: and the Lord, whom ye seek, shall suddenly come to his temple, even the messenger of the covenant, whom ye delight in: behold, he shall come, saith the LORD of hosts.
John 1:7-9 The same came for a witness, to bear witness of the **Light**, that all *men* through him might believe. ⁸ He was not that Light, but *was sent* to bear witness of that Light. ⁹ *That* was the true Light, which lighteth every man that cometh into the world.	**Psalms 27:1** The **LORD** *is* my <u>light</u> and my salvation; whom shall I fear? the LORD is the strength of my life; of whom shall I be afraid? **Isaiah 42:16** And I will bring the blind by a way *that* they knew not; I will lead them in paths *that* they have not known: I will make darkness light before them, and crooked things straight. These things will I do unto them, and not forsake them. **Isaiah 60:1** Arise, shine; for thy light is come, and the glory of the LORD is risen upon thee. **Isaiah 60:19-20** The sun shall be no more thy light by day; neither for brightness shall the moon give light unto thee: but the LORD shall be unto thee an **everlasting light**, and thy God thy glory. 20 Thy sun shall no more go down; neither shall thy moon withdraw itself: for the **LORD shall be thine everlasting <u>light</u>**, and the days of thy mourning shall be ended.

John 1:10 He was in the world, and the world was made by him, and the world knew him not.	**Isaiah 53:3** He is despised and rejected of men; a man of sorrows, and acquainted with grief: and we hid as it were *our* faces from him; he was despised, and we esteemed him not.
John 1:11 He came unto his own, and his own received him not.	**Genesis 37:4** And when his brethren saw that their father loved him more than all his brethren, they hated him, and could not speak peaceably unto him. **Psalms 109:4-5** For my love they are my adversaries: but I *give myself unto* prayer. 5 And they have rewarded me evil for good, and hatred for my love. **Proverb 1:24** Because I have called, and ye refused; I have stretched out my hand, and no man regarded;
John 1:12 But as many as received him, to them gave he power to become the sons of God, *even* to them that believe on his name:	**Isaiah 56:5** Even unto them will I give in mine house and within my walls a place and a name better than of sons and of daughters: I will give them an everlasting name, that shall not be cut off.
John 1:14 And the Word was made **flesh**, and dwelt among us, (and we beheld his glory, the glory as of the only begotten of the Father,) full of grace and truth.	**Genesis 22:2** And he said, Take now thy son, thine only *son* Isaac, whom thou lovest, and get thee into the land of Moriah; and offer him there for a burnt offering upon one of the mountains which I will tell thee of. **Isaiah 7:14** Therefore the Lord himself shall give you a sign; Behold, a virgin shall conceive, and bear a son, and shall call his name Immanuel. **Isaiah 9:6** For unto us a child is born, unto us a son is given: and the government shall be upon his shoulder: and his name shall be called Wonderful, Counseller, The mighty God, The everlasting Father, The Prince of Peace. **Isaiah 40:3-5** The voice of him that crieth in the wilderness, Prepare ye the way of the Lord, make straight in the desert a highway for our God. 4 Every valley shall be exalted, and every mountain and hill shall be made low: and the crooked shall be made straight, and the rough places plain: 5 And the glory of the LORD shall be revealed, and all flesh shall see *it* together: for the mouth of the LORD hath spoken *it*. **Isaiah 42:8** I *am* the LORD: that *is* my name: and **my glory will I not give to another**, neither my praise to graven images. **Isaiah 53:2** For he shall grow up before him as a tender plant, and as a root out of a dry ground: he hath no form nor comeliness; and when we shall see him, *there is* no beauty that we should desire him. **See 1 Thessalonians 5:23** "Body, soul, and spirit"
John 1:17 For the law was given by Moses, *but* grace and truth came by Jesus Christ.	**Exodus 20:1** And God spake all these words, saying, **Leviticus 27:34** These *are* the commandments, which the LORD commanded Moses for the children of Israel in mount Sinai. **Deuteronomy 4:44** And this *is* the law which Moses set before the children of Israel:
John 1:18 No man hath seen God at any time; the only begotten Son, which is in the bosom of the Father, he hath declared *him*.	**Exodus 33:20** And he said, Thou canst not see my face: for there shall no man see me, and live. **Exodus 33:23** And I will take away mine hand, and thou shalt see my back parts: but my face shall not be seen. **Numbers 14:14** And they will tell it to the inhabitants of this land: for they have heard that thou LORD art among this people, that

	thou LORD art seen face to face, and that thy cloud standeth over them, and that thou goest before them, by day time in a pillar of a cloud, and in a pillar of fire by night.
	Deuteronomy 4:12 And the LORD spake unto you out of the midst of the fire: ye heard the voice of the words, but saw no similitude; only *ye heard* a voice.
	Job 42:5 I have heard of thee by the hearing of the ear: but now mine eye seeth thee.
	Judges 13:22 And Manoah said unto his wife, We shall surely die, because we have seen God.
	Isaiah 40:5 And the glory of the LORD shall be revealed, and all flesh shall see *it* together: for the mouth of the LORD hath spoken *it*.
	Isaiah 60:2 For, behold, the darkness shall cover the earth, and gross darkness the people: but the LORD shall arise upon thee, and his glory shall be seen upon thee.
	See 1 Timothy 2:5 "God"
John 1:20 And he confessed, and denied not; but confessed, I am not the Christ.	**Exodus 12:5** Your lamb shall be without blemish, a male of the first year: ye shall take *it* out from the sheep, or from the goats:
John 1:23 He said, I *am* the voice of one crying in the wilderness, Make straight the way of the Lord, as said the prophet Esaias.	**Isaiah 40:3-5** The voice of him that crieth in the wilderness, Prepare ye the way of the Lord, make straight in the desert a highway for our God. Every valley shall be exalted, and every mountain and hill shall be made low: and the crooked shall be made straight, and the rough places plain: And the glory of the LORD shall be revealed, and all flesh shall see *it* together: for the mouth of the LORD hath spoken *it*.
John 1:29 The next day John seeth Jesus coming unto him, and saith, Behold the Lamb of God, which taketh away the sin of the world.	**Leviticus 1:3-5** If his offering *be* a burnt sacrifice of the herd, let him offer a male without blemish: he shall offer it of his own voluntary will at the door of the tabernacle of the congregation before the LORD. 4 And he shall put his hand upon the head of the burnt offering; and it shall be accepted for him to make atonement for him. 5 And he shall kill the bullock before the LORD: and the priests, Aaron's sons, shall bring the blood, and sprinkle the blood round about upon the altar that *is by* the door of the tabernacle of the congregation.
	Exodus 12:3 Speak ye unto all the congregation of Israel, saying, In the tenth *day* of this month they shall take to them every man a lamb, according to the house of *their* fathers, a lamb for an house:
	Exodus 12:5-6 Your lamb shall be without blemish, a male of the first year: ye shall take *it* out from the sheep, or from the goats: 6 And ye shall keep it up until the fourteenth day of the same month: and the whole assembly of the congregation of Israel shall kill it in the evening.
	Exodus 29:10-12 And thou shalt cause a bullock to be brought before the tabernacle of the congregation: and Aaron and his sons shall put their hands upon the head of the bullock. 11 And thou shalt kill the bullock before the LORD, *by* the door of the tabernacle of the congregation. 12 And thou shalt take of the blood of the bullock, and put *it* upon the horns of the altar with thy finger, and pour all the blood beside the bottom of the altar.
	Isaiah 53:5 But he *was* wounded for our transgressions, *he was*

	bruised for our iniquities: the chastisement of our peace *was* upon him; and with his stripes we are healed.
	Isaiah 53:7 He was oppressed, and he was afflicted, yet he opened not his mouth: he is brought as a lamb to the slaughter, and as a sheep before her shearers is dumb, so he openeth not his mouth.
	Isaiah 53:10-11 Yet it pleased the LORD to bruise him; he hath put *him* to grief: when thou shalt make his soul an offering for sin, he shall see *his* seed, he shall prolong *his* days, and the pleasure of the LORD shall prosper in his hand. 11 He shall see of the travail of his soul, *and* shall be satisfied: by his knowledge shall my righteous servant justify many; for he shall bear their iniquities.
	Zechariah 9:11 As for thee also, **by the blood of thy covenant** I have sent forth thy prisoners out of the pit wherein *is* no water.
John 1:34 And I saw, and bare record that this is the Son of God.	**Psalms 2:7** I will declare the decree: the LORD hath said unto me, Thou *art* my **Son**; this day have I begotten thee.
	Psalms 2:12 Kiss the **Son**, lest he be angry, and ye perish *from* the way, when his wrath is kindled but a little. Blessed *are* all they that put their trust in him.
	Isaiah 7:14 Therefore the Lord himself shall give you a sign; Behold, a virgin shall conceive, and bear a **son**, and shall call his name Immanuel.
	Isaiah 9:6 For unto us a child is born, unto us a son is given: and the government shall be upon his shoulder: and his name shall be called Wonderful, Counselor, The mighty God, The everlasting Father, The Prince of Peace.
John 1:36 And looking upon Jesus as he walked, he saith, Behold the Lamb of God!	**Exodus 12:3** Speak ye unto all the congregation of Israel, saying, In the tenth *day* of this month they shall take to them every man a lamb, according to the house of *their* fathers, a lamb for an house:
	Isaiah 53:7 He was oppressed, and he was afflicted, yet he opened not his mouth: he is brought as a lamb to the slaughter, and as a sheep before her shearers is dumb, so he openeth not his mouth.
John 1:45 Philip findeth Nathanael, and saith unto him, We have found him, of whom Moses in the law, and the prophets, did write, Jesus of Nazareth, the son of Joseph.	**Genesis 3:15** And I will put enmity between thee and the woman, and between thy seed and her seed; it shall bruise thy head, and thou shalt bruise his heel.
	Genesis 22:18 And in thy seed shall all the nations of the earth be blessed; because thou hast obeyed my voice.
	Genesis 26:4 And I will make thy seed to multiply as the stars of heaven, and will give unto thy seed all these countries; and in thy seed shall all the nations of the earth be blessed;
	Genesis 49:10 The sceptre shall not depart from Judah, nor a lawgiver from between his feet, until Shiloh come; and unto him *shall* the gathering of the people *be*.
	Deuteronomy 18:18 I will raise them up a Prophet from among their brethren, like unto thee, and will put my words in his mouth; and he shall speak unto them all that I shall command him.
	2 Samuel 7:12 And when thy days be fulfilled, and thou shalt sleep with thy fathers, I will set up thy seed after thee, which shall proceed out of thy bowels, and I will establish his kingdom.
	Isaiah 7:14 Therefore the Lord himself shall give you a sign; Behold, a virgin shall conceive, and bear a son, and shall call his

	name Immanuel. **Isaiah 9:6** For unto us a child is born, unto us a son is given: and the government shall be upon his shoulder: and his name shall be called Wonderful, Counseller, The mighty God, The everlasting Father, The Prince of Peace. **Isaiah 53** **Jeremiah 23:5** Behold, the days come, saith the LORD, that I will raise unto David a righteous Branch, and a King shall reign and prosper, and shall execute judgment and justice in the earth. **Ezekiel 34:23** And I will set up one shepherd over them, and he shall feed them, *even* my servant David; he shall feed them, and he shall be their shepherd.
John 1:47-51 Jesus saw Nathanael coming to him, and saith of him, **Behold an Israelite indeed, in whom is no guile!** 48 Nathanael saith unto him, Whence knowest thou me? Jesus answered and said unto him, **Before that Philip called thee, when thou wast under the fig tree, I saw thee.** 49 Nathanael answered and saith unto him, Rabbi, thou art the Son of God; thou art the King of Israel. 50 Jesus answered and said unto him, Because I said unto thee, I saw thee under the fig tree, believest thou? thou shalt see greater things than these. 51 And he saith unto him, Verily, verily, I say unto you, Hereafter ye shall see heaven open, and the angels of God ascending and descending upon the Son of man.	**See 1 Corinthians 12:8 "Word of Knowledge"**
John 1:49 Nathanael answered and saith unto him, Rabbi, thou art the Son of God; thou art the King of Israel.	**Isaiah 44:6** Thus saith the LORD the King of Israel, and his redeemer the LORD of hosts; I *am* the first, and I *am* the last; and beside me *there is* no God.
John 1:51 And he saith unto him, Verily, verily, I say unto you, Hereafter ye shall see heaven open, and the angels of God ascending and descending upon the Son of man.	**Genesis 28:12** And he dreamed, and behold a ladder set up on the earth, and the top of it reached to heaven: and behold the angels of God ascending and descending on it.
John 2:9 When the ruler of the feast had tasted the water that was made wine, and knew not whence it was: (but the servants which drew the water knew;) the governor of the feast called the bridegroom,	**Exodus 7:20** And Moses and Aaron did so, as the LORD commanded; and he lifted up the rod, and smote the waters that *were* in the river, in the sight of Pharaoh, and in the sight of his servants; and all the waters that *were* in the river were turned to blood. **Psalms 104:15** And wine *that* maketh glad the heart of man, *and* oil to make *his* face to shine, and bread *which* strengtheneth man's heart.
John 2:17 And his disciples remembered that it was written, The zeal of thine house hath eaten me up.	**Psalms 69:9** For the zeal of thine house hath eaten me up; and the reproaches of them that reproached thee are fallen upon me.
John 2:19-22 Jesus answered and said	**Jonah 1:17** Now the LORD had prepared a great fish to swallow up Jonah. And Jonah was in the belly of the fish **three days and**

unto them, Destroy this temple, and in **three days** I will raise it up. 20 Then said the Jews, Forty and six years was this **temple in building**, and wilt thou rear it up in three days? 21 But he spake of the **temple of his body**. 22 When therefore he was risen from the dead, his disciples remembered that he had said this unto them; and they believed the scripture, and the word which Jesus had said.	**three nights**. **Jonah 2:1** Then Jonah prayed unto the LORD his God out of the fish's belly **Ezra 6:3** In the first year of Cyrus the king *the same* Cyrus the king made a decree *concerning* the house of God at Jerusalem, Let the house be builded, the place where they offered sacrifices, and let the foundations thereof be strongly laid; the height thereof threescore cubits, *and* the breadth thereof threescore cubits; **Ezra 6:15** And this house was finished on the third day of the month Adar, which was in the sixth year of the reign of Darius the king. **Psalms 16:10** For thou wilt not leave my soul in hell; neither wilt thou suffer thine Holy One to see corruption. **Psalms 49:15** But God will redeem my soul from the power of the grave: for he shall receive me. Selah.
John 2:24-25 But Jesus did not commit himself unto them, because he knew all *men*, 25 And needed not that any should testify of man: for **he knew what was in man**.	**1 Samuel 16:7** But the LORD said unto Samuel, Look not on his countenance, or on the height of his stature; because I have refused him: for *the LORD seeth* not as man seeth; for man looketh on the outward appearance, but the LORD looketh on the heart. **1 Kings 8:39** Then hear thou in heaven thy dwelling place, and forgive, and do, and give to every man according to his ways, whose heart thou knowest; (for thou, *even* thou only, knowest the hearts of all the children of men;) **1 Chronicles 28:9** And thou, Solomon my son, know thou the God of thy father, and serve him with a perfect heart and with a willing mind: for the LORD searcheth all hearts, and understandeth all the imaginations of the thoughts: if thou seek him, he will be found of thee; but if thou forsake him, he will cast thee off for ever. **Psalms 7:9** Oh let the wickedness of the wicked come to an end; but establish the just: for the righteous God trieth the hearts and reins. **Psalms 26:2** Examine me, O LORD, and prove me; try my reins and my heart. **Jeremiah 11:20** But, O LORD of hosts, that judgest righteously, that triest the reins and the heart, let me see thy vengeance on them: for unto thee have I revealed my cause. **Jeremiah 17:9-10** The **heart** *is* deceitful above all *things*, and desperately wicked: **who can know it?** [10] I the LORD search the heart, *I* try the reins, even to give every man according to his ways, *and* according to the fruit of his doings. **Jeremiah 20:12** But, O LORD of hosts, that triest the righteous, *and* seest the reins and the heart, let me see thy vengeance on them: for unto thee have I opened my cause.
John 3:5 Jesus answered, Verily, verily, I say unto thee, Except a man be born of water and *of* the Spirit, he cannot enter into the kingdom of God.	**Psalms 51:2** Wash me throughly from mine iniquity, and cleanse me from my sin. **Isaiah 1:16** Wash you, make you clean; put away the evil of your doings from before mine eyes; cease to do evil;. **Ezekiel 11:19** And I will give them one heart, and **I will put a new**

	spirit within you; and I will take the stony heart out of their flesh, and will give them an heart of flesh:
	Joel 2:28-29 And it shall come to pass afterward, *that* I will pour out my spirit upon all flesh; and your sons and your daughters shall prophesy, your old men shall dream dreams, your young men shall see visions: 29 And also upon the servants and upon the handmaids in those days will I pour out my spirit.
	Numbers 31:23 Every thing that may abide the fire, **ye shall make** *it* **go through the fire, and** <u>it shall be clean</u>: nevertheless it shall be purified with the water of separation: and all that abideth not the fire ye shall make go through the water.
	See Acts 2:38 "Salvation"
John 3:13 And no man hath ascended up to heaven, but he that came down from heaven, *even* the Son of man which is in heaven.	**Proverb 30:4** Who hath ascended up into heaven, or descended? who hath gathered the wind in his fists? who hath bound the waters in a garment? who hath established all the ends of the earth? what *is* his name, and what *is* his son's name, if thou canst tell?
John 3:14 And as Moses lifted up the serpent in the wilderness, even so must the Son of man be lifted up:	**Numbers 21:8-9** And the LORD said unto Moses, Make thee a fiery serpent, and set it upon a pole: and it shall come to pass, that every one that is bitten, when he looketh upon it, shall live. 9 And Moses made a serpent of brass, and put it upon a pole, and it came to pass, that if a serpent had bitten any man, when he beheld the serpent of brass, he lived.
John 3:16 For God so loved the world, that he gave his only **begotten Son**, that whosoever believeth in him should not perish, but have everlasting life.	**Genesis 22:2** And he said, Take now thy son, thine only *son* Isaac, whom thou lovest, and get thee into the land of Moriah; and offer him there for a burnt offering upon one of the mountains which I will tell thee of. **Psalms 2:7** I will declare the decree: the LORD hath said unto me, Thou *art* my Son; this day have I **begotten thee**. **Psalms 89:27** Also I will make him *my* **firstborn**, higher than the kings of the earth. **Jeremiah 31:9** They shall come with weeping, and with supplications will I lead them: I will cause them to walk by the rivers of waters in a straight way, wherein they shall not stumble: for I am a father to Israel, and Ephraim is my **firstborn**.
John 3:29 He that hath the bride is the bridegroom: but the friend of the bridegroom, which standeth and heareth him, rejoiceth greatly because of the bridegroom's voice: this my joy therefore is fulfilled.	**Isaiah 61:10** I will greatly rejoice in the LORD, my soul shall be joyful in my God; for he hath clothed me with the garments of salvation, he hath covered me with the robe of righteousness, as a bridegroom decketh *himself* with ornaments, and as a bride adorneth *herself* with her jewels. **Isaiah 62:5** For *as* a young man marrieth a virgin, *so* shall thy sons marry thee: and *as* the bridegroom rejoiceth over the bride, *so* shall thy God rejoice over thee. **Jeremiah 2:2** Go and cry in the ears of Jerusalem, saying, Thus saith the LORD; I remember thee, the kindness of thy youth, the love of thine espousals, when thou wentest after me in the wilderness, in a land *that was* not sown. **Joel 2:16** Gather the people, sanctify the congregation, assemble the elders, gather the children, and those that suck the breasts: let the bridegroom go forth of his chamber, and the bride out of her closet.
John 4:1-2 When therefore the Lord	See Acts 2:38 "Salvation"

knew how the Pharisees had heard that Jesus made and baptized more disciples than John, (Though Jesus himself baptized not, but his disciples,)	
John 4:5 Then cometh he to a city of Samaria, which is called Sychar, near to the parcel of ground that Jacob gave to his son Joseph.	**Genesis 33:18-19** And Jacob came to Shalem, a city of Shechem, which *is* in the land of Canaan, when he came from Padanaram; and pitched his tent before the city. **19** And he bought a parcel of a field, where he had spread his tent, at the hand of the children of Hamor, Shechem's father, for an hundred pieces of money. **Joshua 24:32** And the bones of Joseph, which the children of Israel brought up out of Egypt, buried they in Shechem, in a parcel of ground which Jacob bought of the sons of Hamor the father of Shechem for an hundred pieces of silver: and it became the inheritance of the children of Joseph.
John 4:10 Jesus answered and said unto her, If thou knewest the gift of God, and who it is that saith to thee, Give me to drink; thou wouldest have asked of him, and he would have given thee **living water**.	**Exodus 17:6** Behold, I will stand before thee there upon the rock in Horeb; and thou shalt smite the rock, and there shall come water out of it, that the people may drink. And Moses did so in the sight of the elders of Israel. **Numbers 20:11** And Moses lifted up his hand, and with his rod he smote the rock twice: and the water came out abundantly, and the congregation drank, and their beasts *also*. **Psalms 78:15** He clave the rocks in the wilderness, and gave *them* drink as *out of* the great depths. **Psalms 105:41** He opened the rock, and the waters gushed out; they ran in the dry places *like* a river. **Isaiah 9:6** For unto us a child is born, unto us a son is given: and the government shall be upon his shoulder: and his name shall be called Wonderful, Counseller, The mighty God, The everlasting Father, The Prince of Peace. **Isaiah 43:20** The beast of the field shall honour me, the dragons and the owls: because I give waters in the wilderness, *and* rivers in the desert, to give drink to my people, my chosen. **Isaiah 48:21** And they thirsted not *when* he led them through the deserts: he caused the waters to flow out of the rock for them: he clave the rock also, and the waters gushed out. **Isaiah 58:11** And the LORD shall guide thee continually, and satisfy thy soul in drought, and make fat thy bones: and thou shalt be like a watered garden, and like a spring of water, whose waters fail not. **Jeremiah 2:13** For my people have committed two evils; they have forsaken me the fountain of living waters, *and* hewed them out cisterns, broken cisterns, that can hold no water.
John 4:11 The woman saith unto him, Sir, thou hast nothing to draw with, and the well is deep: from whence then hast thou that **living water**?	**Jeremiah 2:13** For my people have committed two evils; they have forsaken me the fountain of **living waters**, *and* hewed them out cisterns, broken cisterns, that can hold no water. **Jeremiah 17:13** O LORD, the hope of Israel, all that forsake thee shall be ashamed, *and* they that depart from me shall be written in the earth, because they have forsaken the LORD, the fountain of **living waters**.
John 4:16-18 Jesus saith unto her, Go, call thy husband, and come hither. 17	**Psalms 139:2** Thou knowest my downsitting and mine uprising, thou understandest my thought afar off.

The woman answered and said, I have no husband. Jesus said unto her, Thou hast well said, I have no husband: 18 For thou hast had five husbands; and he whom thou now hast is not thy husband: in that saidst thou truly.	See 1 Corinthians 12:8 "Word of Knowledge"
John 4:19 The woman saith unto him, Sir, I perceive that thou art a prophet.	**Deuteronomy 18:15** The LORD thy God will raise up unto thee a Prophet from the midst of thee, of thy brethren, like unto me; unto him ye shall hearken;
John 4:20 Our fathers worshipped in this mountain; and ye say, that in Jerusalem is the place where men ought to worship.	**Deuteronomy 12:5** But unto the place which the LORD your God shall choose out of all your tribes to put his name there, *even* unto his habitation shall ye seek, and thither thou shalt come: **Deuteronomy 12:11** Then there shall be a place which the LORD your God shall choose to cause his name to dwell there; thither shall ye bring all that I command you; your burnt offerings, and your sacrifices, your tithes, and the heave offering of your hand, and all your choice vows which ye vow unto the LORD: **1 Kings 9:3** And the LORD said unto him, I have heard thy prayer and thy supplication, that thou hast made before me: I have hallowed this house, which thou hast built, to put my name there for ever; and mine eyes and mine heart shall be there perpetually. **2 Chronicles 7:12** And the LORD appeared to Solomon by night, and said unto him, I have heard thy prayer, and have chosen this place to myself for an house of sacrifice. **Ezra 4:3** But Zerubbabel, and Jeshua, and the rest of the chief of the fathers of Israel, said unto them, Ye have nothing to do with us to build an house unto our God; but we ourselves together will build unto the LORD God of Israel, as king Cyrus the king of Persia hath commanded us.
John 4:22 Ye worship ye know not what: we know what we worship: for salvation is of the Jews.	**2 Kings 17:29** Howbeit every nation made gods of their own, and put *them* in the houses of the high places which the Samaritans had made, every nation in their cities wherein they dwelt. **Deuteronomy 6:4** Hear, O Israel: The LORD our God is one LORD : **Psalms 68:20** *He that is* our God *is* the God of salvation; and unto GOD the Lord *belong* the issues from death. **Isaiah 9:6** For unto us a child is born, unto us a son is given: and the government shall be upon his shoulder: and his name shall be called Wonderful, Counseller, The mighty God, The everlasting Father, The Prince of Peace. **Isaiah 45:15** Verily thou *art* a God that hidest thyself, O God of Israel, the Saviour. **Jeremiah 3:23** Truly in vain *is salvation hoped for* from the hills, *and from* the multitude of mountains: truly in the LORD our God *is* the salvation of Israel. **Jonah 2:9** But I will sacrifice unto thee with the voice of thanksgiving; I will pay *that* that I have vowed. Salvation *is* of the LORD .
John 4:24 God is a Spirit: and they that worship him must **worship** him in spirit and in truth.	**Exodus 33:20** And he said, Thou canst not see my face: for there shall no man see me, and live. **1 Kings 8:22** And Solomon stood before the altar of the LORD in

the presence of all the congregation of Israel, and spread forth his hands toward heaven:

1 Kings 8:54 And it was *so,* that when Solomon had made an end of praying all this prayer and supplication unto the LORD, he arose from before the altar of the LORD, from kneeling on his knees with his hands spread up to heaven.

1 Chronicles 16:29 Give unto the LORD the glory *due* unto his name: bring an offering, and come before him: worship the LORD in the beauty of holiness.

Nehemiah 8:5-8 And Ezra opened the book in the sight of all the people; (for he was above all the people;) and when he opened it, all the people stood up:

6 And Ezra blessed the LORD, the great God. And all the people answered, Amen, Amen, with lifting up their hands: and they bowed their heads, and worshipped the LORD with *their* faces to the ground. 7 Also Jeshua, and Bani, and Sherebiah, Jamin, Akkub, Shabbethai, Hodijah, Maaseiah, Kelita, Azariah, Jozabad, Hanan, Pelaiah, and the Levites, caused the people to understand the law: and the people *stood* in their place. 8 So they read in the book in the law of God distinctly, and gave the sense, and caused *them* to understand the reading.

Nehemiah 9:3-5 And they stood up in their place, and read in the book of the law of the LORD their God *one* fourth part of the day; and *another* fourth part they confessed, and worshipped the LORD their God. 4 Then stood up upon the stairs, of the Levites, Jeshua, and Bani, Kadmiel, Shebaniah, Bunni, Sherebiah, Bani, *and* Chenani, and cried with a loud voice unto the LORD their God. 5 Then the Levites, Jeshua, and Kadmiel, Bani, Hashabniah, Sherebiah, Hodijah, Shebaniah, *and* Pethahiah, said, Stand up *and* bless the LORD your God for ever and ever: and blessed be thy glorious name, which is exalted above all blessing and praise.

Psalms 29:2 Give unto the LORD the glory due unto his name; worship the LORD in the beauty of holiness.

Psalms 33:2-3 Praise the LORD with harp: sing unto him with the psaltery *and* an instrument of ten strings. 3 Sing unto him a new song; play skilfully with a loud noise.

Psalms 47:1 To the chief Musician, A Psalm for the sons of Korah. O clap your hands, all ye people; shout unto God with the voice of triumph.

Psalms 95:1-2 O come, let us sing unto the LORD: let us make a joyful noise to the rock of our salvation. 2 Let us come before his presence with thanksgiving, and make a joyful noise unto him with psalms.

Psalms 96:9 O worship the LORD in the beauty of holiness: fear before him, all the earth.

Psalms 98:4 Make a joyful noise unto the LORD, all the earth: make a loud noise, and rejoice, and sing praise.

Psalms 111:1 Praise ye the LORD. I will praise the LORD with *my* whole heart, in the assembly of the upright, and *in* the congregation.

Psalms 141:2 Let my prayer be set forth before thee *as* incense; *and* the lifting up of my hands *as* the evening sacrifice

	Psalms 149:3 Let them praise his name in the dance: let them sing praises unto him with the timbrel and harp. **Psalms 150:6** Let every thing that hath breath praise the LORD. Praise ye the LORD.
John 4:35 Say not ye, There are yet four months, and *then* cometh harvest? behold, I say unto you, Lift up your eyes, and look on the fields; for they are white already to harvest.	**Leviticus 26:1-13** Ye shall make you no idols nor graven image, neither rear you up a standing image, neither shall ye set up *any* image of stone in your land, to bow down unto it: for I *am* the LORD your God. 2 Ye shall keep my sabbaths, and reverence my sanctuary: I *am* the LORD. 3 If ye walk in my statutes, and keep my commandments, and do them; 4 Then I will give you rain in due season, and the land shall yield her increase, and the trees of the field shall yield their fruit. 5 And your threshing shall reach unto the vintage, and the vintage shall reach unto the sowing time: and ye shall eat your bread to the full, and dwell in your land safely. 6 And I will give peace in the land, and ye shall lie down, and none shall make *you* afraid: and I will rid evil beasts out of the land, neither shall the sword go through your land. 7 And ye shall chase your enemies, and they shall fall before you by the sword. 8 And five of you shall chase an hundred, and an hundred of you shall put ten thousand to flight: and your enemies shall fall before you by the sword. 9 For I will have respect unto you, and make you fruitful, and multiply you, and establish my covenant with you. 10 And ye shall eat old store, and bring forth the old because of the new. 11 And I will set my tabernacle among you: and my soul shall not abhor you. 12 And I will walk among you, and will be your God, and ye shall be my people. 13 I *am* the LORD your God, which brought you forth out of the land of Egypt, that ye should not be their bondmen; and I have broken the bands of your yoke, and made you go upright.
John 4:37 And herein is that saying true, One soweth, and another reapeth.	**Micah 6:15** Thou shalt sow, but thou shalt not reap; thou shalt tread the olives, but thou shalt not anoint thee with oil; and sweet wine, but shalt not drink wine.
John 4:42 And said unto the woman, Now we believe, not because of thy saying: for we have heard *him* ourselves, and know that this is indeed the Christ, the **Saviour** of the world.	**Job 19:25** For I know *that* my redeemer liveth, and *that* he shall stand at the latter *day* upon the earth: **Psalms 106:21** They forgat God their **saviour**, which had done great things in Egypt; **Isaiah 43:3** For I am the LORD thy God, the Holy One of Israel, **thy Saviour**: I gave Egypt for thy ransom, Ethiopia and Seba for thee. **Isaiah 45:21** Tell ye, and bring them near; yea, let them take counsel together: who hath declared this from ancient time? who hath told it from that time? have not I the LORD? and *there is* no God else beside me; a just **God and a Saviour**; *there is* none beside me. **Isaiah 60:16** Thou shalt also suck the milk of the Gentiles, and shalt suck the breast of kings: and thou shalt know that I the LORD *am* thy **Saviour** and thy Redeemer, the mighty One of Jacob.
John 4:48 Then said Jesus unto him, Except ye see **signs** and **wonders**, ye will not believe.	**See Mark 16:17 "Signs"** **Exodus 4:21** And the LORD said unto Moses, When thou goest to return into Egypt, see that thou **do all those wonders** before Pharaoh, which I have put in thine hand: but I will harden his heart, that he shall not let the people go.

	Exodus 11:9-10 And the LORD said unto Moses, Pharaoh shall not hearken unto you; that **my wonders** may be multiplied in the land of Egypt. 10 And Moses and Aaron did all these **wonders** before Pharaoh: and the LORD hardened Pharaoh's heart, so that he would not let the children of Israel go out of his land.
	Joshua 3:5 And Joshua said unto the people, Sanctify yourselves: for to morrow **the LORD will do <u>wonders</u> among you**.
	Joel 2:30 And I will shew **wonders** in the heavens and in the earth, blood, and fire, and pillars of smoke.
John 5:1 After this there was a feast of the Jews; and Jesus went up to Jerusalem.	**Leviticus 23:2** Speak unto the children of Israel, and say unto them, *Concerning* the feasts of the LORD, which ye shall proclaim *to be* holy convocations, *even* these *are* my feasts.
	Numbers 28:16 And in the fourteenth day of the first month *is* the passover of the LORD.
John 5:9 and immediately the man became whole, and he took up his couch, and was walking, and it was a **sabbath** on that day, **John 5:10** The Jews therefore said unto him that was cured, It is the **sabbath** day: it is not lawful for thee to carry *thy* bed.	**Exodus 20:10** But the seventh day *is* the sabbath of the LORD thy God: *in it* thou shalt not do any work, thou, nor thy son, nor thy daughter, thy manservant, nor thy maidservant, nor thy cattle, nor thy stranger that *is* within thy gates: **Deuteronomy 5:13** Six days thou shalt labour, and do all thy work: **Deuteronomy 5:14** But the seventh day *is* the sabbath of the LORD thy God: *in it* thou shalt not do any work, thou, nor thy son, nor thy daughter, nor thy manservant, nor thy maidservant, nor thine ox, nor thine ass, nor any of thy cattle, nor thy stranger that *is* within thy gates; that thy manservant and thy maidservant may rest as well as thou. **Jeremiah 17:21** Thus saith the LORD; Take heed to yourselves, and bear no burden on the sabbath day, nor bring *it* in by the gates of Jerusalem; **See Colossians 2:16 "Sabbath"**
John 5:14 Afterward Jesus findeth him in the temple, and said unto him, Behold, thou art made whole: sin no more, **lest a worse thing come unto thee**.	**Psalm 32:1** A Psalm of David, Maschil. Blessed *is he whose* transgression is forgiven, *whose* sin is covered. **Psalms 107:17-21 Fools because of their transgression, and because of their iniquities, are afflicted.** 18 Their soul abhorreth all manner of meat; and they draw near unto the gates of death. 19 Then they cry unto the LORD in their trouble, *and* he saveth them out of their distresses. 20 **He sent his word, and healed them, and delivered *them* from their destructions.** 21 Oh that *men* would praise the LORD *for* his goodness, and *for* his wonderful works to the children of men!
John 5:16 and because of this were the Jews persecuting Jesus, and seeking to kill him, because these things he was doing on a **sabbath**. **John 5:18** Therefore the Jews sought the more to kill him, because he not only had broken the **sabbath**, but said also that God was his Father, making himself equal with God.	**Psalms 2:7** I will declare the decree: the LORD hath said unto me, Thou *art* my Son; this day have I begotten thee. **See Colossians 2:16 "Sabbath"**
John 5:18 Therefore the Jews sought the more to kill him, because he not only	**Isaiah 9:6** For unto us **a child is born**, unto us a son is given: and the government shall be upon his shoulder: and his name shall be

had broken the Sabbath, but said also that God was his Father, making **himself equal with God**.	called Wonderful, Counsellor, **The mighty God**, The everlasting Father, The Prince of Peace.
John 5:22 For the Father judgeth no man, but hath committed all judgment unto the Son:	**Isaiah 33:22** For the LORD *is* our judge, the LORD *is* our lawgiver, the LORD *is* our king; he will save us.
John 5:23 That all *men* should honour the Son, even as they honour the Father. He that honoureth not the Son honoureth not the Father which hath sent him.	**Isaiah 42:8** I *am* the LORD: that *is* my name: and my **glory** will I not give to another, neither my praise to graven images.
John 5:25 Verily, verily, I say unto you, The hour is coming, and now is, when the dead shall hear the voice of the Son of God: and they that hear shall live.	**Isaiah 26:19** Thy dead *men* shall live, *together with* my dead body shall they arise. Awake and sing, ye that dwell in dust: for thy dew *is as* the dew of herbs, and the earth shall cast out the dead. **Daniel 12:2** And many of them that sleep in the dust of the earth shall awake, some to everlasting life, and some to shame *and* everlasting contempt.
John 5:29 And shall come forth; they that have done good, unto the resurrection of life; and they that have done evil, unto the resurrection of damnation.	**Daniel 12:2** And many of them that sleep in the dust of the earth shall awake, some to everlasting life, and some to shame *and* everlasting contempt.
John 5:32 There is another that beareth witness of me; and I know that the witness which he witnesseth of me is true.	**Isaiah 42:1** Behold my servant, whom I uphold; mine elect, *in whom* my soul delighteth; I have put my spirit upon him: he shall bring forth judgment to the Gentiles.
John 5:37 And the Father himself, which hath sent me, hath borne witness of me. Ye have neither heard his voice at any time, nor seen his shape.	**Exodus 33:20** And he said, Thou canst not see my face: for there shall no man see me, and live. **Deuteronomy 4:12** And the LORD spake unto you out of the midst of the fire: ye heard the voice of the words, but saw no similitude; only *ye heard* a voice.
John 5:39 Search the scriptures; for in them ye think ye have eternal life: and they are they which testify of me.	**Isaiah 34:16** Seek ye out of the book of the LORD, and read: no one of these shall fail, none shall want her mate: for my mouth it hath commanded, and his spirit it hath gathered them. **Deuteronomy 18:18-19** I will raise them up a Prophet from among their brethren, like unto thee, and will put my words in his mouth; and he shall speak unto them all that I shall command him. 19 And it shall come to pass, *that* whosoever will not hearken unto my words which he shall speak in my name, I will require *it* of him. **See Matthew 5:18 "Scriptures"**
John 5:43 I am come in my Father's name, and ye receive me not: if another shall come in his own name, him ye will receive.	**Deuteronomy 6:4** Hear, O Israel: The LORD our God *is* one LORD: **See Matthew 1:21 "Jesus"**
John 5:46 For had ye believed Moses, ye would have believed me: for **he wrote of me**.	**Genesis 22:18** And in thy seed shall all the nations of the earth be blessed; because thou hast obeyed my voice. **Exodus 20:1** AND God spake all these words, saying, **Deuteronomy 9:10** And the LORD delivered unto me two tables of stone written with the finger of God; and on them *was written* according to all the words, which the LORD spake with you in the

	mount out of the midst of the fire in the day of the assembly.
	Deuteronomy 18:18 I will raise them up a Prophet from among their brethren, like unto thee, and will put my words in his mouth; and he shall speak unto them all that I shall command him.
	Deuteronomy 30:14 But the word *is* very nigh unto thee, in thy mouth, and in thy heart, that thou mayest do it.
	Deuteronomy 31:9 And **Moses wrote** this law, and delivered it unto the priests the sons of Levi, which bare the ark of the covenant of the LORD , and unto all the elders of Israel.
	2 Chronicles 17:9 And they taught in Judah, and *had* the book of the law of the LORD with them, and went about throughout all the cities of Judah, and taught the people.
	Isaiah 8:20 To the law and to the testimony: if they speak not according to this word, *it is* because *there is* no light in them.
	See Matthew 5:18 "Scriptures"
John 6:4 And the passover, a feast of the Jews, was nigh.	**Leviticus 23:5** In the fourteenth *day* of the first month at even *is* the LORD's passover.
	Numbers 28:16 And in the fourteenth day of the first month *is* the passover of the LORD.
	Deuteronomy 16:1 Observe the month of Abib, and keep the passover unto the LORD thy God: for in the month of Abib the LORD thy God brought thee forth out of Egypt by night.
John 6:9 There is a lad here, which hath five barley loaves, and two small fishes: but what are they among so many?	**2 Kings 4:43-44** And his servitor said, What, should I set this before an hundred men? He said again, Give the people, that they may eat: for thus saith the LORD, They shall eat, and shall leave *thereof*.
	44 So he set *it* before them, and they did eat, and left *thereof*, according to the word of the LORD.
John 6:19 So when they had rowed about five and twenty or thirty furlongs, they see Jesus walking on the sea, and drawing nigh unto the ship: and they were afraid.	**Exodus 14:21** And Moses stretched out his hand over the sea; and the LORD caused the sea to go *back* by a strong east wind all that night, and made the sea dry *land*, and the waters were divided.
John 6:31 Our fathers did eat manna in the desert; as it is written, He gave them bread from heaven to eat.	**Exodus 16:4** Then said the LORD unto Moses, Behold, I will rain bread from heaven for you; and the people shall go out and gather a certain rate every day, that I may prove them, whether they will walk in my law, or no.
	Exodus 16:14 And when the dew that lay was gone up, behold, upon the face of the wilderness *there lay* a small round thing, *as* small as the hoar frost on the ground.
	Numbers 11:7 And the manna *was* as coriander seed, and the colour thereof as the colour of bdellium.
	Nehemiah 9:15 And gavest them bread from heaven for their hunger, and broughtest forth water for them out of the rock for their thirst, and promisedst them that they should go in to possess the land which thou hadst sworn to give them.
	Psalms 78:24 And had rained down manna upon them to eat, and had given them of the corn of heaven.

	Psalms 105:40 *The people* asked, and he brought quails, and satisfied them with the bread of heaven.
John 6:35 And Jesus said unto them, I am the bread of life: he that cometh to me shall never hunger; and he that believeth on me shall never thirst.	**Isaiah 55:1** Ho, every one that thirsteth, come ye to the waters, and he that hath no money; come ye, buy, and eat; yea, come, buy wine and milk without money and without price.
John 6:45 It is written in the prophets, And they shall be all taught of God. Every man therefore that hath heard, and hath learned of the Father, cometh unto me.	**Isaiah 54:13** And all thy children *shall be* taught of the LORD; and great [shall be] the peace of thy children. **Jeremiah 31:33-34** But this shall be the covenant that I will make with the house of Israel; After those days, saith the LORD, I will put my law in their inward parts, and write it in their hearts; and will be their God, and they shall be my people. 34 And they shall teach no more every man his neighbour, and every man his brother, saying, Know the LORD: for they shall all know me, from the least of them unto the greatest of them, saith the LORD: for I will forgive their iniquity, and I will remember their sin no more.
John 6:49 our fathers did eat manna in the wilderness, and are dead.	**Exodus 16:4** Then said the LORD unto Moses, Behold, I will rain bread from heaven for you; and the people shall go out and gather a certain rate every day, that I may prove them, whether they will walk in my law, or no. **Exodus 16:17** And the children of Israel did so, and gathered, some more, some less.
John 6:53 Then Jesus said unto them, Verily, verily, I say unto you, Except ye **eat the flesh** of the Son of man, and **drink his blood**, ye have no life in you.	**See Matthew 26:28 "Atonement"**
John 6:54-56 Whoso eateth my **flesh**, and drinketh my **blood, hath eternal life**; and I will raise him up at the last day. 55 For my flesh is meat indeed, and my blood is drink indeed. 56 He that eateth my flesh, and drinketh my blood, dwelleth in me, and I in him.	**Leviticus 17:11** For the life of the flesh is in the blood: and I have given it to you upon the altar to make an atonement for your souls: **for it is the blood that maketh an atonement for the soul.**
John 6:63 It is the spirit that quickeneth; the flesh profiteth nothing: **the words that I speak unto you, they are spirit, and they are life.**	**See Matthew 5:18 "Scriptures"**
John 7:2 Now the Jews' feast of tabernacles was at hand.	**Leviticus 23:34** Speak unto the children of Israel, saying, The fifteenth day of this seventh month *shall be* the feast of tabernacles *for* seven days unto the LORD. **Leviticus 23:42-43** Ye shall dwell in booths seven days; all that are Israelites born shall dwell in booths: 43 That your generations may know that I made the children of Israel to dwell in booths, when I brought them out of the land of Egypt: I *am* the LORD your God. **Nehemiah 8:14-15** And they found written in the law which the LORD had commanded by Moses, that the children of Israel should dwell in booths in the feast of the seventh month: 15 And that they should publish and proclaim in all their cities, and in Jerusalem, saying, Go forth unto the mount, and fetch olive branches, and pine branches, and myrtle branches, and palm branches, and branches of thick trees, to make booths, as *it is*

	written.
	Zechariah 14:16 And it shall come to pass, *that* every one that is left of all the nations which came against Jerusalem shall even go up from year to year to worship the King, the LORD of hosts, and to keep the feast of tabernacles.
	Zechariah 14:18-19 And if the family of Egypt go not up, and come not, that *have* no *rain*; there shall be the plague, wherewith the LORD will smite the heathen that come not up to keep the feast of tabernacles. 19 This shall be the punishment of Egypt, and the punishment of all nations that come not up to keep the feast of tabernacles.
John 7:5 For neither did his brethren believe in him.	**Psalms 69:8** I am become a stranger unto my brethren, and an alien unto my mother's children.
John 7:19 Did not Moses give you the law, and *yet* none of you keepeth the law? Why go ye about to kill me?	**Exodus 20:1** And God spake all these words, saying, **Exodus 24:3** And Moses came and told the people all the words of the LORD, and all the judgments: and all the people answered with one voice, and said, All the words which the LORD hath said will we do.
John 7:22 Moses therefore gave unto you circumcision; (not because it is of Moses, but of the fathers;) and ye on the **sabbath** day circumcise a man.	**Genesis 17:10** This *is* my covenant, which ye shall keep, between me and you and thy seed after thee; Every man child among you shall be circumcised. **Leviticus 12:3** And in the eighth day the flesh of his foreskin shall be circumcised. **See Colossians 2:16 "Sabbath"**
John 7:23 if a man doth receive circumcision on a **sabbath** that the law of Moses may not be broken, are ye wroth with me that I made a man all whole on a **sabbath**?	**See Colossians 2:16 "Sabbath"**
John 7:24 Judge not according to the appearance, but judge righteous judgment.	**Leviticus 19:15** Ye shall do no unrighteousness in judgment: thou shalt not respect the person of the poor, nor honour the person of the mighty: *but* in righteousness shalt thou judge thy neighbour. **Deuteronomy 1:16-17** And I charged your judges at that time, saying, Hear *the causes* between your brethren, and judge righteously between *every* man and his brother, and the stranger *that is* with him. 17 Ye shall not respect persons in judgment; *but* ye shall hear the small as well as the great; ye shall not be afraid of the face of man; for the judgment *is* God's: and the cause that is too hard for you, bring *it* unto me, and I will hear it. **Deuteronomy 16:19** Thou shalt not wrest judgment; thou shalt not respect persons, neither take a gift: for a gift doth blind the eyes of the wise, and pervert the words of the righteous. **Proverbs 18:5** *It is* not good to accept the person of the wicked, to overthrow the righteous in judgment. **Proverbs 24:23** These *things* also *belong* to the wise. *It is* not good to have respect of persons in judgment.
John 7:37 In the last day, that great *day* of the feast, Jesus stood and cried, saying, If any man thirst, let him come unto me, and drink.	**Leviticus 23:36** Seven days ye shall offer an offering made by fire unto the LORD: on the eighth day shall be an holy convocation unto you; and ye shall offer an offering made by fire unto the LORD: it *is* a solemn assembly; *and* ye shall do no servile work

	therein. **Leviticus 23:39** Also in the fifteenth day of the seventh month, when ye have gathered in the fruit of the land, ye shall keep a feast unto the LORD seven days: on the first day *shall be* a sabbath, and on the eighth day *shall be* a sabbath. **Isaiah 55:1** Ho, every one that thirsteth, come ye to the waters, and he that hath no money; come ye, buy, and eat; yea, come, buy wine and milk without money and without price.
John 7:38 He that believeth on me, as the scripture hath said, out of his belly shall flow rivers of **living water**.	**Proverb 18:4** The words of a man's mouth *are as* deep waters, *and* the wellspring of wisdom *as* a flowing brook. **Isaiah 12:3** Therefore with joy shall ye draw water out of the wells of salvation. **Isaiah 44:3** For I will pour water upon him that is thirsty, and floods upon the dry ground: I will pour my spirit upon thy seed, and my blessing upon thine offspring: **Isaiah 55:1** Ho, every one that thirsteth, come ye to the waters, and he that hath no money; come ye, buy, and eat; yea, come, buy wine and milk without money and without price. **Isaiah 58:11** And the LORD shall guide thee continually, and satisfy thy soul in drought, and make fat thy bones: and thou shalt be like a watered garden, and like a spring of water, whose waters fail not. **Zechariah 13:1** In that day there shall be a fountain opened to the house of David and to the inhabitants of Jerusalem for sin and for uncleanness. **Zechariah 14:8** And it shall be in that day, *that* living waters shall go out from Jerusalem; half of them toward the former sea, and half of them toward the hinder sea: in summer and in winter shall it be.
John 7:39 (But this spake he of the Spirit, which they that believe on him should receive: for the Holy Ghost was not yet *given;* because that Jesus was not yet glorified.)	**Isaiah 44:3** For I will pour water upon him that is thirsty, and floods upon the dry ground: I will pour my spirit upon thy seed, and my blessing upon thine offspring: **Joel 2:28** And it shall come to pass afterward, *that* I will pour out my spirit upon all flesh; and your sons and your daughters shall prophesy, your old men shall dream dreams, your young men shall see visions:
John 7:40 Many of the people therefore, when they heard this saying, said, Of a truth this is the Prophet.	**Deuteronomy 18:15** The LORD thy God will raise up unto thee a Prophet from the midst of thee, of thy brethren, like unto me; unto him ye shall hearken;
John 7:42 Hath not the scripture said, That Christ cometh of the seed of David, and out of the town of Bethlehem, where David was?	**Genesis 49:10** The sceptre shall not depart from Judah, nor a lawgiver from between his feet, until Shiloh come; and unto him *shall* the gathering of the people *be.* **2 Samuel 7:12** And when thy days be fulfilled, and thou shalt sleep with thy fathers, I will set up thy seed after thee, which shall proceed out of thy bowels, and I will establish his kingdom. **Psalms 89:4** Thy seed will I establish for ever, and build up thy throne to all generations. Selah. **Psalms 132:11** The LORD hath sworn *in* truth unto David; he will not turn from it; Of the fruit of thy body will I set upon thy throne. **Micah 5:1-2** Now gather thyself in troops, O daughter of troops: he hath laid siege against us: they shall smite the judge of Israel

	with a rod upon the cheek. 2 But thou, Bethlehem Ephratah, though thou be little among the thousands of Judah, yet out of thee shall he come forth unto me that is to be ruler in Israel; whose goings forth have been from of old, from everlasting.
John 7:48 Have any of the rulers or of the Pharisees believed on him?	**Isaiah 33:18** Thine heart shall meditate terror. Where *is* the scribe? where *is* the receiver? where *is* he that counted the towers?
John 7:51 Doth our law judge *any* man, before it hear him, and know what he doeth?	**Exodus 23:1** Thou shalt not raise a false report: put not thine hand with the wicked to be an unrighteous witness. **Leviticus 19:15** Ye shall do no unrighteousness in judgment: thou shalt not respect the person of the poor, nor honour the person of the mighty: *but* in righteousness shalt thou judge thy neighbour. **Deuteronomy 1:17** Ye shall not respect persons in judgment; *but* ye shall hear the small as well as the great; ye shall not be afraid of the face of man; for the judgment *is* God's: and the cause that is too hard for you, bring *it* unto me, and I will hear it. **1 Samuel 16:7** But the LORD said unto Samuel, Look not on his countenance, or on the height of his stature; because I have refused him: for *the LORD seeth* not as man seeth; for man looketh on the outward appearance, but the LORD looketh on the heart.
John 8:3 And the scribes and Pharisees brought unto him a woman taken in **adultery**; and when they had set her in the midst,	**See Matthew 5:27 "Adultery"**
John 8:5 Now Moses in the law commanded us, that such should be stoned: but what sayest thou?	**Leviticus 20:10** And the man that committeth adultery with *another* man's wife, *even he* that committeth adultery with his neighbour's wife, the adulterer and the adulteress shall surely be put to death. **Deuteronomy 22:21** Then they shall bring out the damsel to the door of her father's house, and the men of her city shall stone her with stones that she die: because she hath wrought folly in Israel, to play the whore in her father's house: so shalt thou put evil away from among you.
John 8:6 This they said, tempting him, that they might have to accuse him. But Jesus stooped down, and with *his* finger wrote on the ground, *as though he heard them not.*	**Exodus 31:18** And he gave unto Moses, when he had made an end of communing with him upon mount Sinai, two tables of testimony, tables of stone, written with the finger of God. **Daniel 5:5** In the same hour came forth fingers of a man's hand, and wrote over against the candlestick upon the plaister of the wall of the king's palace: and the king saw the part of the hand that wrote.
John 8:7 So when they continued asking him, he lifted up himself, and said unto them, He that is without sin among you, let him first cast a stone at her.	**Deuteronomy 13:9-10** But thou shalt surely kill him; thine hand shall be first upon him to put him to death, and afterwards the hand of all the people. 10 And thou shalt stone him with stones, that he die; because he hath sought to thrust thee away from the LORD thy God, which brought thee out of the land of Egypt, from the house of bondage. **Deuteronomy 17:7** The hands of the witnesses shall be first upon him to put him to death, and afterward the hands of all the people. So thou shalt put the evil away from among you.
John 8:8 And again he stooped down, and wrote on the ground.	**See John 8:6**
John 8:12 Then spake Jesus again unto them, saying, **I am the light of the**	**Psalms 27:1** The **LORD** *is* my <u>light</u> and my salvation; whom shall I fear? the LORD is the strength of my life; of whom shall I be

world: he that followeth me shall not walk in darkness, but shall have the **light of life**.	afraid? **Isaiah 42:16** And I will bring the blind by a way *that* they knew not; I will lead them in paths *that* they have not known: I will make darkness light before them, and crooked things straight. These things will I do unto them, and not forsake them. **Isaiah 60:1** Arise, shine; for thy light is come, and the glory of the LORD is risen upon thee. **Isaiah 60:19-20** The sun shall be no more thy light by day; neither for brightness shall the moon give light unto thee: but the LORD shall be unto thee an **everlasting light**, and thy God thy glory. 20 Thy sun shall no more go down; neither shall thy moon withdraw itself: for the **LORD shall be thine everlasting <u>light</u>**, and the days of thy mourning shall be ended.
John 8:17 It is also written in your law, that the testimony of two men is true.	**Numbers 35:30** Whoso killeth any person, the murderer shall be put to death by the mouth of witnesses: but one witness shall not testify against any person *to cause him* to die. **Deuteronomy 17:6** At the mouth of two witnesses, or three witnesses, shall he that is worthy of death be put to death; *but* at the mouth of one witness he shall not be put to death. **Deuteronomy 19:15** One witness shall not rise up against a man for any iniquity, or for any sin, in any sin that he sinneth: at the mouth of two witnesses, or at the mouth of three witnesses, shall the matter be established.
John 8:24 I said therefore unto you, that ye shall die in your sins: for if ye believe not that I am *he*, ye shall die in your sins.	**Exodus 3:14** And God said unto Moses, **I AM THAT I AM**: and he said, Thus shalt thou say unto the children of Israel, **I AM** hath sent me unto you. 15 And God said moreover unto Moses, Thus shalt thou say unto the children of Israel, The LORD God of your fathers, the God of Abraham, the God of Isaac, and the God of Jacob, hath sent me unto you: this *is* my name forever, and this *is* my memorial unto all generations. **Isaiah 43:10** Ye *are* my witnesses, saith the LORD, and my servant whom I have chosen: that ye may know and believe me, and **understand that I *am* he**: before me there was no God formed, neither shall there be after me.
John 8:28 Then said Jesus unto them, When ye have lifted up the Son of man, then shall ye know that I am *he*, and *that* I do nothing of myself; but as my Father hath taught me, I speak these things.	**Numbers 21:9** And Moses made a serpent of brass, and put it upon a pole, and it came to pass, that if a serpent had bitten any man, when he beheld the serpent of brass, he lived. **Deuteronomy 18:18** I will raise them up a Prophet from among their brethren, like unto thee, and will put my words in his mouth; and he shall speak unto them all that I shall command him. **2 Kings 18:4** He removed the high places, and brake the images, and cut down the groves, and brake in pieces the brasen serpent that Moses had made: for unto those days the children of Israel did burn incense to it: and he called it Nehushtan.
John 8:32 And ye shall know the truth, and the truth shall make you free.	**Hosea 4:6 My people are destroyed for lack of knowledge**: because thou hast rejected knowledge, I will also reject thee, that thou shalt be no priest to me: seeing thou hast forgotten the law of thy God, I will also forget thy children.
John 8:41 Ye do the deeds of your father. Then said they to him, We be not	**1 Chronicles 29:10** Wherefore David blessed the LORD before all the congregation: and David said, Blessed *be* thou, **LORD God**

born of fornication; we have **one Father, even God.**"	of Israel our father, forever and ever." **Psalms 89:26** He shall cry unto me, **Thou *art* my father, my God**, and the rock of my salvation." **Isaiah 9:6** For unto us a child is born, unto us a son is given: and the government shall be upon his shoulder: and his name shall be called Wonderful, Counselor, The mighty God, The everlasting Father, The Prince of Peace. **Isaiah 45:21-22** have not I the LORD? and **there is no God else beside me**; a just God and a Saviour; there is none beside me. 22 Look unto me, and be ye saved, all the ends of the earth: for **I am God, and there is none else.** **Isaiah 63:16** Doubtless thou *art* our father, though Abraham be ignorant of us, and Israel acknowledge us not: thou, **O LORD, *art* our father**, our redeemer; thy name *is* from everlasting **Isaiah 64:8** But now, **O LORD, thou *art* our father**; we *are* the clay, and thou our potter; and we all *are* the work of thy hand." **Malachi 2:10** Have we not all one father? hath not one God created us? why do we deal treacherously every man against his brother, by profaning the covenant of our fathers?
John 8:44 Ye are of *your* father the devil, and the lusts of your father ye will do. He was a murderer from the beginning, and abode not in the truth, because there is no truth in him. When he speaketh a lie, he speaketh of his own: for he is a liar, and the father of it.	**Genesis 3:1** Now the serpent was more subtil than any beast of the field which the LORD God had made. And he said unto the woman, Yea, hath God said, Ye shall not eat of every tree of the garden?
John 8:56 Your father Abraham rejoiced to see my day: and he saw *it*, and was glad.	**Genesis 17:17** Then Abraham fell upon his face, and laughed, and said in his heart, Shall *a child* be born unto him that is an hundred years old? and shall Sarah, that is ninety years old, bear?
John 8:58 Jesus said unto them, Verily, verily, I say unto you, Before Abraham was, I am.	**Exodus 3:14** And God said unto Moses, **I AM THAT I AM**: and he said, Thus shalt thou say unto the children of Israel, **I AM** hath sent me unto you. 15 And God said moreover unto Moses, Thus shalt thou say unto the children of Israel, The LORD God of your fathers, the God of Abraham, the God of Isaac, and the God of Jacob, hath sent me unto you: this *is* my name forever, and this *is* my memorial unto all generations. **Isaiah 9:6** For unto us a child is born, unto us a son is given: and the government shall be upon his shoulder: and his name shall be called Wonderful, Counseller, The mighty God, The everlasting Father, The Prince of Peace. **Zechariah 12:10** And I will pour upon the house of David, and upon the inhabitants of Jerusalem, the spirit of grace and of supplications: and they shall look upon me whom they have pierced, and they shall mourn for him, as one mourneth for *his* only *son*, and shall be in bitterness for him, as one that is in bitterness for *his* firstborn.
John 9:5 As long as I am in the world, I am the light of the world.	**Isaiah 42:6** I the LORD have called thee in righteousness, and will hold thine hand, and will keep thee, and give thee for a covenant of the people, for a light of the Gentiles;
John 9:14 and it was a **sabbath** when Jesus made the clay, and opened his eyes.	**See Colossians 2:16 "Sabbath"**

John 9:16 Of the Pharisees, therefore, certain said, `This man is not from God, because the **sabbath** he doth not keep;' others said, `How is a man--a sinful one--able to do such signs?' and there was a division among them.	
John 9:24 Then again called they the man that was blind, and said unto him, Give God the praise: we know that this man is a sinner.	**Joshua 7:19** And Joshua said unto Achan, My son, give, I pray thee, glory to the LORD God of Israel, and make confession unto him; and tell me now what thou hast done; hide *it* not from me.
John 9:25 He answered and said, Whether he be a sinner or no, I know not: one thing I know, that, whereas I was blind, now I see.	**Isaiah 42:7** To open the blind eyes, to bring out the prisoners from the prison, *and* them that sit in darkness out of the prison house. **Isaiah 61:1-2** The Spirit of the Lord GOD *is* upon me; because the LORD hath anointed me to preach good tidings unto the meek; he hath sent me to bind up the brokenhearted, to proclaim liberty to the captives, and the opening of the prison to *them that* are bound; To proclaim the acceptable year of the LORD, and the day of vengeance of our God; to comfort all that mourn;
John 9:31 Now we know that God heareth not sinners: but if any man be a worshipper of God, and doeth his will, him he heareth.	**Proverb 1:28** Then shall they call upon me, but I will not answer; they shall seek me early, but they shall not find me: **Proverb 15:29** The LORD *is* far from the wicked: but he heareth the prayer of the righteous. **Proverb 28:9** He that turneth away his ear from hearing the law, even his prayer *shall be* abomination. **Isaiah 1:15** And when ye spread forth your hands, I will hide mine eyes from you: yea, when ye make many prayers, I will not hear: your hands are full of blood. **Micah 3:4** Then shall they cry unto the LORD, but he will not hear them: he will even hide his face from them at that time, as they have behaved themselves ill in their doings.
John 9:37-38 And Jesus said unto him, Thou hast both seen him, and it is he that talketh with thee. 38 And he said, Lord, I believe. And he worshipped him.	**Psalms 97:7** Confounded be all they that serve graven images, that boast themselves of idols: worship him, all *ye* gods
John 10:10 The thief cometh not, but for to steal, and to kill, and to destroy: I am come that they might have life, and that they might have *it* more abundantly.	**Genesis 49:24** But his bow abode in strength, and the arms of his hands were made strong by the hands of the mighty God of Jacob; (from thence is the **shepherd**, the stone of Israel:) **1 Kings 22:17** And he said, I saw all Israel scattered upon the hills, as sheep that have not a **shepherd**: and the LORD said, These have no **master**: let them return every man to his house in peace. **Job 2:6-7** And the LORD said unto Satan, Behold, he *is* in thine hand; but save his life. 7 So went **Satan** forth from the presence of the LORD, and **smote Job with sore boils from the sole of his foot unto his crown.** **Psalms 23:1-6** A Psalm of David. The LORD is my **shepherd**; I shall not want. 2 He maketh me to lie down in green pastures: he leadeth me beside the still waters. 3 He restoreth my soul: he leadeth me in the paths of righteousness for his name's sake. 4 Yea, though I walk through the valley of the shadow of death, I will fear no evil: for thou art with me; thy rod and thy staff they comfort me. 5 Thou preparest a table before me in the presence of mine enemies: thou anointest my head with oil; my cup runneth over. 6

Surely goodness and mercy shall follow me all the days of my life: and I will dwell in the house of the LORD for ever.

Psalms 107:20 He sent his word, and healed *them*, and delivered them from their **destructions**.

Ecclesiastes 12:10-11 The preacher sought to find out acceptable words: and that which was written was upright, even words of truth. 11 The words of the wise are as goads, and as nails fastened by the masters of assemblies, which are given from one shepherd.

Isaiah 40:11 He shall **feed** his flock like a shepherd: he shall gather the lambs with his arm, and carry them in his bosom, and shall gently lead those that are with young.

Isaiah 57:11 And of whom hast thou been afraid or feared, that thou hast lied, and hast not remembered me, nor laid *it* to thy heart? have not I held my peace even of old, and thou fearest me not?

Isaiah 56:10-57:15

Isaiah 63:11-12 Then he remembered the days of old, Moses, and his people, saying, Where is he that brought them up out of the sea **with the shepherd of his flock**? where is he that put his holy Spirit within him? 12 That led them by the right hand of Moses with his glorious arm, dividing the water before them, to make himself an everlasting name?

Jeremiah 2:8 The priests said not, Where is the LORD? and they that handle the law knew me not: the **pastors** also transgressed against me, and the prophets prophesied by Baal, and walked after things that do not profit.

Jeremiah 3:15 And I will give you pastors according to mine heart, which shall **feed** you with knowledge and understanding.

Jeremiah 6:2-30

Jeremiah 10:20-25 My tabernacle is spoiled, and all my cords are broken: my children are gone forth of me, and they are not: there is none to stretch forth my tent any more, and to set up my curtains. 21 **For the pastors are become brutish**, and have not sought the LORD: therefore they shall not prosper, and all their flocks shall be scattered. 22 Behold, the noise of the bruit is come, and a great commotion out of the north country, to make the cities of Judah desolate, and a den of dragons. 23 O LORD, I know that the way of man is not in himself: it is not in man that walketh to direct his steps. 24 O LORD, correct me, but with judgment; not in thine anger, lest thou bring me to nothing. 25 Pour out thy fury upon the heathen that know thee not, and upon the families that call not on thy name: for they have eaten up Jacob, and devoured him, and consumed him, and have made his habitation desolate.

Jeremiah 17:16 As for me, I have not hastened from being a **pastor** to follow thee: neither have I desired the woeful day; thou knowest: that which came out of my lips was right before thee.

Jeremiah 22:22-23:2

Jeremiah 22:30 Thus saith the LORD, Write ye this man childless, a man that shall not prosper in his days: for no man of his seed shall prosper, sitting upon the throne of David, and ruling any more in Judah. 1 Woe be unto the pastors that destroy and scatter the sheep of my pasture! saith the LORD. 2 There-fore thus saith the LORD God of Israel against the pastors that feed my people; Ye have scattered my flock, and driven them away, and have not visited them: behold, I will visit upon you the evil of your doings, saith the LORD. 3 And I will gather the remnant of my flock out of all countries whither I have driven them, and will bring them again to their folds; and they shall be fruitful and increase. 4 And I will set up shepherds over them which shall feed them: and they shall fear no more, nor be dismayed, neither shall they be lacking, saith the LORD.

Jeremiah 23:1-4 Woe be unto the pastors that destroy and scatter the sheep of my pasture! saith the LORD. 2 Therefore thus saith the LORD God of Israel against the pastors that feed my people; Ye have scattered my flock, and driven them away, and have not visited them: behold, I will visit upon you the evil of your doings, saith the LORD. 3 And I will gather the remnant of my flock out of all countries whither I have driven them, and will bring them again to their folds; and they shall be fruitful and increase. 4 And I will set up shepherds over them which shall feed them: and they shall fear no more, nor be dismayed, neither shall they be lacking, saith the LORD.

Jeremiah 25:34-38 Howl, ye **shepherds**, and cry; and wallow yourselves in the ashes, ye principal of the flock: for the days of your slaughter and of your dispersions are accomplished; and ye shall fall like a pleasant vessel. 35 And the shepherds shall have no way to flee, nor the principal of the flock to escape. 36 A voice of the cry of the shepherds, and an howling of the principal of the flock, shall be heard: for the LORD hath spoiled their pasture. 37 And the peaceable habitations are cut down because of the fierce anger of the LORD. 38 He hath forsaken his covert, as the lion: for their land is desolate because of the fierceness of the oppressor, and because of his fierce anger.

Jeremiah 31:10 Hear the word of the LORD, O ye nations, and declare it in the isles afar off, and say, He that scattered Israel will gather him, and **keep** him, as a shepherd doth his flock.

Jeremiah 48:10 Cursed *be* he that doeth the work of the LORD deceitfully, and cursed *be* he that keepeth back his sword from blood.

Jeremiah 49:19 Behold, he shall come up like a lion from the swelling of Jordan against the habitation of the strong: but I will suddenly make him run away from her: and who is a chosen man, that I may appoint over her? for who is like me? and who will appoint me the time? and who is that **shepherd that will stand**

	before me?
	Jeremiah 50:6-7 My people hath been lost sheep: their shepherds have caused them to go astray, they have turned them away on the mountains: they have gone from mountain to hill, they have forgotten their restingplace. 7 All that found them have devoured them: and their adversaries said, We offend not, because they have sinned against the LORD, the habitation of justice, even the LORD, the hope of their fathers.
	Ezekiel 34:1-4 And the word of the LORD came unto me, saying, 2 Son of man, prophesy against the shepherds of Israel, prophesy, and say unto them, Thus saith the Lord GOD unto the shepherds; Woe be to the shepherds of Israel that do feed themselves! should not the shepherds feed the flocks? 3 Ye eat the fat, and ye clothe you with the wool, ye kill them that are fed: but ye feed not the flock. 4 **The diseased have ye not strengthened, neither have ye healed that which was sick, neither have ye bound up that which was broken**, neither have ye brought again that which was driven away, neither have ye sought that which was lost; but with force and with cruelty have ye ruled them.
	Ezekiel 34:23 And I will set up one shepherd over them, and he shall feed them, even my servant David; he shall feed them, and he shall be their **shepherd**.
	Ezekiel 34:1-31
	Ezekiel 37:24 And David my servant shall be king over them; and they all shall have one shepherd: they shall also walk in my judgments, and observe my statutes, and do them.
	Micah 5:5 And this One shall be peace. When Assyria shall come into our land; and when he shall walk in our palaces, then we shall raise against him seven shepherds and eight anointed ones of man.
	Zechariah 10:2 For the idols have spoken vanity, and the diviners have seen a lie, and have told false dreams; they **comfort** in vain: therefore they went their way as a flock, they were troubled, because there was no shepherd.
	Zechariah 11:5 ... and their shepherds do not pity them.
	Zechariah 11:8 I also cut off three shepherds in one month. And My soul was impatient with them, and their soul also detested Me.
	Zechariah 11:15-20
	Zechariah 13:7 Awake, O sword, against my shepherd, and against the man that is my fellow, saith the LORD of hosts: **smite the shepherd, and the sheep shall be scattered**: and I will turn mine hand upon the little ones.
John 10:11 I am the good shepherd: the good shepherd giveth his life for the sheep.	**Psalms 23:1** { A Psalm of David. } The LORD *is* my shepherd; I shall not want.
	Isaiah 40:11 He shall feed his flock like a shepherd: he shall gather the lambs with his arm, and carry *them* in his bosom, *and* shall gently lead those that are with young.
	Ezekiel 34:23 And I will set up one shepherd over them, and he shall feed them, *even* my servant David; he shall feed them, and he shall be their shepherd.

John 10:12 But he that is an **hireling**, and not the **shepherd**, whose own the sheep are not, seeth the wolf coming, and leaveth the sheep, and fleeth: and the wolf catcheth them, and scattereth the sheep.	**Ezekiel 34:1-4** And the word of the LORD came unto me, saying, 2 Son of man, prophesy against the **shepherds** of Israel, prophesy, and say unto them, Thus saith the Lord GOD unto the **shepherds**; Woe be to the shepherds of Israel that do feed themselves! should not the **shepherds** feed the flocks? 3 Ye eat the fat, and ye clothe you with the wool, ye kill them that are fed: but ye feed not the flock. 4 The diseased have ye not strengthened, <u>neither have ye healed that</u> which was sick, <u>neither have ye bound up that which was broken</u>, neither have ye brought again that which was driven away, neither have ye sought that which was lost; but with force and with cruelty have ye ruled them.
John 10:14 I am the good **shepherd**, and know my sheep, and am known of mine.	**Isaiah 40:11** He shall feed his flock like a **shepherd**: he shall gather the lambs with his arm, and carry them in his bosom, and shall gently lead those that are with young.
John 10:16 And other sheep I have, which are not of this fold: them also I must bring, and they shall hear my voice; and there shall be one fold, *and* one shepherd.	**Ezekiel 37:22** And I will make them one nation in the land upon the mountains of Israel; and one king shall be king to them all: and they shall be no more two nations, neither shall they be divided into two kingdoms any more at all:
John 10:17 Therefore doth my Father love me, because I lay down my life, that I might take it again.	**Isaiah 53:12** Therefore will I divide him *a portion* with the great, and he shall divide the spoil with the strong; because he hath poured out his soul unto death: and he was numbered with the transgressors; and he bare the sin of many, and made intercession for the transgressors.
John 10:21 Others said, These are not the words of him that hath a devil. Can a devil open the eyes of the blind?	**Exodus 4:11** And the LORD said unto him, Who hath made man's mouth? or who maketh the dumb, or deaf, or the seeing, or the blind? have not I the LORD? **Psalms 146:8** The LORD openeth *the eyes of* the blind: the LORD raiseth them that are bowed down: the LORD loveth the righteous:
John 10:22 And it was at Jerusalem the feast of the dedication, and it was winter.	**Leviticus 23:2** Speak unto the children of Israel, and say unto them, *Concerning* the feasts of the LORD, which ye shall proclaim *to be* holy convocations, *even* these *are* my feasts. **1 Kings 8:63-64** And Solomon offered a sacrifice of peace offerings, which he offered unto the LORD, two and twenty thousand oxen, and an hundred and twenty thousand sheep. So the king and all the children of Israel dedicated the house of the LORD. 64 The same day did the king hallow the middle of the court that *was* before the house of the LORD: for there he offered burnt offerings, and meat offerings, and the fat of the peace offerings: because the brasen altar that *was* before the LORD *was* too little to receive the burnt offerings, and meat offerings, and the fat of the peace offerings. **2 Chronicles 7:5** And king Solomon offered a sacrifice of twenty and two thousand oxen, and an hundred and twenty thousand sheep: so the king and all the people dedicated the house of God. **Ezra 6:16-17** And the children of Israel, the priests, and the Levites, and the rest of the children of the captivity, kept the dedication of this house of God with joy, 17 And offered at the dedication of this house of God an hundred bullocks, two hundred rams, four hundred lambs; and for a sin offering for all Israel, twelve he goats, according to the number of the tribes of Israel.
John 10:23 And Jesus walked in the temple in Solomon's porch.	**1 Kings 6:3** And the porch before the temple of the house, twenty cubits *was* the length thereof, according to the breadth of the

	house; *and* ten cubits *was* the breadth thereof before the house.
John 10:27 My sheep hear my voice, and I know them, and they follow me:	**Psalms 23:3** He restoreth my soul: he leadeth me in the paths of righteousness for his name's sake.
John 10:30-33 I and *my* Father are one. 31 Then the Jews took up stones again to stone him. 33 The Jews answered him, saying, For a good work we stone thee not; but for blasphemy; and because that thou, being a man, makest thyself God.	**Exodus 20:2-3** I am the LORD thy God, which have brought thee out of the land of Egypt, out of the house of bondage. 3 Thou shalt have no other gods before me."

Deuteronomy 6:4 Hear, O Israel: The LORD our God *is* one LORD :

Nehemiah 9:6 Thou, *even* thou, *art* LORD alone; thou hast made heaven, the heaven of heavens, with all their host, the earth, and all *things* that *are* therein, the seas, and all that *is* therein, and thou preservest them all; and the host of heaven worshippeth thee.

Psalms 86:10 For thou *art* great, and doest wondrous things: thou *art* God alone.

Isaiah 43:10-11 Ye *are* my witnesses, saith the LORD, and my servant whom I have chosen: that ye may know and believe me, and understand that I *am* he: before me there was no God formed, neither shall there be after me. 11 I, *even* I, *am* the LORD ; and beside me *there is* no saviour.

Isaiah 44:6 Thus saith the LORD the King of Israel, and his redeemer the LORD of hosts; I *am* the first, and I *am* the last; and beside me *there is* no God.

Isaiah 44:8 Fear ye not, neither be afraid: have not I told thee from that time, and have declared *it*? ye *are* even my witnesses. Is there a God beside me? yea, *there is* no God; I know not *any*.

Isaiah 45:5-6 I am the LORD, and there is none else, **there is no God beside me**: I girded thee, though thou hast not known me: 6 That they may know from the rising of the sun, and from the west, that there is none beside me. I am the LORD, and there is none else.

Isaiah 45:21-22 have not I the LORD? and **there is no God else beside me**; a just God and a Saviour; there is none beside me. 22 Look unto me, and be ye saved, all the ends of the earth: for **I am God, and there is none else**.

Isaiah 54:5 For thy Maker *is* thine husband; the LORD of hosts *is* his name; and thy Redeemer the Holy One of Israel; The God of the whole earth shall he be called.

1 Chronicles 29:10 Wherefore David blessed the LORD before all the congregation: and David said, Blessed *be* thou, **LORD God of Israel our father, forever and ever**."

Psalms 89:26 He shall cry unto me, **Thou *art* my father, my God**, and the rock of my salvation."

Isaiah 9:6 For unto us a child is born, unto us a son is given: and the government shall be upon his shoulder: and his name shall be called Wonderful, Counselor, The mighty God, The everlasting Father, The Prince of Peace.

Isaiah 63:16 Doubtless thou *art* our father, though Abraham be ignorant of us, and Israel acknowledge us not: thou, **O LORD, *art* our father**, our redeemer; thy name *is* from everlasting

Isaiah 64:8 But now, **O LORD, thou *art* our father**; we *are* the |

	clay, and thou our potter; and we all *are* the work of thy hand." **Malachi 2:10** Have we not all one father? hath not one God created us? why do we deal treacherously every man against his brother, by profaning the covenant of our fathers?
John 10:34 Jesus answered them, Is it not written in your law, I said, Ye are gods?	**Psalms 82:6** I have said, Ye *are* gods; and all of you *are* children of the most High.
John 10:35...unto whom <u>the Word of God came</u>, and the **Scripture cannot be broken**;	See Matthew 5:18 "Scripture"
John 11:22 But I know, that even now, whatsoever thou wilt ask of God, God will give it thee.	**2 Chronicles 16:12-13** And Asa in the thirty and ninth year of his reign was diseased in his feet, until his disease *was* exceeding *great*: yet in his disease <u>he sought not to the LORD, but to the physicians</u>. 13 And <u>Asa slept with his fathers</u>, and died in the one and fortieth year of his reign.
John 11:24 Martha saith unto him, I know that he shall rise again in the resurrection at the last day.	**Daniel 12:2** And many of them that sleep in the dust of the earth shall awake, some to everlasting life, and some to shame *and* everlasting contempt.
John 11:33 When Jesus therefore saw her weeping, and the Jews also weeping which came with her, he groaned in the **spirit**, and was troubled.	See 1 Thessalonians 5:23 "Body, soul, and spirit"
John 11:47 Then gathered the chief priests and the Pharisees a council, and said, What do we? for this man doeth many miracles.	**Psalms 2:2** The kings of the earth set themselves, and the rulers take counsel together, against the LORD, and against his anointed, *saying*,
John 11:49 And one of them, *named* Caiaphas, being the high priest that same year, said unto them, Ye know nothing at all,	**Leviticus 21:10-15** And *he that is* the high priest among his brethren, upon whose head the anointing oil was poured, and that is consecrated to put on the garments, shall not uncover his head, nor rend his clothes; 11 Neither shall he go in to any dead body, nor defile himself for his father, or for his mother; 12 Neither shall he go out of the sanctuary, nor profane the sanctuary of his God; for the crown of the anointing oil of his God *is* upon him: I *am* the LORD. 13 And he shall take a wife in her virginity. 14 A widow, or a divorced woman, or profane, *or* an harlot, these shall he not take: but he shall take a virgin of his own people to wife. 15 Neither shall he profane his seed among his people: for I the LORD do sanctify him.
John 11:53 Then from that day forth they took counsel together for to put him to death.	**Psalms 31:13** For I have heard the slander of many: fear *was* on every side: while they took counsel together against me, they devised to take away my life.
John 12:6 This he said, not that he cared for the poor; but because he was a thief, and had the bag, and bare what was put therein.	**Exodus 20:15** Thou shalt not steal. **Deuteronomy 31:29** For I know that after my death ye will utterly corrupt *yourselves*, and turn aside from the way which I have commanded you; and evil will befall you in the latter days; because ye will do evil in the sight of the LORD, to provoke him to anger through the work of your hands. See 1 Thessalonians 4:6 "Defraud"
John 12:8 For the poor always ye have with you; but me ye have not always.	**Deuteronomy 15:11** For the poor shall never cease out of the land: therefore I command thee, saying, Thou shalt open thine hand wide unto thy brother, to thy poor, and to thy needy, in thy land.
John 12:13 Took branches of palm	**Psalms 118:26** Blessed *be* he that cometh in the name of the

trees, and went forth to meet him, and cried, Hosanna: Blessed *is* the King of Israel that cometh in the name of the Lord.	LORD: we have blessed you out of the house of the LORD.
John 12:15 Fear not, daughter of Sion: behold, thy King cometh, sitting on an ass's colt.	**Isaiah 40:9** O Zion, that bringest good tidings, get thee up into the high mountain; O Jerusalem, that bringest good tidings, lift up thy voice with strength; lift *it* up, be not afraid; say unto the cities of Judah, Behold your God! **Isaiah 62:11** Behold, the LORD hath proclaimed unto the end of the world, Say ye to the daughter of Zion, Behold, thy salvation cometh; behold, his reward *is* with him, and his work before him. **Zechariah 9:9** Rejoice greatly, O daughter of Zion; shout, O daughter of Jerusalem: behold, thy King cometh unto thee: he [is] just, and having salvation; lowly, and riding upon an ass, and upon a colt the foal of an ass.
John 12:27 Now is my **soul** troubled; and what shall I say? Father, save me from this hour: but for this cause came I unto this hour.	See 1 Thessalonians 5:23 "Body, soul, and spirit"
John 12:41 These things said Esaias, when he saw his glory, and spake of him.	**Isaiah 6:1** In the year that king Uzziah died I saw also the Lord sitting upon a throne, high and lifted up, and his train filled the temple.
John 12:32 And I, if I be lifted up from the earth, will draw all *men* unto me.	**Numbers 21:9** And Moses made a serpent of brass, and put it upon a pole, and it came to pass, that if a serpent had bitten any man, when he beheld the serpent of brass, he lived. **2 Kings 18:4** He removed the high places, and brake the images, and cut down the groves, and brake in pieces the brasen serpent that Moses had made: for unto those days the children of Israel did burn incense to it: and he called it Nehushtan.
John 12:34 The people answered him, We have heard out of the law that Christ abideth for ever: and how sayest thou, The Son of man must be lifted up? who is this Son of man?	**2 Samuel 7:13** He shall build an house for my name, and I will stablish the throne of his kingdom for ever. **Psalms 89:36-37** His seed shall endure for ever, and his throne as the sun before me. 37 It shall be established for ever as the moon, and as a faithful witness in heaven. Selah. **Psalms 110:4** The LORD hath sworn, and will not repent, Thou *art* a priest for ever after the order of Melchizedek. **Isaiah 9:7** Of the increase of *his* government and peace *there shall be* no end, upon the throne of David, and upon his kingdom, to order it, and to establish it with judgment and with justice from henceforth even for ever. The zeal of the LORD of hosts will perform this. **Isaiah 53:8** He was taken from prison and from judgment: and who shall declare his generation? for he was cut off out of the land of the living: for the transgression of my people was he stricken. **Daniel 7:27** And the kingdom and dominion, and the greatness of the kingdom under the whole heaven, shall be given to the people of the saints of the most High, whose kingdom *is* an everlasting kingdom, and all dominions shall serve and obey him. **Micah 4:7** And I will make her that halted a remnant, and her that was cast far off a strong nation: and the LORD shall reign over them in mount Zion from henceforth, even for ever.

John 12:35 Then Jesus said unto them, Yet a little while is the light with you. Walk while ye have the light, lest darkness come upon you: for he that walketh in darkness knoweth not whither he goeth.	**Isaiah 59:9** Therefore is judgment far from us, neither doth justice overtake us: we wait for light, but behold obscurity; for brightness, *but* we walk in darkness. **Jeremiah 13:16** Give glory to the LORD your God, before he cause darkness, and before your feet stumble upon the dark mountains, and, while ye look for light, he turn it into the shadow of death, *and* make *it* gross darkness.
John 12:38 That the saying of Esaias the prophet might be fulfilled, which he spake, Lord, who hath believed our report? and to whom hath the arm of the Lord been revealed?	**Isaiah 53:1** Who hath believed our report? and to whom is the arm of the LORD revealed? **Amos 3:7** Surely the Lord GOD will do nothing, but he revealeth his secret unto his servants the prophets.
John 12:40 He hath blinded their eyes, and hardened their heart; that they should not see with *their* eyes, nor understand with *their* heart, and be converted, and I should heal them.	**Isaiah 6:9-10** And he said, God, and tell this people, Hear ye indeed, but understand not; and see ye indeed, but perceive not. 10 Make the heart of this people fat, and make their ears heavy, and shut their eyes; lest they see with their eyes, and hear with their ears, and understand with their heart, and convert, and be healed. **Jeremiah 5:21** Hear now this, O foolish people, and without understanding; which have eyes, and see not; which have ears, and hear not: **Ezekiel 12:2** Son of man, thou dwellest in the midst of a rebellious house, which have eyes to see, and see not; they have ears to hear, and hear not: for they *are* a rebellious house.
John 12:41 These things said Esaias, when he saw his glory, and spake of him.	**Isaiah 6:1-3** In the year that king Uzziah died I saw also the Lord sitting upon a throne, high and lifted up, and his train filled the temple. 2 Above it stood the seraphims: each one had six wings; with twain he covered his face, and with twain he covered his feet, and with twain he did fly. 3 And one cried unto another, and said, Holy, holy, holy, is the LORD of hosts: the whole earth is full of his glory.
John 12:46 I am come a light into the world, that whosoever believeth on me should not abide in darkness.	**Isaiah 42:6** I the LORD have called thee in righteousness, and will hold thine hand, and will keep thee, and give thee for a covenant of the people, for a light of the Gentiles; **Isaiah 49:6** And he said, It is a light thing that thou shouldest be my servant to raise up the tribes of Jacob, and to restore the preserved of Israel: I will also give thee for a light to the Gentiles, that thou mayest be my salvation unto the end of the earth.
John 12:48 He that rejecteth me, and **receiveth not my words**, hath one that judgeth him: **the word that I have spoken, the same shall judge him in the last day**.	See Matthew 5:18 "Scriptures"
John 12:49 For I have not spoken of myself; but the Father which sent me, he gave me a commandment, what I should say, and what I should speak.	**Deuteronomy 18:18** I will raise them up a Prophet from among their brethren, like unto thee, and will put my words in his mouth; and he shall speak unto them all that I shall command him.
John 13:18 I speak not of you all: I know whom I have chosen: but that the scripture may be fulfilled, He that eateth bread with me hath lifted up his heel against me.	**Psalms 41:9** Yea, mine own familiar friend, in whom I trusted, which did eat of my bread, hath lifted up [his] heel against me.

John 13:19 Now I tell you before it come, that, when it is come to pass, ye may believe that I am *he*.	**Isaiah 46:9-10** Remember the former things of old: for I *am* God, and *there is* none else; *I am* God, and *there is* none like me, ¹⁰ Declaring the end from the beginning, and from ancient times *the things* that are not *yet* done, saying, My counsel shall stand, and I will do all my pleasure:
John 13:21 When Jesus had thus said, he was troubled in **spirit**, and testified, and said, Verily, verily, I say unto you, that one of you shall betray me.	**See 1 Thessalonians 5:23** "Body, soul, and spirit"
John 13:27 And after the sop Satan entered into him. Then said Jesus unto him, That thou doest, do quickly.	**Genesis 3:4** And the **serpent** said unto the woman, Ye shall not surely die: **Zechariah 3:1-2** And he shewed me Joshua the high priest standing before the angel of the LORD, and **Satan** standing at his right hand to resist him. 2 And the LORD said unto **Satan**, The LORD rebuke thee, O **Satan**; even the LORD that hath chosen Jerusalem rebuke thee: *is* not this a brand plucked out of the fire? **See Matthew 4:10** "satan"
John 13:34 A new commandment I give unto you, That ye love one another; as I have loved you, that ye also love one another.	**Leviticus 19:18** Thou shalt not avenge, nor bear any grudge against the children of thy people, but thou shalt love thy neighbour as thyself: I *am* the LORD.
John 14:3 And if I go and prepare a place for you, I will come again, and receive you unto myself; that where I am, *there* ye may be also.	**See 1 Timothy 2:5** "God"
John 14:6 Jesus saith unto him, I am the way, the truth, and the life: no man cometh unto the Father, but by me.	**Proverb 8:35** For whoso findeth me findeth life, and shall obtain favour of the LORD.
John 14:9-11 Jesus saith unto him, Have I been so long time with you, and yet hast thou not known me, Philip? he that hath seen me hath seen the Father; and how sayest thou then, Shew us the Father? 10 Believest thou not that I am in the Father, and the Father in me? the words that I speak unto you I speak not of myself: but the Father that dwelleth in me, he doeth the works. 11 Believe me that I am in the Father, and the Father in me: or else believe me for the very works' sake.	**1 Chronicles 29:10** Wherefore David blessed the LORD before all the congregation: and David said, Blessed *be* thou, **LORD God of Israel our father, forever and ever**." **Psalms 89:26** He shall cry unto me, **Thou *art* my father, my God**, and the rock of my salvation." **Isaiah 9:6** For unto us a child is born, unto us a son is given: and the government shall be upon his shoulder: and his name shall be called Wonderful, Counselor, The mighty God, The everlasting Father, The Prince of Peace. **Isaiah 45:21-22** have not I the LORD? and **there is no God else beside me**; a just God and a Saviour; there is none beside me. 22 Look unto me, and be ye saved, all the ends of the earth: for **I am God, and there is none else**. **Isaiah 63:16** Doubtless thou *art* our father, though Abraham be ignorant of us, and Israel acknowledge us not: thou, **O LORD, *art* our father**, our redeemer; thy name *is* from everlasting **Isaiah 64:8** But now, **O LORD, thou *art* our father**; we *are* the clay, and thou our potter; and we all *are* the work of thy hand." **Malachi 2:10** Have we not all one father? hath not one God created us? why do we deal treacherously every man against his brother, by profaning the covenant of our fathers?
John 14:13-14 And whatsoever ye shall **ask** in my name, that will I do, that the Father may be glorified in the Son. 14 If	**2 Chronicles 16:12-13** And Asa in the thirty and ninth year of his reign was diseased in his feet, until his disease *was* exceeding *great*: yet in his disease <u>he sought not to the LORD</u>, but to the

ye shall **ask** any thing in my name, I will do it.	physicians. 13 And <u>Asa slept with his fathers</u>, and died in the one and fortieth year of his reign. **Jeremiah 29:12** Then shall ye call upon me, and ye shall go and pray unto me, and I will hearken unto you.
John 14:17 Even the Spirit of truth; whom the world cannot receive, because it seeth him not, neither knoweth him: but ye know him; for he dwelleth with you, and shall be in you.	**Genesis 41:38** And Pharaoh said unto his servants, Can we find such a one as this is, **a man in whom the Spirit of God is**? **Numbers 11:17** And I will come down and talk with thee there: and I will take of **the spirit which is upon thee**, and will put it upon them; and they shall bear the burden of the people with thee, that thou bear it not thyself alone. **Numbers 11:25** And the LORD came down in a cloud, and spake unto him, **and took of the spirit that was upon him, and gave it unto the seventy elders**: and it came to pass, that, when the spirit rested upon them, they prophesied, and did not cease. **Numbers 27:18** And the LORD said unto Moses, Take thee Joshua the son of Nun, a man in whom is the spirit, and lay thine hand upon him; **Isaiah 11:2** And the spirit of the LORD shall rest upon him, the spirit of wisdom and understanding, the spirit of counsel and might, the spirit of knowledge and of the fear of the LORD; **Micah 3:8** But truly I am full of power by the spirit of the LORD, and of judgment, and of might, to declare unto Jacob his transgression, and to Israel his sin.
John 14:23 If a man love me, **he will keep my Words**, and My Father will love him, and we will come unto him and make our abode with him.	**See Matthew 5:18 "Words"**
John 14:26 But the Comforter, *which is* the Holy Ghost, whom the Father will send in my name, **he shall teach you all things**, and bring all things to your remembrance, whatsoever I have said unto you.	**See Ephesians 4:11 "Teach – Teachers"** **See Hebrews 12:14 "Holiness"**
John 14:27 Peace I leave with you, my peace I give unto you: not as the world giveth, give I unto you. Let not your heart be troubled, neither let it be afraid	**Proverbs 4:23** Keep thy heart with all diligence; for out of it are the issues of life. **Proverbs 12:25** Heaviness in the heart of man maketh it stoop: but a good word maketh it glad. **Proverbs 13:12** Hope deferred maketh the heart sick: but when the desire cometh, it is a tree of life. **Proverbs 14:30** A sound heart is the life of the flesh: but envy the rottenness of the bones. **Proverbs 15:13** A merry heart maketh a cheerful countenance: but by sorrow of the heart the spirit is broken. **Proverbs 16:24** Pleasant words are as an honeycomb, sweet to the soul, and health to the bones. **Proverbs 17:22** A merry heart doeth good like a medicine: but a broken spirit drieth the bones. **Proverbs 23:7** For as he thinketh in his heart, so is he: Eat and drink, saith he to thee; but his heart is not with thee.
John 15:3 Now ye are clean through the word which I have spoken unto	**See Hebrews 12:14 "Holiness"**

you.	See Matthew 5:18 "Scriptures"
John 15:6 If a man abide not in me, he is cast forth as a branch, and is withered; and men gather them, and cast *them* into the fire, and they are burned.	**Ezekiel 15:7** And I will set my face against them; they shall go out from *one* fire, and *another* fire shall devour them; and ye shall know that I *am* the LORD, when I set my face against them.
John 15:7 If ye abide in me, and my words abide in you, ye shall **ask** what ye will, and it shall be done unto you.	**2 Chronicles 16:12-13** And Asa in the thirty and ninth year of his reign was diseased in his feet, until his disease [was] exceeding *great*: yet in his disease **he sought not to the LORD**, but to the physicians. 13 And Asa slept with his fathers, and died in the one and fortieth year of his reign. **Jeremiah 29:12** Then shall ye call upon me, and ye shall go and pray unto me, and I will hearken unto you.
John 15:12 This is my commandment, That ye love one another, as I have loved you.	**Leviticus 19:18** Thou shalt not avenge, nor bear any grudge against the children of thy people, but thou shalt love thy neighbour as thyself: I *am* the LORD.
John 15:13 Greater love hath no man than this, that a man lay down his life for his friends.	**Genesis 42:24** And he turned himself about from them, and wept; and returned to them again, and communed with them, and took from them Simeon, and bound him before their eyes. **Genesis 43:30** And Joseph made haste; for his bowels did yearn upon his brother: and he sought *where* to weep; and he entered into *his* chamber, and wept there.
John 15:16 Ye have not chosen me, but I have chosen you, and ordained you, that ye should go and bring forth fruit, and that your fruit should remain: that whatsoever ye shall **ask** of the Father in my name, he may give it you.	**2 Chronicles 16:12-13** And Asa in the thirty and ninth year of his reign was diseased in his feet, until his disease *was* exceeding *great*: yet in his disease **he sought not to the LORD**, but to the physicians. 13 And Asa slept with his fathers, and died in the one and fortieth year of his reign. **Jeremiah 29:12** Then shall ye call upon me, and ye shall go and pray unto me, and I will hearken unto you.
John 15:25 But *this cometh to pass*, that the word might be fulfilled that is written in their law, They hated me without a cause.	**Psalms 35:19** Let not them that are mine enemies wrongfully rejoice over me: *neither* let them wink with the eye that hate me without a cause. **Psalms 69:4** They that hate me without a cause are more than the hairs of mine head: they that would destroy me, *being* mine enemies wrongfully, are mighty: then I restored *that* which I took not away. **Psalms 109:3** They compassed me about also with words of hatred; and fought against me without a cause.
John 15:26 But when the Comforter is come, whom I will send unto you from the Father, *even* the Spirit of truth, which proceedeth from the Father, he shall testify of me:	**Isaiah 11:2** And the spirit of the LORD shall rest upon him, the spirit of wisdom and understanding, the spirit of counsel and might, the spirit of knowledge and of the fear of the LORD; **Joel 2:28-29** And it shall come to pass afterward, *that* I will pour out my spirit upon all flesh; and your sons and your daughters shall prophesy, your old men shall dream dreams, your young men shall see visions: 29 And also upon the servants and upon the handmaids in those days will I pour out my spirit.
John 16:7 Nevertheless I tell you the truth; It is expedient for you that I go away: for if I go not away, the Comforter will not come unto you; but if I depart, I will send him unto you.	**Proverb 1:23** Turn you at my reproof: behold, I will pour out my spirit unto you, I will make known my words unto you.
John 16:13 Howbeit when he, the Spirit	**2 Kings 2:15** And when the sons of the prophets which *were* to

of truth, is come, he will guide you into all truth: for he shall not speak of himself; but whatsoever he shall hear, *that* shall he speak: and he will shew you things to come.	view at Jericho saw him, they said, The spirit of Elijah doth rest on Elisha. And they came to meet him, and bowed themselves to the ground before him.
John 16:21 A woman when she is in travail hath sorrow, because her hour is come: but as soon as she is delivered of the child, she remembereth no more the anguish, for joy that a man is born into the world.	**Isaiah 26:17** Like as a woman with child, *that* draweth near the time of her delivery, is in pain, *and* crieth out in her pangs; so have we been in thy sight, O LORD. **Jeremiah 30:7** Alas! for that day *is* great, so that none *is* like it: it *is* even the time of Jacob's trouble; but he shall be saved out of it.
John 16:23-24 And in that day ye shall **ask** me nothing. Verily, verily, I say unto you, Whatsoever ye shall **ask** the Father in my name, he will give *it* you. 24 Hitherto have ye asked nothing in my name: ask, and ye shall receive, that your joy may be full.	**2 Chronicles 16:12-13** And Asa in the thirty and ninth year of his reign was diseased in his feet, until his disease [was] exceeding *great*: yet in his disease <u>**he sought not to the LORD**, but to the physicians</u>. 13 And <u>Asa slept with his fathers</u>, and died in the one and fortieth year of his reign. **Jeremiah 29:12** Then shall ye call upon me, and ye shall go and pray unto me, and I will hearken unto you.
John 16:30 Now are we sure that **thou knowest all things**, and needest not that any man should ask thee: by this we believe that thou camest forth from God.	**1 Kings 8:39** Then hear thou in heaven thy dwelling place, and forgive, and do, and give to every man according to his ways, whose heart thou knowest; (for thou, *even* thou only, knowest the hearts of all the children of men;) **1 Chronicles 28:9** And thou, Solomon my son, know thou the God of thy father, and serve him with a perfect heart and with a willing mind: for the LORD searcheth all hearts, and understandeth all the imaginations of the thoughts: if thou seek him, he will be found of thee; but if thou forsake him, he will cast thee off for ever. **Jeremiah 17:9-10** The **heart** *is* deceitful above all *things*, and desperately wicked: **who can know it?** 10 I the LORD search the heart, *I* try the reins, even to give every man according to his ways, *and* according to the fruit of his doings.
John 16:32 Behold, the hour cometh, yea, is now come, that ye shall be scattered, every man to his own, and shall leave me alone: and yet I am not alone, because the Father is with me.	**Zechariah 13:7** Awake, O sword, against my shepherd, and against the man *that is* my fellow, saith the LORD of hosts: smite the shepherd, and the sheep shall be scattered: and I will turn mine hand upon the little ones.
John 16:33 These things I have spoken unto you, that in me ye might have peace. In the world ye shall have tribulation: but be of good cheer; I have overcome the world.	**Isaiah 9:6** For unto us a child is born, unto us a son is given: and the government shall be upon his shoulder: and his name shall be called Wonderful, Counseller, The mighty God, The everlasting Father, The Prince of Peace.
John 17:2 As thou hast given him power over all flesh, that he should give eternal life to as many as thou hast given him.	**Psalms 8:6** Thou madest him to have dominion over the works of thy hands; thou hast put all *things* under his feet:
John 17:3 And this is life eternal, that they might know thee the only true God, and Jesus Christ, whom thou hast sent.	**Isaiah 53:11** He shall see of the travail of his soul, *and* shall be satisfied: by his knowledge shall my righteous servant justify many; for he shall bear their iniquities.
John 17:5 And now, O Father, glorify thou me with thine own self with the glory which I had with thee before the world was.	**Genesis 1:1** In the beginning God created the heaven and the earth. **Micah 5:2** But thou, Bethlehem Ephratah, *though* thou be little among the thousands of Judah, *yet* out of thee shall he come forth unto me *that is* to be ruler in Israel; whose goings forth *have been*

	from of old, from everlasting. **Isaiah 40:28** Hast thou not known? hast thou not heard, *that* the everlasting God, the LORD, the Creator of the ends of the earth, fainteth not, neither is weary? *there is* no searching of his understanding.
John 17:12 While I was with them in the world, I kept them in thy name: those that thou gavest me I have kept, and none of them is lost, but the son of perdition; that the scripture might be fulfilled.	**Psalms 41:10** But thou, O LORD, be merciful unto me, and raise me up, that I may requite them. **Psalms 109:8** Let his days be few; *and* let another take his office. **Psalms 109:17** As he loved cursing, so let it come unto him: as he delighted not in blessing, so let it be far from him. **Isaiah 8:18** Behold, I and the children whom the LORD hath given me *are* for signs and for wonders in Israel from the LORD of hosts, which dwelleth in mount Zion.
John 17:17 Sanctify them through thy truth: thy **Word is truth**.	**See Hebrews 12:14 "Holiness"** **See Matthew 5:18 "Scripture"**
John 18:1 When Jesus had spoken these words, he went forth with his disciples over the brook Cedron, where was a garden, into the which he entered, and his disciples.	**2 Samuel 15:23** And all the country wept with a loud voice, and all the people passed over: the king also himself passed over the brook Kidron, and all the people passed over, toward the way of the wilderness.
John 18:11 Then said Jesus unto Peter, Put up thy sword into the sheath: the cup which my Father hath given me, shall I not drink it?	**Psalms 40:8** I delight to do thy will, O my God: yea, thy law *is* within my heart.
John 18:12 Then the band and the captain and officers of the Jews took Jesus, and bound him,	**Genesis 39:20** And Joseph's master took him, and put him into the prison, a place where the king's prisoners *were* bound: and he was there in the prison. **Psalms 105:17-18** He sent a man before them, *even* Joseph, *who* was sold for a servant: 18 Whose feet they hurt with fetters: he was laid in iron:
John 18:14 Now Caiaphas was he, which gave counsel to the Jews, that it was expedient that one man should die for the people.	**Isaiah 53:4-5** Surely he hath borne our griefs, and carried our sorrows: yet we did esteem him stricken, smitten of God, and afflicted. 5 But he *was* wounded for our transgressions, *he was* bruised for our iniquities: the chastisement of our peace *was* upon him; and with his stripes we are healed. **Daniel 9:26** And after threescore and two weeks shall Messiah be cut off, but not for himself: and the people of the prince that shall come shall destroy the city and the sanctuary; and the end thereof *shall be* with a flood, and unto the end of the war desolations are determined.
John 18:22 And when he had thus spoken, one of the officers which stood by struck Jesus with the palm of his hand, saying, Answerest thou the high priest so?	**Jeremiah 20:2** Then Pashur smote Jeremiah the prophet, and put him in the stocks that *were* in the high gate of Benjamin, which *was* by the house of the LORD.
John 18:32 That the saying of Jesus might be fulfilled, which he spake, signifying what death he should die.	**Numbers 21:8** And the LORD said unto Moses, Make thee a fiery serpent, and set it upon a pole: and it shall come to pass, that every one that is bitten, when he looketh upon it, shall live. **Deuteronomy 21:23** His body shall not remain all night upon the tree, but thou shalt in any wise bury him that day; (for he that is hanged *is* accursed of God;) that thy land be not defiled, which the

	LORD thy God giveth thee *for* an inheritance.
	Psalms 22:16 For dogs have compassed me: the assembly of the wicked have inclosed me: they pierced my hands and my feet.
John 19:5 Then came Jesus forth, wearing the crown of thorns, and the purple robe. And *Pilate* saith unto them, **Behold the man!**	**Zechariah 6:12** And speak unto him, saying, Thus speaketh the LORD of hosts, saying, **Behold the man** whose name *is* The BRANCH; and he shall grow up out of his place, and he shall build the temple of the LORD:
John 19:7 The Jews answered him, We have a law, and by our law he ought to die, because he made himself the Son of God.	**Leviticus 24:16** And he that blasphemeth the name of the LORD, he shall surely be put to death, *and* all the congregation shall certainly stone him: as well the stranger, as he that is born in the land, when he blasphemeth the name *of the LORD*, shall be put to death.
John 19:15 But they cried out, Away with *him*, away with *him*, crucify him. Pilate saith unto them, Shall I crucify your King? The chief priests answered, We have no king but Caesar.	**Genesis 49:10** The sceptre shall not depart from Judah, nor a lawgiver from between his feet, until Shiloh come; and unto him *shall* the gathering of the people *be*.
John 19:18 Where they crucified him, and two other with him, on either side one, and Jesus in the midst.	**Genesis 3:15** And I will put enmity between thee and the woman, and between thy seed and her seed; it shall bruise thy head, and thou shalt bruise his heel.
John 19:19 And Pilate wrote a title, and put *it* on the cross. And the writing was, JESUS OF NAZARETH THE KING OF THE JEWS.	**Zechariah 9:9** Rejoice greatly, O daughter of Zion; shout, O daughter of Jerusalem: behold, thy **King** cometh unto thee: he *is* just, and having salvation; lowly, and riding upon an ass, and upon a colt the foal of an ass.
John 19:21 Then said the chief priests of the Jews to Pilate, Write not, The King of the Jews; but that **he said, I am King of the Jews**.	**Psalms 47:7-8** For **God is the King** of all the earth: sing ye praises with understanding. 8 God reigneth over the heathen: God sitteth upon the throne of his holiness. **Isaiah 44:6** Thus saith the LORD the **King of Israel**, and his redeemer the LORD of hosts; I am the first, and I am the last; and beside me there is no God. **Jeremiah 10:10** But the LORD is the true God, he is the living God, and an everlasting **king**: at his wrath the earth shall tremble, and the nations shall not be able to abide his indignation. **Zechariah 9:9** Rejoice greatly, O daughter of Zion; shout, O daughter of Jerusalem: behold, thy **King** cometh unto thee: he *is* just, and having salvation; lowly, and riding upon an ass, and upon a colt the foal of an ass.
John 19:23 Then the soldiers, when they had crucified Jesus, took his garments, and made four parts, to every soldier a part; and also *his* coat: now the coat was without seam, woven from the top throughout.	**Psalms 22:16-18** For dogs have compassed me: the assembly of the wicked have inclosed me: they pierced my hands and my feet. 17 I may tell all my bones: they look and stare upon me. 18 They part my garments among them, and cast lots upon my vesture. **Zechariah 12:10** And I will pour upon the house of David, and upon the inhabitants of Jerusalem, the spirit of grace and of supplications: and they shall look upon me whom they have pierced, and they shall mourn for him, as one mourneth for his only *son*, and shall be in bitterness for him, as one that is in bitterness for his firstborn.
John 19:24 They said therefore among themselves, Let us not rend it, but cast lots for it, whose it shall be: that the scripture might be fulfilled, which saith,	**Psalms 22:18** They part my garments among them, and cast lots upon my vesture.

They parted my raiment among them, and for my vesture they did cast lots. These things therefore the soldiers did.	
John 19:28-29 After this, Jesus knowing that all things were now accomplished, that the scripture might be fulfilled, saith, I thirst. 29 Now there was set a vessel full of vinegar: and they filled a spunge with vinegar, and put it upon hyssop, and put it to his mouth.	**Psalms 22:15** My strength is dried up like a potsherd; and my tongue cleaveth to my jaws; and thou hast brought me into the dust of death. **Psalms 69:21** They gave me also gall for my meat; and in my thirst they gave me vinegar to drink.
John 19:30 When Jesus therefore had received the vinegar, he said, It is finished: and he bowed his head, and gave up the ghost.	**Psalms 22:31** They shall come, and shall declare his righteousness unto a people that shall be born, that he hath done *this*.
John 19:31 The Jews, therefore, that the bodies might not remain on the cross on the sabbath, since it was the preparation, (for that **sabbath** day was a great one,) asked of Pilate that their legs may be broken, and they taken away.	**See Colossians 2:16 "Sabbath"**
John 19:34 But one of the soldiers with a spear pierced his side, and forthwith came there out blood and water.	**Zechriah 12:10** And I will pour upon the house of David, and upon the inhabitants of Jerusalem, the spirit of grace and of supplications: and they shall look upon me whom they have pierced, and they shall mourn for him, as one mourneth for *his* only *son,* and shall be in bitterness for him, as one that is in bitterness for *his* firstborn.
John 19:36 For these things were done, that the scripture should be fulfilled, A bone of him shall not be broken.	**Exodus 12:46** In one house shall it be eaten; thou shalt not carry forth ought of the flesh abroad out of the house; neither shall ye break a bone thereof. **Numbers 9:12** They shall leave none of it unto the morning, nor break any bone of it: according to all the ordinances of the passover they shall keep it. **Psalms 22:14** I am poured out like water, and all my bones are out of joint: my heart is like wax; it is melted in the midst of my bowels. **Psalms 34:20** He keepeth all his bones: not one of them is broken.
John 19:37 And again another scripture saith, They shall look on him whom they pierced.	**Zechariah 12:10** And I will pour upon the house of David, and upon the inhabitants of Jerusalem, the spirit of grace and of supplications: and they shall look upon me whom they have pierced, and they shall mourn for him, as one mourneth for *his* only *son,* and shall be in bitterness for him, as one that is in bitterness for *his* firstborn.
John 20:9 For as yet they knew not the scripture, that he must rise again from the dead.	**Psalms 16:10-11** For thou wilt not leave my soul in hell; neither wilt thou suffer thine Holy One to see corruption. 11 Thou wilt shew me the path of life: in thy presence is fulness of joy; at thy right hand *there* are pleasures for evermore. **Psalms 49:15** But God will redeem my soul from the power of the grave: for he shall receive me. Selah.
John 20:17 Jesus saith unto her, Touch me not; for I am not yet ascended to my Father: but go to my brethren, and say	**Psalms 22:22** I will declare thy name unto my brethren: in the midst of the congregation will I praise thee. **Psalms 68:18** Thou hast ascended on high, thou hast led captivity

unto them, I ascend unto my Father, and your Father; and *to* my God, and your God.	captive: thou hast received gifts for men; yea, *for* the rebellious also, that the LORD God might dwell *among them.*
John 20:19 Then the same day at evening, being the first *day* of the week, when the doors were shut where the disciples were assembled for fear of the Jews, came Jesus and stood in the midst, and saith unto them, Peace *be* unto you.	**Genesis 45:1** Then Joseph could not refrain himself before all them that stood by him; and he cried, Cause every man to go out from me. And there stood no man with him, while Joseph made himself known unto his brethren.
John 20:21 Then said Jesus to them again, Peace *be* unto you: as *my* Father hath sent me, even so send I you.	**Genesis 37:35** And all his sons and all his daughters rose up to comfort him; but he refused to be comforted; and he said, For I will go down into the grave unto my son mourning. Thus his father wept for him.
John 20:28 And Thomas answered and said unto him, My Lord and my God.	**Psalms 35:23** Stir up thyself, and awake to my judgment, *even* unto my cause, my God and my Lord. **Isaiah 7:14** Therefore the Lord himself shall give you a sign; Behold, a virgin shall conceive, and bear a son, and shall call his name Immanuel. **Isaiah 9:6** For unto us a child is born, unto us a son is given: and the government shall be upon his shoulder: and his name shall be called Wonderful, Counsellor, The **mighty God**, The everlasting Father, The Prince of Peace. (Jeremiah 32:18) **Isaiah 25:9** And it shall be said in that day, Lo, this *is* our God; we have waited for him, and he will save us: this *is* the LORD; we have waited for him, we will be glad and rejoice in his salvation. **Isaiah 40:3-5** The voice of him that crieth in the wilderness, Prepare ye the way of the Lord, make straight in the desert a highway for our God. 4 Every valley shall be exalted, and every mountain and hill shall be made low: and the crooked shall be made straight, and the rough places plain: 5 And the glory of the LORD shall be revealed, and all flesh shall see *it* together: for the mouth of the LORD hath spoken *it*. **Jeremiah 32:18** Thou shewest lovingkindness unto thousands, and recompensest the iniquity of the fathers into the bosom of their children after them: the Great, the **Mighty God**, the LORD of hosts, is his name,
John 20:30-31 And many other **signs** truly did Jesus in the presence of his disciples, which are not **written in this book**: 31 But **these are written, that ye might believe that Jesus is the Christ, the Son of God; and that believing ye might have life through His name.**	See Mark 16:17 "Signs" See Matthew 5:18 "Scriptures"
John 21:18 Verily, verily, I say unto thee, When thou wast young, thou girdedst thyself, and walkedst whither thou wouldest: but when thou shalt be old, thou shalt stretch forth thy hands, and another shall gird thee, and carry *thee* whither thou wouldest not.	See 1 Corinthians 12:8 "Word of Knowledge"
Acts 1:1 The former treatise have I made, O Theophilus, of all that **Jesus began both to do and teach,**	See Ephesians 4:11 "Teach – Teachers"

Acts 1:5 For John truly baptized with water; but ye shall be baptized with the Holy Ghost not many days hence.	**Isaiah 44:3** For I will pour water upon him that is thirsty, and floods upon the dry ground: I will pour my spirit upon thy seed, and my blessing upon thine offspring: **Joel 2:28** And it shall come to pass afterward, *that* I will pour out my spirit upon all flesh; and your sons and your daughters shall prophesy, your old men shall dream dreams, your young men shall see visions:
Acts 1:8 But ye shall receive power, after that the Holy Ghost is come upon you: and ye shall be witnesses unto me both in Jerusalem, and in all Judaea, and in Samaria, and unto the uttermost part of the earth.	**Genesis 11:8** So the LORD scattered them abroad from thence upon the face of all the earth: and they left off to build the city. **Isaiah 2:3** And many people shall go and say, Come ye, and let us go up to the mountain of the LORD, to the house of the God of Jacob; and he will teach us of his ways, and we will walk in his paths: for out of Zion shall go forth the law, and the word of the LORD from Jerusalem. **Micah 3:8** But truly I am full of power by the spirit of the LORD, and of judgment, and of might, to declare unto Jacob his transgression, and to Israel his sin.
Acts 1:9-11 And when he had spoken these things, while they beheld, he was taken up; and a cloud received him out of their sight. 10 And while they looked stedfastly toward heaven as he went up, behold, two men stood by them in white apparel; 11 Which also said, Ye men of Galilee, why stand ye gazing up into heaven? this same Jesus, which is taken up from you into heaven, shall so come in like manner as ye have seen him go into heaven.	**Psalms 68:18** Thou hast ascended on high, thou hast led captivity captive: thou hast received gifts for men; yea, *for* the rebellious also, that the LORD God might dwell *among them*. **Daniel 7:13** I saw in the night visions, and, behold, *one* like the Son of man came with the clouds of heaven, and came to the Ancient of days, and they brought him near before him. **Micah 1:3** For, behold, the LORD cometh forth out of his place, and will come down, and tread upon the high places of the earth. **See 1 Timothy 2:5 "God"**
Acts 1:12 Then returned they unto Jerusalem from the **mount called Olivet**, which is from Jerusalem a **sabbath** day's journey.	**Zechariah 14:4** And his feet shall stand in that day upon the mount of Olives, which *is* before Jerusalem on the east, and the **mount of Olives** shall cleave in the midst thereof toward the east and toward the west, *and there shall be* a very great valley; and half of the mountain shall remove toward the north, and half of it toward the south. **See Colossians 2:16 "Sabbath"**
Acts 1:14 These all continued with one accord in prayer and supplication, with the women, and Mary the mother of Jesus, and with his brethren.	**Psalms 133:1** Behold, how good and how pleasant *it is* for brethren to dwell together in unity! **Amos 3:3** Can two walk together, except they be agreed?
Acts 1:16 Men *and* brethren, this scripture must needs have been fulfilled, which the Holy Ghost by the mouth of David spake before concerning Judas, which was guide to them that took Jesus.	**Psalms 41:9** Yea, mine own familiar friend, in whom I trusted, which did eat of my bread, hath lifted up *his* heel against me.
Acts 1:18 Now this man purchased a field with the reward of iniquity; and falling headlong, he burst asunder in the midst, and all his bowels gushed out.	**2 Samuel 17:23** And when Ahithophel saw that his counsel was not followed, he saddled *his* ass, and arose, and gat him home to his house, to his city, and put his household in order, and hanged himself, and died, and was buried in the sepulchre of his father.

Acts 1:20 For it is written in the book of Psalms, Let his habitation be desolate, and let no man dwell therein: and his bishoprick let another take.	**Psalms 69:25** Let their habitation be desolate; *and* let none dwell in their tents. **Psalms 109:8** Let his days be few; *and* let another take his office.
Acts 1:24 And they prayed, and said, Thou, Lord, which knowest the hearts of all *men*, shew whether of these two thou hast chosen,	**Numbers 16:5** And he spake unto Korah and unto all his company, saying, Even to morrow the LORD will shew who *are* his, and *who is* holy; and will cause *him* to come near unto him: even *him* whom he hath chosen will he cause to come near unto him. **Joshua 7:14** In the morning therefore ye shall be brought according to your tribes: and it shall be, *that* the tribe which the LORD taketh shall come according to the families *thereof;* and the family which the LORD shall take shall come by households; and the household which the LORD shall take shall come man by man. **1 Kings 8:39** Then hear thou in heaven thy dwelling place, and forgive, and do, and give to every man according to his ways, whose heart thou knowest; (for thou, *even* thou only, knowest the hearts of all the children of men;) **1 Chronicles 28:9** And thou, Solomon my son, know thou the God of thy father, and serve him with a perfect heart and with a willing mind: for the LORD searcheth all hearts, and understandeth all the imaginations of the thoughts: if thou seek him, he will be found of thee; but if thou forsake him, he will cast thee off for ever. **Jeremiah 17:9-10** The **heart** *is* deceitful above all *things*, and desperately wicked: **who can know it?** [10] I the LORD search the heart, *I* try the reins, even to give every man according to his ways, *and* according to the fruit of his doings.
Acts 2:1 And when the day of Pentecost was fully come, they were all with one accord in one place.	**Leviticus 23:15-16** And ye shall count unto you from the morrow after the sabbath, from the day that ye brought the sheaf of the wave offering; seven sabbaths shall be complete: 16 Even unto the morrow after the seventh sabbath shall ye number fifty days; and ye shall offer a new meat offering unto the LORD. **Deuteronomy 16:9** Seven weeks shalt thou number unto thee: begin to number the seven weeks from *such time as* thou beginnest *to put* the sickle to the corn. **Psalms 133:1** Behold, how good and how pleasant *it is* for brethren to dwell together in unity! **Amos 3:3** Can two walk together, except they be agreed?
Acts 2:3 And there appeared unto them cloven tongues like as of **fire**, and it sat upon each of them.	**Numbers 31:23** Every thing that may abide the fire, **ye shall make *it* go through the fire, and <u>it shall be clean</u>**: nevertheless it shall be purified with the water of separation: and all that abideth not the fire ye shall make go through the water.
Acts 2:4 And they were all filled with the Holy Ghost, and began to speak with other tongues, as the Spirit gave them utterance.	**Genesis 41:38** And Pharaoh said unto his servants, Can we find such a one as this is, **a man in whom the Spirit of God is**? **Numbers 11:17** And I will come down and talk with thee there: and I will take of **the spirit which is upon thee**, and will put it upon them; and they shall bear the burden of the people with thee, that thou bear it not thyself alone. **Numbers 11:25** And the LORD came down in a cloud, and spake unto him, **and took of the spirit that was upon him, and gave it unto the seventy elders**: and it came to pass, that, when the spirit

	rested upon them, they prophesied, and did not cease.
	Numbers 27:18 And the LORD said unto Moses, Take thee Joshua the son of Nun, a man in whom is the spirit, and lay thine hand upon him;
	Isaiah 11:2 And the spirit of the LORD shall rest upon him, the spirit of wisdom and understanding, the spirit of counsel and might, the spirit of knowledge and of the fear of the LORD;
	Micah 3:8 But truly I am full of power by the spirit of the LORD, and of judgment, and of might, to declare unto Jacob his transgression, and to Israel his sin.
Acts 2:5-6 And there were dwelling at Jerusalem Jews, devout men, out of every nation under heaven. 6 Now when this was noised abroad, the multitude came together, and were confounded, because that every man heard them speak in his own language. **Acts 2:8-11** And how hear we every man in our own tongue, wherein we were born? 9 Parthians, and Medes, and Elamites, and the dwellers in Mesopotamia, and in Judaea, and Cappadocia, in Pontus, and Asia, 10 Phrygia, and Pamphylia, in Egypt, and in the parts of **Libya** about Cyrene, and strangers of Rome, Jews and proselytes, 11 Cretes and Arabians, we do hear them speak in our tongues the wonderful works of God.	**Genesis 11:7** Go to, let us go down, and there confound their language, that they may not understand one another's speech. **Genesis 11:9** Therefore is the name of it called Babel; because the LORD did there confound the language of all the earth: and from thence did the LORD scatter them abroad upon the face of all the earth. **Ezekiel 30:5** Ethiopia, and **Libya**, and Lydia, and all the mingled people, and Chub, and the men of the land that is in league, shall fall with them by the sword. **Ezekiel 38:5** Persia, Ethiopia, and **Libya** with them; all of them with shield and helmet:
Acts 2:16 But this is that which was spoken by the prophet Joel;	**Amos 3:7** Surely the Lord GOD will do nothing, but he revealeth his secret unto his servants the prophets.
Acts 2:17 And it shall come to pass in the last days, saith God, I will pour out of my Spirit upon all flesh: and your sons and your daughters shall **prophesy**, and your young men shall see **visions**, and your old men shall dream dreams:	**Genesis 1:2** And the earth was without form, and void; and darkness *was* upon the face of the deep. And the Spirit of God moved upon the face of the waters. **Genesis 41:38** And Pharaoh said unto his servants, Can we find *such a one* as this *is*, a man in whom the Spirit of God *is*? **Job 26:13** By his spirit he hath garnished the heavens; his hand hath formed the crooked serpent. **Psalms 104:30** Thou sendest forth thy spirit, they are created: and thou renewest the face of the earth. **Isaiah 44:3** For I will pour water upon him that is thirsty, and floods upon the dry ground: I will pour my spirit upon thy seed, and my blessing upon thine offspring: **Ezekiel 11:19** And I will give them one heart, and I will put a new spirit within you; and I will take the stony heart out of their flesh, and will give them an heart of flesh: **Ezekiel 36:26-27** A new heart also will I give you, and a new spirit will I put within you: and I will take away the stony heart out of your flesh, and I will give you an heart of flesh. 27 And I will put my spirit within you, and cause you to walk in my statutes, and ye shall keep my judgments, and do *them*.

	Ezekiel 37:14 And shall put my spirit in you, and ye shall live, and I shall place you in your own land: then shall ye know that I the LORD have spoken *it,* and performed *it,* saith the LORD.
	Ezekiel 39:29 Neither will I hide my face any more from them: for I have poured out my spirit upon the house of Israel, saith the Lord GOD.
	Daniel 10:7 And I Daniel alone saw the vision: for the men that were with me saw not the **vision**; but a great quaking fell upon them, so that they fled to hide themselves.
	Zechariah 12:10 And I will pour upon the house of David, and upon the inhabitants of Jerusalem, the spirit of grace and of supplications: and they shall look upon me whom they have pierced, and they shall mourn for him, as one mourneth for *his* only *son,* and shall be in bitterness for him, as one that is in bitterness for *his* firstborn.
	Isaiah 2:2 And it shall come to pass in the **last days**, that the mountain of the LORD'S house shall be established in the top of the mountains, and shall be exalted above the hills; and all nations shall flow unto it.
	Micah 4:1 But in the **last days** it shall come to pass, that the mountain of the house of the LORD shall be established in the top of the mountains, and it shall be exalted above the hills; and people shall flow unto it.
	Joel 2:28 And it shall come to pass afterward, *that* I will pour out my spirit upon all flesh; and your sons and your daughters shall prophesy, your old men shall dream dreams, your young men shall see visions:
	See 1 Corinthians 12:10 "Prophecy"
Acts 2:18 And on my servants and on my handmaidens **I will pour out in those days** of my Spirit; and they shall prophesy:	**Numbers 11:25** And the LORD came down in a cloud, and spake unto him, and took of the **spirit that *was* upon him**, and gave *it* unto the seventy elders: and it came to pass, *that,* when **the spirit rested upon them**, they prophesied, and did not cease.
	Isaiah 32:15 Until the **spirit be poured upon us** from on high, and the wilderness be a fruitful field, and the fruitful field be counted for a forest.
	Ezekiel 39:29 Neither will I hide my face any more from them: for I have **poured out my spirit** upon the house of Israel, saith the Lord GOD.
	Joel 2:29 And also upon the servants and upon the handmaids in those days will **I pour out my spirit**.
Acts 2:19 And I will shew **wonders** in heaven above, and **signs** in the earth beneath; blood, and fire, and vapour of smoke:	**Joel 2:30** And I will shew **wonders** in the heavens and in the earth, blood, and fire, and pillars of smoke.
	See John 4:48 "Wonders"
	See Mark 16:17 "Signs"
Acts 2:20-21 The sun shall be turned into darkness, and the moon into blood, before that great and notable **day of the Lord** come: 21 And it shall come to	**Psalm 50:3-5** Our **God shall come**, and shall not keep silence: a fire shall devour before him, and it shall be very tempestuous round about him. 4 He shall call to the heavens from above, and to the earth, that he may judge his people. 5 Gather my saints together

pass, that whosoever shall call on the name of the Lord shall be saved.	unto me; those that have made a covenant with me by sacrifice. **Isaiah 2:12** For the **day of the LORD** of hosts shall be upon every one that is proud and lofty, and upon every one that is lifted up; and he shall be brought low: **Isaiah 12:1-3** And in that day thou shalt say, O LORD, I will praise thee: though thou wast angry with me, thine anger is turned away, and thou comfortedst me. 2 Behold, God *is* my salvation; I will trust, and not be afraid: for the LORD JEHOVAH *is* my strength and *my* song; he also is become my salvation. 3 Therefore with joy shall ye draw water out of the wells of salvation. **Isaiah 13:6** Howl ye; for the **day of the LORD** is at hand; it shall come as a destruction from the Almighty. **Isaiah 13:9-10** Behold, the **day of the LORD cometh**, cruel both with wrath and fierce anger, to lay the land desolate: and he shall destroy the sinners thereof out of it. 10 For the stars of heaven and the constellations thereof shall not give their light: the sun shall be darkened in his going forth, and the moon shall not cause her light to shine. **Isaiah 34:8** For it is the **day of the LORD'S** vengeance, and the year of recompences for the controversy of Zion. **Jeremiah 46:10** For this is the **day of the Lord** GOD of hosts, a day of vengeance, that he may avenge him of his adversaries: and the sword shall devour, and it shall be satiate and made drunk with their blood: for the Lord GOD of hosts hath a sacrifice in the north country by the river Euphrates. **Lamentations 2:22** Thou hast called as in a solemn day my terrors round about, so that in the **day of the LORD'S** anger none escaped nor remained: those that I have swaddled and brought up hath mine enemy consumed. **Ezekiel 13:5** Ye have not gone up into the gaps, neither made up the hedge for the house of Israel to stand in the battle in the **day of the LORD**. **Ezekiel 30:3** For the day is near, even the **day of the LORD** is near, a cloudy day; it shall be the time of the heathen. **Joel 1:15** Alas for the day! for the **day of the LORD** is at hand, and as a destruction from the Almighty shall it come. **Joel 2:1** Blow ye the trumpet in Zion, and sound an alarm in my holy mountain: let all the inhabitants of the land tremble: for the **day of the LORD** cometh, for it is nigh at hand; **Joel 2:11** And the LORD shall utter his voice before his army: for his camp is very great: for he is strong that executeth his word: for the **day of the LORD** is great and very terrible; and who can abide it? **Joel 2:31-32** The sun shall be turned into darkness, and the moon into blood, before the **great and the terrible day of the LORD** come. 32 And it shall come to pass, *that* whosoever shall call on the name of the LORD shall be delivered: for in mount Zion and in Jerusalem shall be deliverance, as the LORD hath said, and in the remnant whom the LORD shall call. **Joel 3:14** Multitudes, multitudes in the valley of decision: for the **day of the LORD** is near in the valley of decision. **Amos 5:18** Woe unto you that desire the day of the LORD! to

what end is it for you? the **day of the LORD** is darkness, and not light.

Amos 5:20 Shall not the **day of the LORD** be darkness, and not light? even very dark, and no brightness in it?

Obadiah 1:15 For the **day of the LORD** is near upon all the heathen: as thou hast done, it shall be done unto thee: thy reward shall return upon thine own head.

Zephaniah 1:7-8 Hold thy peace at the presence of the Lord GOD: for the **day of the LORD** is at hand: for the LORD hath prepared a sacrifice, he hath bid his guests. 8 And it shall come to pass in the **day of the LORD'S** sacrifice, that I will punish the princes, and the king's children, and all such as are clothed with strange apparel.

Zephaniah 1:14 The great **day of the LORD** is near, it is near, and hasteth greatly, even the voice of the day of the LORD: the mighty man shall cry there bitterly.

Zephaniah 1:18 Neither their silver nor their gold shall be able to deliver them in the **day of the LORD'S** wrath; but the whole land shall be devoured by the fire of his jealousy: for he shall make even a speedy riddance of all them that dwell in the land.

Zephaniah 2:2-3 Before the decree bring forth, before the day pass as the chaff, before the fierce anger of the LORD come upon you, before the **day of the LORD'S** anger come upon you. 3 Seek ye the LORD, all ye meek of the earth, which have wrought his judgment; seek righteousness, seek meekness: it may be ye shall be hid in the **day of the LORD'S** anger.

Zechariah 12:10 And I will pour upon the house of David, and upon the inhabitants of Jerusalem, the spirit of grace and of supplications: and they shall look upon me whom they have pierced, and they shall mourn for him, as one mourneth for *his* only *son*, and shall be in bitterness for him, as one that is in bitterness for *his* firstborn.

Zechariah 14:1 Behold, the **day of the LORD** cometh, and thy spoil shall be divided in the midst of thee.

Malachi 4:5 Behold, I will send you Elijah the prophet before the coming of the **great and dreadful day of the LORD**:

Leviticus 23:27 Also on the tenth *day* of this seventh month *there shall be* a day of atonement: it shall be an holy convocation unto you; and ye shall afflict your souls, and offer an offering made by fire unto the LORD.

Deuteronomy 30:3-5 That then the LORD thy God will turn thy captivity, and have compassion upon thee, and will return and gather thee from all the nations, whither the LORD thy God hath scattered thee.

4 If *any* of thine be driven out unto the outmost *parts* of heaven, from thence will the LORD thy God gather thee, and from thence will he fetch thee: 5 And the LORD thy God will bring thee into the land which thy fathers possessed, and thou shalt possess it; and he will do thee good, and multiply thee above thy fathers.

Jeremiah 32:37-39 Behold, I will gather them out of all countries, whither I have driven them in mine anger, and in my

	fury, and in great wrath; and I will bring them again unto this place, and I will cause them to dwell safely: 38 And they shall be my people, and I will be their God:
	39 And I will give them one heart, and one way, that they may fear me for ever, for the good of them, and of their children after them:
	Isaiah 11:11-12 And it shall come to pass in that day, *that* the Lord shall set his hand again the second time to recover the remnant of his people, which shall be left, from Assyria, and from Egypt, and from Pathros, and from Cush, and from Elam, and from Shinar, and from Hamath, and from the islands of the sea. 12 And he shall set up an ensign for the nations, and shall assemble the outcasts of Israel, and gather together the dispersed of Judah from the four corners of the earth.
Acts 2:22 Ye men of Israel, hear these words; Jesus of Nazareth, a man approved of God among you by miracles and **wonders** and **signs**, which God did by him in the midst of you, as ye yourselves also know:	**Exodus 7:3** And I will harden Pharaoh's heart, and multiply my **signs** and my wonders in the land of Egypt. **See Mark 16:17 "Signs"** **See John 4:48 "Wonders"**
Acts 2:23 Him, being delivered by the determinate counsel and **foreknowledge of God**, ye have taken, and by wicked hands have crucified and slain:	**Job 37:16** Dost thou know the balancings of the clouds, the wondrous works of him which is perfect in knowledge? **Psalms 147:5** Great *is* our Lord, and of great power: his understanding *is* infinite.
Acts 2:25 For David speaketh concerning him, I foresaw the Lord always before my face, for he is on my right hand, that I should not be moved:	**Psalms 8:6** Thou madest him to have dominion over the works of thy hands; thou hast put all *things* under his feet: **Psalms 16:8** I have set the LORD always before me: because *he is* at my right hand, I shall not be moved. **Psalms 110:1** The LORD said unto my Lord, Sit thou at my right hand, until I make thine enemies thy footstool. **Psalms 110:5** The Lord at thy right hand shall strike through kings in the day of his wrath. **Daniel 7:9** I beheld till the thrones were cast down, and the Ancient of days did sit, whose garment *was* white as snow, and the hair of his head like the pure wool: his throne *was like* the fiery flame, *and* his wheels *as* burning fire. **Zechraiah 3:1** And he shewed me Joshua the high priest standing before the angel of the LORD, and Satan standing at his right hand to resist him.
Acts 2:25-28 For David speaketh concerning him, I foresaw the Lord always before my face, for he is on my right hand, that I should not be moved: Therefore did my heart rejoice, and my tongue was glad; moreover also my flesh shall rest in hope: Because thou wilt not leave my soul in **hell**, neither wilt thou suffer thine Holy One to see corruption. Thou hast made known to me the ways of life; thou shalt make me full of joy with thy countenance.	**Psalms 16:8-11** I have set the LORD always before me: because *he is* at my right hand, I shall not be moved. Therefore my heart is glad, and my glory rejoiceth: my flesh also shall rest in hope. For thou wilt not leave my soul in hell; neither wilt thou suffer thine Holy One to see corruption. Thou wilt shew me the path of life: in thy presence *is* fulness of joy; at thy right hand *there are* pleasures for evermore. **See Luke 16:23 "Hell"**
Acts 2:26 Therefore did my heart rejoice, and my tongue was glad;	**Psalms 16:9** Therefore my heart is glad, and my glory rejoiceth: my flesh also shall rest in hope.

moreover also my flesh shall rest in hope:	
Acts 2:27 Because thou wilt not leave my soul in hell, neither wilt thou suffer thine Holy One to see corruption.	**Psalms 16:10** For thou wilt not leave my soul in hell; neither wilt thou suffer thine Holy One to see corruption. **Isaiah 12:6** Cry out and shout, thou inhabitant of Zion: for great *is* the Holy One of Israel in the midst of thee.
Acts 2:28 Thou hast made known to me the ways of life; thou shalt make me full of joy with thy countenance.	**Psalms 16:11** Thou wilt shew me the path of life: in thy presence *is* fulness of joy; at thy right hand *there are* pleasures for evermore.
Acts 2:29 Men *and* brethren, let me freely speak unto you of the patriarch David, that he is both dead and buried, and his sepulchre is with us unto this day.	**1 Kings 2:10** So David slept with his fathers, and was buried in the city of David.
Acts 2:30 Therefore being a prophet, and knowing that God had sworn with an oath to him, that of the fruit of his loins, according to the flesh, he would raise up Christ to sit on his throne;	**2 Samuel 7:12-13** And when thy days be fulfilled, and thou shalt sleep with thy fathers, I will set up thy seed after thee, which shall proceed out of thy bowels, and I will establish his kingdom. 13 He shall build an house for my name, and I will stablish the throne of his kingdom for ever. **Psalms 89:3-4** I have made a covenant with my chosen, I have sworn unto David my servant, 4 Thy seed will I establish for ever, and build up thy throne to all generations. Selah. **Psalms 132:11** The LORD hath sworn *in* truth unto David; he will not turn from it; Of the fruit of thy body will I set upon thy throne.
Acts 2:31 He seeing this before spake of the resurrection of Christ, that his **soul** was not left in **hell**, neither his flesh did see corruption.	**Psalms 16:10** For thou wilt not leave my soul in hell; neither wilt thou suffer thine Holy One to see corruption. **See Luke 16:23 "Hell"** **See 1 Thessalonians 5:23 "Body, soul, and spirit"**
Acts 2:32-33 This Jesus hath God raised up, whereof we all are witnesses. 33 Therefore being by the right hand of God exalted, and having received of the Father the promise of the Holy Ghost, he hath shed forth this, which ye now see and hear.	**Psalms 8:6** Thou madest him to have dominion over the works of thy hands; thou hast put all *things* under his feet: **Psalms 16:8** I have set the LORD always before me: because *he is* at my right hand, I shall not be moved. **Psalms 68:18** Thou hast ascended on high, thou hast led captivity captive: thou hast received gifts for men; yea, *for* the rebellious also, that the LORD God might dwell *among them*. **Psalms 110:1** The LORD said unto my Lord, Sit thou at my right hand, until I make thine enemies thy footstool. **Psalms 110:5** The Lord at thy right hand shall strike through kings in the day of his wrath. **Daniel 7:9** I beheld till the thrones were cast down, and the Ancient of days did sit, whose garment *was* white as snow, and the hair of his head like the pure wool: his throne *was like* the fiery flame, *and* his wheels *as* burning fire. **Zechraiah 3:1** And he shewed me Joshua the high priest standing before the angel of the LORD, and Satan standing at his right hand to resist him.
Acts 2:34-35 For David is not ascended into the heavens: but he saith himself, The LORD said unto my Lord, Sit thou on my right hand, until I make thy foes	**See references above**

thy footstool.	
Acts 2:36 Therefore let all the house of Israel know assuredly, that God hath made that same Jesus, whom ye have crucified, both Lord and Christ.	**Zechariah 14:9** And the LORD shall be king over all the earth: in that day shall there be one LORD, and his name one.
Acts 2:37 Now when they heard *this*, they were pricked in their heart, and said unto Peter and to the rest of the apostles, Men *and* brethren, what shall we do?	**Ezekiel 3:18-19** When I say unto the wicked, Thou shalt surely die; and thou givest him not warning, nor speakest to warn the wicked from his wicked way, to save his life; the same wicked *man* shall die in his iniquity; but his blood will I require at thine hand. 19 Yet if thou warn the wicked, and he turn not from his wickedness, nor from his wicked way, he shall die in his iniquity; but thou hast delivered thy soul. **Zechariah 12:10-11** And I will pour upon the house of David, and upon the inhabitants of Jerusalem, the spirit of grace and of supplications: and they shall look upon me whom they have pierced, and they shall mourn for him, as one mourneth for *his* only *son*, and shall be in bitterness for him, as one that is in bitterness for *his* firstborn. 11 In that day shall there be a great mourning in Jerusalem, as the mourning of Hadadrimmon in the valley of Megiddon.
Acts 2:38 Then Peter said unto them, Repent, and be baptized every one of you in the name of Jesus Christ for the remission of sins, and ye shall receive the gift of the Holy Ghost.	**Job 42:6** Wherefore I abhor myself, and **repent** in dust and ashes. **Ezekiel 14:6** Therefore say unto the house of Israel, Thus saith the Lord GOD; **Repent**, and turn yourselves from your idols; and turn away your faces from all your abominations. **Ezekiel 18:30** Therefore I will judge you, O house of Israel, every one according to his ways, saith the Lord GOD. **Repent**, and turn yourselves from all your transgressions; so iniquity shall not be your ruin. **Genesis 41:38** And Pharaoh said unto his servants, Can we find such a one as this is, **a man in whom the Spirit of God is**? **Numbers 11:17** And I will come down and talk with thee there: and I will take of **the spirit which is upon thee**, and will put it upon them; and they shall bear the burden of the people with thee, that thou bear it not thyself alone. **Numbers 11:25** And the LORD came down in a cloud, and spake unto him, **and took of the spirit that was upon him, and gave it unto the seventy elders**: and it came to pass, that, when the spirit rested upon them, they prophesied, and did not cease. **Numbers 27:18** And the LORD said unto Moses, Take thee Joshua the son of Nun, a man in whom is the **spirit**, and lay thine hand upon him; **Isaiah 11:2** And the spirit of the LORD shall rest upon him, the spirit of wisdom and understanding, the spirit of counsel and might, the spirit of knowledge and of the fear of the LORD **Ezekiel 11:19** And I will give them one heart, and **I will put a new spirit within you**; and I will take the stony heart out of their flesh, and will give them an heart of flesh: **Ezekiel 36:26-27** A new heart also will I give you, and a new spirit will I put within you: and I will take away the stony heart out of your flesh, and I will give you a heart of flesh. 27 And I will put

my spirit within you, and cause you to walk in my statutes, and ye shall keep my judgments, and do *them*.

Joel 2:28-29 And it shall come to pass afterward, *that* I will pour out my spirit upon all flesh; and your sons and your daughters shall prophesy, your old men shall dream dreams, your young men shall see visions: 29 And also upon the servants and upon the handmaids in those days will I pour out my spirit.

Micah 3:8 But truly I am full of power by the spirit of the LORD, and of judgment, and of might, to declare unto Jacob his transgression, and to Israel his sin.

Exodus 29:4-5 And **Aaron and his sons thou shalt bring unto the door of the tabernacle of the congregation**, and shalt **wash them with water**. 5 And thou shalt take the garments, and put upon Aaron the coat, and the robe of the ephod, and the ephod, and the breastplate, and gird him with the curious girdle of the ephod:

Exodus 30:18-21 Thou shalt also make a laver *of* brass, and his foot *also of* brass, to wash *withal*: and thou shalt put it between the tabernacle of the congregation and the altar, and thou shalt put water therein. 19 For Aaron and his sons shall wash their hands and their feet thereat: 20 When they go into the tabernacle of the congregation, they shall wash with water, that they die not; or when they come near to the altar to minister, to burn offering made by fire unto the LORD: 21 So they shall wash their hands and their feet, that they die not: and it shall be a statute for ever to them, *even* to him and to his seed throughout their generations.

Exodus 40:7 And thou shalt set the laver between the tent of the congregation and the altar, and shalt put water therein.

Exodus 40:11-13 And thou shalt anoint the laver and his foot, and sanctify it. 12 And thou shalt bring **Aaron and his sons unto the door of the tabernacle of the congregation, and wash them with water**. 13 And thou shalt put upon Aaron the holy garments, and anoint him, and sanctify him; that he may minister unto me in the priest's office.

Leviticus 14:3-9 And the priest shall go forth out of the camp; and the priest shall look, and, behold, *if* the plague of leprosy be healed in the leper; 4 Then shall the priest command to take for him that is to be cleansed two birds alive *and* clean, and cedar wood, and scarlet, and hyssop: 5 And the priest shall command that one of the birds be killed in an earthen vessel over running **water**: 6 As for the living bird, he shall take it, and the cedar wood, and the scarlet, and the hyssop, and shall dip them and the living bird in the blood of the bird *that was* killed over the running **water**: 7 And he shall sprinkle upon him that is to be cleansed from the leprosy seven times, and shall pronounce him clean, and shall let the living bird loose into the open field. 8 And he that is to be cleansed shall **wash his clothes**, and shave off all his hair, and **wash himself in water, that he may be clean**: and after that he shall come into the camp, and shall tarry abroad out of his tent seven days. 9 But it shall be on the seventh day, that he shall shave all his hair off his head and his beard and his eyebrows, even all his hair he shall shave off: and **he shall wash his clothes, <u>also he shall wash his flesh in water, and he shall be clean</u>**.

Leviticus 14:9-14 But it shall be on the seventh day, that he shall shave all his hair off his head and his beard and his eyebrows, even all his hair he shall shave off: and he shall wash his clothes, <u>**also he shall wash his flesh in water, and he shall be clean**</u>. 10 And on the eighth day he shall take two he lambs without blemish, and **one ewe lamb of the first year without blemish** (type of Jesus), and three tenth deals of fine flour *for* a meat offering, **mingled with oil** (type of Holy Spirit), and one log of oil.

11 And the priest that maketh *him* clean shall present the man that is to be made clean, and those things, before the LORD, *at* the door of the tabernacle of the congregation: 12 And the priest shall take **one he lamb**, and offer him for a trespass offering, and the **log of oil**, and wave them *for* a wave offering before the LORD: 13 And he shall slay the lamb in the place where **he shall kill the sin offering** and the burnt offering, in the holy place: for as the sin offering *is* the priest's, *so is* the trespass offering: it *is* most holy: 14 And the priest shall take *some* of **the blood** of the trespass offering, and the priest shall put *it* upon the tip of the right ear **of him that is to be cleansed**, and upon the thumb of his right hand, and upon the great toe of his right foot:

Leviticus 16:26-28 And he that let go the goat for the scapegoat shall **wash his clothes, and bathe his flesh in water**, and afterward come into the camp. 27 And the bullock *for* the sin offering, and the goat *for* the sin offering, whose blood was brought in to make atonement in the holy *place*, shall *one* carry forth without the camp; and they shall burn in the fire their skins, and their flesh, and their dung. 28 And he that burneth them shall wash **his clothes, and bathe his flesh in water**, and afterward he shall come into the camp.

Leviticus 23:27 Also on the tenth *day* of this seventh month *there shall be* a day of atonement: it shall be an holy convocation unto you; and ye shall afflict your souls, and offer an offering made by fire unto the LORD

Numbers 19:4 And Eleazar the priest shall take of her blood with his finger, and sprinkle of her blood directly before the tabernacle of the congregation seven times:

Numbers 19:9 And a man *that is* clean shall gather up the ashes of the heifer, and lay *them* up without the camp in a clean place, and it shall be kept for the congregation of the children of Israel for a water of separation: it *is* a purification for sin.

Numbers 19:13 Whosoever toucheth the dead body of any man that is dead, and purifieth not himself, defileth the tabernacle of the LORD; and that soul shall be cut off from Israel: because the water of separation was not sprinkled upon him, he shall be unclean; his uncleanness *is* yet upon him.

Numbers 31:21-24 And Eleazar the priest said unto the men of war which went to the battle, This *is* the ordinance of the law which the LORD commanded Moses; 22 Only the gold, and the silver, the brass, the iron, the tin, and the lead, 23 Every thing that may abide **the fire** (baptism of Holy Spirit), ye shall make *it* go through **the fire**, and **it shall be clean**: nevertheless **it shall be purified with the water of separation**: and all that abideth not the fire ye shall make go through the **water**. 24 And ye shall wash your clothes on the seventh day, and **ye shall be clean**, and afterward ye shall come into the camp.

2 Chronicles 4:2-6 Also he made a molten **sea** of ten cubits from brim to brim, round in compass, and five cubits the height thereof;

and a line of thirty cubits did compass it round about. 3 And under it *was* the similitude of oxen, which did compass it round about: ten in a cubit, compassing the sea round about. Two rows of oxen *were* cast, when it was cast. 4 It stood upon twelve oxen, three looking toward the north, and three looking toward the west, and three looking toward the south, and three looking toward the east: and the sea *was set* above upon them, and all their hinder parts *were* inward. 5 And the thickness of it *was* an handbreadth, and the brim of it like the work of the brim of a cup, with flowers of lilies; *and* it received and held three thousand baths. 6 He made also **ten lavers**, and put five on the right hand, and five on the left, to wash in them: such things as they offered for the burnt offering they washed in them; **but the sea *was* for the priests to wash in**.

2 Chronicles 4:10 And he set the **sea** on the right side of the east end, over against the south.

Psalms 51:2 Wash me throughly from mine iniquity, and cleanse me from my sin.

Psalms 51:13 *Then* will I teach transgressors thy ways; and sinners shall be converted unto thee.

Isaiah 1:15-18 And when ye spread forth your hands, I will hide mine eyes from you: yea, when ye make many prayers, I will not hear: your hands are full of blood. 16 **Wash you, make you clean**; put away the evil of your doings from before mine eyes; cease to do evil; 17 Learn to do well; seek judgment, relieve the oppressed, judge the fatherless, plead for the widow. 18 Come now, and let us reason together, saith the LORD: **though your sins be as scarlet, they shall be as white as snow**; though they be red like crimson, they shall be as wool.

Isaiah 44:3 For I will pour water upon him that is thirsty, and floods upon the dry ground: I will pour my spirit upon thy seed, and my blessing upon thine offspring:

Jeremiah 4:14 O Jerusalem, **wash thine heart from wickedness**, that thou mayest be saved. How long shall thy vain thoughts lodge within thee?

Ezekiel 2:2 And the spirit entered into me when he spake unto me, and set me upon my feet, that I heard him that spake unto me.

Ezekiel 36:25-27 Then will I sprinkle clean water upon you, and ye shall be clean: from all your filthiness, and from all your idols, will I cleanse you. 26 A new heart also will I give you, and a new spirit will I put within you: and I will take away the stony heart out of your flesh, and I will give you an heart of flesh. 27 And I will put my spirit within you, and cause you to walk in my statutes, and ye shall keep my judgments, and do them.

Joel 2:28 And it shall come to pass afterward, *that* I will pour out my spirit upon all flesh; and your sons and your daughters shall prophesy, your old men shall dream dreams, your young men shall see visions:

Leviticus 6:8-13 The fire shall ever be burning upon the altar; it shall never go out.

Numbers 31:23 Every thing that may abide the fire, **ye shall make *it* go through the fire, and <u>it shall be clean</u>**: nevertheless it shall be purified with the water of separation: and all that abideth not the fire ye shall make go through the water.

Psalm 66:12 Thou hast caused men to ride over our heads; **we went through <u>fire</u> and through water**: but thou broughtest us out into a wealthy place.

Isaiah 1:25 And I will turn my hand upon thee, and purely purge away thy dross, and take away all thy tin:

Isaiah 4:4 When the Lord shall have **washed away the filth** of the daughters of Zion, and shall have purged the blood of Jerusalem from the midst thereof by the spirit of judgment, and by the **spirit of burning**.

Isaiah 6:6-7 Then flew one of the seraphims unto me, having a live coal in his hand, *which* he had taken with the tongs from off the altar: 7 And he laid *it* upon my mouth, and said, Lo, this hath touched thy lips; and thine iniquity is taken away, and thy sin purged.

Isaiah 33:14 The sinners in Zion are afraid; fearfulness hath surprised the hypocrites. Who among us shall dwell with the devouring fire? who among us shall dwell with everlasting burnings?

Isaiah 43:2-3 When thou passest through the waters, I *will be* with thee; and through the rivers, they shall not overflow thee: when thou **walkest through the fire, thou shalt not be burned; neither shall the flame kindle upon thee**. 3 For I *am* the LORD thy God, the Holy One of Israel, thy Savior: I gave Egypt *for* thy ransom, Ethiopia and Seba for thee.

Jeremiah 23:28-29 The prophet that hath a dream, let him tell a dream; and he that hath my word, let him speak my word faithfully. What *is* the chaff to the wheat? saith the LORD. 29 *Is* **not my word like as a fire? saith the LORD**; and like a hammer *that* breaketh the rock in pieces?

Ezekiel 20:46-48 Son of man, set thy face toward the south, and drop *thy word* toward the south, and prophesy against the forest of the south field; 47 And say to the forest of the south, Hear the word of the LORD; Thus saith the Lord GOD; Behold, I will kindle a **fire** in thee, and it shall devour every green tree in thee, and every dry tree: the **flaming flame shall not be quenched**, and all faces from the south to the north shall be burned therein. 48 And all flesh shall see that **I the LORD have kindled it: it shall not be quenched**.

Ezekiel 24:9-14 Therefore thus saith the Lord GOD; Woe to the bloody city! I will even make the pile for **fire** great. 10 Heap on wood, kindle the **fire**, consume the flesh, and spice it well, and let the bones be burned. 11 Then set it empty upon the coals thereof, that the brass of it may be hot, and may burn, and *that* the filthiness of it may be molten in it, *that* the **scum of it may be consumed**. 12 She hath wearied *herself* with lies, and her great scum went not forth out of her: **her scum *shall be* in the fire**. 13 In thy filthiness *is* lewdness: because **I have purged thee, and thou wast not purged, thou shalt not be purged from thy filthiness any more, till I have caused my fury to rest upon thee**. 14 I the LORD have spoken *it*: it shall come to pass, and I will do *it*; I will not go back, neither will I spare, neither will I repent; according to thy ways, and according to thy doings, shall they judge thee, saith the Lord GOD.

	Zechariah 13:7-9 Awake, O sword, against my shepherd, and against the man *that is* my fellow, saith the LORD of hosts: smite the shepherd, and the sheep shall be scattered: and I will turn mine hand upon the little ones. 8 And
	it shall come to pass, that in all the land, saith the LORD, two parts therein shall be cut off *and* die; but the third shall be left therein. 9 And **I will bring the third part through the fire, and will refine them as silver is refined, and will try them as gold is tried: they shall call on my name, and I will hear them: I will say, It *is* my people: and they shall say, The LORD *is* my God.**
	Malachi 3:1-3 Behold, I will send my messenger, and he shall prepare the way before me: and the Lord, whom ye seek, shall suddenly come to his temple, even the messenger of the covenant, whom ye delight in: behold, he shall come, saith the LORD of hosts. 2 But who may abide the day of his coming? and who shall stand when he appeareth? for he is like a refiner's fire, and like fullers' soap: 3 And he shall sit *as* a refiner and purifier of silver: and he shall purify the sons of Levi, and purge them as gold and silver, that they may offer unto the LORD an offering in righteousness.
Acts 2:39 For the promise is unto you, and to your children, and to all that are afar off, *even* as many as the Lord our God shall call.	**Joel 2:28** And it shall come to pass afterward, *that* I will pour out my spirit upon all flesh; and your sons and your daughters shall prophesy, your old men shall dream dreams, your young men shall see visions:
Acts 2:42 And they continued stedfastly in the apostles' doctrine and fellowship, and in breaking of bread, and in **prayers**.	See Matthew 17:21 "Prayer"
Acts 2:43 And fear came upon every soul: and many wonders and signs were done by the apostles.	See 1 Peter 2:24 "Healing"
Acts 2:44 And all that believed were together, and had all things common;	**Deuteronomy 15:4** Save when there shall be no poor among you; for the LORD shall greatly bless thee in the land which the LORD thy God giveth thee *for* an inheritance to possess it:
Acts 2:45 And sold their possessions and goods, and parted them to all *men*, as every man had need.	**Isaiah 58:7** *Is it* not to deal thy bread to the hungry, and that thou bring the poor that are cast out to thy house? when thou seest the naked, that thou cover him; and that thou hide not thyself from thine own flesh?
Acts 2:46 And they, continuing daily with one accord in the temple, and breaking bread from house to house, did eat their meat with **gladness and singleness of heart**,	**Psalms 133:1** Behold, how good and how pleasant *it is* for brethren to dwell together in unity! **Amos 3:3** Can two walk together, except they be agreed?
Acts 3:1 Now Peter and John went up together into the temple at the hour of **prayer**, *being* the ninth *hour*.	See Matthew 17:21 "Prayer"
Acts 3:3 Who seeing Peter and John about to go into the temple asked an **alms**.	See 1 John 3:17 "Poor"
Acts 3:6 Then **Peter said, Silver and gold have I none**; but such as I have give I thee: In the name of Jesus Christ of Nazareth rise up and walk.	See Matthew 6:24 "Wealth" **Proverbs 18:10** The name of the LORD is a strong tower: the righteous runneth into it, and is safe.
Acts 3:8 And he leaping up stood, and	See John 4:24 "Worship"

walked, and entered with them into the temple, walking, and leaping, and praising God.	
Acts 3:13 The God of Abraham, and of Isaac, and of Jacob, the God of our fathers, hath glorified his Son Jesus; whom ye delivered up, and denied him in the presence of Pilate, when he was determined to let *him* go.	**Exodus 3:6** Moreover he said, I *am* the God of thy father, the God of Abraham, the God of Isaac, and the God of Jacob. And Moses hid his face; for he was afraid to look upon God. **Exodus 3:15** And God said moreover unto Moses, Thus shalt thou say unto the children of Israel, The LORD God of your fathers, the God of Abraham, the God of Isaac, and the God of Jacob, hath sent me unto you: this *is* my name for ever, and this *is* my memorial unto all generations.
Acts 3:16 And his name through faith in his name hath made this man strong, whom ye see and know: yea, the faith which is by him hath given him this perfect soundness in the presence of you all.	**Proverbs 18:10** The name of the LORD is a strong tower: the righteous runneth into it, and is safe.
Acts 3:18 But those things, which God before had shewed by the mouth of all his prophets, that Christ should suffer, he hath so fulfilled.	**Isaiah 50:6** I gave my back to the smiters, and my cheeks to them that plucked off the hair: I hid not my face from shame and spitting. **Isaiah 53:5** But he *was* wounded for our transgressions, *he was* bruised for our iniquities: the chastisement of our peace *was* upon him; and with his stripes we are healed. **Isaiah 53:10** Yet it pleased the LORD to bruise him; he hath put *him* to grief: when thou shalt make his soul an offering for sin, he shall see *his* seed, he shall prolong *his* days, and the pleasure of the LORD shall prosper in his hand.
Acts 3:19 Repent ye therefore, and be converted, that your sins may be blotted out, when the times of refreshing shall come from the presence of the Lord;	**Isaiah 55:7** Let the wicked forsake his way, and the unrighteous man his thoughts: and let him return unto the LORD, and he will have mercy upon him; and to our God, for he will abundantly pardon.
Acts 3:20 And he shall send Jesus Christ, which before was preached unto you:	**Daniel 7:13** I saw in the night visions, and, behold, *one* like the Son of man came with the clouds of heaven, and came to the Ancient of days, and they brought him near before him. **Micah 1:3** For, behold, the LORD cometh forth out of his place, and will come down, and tread upon the high places of the earth. **Zechariah 14:4** And his feet shall stand in that day upon the mount of Olives, which *is* before Jerusalem on the east, and the mount of Olives shall cleave in the midst thereof toward the east and toward the west, *and there shall be* a very great valley; and half of the mountain shall remove toward the north, and half of it toward the south.
Acts 3:22-23 For Moses truly said unto the fathers, A prophet shall the Lord your God raise up unto you of your brethren, like unto me; him shall ye hear in all things whatsoever he shall say unto you. And it shall come to pass, *that* every soul, which will not hear that prophet, shall be destroyed from among the people.	**Deuteronomy 18:15-16** The LORD thy God will raise up unto thee a Prophet from the midst of thee, of thy brethren, like unto me; unto him ye shall hearken; 16 According to all that thou desiredst of the LORD thy God in Horeb in the day of the assembly, saying, Let me not hear again the voice of the LORD my God, neither let me see this great fire any more, that I die not. **Deuteronomy 18:18-19** I will raise them up a Prophet from among their brethren, like unto thee, and will put my words in his mouth; and he shall speak unto them all that I shall command him. And it shall come to pass, [that] whosoever will not hearken unto my words which he shall speak in my name, I will require *it* of him.

	Leviticus 23:29 For whatsoever soul *it be* that shall not be afflicted in that same day, he shall be cut off from among his people.
	Amos 3:7 Surely the Lord GOD will do nothing, but he revealeth his secret unto his servants the prophets.
Acts 3:25 Ye are the children of the prophets, and of the covenant which God made with our fathers, saying unto Abraham, And in thy seed shall all the kindreds of the earth be blessed.	**Genesis 12:3** And I will bless them that bless thee, and curse him that curseth thee: and in thee shall all families of the earth be blessed.
	Genesis 22:18 And in thy seed shall all the nations of the earth be blessed; because thou hast obeyed my voice.
	Genesis 26:4 And I will make thy seed to multiply as the stars of heaven, and will give unto thy seed all these countries; and in thy seed shall all the nations of the earth be blessed;
	Genesis 28:14 And thy seed shall be as the dust of the earth, and thou shalt spread abroad to the west, and to the east, and to the north, and to the south: and in thee and in thy seed shall all the families of the earth be blessed.
	Exodus 6:4 And I have also established my covenant with them, to give them the land of Canaan, the land of their pilgrimage, wherein they were strangers.
Acts 4:6 And Annas the high priest, and Caiaphas, and John, and Alexander, and as many as were of the kindred of the high priest, were gathered together at Jerusalem.	**Leviticus 21:10-15** And *he that is* the high priest among his brethren, upon whose head the anointing oil was poured, and that is consecrated to put on the garments, shall not uncover his head, nor rend his clothes; 11 Neither shall he go in to any dead body, nor defile himself for his father, or for his mother; 12 Neither shall he go out of the sanctuary, nor profane the sanctuary of his God; for the crown of the anointing oil of his God *is* upon him: I *am* the LORD. 13 And he shall take a wife in her virginity. 14 A widow, or a divorced woman, or profane, *or* an harlot, these shall he not take: but he shall take a virgin of his own people to wife. 15 Neither shall he profane his seed among his people: for I the LORD do sanctify him.
Acts 4:7 And when they had set them in the midst, they asked, By what power, or by what name, have ye done this?	**Exodus 2:14** And he said, Who made thee a prince and a judge over us? intendest thou to kill me, as thou killedst the Egyptian? And Moses feared, and said, Surely this thing is known.
	Proverbs 18:10 The name of the LORD is a strong tower: the righteous runneth into it, and is safe.
Acts 4:8 Then Peter, filled with the **Holy Ghost**, said unto them, Ye rulers of the people, and **elders** of Israel,	**Genesis 41:38** And Pharaoh said unto his servants, Can we find such a one as this is, **a man in whom the Spirit of God is**?
	Numbers 11:17 And I will come down and talk with thee there: and I will take of **the spirit which is upon thee**, and will put it upon them; and they shall bear the burden of the people with thee, that thou bear it not thyself alone.
	Numbers 11:25 And the LORD came down in a cloud, and spake unto him, **and took of the spirit that was upon him, and gave it unto the seventy elders**: and it came to pass, that, when the spirit rested upon them, they prophesied, and did not cease.
	Numbers 27:18 And the LORD said unto Moses, Take thee Joshua the son of Nun, a man in whom is the spirit, and lay thine hand upon him;
	Isaiah 11:2 And the spirit of the LORD shall rest upon him, the spirit of wisdom and understanding, the spirit of counsel and

	might, the spirit of knowledge and of the fear of the LORD; **Micah 3:8** But truly I am full of power by the spirit of the LORD, and of judgment, and of might, to declare unto Jacob his transgression, and to Israel his sin. **See 1 Peter 5:1 "Elders"**
Acts 4:10 Be it known unto you all, and to all the people of Israel, that by the name of Jesus Christ of Nazareth, whom ye crucified, whom God raised from the dead, *even* by him doth this man stand here before you whole.	**See 1 Peter 2:24 "Healing"**
Acts 4:11 This is the stone which was set at nought of you builders, which is become the head of the corner.	**Zechariah 4:7** Who *art* thou, O great mountain? before Zerubbabel *thou shalt become* a plain: and he shall bring forth the headstone *thereof with* shoutings, *crying,* Grace, grace unto it. **Psalms 118:22** The stone *which* the builders refused is become the head *stone* of the corner. **Isaiah 8:14** And he shall be for a sanctuary; but for a stone of stumbling and for a rock of offence to both the houses of Israel, for a gin and for a snare to the inhabitants of Jerusalem. **Isaiah 28:16** Therefore thus saith the Lord GOD, Behold, I lay in Zion for a foundation a stone, a tried stone, a precious corner *stone*, a sure foundation: he that believeth shall not make haste. **Isaiah 33:20** Look upon Zion, the city of our solemnities: thine eyes shall see Jerusalem a quiet habitation, a tabernacle *that* shall not be taken down; not one of the stakes thereof shall ever be removed, neither shall any of the cords thereof be broken.
Acts 4:12 Neither is there salvation in any other: for there is none other name under heaven given among men, whereby we must be saved.	**Leviticus 23:27** Also on the tenth *day* of this seventh month *there shall be* a day of atonement: it shall be an holy convocation unto you; and ye shall afflict your souls, and offer an offering made by fire unto the LORD. **Job 19:25** For I know *that* my redeemer liveth, and *that* he shall stand at the latter *day* upon the earth: **Psalms 27:1** { *A Psalm* of David. } The LORD *is* my light and my salvation; whom shall I fear? the LORD *is* the strength of my life; of whom shall I be afraid? **Psalms 72:17** His name shall endure for ever: his name shall be continued as long as the sun: and *men* shall be blessed in him: all nations shall call him blessed. **Isaiah 9:6** For unto us a child is born, unto us a son is given: and the government shall be upon his shoulder: and his name shall be called Wonderful, Counseller, The mighty God, The everlasting Father, The Prince of Peace. **Isaiah 12:2** Behold, God *is* my salvation; I will trust, and not be afraid: for the LORD JEHOVAH *is* my strength and *my* song; he also is become my salvation. **Isaiah 45:21** Tell ye, and bring *them* near; yea, let them take counsel together: who hath declared this from ancient time? *who* hath told it from that time? *have* not I the LORD? and *there is* no God else beside me; a just God and a **Savior**; *there is* none beside me.

	Isaiah 60:16 Thou shalt also suck the milk of the Gentiles, and shalt suck the breast of kings: and thou shalt know that I the LORD *am* thy Saviour and thy Redeemer, the mighty One of Jacob. **Daniel 9:24-25** Seventy weeks are determined upon thy people and upon thy holy city, to finish the transgression, and to make an end of sins, and to make reconciliation for iniquity, and to bring in everlasting righteousness, and to seal up the vision and prophecy, and to anoint the most Holy. 25 Know therefore and understand, *that* from the going forth of the commandment to restore and to build Jerusalem unto the Messiah the Prince *shall be* seven weeks, and threescore and two weeks: the street shall be built again, and the wall, even in troublous times. **Joel 2:31-32** The sun shall be turned into darkness, and the moon into blood, before the great and the terrible day of the LORD come. 32 And it shall come to pass, *that* whosoever shall call on the name of the LORD shall be delivered: for in mount Zion and in Jerusalem shall be deliverance, as the LORD hath said, and in the remnant whom the LORD shall call. **Hosea 13:4** Yet I *am* the LORD thy God from the land of Egypt, and thou shalt know no god but me: for *there is* no saviour beside me. **Zechariah 12:10** And I will pour upon the house of David, and upon the inhabitants of Jerusalem, the spirit of grace and of supplications: and they shall look upon me whom they have pierced, and they shall mourn for him, as one mourneth for *his* only *son*, and shall be in bitterness for him, as one that is in bitterness for *his* firstborn. **Zechariah 14:9** And the LORD shall be king over all the earth: in that day shall there be one LORD, and his name one. **See John 4:42 "Savior"**
Acts 4:14 And beholding the man which was healed standing with them, they could say nothing against it. **Acts 4:16** Saying, What shall we do to these men? for that indeed a notable miracle hath been done by them *is* manifest to all them that dwell in Jerusalem; and we cannot deny *it*.	**See 1 Peter 2:24 "Healing"**
Acts 4:23 And being let go, they went to their own company, and reported all that the chief priests and **elders** had said unto them.	**See 1 Peter 5:1 "Elders"**
Acts 4:24 And when they heard that, they lifted up their voice to God with one accord, and said, Lord, thou *art* God, which hast made heaven, and earth, and the sea, and all that in them is:	**Exodus 20:11** For *in* six days the LORD made heaven and earth, the sea, and all that in them *is,* and rested the seventh day: wherefore the LORD blessed the sabbath day, and hallowed it. **Psalms 146:6** Which made heaven, and earth, the sea, and all that therein *is:* which keepeth truth for ever: **Psalms 133:1** Behold, how good and how pleasant *it is* for brethren to dwell together in unity! **Amos 3:3** Can two walk together, except they be agreed? **See John 4:24 "Worship"**
Acts 4:25-26 Who by the mouth of thy	**Psalms 2:1-2** Why do the heathen rage, and the people imagine a

servant David hast said, Why did the heathen rage, and the people imagine vain things? 26 The kings of the earth stood up, and the rulers were gathered together against the Lord, and against his Christ.	vain thing? The kings of the earth set themselves, and the rulers take counsel together, against the LORD, and against his anointed, *saying*,
Acts 4:27 For of a truth against thy holy child Jesus, whom thou hast **anointed**, both Herod, and Pontius Pilate, with the Gentiles, and the people of Israel, were gathered together,	**See Luke 4:18 "Anointing"**
Acts 4:30 By stretching forth thine hand to heal; and that signs and wonders may be done by the name of thy holy child Jesus.	**Proverbs 18:10** The name of the LORD is a strong tower: the righteous runneth into it, and is safe.
Acts 4:31 And when they had prayed, the place was shaken where they were assembled together; and they were all filled with the Holy Ghost, and they spake the word of God with boldness.	**Genesis 41:38** And Pharaoh said unto his servants, Can we find such a one as this is, **a man in whom the Spirit of God is**? **Numbers 11:17** And I will come down and talk with thee there: and I will take of **the spirit which is upon thee**, and will put it upon them; and they shall bear the burden of the people with thee, that thou bear it not thyself alone. **Numbers 11:25** And the LORD came down in a cloud, and spake unto him, **and took of the spirit that was upon him, and gave it unto the seventy elders**: and it came to pass, that, when the spirit rested upon them, they prophesied, and did not cease. **Numbers 27:18** And the LORD said unto Moses, Take thee Joshua the son of Nun, a man in whom is the spirit, and lay thine hand upon him; **Isaiah 11:2** And the spirit of the LORD shall rest upon him, the spirit of wisdom and understanding, the spirit of counsel and might, the spirit of knowledge and of the fear of the LORD; **Micah 3:8** But truly I am full of power by the spirit of the LORD, and of judgment, and of might, to declare unto Jacob his transgression, and to Israel his sin.
Acts 4:35 And laid *them* down at the apostles' feet: and distribution was made unto every man according as he had need.	**Isaiah 58:7** *Is it* not to deal thy bread to the hungry, and that thou bring the poor that are cast out to thy house? when thou seest the naked, that thou cover him; and that thou hide not thyself from thine own flesh?
Acts 5:3 But Peter said, Ananias, why hath Satan filled thine heart to lie to the Holy Ghost, and to keep back *part* of the price of the land?	**Genesis 3:4** And the **serpent** said unto the woman, Ye shall not surely die: **Zechariah 3:1-2** And he shewed me Joshua the high priest standing before the angel of the LORD, and **Satan** standing at his right hand to resist him. 2 And the LORD said unto **Satan**, The LORD rebuke thee, O **Satan**; even the LORD that hath chosen Jerusalem rebuke thee: *is* not this a brand plucked out of the fire? **See Matthew 4:10 "satan"** **See 1 Corinthians 12:8 "Word of Knowledge"**
Acts 5:9 Then Peter said unto her, How is it that ye have agreed together to tempt the **Spirit of the Lord**? behold, the feet of them which have buried thy husband are at the door, and shall carry	**Isaiah 11:2** And the spirit of the LORD shall rest upon him, the spirit of wisdom and understanding, the spirit of counsel and might, the spirit of knowledge and of the fear of the LORD; **Isaiah 61:1-2** The Spirit of the Lord GOD *is* upon me; because the LORD hath anointed me to preach good tidings unto the meek; he

thee out.	hath sent me to bind up the brokenhearted, to proclaim liberty to the captives, and the opening of the prison to *them that are* bound; To proclaim the acceptable year of the LORD, and the day of vengeance of our God; to comfort all that mourn;
Acts 5:12 And by the hands of the apostles were many signs and wonders wrought among the people; (and they were all with **one accord** in Solomon's porch	**Psalms 133:1** Behold, how good and how pleasant *it is* for brethren to dwell together in unity! **Amos 3:3** Can two walk together, except they be agreed?
Acts 5:16 There came also a multitude *out* of the cities round about unto Jerusalem, bringing sick folks, and them which were vexed with unclean spirits: and **they were healed every one**.	See 1 Peter 2:24 "Healing"
Acts 5:25 Then came one and told them, saying, Behold, the men whom ye put in prison are standing in the temple, and **teaching the people**. **Acts 5:28** Saying, Did not we straitly **command you that ye should not teach in this name**? and, behold, **ye have filled Jerusalem with your doctrine**, and intend to bring this man's blood upon us.	See Ephesians 4:11 "Teach – Teachers"
Acts 5:30 The God of our fathers raised up Jesus, whom ye slew and hanged on a tree.	**Deuteronomy 21:22-23** And if a man have committed a sin worthy of death, and he be to be put to death, and thou hang him on a tree: 23 His body shall not remain all night upon the tree, but thou shalt in any wise bury him that day; (for he that is hanged *is* accursed of God;) that thy land be not defiled, which the LORD thy God giveth thee *for* an inheritance.
Acts 5:31 Him hath God exalted with his right hand *to be* a Prince and a Saviour, for to give repentance to Israel, and forgiveness of sins.	**Job 19:25** For I know *that* my redeemer liveth, and *that* he shall stand at the latter *day* upon the earth: **Psalms 8:6** Thou madest him to have dominion over the works of thy hands; thou hast put all *things* under his feet: **Psalms 16:8** I have set the LORD always before me: because *he is* at my right hand, I shall not be moved. **Psalms 68:18** Thou hast ascended on high, thou hast led captivity captive: thou hast received gifts for men; yea, *for* the rebellious also, that the LORD God might dwell *among them*. **Psalms 110:1** The LORD said unto my Lord, Sit thou at my right hand, until I make thine enemies thy footstool. **Psalms 110:5** The Lord at thy right hand shall strike through kings in the day of his wrath. **Isaiah 9:6** For unto us a child is born, unto us a son is given: and the government shall be upon his shoulder: and his name shall be called Wonderful, Counseller, The mighty God, The everlasting Father, The Prince of Peace. **Isaiah 60:16** Thou shalt also suck the milk of the Gentiles, and shalt suck the breast of kings: and thou shalt know that I the LORD *am* thy Saviour and thy Redeemer, the mighty One of Jacob.

	Daniel 7:9 I beheld till the thrones were cast down, and the Ancient of days did sit, whose garment *was* white as snow, and the hair of his head like the pure wool: his throne *was like* the fiery flame, *and* his wheels *as* burning fire. **Zechraiah 3:1** And he shewed me Joshua the high priest standing before the angel of the LORD, and Satan standing at his right hand to resist him.
Acts 5:38 And now I say unto you, Refrain from these men, and let them alone: for if this counsel or this work be of men, it will come to nought:	**Proverbs 21:30** *There is* no wisdom nor understanding nor counsel against the LORD. **Isaiah 8:10** Take counsel together, and it shall come to nought; speak the word, and it shall not stand: for God *is* with us.
Acts 5:42 And daily in the temple, and in every house, **they ceased not to teach** and preach Jesus Christ.	**See Ephesians 4:11 "Teach – Teachers"**
Acts 6:2 Then the twelve called the multitude of the disciples *unto them*, and said, It is not reason that we should leave the word of God, and serve tables.	**Exodus 18:17-23** And Moses' father in law said unto him, The thing that thou doest *is* not good. 18 Thou wilt surely wear away, both thou, and this people that *is* with thee: for this thing *is* too heavy for thee; thou art not able to perform it thyself alone. 19 Hearken now unto my voice, I will give thee counsel, and God shall be with thee: Be thou for the people to God-ward, that thou mayest bring the causes unto God: 20 And thou shalt teach them ordinances and laws, and shalt shew them the way wherein they must walk, and the work that they must do. 21 Moreover thou shalt provide out of all the people able men, such as fear God, men of truth, hating covetousness; and place *such* over them, *to be* rulers of thousands, *and* rulers of hundreds, rulers of fifties, and rulers of tens: 22 And let them judge the people at all seasons: and it shall be, *that* every great matter they shall bring unto thee, but every small matter they shall judge: so shall it be easier for thyself, and they shall bear *the burden* with thee. 23 If thou shalt do this thing, and God command thee *so*, then thou shalt be able to endure, and all this people shall also go to their place in peace.
Acts 6:3 Wherefore, brethren, look ye out among you seven men of honest report, full of the Holy Ghost and wisdom, whom we may appoint over this business.	**Deuteronomy 1:13** Take you wise men, and understanding, and known among your tribes, and I will make them rulers over you. **Genesis 41:38** And Pharaoh said unto his servants, Can we find such a one as this is, **a man in whom the Spirit of God is**? **Numbers 11:17** And I will come down and talk with thee there: and I will take of **the spirit which is upon thee**, and will put it upon them; and they shall bear the burden of the people with thee, that thou bear it not thyself alone. **Numbers 11:25** And the LORD came down in a cloud, and spake unto him, **and took of the spirit that was upon him, and gave it unto the seventy elders**: and it came to pass, that, when the spirit rested upon them, they prophesied, and did not cease. **Numbers 27:18** And the LORD said unto Moses, Take thee Joshua the son of Nun, a man in whom is the spirit, and lay thine hand upon him; **Isaiah 11:2** And the spirit of the LORD shall rest upon him, the spirit of wisdom and understanding, the spirit of counsel and might, the spirit of knowledge and of the fear of the LORD; **Micah 3:8** But truly I am full of power by the spirit of the LORD, and of judgment, and of might, to declare unto Jacob his

	transgression, and to Israel his sin.
Acts 6:4 But we will give ourselves continually to **prayer**, and to the ministry of the word.	**See Matthew 17:21 "Prayer"**
Acts 6:10 And they were not able to resist the wisdom and the spirit by which he spake.	**Exodus 4:12** Now therefore go, and I will be with thy mouth, and teach thee what thou shalt say. **Isaiah 54:17** No weapon that is formed against thee shall prosper; and every tongue *that* shall rise against thee in judgment thou shalt condemn. This *is* the heritage of the servants of the LORD, and their righteousness *is* of me, saith the LORD.
Acts 6:12 And they stirred up the people, and the **elders**, and the scribes, and came upon him, and caught *him*, and brought *him* to the council,	**See 1 Peter 5:1 "Elders"**
Acts 6:13 And set up false witnesses, which said, This man ceaseth not to speak blasphemous words against this holy place, and the law:	**Exodus 20:16** Thou shalt not bear false witness against thy neighbour. **Leviticus 19:16** Thou shalt not go up and down *as* a talebearer among thy people: neither shalt thou stand against the blood of thy neighbour: I *am* the LORD. **Deutreonomy 5:20** Neither shalt thou bear false witness against thy neighbour. **Psalms 15:3** *He that* backbiteth not with his tongue, nor doeth evil to his neighbour, nor taketh up a reproach against his neighbour.
Acts 7:2 And he said, Men, brethren, and fathers, hearken; The God of glory appeared unto our father Abraham, when he was in Mesopotamia, before he dwelt in Charran,	**Genesis 15:7** And he said unto him, I *am* the LORD that brought thee out of Ur of the Chaldees, to give thee this land to inherit it. **Nehemiah 9:7** Thou *art* the LORD the God, who didst choose Abram, and broughtest him forth out of Ur of the Chaldees, and gavest him the name of Abraham;
Acts 7:3 And said unto him, Get thee out of thy country, and from thy kindred, and come into the land which I shall shew thee.	**Genesis 12:1** Now the LORD had said unto Abram, Get thee out of thy country, and from thy kindred, and from thy father's house, unto a land that I will shew thee:
Acts 7:4 Then came he out of the land of the Chaldaeans, and dwelt in Charran: and from thence, when his father was dead, he removed him into this land, wherein ye now dwell.	**Genesis 11:31** And Terah took Abram his son, and Lot the son of Haran his son's son, and Sarai his daughter in law, his son Abram's wife; and they went forth with them from Ur of the Chaldees, to go into the land of Canaan; and they came unto Haran, and dwelt there. **Genesis 12:4-5** So Abram departed, as the LORD had spoken unto him; and Lot went with him: and Abram was seventy and five years old when he departed out of Haran. 5 And Abram took Sarai his wife, and Lot his brother's son, and all their substance that they had gathered, and the souls that they had gotten in Haran; and they went forth to go into the land of Canaan; and into the land of Canaan they came.
Acts 7:5 And he gave him none inheritance in it, no, not *so much as* to set his foot on: yet he promised that he would give it to him for a possession, and to his seed after him, when *as yet* he had no child.	**Genesis 12:7** And the LORD appeared unto Abram, and said, Unto thy seed will I give this land: and there builded he an altar unto the LORD, who appeared unto him. **Genesis 13:15** For all the land which thou seest, to thee will I give it, and to thy seed for ever. **Genesis 17:8** And I will give unto thee, and to thy seed after thee,

	the land wherein thou art a stranger, all the land of Canaan, for an everlasting possession; and I will be their God.
	Genesis 48:4 And said unto me, Behold, I will make thee fruitful, and multiply thee, and I will make of thee a multitude of people; and will give this land to thy seed after thee *for* an everlasting possession.
Acts 7:6 And God spake on this wise, That his seed should sojourn in a strange land; and that they should bring them into bondage, and entreat *them* evil four hundred years.	**Genesis 15:13** And he said unto Abram, Know of a surety that thy seed shall be a stranger in a land *that is* not theirs, and shall serve them; and they shall afflict them four hundred years; **Exod 12:40** Now the sojourning of the children of Israel, who dwelt in Egypt, *was* four hundred and thirty years.
Acts 7:7 And the nation to whom they shall be in bondage will I judge, said God: and after that shall they come forth, and serve me in this place.	**Genesis 15:14** And also that nation, whom they shall serve, will I judge: and afterward shall they come out with great substance. **Exodus 3:12** And he said, Certainly I will be with thee; and this *shall be* a token unto thee, that I have sent thee: When thou hast brought forth the people out of Egypt, ye shall serve God upon this mountain.
Acts 7:8 And he gave him the covenant of circumcision: and so *Abraham* begat Isaac, and circumcised him the eighth day; and Isaac *begat* Jacob; and Jacob *begat* the twelve patriarchs.	**Genesis 17:10-14** This *is* my covenant, which ye shall keep, between me and you and thy seed after thee; **Every man child among you shall be circumcised.** 11 **And ye shall circumcise the flesh of your foreskin; and it shall be a token of the covenant betwixt me and you.** 12 And he that is eight days old shall be circumcised among you, every man child in your generations, he that is born in the house, or bought with money of any stranger, which *is* not of thy seed. 13 He that is born in thy house, and he that is bought with thy money, must needs be circumcised: and my covenant shall be in your flesh for an everlasting covenant. 14 And **the uncircumcised man child whose flesh of his foreskin is not circumcised, that soul shall be cut off from his people; he hath broken my covenant**. **Genesis 21:3-4** And Abraham called the name of his son that was born unto him, whom Sarah bare to him, Isaac. 4 And Abraham circumcised his son Isaac being eight days old, as God had commanded him. **Genesis 25:26** And after that came his brother out, and his hand took hold on Esau's heel; and his name was called Jacob: and Isaac *was* threescore years old when she bare them. **Genesis 42:13** And they said, Thy servants *are* twelve brethren, the sons of one man in the land of Canaan; and, behold, the youngest *is* this day with our father, and one *is* not. **Deuteronomy 30:6** And the LORD thy God will circumcise thine heart, and the heart of thy seed, to love the LORD thy God with all thine heart, and with all thy soul, that thou mayest live.
Acts 7:9 And the patriarchs, moved with envy, sold Joseph into Egypt: but God was with him,	**Genesis 37:4** And when his brethren saw that their father loved him more than all his brethren, they hated him, and could not speak peaceably unto him. **Genesis 37:11** And his brethren envied him; but his father observed the saying. **Genesis 37:28** Then there passed by Midianites merchantmen; and they drew and lifted up Joseph out of the pit, and sold Joseph to the Ishmeelites for twenty *pieces* of silver: and they brought Joseph into Egypt. **Genesis 39:1-2** And Joseph was brought down to Egypt; and

	Potiphar, an officer of Pharaoh, captain of the guard, an Egyptian, bought him of the hands of the Ishmeelites, which had brought him down thither. 2 And the LORD was with Joseph, and he was a prosperous man; and he was in the house of his master the Egyptian. **Genesis 39:21** But the LORD was with Joseph, and shewed him mercy, and gave him favour in the sight of the keeper of the prison.
Acts 7:10 And delivered him out of all his afflictions, and gave him favour and wisdom in the sight of Pharaoh king of Egypt; and he made him governor over Egypt and all his house.	**Genesis 41:37** And the thing was good in the eyes of Pharaoh, and in the eyes of all his servants. **Genesis 41:40** Thou shalt be over my house, and according unto thy word shall all my people be ruled: only in the throne will I be greater than thou.
Acts 7:11 Now there came a dearth over all the land of Egypt and Chanaan, and great affliction: and our fathers found no sustenance.	**Genesis 41:54** And the seven years of dearth began to come, according as Joseph had said: and the dearth was in all lands; but in all the land of Egypt there was bread. **Psalms 105:16-17** Moreover he called for a famine upon the land: he brake the whole staff of bread. 17 He sent a man before them, *even* Joseph, *who* was sold for a servant:
Acts 7:12 But when Jacob heard that there was corn in Egypt, he sent out our fathers first.	**Genesis 42:2** And he said, Behold, I have heard that there is corn in Egypt: get you down thither, and buy for us from thence; that we may live, and not die.
Acts 7:13 And at the second *time* Joseph was made known to his brethren; and Joseph's kindred was made known unto Pharaoh.	**Genesis 45:1** Then Joseph could not refrain himself before all them that stood by him; and he cried, Cause every man to go out from me. And there stood no man with him, while Joseph made himself known unto his brethren. **Genesis 45:9** Haste ye, and go up to my father, and say unto him, Thus saith thy son Joseph, God hath made me lord of all Egypt: come down unto me, tarry not:
Acts 7:14-15 Then sent Joseph, and called his father Jacob to him, and all his kindred, threescore and fifteen souls. 15 So Jacob went down into Egypt, and died, he, and our fathers,	**Genesis 45:1-28** **Genesis 46:27** And the sons of Joseph, which were born him in Egypt, *were* two souls: all the souls of the house of Jacob, which came into Egypt, *were* threescore and ten. **Exodus 1:5** And all the souls that came out of the loins of Jacob were seventy souls: for Joseph was in Egypt *already*. **Genesis 49:33** And when Jacob had made an end of commanding his sons, he gathered up his feet into the bed, and yielded up the ghost, and was gathered unto his people.
Acts 7:16 And were carried over into Sychem, and laid in the sepulchre that Abraham bought for a sum of money of the sons of Emmor *the father* of Sychem.	**Genesis 50:13** For his sons carried him into the land of Canaan, and buried him in the cave of the field of Machpelah, which Abraham bought with the field for a possession of a buryingplace of Ephron the Hittite, before Mamre. **Exodus 13:19** And Moses took the bones of Joseph with him: for he had straitly sworn the children of Israel, saying, God will surely visit you; and ye shall carry up my bones away hence with you. **Joshua 24:32** And the bones of Joseph, which the children of Israel brought up out of Egypt, buried they in Shechem, in a parcel of ground which Jacob bought of the sons of Hamor the father of Shechem for an hundred pieces of silver: and it became the inheritance of the children of Joseph.
Acts 7:17 But when the time of the promise drew nigh, which God had sworn to Abraham, the people grew and	**Exodus 1:7** And the children of Israel were fruitful, and increased abundantly, and multiplied, and waxed exceeding mighty; and the

multiplied in Egypt,	land was filled with them. **Psalms 105:23-24** Israel also came into Egypt; and Jacob sojourned in the land of Ham. 24 And he increased his people greatly; and made them stronger than their enemies.
Acts 7:18 Till another king arose, which knew not Joseph.	**Exodus 1:8** Now there arose up a new king over Egypt, which knew not Joseph.
Acts 7:19 The same dealt subtilly with our kindred, and evil entreated our fathers, so that they cast out their young children, to the end they might not live.	**Exodus 1:10** Come on, let us deal wisely with them; lest they multiply, and it come to pass, that, when there falleth out any war, they join also unto our enemies, and fight against us, and *so* get them up out of the land. **Exodus 1: 22** And Pharaoh charged all his people, saying, Every son that is born ye shall cast into the river, and every daughter ye shall save alive.
Acts 7:20 In which time Moses was born, and was exceeding fair, and nourished up in his father's house three months:	**Exodus 2:2** And the woman conceived, and bare a son: and when she saw him that he *was a* goodly *child,* she hid him three months. **Exodus 6:20** And Amram took him Jochebed his father's sister to wife; and she bare him Aaron and Moses: and the years of the life of Amram *were* an hundred and thirty and seven years. **Numbers 26:59** And the name of Amram's wife *was* Jochebed, the daughter of Levi, whom *her mother* bare to Levi in Egypt: and she bare unto Amram Aaron and Moses, and Miriam their sister. **1 Chronicles 23:13-14** The sons of Amram; Aaron and Moses: and Aaron was separated, that he should sanctify the most holy things, he and his sons for ever, to burn incense before the LORD, to minister unto him, and to bless in his name for ever. **14** Now *concerning* Moses the man of God, his sons were named of the tribe of Levi.
Acts 7:21 And when he was cast out, Pharaoh's daughter took him up, and nourished him for her own son.	**Exodus 2:3-10** And when she could not longer hide him, she took for him an ark of bulrushes, and daubed it with slime and with pitch, and put the child therein; and she laid it in the flags by the river's brink. 4 And his sister stood afar off, to wit what would be done to him. 5 And the daughter of Pharaoh came down to wash herself at the river; and her maidens walked along by the river's side; and when she saw the ark among the flags, she sent her maid to fetch it. 6 And when she had opened it, she saw the child: and, behold, the babe wept. And she had compassion on him, and said, This is one of the Hebrews' children. 7 Then said his sister to Pharaoh's daughter, Shall I go and call to thee a nurse of the Hebrew women, that she may nurse the child for thee? 8 And Pharaoh's daughter said to her, Go. And the maid went and called the child's mother. 9 And Pharaoh's daughter said unto her, Take this child away, and nurse it for me, and I will give thee thy wages. And the woman took the child, and nursed it. 10 And the child grew, and she brought him unto Pharaoh's daughter, and he became her son. And she called his name Moses: and she said, Because I drew him out of the water.
Acts 7:23 And when he was full forty years old, it came into his heart to visit his brethren the children of Israel.	**Exodus 2:11-14** And it came to pass in those days, when Moses was grown, that he went out unto his brethren, and looked on their burdens: and he spied an Egyptian smiting an Hebrew, one of his brethren. 12 And he looked this way and that way, and when he saw that *there was* no man, he slew the Egyptian, and hid him in the sand. 13 And when he went out the second day, behold, two men of the Hebrews strove together: and he said to him that did the wrong, Wherefore smitest thou thy fellow? 14 And he said, Who

	made thee a prince and a judge over us? intendest thou to kill me, as thou killedst the Egyptian? And Moses feared, and said, Surely this thing is known.
Acts 7:24 And seeing one *of them* suffer wrong, he defended *him,* and avenged him that was oppressed, and smote the Egyptian:	**Exodus 2:11** And it came to pass in those days, when Moses was grown, that he went out unto his brethren, and looked on their burdens: and he spied an Egyptian smiting an Hebrew, one of his brethren.
Acts 7:26-28 And the next day he shewed himself unto them as they strove, and would have set them at one again, saying, Sirs, ye are brethren; why do ye wrong one to another? 27 But he that did his neighbour wrong thrust him away, saying, Who made thee a ruler and a judge over us? 28 Wilt thou kill me, as thou didest the Egyptian yesterday?	**Exodus 2:13-14** And when he went out the second day, behold, two men of the Hebrews strove together: and he said to him that did the wrong, Wherefore smitest thou thy fellow? 14 And he said, Who made thee a prince and a judge over us? intendest thou to kill me, as thou killedst the Egyptian? And Moses feared, and said, Surely this thing is known.
Acts 7:29 Then fled Moses at this saying, and was a stranger in the land of Madian, where he begat two sons.	**Exodus 2:15** Now when Pharaoh heard this thing, he sought to slay Moses. But Moses fled from the face of Pharaoh, and dwelt in the land of Midian: and he sat down by a well. **Exodus 18:3** And her two sons; of which the name of the one *was* Gershom; for he said, I have been an alien in a strange land: 4 And the name of the other *was* Eliezer; for the God of my father, *said he,* was mine help, and delivered me from the sword of Pharaoh:
Acts 7:30 And when forty years were expired, there appeared to him in the wilderness of mount Sina an angel of the Lord in a flame of fire in a bush.	**Exodus 3:2** And the angel of the LORD appeared unto him in a flame of fire out of the midst of a bush: and he looked, and, behold, the bush burned with fire, and the bush *was* not consumed.
Acts 7:32 *Saying*, I *am* the God of thy fathers, the God of Abraham, and the God of Isaac, and the God of Jacob. Then Moses trembled, and durst not behold.	**Exodus 3:6** Moreover he said, I *am* the God of thy father, the God of Abraham, the God of Isaac, and the God of Jacob. And Moses hid his face; for he was afraid to look upon God. **Exodus 3:15** And God said moreover unto Moses, Thus shalt thou say unto the children of Israel, The LORD God of your fathers, the God of Abraham, the God of Isaac, and the God of Jacob, hath sent me unto you: this *is* my name for ever, and this *is* my memorial unto all generations.
Acts 7:33 Then said the Lord to him, Put off thy shoes from thy feet: for the place where thou standest is holy ground.	**Exodus 3:5** And he said, Draw not nigh hither: put off thy shoes from off thy feet, for the place whereon thou standest *is* holy ground. **Joshua 5:15** And the captain of the LORD's host said unto Joshua, Loose thy shoe from off thy foot; for the place whereon thou standest *is* holy. And Joshua did so.
Acts 7:34 I have seen, I have seen the affliction of my people which is in Egypt, and I have heard their **groaning**, and am come down to deliver them. And now come, I will send thee into Egypt.	**Exodus 2:24** And God heard their **groaning**, and God remembered his covenant with Abraham, with Isaac, and with Jacob. **Exodus 3:7-8** And the LORD said, I have surely seen the affliction of my people which *are* in Egypt, and have **heard their cry** by reason of their taskmasters; for I know their sorrows; And I am come down to deliver them out of the hand of the Egyptians, and to bring them up out of that land unto a good land and a large, unto a land flowing with milk and honey; unto the place of the Canaanites, and the Hittites, and the Amorites, and the Perizzites, and the Hivites, and the Jebusites. **Exodus 3:10** Come now therefore, and I will send thee unto Pharaoh, that thou mayest bring forth my people the children of

	Israel out of Egypt.

Psalm 38:8-10 I am feeble and sore broken: I have roared by reason of the **disquietness** of my heart. 9 Lord, all my desire is before thee; and my **groaning** is not hid from thee. 10 My heart panteth, my strength faileth me: as for the light of mine eyes, it also is gone from me. |
| **Acts 7:35** This Moses whom they refused, saying, Who made thee a ruler and a judge? the same did God send *to be* a ruler and a deliverer by the hand of the angel which appeared to him in the bush. | **Exodus 2:14** And he said, Who made thee a prince and a judge over us? intendest thou to kill me, as thou killedst the Egyptian? And Moses feared, and said, Surely this thing is known.

Exodus 3:15-18 And God said moreover unto Moses, Thus shalt thou say unto the children of Israel, The LORD God of your fathers, the God of Abraham, the God of Isaac, and the God of Jacob, hath sent me unto you: this is my name for ever, and this is my memorial unto all generations. 16 Go, and gather the elders of Israel together, and say unto them, The LORD God of your fathers, the God of Abraham, of Isaac, and of Jacob, appeared unto me, saying, I have surely visited you, and seen that which is done to you in Egypt: 17 And I have said, I will bring you up out of the affliction of Egypt unto the land of the Canaanites, and the Hittites, and the Amorites, and the Perizzites, and the Hivites, and the Jebusites, unto a land flowing with milk and honey. 18 And they shall hearken to thy voice: and thou shalt come, thou and the elders of Israel, unto the king of Egypt, and ye shall say unto him, The LORD God of the Hebrews hath met with us: and now let us go, we beseech thee, three days' journey into the wilderness, that we may sacrifice to the LORD our God. |
| **Acts 7:36** He brought them out, after that he had shewed wonders and signs in the land of Egypt, and in the Red sea, and in the wilderness forty years. | **Exodus 7:1-12:51**

Exodus 12:41 And it came to pass at the end of the four hundred and thirty years, even the selfsame day it came to pass, that all the hosts of the LORD went out from the land of Egypt.

Exodus 14:21 And Moses stretched out his hand over the sea; and the LORD caused the sea to go *back* by a strong east wind all that night, and made the sea dry *land,* and the waters were divided.

Exodus 15:23 And when they came to Marah, they could not drink of the waters of Marah, for they *were* bitter: therefore the name of it was called Marah.

Exodus 16:1-36 |
| **Acts 7:37** This is that Moses, which said unto the children of Israel, A prophet shall the Lord your God raise up unto you of your brethren, like unto me; him shall ye hear. | **Deuteronomy 18:15** The LORD thy God will raise up unto thee a Prophet from the midst of thee, of thy brethren, like unto me; unto him ye shall hearken;
Deuteronomy 18:18-19 I will raise them up a Prophet from among their brethren, like unto thee, and will put my words in his mouth; and he shall speak unto them all that I shall command him. And it shall come to pass, *that* whosoever will not hearken unto my words which he shall speak in my name, I will require *it* of him. |
| **Acts 7:38** This is he, that was in the **church** in the wilderness with the angel which spake to him in the mount Sina, and with our fathers: who received the **lively oracles** to give unto us: | **Exodus 12:3** Speak ye unto all the **congregation** of Israel, saying, In the tenth *day* of this month they shall take to them every man a lamb, according to the house of *their* fathers, a lamb for an house:

Exodus 35:20 And all the **congregation** of the children of Israel departed from the presence of Moses.

Numbers 3:25 And the charge of the sons of Gershon in the tabernacle of the **congregation** *shall be* the tabernacle, and the tent, the covering thereof, and the hanging for the door of the |

	tabernacle of the **congregation**, **Exodus 19:2-3** For they were departed from Rephidim, and were come *to* the desert of Sinai, and had pitched in the wilderness; and there Israel camped before the mount. 3 And Moses went up unto God, and the LORD called unto him out of the mountain, saying, Thus shalt thou say to the house of Jacob, and tell the children of Israel; **Exodus 20:1-24:18** See Matthew 5:18 "Scriptures"
Acts 7:39 To whom our fathers would not obey, but thrust him from them, and in their hearts turned back again into Egypt,	**Leviticus 20:23** And ye shall not walk in the manners of the nation, which I cast out before you: for they committed all these things, and therefore I abhorred them. **Psalms 106:40** Therefore was the wrath of the LORD kindled against his people, insomuch that he abhorred his own inheritance.
Acts 7:40 Saying unto Aaron, Make us gods to go before us: for *as for* this Moses, which brought us out of the land of Egypt, we wot not what is become of him.	**Exodus 32:1** And when the people saw that Moses delayed to come down out of the mount, the people gathered themselves together unto Aaron, and said unto him, Up, make us gods, which shall go before us; for *as for* this Moses, the man that brought us up out of the land of Egypt, we wot not what is become of him. **Exodus 32:23** For they said unto me, Make us gods, which shall go before us: for *as for* this Moses, the man that brought us up out of the land of Egypt, we wot not what is become of him.
Acts 7:41 And they made a calf in those days, and offered sacrifice unto the idol, and rejoiced in the works of their own hands.	**Exodus 32:19** And it came to pass, as soon as he came nigh unto the camp, that he saw the calf, and the dancing: and Moses' anger waxed hot, and he cast the tables out of his hands, and brake them beneath the mount. **Deuteronomy 32:17** They sacrificed unto devils, not to God; to gods whom they knew not, to new *gods that* came newly up, whom your fathers feared not.
Acts 7:42-43 Then God turned, and gave them up to worship the host of heaven; as it is written in the book of the prophets, O ye house of Israel, have ye offered to me slain beasts and sacrifices *by the space of* forty years in the wilderness? 43 Yea, ye took up the tabernacle of Moloch, and the star of your god Remphan, figures which ye made to worship them: and I will carry you away beyond Babylon.	**1 Kings 14:15** For the LORD shall smite Israel, as a reed is shaken in the water, and he shall root up Israel out of this good land, which he gave to their fathers, and shall scatter them beyond the river, because they have made their groves, provoking the LORD to anger. **Amos 5:25-27** Have ye offered unto me sacrifices and offerings in the wilderness forty years, O house of Israel? But ye have borne the tabernacle of your Moloch and Chiun your images, the star of your god, which ye made to yourselves. Therefore will I cause you to go into captivity beyond Damascus, saith the LORD, whose name *is* The God of hosts.
Acts 7:44 Our fathers had the tabernacle of witness in the wilderness, as he had appointed, speaking unto Moses, that he should make it according to the fashion that he had seen.	**Exodus 25:40** And look that thou make *them* after their pattern, which was shewed thee in the mount. **Exodus 26:30** And thou shalt rear up the tabernacle according to the fashion thereof which was shewed thee in the mount.
Acts 7:45 Which also our fathers that came after brought in with Jesus into the possession of the Gentiles, whom God drave out before the face of our fathers, unto the days of David;	**Joshua 3:14** And it came to pass, when the people removed from their tents, to pass over Jordan, and the priests bearing the ark of the covenant before the people; **Joshua 18:1** And the whole congregation of the children of Israel assembled together at Shiloh, and set up the tabernacle of the congregation there. And the land was subdued before them.

Acts 7:46 Who found favour before God, and desired to find a tabernacle for the God of Jacob.	**1 Samuel 16:1** And the LORD said unto Samuel, How long wilt thou mourn for Saul, seeing I have rejected him from reigning over Israel? fill thine horn with oil, and go, I will send thee to Jesse the Bethlehemite: for I have provided me a king among his sons. **2 Samuel 7:2** That the king said unto Nathan the prophet, See now, I dwell in an house of cedar, but the ark of God dwelleth within curtains. **1 Chronicles 17:1-2** Now it came to pass, as David sat in his house, that David said to Nathan the prophet, Lo, I dwell in an house of cedars, but the ark of the covenant of the LORD *remaineth* under curtains. **2** Then Nathan said unto David, Do all that *is* in thine heart; for God *is* with thee. **Psalms 89:20** I have found David my servant; with my holy oil have I anointed him: **Psalms 132:5** Until I find out a place for the LORD, an habitation for the mighty *God* of Jacob.
Acts 7:47 But Solomon built him an house.	**1 Kings 5:5** And, behold, I purpose to build an house unto the name of the LORD my God, as the LORD spake unto David my father, saying, Thy son, whom I will set upon thy throne in thy room, he shall build an house unto my name. **1 Kings 6:1** And it came to pass in the four hundred and eightieth year after the children of Israel were come out of the land of Egypt, in the fourth year of Solomon's reign over Israel, in the month Zif, which *is* the second month, that he began to build the house of the LORD. **1 Kings 8:1-66** **1 Chronicles 17:12** He shall build me an house, and I will stablish his throne for ever.
Acts 7:48 Howbeit the most High dwelleth not in temples made with hands; as saith the prophet,	**1 Kings 8:27** But will God indeed dwell on the earth? behold, the heaven and heaven of heavens cannot contain thee; how much less this house that I have builded? **2 Chronicles 2:6** But who is able to build him an house, seeing the heaven and heaven of heavens cannot contain him? who *am* I then, that I should build him an house, save only to burn sacrifice before him? **2 Chronicles 6:18** But will God in very deed dwell with men on the earth? behold, heaven and the heaven of heavens cannot contain thee; how much less this house which I have built! **Isaiah 66:1** Thus saith the LORD, The heaven *is* my throne, and the earth *is* my footstool: where *is* the house that ye build unto me? and where *is* the place of my rest?
Acts 7:49-50 Heaven *is* my throne, and earth *is* my footstool: what house will ye build me? saith the Lord: or what *is* the place of my rest? Hath not my hand made all these things?	**2 Chronicles 6:33** Then hear thou from the heavens, *even* from thy dwelling place, and do according to all that the stranger calleth to thee for; that all people of the earth may know thy name, and fear thee, as *doth* thy people Israel, and may know that this house which I have built is called by thy name. **Isaiah 66:1-2** Thus saith the LORD, The heaven *is* my throne, and the earth *is* my footstool: where *is* the house that ye build unto me? and where *is* the place of my rest? 2 For all those *things* hath mine hand made, and all those *things* have been, saith the LORD: but to

	this *man* will I look, *even* to *him that is* poor and of a contrite spirit, and trembleth at my word.
Acts 7:51 Ye stiffnecked and uncircumcised in heart and ears, ye do always resist the Holy Ghost: as your fathers *did*, so *do* ye.	**Genesis 6:3** And the LORD said, My spirit shall not always strive with man, for that he also *is* flesh: yet his days shall be an hundred and twenty years. **Genesis 6:5-7** And GOD saw that the wickedness of man *was* great in the earth, and *that* every imagination of the thoughts of his heart *was* only evil continually. 6 And it repented the LORD that he had made man on the earth, and it grieved him at his heart. 7 And the LORD said, I will destroy man whom I have created from the face of the earth; both man, and beast, and the creeping thing, and the fowls of the air; for it repenteth me that I have made them. **Psalms 52:3** Thou lovest evil more than good; *and* lying rather than to speak righteousness. Selah. **Proverbs 21:10** The soul of the wicked desireth evil: his neighbour findeth no favour in his eyes. **Isaiah 30:9** That this *is* a rebellious people, lying children, children *that* will not hear the law of the LORD: **Isaiah 55:3** Incline your ear, and come unto me: hear, and your soul shall live; and I will make an everlasting covenant with you, *even* the sure mercies of David. **Jeremiah 4:22** For my people *is* foolish, they have not known me; they *are* sottish children, and they have none understanding: they *are* wise to do evil, but to do good they have no knowledge. **Jeremiah 6:10** To whom shall I speak, and give warning, that they may hear? behold, their ear *is* uncircumcised, and they cannot hearken: behold, the word of the LORD is unto them a reproach; they have no delight in it.
Acts 7:53 Who have received the law by the disposition of angels, and have not kept *it*.	**Exodus 19:3** And Moses went up unto God, and the LORD called unto him out of the mountain, saying, Thus shalt thou say to the house of Jacob, and tell the children of Israel; **Exodus 24:3-4** And Moses came and told the people all the words of the LORD, and all the judgments: and all the people answered with one voice, and said, All the words which the LORD hath said will we do. 4 And Moses wrote all the words of the LORD, and rose up early in the morning, and builded an altar under the hill, and twelve pillars, according to the twelve tribes of Israel.
Acts 7:55-56 But he, being full of the Holy Ghost, looked up stedfastly into heaven, and saw the glory of God, and Jesus standing on the right hand of God, 56 And said, Behold, I see the heavens opened, and the Son of man standing on the right hand of God.	**Job 19:25** For I know *that* my redeemer liveth, and *that* he shall stand at the latter *day* upon the earth: **Psalms 8:6** Thou madest him to have dominion over the works of thy hands; thou hast put all *things* under his feet: **Psalms 16:8** I have set the LORD always before me: because *he is* at my right hand, I shall not be moved. **Psalms 68:18** Thou hast ascended on high, thou hast led captivity captive: thou hast received gifts for men; yea, *for* the rebellious also, that the LORD God might dwell *among them*. **Psalms 110:1** The LORD said unto my Lord, Sit thou at my right hand, until I make thine enemies thy footstool. **Psalms 110:5** The Lord at thy right hand shall strike through kings in the day of his wrath.

	Isaiah 9:6 For unto us a child is born, unto us a son is given: and the government shall be upon his shoulder: and his name shall be called Wonderful, Counseller, The mighty God, The everlasting Father, The Prince of Peace.
	Isaiah 60:16 Thou shalt also suck the milk of the Gentiles, and shalt suck the breast of kings: and thou shalt know that I the LORD *am* thy Saviour and thy Redeemer, the mighty One of Jacob.
	Daniel 7:9 I beheld till the thrones were cast down, and the Ancient of days did sit, whose garment *was* white as snow, and the hair of his head like the pure wool: his throne *was like* the fiery flame, *and* his wheels *as* burning fire.
	Zechraiah 3:1 And he shewed me Joshua the high priest standing before the angel of the LORD, and Satan standing at his right hand to resist him.
	Genesis 41:38 And Pharaoh said unto his servants, Can we find such a one as this is, **a man in whom the Spirit of God is**?
	Numbers 11:17 And I will come down and talk with thee there: and I will take of **the spirit which is upon thee**, and will put it upon them; and they shall bear the burden of the people with thee, that thou bear it not thyself alone.
	Numbers 11:25 And the LORD came down in a cloud, and spake unto him, **and took of the spirit that was upon him, and gave it unto the seventy elders**: and it came to pass, that, when the spirit rested upon them, they prophesied, and did not cease.
	Numbers 27:18 And the LORD said unto Moses, Take thee Joshua the son of Nun, a man in whom is the spirit, and lay thine hand upon him;
	Isaiah 11:2 And the spirit of the LORD shall rest upon him, the spirit of wisdom and understanding, the spirit of counsel and might, the spirit of knowledge and of the fear of the LORD;
	Micah 3:8 But truly I am full of power by the spirit of the LORD, and of judgment, and of might, to declare unto Jacob his transgression, and to Israel his sin.
Acts 7:59 And they stoned Stephen, calling upon *God*, and saying, Lord Jesus, receive my spirit.	**Psalms 31:5** Into thine hand I commit my spirit: thou hast redeemed me, O LORD God of truth. **Ecclesiastes 12:7** Then shall the dust return to the earth as it was: and **the spirit shall return unto God** who gave it. **See 1 Thessalonians 5:23 "Body, soul, and spirit"**
Acts 7:60 And he kneeled down, and cried with a loud voice, Lord, lay not this sin to their charge. And when he had said this, he fell asleep.	**Ezekiel 22:30** And I sought for a man among them, that should make up the hedge, and **stand in the gap** before me for the land, that I should not destroy it: but I found none.
Acts 8:2 And devout men carried Stephen *to his burial*, and made great lamentation over him.	**Genesis 23:2** And Sarah died in Kirjatharba; the same *is* Hebron in the land of Canaan: and Abraham came to mourn for Sarah, and to weep for her. **Genesis 50:10** And they came to the threshingfloor of Atad, which *is* beyond Jordan, and there they mourned with a great and very sore lamentation: and he made a mourning for his father seven days.

	2 Samuel 3:31 And David said to Joab, and to all the people that *were* with him, Rend your clothes, and gird you with sackcloth, and mourn before Abner. And king David *himself* followed the bier.
Acts 8:9 But there was a certain man, called Simon, which beforetime in the same city used sorcery, and bewitched the people of Samaria, giving out that himself was some great one:	**Deuteronomy 18:10-11** There shall not be found among you *any one* that maketh his son or his daughter to pass through the fire, *or* that useth divination, *or* an observer of times, or an enchanter, or a witch, 11 Or a charmer, or a consulter with familiar spirits, or a wizard, or a necromancer.
Acts 8:16 For as yet he was fallen upon none of them: only they were **baptized in the name of the Lord Jesus**.)	See Acts 2:38 "Water baptism"
Acts 8:24 Then answered Simon, and said, Pray ye to the Lord for me, that none of these things which ye have spoken come upon me.	**Numbers 21:7** Therefore the people came to Moses, and said, We have sinned, for we have spoken against the LORD, and against thee; pray unto the LORD, that he take away the serpents from us. And Moses prayed for the people.
Acts 8:27 And he arose and went: and, behold, a man of **Ethiopia**, an eunuch of great authority under Candace queen of the Ethiopians, who had the charge of all her treasure, and had come to Jerusalem for to worship,	**Ezekiel 30:4-5** And the sword shall come upon Egypt, and great pain shall be in **Ethiopia**, when the slain shall fall in Egypt, and they shall take away her multitude, and her foundations shall be broken down. 5 **Ethiopia**, and Libya, and Lydia, and all the mingled people, and Chub, and the men of the land that is in league, shall fall with them by the sword. **Ezekiel 38:5** Persia, **Ethiopia**, and Libya with them; all of them with shield and helmet:
Acts 8:32-33 The place of the scripture which he read was this, He was led as a sheep to the slaughter; and like a lamb dumb before his shearer, so opened he not his mouth: In his humiliation his judgment was taken away: and who shall declare his generation? for his life is taken from the earth.	**Isaiah 53:7-8** He was oppressed, and he was afflicted, yet he opened not his mouth: he is brought as a lamb to the slaughter, and as a sheep before her shearers is dumb, so he openeth not his mouth. He was taken from prison and from judgment: and who shall declare his generation? for he was cut off out of the land of the living: for the transgression of my people was he stricken. **Jeremiah 11:19** But I *was* like a lamb *or* an ox *that* is brought to the slaughter; and I knew not that they had devised devices against me, *saying*, Let us destroy the tree with the fruit thereof, and let us cut him off from the land of the living, that his name may be no more remembered.
Acts 8:39 And when they were come up out of the water, the **Spirit of the Lord** caught away Philip, that the eunuch saw him no more: and he went on his way rejoicing.	**Isaiah 11:2** And the spirit of the LORD shall rest upon him, the spirit of wisdom and understanding, the spirit of counsel and might, the spirit of knowledge and of the fear of the LORD; **Isaiah 61:1-2** The Spirit of the Lord GOD *is* upon me; because the LORD hath anointed me to preach good tidings unto the meek; he hath sent me to bind up the brokenhearted, to proclaim liberty to the captives, and the opening of the prison to *them that are* bound; To proclaim the acceptable year of the LORD, and the day of vengeance of our God; to comfort all that mourn;
Acts 9:5 And he said, Who art thou, Lord? And the Lord said, I am Jesus whom thou persecutest: *it is* hard for thee to kick against the **pricks**.	**Numbers 33:55** But if ye will not drive out the inhabitants of the land from before you; then it shall come to pass, that those which ye let remain of them *shall be* **pricks** in your eyes, and thorns in your sides, and shall vex you in the land wherein ye dwell.
Acts 9:7 And the men which journeyed with him stood speechless, hearing a voice, but seeing no man.	**Daniel 10:7** And I Daniel alone saw the vision: for the men that were with me saw not the vision; but a great quaking fell upon them, so that they fled to hide themselves.
Acts 9:9 And he was **three days** without	See Matthew 17:21 "Fasting"

sight, and **neither did eat nor drink**.	
Acts 9:11 And the **Lord** *said* unto him, Arise, and go into the street which is called Straight, and enquire in the house of Judas for *one* called Saul, of Tarsus: for, behold, he prayeth,	**See 1 Corinthians 12:8 "Word of Knowledge"**
Acts 9:25 Then the disciples took him by night, and let *him* down by the wall in a basket.	**Joshua 2:15** Then she let them down by a cord through the window: for her house *was* upon the town wall, and she dwelt upon the wall. **1 Samuel 19:12** So Michal let David down through a window: and he went, and fled, and escaped.
Acts 9:31 Then had the churches rest throughout all Judaea and Galilee and Samaria, and were edified; and walking in the fear of the Lord, and in the comfort of the Holy Ghost, were multiplied.	**Malachi 3:16** Then they that feared the LORD spake often one to another: and the LORD hearkened, and heard *it,* and a book of remembrance was written before him for them that feared the LORD, and that thought upon his name.
Acts 9:36 Now there was at Joppa a certain disciple named Tabitha, which by interpretation is called Dorcas: this woman was full of good works and **almsdeeds** which she did.	**See 1 John 3:17 "Poor"**
Acts 10:2 *A* devout *man,* and one that feared God with all his house, which **gave much alms to the people**, and prayed to God alway. **Acts 10:4** And when he looked on him, he was afraid, and said, What is it, Lord? And he said unto him, Thy prayers and thine **alms** are come up for a memorial before God.	**See 1 John 3:17 "Poor"**
Acts 10:9 On the morrow, as they went on their journey, and drew nigh unto the city, Peter went up upon the housetop to pray about the sixth hour:	**2 Kings 4:33** He went in therefore, and shut the door upon them twain, and prayed unto the LORD.
Acts 10:10-17 And he became very hungry, and would have eaten: but while they made ready, he fell into a trance, 11 And **saw heaven opened, and a certain vessel descending unto him, as it had been a great sheet knit at the four corners, and let down to the earth:** 12 **Wherein were all manner of fourfooted beasts of the earth, and wild beasts, and creeping things, and fowls of the air.** 13 **And there came a voice to him, Rise, Peter; kill, and eat.** 14 **But Peter said, Not so, Lord; for I have never eaten any thing that is common or <u>unclean</u>.** 15 **And the voice** *spake* **unto him again the second time, What God hath cleansed, *that* call not thou common.** 16 **This was done thrice: and the vessel was received up**	**Leviticus 11:4** Nevertheless these shall ye not eat of them that chew the cud, or of them that divide the hoof: *as* the camel, because he cheweth the cud, but divideth not the hoof; he *is* **unclean** unto you. **Deuteronomy 14:7** Nevertheless these ye shall not eat of them that chew the cud, or of them that divide the cloven hoof; *as* the camel, and the hare, and the coney: for they chew the cud, but divide not the hoof; *therefore* they *are* **unclean** unto you. **Deuteronomy 14:2-21** **Deuteronomy 15:22** Thou shalt eat it within thy gates: **the unclean and the clean** *person shall eat it* alike, as the roebuck, and as the hart. **See 1 Corinthians 12:8 "Word of Knowledge"**

again into heaven. 17 Now while Peter doubted in himself what this vision which he had seen should mean, behold, the men which were sent from Cornelius had made enquiry for Simon's house, and stood before the gate,	
Acts 10:28 And he said unto them, Ye know how that it is an unlawful thing for a man that is a Jew to keep company, or come unto one of another nation; but God hath shewed me that I should not call any man common or unclean.	**Exodus 23:32** Thou shalt make no covenant with them, nor with their gods. **Exodus 34:15** Lest thou make a covenant with the inhabitants of the land, and they go a whoring after their gods, and do sacrifice unto their gods, and *one* call thee, and thou eat of his sacrifice; **Numbers 33:52** Then ye shall drive out all the inhabitants of the land from before you, and destroy all their pictures, and destroy all their molten images, and quite pluck down all their high places: **Deuteronomy 7:2** And when the LORD thy God shall deliver them before thee; thou shalt smite them, *and* utterly destroy them; thou shalt make no covenant with them, nor shew mercy unto them: **Joshua 11:11** And they smote all the souls that *were* therein with the edge of the sword, utterly destroying *them*: there was not any left to breathe: and he burnt Hazor with fire. **Isaiah 52:11-12** Depart ye, depart ye, go ye out from thence, touch no unclean thing; go ye out of the midst of her; be ye clean, that bear the vessels of the LORD. 12 For ye shall not go out with haste, nor go by flight: for the LORD will go before you; and the God of Israel will be your rereward.
Acts 10:30 And Cornelius said, Four days ago I was **fasting** until this hour; and at the ninth hour I prayed in my house, and, behold, a man stood before me in bright clothing,	**See Matthew 17:21 "Fasting"**
Acts 10:31 And said, Cornelius, thy **prayer** is heard, and thine **alms** are had in remembrance in the sight of God.	**See Matthew 17:21 "Prayer"** **See 1 John 3:17 "Poor"**
Acts 10:34 Then Peter opened *his* mouth, and said, Of a truth I perceive that God is no respecter of persons:	**Deuteronomy 10:17** For the LORD your God *is* God of gods, and Lord of lords, a great God, a mighty, and a terrible, which regardeth not persons, nor taketh reward: **2 Chronicles 19:7** Wherefore now let the fear of the LORD be upon you; take heed and do *it*: for *there is* no iniquity with the LORD our God, nor respect of persons, nor taking of gifts. **Job 34:19** *How much less to him* that accepteth not the persons of princes, nor regardeth the rich more than the poor? for they all *are* the work of his hands.
Acts 10:35 But in every nation he that feareth him, and worketh righteousness, is accepted with him.	**Isaiah 56:6** Also the sons of the stranger, that join themselves to the LORD, to serve him, and to love the name of the LORD, to be his servants, every one that keepeth the sabbath from polluting it, and taketh hold of my covenant;
Acts 10:36 The word which *God* sent unto the children of Israel, preaching peace by Jesus Christ: (he is Lord of all:)	**Isaiah 9:6** For unto us a child is born, unto us a son is given: and the government shall be upon his shoulder: and his name shall be called Wonderful, Counseller, The mighty God, The everlasting Father, The Prince of Peace.

	Isaiah 11:2 And the spirit of the LORD shall rest upon him, the spirit of wisdom and understanding, the spirit of counsel and might, the spirit of knowledge and of the fear of the LORD;
	Isaiah 22:22 And the key of the house of David will I lay upon his shoulder; so he shall open, and none shall shut; and he shall shut, and none shall open.
Acts 10:38 How God **anointed** Jesus of Nazareth with the Holy Ghost and with power: who went about doing good, and healing all that were oppressed of the devil; for God was with him.	**Job 2:6-7** And the LORD said unto Satan, Behold, he *is* in thine hand; but save his life. 7 So went **Satan** forth from the presence of the LORD, and **smote Job with sore boils from the sole of his foot unto his crown.**
	Psalms 40:13 Be pleased, O LORD, to deliver me: O LORD, make haste to help me.
	Isaiah 10:27 And it shall come to pass in that day, that his burden shall be taken away from off thy shoulder, and his yoke from off thy neck, and **the yoke shall be destroyed because of the anointing.**
	Isaiah 61:1 The Spirit of the Lord GOD *is* upon me; because the LORD hath anointed me to preach good tidings unto the meek; he hath sent me to bind up the brokenhearted, to proclaim liberty to the captives, and the opening of the prison to *them that are* bound;
Acts 10:42 And he commanded us to preach unto the people, and to testify that it is he which was ordained of God *to be* the **Judge** of quick and dead.	**Isaiah 33:22** For the LORD *is* our **judge**, the LORD *is* our lawgiver, the LORD *is* our king; he will save us.
Acts 10:43 To him give all the prophets witness, that through his name whosoever believeth in him shall receive remission of sins.	**Deuteronomy 18:15** The LORD thy God will raise up unto thee a Prophet from the midst of thee, of thy brethren, like unto me; unto him ye shall hearken;
	Deuteronomy 18:18 I will raise them up a Prophet from among their brethren, like unto thee, and will put my words in his mouth; and he shall speak unto them all that I shall command him.
	Isaiah 7:14 Therefore the Lord himself shall give you a sign; Behold, a virgin shall conceive, and bear a son, and shall call his name Immanuel.
	Isaiah 9:6 For unto us a child is born, unto us a son is given: and the government shall be upon his shoulder: and his name shall be called Wonderful, Counseller, The mighty God, The everlasting Father, The Prince of Peace.
	Isaiah 40:10 Behold, the Lord GOD will come with strong *hand*, and his arm shall rule for him: behold, his reward *is* with him, and his work before him.
	Jeremiah 23:5 Behold, the days come, saith the LORD, that I will raise unto David a righteous Branch, and a King shall reign and prosper, and shall execute judgment and justice in the earth.
	Ezekiel 34:23 And I will set up one shepherd over them, and he shall feed them, *even* my servant David; he shall feed them, and he shall be their shepherd.
	Daniel 9:24 Seventy weeks are determined upon thy people and upon thy holy city, to finish the transgression, and to make an end of sins, and to make reconciliation for iniquity, and to bring in everlasting righteousness, and to seal up the vision and prophecy,

	and to anoint the most Holy.
Acts 10:47 Can any man forbid water, that these should not be baptized, which have received the Holy Ghost as well as we?	**Exodus 40:12** And thou shalt bring Aaron and his sons unto the door of the tabernacle of the congregation, and wash them with water. **See John 3:5 and Acts 2:38**
Acts 11:3 Saying, Thou wentest in to men uncircumcised, and didst eat with them.	**Exodus 23:32** Thou shalt make no covenant with them, nor with their gods. **Exodus 34:15** Lest thou make a covenant with the inhabitants of the land, and they go a whoring after their gods, and do sacrifice unto their gods, and *one* call thee, and thou eat of his sacrifice; **Numbers 33:52** Then ye shall drive out all the inhabitants of the land from before you, and destroy all their pictures, and destroy all their molten images, and quite pluck down all their high places: **Deuteronomy 7:2** And when the LORD thy God shall deliver them before thee; thou shalt smite them, *and* utterly destroy them; thou shalt make no covenant with them, nor shew mercy unto them: **Joshua 11:11** And they smote all the souls that *were* therein with the edge of the sword, utterly destroying *them*: there was not any left to breathe: and he burnt Hazor with fire. **Isaiah 52:11-12** Depart ye, depart ye, go ye out from thence, touch no unclean thing; go ye out of the midst of her; be ye clean, that bear the vessels of the LORD. 12 For ye shall not go out with haste, nor go by flight: for the LORD will go before you; and the God of Israel will be your rereward.
Acts 11:8 But I said, Not so, Lord: for nothing common or unclean hath at any time entered into my mouth.	**Leviticus 11:4** Nevertheless these shall ye not eat of them that chew the cud, or of them that divide the hoof: *as* the camel, because he cheweth the cud, but divideth not the hoof; he *is* unclean unto you. **Deuteronomy 14:7** Nevertheless these ye shall not eat of them that chew the cud, or of them that divide the cloven hoof; *as* the camel, and the hare, and the coney: for they chew the cud, but divide not the hoof; *therefore* they *are* unclean unto you.
Acts 11:26 And when he had found him, he brought him unto Antioch. And it came to pass, that a whole year they assembled themselves with the church, and taught much people. And the disciples were called Christians first in Antioch.	**Numbers 6:27** And they shall put my name upon the children of Israel; and I will bless them. **See Ephesians 4:11 "Teach – Teachers"**
Acts 11:30 Which also they did, and sent it to the **elders** by the hands of Barnabas and Saul.	**See 1 Peter 5:1 "Elders"**
Acts 12:4 And when he had apprehended him, he put *him* in prison, and delivered *him* to four quaternions of soldiers to keep him; intending after **Easter** to bring him forth to the people.	**Leviticus 23:5-6** In the fourteenth *day* of the first month at even *is* the **LORD's passover**. 6 And on the fifteenth day of the same month *is* the feast of unleavened bread unto the LORD: seven days ye must eat unleavened bread.
Acts 12:5 Peter therefore was kept in prison: but **prayer** was made without	**See Matthew 17:21 "Prayer"**

ceasing of the church unto God for him.	
Acts 12:11 And when Peter was come to himself, he said, Now I know of a surety, that the Lord hath sent **his angel**, and hath delivered me out of the hand of Herod, and *from* all the expectation of the people of the Jews.	**Daniel 6:22-23** My God hath sent **his angel**, and hath shut the lions' mouths, that they have not hurt me: forasmuch as before him innocency was found in me; and also before thee, O king, have I done no hurt. 23 Then was the king exceeding glad for him, and commanded that they should take Daniel up out of the den. So Daniel was taken up out of the den, and no manner of hurt was found upon him, because he believed in his God. **See Hebrews 13:2 "Angels"**
Acts 12:23 And immediately the **angel** of the Lord smote him, because he gave not God the glory: and he was eaten of worms, and gave up the ghost.	**See Hebrews 13:2 "Angels"**
Acts 13:2-3 As they ministered to the Lord, and **fasted**, the Holy Ghost said, Separate me Barnabas and Saul for the work whereunto I have called them. 2 And when they had **fasted** and prayed, and laid their hands on them, they sent them away.	**See Matthew 17:21 "Fasting"**
Acts 13:6 And when they had gone through the isle unto Paphos, they found a certain sorcerer, a **false prophet**, a Jew, whose name *was* Barjesus:	**Deuteronomy 18:10-11** There shall not be found among you *any one* that maketh his son or his daughter to pass through the fire, *or* that useth divination, *or* an observer of times, or an enchanter, or a witch, 11 Or a charmer, or a consulter with familiar spirits, or a wizard, or a necromancer. **See 2 Peter 2:1 "False prophets"**
Acts 13:8 But Elymas the sorcerer (for so is his name by interpretation) withstood them, seeking to turn away the deputy from the faith.	**Exodus 7:11-12** Then Pharaoh also called the wise men and the sorcerers: now the magicians of Egypt, they also did in like manner with their enchantments. 12 For they cast down every man his rod, and they became serpents: but Aaron's rod swallowed up their rods.
Acts 13:11 And now, behold, the hand of the Lord *is* upon thee, and thou shalt be blind, not seeing the sun for a season. And immediately there fell on him a mist and a darkness; and he went about seeking some to lead him by the hand.	**2 Kings 2:23-24** And he went up from thence unto Bethel: and as he was going up by the way, there came forth little children out of the city, and mocked him, and said unto him, Go up, thou bald head; go up, thou bald head. 24 And he turned back, and looked on them, and cursed them in the name of the LORD. And there came forth two she bears out of the wood, and tare forty and two children of them.
Acts 13:14 and they having gone through from Perga, came to Antioch of Pisidia, and having gone into the synagogue on the **sabbath**-day, they sat down,	**See Colossians 2:16 "Sabbath"**
Acts 13:17 The God of this people of Israel chose our fathers, and exalted the people when they dwelt as strangers in the land of Egypt, and with an high arm brought he them out of it.	**Exodus 1:1-5** Now these *are* the names of the children of Israel, which came into Egypt; every man and his household came with Jacob. 2 Reuben, Simeon, Levi, and Judah, 3 Issachar, Zebulun, and Benjamin, 4 Dan, and Naphtali, Gad, and Asher. 5 And all the souls that came out of the loins of Jacob were seventy souls: for Joseph was in Egypt *already*. **Exodus 12:37** And the children of Israel journeyed from Rameses to Succoth, about six hundred thousand on foot *that were* men, beside children. **Isaiah 1:2** Hear, O heavens, and give ear, O earth: for the LORD

	hath spoken, I have nourished and brought up children, and they have rebelled against me.
Acts 13:18 And about the time of forty years suffered he their manners in the wilderness.	**Exodus 16:35** And the children of Israel did eat manna forty years, until they came to a land inhabited; they did eat manna, until they came unto the borders of the land of Canaan. **Numbers 14:33** And your children shall wander in the wilderness forty years, and bear your whoredoms, until your carcases be wasted in the wilderness. **Deuteronomy 1:31** And in the wilderness, where thou hast seen how that the LORD thy God bare thee, as a man doth bear his son, in all the way that ye went, until ye came into this place. **Psalm 95:10** Forty years long was I grieved with *this* generation, and said, It *is* a people that do err in their heart, and they have not known my ways:
Acts 13:19 And when he had destroyed seven nations in the land of Chanaan, he divided their land to them by lot.	**Deuteronomy 7:1** When the LORD thy God shall bring thee into the land whither thou goest to possess it, and hath cast out many nations before thee, the Hittites, and the Girgashites, and the Amorites, and the Canaanites, and the Perizzites, and the Hivites, and the Jebusites, seven nations greater and mightier than thou; **Joshua 14:2** By lot *was* their inheritance, as the LORD commanded by the hand of Moses, for the nine tribes, and *for* the half tribe.
Acts 13:20 And after that he gave *unto them* judges about the space of four hundred and fifty years, until Samuel the prophet.	**Judges 2:16** Nevertheless the LORD raised up judges, which delivered them out of the hand of those that spoiled them. **1 Samuel 3:20** And all Israel from Dan even to Beersheba knew that Samuel *was* established *to be* a prophet of the LORD.
Acts 13:21 And afterward they desired a king: and God gave unto them Saul the son of Cis, a man of the tribe of Benjamin, by the space of forty years.	**1 Samuel 8:5** And said unto him, Behold, thou art old, and thy sons walk not in thy ways: now make us a king to judge us like all the nations. **1 Samuel 10:21** When he had caused the tribe of Benjamin to come near by their families, the family of Matri was taken, and Saul the son of Kish was taken: and when they sought him, he could not be found. **Hosea 13:11** I gave thee a king in mine anger, and took *him* away in my wrath.
Acts 13:22 And when he had removed him, he raised up unto them David to be their king; to whom also he gave testimony, and said, I have found David the *son* of Jesse, a man after mine own heart, which shall fulfil all my will.	**1 Samuel 13:14** But now thy kingdom shall not continue: the LORD hath sought him a man after his own heart, and the LORD hath commanded him *to be* captain over his people, because thou hast not kept *that* which the LORD commanded thee. **1 Chronicles 10:14** And enquired not of the LORD: therefore he slew him, and turned the kingdom unto **David the son of Jesse.** **Psalms 89:20** I have found David my servant; with my holy oil have I anointed him: **Isaiah 44:28** That saith of Cyrus, *He is* my shepherd, and shall perform all my pleasure: even saying to Jerusalem, Thou shalt be built; and to the temple, Thy foundation shall be laid.
Acts 13:23 Of this man's seed hath God according to *his* promise raised unto Israel a Saviour, Jesus:	**Job 19:25** For I know *that* my redeemer liveth, and *that* he shall stand at the latter *day* upon the earth: **Isaiah 9:6** For unto us a child is born, unto us a son is given: and the government shall be upon his shoulder: and his name shall be called Wonderful, Counsellor, The mighty God, The everlasting

	Father, The Prince of Peace. **Isaiah 60:16** Thou shalt also suck the milk of the Gentiles, and shalt suck the breast of kings: and thou shalt know that I the LORD *am* thy Saviour and thy Redeemer, the mighty One of Jacob.
Acts 13:27 for those dwelling in Jerusalem, and their chiefs, this one not having known, also the voices of the prophets, which every **sabbath** are being read--having judged *him* --did fulfil,	**See Colossians 2:16 "Sabbath"**
Acts 13:32 And we declare unto you glad tidings, how that the promise which was made unto the fathers,	**Genesis 22:18** And in thy seed shall all the nations of the earth be blessed; because thou hast obeyed my voice. **Isaiah 7:14** Therefore the Lord himself shall give you a sign; Behold, a virgin shall conceive, and bear a son, and shall call his name Immanuel. **Isaiah 9:6** For unto us a child is born, unto us a son is given: and the government shall be upon his shoulder: and his name shall be called Wonderful, Counseller, The mighty God, The everlasting Father, The Prince of Peace. **Jeremiah 23:5** Behold, the days come, saith the LORD, that I will raise unto David a righteous Branch, and a King shall reign and prosper, and shall execute judgment and justice in the earth. **Ezekiel 34:23** And I will set up one shepherd over them, and he shall feed them, *even* my servant David; he shall feed them, and he shall be their shepherd. **Ezekiel 37:24** And David my servant *shall be* king over them; and they all shall have one shepherd: they shall also walk in my judgments, and observe my statutes, and do them. **Daniel 9:24-27** Seventy weeks are determined upon thy people and upon thy holy city, to finish the transgression, and to make an end of sins, and to make reconciliation for iniquity, and to bring in everlasting righteousness, and to seal up the vision and prophecy, and to anoint the most Holy. 25 Know therefore and understand, *that* from the going forth of the commandment to restore and to build Jerusalem unto the Messiah the Prince *shall be* seven weeks, and threescore and two weeks: the street shall be built again, and the wall, even in troublous times. 26 And after threescore and two weeks shall Messiah be cut off, but not for himself: and the people of the prince that shall come shall destroy the city and the sanctuary; and the end thereof *shall be* with a flood, and unto the end of the war desolations are determined. 27 And he shall confirm the covenant with many for one week: and in the midst of the week he shall cause the sacrifice and the oblation to cease, and for the overspreading of abominations he shall make *it* desolate, even until the consummation, and that determined shall be poured upon the desolate.
Acts 13:33 God hath fulfilled the same unto us their children, in that he hath raised up Jesus again; as it is also written in the second psalm, Thou art my Son, **this day have I begotten thee.**	**Psalms 2:7** I will declare the decree: the LORD hath said unto me, Thou *art* my Son; this day have I begotten thee. **Psalms 89:27** Also I will make him *my* **firstborn**, higher than the kings of the earth. **Jeremiah 31:9** They shall come with weeping, and with supplications will I lead them: I will cause them to walk by the rivers of waters in a straight way, wherein they shall not stumble:

	for I am a father to Israel, and Ephraim is my **firstborn**.
Acts 13:34 And as concerning that he raised him up from the dead, *now* no more to return to corruption, he said on this wise, I will give you the sure mercies of David.	**Isaiah 55:3** Incline your ear, and come unto me: hear, and your soul shall live; and I will make an everlasting covenant with you, *even* the sure mercies of David.
Acts 13:35 Wherefore he saith also in another *psalm*, Thou shalt not suffer thine Holy One to see corruption.	**Psalms 16:10** For Thou dost not leave my soul to Sheol, Nor givest thy saintly one to see corruption.
Acts 13:36 For David, after he had served his own generation by the will of God, fell on sleep, and was laid unto his fathers, and saw corruption:	**1 Kings 2:10** So David slept with his fathers, and was buried in the city of David.
Acts 13:41 Behold, ye despisers, and wonder, and perish: for I work a work in your days, a work which ye shall in no wise believe, though a man declare it unto you.	**Isaiah 28:14** Wherefore hear the word of the LORD, ye scornful men, that rule this people which *is* in Jerusalem. **Habakkuk 1:5** Behold ye among the heathen, and regard, and wonder marvellously: for *I* will work a work in your days, *which* ye will not believe, though it be told *you*.
Acts 13:42 And having gone forth out of the synagogue of the Jews, the nations were calling upon *them* that on the next **sabbath** these sayings may be spoken to them, **Acts 13:44** And on the coming **sabbath**, almost all the city was gathered together to hear the word of God,	**See Colossians 2:16** "Sabbath"
Acts 13:46 Then Paul and Barnabas waxed bold, and said, It was necessary that the word of God should first have been spoken to you: but seeing ye put it from you, and judge yourselves unworthy of everlasting life, lo, we turn to the Gentiles.	**Exodus 32:10** Now therefore let me alone, that my wrath may wax hot against them, and that I may consume them: and I will make of thee a great nation. **Isaiah 55:5** Behold, thou shalt call a nation *that* thou knowest not, and nations *that* knew not thee shall run unto thee because of the LORD thy God, and for the Holy One of Israel; for he hath glorified thee.
Acts 13:47 For so hath the Lord commanded us, *saying*, I have set thee to be a light of the Gentiles, that thou shouldest be for salvation unto the ends of the earth.	**Isaiah 11:10** And in that day there shall be a root of Jesse, which shall stand for an ensign of the people; to it shall the Gentiles seek: and his rest shall be glorious. **Isaiah 42:6** I the LORD have called thee in righteousness, and will hold thine hand, and will keep thee, and give thee for a covenant of the people, for a light of the Gentiles; **Isaiah 49:6** And he said, It is a light thing that thou shouldest be my servant to raise up the tribes of Jacob, and to restore the preserved of Israel: I will also give thee for a light to the Gentiles, that thou mayest be my salvation unto the end of the earth.
Acts 14:10 Said with a loud voice, Stand upright on thy feet. And he leaped and walked.	**Isaiah 35:6** Then shall the lame *man* leap as an hart, and the tongue of the dumb sing: for in the wilderness shall waters break out, and streams in the desert.
Acts 14:15 And saying, Sirs, why do ye these things? We also are men of like passions with you, and preach unto you that ye should turn from these vanities unto the living God, which made heaven, and earth, and the sea, and all things that	**Genesis 1:1** In the beginning God created the heaven and the earth. **Exodus 20:11** For *in* six days the LORD made heaven and earth, the sea, and all that in them *is*, and rested the seventh day: wherefore the LORD blessed the sabbath day, and hallowed it.

are therein:	**Psalms 33:6** By the word of the LORD were the heavens made; and all the host of them by the breath of his mouth. **Psalms 124:8** Our help *is* in the name of the LORD, who made heaven and earth. **Psalms 146:6** Which made heaven, and earth, the sea, and all that therein *is:* which keepeth truth for ever: **Exodus 20:5 Thou shalt not bow down thyself to them**, nor serve them: for I the LORD thy God am a jealous God, visiting the iniquity of the fathers upon the children unto the third and fourth generation of them that hate me;
Acts 14:16 Who in times past suffered all nations to walk in their own ways.	**Psalms 81:12** So I gave them up unto their own hearts' lust: *and* they walked in their own counsels.
Acts 14:23 And when they had ordained them **elders** in every church, and had prayed with fasting, they commended them to the Lord, on whom they believed.	**See 1 Peter 5:1 "Elders"** **See Matthew 17:21 "Fasting"**
Acts 15:1 And certain men which came down from Judaea taught the brethren, *and said*, Except ye be circumcised after the manner of Moses, ye cannot be saved.	**Genesis 17:10-14** This *is* my covenant, which ye shall keep, between me and you and thy seed after thee; **Every man child among you shall be circumcised.** 11 **And ye shall circumcise the flesh of your foreskin; and it shall be a token of the covenant betwixt me and you.** 12 And he that is eight days old shall be circumcised among you, every man child in your generations, he that is born in the house, or bought with money of any stranger, which *is* not of thy seed. 13 He that is born in thy house, and he that is bought with thy money, must needs be circumcised: and my covenant shall be in your flesh for an everlasting covenant. 14 And **the uncircumcised man child whose flesh of his foreskin is not circumcised, that soul shall be cut off from his people; he hath broken my covenant.** **Leviticus 12:3** And in the eighth day the flesh of his foreskin shall be circumcised.
Acts 15:2 When therefore Paul and Barnabas had no small dissension and disputation with them, they determined that Paul and Barnabas, and certain other of them, should go up to Jerusalem unto the apostles and **elders** about this question.	**See 1 Peter 5:1 "Elders"**
Acts 15:4 And when they were come to Jerusalem, they were received of the church, and of the apostles and **elders**, and they declared all things that God had done with them.	**See 1 Peter 5:1 "Elders"**
Acts 15:6 And the apostles and **elders** came together for to consider of this matter.	**See 1 Peter 5:1 "Elders"**
Acts 15:8 And God, which knoweth the hearts, bare them witness, giving them the Holy Ghost, even as *he did* unto us;	**1 Chronicles 28:9** And thou, Solomon my son, know thou the God of thy father, and serve him with a perfect heart and with a willing mind: for the LORD searcheth all hearts, and understandeth all the imaginations of the thoughts: if thou seek

	him, he will be found of thee; but if thou forsake him, he will cast thee off for ever.

1 Chronicles 29:17 I know also, my God, that thou triest the heart, and hast pleasure in uprightness. As for me, in the uprightness of mine heart I have willingly offered all these things: and now have I seen with joy thy people, which are present here, to offer willingly unto thee.

Psalms 7:9 Oh let the wickedness of the wicked come to an end; but establish the just: for the righteous God trieth the hearts and reins.

Jeremiah 11:20 But, O LORD of hosts, that judgest righteously, that triest the reins and the heart, let me see thy vengeance on them: for unto thee have I revealed my cause.

Jeremiah 17:10 I the LORD search the heart, *I* try the reins, even to give every man according to his ways, *and* according to the fruit of his doings.

Jeremiah 20:12 But, O LORD of hosts, that triest the righteous, *and* seest the reins and the heart, let me see thy vengeance on them: for unto thee have I opened my cause. |
| **Acts 15:15-17** And to this agree the words of the prophets; as it is written, 16 After this I will return, and will build again **the tabernacle of David**, which is fallen down; and I will build again the ruins thereof, and I will set it up: 17 That the residue of men might seek after the Lord, and all the Gentiles, upon whom my name is called, saith the Lord, who doeth all these things. | **See Revelation 11:1 "Temple"**

Amos 9:11-15 In that day will I raise up the **tabernacle of David** that is fallen, and close up the breaches thereof; and I will raise up his ruins, and I will build it as in the days of old: 12 That they may possess the remnant of Edom, and of all the heathen, which are called by my name, saith the LORD that doeth this. 13 Behold, the days come, saith the LORD, that the plowman shall overtake the reaper, and the treader of grapes him that soweth seed; and the mountains shall drop sweet wine, and all the hills shall melt. 14 And I will bring again the captivity of my people of Israel, and they shall build the waste cities, and inhabit *them*; and they shall plant vineyards, and drink the wine thereof; they shall also make gardens, and eat the fruit of them. 15 And I will plant them upon their land, and **they shall no more be pulled up out of their land which I have given them**, saith the LORD thy God.

Isaiah 45:21   Look below |
| **Acts 15:18** Known unto God are all his works from the beginning of the world. | **Isaiah 45:21** Tell ye, and bring *them* near; yea, let them take counsel together: who hath declared this from ancient time? *who* hath told it from that time? *have* not I the LORD? and *there is* no God else beside me; a just God and a Saviour; *there is* none beside me. |
| **Acts 15:20** But that we write unto them, that they abstain from pollutions of idols, and *from* fornication, and *from* things strangled, and *from* blood. | **Genesis 9:4** But flesh with the life thereof, *which is* the blood thereof, shall ye not eat.

Exodus 20:13 Thou shalt not kill.

Exodus 20:14 Thou shalt not commit adultery.

Leviticus 3:17 *It shall be* a perpetual statute for your generations throughout all your dwellings, that ye eat neither fat nor blood.

Leviticus 7:26 Moreover ye shall eat no manner of blood, *whether it be* of fowl or of beast, in any of your dwellings.

Numbers 25:2 And they called the people unto the sacrifices of their gods: and the people did eat, and bowed down to their gods. |

	Deuteronomy 12:23 Only be sure that thou eat not the blood: for the blood *is* the life; and thou mayest not eat the life with the flesh. See Hebrews 9:22 "Sin remitted by blood" See Romans 1:24 "Sexual perversion"
Acts 15:21 for Moses from former generations in every city hath those preaching him--in the synagogues every sabbath being read.'	See Colossians 2:16 "Sabbath"
Acts 15:22 Then pleased it the apostles and **elders**, with the whole church, to send chosen men of their own company to Antioch with Paul and Barnabas; *namely*, Judas surnamed Barsabas, and Silas, chief men among the brethren:	See 1 Peter 5:1 "Elders"
Acts 15:23 And they wrote *letters* by them after this manner; The apostles and **elders** and brethren *send* greeting unto the brethren which are of the Gentiles in Antioch and Syria and Cilicia:	See 1 Peter 5:1 "Elders"
Acts 15:24 Forasmuch as we have heard, that certain which went out from us have troubled you with words, subverting your souls, saying, *Ye must* be circumcised, and keep the law: to whom we gave no *such* commandment:	**Genesis 17:10-14** This *is* my covenant, which ye shall keep, between me and you and thy seed after thee; **Every man child among you shall be circumcised. 11 And ye shall circumcise the flesh of your foreskin; and it shall be a token of the covenant betwixt me and you.** 12 And he that is eight days old shall be circumcised among you, every man child in your generations, he that is born in the house, or bought with money of any stranger, which *is* not of thy seed. 13 He that is born in thy house, and he that is bought with thy money, must needs be circumcised: and my covenant shall be in your flesh for an everlasting covenant. 14 And **the uncircumcised man child whose flesh of his foreskin is not circumcised, that soul shall be cut off from his people; he hath broken my covenant.**
Acts 15:25 It seemed good unto us, being assembled with **one accord**, to send chosen men unto you with our beloved Barnabas and Paul,	**Psalms 133:1** Behold, how good and how pleasant *it is* for brethren to dwell together in unity! **Amos 3:3** Can two walk together, except they be agreed?
Acts 15:28 For it seemed good to the Holy Ghost, and **to us**, to lay upon you no greater burden than these necessary things;	**Proverbs 11:14** Where no counsel *is,* the people fall: but in the multitude of counsellors *there is* safety. **Ecclesiastes 4:9-12** Two *are* better than one; because they have a good reward for their labour. 10 For if they fall, the one will lift up his fellow: but woe to him *that is* alone when he falleth; for *he hath* not another to help him up. 11 Again, if two lie together, then they have heat: but how can one be warm *alone?* 12 And if one prevail against him, two shall withstand him; and a threefold cord is not quickly broken.
Acts 15:35 Paul also and Barnabas continued in Antioch, **teaching** and preaching the word of the Lord, with many others also.	See Ephesians 4:11 "Teach – Teachers"
Acts 16:4 And as they went through the cities, they delivered them the decrees for to keep, that were ordained of the apostles and **elders** which were at	See 1 Peter 5:1 "Elders"

Jerusalem.	
Acts 16:13 And on the **Sabbath** we went out of the city by a river side, where prayer was wont to be made; and we sat down, and spake unto the women which resorted *thither*.	**See Colossians 2:16** "Sabbath"
Acts 16:15 And when she was baptized, and her household, she besought *us*, saying, If ye have judged me to be faithful to the Lord, come into my house, and abide *there*. And she constrained us.	**Genesis 19:3** And he pressed upon them greatly; and they turned in unto him, and entered into his house; and he made them a feast, and did bake unleavened bread, and they did eat. **Judges 19:21** So he brought him into his house, and gave provender unto the asses: and they washed their feet, and did eat and drink.
Acts 16:16 And it came to pass, as we went to prayer, a certain damsel possessed with a **spirit of divination** met us, which brought her masters much gain by soothsaying:	**Exodus 22:18** Thou shalt not suffer a witch to live **Leviticus 20:27** A man also or woman that hath a familiar spirit, or that is a wizard, shall surely be put to death: they shall stone them with stones: their blood *shall be* upon them. **Deuteronomy 18:10-11** There shall not be found among you any one that maketh his son or his daughter to pass through the fire, or that useth divination, or an observer of times, or an enchanter, or a witch, 11 Or a charmer, or a consulter with familiar spirits, or a wizard, or a necromancer. **1 Samuel 28:7** Then said Saul unto his servants, Seek me a woman that hath a familiar spirit, that I may go to her, and inquire of her. And his servants said to him, Behold, *there is* a woman that hath a familiar spirit at Endor. **Isaiah 8:19** And when they shall say unto you, Seek unto them that have familiar spirits, and unto wizards that peep, and that mutter: should not a people seek unto their God? for the living to the dead? **Isaiah 47:12-14** Stand now with thine enchantments, and with the multitude of thy sorceries, wherein thou hast laboured from thy youth; if so be thou shalt be able to profit, if so be thou mayest prevail. 13 Thou art wearied in the multitude of thy counsels. Let now the astrologers, the stargazers, the monthly prognosticators, stand up, and save thee from *these things* that shall come upon thee. 14 Behold, they shall be as stubble; the fire shall burn them; they shall not deliver themselves from the power of the flame: *there shall* not *be* a coal to warm at, *nor* fire to sit before it. **See Hebrews 13:2** "Good and bad angels"
Acts 16:17 The same followed Paul and us, and cried, saying, These men are the servants of the **most high God**, which shew unto us the way of salvation.	**Genesis 14:18** And Melchizedek king of Salem brought forth bread and wine: and he *was* the priest of the **most high God**. **Psalms 78:56** Yet they tempted and provoked the **most high God**, and kept not his testimonies: **Daniel 3:26** Then Nebuchadnezzar came near to the mouth of the burning fiery furnace, *and* spake, and said, Shadrach, Meshach, and Abednego, ye servants of the **most high God**, come forth, and come *hither*. Then Shadrach, Meshach, and Abednego, came forth of the midst of the fire.
Acts 16:20 And brought them to the magistrates, saying, These men, being Jews, do exceedingly trouble our city,	**1 Kings 18:17** And it came to pass, when Ahab saw Elijah, that Ahab said unto him, *Art* thou he that troubleth Israel? **Amos 7:10** Then Amaziah the priest of Bethel sent to Jeroboam king of Israel, saying, Amos hath conspired against thee in the

	midst of the house of Israel: the land is not able to bear all his words.
Acts 17:2 and according to the custom of Paul, he went in unto them, and for three **sabbaths** he was reasoning with them from the Writings,	**See Colossians 2:16 "Sabbath"**
Acts 17:11 These were more noble than those in Thessalonica, in that they received the word with all readiness of mind, and searched the **scriptures** daily, whether those things were so.	**Isaiah 34:16** Seek ye out of the book of the LORD, and read: no one of these shall fail, none shall want her mate: for my mouth it hath commanded, and his spirit it hath gathered them. **See Matthew 5:18 "Scriptures"**
Acts 17:16 Now while Paul waited for them at Athens, his spirit was stirred in him, when he saw the city wholly given to idolatry.	**Jeremiah 10:2** Thus saith the LORD, Learn not the way of the heathen, and be not dismayed at the signs of heaven; for the heathen are dismayed at them. **Jeremiah 50:38** A drought is upon her waters; and they shall be dried up: for it is the land of graven images, and they are mad upon *their* idols. **See 1 Thessalonians 5:23 "Body, soul, and spirit"**
Acts 17:22 Then Paul stood in the midst of Mars' hill, and said, *Ye* men of Athens, I perceive that in all things ye are too superstitious.	**Leviticus 20:23** And ye shall not walk in the manners of the nation, which I cast out before you: for they committed all these things, and therefore I abhorred them. **Jeremiah 10:2** Thus saith the LORD, Learn not the way of the heathen, and be not dismayed at the signs of heaven; for the heathen are dismayed at them.
Acts 17:24 God that made the world and all things therein, seeing that he is Lord of heaven and earth, dwelleth not in temples made with hands;	**Genesis 1:1** In the beginning God created the heaven and the earth. **Job 38:4** Where wast thou when I laid the foundations of the earth? declare, if thou hast understanding. **Psalms 33:6** By the word of the LORD were the heavens made; and all the host of them by the breath of his mouth. **Psalms 136:5** To him that by wisdom made the heavens: for his mercy *endureth* for ever. **Psalms 146:5-6** Happy *is he* that *hath* the God of Jacob for his help, whose hope *is* in the LORD his God: 6 Which made heaven, and earth, the sea, and all that therein *is*: which keepeth truth for ever: **Proverbs 8:29** When he gave to the sea his decree, that the waters should not pass his commandment: when he appointed the foundations of the earth:
Acts 17:25 Neither is worshipped with men's hands, as though he needed any thing, seeing he giveth to all life, and breath, and all things;	**Genesis 2:7** And the LORD God formed man *of* the dust of the ground, and breathed into his nostrils the breath of life; and man became a living soul.
Acts 17:26 And hath made of one blood all nations of men for to dwell on all the face of the earth, and hath determined the times before appointed, and the bounds of their habitation;	**Deuteronomy 32:8** When the most High divided to the nations their inheritance, when he separated the sons of Adam, he set the bounds of the people according to the number of the children of Israel.
Acts 17:29 Forasmuch then as we are	**Isaiah 40:18** To whom then will ye liken God? or what likeness

the offspring of God, we ought not to think that the Godhead is like unto gold, or silver, or stone, graven by art and man's device.	will ye compare unto him?
Acts 17:31 Because he hath appointed a day, in the which he will judge the world in righteousness by *that* man whom he hath ordained; *whereof* he hath given assurance unto all *men,* in that he hath raised him from the dead.	**Psalm 9:8** And he shall judge the world in righteousness, he shall minister judgment to the people in uprightness. **Psalms 96:13** Before the LORD: for he cometh, for he cometh to judge the earth: he shall judge the world with righteousness, and the people with his truth. **Psalms 98:9** Before the LORD; for he cometh to judge the earth: with righteousness shall he judge the world, and the people with equity. **See 1 Timothy 2:5 "God"**
Acts 18:4 and he was reasoning in the synagogue every sabbath, persuading both Jews and Greeks.	**See Colossians 2:16 "Sabbath"**
Acts 18:11 And he continued *there* a year and six months, **teaching the word of God among them.**	**See Ephesians 4:11 "Teach – Teachers"**
Acts 18:18 And Paul *after this* tarried *there* yet a good while, and then took his leave of the brethren, and sailed thence into Syria, and with him **Priscilla** and Aquila; having shorn *his* head in Cenchrea: for he had a vow.	**Numbers 6:18** And the Nazarite shall shave the head of his separation *at* the door of the tabernacle of the congregation, and shall take the hair of the head of his separation, and put *it* in the fire which *is* under the sacrifice of the peace offerings. **See Acts 18:26 "Woman's role"**
Acts 18:21 But bade them farewell, saying, I must by all means keep this feast that cometh in Jerusalem: but I will return again unto you, if God will. And he sailed from Ephesus.	**Leviticus 23:34** Speak unto the children of Israel, saying, The fifteenth day of this seventh month *shall be* the feast of tabernacles *for* seven days unto the LORD. **Nehemiah 8:14-15** And they found written in the law which the LORD had commanded by Moses, that the children of Israel should dwell in booths in the feast of the seventh month: 15 And that they should publish and proclaim in all their cities, and in Jerusalem, saying, Go forth unto the mount, and fetch olive branches, and pine branches, and myrtle branches, and palm branches, and branches of thick trees, to make booths, as *it is* written. **Zechariah 14:16** And it shall come to pass, *that* every one that is left of all the nations which came against Jerusalem shall even go up from year to year to worship the King, the LORD of hosts, and to keep the feast of tabernacles. **Zechariah 14:18-19** And if the family of Egypt go not up, and come not, that *have* no *rain*; there shall be the plague, wherewith the LORD will smite the heathen that come not up to keep the feast of tabernacles. 19 This shall be the punishment of Egypt, and the punishment of all nations that come not up to keep the feast of tabernacles.
Acts 18:26 And he began to speak boldly in the synagogue: whom when Aquila and **Priscilla** had heard, they took him unto *them,* and expounded unto him the way of God more perfectly.	**Proverbs 31:10-27** Who can find a virtuous woman? for her price *is* far above rubies. 11 The heart of her husband doth safely trust in her, so that he shall have no need of spoil. 12 She will do him good and not evil all the days of her life. 13 She seeketh wool, and flax, and worketh willingly with her hands. 14 She is like the merchants' ships; she bringeth her food from afar.

	15 She riseth also while it is yet night, and giveth meat to her household, and a portion to her maidens. 16 She considereth a field, and buyeth it: with the fruit of her hands she planteth a vineyard. 17 She girdeth her loins with strength, and strengtheneth her arms. 18 She perceiveth that her merchandise *is* good: her candle goeth not out by night. 19 She layeth her hands to the spindle, and her hands hold the distaff. 20 She stretcheth out her hand to the poor; yea, she reacheth forth her hands to the needy. 21 She is not afraid of the snow for her household: for all her household *are* clothed with scarlet. 22 She maketh herself coverings of tapestry; her clothing *is* silk and purple. 23 Her husband is known in the gates, when he sitteth among the elders of the land. 24 She maketh fine linen, and selleth *it;* and delivereth girdles unto the merchant. 25 Strength and honour *are* her clothing; and she shall rejoice in time to come. 26 **She openeth her mouth with wisdom**; and in her tongue *is* the law of kindness. 27 She looketh well to the ways of her household, and eateth not the bread of idleness.
Acts 19:5 When they heard *this,* they were baptized in the name of the Lord Jesus.	**See Acts 2:38 "Salvation"**
Acts 19:6 And when Paul had laid *his* hands upon them, the Holy Ghost came on them; and they spake with tongues, and **prophesied**.	**Genesis 41:38** And Pharaoh said unto his servants, Can we find such a one as this is, **a man in whom the Spirit of God is**? **Numbers 11:17** And I will come down and talk with thee there: and I will take of **the spirit which is upon thee**, and will put it upon them; and they shall bear the burden of the people with thee, that thou bear it not thyself alone. **Numbers 27:18** And the LORD said unto Moses, Take thee Joshua the son of Nun, a man in whom is the spirit, and lay thine hand upon him; **Isaiah 11:2** And the spirit of the LORD shall rest upon him, the spirit of wisdom and understanding, the spirit of counsel and might, the spirit of knowledge and of the fear of the LORD; **Micah 3:8** But truly I am full of power by the spirit of the LORD, and of judgment, and of might, to declare unto Jacob his transgression, and to Israel his sin. **Numbers 11:25** And the LORD came down in a cloud, and spake unto him, **and took of the spirit that was upon him, and gave it unto the seventy elders**: and it came to pass, that, when the spirit rested upon them, they prophesied, and did not cease. See 1 Corinthians 12:10 "Prophecy"
Acts 19:19 Many of them also which used curious arts brought their books together, and burned them before all *men*: and they counted the price of them, and found *it* fifty thousand *pieces* of silver.	**Deuteronomy 18:10-11** There shall not be found among you *any one* that maketh his son or his daughter to pass through the fire, *or* that useth divination, *or* an observer of times, or an enchanter, or a witch, 11 Or a charmer, or a consulter with familiar spirits, or a wizard, or a necromancer.
Acts 19:20 So mightily grew the word of God and prevailed.	**Isaiah 55:11** So shall my word be that goeth forth out of my mouth: it shall not return unto me void, but it shall accomplish that which I please, and it shall prosper *in the thing* whereto I sent it.

Acts 19:21 After these things were ended, Paul purposed in the **spirit**, when he had passed through Macedonia and Achaia, to go to Jerusalem, saying, After I have been there, I must also see Rome.	See 1 Corinthians 12:8 "Word of Knowledge" See 1 Thessalonians 5:23 "Body, soul, and spirit"
Acts 19:26 Moreover ye see and hear, that not alone at Ephesus, but almost throughout all Asia, this Paul hath persuaded and turned away much people, saying that they be no gods, which are made with hands:	**Psalms 115:4-8** Their idols *are* silver and gold, the work of men's hands. 5 They have mouths, but they speak not: eyes have they, but they see not: 6 They have ears, but they hear not: noses have they, but they smell not: 7 They have hands, but they handle not: feet have they, but they walk not: neither speak they through their throat. 8 They that make them are like unto them; *so is* every one that trusteth in them.
Acts 20:6 And we sailed away from Philippi after the days of unleavened bread, and came unto them to Troas in five days; where we abode seven days.	**Leviticus 23:5-6** In the fourteenth *day* of the first month at even *is* the LORD's passover. 6 And on the fifteenth day of the same month *is* the feast of unleavened bread unto the LORD: seven days ye must eat unleavened bread.
Acts 20:10 And Paul went down, and fell on him, and embracing *him* said, Trouble not yourselves; for his life is in him.	**1 Kings 17:21-22** And he stretched himself upon the child three times, and cried unto the LORD, and said, O LORD my God, I pray thee, let this child's soul come into him again. **22** And the LORD heard the voice of Elijah; and the soul of the child came into him again, and he revived. **2 Kings 4:34** And he went up, and lay upon the child, and put his mouth upon his mouth, and his eyes upon his eyes, and his hands upon his hands: and he stretched himself upon the child; and the flesh of the child waxed warm.
Acts 20:16 For Paul had determined to sail by Ephesus, because he would not spend the time in Asia: for he hasted, if it were possible for him, to be at Jerusalem the day of Pentecost.	**Leviticus 23:15-16** And ye shall count unto you from the morrow after the sabbath, from the day that ye brought the sheaf of the wave offering; seven sabbaths shall be complete: 16 Even unto the morrow after the seventh sabbath shall ye number fifty days; and ye shall offer a new meat offering unto the LORD. **Deuteronomy 16:9** Seven weeks shalt thou number unto thee: begin to number the seven weeks from *such time as* thou beginnest *to put* the sickle to the corn.
Acts 20:17 And from Miletus he sent to Ephesus, and called the **elders** of the church.	See 1 Peter 5:1 "Elders"
Acts 20:20 *And* how I kept back nothing that was profitable *unto you*, but have shewed you, and have **taught you publickly, and from house to house,**	See Ephesians 4:11 "Teach – Teachers"
Acts 20:28 Take heed therefore unto yourselves, and to all the flock, over the which the Holy Ghost hath made you overseers, to feed the church of God, which **he hath purchased with his own blood.**	**Leviticus 17:11** For the life of the flesh is in the blood: and I have given it to you upon the altar to make an atonement for your souls: **for it is the blood that maketh an atonement for the soul.** See John 10:10 "Shepherd" See John 4:42 "Saviour" See Matthew 26:28 "Atonement" See 2 Peter 2:1 "False prophets"
Acts 20:35 I have shewed you all things, how that so labouring ye ought to support the weak, and to remember the words of the Lord Jesus, how he said, It is more blessed to give than to	See Luke 6:38 "Prosperity"

receive.	
Acts 21:9 And the same man had four daughters, virgins, which did **prophesy**.	**Joel 2:28** And it shall come to pass afterward, *that* I will pour out my spirit upon all flesh; and your sons and your daughters shall prophesy, your old men shall dream dreams, your young men shall see visions: **See 1 Corinthians 12:10** "Prophecy"
Acts 21:18 And the *day* following Paul went in with us unto James; and all the **elders** were present.	**See 1 Peter 5:1** "Elders"
Acts 21:24 Them take, and purify thyself with them, and be at charges with them, that they may shave *their* heads: and all may know that those things, whereof they were informed concerning thee, are nothing; but *that* thou thyself also walkest orderly, and keepest the law	**Numbers 6:7** He shall not make himself unclean for his father, or for his mother, for his brother, or for his sister, when they die: because the consecration of his God *is* upon his head. **Judges 13:7** But he said unto me, Behold, thou shalt conceive, and bear a son; and now drink no wine nor strong drink, neither eat any unclean *thing:* for the child shall be a Nazarite to God from the womb to the day of his death.
Acts 21:25 As touching the Gentiles which believe, we have written *and* concluded that they observe no such thing, save only that they keep themselves from *things* offered to idols, and from blood, and from strangled, and from fornication.	**Genesis 9:4** But flesh with the life thereof, *which is* the blood thereof, shall ye not eat. **2 Chronicles 21:11** Moreover he made high places in the mountains of Judah, and caused the inhabitants of Jerusalem to commit fornication, and compelled Judah *thereto*.
Acts 22:5 As also the high priest doth bear me witness, and all the estate of the **elder**: from whom also I received letters unto the brethren, and went to Damascus, to bring them which were there bound unto Jerusalem, for to be punished.	**See 1 Peter 5:1** "Elders"
Acts 22:16 And now why tarriest thou? arise, and be baptized, and wash away thy sins, calling on the name of the Lord.	**Psalms 51:2** Wash me throughly from mine iniquity, and cleanse me from my sin. **Isaiah 1:16** Wash you, make you clean; put away the evil of your doings from before mine eyes; cease to do evil; **See Acts 2:38**
Acts 23:2 And the high priest Ananias commanded them that stood by him to smite him on the mouth.	**1 Kings 22:24** But Zedekiah the son of Chenaanah went near, and smote Micaiah on the cheek, and said, Which way went the Spirit of the LORD from me to speak unto thee? **Jeremiah 20:2** Then Pashur smote Jeremiah the prophet, and put him in the stocks that *were* in the high gate of Benjamin, which *was* by the house of the LORD.
Acts 23:3 Then said Paul unto him, God shall smite thee, *thou* whited wall: for sittest thou to judge me after the law, and commandest me to be smitten contrary to the law?	**Deuteronomy 17:9** And thou shalt come unto the priests the Levites, and unto the judge that shall be in those days, and inquire; and they shall shew thee the sentence of judgment:
Acts 23:5 Then said Paul, I wist not, brethren, that he was the high priest: for it is written, Thou shalt not speak evil of the ruler of thy people.	**Exodus 22:28** Thou shalt not revile the gods, nor curse the ruler of thy people.

Acts 23:11 And the night following the Lord stood by him, and said, Be of good cheer, Paul: for as thou hast testified of me in Jerusalem, so must thou bear witness also at Rome.	**See 1 Corinthians 12:8 "Word of Knowledge"**
Acts 23:14 And they came to the chief priests and elders, and said, We have bound ourselves under a great curse, that we will eat nothing until we have slain Paul.	**See 1 Peter 5:1 "Elders"**
Acts 24:1 And after five days Ananias the high priest descended with the **elders**, and *with* a certain orator *named* Tertullus, who informed the governor against Paul.	**See 1 Peter 5:1 "Elders"**
Acts 24:15 And have hope toward God, which they themselves also allow, that there shall be a resurrection of the dead, both of the just and unjust.	**Isaiah 26:19** Thy dead *men* shall live, *together with* my dead body shall they arise. Awake and sing, ye that dwell in dust: for thy dew *is as* the dew of herbs, and the earth shall cast out the dead. **Daniel 12:2** And many of them that sleep in the dust of the earth shall awake, some to everlasting life, and some to shame *and* everlasting contempt.
Acts 24:17 Now after many years **I came to bring alms to my nation**, and offerings.	**See 1 John 3:17 "Poor"**
Acts 25:15 About whom, when I was at Jerusalem, the chief priests and the **elders** of the Jews informed *me*, desiring to *have* judgment against him.	**See 1 Peter 5:1 "Elders"**
Acts 25:16 To whom I answered, It is not the manner of the Romans to deliver any man to die, before that he which is accused have the accusers face to face, and have licence to answer for himself concerning the crime laid against him.	**Deuteronomy 17:4** And it be told thee, and thou hast heard *of it*, and inquired diligently, and, behold, *it be* true, *and* the thing certain, *that* such abomination is wrought in Israel:
Acts 26:6 And now I stand and am judged for the hope of the promise made of God unto our fathers:	**Genesis 3:15** And I will put enmity between thee and the woman, and between thy seed and her seed; it shall bruise thy head, and thou shalt bruise his heel. **Deuteronomy 18:15** The LORD thy God will raise up unto thee a Prophet from the midst of thee, of thy brethren, like unto me; unto him ye shall hearken; **Isaiah 7:14** Therefore the Lord himself shall give you a sign; Behold, a virgin shall conceive, and bear a son, and shall call his name Immanuel. **Isaiah 9:6** For unto us a child is born, unto us a son is given: and the government shall be upon his shoulder: and his name shall be called Wonderful, Counsellor, The mighty God, The everlasting Father, The Prince of Peace. **Jeremiah 23:5** Behold, the days come, saith the LORD, that I will raise unto David a righteous Branch, and a King shall reign and prosper, and shall execute judgment and justice in the earth. **Ezekiel 37:24** And David my servant *shall be* king over them; and they all shall have one shepherd: they shall also walk in my

	judgments, and observe my statutes, and do them. **Daniel 9:24** Seventy weeks are determined upon thy people and upon thy holy city, to finish the transgression, and to make an end of sins, and to make reconciliation for iniquity, and to bring in everlasting righteousness, and to seal up the vision and prophecy, and to anoint the most Holy.
Acts 26:14 And when we were all fallen to the earth, I heard a voice speaking unto me, and saying in the Hebrew tongue, Saul, Saul, why persecutest thou me? *it is* hard for thee to kick against the **pricks**.	**Numbers 33:55** But if ye will not drive out the inhabitants of the land from before you; then it shall come to pass, that those which ye let remain of them *shall be* **pricks** in your eyes, and thorns in your sides, and shall vex you in the land wherein ye dwell.
Acts 26:18 To open their eyes, *and* to turn *them* from darkness to **light**, and *from* the power of **Satan** unto God, that they may **receive forgiveness of sins**, and inheritance among them which are sanctified by faith that is in me.	**Isaiah 60:1-3** Arise, shine; for thy **light** is come, and the glory of the LORD is risen upon thee. **2** For, behold, the darkness shall cover the earth, and gross darkness the people: but the LORD shall arise upon thee, and his glory shall be seen upon thee. **3** And the Gentiles shall come to thy **light**, and kings to the brightness of thy rising. **Genesis 3:4** And the **serpent** said unto the woman, Ye shall not surely die: **Zechariah 3:1-2** And he shewed me Joshua the high priest standing before the angel of the LORD, and **Satan** standing at his right hand to resist him. **2** And the LORD said unto **Satan**, The LORD rebuke thee, O **Satan**; even the LORD that hath chosen Jerusalem rebuke thee: *is* not this a brand plucked out of the fire? **See Matthew 4:10** "satan" **Proverbs 28:13** He that covereth his sins shall not prosper: but whoso confesseth and forsaketh *them* shall have mercy. **Isaiah 55:7** Let the wicked forsake his way, and the unrighteous man his thoughts: and let him return unto the LORD, and he will have mercy upon him; and to our God, for he will abundantly pardon.
Acts 26:28 Then Agrippa said unto Paul, Almost thou persuadest me to be a Christian.	**Numbers 6:27** And they shall put my name upon the children of Israel; and I will bless them.
Acts 27:9 Now when much time was spent, and when sailing was now dangerous, because the fast was now already past, Paul admonished *them*,	**Leviticus 23:27** Also on the tenth *day* of this seventh month *there shall be* a day of atonement: it shall be an holy convocation unto you; and ye shall afflict your souls, and offer an offering made by fire unto the LORD.
Acts 27:23 For there stood by me this night the **angel** of God, whose I am, and whom I serve,	**See Hebrews 13:2** "Angels"
Acts 27:31-34 Paul said to the centurion and to the soldiers, **Except these abide in the ship, ye cannot be saved**. 32 Then the soldiers cut off the ropes of the boat, and let her fall off. 33 And while the day was coming on, Paul besought *them* all to take meat, saying, **This day is the fourteenth day that ye have**	**See 1 Corinthians 12:8** "Word of Knowledge"

tarried and continued fasting, having taken nothing. **34 Wherefore I pray you to take** *some* **meat: for this is for your health: for there shall not an hair fall from the head of any of you.**	
Acts 28:23 And when they had appointed him a day, there came many to him into *his* lodging; to whom he expounded and testified the kingdom of God, persuading them concerning Jesus, both out of the law of Moses, and *out of* the prophets, from morning till evening.	**Genesis 3:15** And I will put enmity between thee and the woman, and between thy seed and her seed; it shall bruise thy head, and thou shalt bruise his heel. **Deuteronomy 18:15** The LORD thy God will raise up unto thee a Prophet from the midst of thee, of thy brethren, like unto me; unto him ye shall hearken; **Isaiah 7:14** Therefore the Lord himself shall give you a sign; Behold, a virgin shall conceive, and bear a son, and shall call his name Immanuel. **Isaiah 9:6** For unto us a child is born, unto us a son is given: and the government shall be upon his shoulder: and his name shall be called Wonderful, Counseller, The mighty God, The everlasting Father, The Prince of Peace. **Jeremiah 23:5** Behold, the days come, saith the LORD, that I will raise unto David a righteous Branch, and a King shall reign and prosper, and shall execute judgment and justice in the earth. **Ezekiel 37:24** And David my servant *shall be* king over them; and they all shall have one shepherd: they shall also walk in my judgments, and observe my statutes, and do them. **Daniel 9:24** Seventy weeks are determined upon thy people and upon thy holy city, to finish the transgression, and to make an end of sins, and to make reconciliation for iniquity, and to bring in everlasting righteousness, and to seal up the vision and prophecy, and to anoint the most Holy.
Acts 28:26-27 Saying, Go unto this people, and say, Hearing ye shall hear, and shall not understand; and seeing ye shall see, and not perceive: For the heart of this people is waxed gross, and their ears are dull of hearing, and their eyes have they closed; lest they should see with [their] eyes, and hear with [their] ears, and understand with [their] heart, and should be converted, and I should heal them.	**Isaiah 6:9-10** And he said, God, and tell this people, Hear ye indeed, but understand not; and see ye indeed, but perceive not. Make the heart of this people fat, and make their ears heavy, and shut their eyes; lest they see with their eyes, and hear with their ears, and understand with their heart, and convert, and be healed. **Jeremiah 5:21** Hear now this, O foolish people, and without understanding; which have eyes, and see not; which have ears, and hear not: **Ezekiel 2:3-8** **Ezekiel 12:2** Son of man, thou dwellest in the midst of a rebellious house, which have eyes to see, and see not; they have ears to hear, and hear not: for they *are* a rebellious house.
Acts 28:28 Be it known therefore unto you, that the salvation of God is sent unto the Gentiles, and *that* they will hear it.	**Psalms 67:2** That thy way may be known upon earth, thy saving health among all nations.
Acts 28:31 Preaching the kingdom of God, and **teaching those things which concern the Lord Jesus Christ, with all confidence**, no man forbidding him.	See Ephesians 4:11 "Teach – Teachers"
Romans 1:2 (Which he had promised afore by his prophets in the holy	**Genesis 3:15** And I will put enmity between thee and the woman, and between thy seed and her seed; it shall bruise thy head, and

scriptures,)	thou shalt bruise his heel.

Deuteronomy 18:15 The LORD thy God will raise up unto thee a Prophet from the midst of thee, of thy brethren, like unto me; unto him ye shall hearken;

Isaiah 7:14 Therefore the Lord himself shall give you a sign; Behold, a virgin shall conceive, and bear a son, and shall call his name Immanuel.

Isaiah 9:6 For unto us a child is born, unto us a son is given: and the government shall be upon his shoulder: and his name shall be called Wonderful, Counseller, The mighty God, The everlasting Father, The Prince of Peace.

Jeremiah 23:5 Behold, the days come, saith the LORD, that I will raise unto David a righteous Branch, and a King shall reign and prosper, and shall execute judgment and justice in the earth.

Ezekiel 37:24 And David my servant *shall be* king over them; and they all shall have one shepherd: they shall also walk in my judgments, and observe my statutes, and do them.

Daniel 9:24 Seventy weeks are determined upon thy people and upon thy holy city, to finish the transgression, and to make an end of sins, and to make reconciliation for iniquity, and to bring in everlasting righteousness, and to seal up the vision and prophecy, and to anoint the most Holy.

See Matthew 5:18 "Scriptures" |
| **Romans 1:4** And declared *to be* the Son of God with power, according to the spirit of holiness, by the resurrection from the dead: | **Isaiah 9:6** For unto us a child is born, unto us a son is given: and the government shall be upon his shoulder: and his name shall be called Wonderful, Counseller, The mighty God, The everlasting Father, The Prince of Peace.

Isaiah 44:6 Thus saith the LORD the King of Israel, and his redeemer the LORD of hosts; I *am* the first, and I *am* the last; and beside me *there is* no God.

Isaiah 54:5 For thy Maker *is* thine husband; the LORD of hosts *is* his name; and thy Redeemer the Holy One of Israel; The God of the whole earth shall he be called. |
| **Romans 1:7** To all that be in Rome, beloved of God, **called** *to be* **saints**: Grace to you and peace from God our Father, and the Lord Jesus Christ. | **Exodus 12:22** And ye shall take a bunch of hyssop, and dip *it* in the blood that *is* in the bason, and strike the lintel and the two side posts with the blood that *is* in the bason; and none of you shall go out at the door of his house until the morning.

Exodus 24:6-8 And Moses took half of the blood, and put *it* in basons; and half of the blood he sprinkled on the altar. 7 And he took the book of the covenant, and read in the audience of the people: and they said, All that the LORD hath said will we do, and be obedient. 8 And Moses took the blood, and sprinkled *it* on the people, and said, Behold the blood of the covenant, which the LORD hath made with you concerning all these words.

Leviticus 5:9 And he shall sprinkle of the blood of the sin offering upon the side of the altar; and the rest of the blood shall be wrung out at the bottom of the altar: it *is* a sin offering.

Isaiah 53:5 But he *was* wounded for our transgressions, *he was* bruised for our iniquities: the chastisement of our peace *was* upon him; and with his stripes we are healed. |

	Daniel 9:24 Seventy weeks are determined upon thy people and upon thy holy city, to finish the transgression, and to make an end of sins, and **to make reconciliation for iniquity**, and to bring in everlasting righteousness, and to seal up the vision and prophecy, and to anoint the most Holy.
Romans 1:16 For I am not ashamed of the gospel of Christ: for it is the power of God unto salvation to every one that believeth; to the Jew first, and also to the Greek.	**Psalms 40:9** I have preached righteousness in the great congregation: lo, I have not refrained my lips, O LORD, thou knowest.
Romans 1:17 For therein is the righteousness of God revealed from faith to faith: as it is written, **The just shall live by faith**.	**Habakkuk 2:4** Behold, his soul *which* is lifted up is not upright in him: but **the just shall live by his faith**.
Romans 1:20 For the invisible things of him from the creation of the world are clearly seen, being understood by the things that are made, *even* his eternal power and Godhead; so that they are without excuse:	**Psalms 19:1** { To the chief Musician, A Psalm of David. } The heavens declare the glory of God; and the firmament sheweth his handywork.
Romans 1:21 Because that, when they knew God, they glorified *him* not as God, neither were thankful; but became vain in their imaginations, and their foolish heart was darkened.	**Deuteronomy 22:5** The woman shall not wear that which pertaineth unto a man, neither shall a man put on a woman's garment: for all that do so *are* abomination unto the LORD thy God. **Deuteronomy 28:28** The LORD shall smite thee with madness, and blindness, and astonishment of heart:
Romans 1:23 And changed the glory of the uncorruptible God into an **image** made like to corruptible man, and to birds, and fourfooted beasts, and creeping things.	**Genesis 1:26** And God said, Let us make man in our image, after our likeness: and let them have dominion over the fish of the sea, and over the fowl of the air, and over the cattle, and over all the earth, and over every creeping thing that creepeth upon the earth. **Psalms 106:20** Thus they changed their glory into the similitude of an ox that eateth grass. **Jeremiah 10:14** Every man is brutish in *his* knowledge: every founder is confounded by the **graven image**: for his molten image *is* falsehood, and *there is* no breath in them. **Jeremiah 51:17-18** Every man is brutish by *his* knowledge; every founder is confounded by the **graven image**: for his **molten image** *is* falsehood, and *there is* no breath in them.18 They *are* vanity, the work of errors: in the time of their visitation they shall perish.
	Genesis 8:21 And Jehovah smelled the delightful odor, and Jehovah said in His heart, I will never again curse the ground for the sake of man, because the <u>imagination</u> of the heart <u>of man is evil from his youth</u>. Yea, I will not again smite every living thing as I have done; **Ezekiel 16:49-50** Behold, this was the iniquity of thy sister Sodom, pride, fulness of bread, and abundance of idleness was in her and in her daughters, neither did she strengthen the hand of the poor and needy. 50 And they were haughty, and committed abomination before me: therefore I took them away as I saw *good*. **Ezekiel 16:17** Thou hast also taken thy fair jewels of my gold and of my silver, which I had given thee, and **madest** to thyself **images of men**, and **didst commit whoredom with them**,

Romans 1:24 Wherefore God also gave them up to uncleanness through the lusts of their own hearts, to dishonour their own bodies between themselves:	**Exodus 22:19** Whosoever lieth with a beast shall surely be put to death. **Leviticus 18:23** Neither shalt thou lie with any beast to defile thyself therewith: neither shall any woman stand before a beast to lie down thereto: it *is* confusion. **Leviticus 20:15-16** And if a man lie with a beast, he shall surely be put to death: and ye shall slay the beast. 16 And if a woman approach unto any beast, and lie down thereto, thou shalt kill the woman, and the beast: they shall surely be put to death; their blood *shall be* upon them. **Exodus 20:26** Neither shalt thou go up by steps unto mine altar, that thy nakedness be not discovered thereon. **Leviticus 18:8** The nakedness of thy father's wife shalt thou not uncover: it *is* thy father's nakedness. **Genesis 49:3-4** Reuben, thou *art* my firstborn, my might, and the beginning of my strength, the excellency of dignity, and the excellency of power: 4 Unstable as water, thou shalt not excel; because **thou wentest up to thy father's bed; then defiledst thou *it***: he went up to my couch. **1 Chronicles 5:1** Now the sons of **Reuben** the firstborn of Israel, (for he *was* the firstborn; but, forasmuch as **he defiled his father's bed**, his birthright was given unto the sons of Joseph the son of Israel: and the genealogy is not to be reckoned after the birthright. **Leviticus 20:11** And the man that lieth with his father's wife hath uncovered his father's nakedness: both of them shall surely be put to death; their blood *shall be* upon them. **Leviticus 20:17** And if a man shall take his sister, his father's daughter, or his mother's daughter, and see her nakedness, and she see his nakedness; it *is* a wicked thing; and they shall be cut off in the sight of their people: he hath uncovered his sister's nakedness; he shall bear his iniquity. **Deuteronomy 22:30** A man shall not take his father's wife, nor discover his father's skirt. **Deuteronomy 27:20** Cursed *be* he that lieth with his father's wife; because he uncovereth his father's skirt. And all the people shall say, Amen. **Job 31:1** I made a covenant with mine eyes; why then should I think upon a maid? **Psalms 119:37** Turn away mine eyes from beholding vanity; *and* quicken thou me in thy way. **Numbers 25:1-3** And Israel abode in Shittim, and the people began to **commit whoredom with the daughters of Moab**. 2 And **they called the people unto the sacrifices of their gods**: and the people did eat, and bowed down to their gods. 3 And **Israel joined himself unto Baalpeor**: and the anger of the LORD was kindled

	against Israel.
	Hosea 2:13 And I will visit upon her the days of Baalim, wherein she burned incense to them, and she decked herself with her earrings and her jewels, and **she went after her lovers**, and forgot me, saith the LORD.
	Deuteronomy 22:5 The woman shall not wear that which pertaineth unto a man, neither shall a man put on a woman's garment: for all that do so are abomination unto the Lord thy God.
	Deuteronomy 23:17-18 There shall be **no whore** of the daughters of Israel, **nor a sodomite** of the sons of Israel. 18 Thou shalt not bring the hire of a **whore**, or **the price of a dog**, into the house of the LORD thy God for any vow: for even both these *are* abomination unto the LORD thy God.
	Leviticus 18:6-30
	See Matthew 5:27 "Adultery"
	See 1 Timothy 2:9 "Adornment"
Romans 1:26 For this cause God gave them up unto vile affections: for even their women did change the natural use into that which is against nature:	**Exodus 22:19** Whosoever lieth with a beast shall surely be put to death.
	Leviticus 18:22-23 Thou shalt not lie with mankind, as with womankind: it *is* abomination. 23 Neither shalt thou lie with any beast to defile thyself therewith: neither shall any woman stand before a beast to lie down thereto: it *is* confusion.
	Leviticus 20:15-16 And if a man lie with a beast, he shall surely be put to death: and ye shall slay the beast. 16 And if a woman approach unto any beast, and lie down thereto, thou shalt kill the woman, and the beast: they shall surely be put to death; their blood *shall be* upon them.
	Deuteronomy 27:21 Cursed *be* he that lieth with any manner of beast. And all the people shall say, Amen.
Romans 1:27 And likewise also the men, leaving the natural use of the woman, burned in their lust one toward another; men with men working that which is unseemly, and receiving in themselves that recompence of their error which was meet.	**Genesis 9:21-25** And he drank of the wine, and was drunken; and he was uncovered within his tent. 22 And Ham, the father of Canaan, saw the nakedness of his father, and told his two brethren without. 23 And Shem and Japheth took a garment, and laid *it* upon both their shoulders, and went backward, and covered the nakedness of their father; and their faces *were* backward, and they saw not their father's nakedness. 24 And Noah awoke from his wine, and knew what his younger son had done unto him. 25 And he said, Cursed *be* Canaan; a servant of servants shall he be unto his brethren.
	Genesis 19:4-7 Before they had laid down, even the men of the city, the men of **Sodom**, surrounded the house; from the young to the aged, all the people from the limits. And they called to Lot and said to him, Where are the men who came to you tonight? Bring them out to us that we may know them. And Lot went out to them, to the door, and he closed the door behind him. And he said, My brothers, please do not act evilly.
	Genesis 19:24-26 And Jehovah rained brimstone and fire on

Sodom and Gomorrah, from Jehovah out of the heavens. And He overthrew those cities, and all the plain, and all those living in the cities, and the produce of the ground. And his wife looked back from behind him, and she became a pillar of salt.

Leviticus 18:22 Thou shalt not lie with mankind, as with womankind: it is abomination.

Leviticus 20:13 And a man who lies with a male as one lies with a woman, both of them have done a disgusting thing; they shall certainly be put to death; their blood *shall* be on them.

Leviticus 20:22 And a man who lies with a male as one lies with a woman, both of them have done a disgusting thing; they shall certainly be put to death; their blood *shall* be on them.

Deuteronomy 23:17 ... , nor a sodomite of the sons of Israel.

Deuteronomy 27:22-23 Cursed *be* he that lieth with his sister, the daughter of his father, or the daughter of his mother. And all the people shall say, Amen. 23 Cursed *be* he that lieth with his mother in law. And all the people shall say, Amen.

Judges 19:22-25 *Now* as they were making their hearts merry, behold, the men of the city, certain sons of Belial, beset the house round about, *and* beat at the door, and spake to the master of the house, the old man, saying, **Bring forth the man that came into thine house, that we may know him**. 23 And the man, the master of the house, went out unto them, and said unto them, Nay, my brethren, *nay,* I pray you, **do not** *so* **wickedly**; seeing that this man is come into mine house, **do not this folly**. 24 Behold, *here is* my daughter a maiden, and his concubine; them I will bring out now, and humble ye them, and do with them what seemeth good unto you: but unto this man do not so vile a thing. 25 But the men would not hearken to him: so the man took his concubine, and brought her forth unto them; and they knew her, and abused her all the night until the morning: and when the day began to spring, they let her go.

1 Kings 15:12 And **he took away the sodomites out of the land**, and removed all the idols that his fathers had made.

1 Kings 22:46 And **the remnant of the sodomites**, which remained in the days of his father Asa, **he took out of the land**.

2 Kings 23:7 And he broke down the houses of the **sodomites**, that *were* by the house of the LORD, where the women wove hangings for the grove.

Job 36:14 They die in youth, and their life *is* among the unclean.

Psalms 11:6 Upon the wicked he shall rain snares, fire and brimstone, and an horrible tempest: *this shall be* the portion of their cup.

Ezekiel 16:48-49 *As* I live, saith the Lord GOD, Sodom thy sister hath not done, she nor her daughters, as thou hast done, thou and thy daughters. 49 Behold, this was **the iniquity of thy sister Sodom, pride, fulness of bread, and abundance of idleness was in her and in her daughters, neither did she strengthen the hand of the poor and needy**.

Romans 1:28-32 And even as they did not like to retain God in *their* knowledge, God gave them over to a reprobate mind, to do those things which	**Deuteronomy 22:25** But if a man find a betrothed damsel in the field, and the man force her, and lie with her: then the man only that lay with her shall die: **Job 31:1** I made a covenant with mine eyes; why then should I

are not convenient; 29 Being filled with all unrighteousness, fornication, wickedness, covetousness, maliciousness; full of envy, murder, debate, deceit, malignity; whisperers, 30 Backbiters, haters of God, despiteful, proud, boasters, inventors of evil things, disobedient to parents, 31 Without understanding, covenant breakers, without natural affection, implacable, unmerciful: 32 Who knowing the judgment of God, that they which commit such things are worthy of death, not only do the same, but have pleasure in them that do them.	think upon a maid? **Psalms 15:2-3** He that walketh uprightly, and worketh righteousness, and speaketh the truth in his heart. 3 *He that* backbiteth not with his tongue, nor doeth evil to his neighbour, nor taketh up a reproach against his neighbour. **Psalms 19:14** Let the words of my mouth, and the meditation of my heart, be acceptable in thy sight, O LORD, my strength, and my redeemer. **Psalms 97:10** Ye that love the LORD, **hate evil**: he preserveth the souls of his saints; he delivereth them out of the hand of the wicked. **Psalms 101:3 I will set no wicked thing before mine eyes**: I hate the work of them that turn aside; *it* shall not cleave to me. **Psalms 119:36-37** Incline my heart unto thy testimonies, and not to covetousness. 37 **Turn away mine eyes from beholding vanity**; *and* quicken thou me in thy way. **Proverbs 25:23** The north wind driveth away rain: so *doth* an angry countenance a backbiting **tongue**. **Isaiah 33:15-16** He that walketh righteously, and speaketh uprightly; he that despiseth the gain of oppressions, that shaketh his hands from holding of bribes, that stoppeth his ears from hearing of blood, and **shutteth his eyes from seeing evil**; 16 He shall dwell on high: his place of defense *shall be* the munitions of rocks: bread shall be given him; his waters *shall be* sure. **See Hebrews 12:14 "Holiness"**
Romans 2:1 Therefore thou art inexcusable, O man, whosoever thou art that judgest: for wherein thou judgest another, thou condemnest thyself; for thou that judgest doest the same things.	**2 Samuel 12:5** And David's anger was greatly kindled against the man; and he said to Nathan, As the LORD liveth, the man that hath done this *thing* shall surely die:
Romans 2:4 Or despisest thou the riches of his goodness and forbearance and longsuffering; not knowing that the goodness of God leadeth thee to repentance?	**Proverbs 28:13** He that covereth his sins shall not prosper: but whoso confesseth and forsaketh *them* shall have mercy. **Isaiah 30:18** And therefore will the LORD wait, that he may be gracious unto you, and therefore will he be exalted, that he may have mercy upon you: for the LORD *is* a God of judgment: blessed *are* all they that wait for him. **Isaiah 55:7** Let the wicked forsake his way, and the unrighteous man his thoughts: and let him return unto the LORD, and he will have mercy upon him; and to our God, for he will abundantly pardon.
Romans 2:6 Who will render to every man according to his deeds:	**Psalms 62:12** Also unto thee, O Lord, *belongeth* mercy: for thou renderest to every man according to his work. **Proverbs 24:12** If thou sayest, Behold, we knew it not; doth not he that pondereth the heart consider *it*? and he that keepeth thy soul, doth [not] he know [it]? and shall [not] he render to *every* man according to his works? **Jeremiah 17:10** I the LORD search the heart, *I* try the reins, even to give every man according to his ways, *and* according to the fruit of his doings. **Jeremiah 32:19** Great in counsel, and mighty in work: for thine eyes *are* open upon all the ways of the sons of men: to give every one according to his ways, and according to the fruit of his doings:
Romans 2:8-9 But unto them that are	**Deuteronomy 28:14-16** And **thou shalt not go aside from any of**

contentious, and do not obey the truth, but obey unrighteousness, indignation and wrath, 9 **Tribulation and anguish, upon every soul of man that doeth evil**, of the Jew first, and also of the Gentile;	**the words which I command thee this day, to the right hand, or to the left, to go after other gods to serve them.** 15 But it shall come to pass, **if thou wilt not hearken unto the voice of the LORD thy God, to observe to do all his commandments and his statutes** which I command thee this day; that all these curses shall come upon thee, and overtake thee: 16 **Cursed shalt thou be** in the city, and cursed shalt thou be in the field. **Nahum 1:2-3** God *is* jealous, and the LORD revengeth; the LORD revengeth, and *is* furious; **the LORD will take vengeance on his adversaries**, and **he reserveth** *wrath* **for his enemies.** 3 The LORD *is* slow to anger, and great in power, and **will not at all acquit** *the wicked*: the LORD hath his way in the whirlwind and in the storm, and the clouds *are* the dust of his feet.
Romans 2:11 For there is no respect of persons with God.	**Deuteronomy 10:17** For the LORD your God *is* God of gods, and Lord of lords, a great God, a mighty, and a terrible, which regardeth not persons, nor taketh reward: **Deuteronomy 16:18-19** Judges and officers shalt thou make thee in all thy gates, which the LORD thy God giveth thee, throughout thy tribes: and they shall judge the people with just judgment. 19 Thou shalt not wrest judgment; thou shalt not respect persons, neither take a gift: for a gift doth blind the eyes of the wise, and pervert the words of the righteous. **2 Chronicles 19:7** Wherefore now let the fear of the LORD be upon you; take heed and do *it*: for *there is* no iniquity with the LORD our God, nor respect of persons, nor taking of gifts. **Job 34:19** *How much less to him* that accepteth not the persons of princes, nor regardeth the rich more than the poor? for they all *are* the work of his hands. **Proverbs 24:23** These *things* also *belong* to the wise. *It is* not good to have respect of persons in judgment.
Romans 2:13 (For not the hearers of the law *are* just before God, but the doers of the law shall be justified.	**Jeremiah 11:6** Then the LORD said unto me, Proclaim all these words in the cities of Judah, and in the streets of Jerusalem, saying, Hear ye the words of this covenant, and do them.
Romans 2:21 Thou therefore which teachest another, teachest thou not thyself? thou that preachest a man should not steal, dost thou steal?	**Leviticus 19:11** Ye shall not steal, neither deal falsely, neither lie one to another.
Romans 2:22 Thou that sayest a man should not commit **adultery**, dost thou commit **adultery**? thou that abhorrest idols, dost thou commit sacrilege?	**See Matthew 5:27 "Adultery"**
Romans 2:24 For the name of God is blasphemed among the Gentiles through you, as it is written.	**Isaiah 52:5** Now therefore, what have I here, saith the LORD, that my people is taken away for nought? they that rule over them make them to howl, saith the LORD; and my name continually every day *is* blasphemed. **Isaiah 65:7** Your iniquities, and the iniquities of your fathers together, saith the LORD, which have burned incense upon the mountains, and blasphemed me upon the hills: therefore will I measure their former work into their bosom. **Ezekiel 36:23** And I will sanctify my great name, which was profaned among the heathen, which ye have profaned in the midst of them; and the heathen shall know that I *am* the LORD, saith the

	Lord GOD, when I shall be sanctified in you before their eyes.
Romans 2:25 For circumcision verily profiteth, if thou keep the law: but if thou be a breaker of the law, thy circumcision is made uncircumcision.	**Genesis 17:10-14** This *is* my covenant, which ye shall keep, between me and you and thy seed after thee; **Every man child among you shall be circumcised.** 11 **And ye shall circumcise the flesh of your foreskin; and it shall be a token of the covenant betwixt me and you.** 12 And he that is eight days old shall be circumcised among you, every man child in your generations, he that is born in the house, or bought with money of any stranger, which *is* not of thy seed. 13 He that is born in thy house, and he that is bought with thy money, must needs be circumcised: and my covenant shall be in your flesh for an everlasting covenant. 14 And **the uncircumcised man child whose flesh of his foreskin is not circumcised, that soul shall be cut off from his people; he hath broken my covenant.** **Ezekiel 36:22** Therefore say unto the house of Israel, Thus saith the Lord GOD; I do not this for your sakes, O house of Israel, but for mine holy name's sake, which ye have profaned among the heathen, whither ye went. **Ezekiel 36:23** And I will sanctify my great name, which was profaned among the heathen, which ye have profaned in the midst of them; and the heathen shall know that I *am* the LORD, saith the Lord GOD, when I shall be sanctified in you before their eyes. Ezekiel 36:24 For I will take you from among the heathen, and gather you out of all countries, and will bring you into your own land. Ezekiel 36:25 Then will **I sprinkle clean water upon you, and ye shall be clean: from all your filthiness**, and from all your idols, will I cleanse you. **Ezekiel 36:26** A new heart also will I give you, and **a new spirit will I put within you**: and I will take away the stony heart out of your flesh, and I will give you a heart of flesh. **Ezekiel 36:27** And **I will put my spirit within you**, and cause you to walk in my statutes, and ye shall keep my judgments, and do *them*. Ezekiel 36:28 And ye shall dwell in the land that I gave to your fathers; and ye shall be my people, and I will be your God.
Romans 2:29 But he *is* a Jew, which is one inwardly; and circumcision *is that* of the heart, in the spirit, *and* not in the letter; whose praise *is* not of men, but of God.	**Deuteronomy 10:16** Circumcise therefore the foreskin of your heart, and be no more stiffnecked. **Jeremiah 4:4** Circumcise yourselves to the LORD, and take away the foreskins of your heart, ye men of Judah and inhabitants of Jerusalem: lest my fury come forth like fire, and burn that none can quench *it*, because of the evil of your doings.
Romans 3:2 Much every way: chiefly, because that unto them were committed the oracles of God.	**Psalms 147:19** He sheweth his word unto Jacob, his statutes and his judgments unto Israel. **See Matthew 5:18 "Scriptures"**
Romans 3:3 For what if some did not believe? shall their unbelief make the faith of God without effect?	**Deuteronomy 32:20** And he said, I will hide my face from them, I will see what their end *shall be*: for they *are* a very froward generation, **children in whom *is* no faith**.
Romans 3:4 God forbid: yea, let God be true, but every man a liar; as it is written, That thou mightest be justified in thy sayings, and mightest overcome when	**Psalms 51:4** Against thee, thee only, have I sinned, and done [this] evil in thy sight: that thou mightest be justified when thou speakest, [and] be clear when thou judgest.

thou art judged.	**Psalms 116:11** I said in my haste, All men *are* liars.
Romans 3:10 As it is written, There is none righteous, no, not one:	**Ecclesiastes 7:20** For *there is* not a just man upon earth, that doeth good, and sinneth not. **Psalms 14:3** They are all gone aside, they are *all* together become filthy: *there is* none that doeth good, no, not one. **Psalms 53:1-3** { To the chief Musician upon Mahalath, Maschil, *A Psalm* of David. } The fool hath said in his heart, *There is* no God. Corrupt are they, and have done abominable iniquity: *there is* none that doeth good. 2 God looked down from heaven upon the children of men, to see if there were *any* that did understand, that did seek God. 3 Every one of them is gone back: they are altogether become filthy; *there is* none that doeth good, no, not one.
Romans 3:11 There is none that understandeth, there is none that seeketh after God	**Psalm 14:2** The LORD looked down from heaven upon the children of men, to see if there were any that did understand, *and* seek God. **Proverb 1:22** How long, ye simple ones, will ye love simplicity? and the scorners delight in their scorning, and fools hate knowledge?
Romans 3:12 They are all gone out of the way, they are together become unprofitable; there is none that doeth good, no, not one.	**Psalms 14:1** To the chief Musician, *A Psalm* of David. The fool hath said in his heart, *There is* no God. They are corrupt, they have done abominable works, *there is* none that doeth good. **Psalms 14:3** They are all gone aside, they are *all* together become filthy: *there is* none that doeth good, no, not one.
Romans 3:13 Their throat is an open sepulchre; with their tongues they have used deceit; the poison of asps is under their lips:	**Psalm 5:9** For *there is* no faithfulness in their mouth; their inward part *is* very wickedness; their throat *is* an open sepulchre; they flatter with their tongue. **Psalms 140:3** They have sharpened their tongues like a serpent; adders' poison *is* under their lips. Selah.
Romans 3:14 Whose mouth is full of cursing and bitterness:	**Psalms 10:7** His mouth is full of cursing and deceit and fraud: under his tongue *is* mischief and vanity. **Isaiah 57:19** I create the fruit of the lips; Peace, peace to *him that is* far off, and to *him that is* near, saith the LORD; and I will heal him.
Romans 3:15-16 Their feet are swift to shed blood: 16 Destruction and misery are in their ways:	**Proverbs 1:16** For their feet run to evil, and make haste to shed blood. **Isaiah 59:7** Behold, they belch out with their mouth: swords *are* in their lips: for who, *say they,* doth hear?
Romans 3:17 And the way of peace have they not known:	**Isaiah 59:8** The way of peace they know not; and *there is* no judgment in their goings: they have made them crooked paths: whosoever goeth therein shall not know peace.
Romans 3:18 There is no fear of God before their eyes.	**Psalms 36:1** To the chief Musician, *A Psalm* of David the servant of the LORD. The transgression of the wicked saith within my heart, *that there is* no fear of God before his eyes.
Romans 3:20 Therefore by the deeds of the law there shall no flesh be justified in his sight: for by the **law** *is* the knowledge of sin.	**Psalms 143:2** And enter not into judgment with thy servant: for in thy sight shall no man living be justified. **See Romans 1:24-26 "Sin in the law"**
Romans 3:23 For all have sinned, and come short of the glory of God;	**Ezekiel 18:4** Behold, all souls are mine; as the soul of the father, so also the soul of the son is mine: the soul that sinneth, it shall die.

Romans 3:24 Being justified freely by his grace through the redemption that is in Christ Jesus:	**Isaiah 53:5** But he *was* wounded for our transgressions, *he was* bruised for our iniquities: the chastisement of our peace *was* upon him; and with his stripes we are healed.
Romans 3:25 Whom God hath set forth *to be* a propitiation through faith in his blood, to declare his righteousness for the remission of sins that are past, through the forbearance of God;	**Exodus 25:17** And thou shalt make a mercy seat *of* pure gold: two cubits and a half *shall be* the length thereof, and a cubit and a half the breadth thereof. **Leviticus 17:11** For the life of the flesh is in the blood: and I have given it to you upon the altar to make an atonement for your souls: **for it is the blood that maketh an atonement for the soul**. **See Matthew 26:28 "Atonement"**
Romans 3:30 Seeing *it is* one God, which shall justify the circumcision by faith, and uncircumcision through faith.	**Deuteronomy 6:4** Hear, O Israel: The LORD our God *is* one LORD: Tell ye, and bring them near; yea, let them take counsel together: who hath declared this from ancient time? who hath told it from that time? **Isaiah 45:5-6** I am the LORD, and there is none else, **there is no God beside me**: I girded thee, though thou hast not known me: 6 That they may know from the rising of the sun, and from the west, that there is none beside me. I am the LORD, and there is none else. **Isaiah 45:21-22** have not I the LORD? and **there is no God else beside me**; a just God and a Saviour; there is none beside me. 22 Look unto me, and be ye saved, all the ends of the earth: for **I am God, and there is none else**. **Deuteronomy 32:39; 2 Samuel 7:22; 1 Chronicles 17:20; Psalm86:10; Isaiah 44:6, 8-10; Isaiah 45:21-23; Isaiah 46:9; Malachi 2:10**
Romans 4:1 What shall we say then that Abraham our father, as pertaining to the flesh, hath found?	**Isaiah 51:2** Look unto Abraham your father, and unto Sarah *that* bare you: for I called him alone, and blessed him, and increased him.
Romans 4:3 For what saith the scripture? Abraham believed God, and it was counted unto him for righteousness.	**Genesis 15:6** And he believed in the LORD; and he counted it to him for righteousness.
Romans 4:5-6 But to him that worketh not, but believeth on him that justifieth the ungodly, his faith is counted for **righteousness**. 6 Even as David also describeth the blessedness of the man, unto whom God imputeth **righteousness** without works,	**Isaiah 64:6** But we are all as an unclean *thing,* and all our **righteousnesses** *are* as filthy rags; and we all do fade as a leaf; and our iniquities, like the wind, have taken us away.
Romans 4:7-8 *Saying*, Blessed *are* they whose iniquities are forgiven, and whose sins are covered. Blessed *is* the man to whom the Lord will not impute sin.	**Psalms 32:1-2** Blessed *is he whose* transgression *is* forgiven, *whose* sin *is* covered. Blessed *is* the man unto whom the LORD imputeth not iniquity, and in whose spirit *there is* no guile.
Romans 4:9 *Cometh* this blessedness then upon the circumcision *only,* or upon the uncircumcision also? for we say that faith was reckoned to Abraham for righteousness.	**Genesis 12:3** And I will bless them that bless thee, and curse him that curseth thee: and in thee shall all families of the earth be blessed. **Genesis 15:6** And he believed in the LORD; and he counted it to him for righteousness. **Habakkuk 2:4** Behold, his soul *which* is lifted up is not upright in him: but the just shall live by his faith.

Romans 4:11 And he received the sign of circumcision, a seal of the righteousness of the faith which *he had yet* being uncircumcised: that he might be the father of all them that believe, though they be not circumcised; that righteousness might be imputed unto them also:	**Genesis 17:11** And ye shall circumcise the flesh of your foreskin; and it shall be a token of the covenant betwixt me and you.
Romans 4:16 Therefore *it is* of faith, that *it might be* by grace; to the end the promise might be sure to all the seed; not to that only which is of the law, but to that also which is of the faith of Abraham; who is the father of us all,	**Isaiah 51:2** Look unto Abraham your father, and unto Sarah *that* bare you: for I called him alone, and blessed him, and increased him.
Romans 4:17 (As it is written, I have made thee a father of many nations,) before him whom he believed, *even* God, who quickeneth the dead, and calleth those things which be not as though they were.	**Genesis 17:5** Neither shall thy name any more be called Abram, but thy name shall be Abraham; for a father of many nations have I made thee.
Romans 4:19 And being not weak in faith, he considered not his own body now dead, when he was about an hundred years old, neither yet the deadness of Sara's womb:	**Genesis 17:17** Then Abraham fell upon his face, and laughed, and said in his heart, Shall *a child* be born unto him that is an hundred years old? and shall Sarah, that is ninety years old, bear? **Genesis 18:12** Therefore Sarah laughed within herself, saying, After I am waxed old shall I have pleasure, my lord being old also?
Romans 4:18 Who against hope believed in hope, that he might become the father of many nations, according to that which was spoken, So shall thy seed be.	**Genesis 15:4-5** As for me, behold, my covenant *is* with thee, and thou shalt be a father of many nations. 5 And he brought him forth abroad, and said, Look now toward heaven, and tell the stars, if thou be able to number them: and he said unto him, So shall thy seed be.
Romans 4:21 And being fully persuaded that, what he had promised, he was able also to perform.	**Psalms 115:3** But our God *is* in the heavens: he hath done whatsoever he hath pleased.
Romans 4:22 And therefore it was imputed to him for righteousness.	**Genesis 15:6** And he believed in the LORD; and he counted it to him for righteousness.
Romans 4:24 But for us also, to whom it shall be imputed, if we believe on him that raised up Jesus our Lord from the dead; 25 Who was delivered for our offences, and was raised again for our justification	**Exodus 12:22** And ye shall take a bunch of hyssop, and dip *it* in the blood that *is* in the bason, and strike the lintel and the two side posts with the blood that *is* in the bason; and none of you shall go out at the door of his house until the morning. **Exodus 24:6-8** And Moses took half of the blood, and put *it* in basons; and half of the blood he sprinkled on the altar. 7 And he took the book of the covenant, and read in the audience of the people: and they said, All that the LORD hath said will we do, and be obedient. 8 And Moses took the blood, and sprinkled *it* on the people, and said, Behold the blood of the covenant, which the LORD hath made with you concerning all these words. **Leviticus 5:9** And he shall sprinkle of the blood of the sin offering upon the side of the altar; and the rest of the blood shall be wrung out at the bottom of the altar: it *is* a sin offering. **Psalms 103:3** Who forgiveth all thine iniquities; who healeth all thy diseases; **Psalms 130:7-8** Let Israel hope in the LORD: for with the LORD *there is* mercy, and with him *is* plenteous redemption. 8 And he

	shall redeem Israel from all his iniquities
	Isaiah 53:5 But he *was* wounded for our transgressions, *he was* bruised for our iniquities: the chastisement of our peace *was* upon him; and with his stripes we are healed.
	Daniel 9:24 Seventy weeks are determined upon thy people and upon thy holy city, to finish the transgression, and to make an end of sins, and **to make reconciliation for iniquity**, and to bring in everlasting righteousness, and to seal up the vision and prophecy, and to anoint the most Holy.
Romans 4:25 Who was delivered for our offences, and was raised again for our justification.	**Isaiah 53:4-5** Surely he hath borne our griefs, and carried our sorrows: yet we did esteem him stricken, smitten of God, and afflicted. 5 But he *was* wounded for our transgressions, *he was* bruised for our iniquities: the chastisement of our peace *was* upon him; and with his stripes we are healed.
Romans 5:1 Therefore being justified by faith, we have peace with God through our Lord Jesus Christ:	**Isaiah 32:17** And the work of righteousness shall be peace; and the effect of righteousness quietness and assurance for ever.
Romans 5:9 Much more then, **being now justified by his blood**, we shall be saved from wrath through him.	**Leviticus 17:11** For the life of the flesh is in the blood: and I have given it to you upon the altar to make an atonement for your souls: **for it is the blood that maketh an atonement for the soul**. **See Matthew 26:28 "Atonement"**
Romans 5:11 And not only *so*, but we also joy in God through our Lord Jesus Christ, by whom we have now received the atonement.	**Leviticus 6:7** And the priest shall make an atonement for him before the LORD: and it shall be forgiven him for any thing of all that he hath done in trespassing therein **Nehemiah 10:33** For the shewbread, and for the continual meat offering, and for the continual burnt offering, of the sabbaths, of the new moons, for the set feasts, and for the holy *things,* and for the sin offerings to make an atonement for Israel, and *for* all the work of the house of our God. **2 Chronicles 29:24** And the priests killed them, and they made reconciliation with their blood upon the altar, to make an atonement for all Israel: for the king commanded *that* the burnt offering and the sin offering *should be made* for all Israel. **Isaiah 53:4-5** Surely he hath borne our griefs, and carried our sorrows: yet we did esteem him stricken, smitten of God, and afflicted. 5 But <u>he was wounded for our transgressions, he was bruised for our iniquities</u>: <u>the chastisement of our peace was upon him</u>; and <u>with his stripes we are healed</u>.
Romans 5:12 Wherefore, as by one man sin entered into the world, and death by sin; and so death passed upon all men, for that all have sinned:	**Genesis 2:17** But of the tree of the knowledge of good and evil, thou shalt not eat of it: for in the day that thou eatest thereof thou shalt surely die. **Genesis 3:6** And when the woman saw that the tree *was* good for food, and that it *was* pleasant to the eyes, and a tree to be desired to make *one* wise, she took of the fruit thereof, and did eat, and gave also unto her husband with her; and he did eat. own likeness, after his image; and called his name Seth: **Genesis 3:19** In the sweat of thy face shalt thou eat bread, till thou return unto the ground; for out of it wast thou taken: for dust thou *art*, and unto dust shalt thou return. **Genesis 5:3** And Adam lived an hundred and thirty years, and begat *a son* in his own likeness, after his image; and called his

	name Seth:
	Genesis 5:5 And all the days that Adam lived were nine hundred and thirty years: and he died.
	Psalms 51:5 Behold, I was shapen in iniquity; and in sin did my mother conceive me.
	Isaiah 43:27 Thy first father hath sinned, and thy teachers have transgressed against me.
	Ezekiel 18:4 Behold, all souls are mine; as the soul of the father, so also the soul of the son is mine: the soul that sinneth, it shall die.
Romans 5:18-19 Therefore as by the offence of one *judgment came* upon all men to condemnation; even so by the righteousness of one *the free gift came* upon all men unto justification of life. 19 For as by one man's disobedience many were made sinners, so by the obedience of one shall many be made righteous.	**Isaiah 53:11** He shall see of the travail of his soul, *and* shall be satisfied: by his knowledge shall my righteous servant justify many; for he shall bear their iniquities. **See Romans 5:12**
Romans 6:2 God forbid. How shall we, that are dead to sin, live any longer therein?	**See Hebrew 12:14** "Holiness"
Romans 6:5 For if we have been planted together in the likeness of his death, we shall be also *in the likeness* of *his* resurrection:	**Psalm 51:2** Wash me throughly from mine iniquity, and cleanse me from my sin. **Isaiah 1:16** Wash you, make you clean; put away the evil of your doings from before mine eyes; cease to do evil; **See Acts 2:38 "Salvation"**
Romans 6:10 For in that he died, he died unto sin once: but in that he liveth, he liveth unto God.	**Isaiah 53:12** Therefore will I divide him *a portion* with the great, and he shall divide the spoil with the strong; because he hath poured out his soul unto death: and he was numbered with the transgressors; and he bare the sin of many, and made intercession for the transgressors.
Romans 6:12-13 Let not sin therefore reign in your mortal body, that ye should obey it in the lusts thereof. 13 Neither yield ye your members *as instruments* of unrighteousness unto sin: but yield yourselves unto God, as those that are alive from the dead, and your members *as* instruments of righteousness unto God.	**See Romans 1:26-27 "Sexual sins"**
Romans 6:23 For the wages of sin *is* death; but the gift of God *is* eternal life through Jesus Christ our Lord.	**Genesis 2:17** But of the tree of the knowledge of good and evil, thou shalt not eat of it: for in the day that thou eatest thereof thou shalt surely die. **Psalms 103:12** As far as the east is from the west, *so* far hath he removed our transgressions from us. **Ezekiel 18:4** Behold, all souls are mine; as the soul of the father, so also the soul of the son is mine: the soul that sinneth, it shall die.
Romans 7:3 So then if, while *her* husband liveth, she be married to another man, she shall be called an adulteress: but if her husband be dead, she is free from that law; so that she is no adulteress, though she be married to	**Exodus 20:14** Thou shalt not commit adultery. **Leviticus 20:10** And the man that committeth adultery with *another* man's wife, *even he* that committeth adultery with his neighbour's wife, the adulterer and the adulteress shall surely be put to death.

another man.	**Deuteronomy 5:18** Neither shalt thou commit adultery. **Proverbs 6:32** *But* whoso committeth adultery with a woman lacketh understanding: he *that* doeth it destroyeth his own soul. **See Matthew 5:27** "Adultery"
Romans 7:7 What shall we say then? *Is* the law sin? God forbid. Nay, I had not known sin, but by the law: for I had not known lust, except the law had said, Thou shalt not covet.	**Exodus 20:17** Thou shalt not covet thy neighbour's house, thou shalt not covet thy neighbour's wife, nor his manservant, nor his maidservant, nor his ox, nor his ass, nor any thing that *is* thy neighbour's. **Deuteronomy 5:21** Neither shalt thou desire thy neighbour's wife, neither shalt thou covet thy neighbour's house, his field, or his manservant, or his maidservant, his ox, or his ass, or any *thing* that *is* thy neighbour's.
Romans 7:18 For I know that in me (that is, in my flesh,) dwelleth no good thing: for to will is present with me; but *how* to perform that which is good I find not.	**Genesis 6:5** And GOD saw that the wickedness of man *was* great in the earth, and *that* every imagination of the thoughts of his heart *was* only evil continually. **Genesis 8:21** And the LORD smelled a sweet savour; and the LORD said in his heart, I will not again curse the ground any more for man's sake; for the imagination of man's heart *is* evil from his youth; neither will I again smite any more every thing living, as I have done. **Job 15:16** How much more abominable and filthy *is* man, which drinketh iniquity like water? **Proverb 6:14** Frowardness *is* in his heart, he deviseth mischief continually; he soweth discord. **Jeremiah 17:9** The heart *is* deceitful above all *things*, and desperately wicked: who can know it?
Romans 8:4 That the righteousness of the law might be fulfilled in us, who walk not after the flesh, but after the Spirit.	**See Hebrews 12:14** "Holiness" **Psalms 97:10** Ye that love the LORD, hate evil: he preserveth the souls of his saints; he delivereth them out of the hand of the wicked. **Proverbs 8:13** The fear of the LORD *is* to hate evil: pride, and arrogancy, and the evil way, and the froward mouth, do I hate.
Romans 8:9 But ye are not in the flesh, but in the Spirit, if so be that the **Spirit of God** dwell in you. Now if any man have not the Spirit of Christ, he is none of his.	**Genesis 41:38** And Pharaoh said unto his servants, Can we find *such a one* as this *is*, a man in whom the **Spirit of God** *is*? **Exodus 31:3** And I have filled him with the **spirit of God**, in wisdom, and in understanding, and in knowledge, and in all manner of workmanship, **1 Samuel 10:10** And when they came thither to the hill, behold, a company of prophets met him; and the **Spirit of God** came upon him, and he prophesied among them. **Isaiah 9:6** For unto us a child is born, unto us a son is given: and the government shall be upon his shoulder: and his name shall be called Wonderful, Counsellor, The mighty God, The everlasting Father, The Prince of Peace. **Isaiah 11:2** And the spirit of the LORD shall rest upon him, the spirit of wisdom and understanding, the spirit of counsel and might, the spirit of knowledge and of the fear of the LORD; **Isaiah 42:1** Behold my servant, whom I uphold; mine elect, *in whom* my soul delighteth; I have put my spirit upon him: he shall

	bring forth judgment to the Gentiles.
Romans 8:9-11 But ye are not in the flesh, but in the Spirit, **if** so be that the Spirit of God dwell in you. Now **if** any man have not the Spirit of Christ, he is none of his. 10 And if Christ be in you, the body is dead because of sin; but the Spirit is life because of righteousness. 11 But **if** the Spirit of him that raised up Jesus from the dead dwell in you, he that raised up Christ from the dead shall also quicken your mortal bodies by his Spirit that dwelleth in you.	**Numbers 11:17** And I will come down and talk with thee there: and I will take of the spirit which *is* upon thee, and will put *it* upon them; and they shall bear the burden of the people with thee, that thou bear *it* not thyself alone. **Psalms 51:11** Cast me not away from thy presence; and take not thy holy spirit from me. **Isaiah 59:21** As for me, this *is* my covenant with them, saith the LORD; My spirit that *is* upon thee, and my words which I have put in thy mouth, shall not depart out of thy mouth, nor out of the mouth of thy seed, nor out of the mouth of thy seed's seed, saith the LORD, from henceforth and for ever. **See John 3:5 and Acts 2:38**
Romans 8:15 For ye have not received the spirit of bondage again to fear; but ye have received the Spirit of adoption, whereby we cry, Abba, Father.	**Proverb 29:25** The fear of man bringeth a snare: but whoso putteth his trust in the LORD shall be safe. **Isaiah 51:12** I, *even* I, *am* he that comforteth you: who *art* thou, that thou shouldest be afraid of a man *that* shall die, and of the son of man *which* shall be made *as* grass; **Isaiah 56:5** Even unto them will I give in mine house and within my walls a place and a name better than of sons and of daughters: I will give them an everlasting name, that shall not be cut off. **See Hebrews 13:2 "Good and bad angels"**
Romans 8:23 And not only *they*, but ourselves also, which have the firstfruits of the Spirit, even we ourselves **groan** within ourselves, waiting for the adoption, *to wit*, the redemption of our body.	**Exodus 2:24** And God heard their **groaning**, and God remembered his covenant with Abraham, with Isaac, and with Jacob. **Psalm 38:8-10** I am feeble and sore broken: I have roared by reason of the **disquietness** of my heart. 9 Lord, all my desire is before thee; and my **groaning** is not hid from thee. 10 My heart panteth, my strength faileth me: as for the light of mine eyes, it also is gone from me.
Romans 8:23 And not only *they*, but ourselves also, which have the **firstfruits** of the Spirit, even we ourselves groan within ourselves, waiting for the adoption, *to wit*, the redemption of our body. **Romans 8:29** For whom he did foreknow, he also did predestinate *to be* conformed to the image of his Son, that he might be the **firstborn** among many brethren.	**Exodus 22:29** Thou shalt not delay *to offer* the **first** of thy ripe **fruits**, and of thy liquors: the firstborn of thy sons shalt thou give unto me. **Exodus 23:16** And the feast of harvest, the **firstfruits** of thy labors, which thou hast sown in the field: and the feast of ingathering, *which is* in the end of the year, when thou hast gathered in thy labors out of the field. **Exodus 23:19** The first of the **firstfruits** of thy land thou shalt bring into the house of the LORD thy God. Thou shalt not seethe a kid in his mother's milk. **Exodus 34:22** And thou shalt observe the feast of weeks, of the **firstfruits** of wheat harvest, and the feast of ingathering at the year's end. **Leviticus 2:12** As for the oblation of the **firstfruits**, ye shall offer them unto the LORD: but they shall not be burnt on the altar for a sweet savour. **Leviticus 23:10** Speak unto the children of Israel, and say unto them, When ye be come into the land which I give unto you, and shall reap the harvest thereof, then ye shall bring a sheaf of the **firstfruits of your harvest unto the priest**: **Numbers 18:12-13** All the best of the oil, and all the best of the wine, and of the wheat, the firstfruits of them which they shall

	offer unto the LORD, them have I given thee.13 *And* whatsoever is **first ripe** in the land, which they shall bring unto the LORD, shall be thine; every one that is clean in thine house shall eat *of* it. **Deuteronomy 18:4** The **firstfruit** *also* of thy corn, of thy wine, and of thine oil, and the first of the fleece of thy sheep, shalt thou give him." **Deuteronomy 26:2** That thou shalt take of the **first** of all the **fruit** of the earth, which thou shalt bring of thy land that the LORD thy God giveth thee, and shalt put *it* in a basket, and shalt go unto the place which the LORD thy God shall choose to place his name there. **Nehemiah 12:44** And at that time were some appointed over the chambers for the treasures, for the offerings, for the **firstfruits**, and for the tithes, to gather into them out of the fields of the cities the portions of the law for the priests and Levites: for Judah rejoiced for the priests and for the Levites that waited. **Proverbs 3:8-11** It shall be health to thy navel, and marrow to thy bones. 9 Honour the LORD with thy substance, and with the **firstfruits** of all thine increase: 10 So shall thy barns be filled with plenty, and thy presses shall burst out with new wine. 11 My son, despise not the chastening of the LORD; neither be weary of his correction:
Romans 8:26 Likewise the **Spirit also helpeth our infirmities**: for we know not what we should pray for as we ought: but the **Spirit itself maketh intercession** for us with **groanings** which cannot be uttered.	**See 1 Peter 2:24 "Healing"** **Isaiah 53:12** Therefore will I divide him *a portion* with the great, and he shall divide the spoil with the strong; because he hath poured out his soul unto death: and he was numbered with the transgressors; and **he** bare the sin of many, and **made intercession for the transgressors**. **See Romans 8:23 "Groanings"** **See John 4:24 "Worship"**
Romans 8:29 For whom he did foreknow, he also did predestinate *to be* conformed to the image of his Son, that he might be the firstborn among many brethren.	**See Hebrews 12:14 "Holiness"**
Romans 8:31 What shall we then say to these things? If God *be* for us, who *can be* against us?	**Numbers 14:8** If the LORD delight in us, then he will bring us into this land, and give it us; a land which floweth with milk and honey.
Romans 8:32 He that spared not his own Son, but delivered him up for us all, how shall he not with him also freely give us all things?	**Genesis 22:12** And he said, Lay not thine hand upon the lad, neither do thou any thing unto him: for now I know that thou fearest God, seeing thou hast not withheld thy son, thine only *son* from me.
Romans 8:33 Who shall lay any thing to the charge of God's elect? *It is* God that justifieth.	**Isaiah 50:8** *He is* near that justifieth me; who will contend with me? let us stand together: who *is* mine adversary? let him come near to me.
Romans 8:34 Who is he that condemneth? It is Christ that died, yea rather, that is risen again, who is even at the right hand of God, who also maketh intercession for us.	**Job 19:25** For I know *that* my redeemer liveth, and *that* he shall stand at the latter *day* upon the earth: **Psalms 8:6** Thou madest him to have dominion over the works of thy hands; thou hast put all *things* under his feet: **Psalms 16:8** I have set the LORD always before me: because *he is* at my right hand, I shall not be moved.

	Psalms 68:18 Thou hast ascended on high, thou hast led captivity captive: thou hast received gifts for men; yea, *for* the rebellious also, that the LORD God might dwell *among them*.
	Psalms 110:1 The LORD said unto my Lord, Sit thou at my right hand, until I make thine enemies thy footstool.
	Psalms 110:5 The Lord at thy right hand shall strike through kings in the day of his wrath.
	Isaiah 9:6 For unto us a child is born, unto us a son is given: and the government shall be upon his shoulder: and his name shall be called Wonderful, Counseller, The mighty God, The everlasting Father, The Prince of Peace.
	Isaiah 60:16 Thou shalt also suck the milk of the Gentiles, and shalt suck the breast of kings: and thou shalt know that I the LORD *am* thy Saviour and thy Redeemer, the mighty One of Jacob.
	Daniel 7:9 I beheld till the thrones were cast down, and the Ancient of days did sit, whose garment *was* white as snow, and the hair of his head like the pure wool: his throne *was like* the fiery flame, *and* his wheels *as* burning fire.
	Zechraiah 3:1 And he shewed me Joshua the high priest standing before the angel of the LORD, and Satan standing at his right hand to resist him.
Romans 8:36 As it is written, For thy sake we are killed all the day long; we are accounted as sheep for the slaughter.	**Psalm 44:22** Yea, for thy sake are we killed all the day long; we are counted as sheep for the slaughter.
Romans 9:3 For I could wish that myself were accursed from Christ for my brethren, my kinsmen according to the flesh:	**Exodus 32:32** Yet now, if thou wilt forgive their sin—; and if not, blot me, I pray thee, out of thy book which thou hast written.
Romans 9:4 Who are Israelites; to whom *pertaineth* the adoption, and the glory, and the **covenants**, and the giving of the law, and the service *of God*, and the promises;	**Genesis 3:21** Unto Adam also and to his wife did the LORD God make coats of skins, and clothed them.
	Genesis 9:8-9 And God spake unto Noah, and to his sons with him, saying, 9 And I, behold, I establish my covenant with you, and with your seed after you;
	Exodus 2:24 And God heard their groaning, and God remembered his covenant with Abraham, with Isaac, and with Jacob.
	Exodus 19:5 Now therefore, if ye will obey my voice indeed, and keep my covenant, then ye shall be a peculiar treasure unto me above all people: for all the earth *is* mine:
	Numbers 18:19 All the heave offerings of the holy things, which the children of Israel offer unto the LORD, have I given thee, and thy sons and thy daughters with thee, by a statute for ever: it *is* a covenant of salt for ever before the LORD unto thee and to thy seed with thee.
	Numbers 25:12-13 Wherefore say, Behold, I give unto him my covenant of peace: 13 And he shall have it, and his seed after him, *even* the covenant of an everlasting priesthood; because he was zealous for his God, and made an atonement for the children of Israel.
	Deuteronomy 7:6 For thou *art* an holy people unto the LORD thy God: the LORD thy God hath chosen thee to be a special people

	unto himself, above all people that *are* upon the face of the earth.
	Deuteronomy 10:14-15 Behold, the heaven and the heaven of heavens *is* the LORD's thy God, the earth *also*, with all that therein *is*. 15 Only the LORD had a delight in thy fathers to love them, and he chose their seed after them, *even* you above all people, as *it is* this day.
	2 Samuel 23:5 Although my house *be* not so with God; yet he hath made with me an everlasting covenant, ordered in all *things*, and sure: for *this is* all my salvation, and all *my* desire, although he make *it* not to grow.
Romans 9:5 Whose *are* the fathers, and of whom as concerning the flesh Christ *came*, who is over all, God blessed for ever. Amen.	**Jeremiah 23:6** In his days Judah shall be saved, and Israel shall dwell safely: and this *is* his name whereby he shall be called, THE LORD OUR RIGHTEOUSNESS.
Romans 9:6 Not as though the word of God hath taken none effect. For they *are* not all Israel, which are of Israel:	**Numbers 23:19** God *is* not a man, that he should lie; neither the son of man, that he should repent: hath he said, and shall he not do *it*? or hath he spoken, and shall he not make it good?
	1 Samuel 15:29 And also the Strength of Israel will not lie nor repent: for he *is* not a man, that he should repent.
Romans 9:7 Neither, because they are the seed of Abraham, *are they* all children: but, In Isaac shall thy seed be called.	**Genesis 21:12** And God said unto Abraham, Let it not be grievous in thy sight because of the lad, and because of thy bondwoman; in all that Sarah hath said unto thee, hearken unto her voice; for in Isaac shall thy seed be called.
Romans 9:9 For this *is* the word of promise, At this time will I come, and Sara shall have a son.	**Genesis 17:17** Then Abraham fell upon his face, and laughed, and said in his heart, Shall *a child* be born unto him that is an hundred years old? and shall Sarah, that is ninety years old, bear?
	Genesis 18:10 And he said, I will certainly return unto thee according to the time of life; and, lo, Sarah thy wife shall have a son. And Sarah heard *it* in the tent door, which *was* behind him.
	Genesis 18:12 Therefore Sarah laughed within herself, saying, After I am waxed old shall I have pleasure, my lord being old also? **Genesis 18:14** Is any thing too hard for the LORD? At the time appointed I will return unto thee, according to the time of life, and Sarah shall have a son.
Romans 9:10 And not only *this*; but when Rebecca also had conceived by one, *even* by our father Isaac;	**Genesis 25:21** And Isaac intreated the LORD for his wife, because she *was* barren: and the LORD was intreated of him, and Rebekah his wife conceived.
Romans 9:12 It was said unto her, The elder shall serve the younger.	**Genesis 25:23** And the LORD said unto her, Two nations *are* in thy womb, and two manner of people shall be separated from thy bowels; and *the one* people shall be stronger than *the other* people; and the elder shall serve the younger.
Romans 9:13 As it is written, Jacob have I loved, but Esau have I hated.	**Malachi 1:2-3** I have loved you, saith the LORD. Yet ye say, Wherein hast thou loved us? *Was* not Esau Jacob's brother? saith the LORD: yet I loved Jacob, And I hated Esau, and laid his mountains and his heritage waste for the dragons of the wilderness.
Romans 9:14 What shall we say then? *Is there* unrighteousness with God? God forbid.	**Deuteronomy 32:4** *He is* the Rock, his work *is* perfect: for all his ways *are* judgment: a God of truth and without iniquity, just and right *is* he.
	2 Chronicles 19:7 Wherefore now let the fear of the LORD be upon you; take heed and do *it*: for *there is* no iniquity with the LORD our God, nor respect of persons, nor taking of gifts.

	Job 34:10 Therefore hearken unto me, ye men of understanding: far be it from God, *that he should do* wickedness; and *from* the Almighty, *that he should commit* iniquity.
Romans 9:15 For he saith to Moses, **I will have mercy on whom I will have mercy**, and I will have compassion on whom I will have compassion.	**Exodus 33:19** And he said, I will make all my goodness pass before thee, and I will proclaim the name of the LORD before thee; and will be gracious to whom I will be gracious, and **will shew mercy on whom I will shew mercy**. **Jonah 4:2** And he prayed unto the LORD, and said, I pray thee, O LORD, *was* not this my saying, when I was yet in my country? Therefore I fled before unto Tarshish: for I knew that **thou *art* a gracious God, and merciful, slow to anger, and of great kindness**, and repentest thee of the evil.
Romans 9:17 For the scripture saith unto Pharaoh, Even for this same purpose have I raised thee up, that I might shew my power in thee, and that my name might be declared throughout all the earth.	**Exodus 9:16** And in very deed for this *cause* have I raised thee up, for to shew *in* thee my power; and that my name may be declared throughout all the earth.
Romans 9:20 Nay but, O man, who art thou that repliest against God? Shall the thing formed say to him that formed *it*, Why hast thou made me thus?	**Isaiah 29:16** Surely your turning of things upside down shall be esteemed as the potter's clay: for shall the work say of him that made it, He made me not? or shall the thing framed say of him that framed it, He had no understanding? **Isaiah 45:9** Woe unto him that striveth with his Maker! *Let* the potsherd [strive] with the potsherds of the earth. Shall the clay say to him that fashioneth it, What makest thou? or thy work, He hath no hands? **Jeremiah 18:6** O house of Israel, cannot I do with you as this potter? saith the LORD. Behold, as the clay *is* in the potter's hand, so *are* ye in mine hand, O house of Israel.
Romans 9:21 Hath not the potter power over the clay, of the same lump to make one vessel unto honour, and another unto dishonour?	**Jeremiah 18:6** O house of Israel, cannot I do with you as this potter? saith the LORD. Behold, as the clay *is* in the potter's hand, so *are* ye in mine hand, O house of Israel.
Romans 9:22-24 *What* if God, willing to shew *his* wrath, and to make his power known, endured with much longsuffering the vessels of wrath fitted to destruction: 23 And that he might make known the riches of his glory on the vessels of mercy, which he had afore prepared unto glory, 24 Even us, whom he hath called, not of the Jews only, but also of the Gentiles?	See 1 Thessalonians 5:23 "Body, soul, and spirit"
Romans 9:25 As he saith also in Osee, I will call them my people, which were not my people; and her beloved, which was not beloved.	**Hosea 2:23** And I will sow her unto me in the earth; and I will have mercy upon her that had not obtained mercy; and I will say to *them which were* not my people, Thou *art* my people; and they shall say, *Thou art* my God.
Romans 9:26 And it shall come to pass, *that* in the place where it was said unto them, Ye *are* not my people; there shall they be called the children of the living God.	**Hosea 1:10** Yet the number of the children of Israel shall be as the sand of the sea, which cannot be measured nor numbered; and it shall come to pass, [that] in the place where it was said unto them, Ye [are] not my people, [there] it shall be said unto them, *Ye are* the sons of the living God.
Romans 9:27-28 Esaias also crieth concerning Israel, Though the number of	**Isaiah 10:22-23** For though thy people Israel be as the sand of the sea, *yet* a remnant of them shall return: the consumption decreed

the children of Israel be as the sand of the sea, a remnant shall be saved: For he will finish the work, and cut *it* short in righteousness: because a short work will the Lord make upon the earth.	shall overflow with righteousness. For the Lord GOD of hosts shall make a consumption, even determined, in the midst of all the land. **Hosea 1:10** Yet the number of the children of Israel shall be as the sand of the sea, which cannot be measured nor numbered; and it shall come to pass, *that* in the place where it was said unto them, Ye *are* not my people, *there* it shall be said unto them, *Ye are* the sons of the living God.
Romans 9:29 And as Esaias said before, Except the Lord of Sabaoth had left us a seed, we had been as Sodoma, and been made like unto Gomorrha.	**Genesis 19:24** Then the LORD rained upon Sodom and upon Gomorrah brimstone and fire from the LORD out of heaven; **Deuteronomy 29:23** *And that* the whole land thereof *is* brimstone, and salt, *and* burning, *that* it is not sown, nor beareth, nor any grass groweth therein, like the overthrow of Sodom, and Gomorrah, Admah, and Zeboim, which the LORD overthrew in his anger, and in his wrath: **Isaiah 1:9** Except the LORD of hosts had left unto us a very small remnant, we should have been as Sodom, *and* we should have been like unto Gomorrah. **Isaiah 13:19** And Babylon, the glory of kingdoms, the beauty of the Chaldees' excellency, shall be as when God overthrew Sodom and Gomorrah. **Jeremiah 50:40** As God overthrew Sodom and Gomorrah and the neighbour *cities* thereof, saith the LORD; *so* shall no man abide there, neither shall any son of man dwell therein. **Ezekiel 16:46** And thine elder sister *is* Samaria, she and her daughters that dwell at thy left hand: and thy younger sister, that dwelleth at thy right hand, *is* Sodom and her daughters.
Romans 9:32-33 Wherefore? Because *they sought it* not by faith, but as it were by the works of the law. For they stumbled at that stumblingstone; 33 As it is written, Behold, I lay in Sion a stumblingstone and rock of offence: and whosoever believeth on him shall not be ashamed.	**Psalms 2:12** Kiss the Son, lest he be angry, and ye perish *from* the way, when his wrath is kindled but a little. Blessed *are* all they that put their trust in him. **Psalms 118:22** The stone *which* the builders refused is become the head *stone* of the corner. **Proverb 16:20** He that handleth a matter wisely shall find good: and whoso trusteth in the LORD, happy *is* he. **Isaiah 8:14** And he shall be for a sanctuary; but for a stone of stumbling and for a rock of offence to both the houses of Israel, for a gin and for a snare to the inhabitants of Jerusalem. **Isaiah 28:16** Therefore thus saith the Lord GOD, Behold, I lay in Zion for a foundation a stone, a tried stone, a precious corner *stone*, a sure foundation: he that believeth shall not make haste. **Jeremiah 17:7** Blessed *is* the man that trusteth in the LORD, and whose hope the LORD is.
Romans 10:5 For Moses describeth the righteousness which is of the law, That the man which doeth those things shall live by them.	**Leviticus 18:5** Ye shall therefore keep my statutes, and my judgments: which if a man do, he shall live in them: I *am* the LORD. **Ezekiel 20:11** And I gave them my statutes, and shewed them my judgments, which *if* a man do, he shall even live in them.
Romans 10:6 But the righteousness which is of faith speaketh on this wise, Say not in thine heart, Who shall ascend into heaven? (that is, to bring Christ down *from above:*)	**Deuteronomy 9:4** Speak not thou in thine heart, after that the LORD thy God hath cast them out from before thee, saying, For my righteousness the LORD hath brought me in to possess this land: but for the wickedness of these nations the LORD doth drive them out from before thee.

	Deuteronomy 30:12 It *is* not in heaven, that thou shouldest say, Who shall go up for us to heaven, and bring it unto us, that we may hear it, and do it?
Romans 10:7 Or, Who shall descend into the deep? (that is, to bring up Christ again from the dead.)	**Deuteronomy 30:13** Neither *is* it beyond the sea, that thou shouldest say, Who shall go over the sea for us, and bring it unto us, that we may hear it, and do it?
Romans 10:8 But what saith it? The word is nigh thee, *even* in thy mouth, and in thy heart: that is, the word of faith, which we preach;	**Deuteronomy 30:14** But the word *is* very nigh unto thee, in thy mouth, and in thy heart, that thou mayest do it.
Romans 10:9-10 That if thou shalt confess with thy mouth the Lord Jesus, and shalt believe in thine heart that God hath raised him from the dead, thou shalt be saved. 10 For with the heart man believeth unto righteousness; and with the mouth confession is made unto salvation. **(Romans 6:5 and Romans 8:9-11)**	**1 Kings 8:35-36** When heaven is shut up, and there is no rain, because they have sinned against thee; if they pray toward this place, and confess thy name, and turn from their sin, when thou afflictest them: 36 Then hear thou in heaven, and forgive the sin of thy servants, and of thy people Israel, that thou teach them the good way wherein they should walk, and give rain upon thy land, which thou hast given to thy people for an inheritance.
Romans 10:11 For the scripture saith, Whosoever believeth on him shall not be ashamed.	**Isaiah 8:14** And he shall be for a sanctuary; but for a stone of stumbling and for a rock of offence to both the houses of Israel, for a gin and for a snare to the inhabitants of Jerusalem. **Isaiah 28:16** Therefore thus saith the Lord GOD, Behold, I lay in Zion for a foundation a stone, a tried stone, a precious corner *stone*, a sure foundation: he that believeth shall not make haste.
Romans 10:13 For whosoever shall call upon the name of the Lord shall be saved.	**Psalms 34:17** *The righteous* cry, and the LORD heareth, and delivereth them out of all their troubles. **Psalms 50:15** And call upon me in the day of trouble: I will deliver thee, and thou shalt glorify me. **Joel 2:32** And it shall come to pass, *that* whosoever shall call on the name of the LORD shall be delivered: for in mount Zion and in Jerusalem shall be deliverance, as the LORD hath said, and in the remnant whom the LORD shall call. **Zechariah 13:9** And I will bring the third part through the fire, and will refine them as silver is refined, and will try them as gold is tried: they shall call on my name, and I will hear them: I will say, It *is* my people: and they shall say, The LORD *is* my God.
Romans 10:15 And how shall they preach, except they be sent? as it is written, How beautiful are the feet of them that preach the gospel of peace, and bring glad tidings of good things!	**Isaiah 52:7** How beautiful upon the mountains are the feet of him that bringeth good tidings, that publisheth peace; that bringeth good tidings of good, that saith unto Zion, Thy God reigneth! **Nahum 1:15** Behold upon the mountains the feet of him that bringeth good tidings, that publisheth peace! O Judah, keep thy solemn feasts, perform thy vows: for the wicked shall no more pass through thee; he is utterly cut off.
Romans 10:16 But they have not all obeyed the gospel. For Esaias saith, Lord, who hath believed our report?	**Isaiah 53:1** Who hath believed our report? and to whom is the arm of the LORD revealed?
Romans 10:17 So then **faith *cometh* by hearing, and hearing by the Word of God**.	See Matthew 5:18 "Scriptures"
Romans 10:18 But I say, Have they not	**Psalms 19:4** Their line is gone out through all the earth, and their

heard? Yes verily, their sound went into all the earth, and their words unto the ends of the world.	words to the end of the world. In them hath he set a tabernacle for the sun,
Romans 10:19 But I say, Did not Israel know? First Moses saith, I will provoke you to jealousy by *them that are* no people, *and* by a foolish nation I will anger you.	**Deuteronomy 32:21** They have moved me to jealousy with *that which is* not God; they have provoked me to anger with their vanities: and I will move them to jealousy with *those which are* not a people; I will provoke them to anger with a foolish nation.
Romans 10:20 But Esaias is very bold, and saith, I was found of them that sought me not; I was made manifest unto them that asked not after me.	**Isaiah 65:1** I am sought of *them that* asked not *for me*; I am found of *them that* sought me not: I said, Behold me, behold me, unto a nation *that* was not called by my name.
Romans 10:20-21 But Esaias is very bold, and said, I was found of them that sought me not; I was made manifest to them that asked not after me. 21 But to Israel he saith, All day long I have stretched forth my hands unto a disobedient and gainsaying people.	**Isaiah 65:1-2** I am sought of them that asked not for me; I am found of them that sought me not: I said, Behold me, behold me, to a nation that was not called by my name. 2 I have spread out my hands all the day unto a rebellious people, which walketh in a way *that was* not good, after their own thoughts;
Romans 11:1 I say then, Hath God cast away his people? God forbid. For I also am an Israelite, of the seed of Abraham, *of* the tribe of Benjamin.	**Jeremiah 31:37** Thus saith the LORD; If heaven above can be measured, and the foundations of the earth searched out beneath, I will also cast off all the seed of Israel for all that they have done, saith the LORD.
Romans 11:2 God hath not cast away his people which he foreknew. Wot ye not what the scripture saith of Elias? how he maketh intercession to God against Israel, saying,	**1 Samuel 12:22** For the LORD will not forsake his people for his great name's sake: because it hath pleased the LORD to make you his people. **Psalms 94:14** For the LORD will not cast off his people, neither will he forsake his inheritance.
Romans 11:3 Lord, they have killed thy prophets, and digged down thine altars; and I am left alone, and they seek my life.	**1 Kings 19:10** And he said, I have been very jealous for the LORD God of hosts: for the children of Israel have forsaken thy covenant, thrown down thine altars, and slain thy prophets with the sword; and I, *even* I only, am left; and they seek my life, to take it away. **1 Kings 19:14** And he said, I have been very jealous for the LORD God of hosts: because the children of Israel have forsaken thy covenant, thrown down thine altars, and slain thy prophets with the sword; and I, *even* I only, am left; and they seek my life, to take it away.
Romans 11:4 But what saith the answer of God unto him? I have reserved to myself seven thousand men, who have not bowed the knee to *the image of* Baal.	**1 Kings 19:18** Yet I have left *me* seven thousand in Israel, all the knees which have not bowed unto Baal, and every mouth which hath not kissed him.
Romans 11:8 (According as it is written, God hath given them the spirit of slumber, eyes that they should not see, and ears that they should not hear;) unto this day.	**Deuteronomy 29:3-4** The great temptations which thine eyes have seen, the signs, and those great miracles: 4 Yet the LORD hath not given you an heart to perceive, and eyes to see, and ears to hear, unto this day. **Isaiah 6:9** And he said, Go, and tell this people, Hear ye indeed, but understand not; and see ye indeed, but perceive not. **Isaiah 29:10** For the LORD hath poured out upon you the spirit of deep sleep, and hath closed your eyes: the prophets and your rulers, the seers hath he covered. **Ezekiel 12:2** Son of man, thou dwellest in the midst of a rebellious house, which have eyes to see, and see not; they have ears to hear, and hear not: for they *are* a rebellious house.

Romans 11:9-10 And David saith, Let their table be made a snare, and a trap, and a stumblingblock, and a recompence unto them: 10 Let their eyes be darkened, that they may not see, and bow down their back alway.	**Psalms 69:22-23** Let their table become a snare before them: and *that which should have been* for *their* welfare, *let it become* a trap. Let their eyes be darkened, that they see not; and make their loins continually to shake.
Romans 11:16 For if the **firstfruit** *be* holy, the lump *is* also *holy*: and if the root *be* holy, so *are* the branches.	**See Romans 8:23 "first fruit"**
Romans 11:17 And if some of the branches be broken off, and thou, being a wild olive tree, wert graffed in among them, and with them partakest of the root and fatness of the olive tree;	**Proverbs 12:3** A man shall not be established by wickedness: but the **root of the righteous** shall not be moved. **Proverb 12:12** The wicked desireth the net of evil men: but the **root of the righteous** yieldeth fruit. **Jeremiah 11:16** The LORD called thy name, A green olive tree, fair, *and* of goodly fruit: with the noise of a great tumult he hath kindled fire upon it, and the branches of it are broken.
Romans 11:22 Behold therefore the **goodness** and severity of God: on them which fell, severity; but toward thee, **goodness**, if thou continue in *his* goodness: otherwise thou also shalt be cut off.	**Isaiah 64:6** But we are all as an unclean *thing,* and all our **righteousnesses** *are* as filthy rags; and we all do fade as a leaf; and our iniquities, like the wind, have taken us away.
Romans 11:26 And so all Israel shall be saved: as it is written, There shall come out of Sion the Deliverer, and shall turn away ungodliness from Jacob:	**Leviticus 16:30-33** For on that day shall *the priest* make an atonement for you, to cleanse you, *that* ye may be clean from all your sins before the LORD. 31 It *shall be* a sabbath of rest unto you, and ye shall afflict your souls, by a statute for ever. 32 And the priest, whom he shall anoint, and whom he shall consecrate to minister in the priest's office in his father's stead, shall make the atonement, and shall put on the linen clothes, *even* the holy garments: 33 And he shall make an atonement for the holy sanctuary, and he shall make an atonement for the tabernacle of the congregation, and for the altar, and he shall make an atonement for the priests, and for all the people of the congregation. **Leviticus 23:27** Also on the tenth *day* of this seventh month *there shall be* a day of atonement: it shall be an holy convocation unto you; and ye shall afflict your souls, and offer an offering made by fire unto the LORD. **Psalms 14:7** Oh that the salvation of Israel *were* come out of Zion! when the LORD bringeth back the captivity of his people, Jacob shall rejoice, *and* Israel shall be glad. **Psalms 34:7** The angel of the LORD encampeth round about them that fear him, and delivereth them. **Isaiah 27:9** By this therefore shall the iniquity of Jacob be purged; and this *is* all the fruit to take away his sin; when he maketh all the stones of the altar as chalkstones that are beaten in sunder, the groves and images shall not stand up.
Romans 11:27 For this *is* my covenant unto them, when I shall take away their sins.	**See Isaiah 59:20-21 and Jeremiah 31:31-33 and Ezekiel 34:22-31**
Romans 11:29 For the gifts and calling of God *are* without repentance.	**Psalm 33:11** The counsel of the LORD standeth forever, the thoughts of his heart to all generations.

	Psalm 102:27 But thou *art* the same, and thy years shall have no end.
	Malachi 3:6 For I *am* the LORD, I change not; therefore ye sons of Jacob are not consumed.
Romans 11:32 For God hath concluded them all in unbelief, that **he might have mercy** upon all.	**Exodus 33:19** And he said, I will make all my goodness pass before thee, and I will proclaim the name of the LORD before thee; and will be gracious to whom I will be gracious, and **will shew mercy on whom I will shew mercy**.
	Jonah 4:2 And he prayed unto the LORD, and said, I pray thee, O LORD, *was* not this my saying, when I was yet in my country? Therefore I fled before unto Tarshish: for I knew that **thou *art* a gracious God, and merciful, slow to anger, and of great kindness**, and repentest thee of the evil.
Romans 11:33 O the depth of the riches both of the wisdom and knowledge of God! how unsearchable *are* his judgments, and his ways past finding out!	**Psalms 36:6** Thy righteousness *is* like the great mountains; thy judgments *are* a great deep: O LORD, thou preservest man and beast.
	Isaiah 55:8-9 For my thoughts *are* not your thoughts, neither *are* your ways my ways, saith the LORD. ⁹ For *as* the heavens are higher than the earth, so are my ways higher than your ways, and my thoughts than your thoughts.
Romans 11:34-35 For who hath known the mind of the Lord? or who hath been his counsellor? 35 Or who hath first given to him, and it shall be recompensed unto him again?	**Isaiah 40:13-14** Who hath directed the Spirit of the LORD, or *being* his counsellor hath taught him? 14 With whom took he counsel, and *who* instructed him, and taught him in the path of judgment, and taught him knowledge, and shewed to him the way of understanding?
Romans 11:35 Or who hath first given to him, and it shall be recompensed unto him again?	**Job 41:11** Who hath prevented me, that I should repay *him? whatsoever is* under the whole heaven is mine.
Romans 11:36 For of him, and through him, and to him, *are* all things: to whom *be* glory for ever. Amen.	**Proverb 16:4** The LORD hath made all *things* for himself: yea, even the wicked for the day of evil.
Romans 12:1-2 I beseech you therefore, brethren, by the mercies of God, that ye present your bodies a living sacrifice, holy, acceptable unto God, which is your reasonable service. 2 And be not conformed to this world: but be ye transformed by the renewing of your mind, that ye may prove what is that good, and acceptable, and perfect, will of God.	**Ezra 7:10** For Ezra had prepared his heart to seek the law of the LORD, and to do *it*, and to teach in Israel statutes and judgments.
	1 Samuel 7:3-4 And Samuel spake unto all the house of Israel, saying, If ye do return unto the Lord with all your hearts, then put away the strange gods and Ashtaroth from among you, and prepare your hearts unto the Lord, and serve him only: and he will deliver you out of the hand of the Philistines. 4 Then the children of Israel did put away Baalim and Ashtaroth, and served the Lord only.
	1 Chronicles 29:18 O LORD God of Abraham, Isaac, and of Israel, our fathers, keep this forever in the imagination of the thoughts of the heart of thy people, and prepare their heart unto thee:
	2 Chronicles 12:14 And he did evil, because he prepared not his heart to seek the LORD.
	2 Chronicles 19:3 Nevertheless there are good things found in thee, in that thou hast taken away the groves out of the land, and hast prepared thine heart to seek God.
	Job 11:13 If thou prepare thine heart, and stretch out thine hands toward him;
	Psalm 10:17 LORD, thou hast heard the desire of the humble: thou

	wilt prepare their heart, thou wilt cause thine ear to hear:
	Psalms 51:10 Create in me a clean heart, O God; and **renew** a right spirit within me.
	Psalm 57:7 My heart is fixed, O God, my heart is fixed: I will sing and give praise.
	Proverbs 16:1 The preparations of the heart in man, and the answer of the tongue, *is* from the LORD.
	See Hebrews 12:14 "Holiness"
Romans 12:6 Having then gifts differing according to the grace that is given to us, whether **prophecy**, *let us prophesy* according to the proportion of faith;	**See 1 Corinthians 12:10 "Prophecy"**
Romans 12:7 Or ministry, *let us wait* on *our* ministering: or he that **teacheth**, on teaching;	**2 Chronicles 15:3** Now for a long season Israel *hath been* without the true God, and without a **teaching priest**, and without law.
	2 Chronicles 30:22 And Hezekiah spake comfortably unto all the **Levites that taught the good knowledge of the LORD**: and they did eat throughout the feast seven days, offering peace offerings, and making confession to the LORD God of their fathers.
	Jeremiah 32:33 And they have turned unto me the back, and not the face: though **I taught them**, rising up early and **teaching** *them*, yet they have not hearkened to receive instruction.
	Hosea 4:6 My people are destroyed for lack of knowledge: because thou hast rejected knowledge, I will also reject thee, that thou shalt be no priest to me: seeing thou hast forgotten the law of thy God, I will also forget thy children.
Romans 12:8 Or he that exhorteth, on exhortation: he that giveth, *let him do it* with simplicity; he that ruleth, with diligence; he that sheweth mercy, with cheerfulness.	**Deuteronomy 15:7** If there be among you a poor man of one of thy brethren within any of thy gates in thy land which the LORD thy God giveth thee, thou shalt not harden thine heart, nor shut thine hand from thy poor brother:
Romans 12:9 *Let* love be without dissimulation. Abhor that which is evil; cleave to that which is good.	**Psalms 97:10** Ye that love the LORD, hate evil: he preserveth the souls of his saints; he delivereth them out of the hand of the wicked.
	Amos 5:15 Hate the evil, and love the good, and establish judgment in the gate: it may be that the LORD God of hosts will be gracious unto the remnant of Joseph.
Romans 12:12 Rejoicing in hope; patient in tribulation; continuing instant in **prayer**;	**See Matthew 17:21 "Prayer"**
Romans 12:16 *Be* of the same mind one toward another. Mind not high things, but condescend to men of low estate. Be not wise in your own conceits.	**Proverb 3:7** Be not wise in thine own eyes: fear the LORD, and depart from evil.
	Isaiah 5:21 Woe unto *them that are* wise in their own eyes, and prudent in their own sight!
Romans 12:17 Recompense to no man evil for evil. Provide things honest in the sight of all men.	**Leviticus 19:18** Thou shalt not avenge, nor bear any grudge against the children of thy people, but thou shalt love thy neighbour as thyself: I *am* the LORD.
	Proverbs 20:22 Say not thou, I will recompense evil; *but* wait on the LORD, and he shall save thee.
	Proverbs 24:29 Say not, I will do so to him as he hath done to me:

	I will render to the man according to his work. **Proverbs 3:4** So shalt thou find favour and good understanding in the sight of God and man.
Romans 12:19 Dearly beloved, avenge not yourselves, but *rather* give place unto wrath: for it is written, Vengeance *is* mine; I will repay, saith the Lord.	**Leviticus 19:18** Thou shalt not avenge, nor bear any grudge against the children of thy people, but thou shalt love thy neighbour as thyself: I *am* the LORD. **Deuteronomy 32:35** To me *belongeth* vengeance, and recompence; their foot shall slide in *due* time: for the day of their calamity *is* at hand, and the things that shall come upon them make haste.
Romans 12:20 Therefore if thine enemy hunger, feed him; if he thirst, give him drink: for in so doing thou shalt heap coals of fire on his head.	**Proverbs 25:21-22** If thine enemy be hungry, give him bread to eat; and if he be thirsty, give him water to drink: For thou shalt heap coals of fire upon his head, and the LORD shall reward thee.
Romans 13:1 Let every soul be subject unto the higher powers. For there is no power but of God: the powers that be are ordained of God.	**Proverb 8:15** By me kings reign, and princes decree justice. **Daniel 4:32** And they shall drive thee from men, and thy dwelling *shall be* with the beasts of the field: they shall make thee to eat grass as oxen, and seven times shall pass over thee, until thou know that the most High ruleth in the kingdom of men, and giveth it to whomsoever he will.
Romans 13:8 Owe no man any thing, but to love one another: for he that loveth another hath fulfilled the law.	**Exodus 22:25** If thou lend money to *any of* my people *that is* poor by thee, thou shalt not be to him as an usurer, neither shalt thou lay upon him usury. **Exodus 22:26-27** If thou at all take thy neighbour's raiment to pledge, thou shalt deliver it unto him by that the sun goeth down: 27 For that *is* his covering only, it *is* his raiment for his skin: wherein shall he sleep? and it shall come to pass, when he crieth unto me, that I will hear; for I *am* gracious. **Leviticus 19:13** Thou shalt not defraud thy neighbour, neither rob him: the wages of him that is hired shall not abide with thee all night until the morning. **Deuteronomy 23:19-20** Thou shalt not lend upon usury to thy brother; usury of money, usury of victuals, usury of any thing that is lent upon usury: 20 Unto a stranger thou mayest lend upon usury; but unto thy brother thou shalt not lend upon usury: that the LORD thy God may bless thee in all that thou settest thine hand to in the land whither thou goest to possess it. **Psalms 15:5** *He that* putteth not out his money to usury, nor taketh reward against the innocent. He that doeth these *things* shall never be moved. **Proverbs 28:8** He that by usury and unjust gain increaseth his substance, he shall gather it for him that will pity the poor. **Ezekiel 18:8** He *that* hath not given forth upon usury, neither hath taken any increase, *that* hath withdrawn his hand from iniquity, hath executed true judgment between man and man, **Ezekiel 18:13** Hath given forth upon usury, and hath taken increase: shall he then live? he shall not live: he hath done all these abominations; he shall surely die; his blood shall be upon him. **Ezekiel 18:17** *That* hath taken off his hand from the poor, *that* hath not received usury nor increase, hath executed my judgments, hath walked in my statutes; he shall not die for the iniquity of his father,

	he shall surely live. **Ezekiel 22:12** In thee have they taken gifts to shed blood; thou hast taken usury and increase, and thou hast greedily gained of thy neighbours by extortion, and hast forgotten me, saith the Lord GOD.
Romans 13:9 For this, Thou shalt not commit adultery, Thou shalt not kill, Thou shalt not steal, Thou shalt not bear false witness, Thou shalt not covet; and if *there be* any other commandment, it is briefly comprehended in this saying, namely, Thou shalt love thy neighbour as thyself.	**Exodus 20:13-17** Thou shalt not kill. 14 Thou shalt not commit adultery. 15 Thou shalt not steal. 16 Thou shalt not bear false witness against thy neighbour. 17 Thou shalt not covet thy neighbour's house, thou shalt not covet thy neighbour's wife, nor his manservant, nor his maidservant, nor his ox, nor his ass, nor any thing that is thy neighbour's. **Leviticus 19:11** Ye shall not steal, neither deal falsely, neither lie one to another. **Leviticus 19:18** Thou shalt not avenge, nor bear any grudge against the children of thy people, but thou shalt love thy neighbour as thyself: I *am* the LORD. **Deuteronomy 5:17-21** Thou shalt not kill. 18 Neither shalt thou commit adultery. 19 Neither shalt thou steal. 20 Neither shalt thou bear false witness against thy neighbour. 21 Neither shalt thou desire thy neighbour's wife, neither shalt thou covet thy neighbour's house, his field, or his manservant, or his maidservant, his ox, or his ass, or any thing that is thy neighbour's. **See Matthew 5:27 "Adultery"**
Romans 13:10 Love worketh no ill to his neighbour: therefore love *is* the fulfilling of the law.	**Leviticus 19:18** Thou shalt not avenge, nor bear any grudge against the children of thy people, but thou shalt love thy neighbour as thyself: I *am* the LORD.
Romans 13:13-14 Let us walk honestly, as in the day; not in rioting and **drunkenness, not in chambering and wantonness**, not in **strife** and envying. 14 But put ye on the Lord Jesus Christ, and make not provision for the flesh, to *fulfil* the lusts *thereof.*	**See Ephesians 5:18 "Drunkards"** **See Romans 1:26-27 "Sexual sins"** **Psalms 31:20** Thou shalt hide them in the secret of thy presence from the pride of man: thou shalt keep them secretly in a pavilion from the **strife** of tongues.
Romans 14:10 But why dost thou judge thy brother? or why dost thou set at nought thy brother? for we shall all stand before the **judgment** seat of Christ.	**See 2 Timothy 4:1 "Judge"**
Romans 14:11 For it is written, [As] I live, saith the Lord, every knee shall bow to me, and every tongue shall confess to God.	**Isaiah 45:23** I have sworn by myself, the word is gone out of my mouth *in* righteousness, and shall not return, That unto me every knee shall bow, every tongue shall swear. **Isaiah 49:18** Lift up thine eyes round about, and behold: all these gather themselves together, *and* come to thee. *As* I live, saith the LORD, thou shalt surely clothe thee with them all, as with an ornament, and bind them *on thee,* as a bride *doeth.*
Romans 14:12 So then every one of us shall give account of himself to God.	**Job 34:21** For his eyes *are* upon the ways of man, and he seeth all his goings. **Psalms 62:12** Also unto thee, O Lord, *belongeth* mercy: for thou renderest to every man according to his work. **Proverb 15:3** The eyes of the LORD *are* in every place, beholding the evil and the good. **Ecclesiastes 11:9-10** Rejoice, O young man, in thy youth; and let

	thy heart cheer thee in the days of thy youth, and walk in the ways of thine heart, and in the sight of thine eyes: but know thou, that for all these things God will bring thee into judgment. 10 Therefore remove sorrow from thy heart, and put away evil from thy flesh: for childhood and youth are vanity. **Jeremiah 17:10** I the LORD search the heart, *I* try the reins, even to give every man according to his ways, *and* according to the fruit of his doings. **Jeremiah 32:19** Great in counsel, and mighty in work: for thine eyes *are* open upon all the ways of the sons of men: to give every one according to his ways, and according to the fruit of his doings:
Romans 14:17 For the kingdom of God is not meat and drink; but righteousness, and **peace**, and **joy** in the Holy Ghost.	**Isaiah 26:3** Thou wilt keep *him* in perfect **peace**, *whose* mind *is* stayed *on thee:* because he trusteth in thee. **Isaiah 12:3-4** Therefore with **joy** shall ye draw water out of the wells of salvation. 4 And in that day shall ye say, Praise the LORD, call upon his name, declare his doings among the people, make mention that his name is exalted. **Habakkuk 3:17** Although the fig tree shall not blossom, neither *shall* fruit *be* in the vines; the labour of the olive shall fail, and the fields shall yield no meat; the flock shall be cut off from the fold, and *there shall be* no herd in the stalls: 18 Yet I will **rejoice** in the LORD, I will **joy** in the God of my salvation.
Romans 15:3 For even Christ pleased not himself; but, as it is written, The reproaches of them that reproached thee fell on me.	**Psalms 69:9** For the zeal of thine house hath eaten me up; and the reproaches of them that reproached thee are fallen upon me. **Isaiah 53:4-5** Surely he hath borne our griefs, and carried our sorrows: yet we did esteem him stricken, smitten of God, and afflicted. 5 But he *was* wounded for our transgressions, *he was* bruised for our iniquities: the chastisement of our peace *was* upon him; and with his stripes we are healed.
Romans 15:4 For whatsoever things **were written aforetime were written** for our learning, that we through patience and comfort of the **Scriptures** might have hope.	**See Matthew 5:18 "Scriptures"**
Romans 15:5-6 Now the God of patience and consolation grant you to be **likeminded** one toward another according to Christ Jesus: 6 That ye may with **one mind** *and* one mouth glorify God, even the Father of our Lord Jesus Christ.	**Psalms 133:1** Behold, how good and how pleasant *it is* for brethren to dwell together in unity! **Amos 3:3** Can two walk together, except they be agreed?
Romans 15:9 And that the Gentiles might glorify God for *his* mercy; as it is written, For this cause I will confess to thee among the Gentiles, and sing unto thy name.	**2 Samuel 22:50** Therefore I will give thanks unto thee, O LORD, among the heathen, and I will sing praises unto thy name. **Psalms 18:49** Therefore will I give thanks unto thee, O LORD, among the heathen, and sing praises unto thy name.
Romans 15:10 And again he saith, Rejoice, ye Gentiles, with his people.	**Deuteronomy 32:43** Rejoice, O ye nations, *with* his people: for he will avenge the blood of his servants, and will render vengeance to his adversaries, and will be merciful unto his land, *and* to his people.
Romans 15:11 And again, Praise the	**Psalms 117:1** O praise the LORD, all ye nations: praise him, all ye

Lord, all ye Gentiles; and laud him, all ye people.	people.
Romans 15:12 And again, Esaias saith, There shall be a root of Jesse, and he that shall rise to reign over the Gentiles; in him shall the Gentiles trust.	**Isaiah 11:10** And in that day there shall be a root of Jesse, which shall stand for an ensign of the people; to it shall the Gentiles seek: and his rest shall be glorious.
Romans 15:21 But as it is written, To whom he was not spoken of, they shall see: and they that have not heard shall understand.	**Isaiah 52:15** So shall he sprinkle many nations; the kings shall shut their mouths at him: for *that* which had not been told them shall they see; and [that] which they had not heard shall they consider.
Romans 15:26 For it hath pleased them of Macedonia and Achaia to make a certain contribution for the poor saints which are at Jerusalem.	**Deuteronomy 15:11** For the poor shall never cease out of the land: therefore I command thee, saying, Thou shalt open thine hand wide unto thy brother, to thy poor, and to thy needy, in thy land.
Romans 16:1 I commend unto you Phebe our sister, which is **a servant of the church** which is at Cenchrea:	**Judges 4:4** And Deborah, a **prophetess**, the wife of Lapidoth, she judged Israel at that time. **Isaiah 8:3** And I went unto the **prophetess**; and she conceived, and bare a son. Then said the LORD to me, Call his name Mahershalalhashbaz.
Romans 16:3 Greet **Priscilla** and Aquila my helpers in Christ Jesus:	**See Acts 18:26** "Woman's role"
Romans 16:5 Likewise *greet* the church that is in their house. Salute my well-beloved Epaenetus, who is the **firstfruits** of Achaia unto Christ.	**See Romans 8:23** "Firstfruits"
Romans 16:17-18 Now I beseech you, brethren, mark them which cause divisions and offences contrary to the doctrine which ye have learned; and avoid them. 18 For they that are such serve not our Lord Jesus Christ, but their own belly; and by good words and fair speeches deceive the hearts of the **simple**.	**Deuteronomy 23:10** If there be among you any man, that is not clean by reason of uncleanness that chanceth him by night, then shall he go abroad out of the camp, he shall not come within the camp: **Proverbs 14:15** The **simple** believeth every word: but the prudent *man* looketh well to his going. **Proverbs 22:3** A prudent *man* foreseeth the evil, and hideth himself: but the **simple** pass on, and are punished. **Proverbs 22:24-25** Make no friendship with an angry man; and with a furious man thou shalt not go: 25 Lest thou learn his ways, and get a snare to thy soul. **Isaiah 5:20** Woe unto them that call evil good, and good evil; that put darkness for light, and light for **darkness**; that put bitter for sweet, and sweet for bitter! **Ezekiel 13:18** And say, Thus saith the Lord GOD; Woe to the *women* that sew pillows to all armholes, and make kerchiefs upon the head of every stature to hunt souls! Will ye hunt the souls of my people, and will ye save the souls alive *that come* unto you?
Romans 16:20 And the God of peace shall bruise **Satan** under your feet shortly. The grace of our Lord Jesus Christ *be* with you. Amen.	**Genesis 3:4** And the **serpent** said unto the woman, Ye shall not surely die: **Zechariah 3:1-2** And he shewed me Joshua the high priest standing before the angel of the LORD, and **Satan** standing at his right hand to resist him. 2 And the LORD said unto **Satan,** The LORD rebuke thee, O **Satan**; even the LORD that hath chosen Jerusalem rebuke thee: *is* not this a brand plucked out of the fire? **See Matthew 4:10** "satan"

1 Corinthians 1:2 Unto the church of God which is at Corinth, to them that are sanctified in Christ Jesus, called *to be* saints, with all that in every place call upon the name of Jesus Christ our Lord, both theirs and ours:	**Exodus 12:22** And ye shall take a bunch of hyssop, and dip *it* in the blood that *is* in the bason, and strike the lintel and the two side posts with the blood that *is* in the bason; and none of you shall go out at the door of his house until the morning. **Exodus 24:6-8** And Moses took half of the blood, and put *it* in basons; and half of the blood he sprinkled on the altar. 7 And he took the book of the covenant, and read in the audience of the people: and they said, All that the LORD hath said will we do, and be obedient. 8 And Moses took the blood, and sprinkled *it* on the people, and said, Behold the blood of the covenant, which the LORD hath made with you concerning all these words. **Leviticus 5:9** And he shall sprinkle of the blood of the sin offering upon the side of the altar; and the rest of the blood shall be wrung out at the bottom of the altar: it *is* a sin offering. **Isaiah 53:5** But he *was* wounded for our transgressions, *he was* bruised for our iniquities: the chastisement of our peace *was* upon him; and with his stripes we are healed. **Daniel 9:24** Seventy weeks are determined upon thy people and upon thy holy city, to finish the transgression, and to make an end of sins, and **to make reconciliation for iniquity**, and to bring in everlasting righteousness, and to seal up the vision and prophecy, and to anoint the most Holy.
1 Corinthians 1:10 Now I beseech you, brethren, by the name of our Lord Jesus Christ, that ye all speak the same thing, and *that* there be **no divisions among you**; but *that* ye be perfectly joined together in the same mind and in the same judgment.	**Numbers 16:10** And he hath brought thee near *to him*, and all thy brethren the sons of Levi with thee: and **seek ye the priesthood also?** **Numbers 16:26** And he spake unto the congregation, saying, **Depart**, I pray you, from the tents of these wicked men, and touch nothing of theirs, **lest ye be consumed in all their sins**. **Numbers 16:28** And Moses said, Hereby ye shall know that the Lord hath sent me to do all these works; for I have not done them of mine own mind. **Numbers 16:32-34** And the earth opened her mouth, and swallowed them up, and their houses, and all the men that appertained unto Korah, and all their goods. 33 They, and all that appertained to them, went down alive into the pit, and the earth closed upon them: and they perished from among the congregation. 34 And all Israel that were round about them fled at the cry of them: for they said, Lest the earth swallow us up also.
1 Corinthians 1:12 Now this I say, that every one of you saith, I am of Paul; and I of Apollos; and I of Cephas; and I of Christ.	**Psalms 133:1** Behold, how good and how pleasant *it is* for brethren to dwell together in unity! **Amos 3:3** Can two walk together, except they be agreed?
1 Corinthians 1:19 For it is written, I will destroy the wisdom of the wise, and will bring to nothing the understanding of the prudent.	**Nehemiah 4:15** And it came to pass, when our enemies heard that it was known unto us, and God had brought their counsel to nought, that we returned all of us to the wall, every one unto his work. **Job 5:12** He disappointeth the devices of the crafty, so that their hands cannot perform *their* enterprise. **Psalms 33:10** The LORD bringeth the counsel of the heathen to nought: he maketh the devices of the people of none effect. **Isaiah 19:3** And the spirit of Egypt shall fail in the midst thereof; and I will destroy the counsel thereof: and they shall seek to the idols, and to the charmers, and to them that have familiar spirits,

	and to the wizards. **Isaiah 29:14** Therefore, behold, I will proceed to do a marvellous work among this people, [even] a marvellous work and a wonder: for the wisdom of their wise *men* shall perish, and the understanding of their prudent [men] shall be hid.
1 Corinthians 1:20 Where *is* the wise? where *is* the scribe? where *is* the disputer of this world? hath not God made foolish the wisdom of this world?	**Jeremiah 4:22** For my people *is* foolish, they have not known me; they *are* sottish children, and they have none understanding: they *are* wise to do evil, but to do good they have no knowledge.
1 Corinthians 1:30 But of him are ye in Christ Jesus, who of God is made unto us wisdom, and righteousness, and sanctification, and redemption:	**Jeremiah23:5** Behold, the days come, saith the LORD, that I will raise unto David a righteous Branch, and a King shall reign and prosper, and shall execute judgment and justice in the earth. **Jeremiah 33:14-15** Behold, the days come, saith the LORD, that I will perform that good thing which I have promised unto the house of Israel and to the house of Judah. 15 In those days, and at that time, will I cause the Branch of righteousness to grow up unto David; and he shall execute judgment and righteousness in the land.
1 Corinthians 1:31 That, according as it is written, He that glorieth, let him glory in the Lord.	**Jeremiah 9:23-24** Thus saith the LORD, Let not the wise *man* glory in his wisdom, neither let the mighty *man* glory in his might, let not the rich *man* glory in his riches: 24 But let him that glorieth glory in this, that he understandeth and knoweth me, that I [am] the LORD which exercise lovingkindness, judgment, and righteousness, in the earth: for in these *things* I delight, saith the LORD.
1 Corinthians 2:5 That your faith should not stand in the wisdom of men, but in the **power** of God.	**See Luke 4:18 "Anointing"**
1 Corinthians 2:6 Howbeit we speak wisdom among them that are perfect: yet not the wisdom of this world, nor of the **princes of this world**, that come to nought:	**Job 28:20-21** Whence then cometh wisdom? and where *is* the place of understanding? 21 Seeing it is hid from the eyes of all living, and kept close from the fowls of the air. **See Hebrews 13:2 "Angels"**
1 Corinthians 2:8 Which none of the **princes of this world** knew: for had they known *it,* they would not have crucified the Lord of glory.	**Psalms 24:10** Who is this King of glory? The LORD of hosts, he *is* the King of glory. Selah. **See Hebrews 13:2 "Angels"**
1 Corinthians 2:9 But as it is written, Eye hath not seen, nor ear heard, neither have entered into the heart of man, the things which God hath prepared for them that love him.	**Isaiah 52:15** So shall he sprinkle many nations; the kings shall shut their mouths at him: for *that* which had not been told them shall they see; and *that* which they had not heard shall they consider. **Isaiah 64:4** For since the beginning of the world [men] have not heard, nor perceived by the ear, neither hath the eye seen, O God, beside thee, [what] he hath prepared for him that waiteth for him. Jeremiah 3:16 And it shall come to pass, when ye be multiplied and increased in the land, in those days, saith the LORD, they shall say no more, The ark of the covenant of the LORD: neither shall it come to mind: neither shall they remember it; neither shall they visit *it;* neither shall *that* be done any more.
1 Corinthians 2:11 For what man knoweth the things of a man, save the spirit of man which is in him? even so the things of God knoweth no man, but	**Jerermiah 17:9** The heart *is* deceitful above all *things*, and desperately wicked: who can know it?

the Spirit of God.	
1 Corinthians 2:16 For who hath known the mind of the Lord, that he may instruct him? But we have the mind of Christ.	**Isaiah 40:13-14** Who hath directed the Spirit of the LORD, or *being* his counsellor hath taught him? 14 With whom took he counsel, and *who* instructed him, and taught him in the path of judgment, and taught him knowledge, and shewed to him the way of understanding?
1 Corinthians 2:17 For we are not as many, **which corrupt the word of God**: but as of sincerity, but as of God, in the sight of God speak we in Christ.	**See Matthew 5:18 "Scriptures"**
1 Corinthians 3:3 For ye are yet carnal: for whereas *there is* among you envying, and **strife**, and divisions, are ye not carnal, and walk as men?	**Psalms 31:20** Thou shalt hide them in the secret of thy presence from the pride of man: thou shalt keep them secretly in a pavilion from the **strife** of tongues.
1 Corinthians 3:8 Now he that planteth and he that watereth are one: and every man shall receive his own reward according to his own labour.	**Job 34:11** For the work of a man shall he render unto him, and cause every man to find according to *his* ways. **Psalms 62:12** Also unto thee, O Lord, *belongeth* mercy: for thou renderest to every man according to his work. **Proverb 24:12** If thou sayest, Behold, we knew it not; doth not he that pondereth the heart consider *it*? and he that keepeth thy soul, doth *not* he know *it*? and shall *not* he render to *every* man according to his works? **Jeremiah 32:19** Great in counsel, and mighty in work: for thine eyes *are* open upon all the ways of the sons of men: to give every one according to his ways, and according to the fruit of his doings:
1 Corinthians 3:11 For other foundation can no man lay than that is laid, which is Jesus Christ.	**Psalms 118:22** The stone *which* the builders refused is become the head *stone* of the corner. **Isaiah 8:14** And he shall be for a sanctuary; but for a stone of stumbling and for a rock of offence to both the houses of Israel, for a gin and for a snare to the inhabitants of Jerusalem. **Isaiah 28:16** Therefore thus saith the Lord GOD, Behold, I lay in Zion for a foundation a stone, a tried stone, a precious corner *stone*, a sure foundation: he that believeth shall not make haste. **Isaiah 33:20** Look upon Zion, the city of our solemnities: thine eyes shall see Jerusalem a quiet habitation, a tabernacle *that* shall not be taken down; not one of the stakes thereof shall ever be removed, neither shall any of the cords thereof be broken.
1 Corinthians 3:13 Every man's work shall be made manifest: for the day shall declare it, because it shall be revealed by fire; and the fire shall try every man's work of what sort it is.	**Isaiah 8:20** To the law and to the testimony: if they speak not according to this word, *it is* because *there is* no light in them. **Isaiah 48:10** Behold, I have refined thee, but not with silver; I have chosen thee in the furnace of affliction. **Jeremiah 23:29** *Is* not my word like as a fire? saith the LORD; and like a hammer *that* breaketh the rock in pieces?
1 Corinthians 3:16-17 Know ye not that ye are the temple of God, and *that* the Spirit of God dwelleth in you? 17 If any man defile the temple of God, him shall God destroy; for the temple of God is holy, which *temple* ye are."	**Genesis 41:38** And Pharaoh said unto his servants, Can we find such a one as this is, **a man in whom the Spirit of God is**? **Numbers 11:17** And I will come down and talk with thee there: and I will take of **the spirit which is upon thee**, and will put it upon them; and they shall bear the burden of the people with thee, that thou bear it not thyself alone. **Numbers 11:25** And the LORD came down in a cloud, and spake

	unto him, **and took of the spirit that was upon him, and gave it unto the seventy elders**: and it came to pass, that, when the spirit rested upon them, they prophesied, and did not cease. **Numbers 27:18** And the LORD said unto Moses, Take thee Joshua the son of Nun, a man in whom is the spirit, and lay thine hand upon him; **Numbers 31:23** Every thing that may abide the fire, **ye shall make** *it* **go through the fire, and** <u>**it shall be clean**</u>: nevertheless it shall be purified with the water of separation: and all that abideth not the fire ye shall make go through the water. **Isaiah 11:2** And the spirit of the LORD shall rest upon him, the spirit of wisdom and understanding, the spirit of counsel and might, the spirit of knowledge and of the fear of the LORD; **Micah 3:8** But truly I am full of power by the spirit of the LORD, and of judgment, and of might, to declare unto Jacob his transgression, and to Israel his sin.
1 Corinthians 3:18 Let no man deceive himself. If any man among you seemeth to be wise in this world, let him become a fool, that he may be wise.	**Proverb 3:7** Be not wise in thine own eyes: fear the LORD, and depart from evil. **Isaiah 5:21** Woe unto *them that are* wise in their own eyes, and prudent in their own sight!
1 Corinthians 3:19 For the wisdom of this world is foolishness with God. For it is written, He taketh the wise in their own craftiness.	**Job 5:13** He taketh the wise in their own craftiness: and the counsel of the froward is carried headlong.
1 Corinthians 3:20 And again, The Lord knoweth the thoughts of the wise, that they are vain.	**Psalms 94:11** The LORD knoweth the thoughts of man, that they [are] vanity.
1 Corinthians 4:4 For I know nothing by myself; yet am I not hereby justified: but he that judgeth me is the Lord.	**Exodus 34:7** Keeping mercy for thousands, forgiving iniquity and transgression and sin, and that will by no means clear *the guilty*; visiting the iniquity of the fathers upon the children, and upon the children's children, unto the third and to the fourth *generation*. **Psalms 143:2** And enter not into judgment with thy servant: for in thy sight shall no man living be justified. **Daniel 7:10** A fiery stream issued and came forth from before him: thousand thousands ministered unto him, and ten thousand times ten thousand stood before him: the judgment was set, and the books were opened.
1 Corinthians 4:6 And these things, brethren, I have in a figure transferred to myself and *to* Apollos for your sakes; that ye might learn in us not to think *of men* above that which is written, that no one of you be puffed up for one against another.	**Proverbs 3:7** Be not wise in thine own eyes: fear the LORD, and depart from evil.
1 Corinthians 4:9 For I think that God hath set forth us the apostles last, as it were appointed to death: for we are made a spectacle unto the world, and to angels, and to men.	**Psalms 44:22** Yea, for thy sake are we killed all the day long; we are counted as sheep for the slaughter.
1 Corinthians 4:17 For this cause have I sent unto you Timotheus, who is my	**See Ephesians 4:11 "Teach – Teachers"**

beloved son, and faithful in the Lord, who shall bring you into remembrance of my ways which be in Christ, as **I teach every where in every church.**	
1 Corinthians 5:1 It is reported commonly *that there is* fornication among you, and such fornication as is not so much as named among the Gentiles, that one should have his father's wife.	**Leviticus 18:8** The nakedness of thy father's wife shalt thou not uncover: it *is* thy father's nakedness. **Leviticus 20:11** And the man that lieth with his father's wife hath uncovered his father's nakedness: both of them shall surely be put to death; their blood *shall be* upon them. **Deuteronomy 22:30** A man shall not take his father's wife, nor discover his father's skirt. **Deuteronomy 27:20** Cursed *be* he that lieth with his father's wife; because he uncovereth his father's skirt. And all the people shall say, Amen.
1 Corinthians 5:3-4 For I verily, as absent in **body**, but present in **spirit**, have judged already, as though I were present, *concerning* him that hath so done this deed. 4 In the name of our Lord Jesus Christ, when ye are gathered together, and my **spirit**, with the power of our Lord Jesus Christ,	**See 1 Thessalonians 5:23 "Body, soul, and spirit"**
1 Corinthians 5:5 To deliver such an one unto Satan for the destruction of the flesh, that the spirit may be saved in the **day of the Lord** Jesus.	**Ezekiel 3:20** Again, When a righteous *man* doth turn from his righteousness, and commit iniquity, and I lay a stumblingblock before him, he shall die: because thou hast not given him warning, he shall die in his sin, and his righteousness which he hath done shall not be remembered; but his blood will I require at thine hand. **Leviticus 23:27** Also on the tenth *day* of this seventh month *there shall be* a day of atonement: it shall be an holy convocation unto you; and ye shall afflict your souls, and offer an offering made by fire unto the LORD. **Joel 2:31-32** The sun shall be turned into darkness, and the moon into blood, before the great and the terrible day of the LORD come. 32 And it shall come to pass, *that* whosoever shall call on the name of the LORD shall be delivered: for in mount Zion and in Jerusalem shall be deliverance, as the LORD hath said, and in the remnant whom the LORD shall call. **Zechariah 12:10** And I will pour upon the house of David, and upon the inhabitants of Jerusalem, the spirit of grace and of supplications: and they shall look upon me whom they have pierced, and they shall mourn for him, as one mourneth for *his* only *son*, and shall be in bitterness for him, as one that is in bitterness for *his* firstborn. **See Acts 2:20 "Day of the Lord"** **Genesis 3:4** And the **serpent** said unto the woman, Ye shall not surely die: **Zechariah 3:1-2** And he shewed me Joshua the high priest standing before the angel of the LORD, and **Satan** standing at his right hand to resist him. 2 And the LORD said unto **Satan,** The

	LORD rebuke thee, O **Satan**; even the LORD that hath chosen Jerusalem rebuke thee: *is* not this a brand plucked out of the fire?
	See Matthew 4:10 "satan"
	See Hebrew 12:14 "Holiness"
1 Corinthians 5:7 Purge out therefore the old leaven, that ye may be a new lump, as ye are unleavened. For even Christ our passover is sacrificed for us:	**Leviticus 1:3** If his offering *be* a burnt sacrifice of the herd, let him offer a male without blemish: he shall offer it of his own voluntary will at the door of the tabernacle of the congregation before the LORD. **Leviticus 23:5-6** In the fourteenth *day* of the first month at even *is* the LORD's passover. 6 And on the fifteenth day of the same month *is* the feast of unleavened bread unto the LORD: seven days ye must eat unleavened bread. **Exodus 12:21-22** Then Moses called for all the elders of Israel, and said unto them, Draw out and take you a lamb according to your families, and kill the passover. 22 And ye shall take a bunch of hyssop, and dip it in the blood that *is* in the bason, and strike the lintel and the two side posts with the blood that *is* in the bason; and none of you shall go out at the door of his house until the morning. **Isaiah 53:7** He was oppressed, and he was afflicted, yet he opened not his mouth: he is brought as a lamb to the slaughter, and as a sheep before her shearers is dumb, so he openeth not his mouth.
1 Corinthians 5:8 Therefore let us **keep the feast**, not with old leaven, neither with the leaven of malice and wickedness; but with the unleavened *bread* of sincerity and truth.	**Exodus 12:3** Speak ye unto all the congregation of Israel, saying, In the tenth *day* of this month they shall take to them every man a lamb, according to the house of *their* fathers, a lamb for an house: **Exodus 12:14-15** And this day shall be unto you for a memorial; and ye shall keep it a feast to the LORD throughout your generations; ye shall **keep it a feast by an ordinance forever**. 15 Seven days shall ye eat unleavened bread; even the first day ye shall put away leaven out of your houses: for whosoever eateth leavened bread from the first day until the seventh day, that soul shall be cut off from Israel. **Leviticus 23:5-6** In the fourteenth *day* of the first month at even *is* the LORD's passover. 6 And on the fifteenth day of the same month *is* the feast of unleavened bread unto the LORD: seven days ye must eat unleavened bread. **Deuteronomy 16:3** Thou shalt eat no leavened bread with it; seven days shalt thou eat unleavened bread therewith, *even* the bread of affliction; for thou camest forth out of the land of Egypt in haste: that thou mayest remember the day when thou camest forth out of the land of Egypt all the days of thy life.
1 Corinthians 5:9 I wrote unto you in an epistle not to company with fornicators:	**Deuteronomy 7:2-3** And when the LORD thy God shall deliver them before thee; thou shalt smite them, *and* utterly destroy them; thou shalt make no covenant with them, nor shew mercy unto them: 3 Neither shalt thou make marriages with them; thy daughter thou shalt not give unto his son, nor his daughter shalt thou take unto thy son. **Numbers 33:52** Then ye shall drive out all the inhabitants of the land from before you, and destroy all their pictures, and destroy all their molten images, and quite pluck down all their high places:

	Joshua 11:11 And they smote all the souls that *were* therein with the edge of the sword, utterly destroying *them*: there was not any left to breathe: and he burnt Hazor with fire.
1 Corinthians 5:11 But now I have written unto you not to keep company, if any man that is called a brother be a fornicator, or covetous, or an idolater, or a railer, or a drunkard, or an extortioner; with such an one no not to eat.	**Deuteronomy 23:10** If there be among you any man, that is not clean by reason of uncleanness that chanceth him by night, then shall he go abroad out of the camp, he shall not come within the camp: **Proverbs 22:24-25** Make no friendship with an angry man; and with a furious man thou shalt not go: 25 Lest thou learn his ways, and get a snare to thy soul. **Isaiah 5:20** Woe unto them that call evil good, and good evil; that put darkness for light, and light for **darkness**; that put bitter for sweet, and sweet for bitter!
1 Corinthians 5:13 But them that are without God judgeth. Therefore put away from among yourselves that wicked person.	**Deuteronomy 13:5** And that prophet, or that dreamer of dreams, shall be put to death; because he hath spoken to turn *you* away from the LORD your God, which brought you out of the land of Egypt, and redeemed you out of the house of bondage, to thrust thee out of the way which the LORD thy God commanded thee to walk in. So shalt thou put the evil away from the midst of thee. **Deuteronomy 17:7** The hands of the witnesses shall be first upon him to put him to death, and afterward the hands of all the people. So thou shalt put the evil away from among you. **Deuteronomy 19:19** Then shall ye do unto him, as he had thought to have done unto his brother: so shalt thou put the evil away from among you. **Deuteronomy 22:21-22** Then they shall bring out the damsel to the door of her father's house, and the men of her city shall stone her with stones that she die: because she hath wrought folly in Israel, to play the whore in her father's house: so shalt thou put evil away from among you. 22 If a man be found lying with a woman married to a husband, then they shall **both of them die**, *both* the man that lay with the woman, and the woman: so shalt thou put away evil from Israel. **Deuteronomy 22:24** Then ye shall bring them both out unto the gate of that city, and ye shall stone them with stones that they die; the damsel, because she cried not, *being* in the city; and the man, because he hath humbled his neighbour's wife: so thou shalt put away evil from among you. **Deuteronomy 24:7** If a man be found stealing any of his brethren of the children of Israel, and maketh merchandise of him, or selleth him; then that thief shall die; and thou shalt put evil away from among you.
1 Corinthians 6:7 Now therefore there is utterly a fault among you, because ye go to law one with another. Why do ye not rather take wrong? why do ye not rather *suffer yourselves to* be defrauded?	**Deuteronomy 32:35** To me *belongeth* vengeance, and recompence; their foot shall slide in *due* time: for the day of their calamity *is* at hand, and the things that shall come upon them make haste. **Proverb 20:22** Say not thou, I will recompense evil; *but* wait on the LORD, and he shall save thee. **Proverb 24:29** Say not, I will do so to him as he hath done to me: I will render to the man according to his work.
1 Corinthians 6:8 Nay, ye do wrong, and defraud, and that *your* brethren.	**Leviticus 19:13** Thou shalt not defraud thy neighbour, neither rob *him:* the wages of him that is hired shall not abide with thee all

	night until the morning.
1 Corinthians 6:9-10 Know ye not that the unrighteous shall not inherit the kingdom of God? Be not deceived: neither fornicators, nor idolaters, **nor adulterers**, nor effeminate, nor abusers of themselves with mankind, 10 **Nor thieves**, nor covetous, **nor drunkards**, nor revilers, nor extortioners, shall inherit the kingdom of God.	**Exodus 20:15** Thou shalt not steal. **Deuteronomy 31:29** For I know that after my death ye will utterly corrupt *yourselves*, and turn aside from the way which I have commanded you; and evil will befall you in the latter days; because ye will do evil in the sight of the LORD, to provoke him to anger through the work of your hands. See Matthew 5:27 "Adultery" See Ephesians 5:18 "Drunkards"
1 Corinthians 6:11 ...ye are washed, but ye are sanctified, but ye are justified in the name of the Lord Jesus, and by the Spirit of our God.	See Acts 2:38 "Salvation"
1 Corinthians 6:12 All things are lawful unto me, but all things are not expedient: all things are lawful for me, but I will not be brought under the power of any.	**Deuteronomy 14:26** And thou shalt bestow that money for whatsoever thy soul lusteth after, for oxen, or for sheep, or for wine, or for strong drink, or for whatsoever thy soul desireth: and thou shalt eat there before the LORD thy God, and thou shalt rejoice, thou, and thine household, **Proverbs 20:1** Wine *is* a mocker, strong drink *is* raging: and whosoever is deceived thereby is not wise. **Isaiah 5:11** Woe unto them that rise up early in the morning, *that* they may follow strong drink; that continue until night, *till* wine inflame them!
1 Corinthians 6:15-16 Know ye not that your bodies are the members of Christ? shall I then take the members of Christ, and make *them* the members of an **harlot**? God forbid.16 What? know ye not that he which is joined to an **harlot** is one body? for two, saith he, shall be one flesh.	**Genesis 2:24** Therefore shall a man leave his father and his mother, and shall cleave unto his wife: and **they shall be one flesh**. **Deuteronomy 7:2** And when the LORD thy God shall deliver them before thee; thou shalt smite them, *and* utterly destroy them; thou shalt make no covenant with them, nor shew mercy unto them: **Exodus 23:32** Thou shalt make no covenant with them, nor with their gods. **Exodus 34:12** Take heed to thyself, lest thou make a covenant with the inhabitants of the land whither thou goest, lest it be for a snare in the midst of thee: See Matthew 5:27 "Adultery" See Romans 1:26-27 "Sexual sins" See Matthew 19:5 "Shall be one flesh" See Hebrews 12:14 "Holiness"
1 Corinthians 6:19 What? know ye not that your body is the temple of the Holy Ghost *which is* in you, which ye have of God, and ye are not your own?	**Psalms 12:4** Who have said, With our tongue will we prevail; our lips *are* our own: **who *is* lord over us?** **Psalms 100:3** Know ye that the LORD he *is* God: ***it is* he *that* hath made us**, and not we ourselves; *we are* his people, and the sheep of his pasture. **Jeremiah 2:31** O generation, see ye the word of the LORD. Have I been a wilderness unto Israel? a land of darkness? wherefore say **my people**, We are lords; we will come no more unto thee? **Daniel 3:15** Now if ye be ready that at what time ye hear the sound of the cornet, flute, harp, sackbut, psaltery, and dulcimer, and all

	kinds of musick, ye fall down and worship the image which I have made; *well:* but if ye worship not, ye shall be cast the same hour into the midst of a burning fiery furnace; and **who *is* that God that shall deliver you out of my hands?**
1 Corinthians 6:20 For ye are bought with a price: therefore glorify God in your body, and in your **spirit, which are God's**.	**Job 34:14** If he set his heart upon man, if **he gather unto himself his spirit** and his breath; **Ecclesiastes 3:21** Who knoweth the **spirit of man that goeth upward**, and the spirit of the beast that goeth downward to the earth? **Ecclesiastes 12:7** Then shall the dust return to the earth as it was: and the **spirit shall return unto God** who gave it. **See 1 Thessalonians 5:23** "Body, soul, and spirit"
1 Corinthians 7:2 Nevertheless, *to avoid* fornication, let every man have his own **wife**, and let every woman have her own husband.	**Genesis 2:18** And the LORD God said, *It is* not good that the man should be alone; I will make him a help meet for him. **Genesis 12:3** And I will bless them that bless thee, and curse him that curseth thee: and in thee shall all families of the earth be blessed. **Deuteronomy 22:20-21** But if this thing be true, *and the tokens of* virginity be not found for the damsel: 21 Then they shall bring out the damsel to the door of her father's house, and the men of her city shall stone her with stones that she die: because she hath wrought folly in Israel, to play the whore in her father's house: so shalt thou put evil away from among you. **Deuteronomy 22:22** If a man be found lying with a woman married to an husband, then they shall both of them die, *both* the man that lay with the woman, and the woman: so shalt thou put away evil from Israel. **Proverbs 18:22** *Whoso* findeth a **wife** findeth a good *thing*, and obtaineth favour of the LORD. **Proverb 31:10** Who can find a **virtuous woman**? for her price *is* far above rubies. **Proverbs 31:28** Her children arise up, and call her blessed; her husband *also*, and he praiseth her. **Numbers 25:1-3** And Israel abode in Shittim, and the people began to **commit whoredom with the daughters of Moab**. 2 And **they called the people unto the sacrifices of their gods**: and the people did eat, and bowed down to their gods. 3 And **Israel joined himself unto Baalpeor**: and the anger of the LORD was kindled against Israel. **Hosea 2:13** And I will visit upon her the days of Baalim, wherein she burned incense to them, and she decked herself with her earrings and her jewels, and **she went after her lovers**, and forgot me, saith the LORD.
1 Corinthians 7:5 Defraud ye not one the other, except *it be* with consent for a time, that ye may give yourselves to **fasting** and prayer; and come together again, that **Satan** tempt you not for your incontinency.	**Genesis 3:4** And the **serpent** said unto the woman, Ye shall not surely die: **Joel 2:16** Gather the people, sanctify the congregation, assemble the elders, gather the children, and those that suck the breasts: let the bridegroom go forth of his chamber, and the bride out of her closet.

	Zechariah 3:1-2 And he shewed me Joshua the high priest standing before the angel of the LORD, and **Satan** standing at his right hand to resist him. 2 And the LORD said unto **Satan,** The LORD rebuke thee, O **Satan**; even the LORD that hath chosen Jerusalem rebuke thee: *is* not this a brand plucked out of the fire? **See Matthew 4:10 "satan"** **See Matthew 17:21 "Fasting"**
1 Corinthians 7:10 And unto the married I **command**, *yet* not I, but the Lord, Let not the wife depart from *her* husband:	**Malachi 2:14** Yet ye say, Wherefore? Because the LORD hath been witness between thee and the wife of thy youth, against whom thou hast dealt treacherously: yet *is* she thy companion, and the wife of thy covenant. **Exodus 7:2** Thou shalt speak **all that I command thee**: and Aaron thy brother shall speak unto Pharaoh, that he send the children of Israel out of his land. **Exodus 27:20** And thou shalt **command** the children of Israel, that they bring thee pure oil olive beaten for the light, to cause the lamp to burn always. **Joshua 11:15** As the LORD **commanded** Moses his servant, so did Moses **command** Joshua, and so did Joshua; he left nothing undone of all that the LORD **commanded** Moses. 16 So Joshua took all that land, the hills, and all the south country, and all the land of Goshen, and the valley, and the plain, and the mountain of Israel, and the valley of the same; **See Hebrews 13:7 "rule"**
1 Corinthians 8:4 As concerning therefore the eating of those things that are offered in sacrifice unto idols, we know that an idol is nothing in the world, and that **there is none other God but one.** **1 Corinthians 8:6** But to us *there is but* one God, the Father, of whom *are* all things, and we in him; and one Lord Jesus Christ, by whom *are* all things, and we by him.	**Exodus 20:2-3** I am the LORD thy God, which have brought thee out of the land of Egypt, out of the house of bondage. 3 Thou shalt have no other gods before me." **Deuteronomy 6:4** Hear, O Israel: The LORD our God *is* one LORD : **Deuteronomy 32:17** They sacrificed unto devils, not to God; to gods whom they knew not, to new *gods that* came newly up, whom your fathers feared not. **1 Chronicles 29:10** Wherefore David blessed the LORD before all the congregation: and David said, Blessed *be* thou, **LORD God of Israel our father, forever and ever**. **Judges 16:23** Then the lords of the Philistines gathered them together for to offer a great sacrifice unto Dagon their god, and to rejoice: for they said, Our god hath delivered Samson our enemy into our hand. **Nehemiah 9:6** Thou, *even* thou, *art* LORD alone; thou hast made heaven, the heaven of heavens, with all their host, the earth, and all *things* that *are* therein, the seas, and all that *is* therein, and thou preservest them all; and the host of heaven worshippeth thee. **Psalms 86:10** For thou *art* great, and doest wondrous things: thou *art* God alone. **Psalms 89:26** He shall cry unto me, **Thou *art* my father, my God**, and the rock of my salvation. **Psalms 96:5** For all the gods of the nations *are* idols: but the LORD made the heavens. **Isaiah 9:6** For unto us a child is born, unto us a son is given: and

	the government shall be upon his shoulder: and his name shall be called Wonderful, Counselor, The mighty God, The everlasting Father, The Prince of Peace. **Isaiah 43:10-11** Ye *are* my witnesses, saith the LORD, and my servant whom I have chosen: that ye may know and believe me, and understand that I *am* he: before me there was no God formed, neither shall there be after me. 11 I, *even* I, *am* the LORD ; and beside me *there is* no saviour. **Isaiah 44:6** Thus saith the LORD the King of Israel, and his redeemer the LORD of hosts; I *am* the first, and I *am* the last; and beside me *there is* no God. **Isaiah 44:8** Fear ye not, neither be afraid: have not I told thee from that time, and have declared *it*? ye *are* even my witnesses. Is there a God beside me? yea, *there is* no God; I know not *any*. **Isaiah 45:5-6** I am the LORD, and there is none else, **there is no God beside me**: I girded thee, though thou hast not known me: {6} That they may know from the rising of the sun, and from the west, that there is none beside me. I am the LORD, and there is none else. **Isaiah 45:21-22** have not I the LORD? and **there is no God else beside me**; a just God and a Saviour; there is none beside me. 22 Look unto me, and be ye saved, all the ends of the earth: for **I am God, and there is none else**. **Isaiah 54:5** For thy Maker *is* thine husband; the LORD of hosts *is* his name; and thy Redeemer the Holy One of Israel; The God of the whole earth shall he be called. **Isaiah 63:16** Doubtless thou *art* our father, though Abraham be ignorant of us, and Israel acknowledge us not: thou, **O LORD, *art* our father**, our redeemer; thy name *is* from everlasting **Isaiah 64:8** But now, **O LORD, thou *art* our father**; we *are* the clay, and thou our potter; and we all *are* the work of thy hand. **Daniel 5:23** But hast lifted up thyself against the Lord of heaven; and they have brought the vessels of his house before thee, and thou, and thy lords, thy wives, and thy concubines, have drunk wine in them; and thou hast praised the gods of silver, and gold, of brass, iron, wood, and stone, which see not, nor hear, nor know: and the God in whose hand thy breath *is,* and whose *are* all thy ways, hast thou not glorified: **Malachi 2:10** Have we not all one father? hath not one God created us? why do we deal treacherously every man against his brother, by profaning the covenant of our fathers?
1 Corinthians 9:9 For it is written in the law of Moses, Thou shalt not muzzle the mouth of the ox that treadeth out the corn. Doth God take care for oxen?	**Deuteronomy 25:4** Thou shalt not muzzle the ox when he treadeth out *the corn*.
1 Corinthians 9:13 Do ye not know that they which minister about holy things live *of the things* of the temple? and they which wait at the altar are partakers with the altar?	**Numbers 18:20** And the LORD spake unto Aaron, Thou shalt have no inheritance in their land, neither shalt thou have any part among them: I *am* thy part and thine inheritance among the children of Israel. **Deuteronomy 10:9** Wherefore Levi hath no part nor inheritance with his brethren; the LORD *is* his inheritance, according as the LORD thy God promised him.

	Deuteronomy 18:1 The priests the Levites, *and* all the tribe of Levi, shall have no part nor inheritance with Israel: they shall eat the offerings of the LORD made by fire, and his inheritance.
	Deuteronomy 24:14 Thou shalt not oppress an hired servant *that is* poor and needy, *whether he be* of thy brethren, or of thy strangers that *are* in thy land within thy gates:
	Ezekiel 44:28 And it shall be unto them for an inheritance: I *am* their inheritance: and ye shall give them no possession in Israel: I *am* their possession.
1 Corinthians 9:14 Even so hath the Lord ordained that they which preach the gospel should live of the gospel.	**Leviticus 19:13** Thou shalt not defraud thy neighbour, neither rob *him*: the wages of him that is hired shall not abide with thee all night until the morning.
	Deuteronomy 25:4 Thou shalt not muzzle the ox when he treadeth out *the corn*.
1 Corinthians 9:25 And every man that striveth for the mastery is **temperate in all things**. Now they *do it* to obtain a corruptible crown; but we an incorruptible.	**Deuteronomy 21:20** And they shall say unto the elders of his city, This our son *is* stubborn and rebellious, he will not obey our voice; *he is* **a glutton**, and a drunkard.
	Proverbs 23:21 For the drunkard and the **glutton** shall come to poverty: and drowsiness shall clothe *a man* with rags.
	Proverbs 25:16 Hast thou found honey? eat so much as is sufficient for thee, lest thou be filled therewith, and vomit it.
	Psalms 78:29-31 So they did eat, and were well filled: for he gave them their own desire; 30 They were not estranged from their lust. But while their meat *was* yet in their mouths, 31 The wrath of God came upon them, and **slew the fattest of them**, and smote down the chosen *men* of Israel.
	See Hebrews 12:14 "Holiness"
1 Corinthians 10:1 Moreover, brethren, I would not that ye should be ignorant, how that all our fathers were under the cloud, and all passed through the sea;	**Exodus 13:21** And the LORD went before them by day in a pillar of a cloud, to lead them the way; and by night in a pillar of fire, to give them light; to go by day and night:
	Exodus 14:22 And the children of Israel went into the midst of the sea upon the dry *ground*: and the waters *were* a wall unto them on their right hand, and on their left.
	Psalms 78:13 He divided the sea, and caused them to pass through; and he made the waters to stand as an heap.
	Numbers 9:18 At the commandment of the LORD the children of Israel journeyed, and at the commandment of the LORD they pitched: as long as the cloud abode upon the tabernacle they rested in their tents.
	Deuteronomy 1:33 Who went in the way before you, to search you out a place to pitch your tents *in*, in fire by night, to shew you by what way ye should go, and in a cloud by day.
	Joshua 4:23 For the LORD your God dried up the waters of Jordan from before you, until ye were passed over, as the LORD your God did to the Red sea, which he dried up from before us, until we were gone over:
	Nehemiah 9:12 Moreover thou leddest them in the day by a cloudy pillar; and in the night by a pillar of fire, to give them light in the way wherein they should go.

	Nehemiah 9:19 Yet thou in thy manifold mercies forsookest them not in the wilderness: the pillar of the cloud departed not from them by day, to lead them in the way; neither the pillar of fire by night, to shew them light, and the way wherein they should go.

Psalms 78:14 In the daytime also he led them with a cloud, and all the night with a light of fire.

Psalms 105:39 He spread a cloud for a covering; and fire to give light in the night.

See Acts 2:38 "Salvation" |
| **1 Corinthians 10:3** And did all eat the same spiritual meat; | **Exodus 16:15** And when the children of Israel saw *it*, they said one to another, It *is* manna: for they wist not what it *was*. And Moses said unto them, This *is* the bread which the LORD hath given you to eat. |
| **1 Corinthians 10:4** And did all drink the same spiritual drink: for they drank of that spiritual **Rock** that followed them: and that **Rock** was Christ. | **Exodus 17:6** Behold, I will stand before thee there upon the **rock** in Horeb; and thou shalt smite the **rock**, and there shall come water out of it, that the people may drink. And Moses did so in the sight of the elders of Israel.

Numbers 20:11 And Moses lifted up his hand, and with his rod he smote the **rock** twice: and the water came out abundantly, and the congregation drank, and their beasts *also*.

Deuteronomy 32:3-4 Because I will publish the name of the LORD: ascribe ye greatness unto our God. 4 *He is* the **Rock**, his work *is* perfect: for all his ways a*re* judgment: a God of truth and without iniquity, just and right *is* he.

2 Samuel 22:32 For who is God, save the LORD? and who is a **rock**, save our God?

Psalms 18:31 For who *is* God save the LORD? or who *is* a **rock** save our God?

Psalms 27:5 For in the time of trouble he shall hide me in his pavilion: in the secret of his tabernacle shall he hide me; he shall set me up upon a **rock**.

Psalms 40:2 He brought me up also out of an horrible pit, out of the miry clay, and set my feet upon a **rock**, *and* established my goings.

Psalms 78:15 He clave the **rock**s in the wilderness, and gave *them* drink as *out of* the great depths.

Psalms 105:41 He opened the **rock**, and the waters gushed out; they ran in the dry places *like* a river.

Psalms 114:8 Which turned the **rock** *into* a standing water, the flint into a fountain of waters.

Isaiah 17:10 Because thou hast forgotten the God of thy salvation, and hast not been mindful of the **rock** of thy strength, therefore shalt thou plant pleasant plants, and shalt set it with strange slips: |
| **1 Corinthians 10:5** But with many of them God was not well pleased: for they were overthrown in the wilderness. | **Numbers 14:16** Because the LORD was not able to bring this people into the land which he sware unto them, therefore he hath slain them in the wilderness.

Numbers 26:65 For the LORD had said of them, They shall surely die in the wilderness. And there was not left a man of them, save Caleb the son of Jephunneh, and Joshua the son of Nun. |

1 Corinthians 10:6 Now these things were our examples, to the intent we should not lust after evil things, as they also lusted.	**Numbers 11:4** And the mixt multitude that *was* among them fell a lusting: and the children of Israel also wept again, and said, Who shall give us flesh to eat? **Numbers 11:33-34** And while the flesh *was* yet between their teeth, ere it was chewed, the wrath of the LORD was kindled against the people, and the LORD smote the people with a very great plague. 34 And he called the name of that place Kibrothhattaavah: because there they buried the people that lusted.
1 Corinthians 10:7 Neither be ye idolaters, as [were] some of them; as it is written, The people sat down to eat and drink, and rose up to play.	**Exodus 32:6** And they rose up early on the morrow, and offered burnt offerings, and brought peace offerings; and the people sat down to eat and to drink, and rose up to play.
1 Corinthians 10:8 Neither let us commit fornication, as some of them committed, and fell in one day three and twenty thousand.	**Numbers 25:1** And Israel abode in Shittim, and the people began to commit whoredom with the daughters of Moab. **Numbers 25:9** And those that died in the plague were twenty and four thousand. **Psalms 106:29-30** Thus they provoked *him* to anger with their inventions: and the plague brake in upon them. 30 Then stood up Phinehas, and executed judgment: and *so* the plague was stayed.
1 Corintians 10:9 Neither let us tempt Christ, as some of them also tempted, and were destroyed of serpents.	**Numbers 21:5-7** And the people spake against God, and against Moses, Wherefore have ye brought us up out of Egypt to die in the wilderness? for *there is* no bread, neither *is there any* water; and our soul loatheth this light bread. 6 And the LORD sent fiery serpents among the people, and they bit the people; and much people of Israel died. 7 Therefore the people came to Moses, and said, We have sinned, for we have spoken against the LORD, and against thee; pray unto the LORD, that he take away the serpents from us. And Moses prayed for the people. **Psalms 106:14** But lusted exceedingly in the wilderness, and tempted God in the desert.
1 Corinthians 10:10 Neither murmur ye, as some of them also murmured, and were destroyed of the destroyer.	**Exodus 16:2** And the whole congregation of the children of Israel murmured against Moses and Aaron in the wilderness: **Exodus 17:2** Wherefore the people did chide with Moses, and said, Give us water that we may drink. And Moses said unto them, Why chide ye with me? wherefore do ye tempt the LORD? **Numbers 14:36** And the men, which Moses sent to search the land, who returned, and made all the congregation to murmur against him, by bringing up a slander upon the land, **Psalms 106:25** But murmured in their tents, *and* hearkened not unto the voice of the LORD.
1 Corinthians 10:16 The cup of blessing which we bless, is it not the **communion of the blood of Christ**? The bread which we break, is it not the **communion of the body of Christ**?	**Leviticus 17:11** For the life of the flesh is in the blood: and I have given it to you upon the altar to make an atonement for your souls: **for it is the blood that maketh an atonement for the soul**. See Matthew 26:28 "Atonement"
1 Corinthians 10:20 But *I say,* that the things which the Gentiles sacrifice, they sacrifice to devils, and not to God: and I would not that ye should have fellowship with devils.	**Leviticus 17:7** And they shall no more offer their sacrifices unto devils, after whom they have gone a whoring. This shall be a statute for ever unto them throughout their generations. **Deuteronomy 32:17** They sacrificed unto devils, not to God; to

	gods whom they knew not, to new *gods that* came newly up, whom your fathers feared not.
1 Corinthians 10:22 Do we provoke the Lord to jealousy? are we stronger than he?	**Deuteronomy 32:21** They have moved me to jealousy with *that which is* not God; they have provoked me to anger with their vanities: and I will move them to jealousy with *those which are* not a people; I will provoke them to anger with a foolish nation.
1 Corinthians 10:26 For the earth *is* the Lord's, and the fulness thereof.	**Exodus 19:5** Now therefore, if ye will obey my voice indeed, and keep my covenant, then ye shall be a peculiar treasure unto me above all people: for all the earth *is* mine: **Deuteronomy 10:14** Behold, the heaven and the heaven of heavens *is* the LORD'S thy God, the earth *also*, with all that therein *is*. **Psalms 24:1** The earth *is* the LORD'S, and the fulness thereof; the world, and they that dwell therein. **Psalms 50:12** If I were hungry, I would not tell thee: for the world *is* mine, and the fulness thereof.
1 Corinthians 10:28 But if any man say unto you, This is offered in sacrifice unto idols, eat not for his sake that shewed it, and for conscience sake: for the earth *is* the Lord's, and the fulness thereof:	**Deuteronomy 10:14** Behold, the heaven and the heaven of heavens *is* the LORD'S thy God, the earth *also*, with all that therein *is*. **Psalms 24:1** The earth *is* the LORD'S, and the fulness thereof; the world, and they that dwell therein.
1 Corinthians 10:31 Whether therefore ye eat, or drink, or whatsoever ye do, do all to the glory of God.	**Deuteronomy 14:26** And thou shalt bestow that money for whatsoever thy soul lusteth after, for oxen, or for sheep, or for wine, or for strong drink, or for whatsoever thy soul desireth: and thou shalt eat there before the LORD thy God, and thou shalt rejoice, thou, and thine household, **Proverbs 20:1** Wine *is* a mocker, strong drink *is* raging: and whosoever is deceived thereby is not wise. **Isaiah 5:11** Woe unto them that rise up early in the morning, *that* they may follow strong drink; that continue until night, *till* wine inflame them!
1 Corinthians 11:5 But every woman that prayeth or **prophesieth** with her head uncovered dishonoureth her head: for that is even all one as if she were shaven.	**See 1 Corinthians 12:10** "Prophecy"
1 Corinthians 11:6 For if the woman be not covered, let her also be shorn: but if it be a shame for a woman to be shorn or shaven, let her be covered.	**Numbers 5:18** And the priest shall set the woman before the LORD, and uncover the woman's head, and put the offering of memorial in her hands, which *is* the jealousy offering: and the priest shall have in his hand the bitter water that causeth the curse: **Deuteronomy 22:5** The woman shall not wear that which pertaineth unto a man, neither shall a man put on a woman's garment: for all that do so *are* abomination unto the LORD thy God. **Nehemiah 13:25** And I contended with them, and cursed them, and smote certain of them, and plucked off their hair, and made them swear by God, *saying*, Ye shall not give your daughters unto their sons, nor take their daughters unto your sons, or for yourselves. **Proverbs 16:31** The hoary head *is* a crown of glory, *if* it be found in the way of righteousness.

	Isaiah 3:24 And it shall come to pass, *that* instead of sweet smell there shall be stink; and instead of a girdle a rent; and instead of well set hair baldness; and instead of a stomacher a girding of sackcloth; *and* burning instead of beauty. **Jeremiah 7:28-29** But thou shalt say unto them, This *is* a nation that obeyeth not the voice of the LORD their God, nor receiveth correction: truth is perished, and is cut off from their mouth. 29 Cut off thine hair, *O Jerusalem,* and cast *it* away, and take up a lamentation on high places; for the LORD hath rejected and forsaken the generation of his wrath. **Jeremiah 47:5** Baldness is come upon Gaza; Ashkelon is cut off *with* the remnant of their valley: how long wilt thou cut thyself? **Ezekiel 7:17-18** All hands shall be feeble, and all knees shall be weak *as* water. 18 They shall also gird *themselves* with sackcloth, and horror shall cover them; and shame *shall be* upon all faces, and baldness upon all their heads. **Ezekiel 16:7** I have caused thee to multiply as the bud of the field, and thou hast increased and waxen great, and thou art come to excellent ornaments: *thy* breasts are fashioned, and thine hair is grown, whereas thou *wast* naked and bare. **Amos 8:10** And I will turn your feasts into mourning, and all your songs into lamentation; and I will bring up sackcloth upon all loins, and baldness upon every head; and I will make it as the mourning of an only *son,* and the end thereof as a bitter day.
1 Corinthians 11:7 For a man indeed ought not to cover *his* head, forasmuch as he is the image and glory of God: but the woman is the glory of the man.	**Genesis 1:26-27** And God said, Let us make man in our image, after our likeness: and let them have dominion over the fish of the sea, and over the fowl of the air, and over the cattle, and over all the earth, and over every creeping thing that creepeth upon the earth. 27 So God created man in his *own* image, in the image of God created he him; male and female created he them. **Genesis 5:1** This *is* the book of the generations of Adam. In the day that God created man, in the likeness of God made he him; **Genesis 9:6** Whoso sheddeth man's blood, by man shall his blood be shed: for in the image of God made he man.
1 Corinthians 11:8 For the man is not of the woman; but the woman of the man.	**Genesis 2:18** And the LORD God said, *It is* not good that the man should be alone; I will make him an help meet for him. **Genesis 2:21-22** And the LORD God caused a deep sleep to fall upon Adam, and he slept: and he took one of his ribs, and closed up the flesh instead thereof; 22 And the rib, which the LORD God had taken from man, made he a woman, and brought her unto the man.
1 Corinthians 11:25 After the same manner also *he took* the cup, when he had supped, saying, This cup is the new testament in my blood: this do ye, as oft as ye drink *it,* in remembrance of me.	**Jeremiah 31:31** Behold, the days come, saith the LORD, that **I will make a new covenant with the house of Israel**, and with the house of Judah: **Leviticus 17:11** For the life of the flesh is in the blood: and I have given it to you upon the altar to make an atonement for your souls: **for it is the blood that maketh an atonement for the soul**. **See Matthew 26:28 "Atonement"**
1 Corinthians 11:27 Wherefore whosoever shall eat this bread, and drink *this* cup of the Lord, unworthily, shall be guilty of the body and blood of the Lord.	**Genesis 14:18** And Melchizedek king of Salem brought forth bread and wine: and he *was* the priest of the most high God. **Numbers 9:10** Speak unto the children of Israel, saying, If any

	man of you or of your posterity shall be unclean by reason of a dead body, or *be* in a journey afar off, yet he shall keep the passover unto the LORD. **Numbers 9:13** But the man that *is* clean, and is not in a journey, and forbeareth to keep the passover, even the same soul shall be cut off from among his people: because he brought not the offering of the LORD in his appointed season, that man shall bear his sin. **Judge 19:19** Yet there is both straw and provender for our asses; and there is bread and wine also for me, and for thy handmaid, and for the young man *which is* with thy servants: *there is* no want of any thing. **Proverb 9:5** Come, eat of my bread, and drink of the wine *which* I have mingled. **See Matthew 26:28 "Atonement"**
1 Corinthians 11:31 For if we would judge ourselves, we should not be judged.	**Psalms 32:5** I acknowledged my sin unto thee, and mine iniquity have I not hid. I said, I will confess my transgressions unto the LORD; and thou forgavest the iniquity of my sin. Selah. **Proverb 18:17** *He that is* first in his own cause *seemeth* just; but his neighbour cometh and searcheth him. **Proverb 28:13** He that covereth his sins shall not prosper: but whoso confesseth and forsaketh *them* shall have mercy.
1 Corinthians 12:8 For to one is given by the Spirit the **word of wisdom**; to another the **word of knowledge** by the same Spirit;	**1 Kings 3:16-28** … 27 **Then the king answered and said, Give her the living child, and in no wise slay it: she *is* the mother thereof.** 28 And all Israel heard of the judgment which the king had judged; and they feared the king: for they saw that the wisdom of God *was* in him, to do judgment. **1 Samuel 9:15-20** Now the <u>LORD had told Samuel in his ear a day before Saul came, saying,</u> … 19 And Samuel answered Saul, and said, I *am* the seer: go up before me unto the high place; for ye shall eat with me to day, and to morrow I will let thee go, and **will tell thee all that *is* in thine heart**. 20 And as for thine asses that were lost three days ago, set not thy mind on them; for they are found. And on whom *is* all the desire of Israel? *Is it* not on thee, and on all thy father's house? **1 Samuel 10:1-9** **1 Samuel 10:21-22** When he had caused the tribe of Benjamin to come near by their families, the family of Matri was taken, and Saul the son of Kish was taken: and when they sought him, he could not be found. 22 Therefore **they enquired of the LORD further**, if the man should yet come thither. And the LORD answered, **Behold, he hath hid himself among the stuff**. **2 Kings 3:12** And Jehoshaphat said, **The word of the LORD is with him**. So the king of Israel and Jehoshaphat and the king of Edom went down to him. **2 Kings 3:15-19** But now bring me a minstrel. And it came to pass, when the minstrel played, that the hand of the LORD came upon him. 16 And he said, Thus saith the LORD, Make this valley full of ditches. 17 For thus saith the LORD, Ye shall not see wind, neither shall ye see rain; yet that valley shall be filled with water, that ye may drink, both ye, and your cattle, and your beasts. 18

	And this is *but* a light thing in the sight of the LORD: he will deliver the Moabites also into your hand. 19 And ye shall smite every fenced city, and every choice city, and shall fell every good tree, and stop all wells of water, and mar every good piece of land with stones.
1 Corinthians 12:10 To another the working of miracles; to another prophecy; to another discerning of **spirits**; to another *divers* kinds of tongues; to another the interpretation of tongues:	**Numbers 11:25** And the LORD came down in a cloud, and spake unto him, and took of the spirit that *was* upon him, and gave *it* unto the seventy elders: and it came to pass, *that*, when the spirit rested upon them, they prophesied, and did not cease. **Numbers 11:27** And there ran a young man, and told Moses, and said, Eldad and Medad do prophesy in the camp. And the Spirit of the LORD will come upon thee, and thou shalt prophesy with them, and shalt be turned into another man **1 Samuel 10:6** And the Spirit of the LORD will come upon thee, and thou shalt prophesy with them, and shalt be turned into another man **1 Samuel 10:9-13** And it was *so*, that when he had turned his back to go from Samuel, God gave him another heart: and all those signs came to pass that day. 10 And when they came thither to the hill, behold, a company of prophets met him; and the Spirit of God came upon him, and he prophesied among them. 11 And it came to pass, when all that knew him beforetime saw that, behold, he prophesied among the prophets, then the people said one to another, What *is* this *that* is come unto the son of Kish? *Is* Saul also among the prophets? 12 And one of the same place answered and said, But who *is* their father? Therefore it became a proverb, *Is* Saul also among the prophets? 13 And when he had made an end of prophesying, he came to the high place. **Malachi 3:18** Then shall ye return, and discern between the righteous and the wicked, between him that serveth God and him that serveth him not. **See Hebrews 13:2 "Good and bad angels"**
1 Corinthians 12:13 For by one Spirit are we all baptized into one body, whether we be Jews or Gentiles, whether we be bond or free; and have been all made to drink into one Spirit.	**Psalms 139:7** Whither shall I go from thy spirit? or whither shall I flee from thy presence?
1 Corinthians 13:4 Charity suffereth long, *and* is kind; charity envieth not; charity vaunteth not itself, is not puffed up,	**Proverb 10:12** Hatred stirreth up strifes: but love covereth all sins.
1 Corinthians 13:8 Charity never faileth: but whether *there be* **prophecies**, they shall fail; whether *there be* tongues, they shall cease; whether *there be* knowledge, it shall vanish away.	**See 1 Corinthians 12:10 "Prophecy"**
1 Corinthians 14:1 Follow after charity, and desire spiritual *gifts*, but rather that ye may **prophesy**.	**See 1 Corinthians 12:10 "Prophecy"**
1 Corinthians 14:15 What is it then? I will pray with the spirit, and I will pray with the understanding also: I will sing with the spirit, and I will sing with the	**See John 4:24 "Worship"** **See Colossians 3:16 "Music"**

understanding also.	
1 Corinthians 14:21 In the law it is written, With *men of* other tongues and other lips will I speak unto this people; and yet for all that will they not hear me, saith the Lord.	**Isaiah 28:11-12** For with stammering lips and another tongue will he speak to this people. 12 To whom he said, This *is* the rest *wherewith* ye may cause the weary to rest; and this *is* the refreshing: yet they would not hear.
1 Corinthians 14:26 How is it then, brethren? when ye come together, every one of you hath a psalm, hath a doctrine, hath a tongue, hath a revelation, hath an interpretation. Let all things be done unto edifying. **1 Corinthians 14:40** Let all things be done decently and in order.	**Leviticus 10:1-3** And Nadab and Abihu, the sons of Aaron, took either of them his censer, and put fire therein, and put incense thereon, and **offered strange fire before the Lord, which he commanded them not**. 2 And there went out fire from the Lord, and devoured them, and **they died before the Lord**. 3 Then Moses said unto Aaron, This is it that the Lord spake, saying, I will be sanctified in them that come nigh me, and before all the people I will be glorified. And Aaron held his peace. **See John 4:24 "Worship"** **See Colossians 3:16 "Music"**
1 Corinthians 15:3 For I delivered unto you first of all that which I also received, how that Christ died for our sins according to the **scriptures**;	**Isaiah 53:7** He was oppressed, and he was afflicted, yet he opened not his mouth: he is brought as a lamb to the slaughter, and as a sheep before her shearers is dumb, so he openeth not his mouth. **Daniel 9:24** Seventy weeks are determined upon thy people and upon thy holy city, to finish the transgression, and to make an end of sins, and to make reconciliation for iniquity, and to bring in everlasting righteousness, and to seal up the vision and prophecy, and to anoint the most Holy. **Daniel 9:26** And after threescore and two weeks shall Messiah be cut off, but not for himself: and the people of the prince that shall come shall destroy the city and the sanctuary; and the end thereof *shall be* with a flood, and unto the end of the war desolations are determined. **See Matthew 5:18 "Scriptures"**
1 Corinthians 15:4 And that he was buried, and that he rose again the third day according to the **scriptures**:	**Psalms 16:10** For thou wilt not leave my soul in hell; neither wilt thou suffer thine Holy One to see corruption. **Psalms 68:18** Thou hast ascended on high, thou hast led captivity captive: thou hast received gifts for men; yea, *for* the rebellious also, that the LORD God might dwell *among them*. **Isaiah 53:9** And he made his grave with the wicked, and with the rich in his death; because he had done no violence, neither *was any* deceit in his mouth. **Jonah 1:17** Now the LORD had prepared a great fish to swallow up Jonah. And Jonah was in the belly of the fish three days and three nights. **See Matthew 5:18 "Scriptures"**
1 Corinthians 15:20 But now is Christ risen from the dead, *and* become the **firstfruits** of them that slept.	**Leviticus 23:10** Speak unto the children of Israel, and say unto them, When ye be come into the land which I give unto you, and shall reap the harvest thereof, then ye shall bring a sheaf of the firstfruits of your harvest unto the priest: **See Romans 8:23 "Firstfruits"**
1 Corinthians 15:21 For since by man *came* death, by man *came* also the resurrection of the dead.	**Genesis 2:17** But of the tree of the knowledge of good and evil, thou shalt not eat of it: for in the day that thou eatest thereof thou shalt surely die.

	Genesis 3:6 And when the woman saw that the tree *was* good for food, and that it *was* pleasant to the eyes, and a tree to be desired to make *one* wise, she took of the fruit thereof, and did eat, and gave also unto her husband with her; and he did eat.
1 Corinthians 15:22 For as in Adam all die, even so in Christ shall all be made alive.	**Genesis 3:19** In the sweat of thy face shalt thou eat bread, till thou return unto the ground; for out of it wast thou taken: for dust thou *art*, and unto dust shalt thou return.
1 Corinthians 15:23 But every man in his own order: Christ the firstfruits; afterward they that are Christ's at his coming.	**Leviticus 23:16** Even unto the morrow after the seventh sabbath shall ye number fifty days; and ye shall offer a new meat offering unto the LORD. **Deuteronomy 16:9-10** Seven weeks shalt thou number unto thee: begin to number the seven weeks from *such time as* thou beginnest *to put* the sickle to the corn. **10** And thou shalt keep the feast of weeks unto the LORD thy God with a tribute of a freewill offering of thine hand, which thou shalt give *unto the LORD thy God*, according as the LORD thy God hath blessed thee:
1 Corinthians 15:25 For he must reign, till he hath put all enemies under his feet.	**Psalms 110:1** A Psalm of David. The LORD said unto my Lord, Sit thou at my right hand, until I make thine enemies thy footstool. **Isaiah 56:12** Come ye, *say they*, I will fetch wine, and we will fill ourselves with strong drink; and to morrow shall be as this day, *and* much more abundant.
1 Corinthians 15:27 For he hath put all things under his feet. But when he saith all things are put under *him, it* is manifest that he is excepted, which did put all things under him.	**Psalms 8:4-6** What is man, that thou art mindful of him? and the son of man, that thou visitest him? For thou hast made him a little lower than the angels, and hast crowned him with glory and honour. Thou madest him to have dominion over the works of thy hands; thou hast put all *things* under his feet:
1 Corinthians 15:32 If after the manner of men I have fought with beasts at Ephesus, what advantageth it me, if the dead rise not? let us eat and drink; for to morrow we die.	**Isaiah 22:13** And behold joy and gladness, slaying oxen, and killing sheep, eating flesh, and drinking wine: let us eat and drink; for to morrow we shall die.
1 Corinthians 15:33 Be not deceived: evil communications corrupt good manners.	**Proverbs 22:24-25** Make no friendship with an angry man; and with a furious man thou shalt not go: 25 Lest thou learn his ways, and get a snare to thy soul. **Isaiah 5:20** Woe unto them that call evil good, and good evil; that put darkness for light, and light for **darkness**; that put bitter for sweet, and sweet for bitter!
1 Corinthians 15:35 But some *man* will say, How are the dead raised up? and with what body do they come?	**Ezekiel 37:3** And he said unto me, Son of man, can these bones live? And I answered, O Lord GOD, thou knowest. **Ezekiel 37:7-8** So I prophesied as I was commanded: and as I prophesied, there was a noise, and behold a shaking, and the bones came together, bone to his bone. 8 And when I beheld, lo, the sinews and the flesh came up upon them, and the skin covered them above: but *there was* no breath in them. **Ezekiel 37:10** So I prophesied as he commanded me, and the breath came into them, and they lived, and stood up upon their feet, an exceeding great army.
1 Corinthians 15:42 So also *is* the resurrection of the dead. It is sown in corruption; it is raised in incorruption:	**Job 14:12-14** So man lieth down, and riseth not: till the heavens be no more, they shall not awake, nor be raised out of their sleep. 13 O that thou wouldest hide me in the grave, that thou wouldest keep me secret, until thy wrath be past, that thou wouldest appoint me a set time, and remember me! 14 If a man die, shall he live

	again? all the days of my appointed time will I wait, till my change come.
	Isaiah 26:19 Thy dead *men* shall live, *together with* my dead body shall they arise. Awake and sing, ye that dwell in dust: for thy dew *is as* the dew of herbs, and the earth shall cast out the dead.
	Daniel 12:3 And they that be wise shall shine as the brightness of the firmament; and they that turn many to righteousness as the stars for ever and ever.
1 Corinthians 15:45 And so it is written, The first man Adam was made a living **soul**; the last Adam *was made* a quickening **spirit**.	**Genesis 2:7** And the LORD God formed man *of* the dust of the ground, and breathed into his nostrils the breath of life; and man became a living soul. **See 1 Thessalonians 5:23 "Body, soul, and spirit"**
1 Corinthians 15:47 The first man *is* of the earth, earthy: the second man *is* the Lord from heaven.	**Genesis 2:7** And the LORD God formed man *of* the dust of the ground, and breathed into his nostrils the breath of life; and man became a living soul. **See 1 Timothy 2:5 "God"**
1 Corinthians 15:49 And as we have borne the image of the earthy, we shall also bear the image of the heavenly.	**Genesis 1:26** And God said, Let us make man in our image, after our likeness: and let them have dominion over the fish of the sea, and over the fowl of the air, and over the cattle, and over all the earth, and over every creeping thing that creepeth upon the earth.
1 Corinthians 15:52 In a moment, in the twinkling of an eye, at the last trump: for the trumpet shall sound, and the dead shall be raised incorruptible, and we shall be changed.	**Genesis 5:24** And Enoch walked with God: and he *was* not; for God took him. **Exodus 19:19-20** And when the voice of the **trumpet** sounded long, and waxed louder and louder, Moses spake, and God answered him by a voice. 20 And the LORD came down upon mount Sinai, on the top of the mount: and the LORD called Moses *up* to the top of the mount; and **Moses went up**. **Leviticus 23:24** Speak unto the children of Israel, saying, In the seventh month, in the first *day* of the month, shall ye have a sabbath, a memorial of blowing of trumpets, an holy convocation. **Numbers 10:9** And if ye go to war in your land against the enemy that oppresseth you, then ye shall blow an alarm with the trumpets; and ye shall be remembered before the LORD your God, and ye shall be saved from your enemies. **Numbers 29:1** And in the seventh month, on the first *day* of the month, ye shall have an holy convocation; ye shall do no servile work: it is a day of blowing the trumpets unto you. **2 Kings 2:11** And it came to pass, as they still went on, and talked, that, behold, there appeared a chariot of fire, and horses of fire, and parted them both asunder; and **Elijah went up** by a whirlwind into heaven. **Psalms 50:5** Gather my saints together unto me; those that have made a covenant with me by sacrifice. **Isaiah 11:12** And he shall set up an ensign for the nations, and shall assemble the outcasts of Israel, and gather together the dispersed of Judah from the four corners of the earth. **Isaiah 26:19** Thy dead *men* shall live, *together with* my dead body shall they arise. Awake and sing, ye that dwell in dust: for thy dew *is as* the dew of herbs, and the earth shall cast out the dead. **Isaiah 27:13** And it shall come to pass in that day, *that* the great

	trumpet shall be blown, and they shall come which were ready to perish in the land of Assyria, and the outcasts in the land of Egypt, and shall worship the LORD in the holy mount at Jerusalem.
1 Corinthians 15:54 So when this corruptible shall have put on incorruption, and this mortal shall have put on immortality, then shall be brought to pass the saying that is written, Death is swallowed up in victory.	**Isaiah 22:13** And behold joy and gladness, slaying oxen, and killing sheep, eating flesh, and drinking wine: let us eat and drink; for to morrow we shall die. **Isaiah 25:8** He will swallow up death in victory; and the Lord GOD will wipe away tears from off all faces; and the rebuke of his people shall he take away from off all the earth: for the LORD hath spoken *it*. **See 1 Thessalonians 5:23 "Body, soul, and spirit"**
1 Corinthians 15:55 O death, where *is* thy sting? O grave, where *is* thy victory?	**Hosea 13:14** I will ransom them from the power of the grave; I will redeem them from death: O death, I will be thy plagues; O grave, I will be thy destruction: repentance shall be hid from mine eyes.
1 Corinthians 16:1-3 Now concerning the collection for the saints, as I have given order to the churches of Galatia, even so do ye. 2 Upon the first *day* of the week let every one of you lay by him in store, **as** *God* **hath prospered him**, that there be no gatherings when I come. 3 And when I come, whomsoever ye shall approve by *your* letters, them will I send to bring your liberality unto Jerusalem.	**Genesis 2:15** And the LORD God took the man, and put him into the garden of Eden **to dress it and to keep it**. **Deuteronomy 8:18** But thou shalt remember the LORD thy God: for *it is* he that giveth thee power to get wealth, that he may establish his covenant which he sware unto thy fathers, as *it is* this day. **Haggai 2:8** The silver *is* mine, and the gold *is* mine, saith the LORD of hosts.
1 Corinthians 16:8 But I will tarry at Ephesus until Pentecost.	**Leviticus 23:15-16** And ye shall count unto you from the morrow after the sabbath, from the day that ye brought the sheaf of the wave offering; seven sabbaths shall be complete: 16 Even unto the morrow after the seventh sabbath shall ye number fifty days; and ye shall offer a new meat offering unto the LORD. **Deuteronomy 16:9** Seven weeks shalt thou number unto thee: begin to number the seven weeks from *such time as* thou beginnest *to put* the sickle to the corn.
1 Corinthians 16:15 I beseech you, brethren, (ye know the house of Stephanas, that it is the **firstfruits** of Achaia, and *that* they have addicted themselves to the ministry of the saints,)	**See Romans 8:23 "Firstfruits"**
2 Corinthians 1:5 For as the sufferings of Christ abound in us, so our consolation also aboundeth by Christ.	**Psalms 34:19** Many *are* the afflictions of the righteous: but the LORD delivereth him out of them all. **Psalms 94:19** In the multitude of my thoughts within me thy comforts delight my soul.
2 Corinthians 1:9 But we had the sentence of death in ourselves, that we should not trust in ourselves, but in God which raiseth the dead:	**1 Samuel 2:6** The LORD killeth, and maketh alive: he bringeth down to the grave, and bringeth up. **2 Samuel 12:23** But now he is dead, wherefore should I fast? can I bring him back again? I shall go to him, but he shall not return to me. **2 Kings 2:11** And it came to pass, as they still went on, and talked, that, behold, there appeared a chariot of fire, and horses of fire, and parted them both asunder; and Elijah went up by a whirlwind into heaven. **Job 33:30** To bring back his soul from the pit, to be enlightened

	with the light of the living.
Psalms 30:3 O LORD, thou hast brought up my soul from the grave: thou hast kept me alive, that I should not go down to the pit.
Psalms 31:5 Into thine hand I commit my spirit: thou hast redeemed me, O LORD God of truth.
Psalms 49:15 But God will redeem my soul from the power of the grave: for he shall receive me. Selah.
Psalms 56:13 For thou hast delivered my soul from death: *wilt* not *thou deliver* my feet from falling, that I may walk before God in the light of the living?
Psalms 71:20 *Thou*, which hast shewed me great and sore troubles, shalt quicken me again, and shalt bring me up again from the depths of the earth.
Psalms 86:13 For great *is* thy mercy toward me: and thou hast delivered my soul from the lowest hell.
Psalms 116:8 For thou hast delivered my soul from death, mine eyes from tears, *and* my feet from falling.
Isaiah 26:19 Thy dead men shall live, together with my dead body shall they arise. Awake and sing, ye that dwell in dust: for thy dew is as the dew of herbs, and the earth shall cast out the dead.
Jeremiah 17:5 Thus saith the LORD; Cursed *be* the man that trusteth in man, and maketh flesh his arm, and whose heart departeth from the LORD.
Jeremiah 17:7 Blessed *is* the man that trusteth in the LORD, and whose hope the LORD is.
Hosea 13:14 I will ransom them from the power of the grave; I will redeem them from death: O death, I will be thy plagues; O grave, I will be thy destruction: repentance shall be hid from mine eyes.
2 Corinthians 1:14 As also ye have acknowledged us in part, that we are your rejoicing, even as ye also *are* ours in the day of the Lord Jesus.	**Leviticus 23:27** Also on the tenth *day* of this seventh month *there shall be* a day of atonement: it shall be an holy convocation unto you; and ye shall afflict your souls, and offer an offering made by fire unto the LORD.
Joel 2:31-32 The sun shall be turned into darkness, and the moon into blood, before the great and the terrible day of the LORD come. 32 And it shall come to pass, *that* whosoever shall call on the name of the LORD shall be delivered: for in mount Zion and in Jerusalem shall be deliverance, as the LORD hath said, and in the remnant whom the LORD shall call.
Zechariah 12:10 And I will pour upon the house of David, and upon the inhabitants of Jerusalem, the spirit of grace and of supplications: and they shall look upon me whom they have pierced, and they shall mourn for him, as one mourneth for *his* only *son*, and shall be in bitterness for him, as one that is in bitterness for *his* firstborn.
See Acts 2:20 "Day of the Lord"
2 Corinthians 1:21 Now He which	**1 Chronicles 16:22 Touch not Mine anointed**, and do My

stablisheth us with you in Christ, and **hath anointed us**, *is* God;	prophets no harm. **Isaiah 10:27** And it shall come to pass in that day, *that* his burden shall be taken away from off thy shoulder, and his yoke from off thy neck, and **the yoke shall be destroyed because of the anointing**. See Luke 4:18 "Anointing"
2 Corinthians 1:23 Moreover I call God for a record upon my **soul**, that to spare you I came not as yet unto Corinth.	See 1 Thessalonians 5:23 "Body, soul, and spirit"
2 Corinthians 2:11 Lest Satan should get an advantage of us: for we are not ignorant of his devices.	**Genesis 3:4** And the **serpent** said unto the woman, Ye shall not surely die: **Zechariah 3:1-2** And he shewed me Joshua the high priest standing before the angel of the LORD, and **Satan** standing at his right hand to resist him. 2 And the LORD said unto **Satan,** The LORD rebuke thee, O **Satan**; even the LORD that hath chosen Jerusalem rebuke thee: *is* not this a brand plucked out of the fire? See Matthew 4:10 "satan"
2 Corinthians 2:17 For we are not as many, which **corrupt** the **word of God**: but as of sincerity, but as of God, in the sight of God speak we in Christ.	**Jeremiah 23:36** And the burden of the LORD shall ye mention no more: for every man's word shall be his burden; for ye have **perverted** the **words of the living God**, of the LORD of hosts our God. See Matthew 5:18 "Scripture"
2 Corinthians 3:3 *Forasmuch as ye are* manifestly declared to be the epistle of Christ ministered by us, written not with ink, but with the Spirit of the living God; not in tables of stone, but in fleshy tables of the heart.	**Exodus 24:12** And the LORD said unto Moses, Come up to me into the mount, and be there: and I will give thee tables of stone, and a law, and commandments which I have written; that thou mayest teach them. **Exodus 34:1** And the LORD said unto Moses, Hew thee two tables of stone like unto the first: and I will write upon *these* tables the words that were in the first tables, which thou brakest. **Jeremiah 31:33** But this *shall be* the covenant that I will make with the house of Israel; After those days, saith the LORD, I will put my law in their inward parts, and write it in their hearts; and will be their God, and they shall be my people. **Ezekiel 11:19** And I will give them one heart, and I will put a new spirit within you; and I will take the stony heart out of their flesh, and will give them an heart of flesh: **Ezekiel 36:26** A new heart also will I give you, and a new spirit will I put within you: and I will take away the stony heart out of your flesh, and I will give you an heart of flesh.
2 Corinthians 3:6 Who also hath made us able ministers of the new testament; not of the letter, but of the spirit: for the letter killeth, but the spirit giveth life.	**Isaiah 59:20-21** And the Redeemer shall come to Zion, and unto them that turn from transgression in Jacob, saith the LORD. 21 As for me, this *is* my covenant with them, saith the LORD; My spirit that *is* upon thee, and my words which I have put in thy mouth, shall not depart out of thy mouth, nor out of the mouth of thy seed, nor out of the mouth of thy seed's seed, saith the LORD, from henceforth and for ever. **Jeremiah 31:31-33** Behold, the days come, saith the LORD, that **I will make a new covenant with the house of Israel,** and with the house of Judah: 32 Not according to the covenant that I made with their fathers in the day *that* I took them by the hand to bring them

	out of the land of Egypt; which my covenant they brake, although I was an husband unto them, saith the LORD: 33 But this *shall be* the covenant that I will make with the house of Israel; After those days, saith the LORD, I will put my law in their inward parts, and write it in their hearts; and will be their God, and they shall be my people. 34 And they shall teach no more every man his neighbour, and every man his brother, saying, Know the LORD: for they shall all know me, from the least of them unto the greatest of them, saith the LORD: for I will forgive their iniquity, and I will remember their sin no more.
2 Corinthians 3:7 But if the ministration of death, written *and* engraven in stones, was glorious, so that the children of Israel could not stedfastly behold the face of Moses for the glory of his countenance; which *glory* was to be done away:	**Exodus 24:12** And the LORD said unto Moses, Come up to me into the mount, and be there: and I will give thee tables of stone, and a law, and commandments which I have written; that thou mayest teach them. **Exodus 34:30** And when Aaron and all the children of Israel saw Moses, behold, the skin of his face shone; and they were afraid to come nigh him. **Exodus 34:35** And the children of Israel saw the face of Moses, that the skin of Moses' face shone: and Moses put the vail upon his face again, until he went in to speak with him.
2 Corinthians 3:13 And not as Moses, *which* put a vail over his face, that the children of Israel could not stedfastly look to the end of that which is abolished:	**Exodus 34:35** And the children of Israel saw the face of Moses, that the skin of Moses' face shone: and Moses put the vail upon his face again, until he went in to speak with him.
2 Corinthians 3:14 But their minds were blinded: for until this day remaineth the same vail untaken away in the reading of the old testament; which *vail* is done away in Christ.	**Isaiah 6:9-10** And he said, Go, and tell this people, Hear ye indeed, but understand not; and see ye indeed, but perceive not. 10 Make the heart of this people fat, and make their ears heavy, and shut their eyes; lest they see with their eyes, and hear with their ears, and understand with their heart, and convert, and be healed. **Jeremiah 5:21** Hear now this, O foolish people, and without understanding; which have eyes, and see not; which have ears, and hear not: **Ezekiel 12:2** Son of man, thou dwellest in the midst of a rebellious house, which have eyes to see, and see not; they have ears to hear, and hear not: for they *are* a rebellious house.
2 Corinthians 3:16 Nevertheless when it shall turn to the Lord, the vail shall be taken away.	**Exodus 34:34** But when Moses went in before the LORD to speak with him, he took the vail off, until he came out. And he came out, and spake unto the children of Israel *that* which he was commanded.
2 Corinthians 3:17 Now the Lord is that Spirit: and where the Spirit of the Lord *is,* there *is* liberty.	**See John 4:24 "Worship"**
2 Corinthians 3:18 But we all, with open face beholding as in a glass the glory of the Lord, are changed into the same image from glory to glory, *even* as by the Spirit of the Lord.	**Isaiah 11:2** And the spirit of the LORD shall rest upon him, the spirit of wisdom and understanding, the spirit of counsel and might, the spirit of knowledge and of the fear of the LORD; **Isaiah 61:1-2** The Spirit of the Lord GOD *is* upon me; because the LORD hath anointed me to preach good tidings unto the meek; he hath sent me to bind up the brokenhearted, to proclaim liberty to the captives, and the opening of the prison to *them that are* bound; To proclaim the acceptable year of the LORD, and the day of vengeance of our God; to comfort all that mourn;

	See Hebrews 12:14 "Holiness"
2 Corinthians 4:4 In whom the god of this world hath blinded the minds of them which believe not, lest the light of the glorious gospel of Christ, who is the image of God, should shine unto them.	**Genesis 1:26** And God said, Let us make man in our image, after our likeness: and let them have dominion over the fish of the sea, and over the fowl of the air, and over the cattle, and over all the earth, and over every creeping thing that creepeth upon the earth. **Isaiah 6:10** Make the heart of this people fat, and make their ears heavy, and shut their eyes; lest they see with their eyes, and hear with their ears, and understand with their heart, and convert, and be healed.
2 Corinthians 4:6 For God, who commanded the light to shine out of darkness, hath shined in our hearts, to *give* the light of the knowledge of the glory of God in the face of Jesus Christ.	**Genesis 1:3** And God said, Let there be light: and there was light. **Isaiah 40:5** And the glory of the LORD shall be revealed, and all flesh shall see *it* together: for the mouth of the LORD hath spoken *it*.
2 Corinthians 4:11 For we which live are alway delivered unto death for Jesus' sake, that the life also of Jesus might be made manifest in our mortal flesh.	**Psalms 44:22** Yea, for thy sake are we killed all the day long; we are counted as sheep for the slaughter.
2 Corinthians 4:13 We having the same spirit of faith, according as it is written, I believed, and therefore have I spoken; we also believe, and therefore speak;	**Psalms 116:10** I believed, therefore have I spoken: I was greatly afflicted:
2 Corinthians 4:17 For our light affliction, which is but for a moment, worketh for us a far more exceeding *and* eternal weight of glory;	**Psalms 30:5** For his anger *endureth but* a moment; in his favour *is* life: weeping may endure for a night, but joy *cometh* in the morning.
2 Corinthians 5:2-4 For in this we **groan**, earnestly desiring to be clothed upon with our house which is from heaven: 3 If so be that being clothed we shall not be found naked. 4 For we that are in this tabernacle do **groan**, being burdened: not for that we would be unclothed, but clothed upon, that mortality might be swallowed up of life.	**Exodus 2:24** And God heard their **groaning**, and God remembered his covenant with Abraham, with Isaac, and with Jacob. **Psalm 38:8-10** I am feeble and sore broken: I have roared by reason of the **disquietness** of my heart. 9 Lord, all my desire is before thee; and my **groaning** is not hid from thee. 10 My heart panteth, my strength faileth me: as for the light of mine eyes, it also is gone from me.
2 Corinthians 5:8 We are confident, *I say,* and willing rather to be absent from the **body**, and to be present with the Lord.	See 1 Thessalonians 5:23 "Body, soul, and spirit"
2 Corinthians 5:10 For we must all appear before the **judgment** seat of Christ; that every one may receive the things done in his body, according to that he hath done, whether it be good or bad.	See 2 Timothy 4:1 "Judge"
2 Corinthians 5:17 Therefore if any man *be* in Christ, *he is* a new creature: old things are passed away; behold, all things are become new.	**Isaiah 43:18-19** Remember ye not the former things, neither consider the things of old. 19 Behold, I will do a new thing; now it shall spring forth; shall ye not know it? I will even make a way in the wilderness, and rivers in the desert.
2 Corinthians 5:18-19 And all things *are* of God, who hath reconciled us to himself by Jesus Christ, and hath given to us the ministry of reconciliation;19 To	**Daniel 9:24** Seventy weeks are determined upon thy people and upon thy holy city, to finish the transgression, and to make an end of sins, and to make reconciliation for iniquity, and to bring in everlasting righteousness, and to seal up the vision and prophecy,

wit, that **God was in Christ**, reconciling the world unto himself, not imputing their trespasses unto them; and hath committed unto us the word of reconciliation.	and to anoint the most Holy. **See 1 Timothy 2:5 "God"**
2 Corinthians 5:21 For he hath made him *to be* sin for us, who knew no sin; that we might be made the righteousness of God in him.	**Leviticus 6:7** And the priest shall make an atonement for him before the LORD: and it shall be forgiven him for any thing of all that he hath done in trespassing therein **Deuteronomy 16:5** Thou mayest not sacrifice the passover within any of thy gates, which the LORD thy God giveth thee: **2 Chronicles 29:24** And the priests killed them, and they made reconciliation with their blood upon the altar, to make an atonement for all Israel: for the king commanded *that* the burnt offering and the sin offering *should be made* for all Israel. **Nehemiah 10:33** For the shewbread, and for the continual meat offering, and for the continual burnt offering, of the sabbaths, of the new moons, for the set feasts, and for the holy *things,* and for the sin offerings to make an atonement for Israel, and *for* all the work of the house of our God. **Psalms 40:6** Sacrifice and offering thou didst not desire; mine ears hast thou opened: burnt offering and sin offering hast thou not required. **Isaiah 53:10-11** Yet it pleased the LORD to bruise him; he hath put *him* to grief: when thou shalt make his soul an offering for sin, he shall see *his* seed, he shall prolong *his* days, and the pleasure of the LORD shall prosper in his hand. 11 He shall see of the travail of his soul, *and* shall be satisfied: by his knowledge shall my righteous servant justify many; for he shall bear their iniquities.
2 Corinthians 6:2 (For he saith, I have heard thee in a time accepted, and in the day of salvation have I succoured thee: behold, now *is* the accepted time; behold, now *is* the day of salvation.)	**Isaiah 49:8** Thus saith the LORD, In an acceptable time have I heard thee, and in a day of salvation have I helped thee: and I will preserve thee, and give thee for a covenant of the people, to establish the earth, to cause to inherit the desolate heritages;
2 Corinthians 6:4-5 But in all *things* **approving ourselves as the ministers of God**, in much patience, in afflictions, in necessities, in distresses, 5 In stripes, in imprisonments, in tumults, in labours, in watchings, **in fastings**;	**See Matthew 17:21 "Fasting"**
2 Corinthians 6:9 As unknown, and *yet* well known; as dying, and, behold, we live; as chastened, and not killed;	**Psalms 118:18** The LORD hath chastened me sore: but he hath not given me over unto death. **Isaiah 26:19** Thy dead *men* shall live, *together with* my dead body shall they arise. Awake and sing, ye that dwell in dust: for thy dew *is as* the dew of herbs, and the earth shall cast out the dead.
2 Corinthians 6:14 Be ye not unequally yoked together with unbelievers: for what fellowship hath righteousness with unrighteousness? and what communion hath light with darkness?	**Genesis 2:24** Therefore shall a man leave his father and his mother, and shall cleave unto his wife: and **they shall be one flesh**. **Deuteronomy 7:2** And when the LORD thy God shall deliver them before thee; thou shalt smite them, *and* utterly destroy them; thou shalt make no covenant with them, nor shew mercy unto them: **Exodus 23:32** Thou shalt make no covenant with them, nor with their gods.

	Exodus 34:12 Take heed to thyself, lest thou make a covenant with the inhabitants of the land whither thou goest, lest it be for a snare in the midst of thee:
	Nehemiah 13:27 Shall we then hearken unto you to do all this great evil, to transgress against our God in marrying strange wives?
	Proverbs 22:24-25 Make no friendship with an angry man; and with a furious man thou shalt not go: 25 Lest thou learn his ways, and get a snare to thy soul.
	Isaiah 5:20 Woe unto them that call evil good, and good evil; that put darkness for light, and light for **darkness**; that put bitter for sweet, and sweet for bitter!
2 Corinthians 6:16 And what agreement hath the temple of God with idols? for ye are the temple of the living God; as God hath said, I will dwell in them, and walk in [them]; and I will be their God, and they shall be my people.	**Psalms 133:1** Behold, how good and how pleasant *it is* for brethren to dwell together in unity!
	Amos 3:3 Can two walk together, except they be agreed?
	Exodus 29:45 And I will dwell among the children of Israel, and will be their God.
	Leviticus 26:11-12 And I will set my tabernacle among you: and my soul shall not abhor you. 12 And I will walk among you, and will be your God, and ye shall be my people.
	Jeremiah 30:22 And ye shall be my people, and I will be your God. **Jeremiah 31:1** At the same time, saith the LORD, will I be the God of all the families of Israel, and they shall be my people.
	Jeremiah 32:38 And they shall be my people, and I will be their God:
	Zechariah 2:10 Sing and rejoice, O daughter of Zion: for, lo, I come, and I will dwell in the midst of thee, saith the LORD.
	Zechariah 8:8 And I will bring them, and they shall dwell in the midst of Jerusalem: and they shall be my people, and I will be their God, in truth and in righteousness.
	Ezekiel 37:26-27 Moreover I will make a covenant of peace with them; it shall be an everlasting covenant with them: and I will place them, and multiply them, and will set my sanctuary in the midst of them for evermore. 27 My tabernacle also shall be with them: yea, I will be their God, and they shall be my people.
2 Corinthians 6:17-18 Wherefore come out from among them, and be ye separate, saith the Lord, and touch not the unclean *thing*; and I will receive you, And will be a Father unto you, and ye shall be my sons and daughters, saith the Lord Almighty.	**Leviticus 11:8** Of their flesh shall ye not eat, and their carcase shall ye not touch; they *are* **unclean** to you.
	Isaiah 52:11 Depart ye, depart ye, go ye out from thence, **touch no unclean** *thing*; go ye out of the midst of her; be ye clean, that bear the vessels of the LORD. **Jeremiah 31:9** They shall come with weeping, and with supplications will I lead them: I will cause them to walk by the rivers of waters in a straight way, wherein they shall not stumble: for I am a father to Israel, and Ephraim *is* my firstborn.
	Jeremiah 31:1 At the same time, saith the LORD, will I be the God of all the families of Israel, and they shall be my people.
	Jeremiah 51:45 My people, go ye out of the midst of her, and deliver ye every man his soul from the fierce anger of the LORD.
	Ezekiel 20:34 And I will bring you out from the people, and will gather you out of the countries wherein ye are scattered, with a mighty hand, and with a stretched out arm, and with fury poured

	out. **See Hebrews 12:14** "Holiness"
2 Corinthians 6:18 And will be a Father unto you, and ye shall be my sons and daughters, saith the Lord Almighty.	**2 Samuel 7:8** Now therefore so shalt thou say unto my servant David, Thus saith the LORD of hosts, I took thee from the sheepcote, from following the sheep, to be ruler over my people, over Israel: **2 Samuel 7:14** I will be his father, and he shall be my son. If he commit iniquity, I will chasten him with the rod of men, and with the stripes of the children of men: **Isaiah 43:6** I will say to the north, Give up; and to the south, Keep not back: bring my sons from far, and my daughters from the ends of the earth;
2 Corinthians 7:1 Having therefore these promises, dearly beloved, let us cleanse ourselves from all filthiness of the flesh and spirit, perfecting holiness in the fear of God.	**See Hebrews 12:14** "Holiness"
2 Corinthians 7:9 Now I rejoice, not that ye were made sorry, but that ye sorrowed to repentance: for ye were made sorry after a godly manner, that ye might receive damage by us in nothing.	**Proverbs 28:13** He that covereth his sins shall not prosper: but whoso confesseth and forsaketh *them* shall have mercy. **Isaiah 55:7** Let the wicked forsake his way, and the unrighteous man his thoughts: and let him return unto the LORD, and he will have mercy upon him; and to our God, for he will abundantly pardon.
2 Corinthians 8:9 For ye know the grace of our Lord Jesus Christ, that, though he was rich, yet for your sakes he became poor, that **ye through his poverty might be rich**.	**See Matthew 6:24** "Wealth"
2 Corinthians 8:15 As it is written, He that [had gathered] much had nothing over; and he that [had gathered] little had no lack.	**Exodus 16:18** And when they did mete *it* with an omer, he that gathered much had nothing over, and he that gathered little had no lack; they gathered every man according to his eating.
2 Corinthians 8:21 Providing for honest things, not only in the sight of the Lord, but also in the sight of men.	**Proverbs 3:4** So shalt thou find favour and good understanding in the sight of God and man.
2 Corinthians 9:6 But this *I say*, He which soweth sparingly shall reap also sparingly; and he which soweth bountifully shall reap also bountifully.	**Proverb 11:24** There is that scattereth, and yet increaseth; and *there is* that withholdeth more than is meet, but *it tendeth* to poverty. **See Luke 6:38** "Prosperity"
2 Corinthians 9:7 Every man according as he purposeth in his heart, *so let him give;* not grudgingly, or of necessity: for God loveth a cheerful giver.	**Exodus 25:2** Speak unto the children of Israel, that they bring me an offering: of every man that giveth it willingly with his heart ye shall take my offering. **Exodus 35:5** Take ye from among you an offering unto the LORD: whosoever *is* of a willing heart, let him bring it, an offering of the LORD; gold, and silver, and brass, **Deuteronomy 15:7** If there be among you a poor man of one of thy brethren within any of thy gates in thy land which the LORD thy God giveth thee, thou shalt not harden thine heart, nor shut thine hand from thy poor brother: **1 Chronicles 29:3** Moreover, because I have set my affection to the house of my God, I have of mine own proper good, of gold and

	silver, *which* I have given to the house of my God, over and above all that I have prepared for the holy house,
	1 Chronicles 29:9 Then the people rejoiced, for that they offered willingly, because with perfect heart they offered willingly to the LORD: and David the king also rejoiced with great joy.
	Proverbs 22:8 He that soweth iniquity shall reap vanity: and the rod of his anger shall fail.
2 Corinthians 9:8 And God *is* able to make all grace abound toward you; that ye, always having all sufficiency in all *things*, may abound to every good work:	**See Luke 6:38 "Prosperity"**
2 Corinthians 9:9 (As it is written, He hath dispersed abroad; he hath given to the poor: his righteousness remaineth for ever.	**Psalms 112:9** He hath dispersed, he hath given to the poor; his righteousness endureth for ever; his horn shall be exalted with honour.
2 Corinthians 9:10 Now he that ministereth seed to the sower both minister bread for *your* food, and multiply your seed sown, and increase the fruits of your righteousness;)	**Isaiah 55:10** For as the rain cometh down, and the snow from heaven, and returneth not thither, but watereth the earth, and maketh it bring forth and bud, that it may give seed to the sower, and bread to the eater:
2 Corinthians 9:11 Being enriched in every thing to all bountifulness, which causeth through us thanksgiving to God.	**Genesis 2:15** And the LORD God took the man, and put him into the garden of Eden **to dress it and to keep it**.
	Deuteronomy 8:18 But thou shalt remember the LORD thy God: for *it is* he that giveth thee power to get wealth, that he may establish his covenant which he sware unto thy fathers, as *it is* this day.
	Haggai 2:8 The silver *is* mine, and the gold *is* mine, saith the LORD of hosts.
2 Corinthians 10:17 But he that glorieth, let him glory in the Lord.	**Jeremiah 9:24** But let him that glorieth glory in this, that he understandeth and knoweth me, that I [am] the LORD which exercise lovingkindness, judgment, and righteousness, in the earth: for in these *things* I delight, saith the LORD.
2 Corinthians 10:18 For not he that commendeth himself is approved, but whom the Lord commendeth.	**Proverb 12:8** A man shall be commended according to his wisdom: but he that is of a perverse heart shall be despised.
	Proverb 27:2 Let another man praise thee, and not thine own mouth; a stranger, and not thine own lips.
2 Corinthians 11:2 For I am jealous over you with godly jealousy: for I have espoused you to one husband, that I may present *you as* a chaste virgin to Christ.	**Leviticus 21:13** And he shall take a wife in her virginity.
	Isaiah 61:10 I will greatly rejoice in the LORD, my soul shall be joyful in my God; for he hath clothed me with the garments of salvation, he hath covered me with the robe of righteousness, as a bridegroom decketh *himself* with ornaments, and as a bride adorneth *herself* with her jewels.
	Isaiah 62:5 For *as* a young man marrieth a virgin, *so* shall thy sons marry thee: and *as* the bridegroom rejoiceth over the bride, *so* shall thy God rejoice over thee.
	Jeremiah 2:2 Go and cry in the ears of Jerusalem, saying, Thus saith the LORD; I remember thee, the kindness of thy youth, the love of thine espousals, when thou wentest after me in the wilderness, in a land *that was* not sown.
	Jeremiah 31:32 Not according to the covenant that I made with

	their fathers in the day *that* I took them by the hand to bring them out of the land of Egypt; which my covenant they broke, although I was a **husband** unto them, saith the LORD: **Joel 2:16** Gather the people, sanctify the congregation, assemble the elders, gather the children, and those that suck the breasts: let the bridegroom go forth of his chamber, and the bride out of her closet.
2 Corinthians 11:3 But I fear, lest by any means, as the serpent beguiled Eve through his subtilty, so your minds should be corrupted from the simplicity that is in Christ.	**Genesis 3:4** And the serpent said unto the woman, Ye shall not surely die: **Genesis 3:5** For God doth know that in the day ye eat thereof, then your eyes shall be opened, and ye shall be as gods, knowing good and evil.
2 Corinthians 11:13 For such *are* false apostles, deceitful workers, transforming themselves into the apostles of Christ.	**See 2 Peter 2:1 "False prophets"**
2 Corinthians 11:14 And no marvel; for Satan himself is transformed into an angel of light. **2 Corinthians 11:15** Therefore *it is* no great thing if his **ministers** also be transformed as the ministers of righteousness; whose end shall be according to their works. **2 Corinthians 11:23** Are they **ministers** of Christ? I (speak as a fool) I *am* more; in labors more abundant, in stripes above measure, in prisons more frequent, in deaths oft.	**Genesis 3:4** And the **serpent** said unto the woman, Ye shall not surely die: **Zechariah 3:1-2** And he shewed me Joshua the high priest standing before the angel of the LORD, and **Satan** standing at his right hand to resist him. 2 And the LORD said unto **Satan**, The LORD rebuke thee, O **Satan**; even the LORD that hath chosen Jerusalem rebuke thee: *is* not this a brand plucked out of the fire? **See Matthew 4:10 "satan"**
2 Corinthians 11:24 Of the Jews five times received I forty *stripes* save one.	**Deuteronomy 25:3** Forty stripes he may give him, *and* not exceed: lest, *if* he should exceed, and beat him above these with many stripes, then thy brother should seem vile unto thee.
2 Corinthians 11:27 In weariness and painfulness, in watchings often, in hunger and thirst, **in fastings often**, in cold and nakedness.	**See Matthew 17:21 "fasting"**
2 Corinthians 12:7 And lest I should be exalted above measure through the abundance of the revelations, there was given to me a **thorn in the flesh**, the messenger of Satan to buffet me, lest I should be exalted above measure.	**Numbers 33:55** But if ye will not drive out the inhabitants of the land from before you; then it shall come to pass, that those which ye let remain of them *shall be* pricks in your eyes, and **thorns in your sides**, and shall vex you in the land wherein ye dwell. **Joshua 23:13** Know for a certainty that the LORD your God will no more drive out any of these nations from before you; but they shall be snares and traps unto you, and **scourges in your sides**, and **thorns** in your eyes, until ye perish from off this good land which the LORD your God hath given you. **Judges 2:3** Wherefore I also said, I will not drive them out from before you; but **they shall be *as thorns* in your sides**, and their gods shall be a snare unto you. **Job 2:6** And the LORD said unto **Satan**, Behold, he *is* in thine hand; but save his life. **Genesis 3:4** And the **serpent** said unto the woman, Ye shall not surely die: **Zechariah 3:1-2** And he shewed me Joshua the high priest

	standing before the angel of the LORD, and **Satan** standing at his right hand to resist him. 2 And the LORD said unto **Satan,** The LORD rebuke thee, O **Satan**; even the LORD that hath chosen Jerusalem rebuke thee: *is* not this a brand plucked out of the fire? **See Matthew 4:10** "satan"
2 Corinthians 12:21 *And* lest, when I come again, my God will humble me among you, and *that* I shall bewail many which have sinned already, and **have not repented of the uncleanness and fornication and lasciviousness which they have committed**.	**See Romans 1:26-27** "Sexual sins"
2 Corinthians 13:1 This *is* the third *time* I am coming to you. In the mouth of two or three witnesses shall every word be established.	**Numbers 35:30** Whoso killeth any person, the murderer shall be put to death by the mouth of witnesses: but one witness shall not testify against any person *to cause him* to die. **Deuteronomy 17:6** At the mouth of two witnesses, or three witnesses, shall he that is worthy of death be put to death; *but* at the mouth of one witness he shall not be put to death. **Deuteronomy 19:15** One witness shall not rise up against a man for any iniquity, or for any sin, in any sin that he sinneth: at the mouth of two witnesses, or at the mouth of three witnesses, shall the matter be established.
2 Corinthians 13:11 Finally, brethren, farewell. Be perfect, be of good comfort, be of one mind, live in peace; and the God of love and peace shall be with you.	**See Hebrews 12:14** "Holiness"
Galatians 1:4 Who gave himself for our sins, that he might deliver us from this present evil world, according to the will of God and our Father:	**Exodus 12:22** And ye shall take a bunch of hyssop, and dip *it* in the blood that *is* in the bason, and strike the lintel and the two side posts with the blood that *is* in the bason; and none of you shall go out at the door of his house until the morning. **Exodus 24:6-8** And Moses took half of the blood, and put *it* in basons; and half of the blood he sprinkled on the altar. 7 And he took the book of the covenant, and read in the audience of the people: and they said, All that the LORD hath said will we do, and be obedient. 8 And Moses took the blood, and sprinkled *it* on the people, and said, Behold the blood of the covenant, which the LORD hath made with you concerning all these words. **Leviticus 5:9** And he shall sprinkle of the blood of the sin offering upon the side of the altar; and the rest of the blood shall be wrung out at the bottom of the altar: it *is* a sin offering. **Isaiah 53:5** But he *was* wounded for our transgressions, *he was* bruised for our iniquities: the chastisement of our peace *was* upon him; and with his stripes we are healed. **Daniel 9:24** Seventy weeks are determined upon thy people and upon thy holy city, to finish the transgression, and to make an end of sins, and **to make reconciliation for iniquity**, and to bring in everlasting righteousness, and to seal up the vision and prophecy, and to anoint the most Holy.
Galatians 1:6-9 I marvel that ye are so soon removed from him that called you into the grace of Christ unto another gospel: 7 Which is not another; but there be some that trouble you, and would	**Psalms 119:104** Through thy precepts I get understanding: therefore I hate every false way. **Psalms 119:127-128** Therefore I love thy commandments above gold; yea, above fine gold. 128 Therefore I esteem all *thy* precepts

pervert the gospel of Christ. 8 But though we, or an angel from heaven, preach any other gospel unto you than that which we have preached unto you, let him be accursed. 9 As we said before, so say I now again, If any *man* preach any other gospel unto you than that ye have received, let him be accursed.	*concerning* all *things to be* right; *and* I hate every false way. **Psalms 119:30** I have chosen the way of truth: thy judgments have I laid *before me.*
Galatians 1:12 For I neither received it of man, neither was I **taught** *it*, but by the revelation of Jesus Christ.	**See Ephesians 4:11 "Teach-Teaching"**
Galatians 1:15 But when it pleased God, who separated me from my mother's womb, and called *me* by his grace,	**Isaiah 49:1** Listen, O isles, unto me; and hearken, ye people, from far; The LORD hath called me from the womb; from the bowels of my mother hath he made mention of my name. **Jeremiah 1:5** Before I formed thee in the belly I knew thee; and before thou camest forth out of the womb I sanctified thee, *and* I ordained thee a prophet unto the nations.
Galatians 2:10 Only *they would* that we should remember the poor; the same which I also was forward to do.	**Deuteronomy 15:11** For the poor shall never cease out of the land: therefore I command thee, saying, Thou shalt open thine hand wide unto thy brother, to thy poor, and to thy needy, in thy land.
Galalatians 2:14 But when I saw that they walked not uprightly according to the truth of the gospel, I said unto Peter before *them* all, If thou, being a Jew, livest after the manner of Gentiles, and not as do the Jews, why compellest thou the Gentiles to live as do the Jews?	**Proverbs 9:9** Give *instruction* to a wise *man,* and he will be yet wiser: teach a just *man,* and he will increase in learning. **Proverbs 17:10** A reproof entereth more into a wise man than an hundred stripes into a fool.
Galatians 2:16 Knowing that a man is not justified by the works of the law, but by the faith of Jesus Christ, even we have believed in Jesus Christ, that we might be justified by the faith of Christ, and not by the works of the law: for by the works of the law shall no flesh be justified.	**2 Chronicles 13:8** Neither will I any more remove the foot of Israel from out of the land which I have appointed for your fathers; so that they will take heed to do all that I have commanded them, according to the whole **law** and the **statutes** and the **ordinances** by the hand of Moses. **Psalms 123:2** Behold, as the eyes of servants *look* unto the hand of their masters, *and* as the eyes of a maiden unto the hand of her mistress; so our eyes *wait* upon the LORD our God, until that he have mercy upon us. **Psalms 143:2** And enter not into judgment with thy servant: for in thy sight shall no man living be justified.
Galatians 3:6 Even as Abraham believed God, and it was accounted to him for righteousness.	**Genesis 15:6** And he believed in the LORD; and he counted it to him for righteousness.
Galatians 3:8 And the scripture, foreseeing that God would justify the heathen through faith, preached before the gospel unto Abraham, *saying,* In thee shall all nations be blessed.	**Genesis 12:3** And I will bless them that bless thee, and curse him that curseth thee: and in thee shall all families of the earth be blessed. **Genesis 17:7** And I will establish My covenant between Me and thee and thy seed after thee in their generations for an everlasting covenant, to be God unto thee, and to thy seed after thee. **Genesis 18:18** Seeing that Abraham shall surely become a great and mighty nation, and all the nations of the earth shall be blessed in him? **Genesis 22:18** And in thy seed shall all the nations of the earth be blessed; because thou hast obeyed my voice.

	Genesis 26:4 And I will make thy seed to multiply as the stars of heaven, and will give unto thy seed all these countries; and in thy seed shall all the nations of the earth be blessed;
	Genesis 28:14 And thy seed shall be as the dust of the earth, and thou shalt spread abroad to the west, and to the east, and to the north, and to the south: and in thee and in thy seed shall all the families of the earth be blessed.
	Jeremiah 34:8 *This is* the word that came unto Jeremiah from the LORD, after that the king Zedekiah had made a covenant with all the people which *were* at Jerusalem, to proclaim liberty unto them;
Galatians 3:9 So then they which be of faith are blessed with faithful Abraham.	**Genesis 12:3c** … in thee shall all families of the earth be blessed.
Galatians 3:10 For as many as are of the works of the law are under the curse: for it is written, Cursed *is* every one that continueth not in all things which are written in the book of the law to do them.	**Deuteronomy 21:23** His body shall not remain all night upon the tree, but thou shalt in any wise bury him that day; (for **he that is hanged is accursed of God**;) that thy land be not defiled, which the LORD thy God giveth thee for an inheritance.
	Deuteronomy 27:26 Cursed [be] he that confirmeth not *all* the words of this law to do them. And all the people shall say, Amen.
Galatians 3:11 But that no man is justified by the law in the sight of God, *it is* evident: for, **The just shall live by faith**.	**Habakkuk 2:4** Behold, his soul *which* is lifted up is not upright in him: but **the just shall live by his faith**.
Galatians 3:12 And the law is not of faith: but, The man that doeth them shall live in them.	**Leviticus 18:5** Ye shall therefore keep my statutes, and my judgments: which if a man do, he shall live in them: I *am* the LORD.
	Ezekiel 20:11 And I gave them my statutes, and shewed them my judgments, which *if* a man do, he shall even live in them.
Galatians 3:13 Christ hath redeemed us from the curse of the law, being made a curse for us: for it is written, Cursed [is] every one that hangeth on a tree:	**Genesis 12:3** And I will bless them that bless thee, and curse him that curseth thee: and in thee shall all families of the earth be blessed.
	Genesis 22:16 And said, By myself have I sworn, saith the LORD, for because thou hast done this thing, and hast not withheld thy son, thine only *son:*
	Deuteronomy 21:23 His body shall not remain all night upon the tree, but thou shalt in any wise bury him that day; (for he that is hanged [is] accursed of God;) that thy land be not defiled, which the LORD thy God giveth thee [for] an inheritance.
	Deuteronomy 28:45-46 Moreover all these curses shall come upon thee, and shall pursue thee, and overtake thee, till thou be destroyed; because thou hearkenedst not unto the voice of the LORD thy God, to keep His commandments and His statutes which He commanded thee: 46 And they shall be upon thee for a sign and for a wonder, and **upon thy seed for ever**.
	Isaiah 44:6 Thus saith the LORD the King of Israel, and his **redeemer** the LORD of hosts; I *am* the first, and I *am* the last; and beside me *there is* no God.
	Isaiah 53:4-5 Surely he hath borne our griefs, and carried our sorrows: yet we did esteem him stricken, smitten of God, and afflicted. 5 But he *was* wounded for our transgressions, *he was* bruised for our iniquities: the chastisement of our peace *was* upon him; and with his stripes we are healed.
	Isaiah 54:5 For thy Maker *is* thine husband; the LORD of hosts *is*

	his name; and thy Redeemer the Holy One of Israel; The God of the whole earth shall he be called. **Isaiah 60:16** Thou shalt also suck the milk of the Gentiles, and shalt suck the breast of kings: and thou shalt know that I the LORD *am* thy Saviour and thy Redeemer, the mighty One of Jacob.
Galatians 3:14 That the blessing of Abraham might come on the Gentiles through Jesus Christ; that we might receive the promise of the Spirit through faith.	**Genesis 12:3** And I will bless them that bless thee, and curse him that curseth thee: and in thee shall all families of the earth be blessed. **Genesis 17:7** And I will establish my covenant between me and thee and thy seed after thee in their generations for an everlasting covenant, to be a God unto thee, and to thy seed after thee. **Genesis 18:18** Seeing that Abraham shall surely become a great and mighty nation, and all the nations of the earth shall be blessed in him? **Genesis 28:4** And give thee the blessing of Abraham, to thee, and to thy seed with thee; that thou mayest inherit the land wherein thou art a stranger, which God gave unto Abraham.
Galatians 3:16 Now to Abraham and his seed were the promises made. He saith not, And to seeds, as of many; but as of one, And to thy seed, which is Christ.	**Genesis 12:7** And the LORD appeared unto Abram, and said, Unto thy seed will I give this land: and there builded he an altar unto the LORD, who appeared unto him. **Genesis 13:15** For all the land which thou seest, to thee will I give it, and to thy seed for ever. **Genesis 17:7-8** And I will establish my covenant between me and thee and thy seed after thee in their generations for an everlasting covenant, to be a God unto thee, and to thy seed after thee. 8 And I will give unto thee, and to thy seed after thee, the land wherein thou art a stranger, all the land of Canaan, for an everlasting possession; and I will be their God. **Genesis 24:7** The LORD God of heaven, which took me from my father's house, and from the land of my kindred, and which spake unto me, and that sware unto me, saying, Unto thy seed will I give this land; he shall send his angel before thee, and thou shalt take a wife unto my son from thence.
Galatians 3:17 And this I say, *that* the covenant, that was confirmed before of God in Christ, the law, which was four hundred and thirty years after, cannot disannul, that it should make the promise of none effect.	**Genesis 15:13** And he said unto Abram, Know of a surety that thy seed shall be a stranger in a land *that is* not theirs, and shall serve them; and they shall afflict them four hundred years; **Exodus 12:40** Now the sojourning of the children of Israel, who dwelt in Egypt, *was* four hundred and thirty years.
Galatians 3:19 Wherefore then *serveth* the law? It was added because of transgressions, till the seed should come to whom the promise was made; *and it was* ordained by angels in the hand of a mediator.	**Exodus 24:3** And Moses came and told the people all the words of the LORD, and all the judgments: and all the people answered with one voice, and said, All the words which the LORD hath said will we do. **Deuteronomy 18:18** I will raise them up a Prophet from among their brethren, like unto thee, and will put my words in his mouth; and he shall speak unto them all that I shall command him. **Isaiah 53:12** Therefore will I divide him *a portion* with the great, and he shall divide the spoil with the strong; because he hath poured out his soul unto death: and he was numbered with the transgressors; and he bare the sin of many, and made intercession for the transgressors.
Galatians 3:20 Now a mediator is not	**Exodus 20:2-3** I am the LORD thy God, which have brought thee

a mediator of one, but God is one.	out of the land of Egypt, out of the house of bondage. 3 Thou shalt have no other gods before me."

Deuteronomy 6:4 Hear, O Israel: The LORD our God *is* one LORD :

Nehemiah 9:6 Thou, *even* thou, *art* LORD alone; thou hast made heaven, the heaven of heavens, with all their host, the earth, and all *things* that *are* therein, the seas, and all that *is* therein, and thou preservest them all; and the host of heaven worshippeth thee.

Psalms 86:10 For thou *art* great, and doest wondrous things: thou *art* God alone.

Isaiah 9:6 For unto us a child is born, unto us a son is given: and the government shall be upon his shoulder: and his name shall be called Wonderful, Counselor, The mighty God, The everlasting Father, The Prince of Peace.

Isaiah 43:10-11 Ye *are* my witnesses, saith the LORD, and my servant whom I have chosen: that ye may know and believe me, and understand that I *am* he: before me there was no God formed, neither shall there be after me. 11 I, *even* I, *am* the LORD ; and beside me *there is* no saviour.

Isaiah 44:6 Thus saith the LORD the King of Israel, and his redeemer the LORD of hosts; I *am* the first, and I *am* the last; and beside me *there is* no God.

Isaiah 44:8 Fear ye not, neither be afraid: have not I told thee from that time, and have declared *it*? ye *are* even my witnesses. Is there a God beside me? yea, *there is* no God; I know not *any*.

Isaiah 45:5-6 I am the LORD, and there is none else, **there is no God beside me**: I girded thee, though thou hast not known me: 6 That they may know from the rising of the sun, and from the west, that there is none beside me. I am the LORD, and there is none else.

Isaiah 45:21-22 have not I the LORD? and **there is no God else beside me**; a just God and a Saviour; there is none beside me. 22 Look unto me, and be ye saved, all the ends of the earth: for **I am God, and there is none else**.

Isaiah 54:5 For thy Maker *is* thine husband; the LORD of hosts *is* his name; and thy Redeemer the Holy One of Israel; The God of the whole earth shall he be called.

Malachi 2:10 Have we not all one father? hath not one God created us? why do we deal treacherously every man against his brother, by profaning the covenant of our fathers? |
Galatians 3:22 But the **Scripture hath concluded all under sin**, that the promise by faith of Jesus Christ might be given to them that believe.	**See Matthew 5:18 "Scripture"**
Galatians 3:26 For ye are all the children of God by faith in Christ Jesus.	**Isaiah 56:5** Even unto them will I give in mine house and within my walls a place and a name better than of sons and of daughters: I will give them an everlasting name, that shall not be cut off.
Galatians 3:27 For as many of you as have been **baptized into Christ have put on Christ**.	**See Acts 3:5 "Salvation"**
Galatians 3:28 There is neither Jew nor Greek, there is neither bond nor free,	**Judges 4:4** And Deborah, a **prophetess**, the wife of Lapidoth, she

there is neither male **nor female**: for ye are all one in Christ Jesus.	judged Israel at that time. **Isaiah 8:3** And I went unto the **prophetess**; and she conceived, and bare a son. Then said the LORD to me, Call his name Mahershalalhashbaz.
Galatians 3:29 And if ye *be* Christ's, then are ye Abraham's seed, and heirs according to the promise.	**Genesis 21:12** And God said unto Abraham, Let it not be grievous in thy sight because of the lad, and because of thy bondwoman; in all that Sarah hath said unto thee, hearken unto her voice; for in Isaac shall thy seed be called.
Galatians 4:4-5 But when the fulness of the time was come, God sent forth his Son, made of a woman, made under the law, 5 To redeem them that were under the law, that we might receive the adoption of sons.	**Genesis 3:15** And I will put enmity between thee and the woman, and between thy seed and her seed; it shall bruise thy head, and thou shalt bruise his heel. **Genesis 49:10** The sceptre shall not depart from Judah, nor a lawgiver from between his feet, until Shiloh come; and unto him *shall* the gathering of the people *be*. **Leviticus 25:25** If thy brother be waxen poor, and hath sold away *some* of his possession, and if any of his kin come to redeem it, then shall he redeem that which his brother sold. **Job 19:25** For I know *that* my redeemer liveth, and *that* he shall stand at the latter *day* upon the earth: **Psalms 19:14** Let the words of my mouth, and the meditation of my heart, be acceptable in thy sight, O LORD , my strength, and my redeemer. **Jeremiah 50:34** Their Redeemer *is* strong; the LORD of hosts *is* his name: he shall throughly plead their cause, that he may give rest to the land, and disquiet the inhabitants of Babylon. **Daniel 9:24** Seventy weeks are determined upon thy people and upon thy holy city, to finish the transgression, and to make an end of sins, and to make reconciliation for iniquity, and to bring in everlasting righteousness, and to seal up the vision and prophecy, and to anoint the most Holy.
Galatians 4:22 For it is written, that Abraham had two sons, the one by a bondmaid, the other by a freewoman.	**Genesis 16:2** And Sarai said unto Abram, Behold now, the LORD hath restrained me from bearing: I pray thee, go in unto my maid; it may be that I may obtain children by her. And Abram hearkened to the voice of Sarai. **Genesis 16:15** And Hagar bare Abram a son: and Abram called his son's name, which Hagar bare, Ishmael. **Genesis 21:3** And Abraham called the name of his son that was born unto him, whom Sarah bare to him, Isaac.
Galatians 4:24-25 Which things are an allegory: for these are the two **covenants**; the one from the mount Sinai, which gendereth to bondage, which is Agar.25 For this Agar is mount Sinai in Arabia, and answereth to Jerusalem which now is, and is in bondage with her children.	**Genesis 3:21** Unto Adam also and to his wife did the LORD God make coats of skins, and clothed them. **Genesis 9:8-9** And God spake unto Noah, and to his sons with him, saying, 9 And I, behold, I establish my covenant with you, and with your seed after you; **Exodus 2:24** And God heard their groaning, and God remembered his covenant with Abraham, with Isaac, and with Jacob. **Exodus 19:5** Now therefore, if ye will obey my voice indeed, and keep my covenant, then ye shall be a peculiar treasure unto me above all people: for all the earth *is* mine: **Numbers 18:19** All the heave offerings of the holy things, which

	the children of Israel offer unto the LORD, have I given thee, and thy sons and thy daughters with thee, by a statute for ever: it *is* a covenant of salt for ever before the LORD unto thee and to thy seed with thee.
	Numbers 25:12-13 Wherefore say, Behold, I give unto him my covenant of peace: 13 And he shall have it, and his seed after him, *even* the covenant of an everlasting priesthood; because he was zealous for his God, and made an atonement for the children of Israel.
	Deuteronomy 7:6 For thou *art* an holy people unto the LORD thy God: the LORD thy God hath chosen thee to be a special people unto himself, above all people that *are* upon the face of the earth.
	Deuteronomy 10:14-15 Behold, the heaven and the heaven of heavens *is* the LORD's thy God, the earth *also*, with all that therein *is*. 15 Only the LORD had a delight in thy fathers to love them, and he chose their seed after them, *even* you above all people, as *it is* this day.
	2 Samuel 23:5 Although my house *be* not so with God; yet he hath made with me an everlasting covenant, ordered in all *things*, and sure: for *this is* all my salvation, and all *my* desire, although he make *it* not to grow.
Galatians 4:26 But Jerusalem which is above is free, which is the mother of us all.	**Psalms 135:21** Blessed be the LORD out of Zion, which dwelleth at Jerusalem. Praise ye the LORD. **Isaiah 60:14** The sons also of them that afflicted thee shall come bending unto thee; and all they that despised thee shall bow themselves down at the soles of thy feet; and they shall call thee, The city of the LORD, The Zion of the Holy One of Israel.
Galatians 4:27 For it is written, Rejoice, *thou* barren that bearest not; break forth and cry, thou that travailest not: for the desolate hath many more children than she which hath an husband.	**Isaiah 54:1** Sing, O barren, thou *that* didst not bear; break forth into singing, and cry aloud, thou *that* didst not travail with child: for more *are* the children of the desolate than the children of the married wife, saith the LORD.
Galatians 4:28 Now we, brethren, as Isaac was, are the children of promise.	**Genesis 21:5-7** And Abraham was an hundred years old, when his son Isaac was born unto him. 6 And Sarah said, God hath made me to laugh, *so that* all that hear will laugh with me. 7 And she said, Who would have said unto Abraham, that Sarah should have given children suck? for I have born *him* a son in his old age.
Galatians 4:29 But as then he that was born after the flesh persecuted him *that was born* after the Spirit, even so *it is* now.	**Genesis 21:9** And Sarah saw the son of Hagar the Egyptian, which she had born unto Abraham, mocking.
Galatians 4:30 Nevertheless what saith the scripture? Cast out the bondwoman and her son: for the son of the bondwoman shall not be heir with the son of the freewoman.	**Genesis 21:10** Wherefore she said unto Abraham, Cast out this bondwoman and her son: for the son of this bondwoman shall not be heir with my son, [even] with Isaac.
Galatians 5:1 Stand fast therefore in the liberty wherewith **Christ hath made us free**, and be not entangled again with the yoke of bondage.	**Psalms 107:2** Let the redeemed of the LORD say *so*, whom **he hath redeemed from the hand of the enemy**;
Galatians 5:2-3 Behold, I Paul say unto you, that if ye be circumcised, Christ shall profit you nothing. 3 For I testify	**Genesis 17:10-14** This *is* my covenant, which ye shall keep, between me and you and thy seed after thee; **Every man child among you shall be circumcised.** 11 **And ye shall circumcise the**

again to every man that is circumcised, that he is a debtor to do the whole law. **Galatians 5:6** For in Jesus Christ neither circumcision availeth any thing, nor uncircumcision; but faith which worketh by love.	**flesh of your foreskin; and it shall be a token of the covenant betwixt me and you.** 12 And he that is eight days old shall be circumcised among you, every man child in your generations, he that is born in the house, or bought with money of any stranger, which *is* not of thy seed. 13 He that is born in thy house, and he that is bought with thy money, must needs be circumcised: and my covenant shall be in your flesh for an everlasting covenant. 14 And **the uncircumcised man child whose flesh of his foreskin is not circumcised, that soul shall be cut off from his people; he hath broken my covenant**.
Galatians 5:12 I would they were even cut off which trouble you.	**Joshua 7:25** And Joshua said, Why hast thou troubled us? the LORD shall trouble thee this day. And all Israel stoned him with stones, and burned them with fire, after they had stoned them with stones.
Galatians 5:14 For all the law is fulfilled in one word, *even* in this; Thou shalt love thy neighbour as thyself.	**Leviticus 19:18** Thou shalt not avenge, nor bear any grudge against the children of thy people, but thou shalt love thy neighbour as thyself: I [am] the LORD.
Galatians 5:16-17 But I say, **Walk in *the* Spirit, and you will not fulfill *the* lust of *the* flesh**, 17 For the flesh lusts against the Spirit, and the Spirit against the flesh; and these are contrary to one another; lest whatever you may will, these things you do.	**Job 31:1** I made a covenant with mine eyes; why then should I think upon a maid? **Psalms 119:37** Turn away mine eyes from beholding vanity; *and* quicken thou me in thy way. **See Romans 1:26-27 "Sexual sins"**
Galatians 5:19-21 Now the works of the flesh are manifest, which are *these*; Adultery, fornication, uncleanness, lasciviousness, 20 Idolatry, **witchcraft**, hatred, variance, emulations, wrath, strife, seditions, heresies, 21 Envyings, murders, **drunkenness**, revellings, and such like: of the which I tell you before, as I have also told *you* in time past, that they which do such things shall not inherit the kingdom of God.	**Exodus 20:13-17** Thou shalt not kill. 14 Thou shalt not commit **adultery**. 15 Thou shalt not steal. 16 Thou shalt not bear false witness against thy neighbour. 17 Thou shalt not covet thy neighbour's house, thou shalt not covet thy neighbour's wife, nor his manservant, nor his maidservant, nor his ox, nor his ass, nor any thing that *is* thy neighbour's. **Deuteronomy 17:17 Neither shall he multiply wives to himself**, that his heart turn not away: neither shall he greatly multiply to himself silver and gold. **Deuteronomy 22:22** If a man be found lying with a woman married to an husband, then **they shall both of them die**, *both* the man that lay with the woman, and the woman: so shalt thou put away evil from Israel. **See Matthew 5:27 "Adultery"** **Exodus 22:18** Thou shalt not suffer a witch to live. **Leviticus 20:27** A man also or woman that hath a familiar spirit, or that is a wizard, shall surely be put to death: they shall stone them with stones: their blood *shall be* upon them. **Deutoronomy 18:10-11** There shall not be found among you *any one* that maketh his son or his daughter to pass through the fire, *or* that useth divination, *or* an observer of times, or an enchanter, or a witch, 11 Or a charmer, or a consulter with familiar spirits, or a wizard, or a necromancer. **Isaiah 8:19** And when they shall say unto you, Seek unto them that have familiar spirits, and unto wizards that peep, and that mutter: should not a people seek unto their God? for the living to the dead? **See Romans 1:26 "Sexual sins"**

	See Ephesians 5:18 "Drunkenness"
Galatians 6:5 For every man shall bear his own burden.	**Jeremiah 23:36** And the burden of the LORD shall ye mention no more: for every man's word shall be his burden; for ye have perverted the words of the living God, of the LORD of hosts our God.
Galatians 6:6 Let **him that is taught in the word** communicate unto him that teacheth in all good things.	**See Matthew 5:18 "Word"**
Galatians 6:8-9 For he **that soweth to his flesh shall of the flesh reap corruption**; but he that soweth to the Spirit shall of the Spirit reap life everlasting. 9 And let us not be weary in well doing: for in due season we shall reap, if we faint not.	**See Romans 1:26-27 "Sexual sins"**
Galatians 6:16 And as many as walk according to this rule, peace *be* on them, and mercy, and upon the Israel of God.	**Psalms 125:5** As for such as turn aside unto their crooked ways, the LORD shall lead them forth with the workers of iniquity: *but* peace *shall be* upon Israel.
Ephesians 1:7 In whom **we have redemption through his blood**, the forgiveness of sins, according to the riches of his grace;	**Psalms 103:3** Who forgiveth all thine iniquities; who healeth all thy diseases; **Psalms 130:7-8** Let Israel hope in the LORD: for with the LORD *there is* mercy, and with him *is* plenteous redemption. 8 And he shall redeem Israel from all his iniquities **Isaiah 53:5** But he *was* wounded for our transgressions, *he was* bruised for our iniquities: the chastisement of our peace *was* upon him; and with his stripes we are healed. **Daniel 9:24** Seventy weeks are determined upon thy people and upon thy holy city, to finish the transgression, and to make an end of sins, and **to make reconciliation for iniquity**, and to bring in everlasting righteousness, and to seal up the vision and prophecy, and to anoint the most Holy. **See Matthew 26:28 "Atonement"**
Ephesians 1:10 That in the dispensation of the fulness of times he might gather together in one all things in Christ, both which are in heaven, and which are on earth; *even* in him:	**Genesis 49:10** The sceptre shall not depart from Judah, nor a lawgiver from between his feet, until Shiloh come; and unto him *shall* the gathering of the people *be*. **Daniel 9:24** Seventy weeks are determined upon thy people and upon thy holy city, to finish the transgression, and to make an end of sins, and to make reconciliation for iniquity, and to bring in everlasting righteousness, and to seal up the vision and prophecy, and to anoint the most Holy.
Ephesians 1:11 In whom also we have obtained an inheritance, being predestinated according to the purpose of him who worketh all things after the counsel of his own will:	**Psalms 91:9-12** Because thou hast made the LORD, *which is* my refuge, *even* the most High, thy habitation; 10 There shall no evil befall thee, neither shall any plague come nigh thy dwelling. 11 For he shall give his angels charge over thee, to keep thee in all thy ways. 12 They shall bear thee up in *their* hands, lest thou dash thy foot against a stone.
Ephesians 1:14 Which is the earnest of our inheritance until the redemption of the purchased possession, unto the praise of his glory.	**Exodus 19:5** Now therefore, if ye will obey my voice indeed, and keep my covenant, then ye shall be a peculiar treasure unto me above all people: for all the earth *is* mine: **Deuteronomy 7:6** For thou *art* an holy people unto the LORD thy God: the LORD thy God hath chosen thee to be a special people

	unto himself, above all people that *are* upon the face of the earth.
Deuteronomy 14:2 For thou *art* an holy people unto the LORD thy God, and the LORD hath chosen thee to be a peculiar people unto himself, above all the nations that *are* upon the earth.
Deuteronomy 26:18 And the LORD hath avouched thee this day to be his peculiar people, as he hath promised thee, and that *thou* shouldest keep all his commandments;
Ephesians 1:17 that the God of our Lord Jesus Christ, the Father of glory, may give to you a spirit of **wisdom** and revelation in the knowledge of Him,	**See 1 Corinthians 12:8 "Word of Wisdom"**
Ephesians 1:20 Which he wrought in Christ, when he raised him from the dead, and set *him* at his own right hand in the heavenly *places,*	**Job 19:25** For I know *that* my redeemer liveth, and *that* he shall stand at the latter *day* upon the earth:
Psalms 8:6 Thou madest him to have dominion over the works of thy hands; thou hast put all *things* under his feet:
Psalms 16:8 I have set the LORD always before me: because *he is* at my right hand, I shall not be moved.
Psalms 68:18 Thou hast ascended on high, thou hast led captivity captive: thou hast received gifts for men; yea, *for* the rebellious also, that the LORD God might dwell *among them.*
Psalms 110:1 The LORD said unto my Lord, Sit thou at my right hand, until I make thine enemies thy footstool.
Psalms 110:5 The Lord at thy right hand shall strike through kings in the day of his wrath.
Isaiah 9:6 For unto us a child is born, unto us a son is given: and the government shall be upon his shoulder: and his name shall be called Wonderful, Counseller, The mighty God, The everlasting Father, The Prince of Peace.
Isaiah 60:16 Thou shalt also suck the milk of the Gentiles, and shalt suck the breast of kings: and thou shalt know that I the LORD *am* thy Saviour and thy Redeemer, the mighty One of Jacob.
Daniel 7:9 I beheld till the thrones were cast down, and the Ancient of days did sit, whose garment *was* white as snow, and the hair of his head like the pure wool: his throne *was like* the fiery flame, *and* his wheels *as* burning fire.
Zechraiah 3:1 And he shewed me Joshua the high priest standing before the angel of the LORD, and Satan standing at his right hand to resist him.
Ephesians 1:21 Far above all principality, and power, and might, and dominion, and every name that is named, not only in this world, but also in that which is to come:	**Proverbs 18:10** The name of the LORD is a strong tower: the righteous runneth into it, and is safe.
Ephesians 1:22 And hath put all *things* under his feet, and gave him *to be* the head over all *things* to the church,	**1 Samuel 8:4-7** Then all the elders of Israel gathered themselves together, and came to Samuel unto Ramah, 5 And said unto him, Behold, thou art old, and thy sons walk not in thy ways: now make us a king to judge us like all the nations. 6 But the thing displeased Samuel, when they said, Give us a king to judge us. And Samuel prayed unto the Lord. 7 And the Lord said unto Samuel, Hearken unto the voice of the people in all that they say unto thee: for they have not rejected thee, but **they have rejected me, that I should**

	not reign over them.
Psalms 8:6 Thou madest him to have dominion over the works of thy hands; thou hast put all *things* under his feet:
Ephesians 2:1 And you *hath he quickened,* who were dead in trespasses and sins;	**Psalms 51:5** Behold, I was shapen in iniquity; and in sin did my mother conceive me.
Ephesians 2:2 Wherein in time past ye walked according to the course of this world, according to the prince of the power of the air, the spirit that now worketh in the **children of disobedience**:	**Exodus 21:15** And he that smiteth his father, or his mother, shall be surely put to death.
Deuteronomy 21:18-21 If a man have a stubborn and rebellious son, which will not obey the voice of his father, or the voice of his mother, and that, when they have chastened him, will not hearken unto them: 19 Then shall his father and his mother lay hold on him, and bring him out unto the elders of his city, and unto the gate of his place; 20 And they shall say unto the elders of his city, This our son is stubborn and rebellious, he will not obey our voice; he is a glutton, and a drunkard. 21 And all the men of his city shall stone him with stones, that he die: so shalt thou put evil away from among you; and all Israel shall hear, and fear.
Proverbs 1:8-10 My son, hear the instruction of thy father, and forsake not the law of thy mother: 9 For they shall be an ornament of grace unto thy head, and chains about thy neck. 10 My son, if sinners entice thee, consent thou not.
Proverbs 10:1 The proverbs of Solomon. A wise son maketh a glad father: but a foolish son is the heaviness of his mother.
Proverbs 10:5 He that gathereth in summer is a wise son: but he that sleepeth in harvest is a son that causeth shame.
Proverbs 19:26 He that wasteth his father, and chaseth away his mother, is a son that causeth shame, and bringeth reproach.
Proverbs 28:7 Whoso keepeth the law is a wise son: but he that is a companion of riotous men shameth his father.
Proverbs 28:24 Whoso robbeth his father or his mother, and saith, It is no transgression; the same is the companion of a destroyer.
Proverbs 30:17 The eye that mocketh at his father, and despiseth to obey his mother, the ravens of the valley shall pick it out, and the young eagles shall eat it.
Ephesians 2:12 That at that time ye were without Christ, being aliens from the commonwealth of Israel, and strangers from the **covenants** of promise, having no hope, and without God in the world:	**Genesis 3:21** Unto Adam also and to his wife did the LORD God make coats of skins, and clothed them.
Genesis 9:8-9 And God spake unto Noah, and to his sons with him, saying, 9 And I, behold, I establish my covenant with you, and with your seed after you;
Exodus 2:24 And God heard their groaning, and God remembered his covenant with Abraham, with Isaac, and with Jacob.
Exodus 19:5 Now therefore, if ye will obey my voice indeed, and keep my covenant, then ye shall be a peculiar treasure unto me above all people: for all the earth *is* mine:
Numbers 18:19 All the heave offerings of the holy things, which the children of Israel offer unto the LORD, have I given thee, and thy sons and thy daughters with thee, by a statute for ever: it *is* a covenant of salt for ever before the LORD unto thee and to thy seed with thee.

	Numbers 25:12-13 Wherefore say, Behold, I give unto him my covenant of peace: 13 And he shall have it, and his seed after him, *even* the covenant of an everlasting priesthood; because he was zealous for his God, and made an atonement for the children of Israel.
	Deuteronomy 7:6 For thou *art* an holy people unto the LORD thy God: the LORD thy God hath chosen thee to be a special people unto himself, above all people that *are* upon the face of the earth.
	Deuteronomy 10:14-15 Behold, the heaven and the heaven of heavens *is* the LORD's thy God, the earth *also*, with all that therein *is*. 15 Only the LORD had a delight in thy fathers to love them, and he chose their seed after them, *even* you above all people, as *it is* this day.
	2 Samuel 23:5 Although my house *be* not so with God; yet he hath made with me an everlasting covenant, ordered in all *things*, and sure: for *this is* all my salvation, and all *my* desire, although he make *it* not to grow.
Ephesians 2:13 But now in Christ Jesus ye who sometimes were far off are made nigh by the blood of Christ.	**Isaiah 9:6** For unto us a child is born, unto us a son is given: and the government shall be upon his shoulder: and his name shall be called Wonderful, Counsellor, The mighty God, The everlasting Father, The Prince of Peace. **See Matthew 26:28 "Atonement"**
Ephesians 2:17 And came and preached peace to you which were afar off, and to them that were nigh.	**Isaiah 57:19** I create the fruit of the lips; Peace, peace to *him that is* far off, and to *him that is* near, saith the LORD; and I will heal him.
Ephesians 2:20 And are built upon the foundation of the apostles and prophets, Jesus Christ himself being the chief corner *stone*;	**Psalms 118:22** The stone *which* the builders refused is become the head *stone* of the corner. **Isaiah 28:16** Therefore thus saith the Lord GOD, Behold, I lay in Zion for a foundation a stone, a tried stone, a precious corner *stone*, a sure foundation: he that believeth shall not make haste. **Isaiah 33:20** Look upon Zion, the city of our solemnities: thine eyes shall see Jerusalem a quiet habitation, a tabernacle *that* shall not be taken down; not one of the stakes thereof shall ever be removed, neither shall any of the cords thereof be broken.
Ephesians 3:19 And to know the love of Christ, which passeth knowledge, that ye might be **filled with all the fulness of God**.	**Numbers 11:25** And the LORD came down in a cloud, and spake unto him, and took of the **spirit that *was* upon him**, and gave *it* unto the seventy elders: and it came to pass, *that,* when **the spirit rested upon them**, they prophesied, and did not cease. **Isaiah 32:15** Until the **spirit be poured upon us** from on high, and the wilderness be a fruitful field, and the fruitful field be counted for a forest. **Ezekiel 39:29** Neither will I hide my face any more from them: for I have **poured out my spirit** upon the house of Israel, saith the Lord GOD. **Joel 2:29** And also upon the servants and upon the handmaids in those days will **I pour out my spirit**.
Ephesians 3:20 Now unto him that is able to do exceeding abundantly above all that we **ask** or think, according to the power that worketh in us,	**2 Chronicles 16:12-13** And Asa in the thirty and ninth year of his reign was diseased in his feet, until his disease [was] exceeding *great*: yet in his disease <u>**he sought not to the LORD**</u>, <u>but to the physicians</u>. 13 And <u>Asa slept with his fathers</u>, and died in the one and fortieth year of his reign.

	Jeremiah 29:12 Then shall ye call upon me, and ye shall go and pray unto me, and I will hearken unto you.
Ephesians 4:1 I therefore, the prisoner of the Lord, beseech you that ye walk worthy of the vocation wherewith ye are called,	**Genesis 5:22** And Enoch walked with God after he begat Methuselah three hundred years, and begat sons and daughters: **Genesis 17:1** And when Abram was ninety years old and nine, the LORD appeared to Abram, and said unto him, I *am* the Almighty God; walk before me, and be thou perfect.
Ephesians 4:3 Endeavouring to keep the **unity** of the Spirit in the bond of peace.	**Psalms 133:1** Behold, how good and how pleasant *it is* for brethren to dwell together in unity! **Amos 3:3** Can two walk together, except they be agreed?
Ephesians 4:5 One Lord, one faith, one baptism,	**Deuteronomy 6:4** Hear, O Israel: The LORD our God *is* one LORD : **Nehemiah 9:6** Thou, *even* thou, *art* LORD alone; thou hast made heaven, the heaven of heavens, with all their host, the earth, and all *things* that *are* therein, the seas, and all that *is* therein, and thou preservest them all; and the host of heaven worshippeth thee. **Psalms 86:10** For thou *art* great, and doest wondrous things: thou *art* God alone. **Isaiah 43:10-11** Ye *are* my witnesses, saith the LORD, and my servant whom I have chosen: that ye may know and believe me, and understand that I *am* he: before me there was no God formed, neither shall there be after me. 11 I, *even* I, *am* the LORD ; and beside me *there is* no saviour. **Isaiah 44:6** Thus saith the LORD the King of Israel, and his redeemer the LORD of hosts; I *am* the first, and I *am* the last; and beside me *there is* no God. **Isaiah 44:8** Fear ye not, neither be afraid: have not I told thee from that time, and have declared *it*? ye *are* even my witnesses. Is there a God beside me? yea, *there is* no God; I know not *any*. **Isaiah 45:5** I *am* the LORD, and *there is* none else, *there is* no God beside me: I girded thee, though thou hast not known me: **Isaiah 45:21** Tell ye, and bring *them* near; yea, let them take counsel together: who hath declared this from ancient time? *who* hath told it from that time? *have* not I the LORD? and *there is* no God else beside me; a just God and a Saviour; *there is* none beside me. **Isaiah 54:5** For thy Maker *is* thine husband; the LORD of hosts *is* his name; and thy Redeemer the Holy One of Israel; The God of the whole earth shall he be called.
Ephesians 4:6 One God and **Father** of all, who is above all, and through all, and in you all.	**Deuteronomy 6:4** Hear, O Israel: The LORD our God *is* one LORD: Tell ye, and bring them near; yea, let them take counsel together: who hath declared this from ancient time? who hath told it from that time? **Nehemiah 9:6** Thou, *even* thou, *art* LORD alone; thou hast made heaven, the heaven of heavens, with all their host, the earth, and all *things* that *are* therein, the seas, and all that *is* therein, and thou preservest them all; and the host of heaven worshippeth thee. **Isaiah 9:6** For unto us a child is born, unto us a son is given: and the government shall be upon his shoulder: and his name shall be

	called Wonderful, Counselor, The mighty God, The everlasting Father, The Prince of Peace
	Isaiah 43:10-11 Ye *are* my witnesses, saith the LORD, and my servant whom I have chosen: that ye may know and believe me, and understand that I *am* he: before me there was no God formed, neither shall there be after me. 11 I, *even* I, *am* the LORD ; and beside me *there is* no saviour.
	Isaiah 44:6 Thus saith the LORD the King of Israel, and his redeemer the LORD of hosts; I *am* the first, and I *am* the last; and beside me *there is* no God.
	Isaiah 44:8 Fear ye not, neither be afraid: have not I told thee from that time, and have declared *it*? ye *are* even my witnesses. Is there a God beside me? yea, *there is* no God; I know not *any*.
	Isaiah 45:5-6 I am the LORD, and there is none else, **there is no God beside me**: I girded thee, though thou hast not known me: 6 That they may know from the rising of the sun, and from the west, that there is none beside me. I am the LORD, and there is none else.
	Isaiah 45:21-22 have not I the LORD? and **there is no God else beside me**; a just God and a Saviour; there is none beside me. 22 Look unto me, and be ye saved, all the ends of the earth: for **I am God, and there is none else**.
	Deuteronomy 32:39; 2 Samuel 7:22; 1 Chronicles 17:20; Psalm86:10; Isaiah 44:6, 8-10; Isaiah 45:21-23; Isaiah 46:9; Isaiah 54:5; Malachi 2:10.
	1 Chronicles 29:10 Wherefore David blessed the LORD before all the congregation: and David said, Blessed *be* thou, **LORD God of Israel our father, forever and ever**."
	Psalms 89:26 He shall cry unto me, **Thou *art* my father, my God**, and the rock of my salvation."
	Isaiah 9:6 For unto us a child is born, unto us a son is given: and the government shall be upon his shoulder: and his name shall be called Wonderful, Counselor, The mighty God, The everlasting Father, The Prince of Peace.
	Isaiah 45:21-22 have not I the LORD? and **there is no God else beside me**; a just God and a Saviour; there is none beside me. 22 Look unto me, and be ye saved, all the ends of the earth: for **I am God, and there is none else**.
	Isaiah 63:16 Doubtless thou *art* our father, though Abraham be ignorant of us, and Israel acknowledge us not: thou, **O LORD, *art* our father**, our redeemer; thy name *is* from everlasting
	Isaiah 64:8 But now, **O LORD, thou *art* our father**; we *are* the clay, and thou our potter; and we all *are* the work of thy hand."
	Malachi 2:10 Have we not all one father? hath not one God created us? why do we deal treacherously every man against his brother, by profaning the covenant of our fathers?
Ephesians 4:8 Wherefore he saith, When he ascended up on high, he led captivity captive, and gave gifts unto men.	**Psalms 68:18** Thou hast ascended on high, thou hast led captivity captive: thou hast received gifts for men; yea, *for* the rebellious also, that the LORD God might dwell *among them*.
	Psalms 68:18-20 Thou hast ascended on high, thou hast **led**

	captivity captive: thou hast received gifts for men; yea, *for* the rebellious also, that the LORD God might dwell *among them*. ¹⁹ Blessed *be* the Lord, *who* daily loadeth us *with benefits, even* the God of our salvation. Selah. ²⁰ *He that is* our God *is* the God of salvation; and unto GOD the Lord *belong* the issues from death.
Ephesians 4:9 (Now that he ascended, what is it but that he also descended first into the lower parts of the earth?	**Psalm 63:9** But those *that* seek my soul, to destroy *it*, shall go into the lower parts of the earth.
Ephesians 4:11 And he gave some, apostles; and some, **prophets**; and some, evangelists; and some, **pastors** and **teachers**;	**2 Chronicles 15:3** Now for a long season Israel *hath been* without the true God, and without a **teaching priest**, and without law.

2 Chronicles 30:22 And Hezekiah spake comfortably unto all the **Levites that taught the good knowledge of the LORD**: and they did eat throughout the feast seven days, offering peace offerings, and making confession to the LORD God of their fathers.

Jeremiah 32:33 And they have turned unto me the back, and not the face: though **I taught them**, rising up early and **teaching** *them*, yet they have not hearkened to receive instruction.

Hosea 4:6 My people are destroyed for lack of knowledge: because thou hast rejected knowledge, I will also reject thee, that thou shalt be no priest to me: seeing thou hast forgotten the law of thy God, I will also forget thy children.

Exodus 15:20 And **Miriam the prophetess**, the sister of Aaron, took a timbrel in her hand; and all the women went out after her with timbrels and with dances.

Judges 4:4 And **Deborah, a prophetess**, the wife of Lapidoth, she judged Israel at that time.

2 Kings 22:14 So Hilkiah the priest, and Ahikam, and Achbor, and Shaphan, and Asahiah, went unto **Huldah the prophetess**,

Nehemiah 6:14 My God, think thou upon Tobiah and Sanballat according to these their works, and on the **prophetess Noadiah**, and the **rest of the prophets**, that would have put me in fear.

Isaiah 8:3 And I went unto the **prophetess**; and she conceived, and bare a son. Then said the LORD to me, Call his name Mahershalalhashbaz.

Jeremiah 3:15 And I will give you **pastors** according to mine heart, which shall feed you with knowledge and understanding.

Jeremiah 23:4 And I will set up **shepherds** over them which shall feed them: and they shall fear no more, nor be dismayed, neither shall they be lacking, saith the LORD.

Ezekiel 34:1-4 And the word of the LORD came unto me, saying, 2 Son of man, prophesy against the shepherds of Israel, prophesy, and say unto them, Thus saith the Lord GOD unto the shepherds; Woe be to the shepherds of Israel that do feed themselves! should not the shepherds feed the flocks? 3 Ye eat the fat, and ye clothe you with the wool, ye kill them that are fed: but ye feed not the flock. 4 The diseased have ye not strengthened, <u>neither have ye healed that which was sick</u>, <u>neither have ye bound up that which was broken</u>, neither have ye brought again that which was driven away, neither have ye sought that which was lost; but with force |

	and with cruelty have ye ruled them. **Ezeziel 34:10** Thus saith the Lord GOD; Behold, I am against the **shepherds**; and I will require my flock at their hand, and cause them to cease from feeding the flock; neither shall the **shepherds** feed themselves any more; for I will deliver my flock from their mouth, that they may not be meat for them.
Ephesians 4:12 For the perfecting of the saints, for the work of the ministry, for the edifying of the body of Christ:	**See Hebrews 12:14 "Holiness"** **Ezekiel 3:17-19** Son of man, I have made thee a watchman unto the house of Israel: therefore hear the word at my mouth, and give them warning from me. 18 When I say unto the wicked, Thou shalt surely die; and thou givest him not warning, nor speakest to warn the wicked from his wicked way, to save his life; the same wicked *man* shall die in his iniquity; but his blood will I require at thine hand. 19 Yet if thou warn the wicked, and he turn not from his wickedness, nor from his wicked way, he shall die in his iniquity; but thou hast delivered thy soul.
Ephesians 4:18 Having the understanding darkened, being alienated from the life of God through the ignorance that is in them, because of the blindness of their **heart**:	**Isaiah 44:18** They have not known nor understood: for he hath shut their eyes, that they cannot see; *and* their **hearts**, that they cannot understand. **Jeremiah 17:9** The **heart** *is* deceitful above all *things,* and desperately wicked: who can know it?
Ephesians 4:23 And be **renewed** in the spirit of your mind;	**Psalms 51:10** Create in me a clean heart, O God; and **renew** a right spirit within me.
Ephesians 4:25 Wherefore putting away lying, speak every man truth with his neighbour: for we are members one of another.	**Zechariah 8:16** These *are* the things that ye shall do; Speak ye every man the truth to his neighbour; execute the judgment of truth and peace in your gates:
Ephesians 4:26 Be ye angry, and sin not: let not the sun go down upon your wrath:	**Psalms 4:4** Stand in awe, and sin not: commune with your own heart upon your bed, and be still. Selah.
Ephesians 4:27 Neither give place to the **devil**.	**See Matthew 4:10 "satan"**
Ephesians 4:28 Let him that stole steal no more: but rather let him labour, working with *his* hands the thing which is good, that he may have to give to him that needeth.	**Exodus 20:15** Thou shalt not steal. **Leviticus 19:11** Ye shall not steal, neither deal falsely, neither lie one to another. **Deuteronomy 31:29** For I know that after my death ye will utterly corrupt *yourselves,* and turn aside from the way which I have commanded you; and evil will befall you in the latter days; because ye will do evil in the sight of the LORD, to provoke him to anger through the work of your hands.
Ephesians 4:29 Let no corrupt communication proceed out of your mouth, but that which is good to the use of edifying, that it may minister grace unto the hearers.	**Psalms 10:7** His mouth is full of cursing and deceit and fraud: under his tongue *is* mischief and vanity. **Psalms 12:3-4** The LORD shall cut off all flattering lips, *and* the tongue that speaketh proud things: 4 Who have said, With our tongue will we prevail; our lips *are* our own: who *is* lord over us? **Psalms 34:13** Keep thy tongue from evil, and thy lips from speaking guile. **Psalms 35:28** And my tongue shall speak of thy righteousness

	[and] of thy praise all the day long.
	Psalms 37:30 The mouth of the righteous speaketh wisdom, and his tongue talketh of judgment.
	Psalms 39:1 I said, I will take heed to my ways, that I sin not with my tongue: I will keep my mouth with a bridle, while the wicked is before me.
	Ecclesiastes 10:12-14 The words of a wise man's mouth *are* gracious; but the lips of a fool will swallow up himself. 13 The beginning of the words of his mouth *is* foolishness: and the end of his talk *is* mischievous madness.14 A fool also is full of words: a man cannot tell what shall be; and what shall be after him, who can tell him?
Ephesians 4:31 Let all bitterness, and wrath, and anger, and clamour, and evil speaking, be put away from you, with all malice:	**Psalms 37:8** Cease from anger, and forsake wrath: fret not thyself in any wise to do evil.
Ephesians 5:2 And walk in love, as Christ also hath loved us, and hath given himself for us an offering and a sacrifice to God for a sweetsmelling savour.	**Genesis 8:20-21** And Noah builded an altar unto the LORD; and took of every clean beast, and of every clean fowl, and offered burnt offerings on the altar. 21 And the LORD smelled a sweet savour; and the LORD said in his heart, I will not again curse the ground any more for man's sake; for the imagination of man's heart *is* evil from his youth; neither will I again smite any more every thing living, as I have done. **Genesis 22:2** And he said, Take now thy son, thine only *son* Isaac, whom thou lovest, and get thee into the land of Moriah; and offer him there for a burnt offering upon one of the mountains which I will tell thee of.
Ephesians 5:3-5 But fornication, and all uncleanness, or covetousness, let it not be once named among you, as becometh saints; 4 Neither filthiness, nor foolish talking, nor jesting, which are not convenient: but rather giving of thanks. 5 For this ye know, that no whoremonger, nor unclean person, nor covetous man, who is an idolater, hath any inheritance in the kingdom of Christ and of God.	**Exodus 20:13-17** Thou shalt not kill. 14 Thou shalt not commit **adultery**. 15 Thou shalt not steal. 16 Thou shalt not bear false witness against thy neighbour. 17 Thou shalt not covet thy neighbour's house, thou shalt not covet thy neighbour's wife, nor his manservant, nor his maidservant, nor his ox, nor his ass, nor any thing that *is* thy neighbour's. **Deuteronomy 17:17 Neither shall he multiply wives to himself**, that his heart turn not away: neither shall he greatly multiply to himself silver and gold. **Deuteronomy 22:22** If a man be found lying with a woman married to an husband, then **they shall both of them die**, *both* the man that lay with the woman, and the woman: so shalt thou put away evil from Israel. **See Romans 1:26-27 "Sexual sins"**
Ephesians 5:5-8 For be knowing this, that every **fornicator**, or unclean one, or covetous *one*, who is an idolater, has no inheritance in the kingdom of Christ and of God. Let no one deceive you with empty words, for through these the wrath of God comes on the sons of disobedience. Then do not be partners with them; for you then were darkness, but now light in *the* Lord - walk as children of light.	**Numbers 25:1-3** And Israel abode in Shittim, and the people began to **commit whoredom with the daughters of Moab**. 2 And **they called the people unto the sacrifices of their gods**: and the people did eat, and bowed down to their gods. 3 And **Israel joined himself unto Baalpeor**: and the anger of the LORD was kindled against Israel. **Hosea 2:13** And I will visit upon her the days of Baalim, wherein she burned incense to them, and she decked herself with her earrings and her jewels, and **she went after her lovers**, and forgot me, saith the LORD.
Ephesians 5:6 Let no man deceive you	**Jeremiah 29:4** Thus saith the LORD of hosts, the God of Israel,

with vain words: for because of these things cometh the wrath of God upon the children of disobedience.	unto all that are carried away captives, whom I have caused to be carried away from Jerusalem unto Babylon;
Ephesians 5:11-12 And have no fellowship with the unfruitful works of **darkness**, but rather reprove *them*. 12 For it is a shame even to speak of those things which are done of them in secret.	**Proverbs 22:24-25** Make no friendship with an angry man; and with a furious man thou shalt not go: 25 Lest thou learn his ways, and get a snare to thy soul. **Isaiah 5:20** Woe unto them that call evil good, and good evil; that put darkness for light, and light for **darkness**; that put bitter for sweet, and sweet for bitter!
Ephesians 5:14 Wherefore he saith, Awake thou that sleepest, and arise from the dead, and Christ shall give thee light.	**Isaiah 60:1** Arise, shine; for thy light is come, and the glory of the LORD is risen upon thee.
Ephesians 5:18 And be not drunk with wine, wherein is excess; but be filled with the Spirit;	**Leviticus 10:9** **Do not drink wine nor strong drink**, thou, nor thy sons with thee, when ye go into the tabernacle of the congregation, lest ye die: *it shall be* a statute for ever throughout your generations: **Numbers 6:2-3** Speak unto the children of Israel, and say unto them, When either man or woman shall separate *themselves* to vow a vow of a **Nazarite**, to separate *themselves* unto the LORD: 3 **He shall separate *himself* from wine** and strong drink, and shall drink no vinegar of wine, or vinegar of strong drink, neither shall he drink any liquor of grapes, nor eat moist grapes, or dried. **Deuteronomy 14:26** And thou shalt bestow that **money** for whatsoever thy soul lusteth after, for oxen, or for sheep, or **for wine**, or for strong drink, or for whatsoever thy soul desireth: and thou shalt eat there before the LORD thy God, and thou shalt rejoice, thou, and thine household, **Psalms 104:15** And wine *that* maketh glad the heart of man, *and* oil to make *his* face to shine, and bread *which* strengtheneth man's heart. **Proverbs 4:17** For they eat the bread of wickedness, and drink the wine of violence. **Proverbs 20:1** Wine *is* a mocker, strong drink *is* raging: and whosoever is deceived thereby is not wise. **Proverbs 21:17** He that loveth pleasure *shall be* a poor man: he that loveth wine and oil shall not be rich. **Proverbs 23:31** Look not thou upon the wine when it is red, when it giveth his colour in the cup, *when* it moveth itself aright. **Proverbs 31:4** *It is* not for kings, O Lemuel, *it is* not for kings to drink wine; nor for princes strong drink: **Proverbs 31:6** Give strong drink unto him that is ready to perish, and wine unto those that be of heavy hearts. **Isaiah 5:11** Woe unto them that rise up early in the morning, *that* they may follow strong drink; that continue until night, *till* wine inflame them! **Hosea 4:11** Whoredom and wine and new wine take away the heart. **Habakkuk 2:15** Woe unto him that giveth his neighbour drink, that puttest thy bottle to *him,* and makest *him* drunken also, that thou mayest look on their nakedness!

	Genesis 41:38 And Pharaoh said unto his servants, Can we find such a one as this is, **a man in whom the Spirit of God is**?
	Numbers 11:17 And I will come down and talk with thee there: and I will take of **the spirit which is upon thee**, and will put it upon them; and they shall bear the burden of the people with thee, that thou bear it not thyself alone.
	Numbers 11:25 And the LORD came down in a cloud, and spake unto him, **and took of the spirit that was upon him, and gave it unto the seventy elders**: and it came to pass, that, when the spirit rested upon them, they prophesied, and did not cease.
	Numbers 27:18 And the LORD said unto Moses, Take thee Joshua the son of Nun, a man in whom is the spirit, and lay thine hand upon him;
	Isaiah 11:2 And the spirit of the LORD shall rest upon him, the spirit of wisdom and understanding, the spirit of counsel and might, the spirit of knowledge and of the fear of the LORD;
	Micah 3:8 But truly I am full of power by the spirit of the LORD, and of judgment, and of might, to declare unto Jacob his transgression, and to Israel his sin.
Ephesians 5:19 Speaking to yourselves in psalms and hymns and spiritual songs, singing and making melody in your heart to the Lord;	**See Colossians 3:16 "Music"**
Ephesians 5:22 Wives, submit yourselves unto your own husbands, as unto the Lord.	**Genesis 3:16** Unto the woman he said, I will greatly multiply thy sorrow and thy conception; in sorrow thou shalt bring forth children; and thy desire *shall be* to thy husband, and he shall rule over thee.
Ephesians 5:23-24 For the husband is the head of the wife, even as Christ is the head of the church: and he is the saviour of the body. 24 Therefore as **the church is subject unto Christ**, so let the wives be to their own husbands in every thing.	**1 Samuel 8:4-7** Then all the elders of Israel gathered themselves together, and came to Samuel unto Ramah, 5 And said unto him, Behold, thou art old, and thy sons walk not in thy ways: now make us a king to judge us like all the nations. 6 But the thing displeased Samuel, when they said, Give us a king to judge us. And Samuel prayed unto the Lord. 7 And the Lord said unto Samuel, Hearken unto the voice of the people in all that they say unto thee: for they have not rejected thee, but **they have rejected me, that I should not reign over them**. **Job 19:25** For I know *that* my redeemer liveth, and *that* he shall stand at the latter *day* upon the earth: **Isaiah 9:6** For unto us a child is born, unto us a son is given: and the government shall be upon his shoulder: and his name shall be called Wonderful, Counsellor, The mighty God, The everlasting Father, The Prince of Peace. **Isaiah 60:16** Thou shalt also suck the milk of the Gentiles, and shalt suck the breast of kings: and thou shalt know that I the LORD *am* thy Saviour and thy Redeemer, the mighty One of Jacob.
Ephsians 5:25 Husbands, **love your wives**, even as Christ also loved the church, and gave himself for it;	**Genesis 26:8** And it came to pass, when he had been there a long time, that Abimelech king of the Philistines looked out at a window, and saw, and, behold, **Isaac *was* sporting with Rebekah his wife**. **Proverbs 20:6** Most men will proclaim every one his own

	goodness: but **a faithful man who can find?**
Ephesians 5:26 That he might **sanctify and cleanse it with the washing of water by the word,**	See Matthew 5:18 "Word" See Hebrews 12:14 "Holiness"
Ephesians 5:27 That he might present it to himself a glorious church, not having spot, or wrinkle, or any such thing; but that it should be holy and without blemish.	See Hebrews 12:14 "Holiness"
Ephesians 5:31 For this cause shall a man leave his father and mother, and shall be joined unto his wife, and they two shall be one flesh.	**Genesis 2:24** Therefore shall a man leave his father and his mother, and shall cleave unto his wife: and they shall be one flesh.
Ephesians 6:1 Children, obey your parents in the Lord: for this is right.	**Exodus 20:12** Honour thy father and thy mother: that thy days may be long upon the land which the LORD thy God giveth thee. **Deuteronomy 5:16** Honour thy father and thy mother, as the LORD thy God hath commanded thee; that thy days may be prolonged, and that it may go well with thee, in the land which the LORD thy God giveth thee. **Proverbs 23:22** Hearken unto thy father that begat thee, and despise not thy mother when she is old. See Ephesians 2:2 "Children of disobedience"
Ephesians 6:2-3 Honour thy father and mother; (which is the first commandment with promise;) That it may be well with thee, and thou mayest live long on the earth.	**Exodus 20:12** Honour thy father and thy mother: that thy days may be long upon the land which the LORD thy God giveth thee. **Deuteronomy 5:16** Honour thy father and thy mother, as the LORD thy God hath commanded thee; that thy days may be prolonged, and that it may go well with thee, in the land which the LORD thy God giveth thee.
Ephesians 6:4 And, ye fathers, provoke not your children to wrath: but bring them up in the nurture and admonition of the Lord.	**Deuteronomy 6:7** And thou shalt teach them diligently unto thy children, and shalt talk of them when thou sittest in thine house, and when thou walkest by the way, and when thou liest down, and when thou risest up. **Deuteronomy 6:20-23** *And* when thy son asketh thee in time to come, saying, What *mean* the testimonies, and the statutes, and the judgments, which the LORD our God hath commanded you? 21 Then thou shalt say unto thy son, We were Pharaoh's bondmen in Egypt; and the LORD brought us out of Egypt with a mighty hand: 22 And the LORD shewed signs and wonders, great and sore, upon Egypt, upon Pharaoh, and upon all his household, before our eyes: 23 And he brought us out from thence, that he might bring us in, to give us the land which he sware unto our fathers. **Deuteronomy 11:18-19** Therefore shall ye lay up these my words in your heart and in your soul, and bind them for a sign upon your hand, that they may be as frontlets between your eyes. :19 And ye shall teach them your children, speaking of them when thou sittest in thine house, and when thou walkest by the way, when thou liest down, and when thou risest up. **Psalms 78:4** We will not hide *them* from their children, shewing to the generation to come the praises of the LORD, and his strength, and his wonderful works that he hath done.

	Proverb 13:24 He that spareth his rod hateth his son: but he that loveth him chasteneth him betimes.
	Proverb 19:8 He that getteth wisdom loveth his own soul: he that keepeth understanding shall find good.
	Proverb 19:18 Chasten thy son while there is hope, and let not thy soul spare for his crying.
	Proverb 22:6 Train up a child in the way he should go: and when he is old, he will not depart from it.
	Proverb 23:13 Withhold not correction from the child: for *if* thou beatest him with the rod, he shall not die.
	Proverb 29:17 Correct thy son, and he shall give thee rest; yea, he shall give delight unto thy soul.
Ephesians 6:9 And, ye masters, do the same things unto them, forbearing threatening: knowing that your Master also is in heaven; neither is there respect of persons with him.	**Leviticus 25:43** Thou shalt not rule over him with rigour; but shalt fear thy God. **Deuteronomy 10:17** For the LORD your God *is* God of gods, and Lord of lords, a great God, a mighty, and a terrible, which regardeth not persons, nor taketh reward: **2 Chronicles 19:7** Wherefore now let the fear of the LORD be upon you; take heed and do *it*: for *there is* no iniquity with the LORD our God, nor respect of persons, nor taking of gifts.
Ephesians 6:12 For we wrestle not against flesh and blood, but against principalities, against powers, against the rulers of the darkness of this world, against spiritual wickedness in high *places*.	**1 Samuel 17:47** And all this assembly shall know that the LORD saveth not with sword and spear: for the battle is the LORD's, and he will give you into our hands. **2 Chronicles 20:17** Ye shall not *need* to fight in this *battle*: set yourselves, stand ye *still*, and see the salvation of the LORD with you, O Judah and Jerusalem: fear not, nor be dismayed; tomorrow go out against them: for the LORD *will be* with you. **Joshua 23:10** One man of you shall chase a thousand: for the LORD your God, he *it is* that fighteth for you, as he hath promised you.
Ephesians 6:13 Wherefore take unto you the whole armour of God, that ye may be able to withstand in the evil day, and having done all, to stand.	**Isaiah 54:17** No weapon that is formed against thee shall prosper; and every tongue *that* shall rise against thee in judgment thou shalt condemn. This *is* the heritage of the servants of the LORD, and their righteousness *is* of me, saith the LORD.
Ephesians 6:14 Stand therefore, having your loins girt about with truth, and having on the breastplate of righteousness;	**Isaiah 11:5** And righteousness shall be the girdle of his loins, and faithfulness the girdle of his reins. **Isaiah 59:17** For he put on righteousness as a breastplate, and an helmet of salvation upon his head; and he put on the garments of vengeance *for* clothing, and was clad with zeal as a cloke.
Ephesians 6:15 And your feet shod with the preparation of the gospel of peace;	**Isaiah 52:7** How beautiful upon the mountains are the feet of him that bringeth good tidings, that publisheth peace; that bringeth good tidings of good, that publisheth salvation; that saith unto Zion, Thy God reigneth!
Ephesians 6:17 And take the helmet of salvation, and the sword of the Spirit, which is the word of God:	**Isaiah 11:4** But with righteousness shall he judge the poor, and reprove with equity for the meek of the earth: and he shall smite the earth with the rod of his mouth, and with the breath of his lips shall he slay the wicked. **Isaiah 49:2** And he hath made my mouth like a sharp sword; in the shadow of his hand hath he hid me, and made me a polished shaft; in his quiver hath he hid me;

	Isaiah 59:17 For he put on righteousness as a breastplate, and an helmet of salvation upon his head; and he put on the garments of vengeance *for* clothing, and was clad with zeal as a cloke. **Hosea 6:5** Therefore have I hewed *them* by the prophets; I have slain them by the words of my mouth: and thy judgments *are as* the light *that* goeth forth.
Ephesians 6:18 Praying always with all prayer and supplication in the Spirit, and watching thereunto with all perseverance and supplication for all saints;	**Job 5:20** In famine he shall redeem thee from death: and in war from the power of the sword. **Job 5:22** At destruction and famine thou shalt laugh: neither shalt thou be afraid of the beasts of the earth.
Philippians 1:15 Some indeed preach Christ even of envy and **strife**; and some also of good will:	**Psalms 31:20** Thou shalt hide them in the secret of thy presence from the pride of man: thou shalt keep them secretly in a pavilion from the **strife** of tongues.
Philippians 1:17 But the other of love, knowing that I am set for the defence of the gospel.	**Psalms 119:63** I *am* a companion of all *them* that fear thee, and of them that keep thy precepts.
Philippians 1:19 For I know that this shall turn to my salvation through your prayer, and the supply of the Spirit of Jesus Christ,	**Job 13:16** He also *shall be* my salvation: for an hypocrite shall not come before him.
Philippians 1:25 And having this confidence, I know that I shall abide and continue with you all **for your furtherance and joy of faith**;	**Psalms 31:23** O love the LORD, all ye his saints: *for* **the LORD preserveth the faithful**, and plentifully rewardeth the proud doer. **Hosea 2:20 I will even betroth thee unto me in faithfulness**: and thou shalt know the LORD.
Philippians 1:27 Only let your conversation be as it becometh the gospel of Christ: that whether I come and see you, or else be absent, I may hear of your affairs, that ye stand fast in one spirit, with **one mind** striving together for the faith of the gospel;	**Genesis 17:1** And when Abram was ninety years old and nine, the LORD appeared to Abram, and said unto him, I *am* the Almighty God; walk before me, and be thou perfect. **Genesis 5:22** And Enoch walked with God after he begat Methuselah three hundred years, and begat sons and daughters: **Psalms 133:1** Behold, how good and how pleasant *it is* for brethren to dwell together in unity! **Amos 3:3** Can two walk together, except they be agreed?
Philippians 2:3 *Let* nothing *be done* through **strife** or vainglory; but in lowliness of mind let each esteem other better than themselves.	**Psalms 31:20** Thou shalt hide them in the secret of thy presence from the pride of man: thou shalt keep them secretly in a pavilion from the **strife** of tongues.
Philippians 2:7 But made himself of no reputation, and took upon him the form of a servant, and was made in the likeness of men:	**Psalms 8:5** For thou hast made him a little lower than the angels, and hast crowned him with glory and honour.
Philippians 2:8 And being found in fashion as a man, he humbled himself, and became obedient unto death, even the death of the cross.	**2 Chronicles 7:14** If my people, which are called by my name, shall humble themselves, and pray, and seek my face, and turn from their wicked ways; then will I hear from heaven, and will forgive their sin, and will heal their land. **Psalms 25:9** The meek will he guide in judgment: and the meek will he teach his way. **Psalms 37:11** But the meek shall inherit the earth; and shall delight themselves in the abundance of peace. **Proverbs 3:34** Surely he scorneth the scorners: but he giveth grace unto the lowly.

	See 1 Timothy 2:5 "God"
Philippians 2:9 Wherefore God also hath highly exalted him, and given him a name which is above every name:	**Isaiah 52:13** Behold, my servant shall deal prudently, he shall be exalted and extolled, and be very high.
Philippians 2:10-11 that at the name of Jesus every knee should bow, of things in heaven, and things in earth, and things under the earth; and that every tongue should confess that Jesus Christ is Lord, to the glory of God the Father.	**Psalms 22:29** All *they that be* fat upon earth shall eat and worship: all they that go down to the dust shall bow before him: and none can keep alive his own soul. **Isaiah 45:23** I have sworn by myself, the word is gone out of my mouth in righteousness, and shall not return, That unto me every knee shall bow, every tongue shall swear. See 1 Timothy 2:5 "God"
Phippians 2:12 Wherefore, my beloved, as ye have always obeyed, not as in my presence only, but now much more in my absence, work out your own salvation with fear and trembling.	See Hebrews 12:14 "Holiness"
Philippians 2:14 Do all things without **murmurings** and disputings:	**Numbers 14:27-30** How long *shall I bear with* this evil congregation, which **murmur** against me? I have heard the **murmurings** of the children of Israel, which they **murmur** against me. 28 Say unto them, *As truly as* I live, saith the LORD, as ye have spoken in mine ears, so will I do to you: 29 Your carcases shall fall in this wilderness; and all that were numbered of you, according to your whole number, from twenty years old and upward, which have **murmured** against me, 30 Doubtless ye shall not come into the land, *concerning* which I sware to make you dwell therein, save Caleb the son of Jephunneh, and Joshua the son of Nun. **Psalms 106:25** But murmured in their tents, *and* hearkened not unto the voice of the LORD.
Philippians 2:15 That ye may be blameless and harmless, the sons of God, without rebuke, in the midst of a crooked and perverse nation, among whom ye shine as lights in the world;	**Proverb 4:18** But the path of the just *is* as the shining light, that shineth more and more unto the perfect day.
Philippians 3:2 Beware of dogs, beware of evil workers, beware of the concision.	**Isaiah 56:10** His watchmen *are* blind: they are all ignorant, they *are* all dumb dogs, they cannot bark; sleeping, lying down, loving to slumber.
Philippians 3:3 For we are the circumcision, which worship God in the spirit, and rejoice in Christ Jesus, and have no confidence in the flesh.	**Deuteronomy 10:16** Circumcise therefore the foreskin of your heart, and be no more stiffnecked. **Deuteronomy 30:6** And the LORD thy God will circumcise thine heart, and the heart of thy seed, to love the LORD thy God with all thine heart, and with all thy soul, that thou mayest live. **Jeremiah 4:4** Circumcise yourselves to the LORD, and take away the foreskins of your heart, ye men of Judah and inhabitants of Jerusalem: lest my fury come forth like fire, and burn that none can quench *it*, because of the evil of your doings.
Philippians 3:8 Yea doubtless, and I count all things *but* loss for the excellency of the knowledge of Christ Jesus my Lord: for whom I have suffered the loss of all things, and do count them *but* dung, that I may win Christ,	**Isaiah 53:11** He shall see of the travail of his soul, *and* shall be satisfied: by his knowledge shall my righteous servant justify many; for he shall bear their iniquities. **Jeremiah 9:23** Thus saith the LORD, Let not the wise *man* glory in his wisdom, neither let the mighty *man* glory in his might, let

	not the rich *man* glory in his riches:
Philippians 3:9 And be found in him, not having mine own righteousness, which is of the law, but that which is through the faith of Christ, the righteousness which is of God by faith:	**Jeremiah 23:6** In his days Judah shall be saved, and Israel shall dwell safely: and this *is* his name whereby he shall be called, THE LORD OUR RIGHTEOUSNESS.
Philippians 3:15 Let us therefore, as many as be perfect, be thus minded: and if in any thing ye be otherwise minded, God shall reveal even this unto you.	**See Hebrews 12:14 "Holiness"**
Philippians 3:20 For our conversation is in heaven; from whence also we look for the Saviour, the Lord Jesus Christ:	**Job 19:25** For I know *that* my redeemer liveth, and *that* he shall stand at the latter *day* upon the earth: **Isaiah 9:6** For unto us a child is born, unto us a son is given: and the government shall be upon his shoulder: and his name shall be called Wonderful, Counseller, The mighty God, The everlasting Father, The Prince of Peace. **Isaiah 60:16** Thou shalt also suck the milk of the Gentiles, and shalt suck the breast of kings: and thou shalt know that I the LORD *am* thy Saviour and thy Redeemer, the mighty One of Jacob.
Philippians 3:21 Who shall change our vile body, that it may be fashioned like unto his glorious body, according to the working whereby he is able even to subdue all things unto himself.	**Isaiah 26:19** Thy dead *men* shall live, *together with* my dead body shall they arise. Awake and sing, ye that dwell in dust: for thy dew *is as* the dew of herbs, and the earth shall cast out the dead. **Job 14:14** If a man die, shall he live *again*? all the days of my appointed time will I wait, till my change come. **See 1 Thessalonians 5:23 "Body, soul, and spirit"**
Philippians 4:3 And I intreat thee also, true yokefellow, help those **women which laboured** with me in the gospel, with Clement also, and *with* other my fellowlabourers, whose names are in the **book of life**.	**Exodus 32:32-33** Yet now, if thou wilt forgive their sin--; and if not, blot me, I pray thee, out of thy **book** which thou hast written. 33 And the LORD said unto Moses, Whosoever hath sinned against me, him will I blot out of my **book**. **Psalms 69:28** Let them be blotted out of the **book of the living**, and not be written with the righteous. **Daniel 7:10** A fiery stream issued and came forth from before him: thousand thousands ministered unto him, and ten thousand times ten thousand stood before him: the judgment was set, and the **books** were opened. **Daniel 12:1** And at that time shall Michael stand up, the great prince which standeth for the children of thy people: and there shall be a time of trouble, such as never was since there was a nation even to that same time: and at that time thy people shall be delivered, every one that shall be found written in the **book**. **See Revelations 3:5 "Book of life"** **Judges 4:4** And Deborah, a **prophetess**, the wife of Lapidoth, she judged Israel at that time. **Isaiah 8:3** And I went unto the **prophetess**; and she conceived, and bare a son. Then said the LORD to me, Call his name Mahershalalhashbaz.
Philippians 4:6 Be careful for nothing; but in every thing by prayer and supplication with thanksgiving let your requests be made known unto God.	**Psalms 55:22** Cast thy burden upon the LORD, and he shall sustain thee: he shall never suffer the righteous to be moved. **See Matthew 17:21 "Prayer"**

Philippians 4:7 And the **peace** of God, which passeth all understanding, **shall keep** your hearts and minds through Christ Jesus.	**Psalms 97:10** Ye that love the LORD, hate evil: **he preserveth** the souls of his saints; he delivereth them out of the hand of the wicked. **Psalms 119:165** Great **peace** have they which love thy law: and nothing shall offend them. **Isaiah 26:3** Thou wilt keep *him* in perfect **peace**, *whose* mind *is* stayed *on thee*: because he trusteth in thee.
Philippians 4:8 Finally, brethren, whatsoever things are true, whatsoever things *are* honest, whatsoever things *are* just, whatsoever things *are* pure, whatsoever things *are* lovely, whatsoever things *are* of good report; if *there be* any virtue, and if *there be* any praise, **think on these things**.	**Psalms 101:3 I will set no wicked thing before mine eyes**: I hate the work of them that turn aside; *it* shall not cleave to me. **Psalms 19:14** Let the words of my mouth, and the meditation of my heart, be acceptable in thy sight, O LORD, my strength, and my redeemer. **Psalms 119:11** Thy word have I hid in mine heart, that I might not sin against thee. **Psalms 119:36-37** Incline my heart unto thy testimonies, and not to covetousness. 37 **Turn away mine eyes from beholding vanity**; *and* quicken thou me in thy way. **Proverbs 23:7** For **as he thinketh in his heart, so *is* he**: Eat and drink, saith he to thee; but his heart *is* not with thee. **Job 31:1 I made a covenant with mine eyes**; why then should I think upon a maid? **Isaiah 33:15-16** He that walketh righteously, and speaketh uprightly; he that despiseth the gain of oppressions, that shaketh his hands from holding of bribes, that stoppeth his ears from hearing of blood, and **shutteth his eyes from seeing evil**; 16 He shall dwell on high: his place of defense *shall be* the munitions of rocks: bread shall be given him; his waters *shall be* sure.
Philippians 4:11 Not that I speak in respect of want: for I have learned, in whatsoever state I am, *therewith* to be content.	**Exodus 16:2-3** And the whole congregation of the children of Israel **murmured** against Moses and Aaron in the wilderness: 3 And the children of Israel said unto them, Would to God we had died by the hand of the LORD in the land of Egypt, when we sat by the flesh pots, *and* when we did eat bread to the full; for ye have brought us forth into this wilderness, to kill this whole assembly with hunger. **Numbers 12:2-3** And they said, Hath the LORD indeed spoken only by Moses? hath he not spoken also by us? And the LORD heard *it*. 3 (Now the man Moses *was* very meek, above all the men which *were* upon the face of the earth.)
Philippians 4:15-19 Now ye Philippians know also, that in the beginning of the gospel, when I departed from Macedonia, no church communicated with me as concerning giving and receiving, but ye only. 16 For even in Thessalonica ye sent once and again unto my necessity. 17 Not because I desire a gift: but I desire fruit that may abound to your account. 18 But I have all, and abound: I am full, having received of Epaphroditus the things *which were sent* from you, an odour of a sweet smell, a sacrifice acceptable, wellpleasing to God. 19 But my God	**See Luke 6:38 "Prosperity"** **See Matthew 6:24 "Wealth"**

shall supply all your need according to his riches in glory by Christ Jesus.	
Colossians 1:9 For this cause we also, since the day we heard it, do not cease to pray for you, and to desire **that ye might be filled with the knowledge of his will in all wisdom and spiritual understanding**;	**Hosea 4:6** My people are destroyed for lack of knowledge: ...
Colossians 1:10 That ye might walk worthy of the Lord unto all pleasing, being fruitful in every good work, and increasing in the knowledge of God;	**Genesis 17:1** And when Abram was ninety years old and nine, the LORD appeared to Abram, and said unto him, I *am* the Almighty God; walk before me, and be thou perfect. **Genesis 5:22-24** And Enoch walked with God after he begat Methuselah three hundred years, and begat sons and daughters: 23 And all the days of Enoch were three hundred sixty and five years: 24 And Enoch walked with God: and he *was* not; for God took him.
Colossians 1:14 In whom **we have redemption through his blood, even the forgiveness of sins**:	**Leviticus 17:11** For the life of the flesh is in the blood: and I have given it to you upon the altar to make an atonement for your souls: **for it is the blood that maketh an atonement for the soul**. **See Matthew 26:28 "Atonement"**
Colossians 1:15 Who is the image of the invisible God, the **firstborn** of every creature:	**Psalms 89:26-27** He shall cry unto me, Thou art my father, my God, and the rock of my salvation. 27 Also I will make him my **firstborn**, higher than the kings of the earth. **Jeremiah 31:9** They shall come with weeping, and with supplications will I lead them: I will cause them to walk by the rivers of waters in a straight way, wherein they shall not stumble: for I am a father to Israel, and **Ephraim is my firstborn**. **See 1 Timothy 2:5 "God"**
Colossians 1:16-17 For by him were all things created, that are in heaven, and that are in earth, visible and invisible, whether *they be* thrones, or dominions, or principalities, or powers: **all things** were created by him, and for him: 17 And he is before all things, and by him all things consist.	**Isaiah 40:28** Hast thou not known? hast thou not heard, *that* the everlasting God, the LORD, the **Creator** of the ends of the earth, fainteth not, neither is weary? *there is* no searching of his understanding. **Isaiah 44:24** Thus saith the LORD, thy redeemer, and he that formed thee from the womb, I *am* the LORD that maketh all *things*; that stretcheth forth the heavens alone; that spreadeth abroad the earth by myself; **See John 1:3 "Creation"**
Colossians 1:18 And he is the head of the body, the church: who is the beginning, the firstborn from the dead; that in all things he might have the preeminence.	**1 Samuel 8:4-7** Then all the elders of Israel gathered themselves together, and came to Samuel unto Ramah, 5 And said unto him, Behold, thou art old, and thy sons walk not in thy ways: now make us a king to judge us like all the nations. 6 But the thing displeased Samuel, when they said, Give us a king to judge us. And Samuel prayed unto the Lord. 7 And the Lord said unto Samuel, Hearken unto the voice of the people in all that they say unto thee: for they have not rejected thee, but **they have rejected me, that I should not reign over them**. **1 Chronicles 29:11** Thine, O LORD, ... and thou art exalted as head above all. **See Colossians 1:16**
Colossians 1:20 And, having made	**Exodus 15:23** And when they came to Marah, they could not

peace through the blood of his cross, by him to reconcile all things unto himself; by him, *I say,* whether *they be* things in earth, or things in heaven.	drink of the waters of Marah, for they *were* bitter: therefore the name of it was called Marah. **Exodus 15:25** And he cried unto the LORD; and the LORD shewed him a tree, *which* when he had cast into the waters, the waters were made sweet: there he made for them a statute and an ordinance, and there he proved them, **Leviticus 17:11** For the life of the flesh is in the blood: and I have given it to you upon the altar to make an atonement for your souls: **for it is the blood that maketh an atonement for the soul**. See Matthew 26:28 "Atonement"
Colossians 1:28 Whom we preach, warning every man, and **teaching** every man in all wisdom; that we may present every man perfect in Christ Jesus:	**See Ephesians 4:11 "Teach-Teaching"**
Colossians 2:2 That their hearts might be comforted, being **knit together** in love, and unto all riches of the full assurance of understanding, to the acknowledgement of the mystery of God, and of the Father, and of Christ;	**Isaiah 53:11** He shall see of the travail of his soul, *and* shall be satisfied: by his knowledge shall my righteous servant justify many; for he shall bear their iniquities. **Jeremiah 9:23** Thus saith the LORD, Let not the wise *man* glory in his wisdom, neither let the mighty *man* glory in his might, let not the rich *man* glory in his riches: **Genesis 2:24** Therefore shall a man leave his father and his mother, and shall cleave unto his wife: and **they shall be one flesh**. **1 Samuel 18:1** And it came to pass, when he had made an end of speaking unto Saul, that the soul of Jonathan was knit with the soul of David, and Jonathan loved him as his own soul. **1 Chronicles 12:17** And David went out to meet them, and answered and said unto them, If ye be come peaceably unto me to help me, **mine heart shall be knit unto you**: but if ye be come to betray me to mine enemies, seeing there is no wrong in mine hands, the God of our fathers look thereon, and rebuke it. **Hosea 4:17 Ephraim is joined to idols**: let him alone. **Malachi 2:15** And did not he make one? Yet had he the residue of the spirit. And wherefore one? That he might seek a godly seed. Therefore take heed to your spirit, and let none deal treacherously against the wife of his youth.
Colossians 2:3 In whom are hid all the treasures of wisdom and knowledge.	**Isaiah 11:2** And the spirit of the LORD shall rest upon him, the spirit of wisdom and understanding, the spirit of counsel and might, the spirit of knowledge and of the fear of the LORD;
Colossians 2:9 For in him dwelleth all the fulness of the Godhead bodily.	**Isaiah 9:6** For unto us a child is born, unto us a son is given: and the government shall be upon his shoulder: and his name shall be called Wonderful, Counseller, The mighty God, The everlasting Father, The Prince of Peace. **Isaiah 40:3-5** The voice of him that crieth in the wilderness, Prepare ye the way of the Lord, make straight in the desert a highway for our God. 4 Every valley shall be exalted, and every mountain and hill shall be made low: and the crooked shall be made straight, and the rough places plain: 5 And the glory of the LORD shall be revealed, and all flesh shall see *it* together: for the mouth of the LORD hath spoken *it*.

	See 1 Timothy 2:5 "God"
Colossians 2:11 In whom also ye are circumcised with the circumcision made without hands, in putting off the body of the sins of the flesh by the circumcision of Christ:	**Deuteronomy 10:16** Circumcise therefore the foreskin of your heart, and be no more stiffnecked. **Jeremiah 4:4** Circumcise yourselves to the LORD, and take away the foreskins of your heart, ye men of Judah and inhabitants of Jerusalem: lest my fury come forth like fire, and burn that none can quench *it*, because of the evil of your doings.
Colossians 2:12 Buried with him in baptism, wherein also ye are risen with *him* through the faith of the operation of God, who hath raised him from the dead.	**See Acts 2:38** "Salvation"
Colossians 2:15 *And* having spoiled principalities and powers, he made a shew of them openly, triumphing over them in it.	**Genesis 3:15** And I will put enmity between thee and the woman, and between thy seed and her seed; it shall bruise thy head, and thou shalt bruise his heel.
Colossians 2:16 Let no man therefore judge you in meat, or in drink, or in respect of an holyday, or of the new moon, or of the **sabbath** *days*:	**Leviticus 11:2** Speak unto the children of Israel, saying, These *are* the beasts which ye shall eat among all the beasts that *are* on the earth. **Leviticus 23:2** Speak unto the children of Israel, and say unto them, *Concerning* the feasts of the LORD, which ye shall proclaim *to be* holy convocations, *even* these *are* my feasts. **Genesis 2:2** And on the seventh day God ended his work which he had made; and he rested on the seventh day from all his work which he had made. **Exodus 16:22-23** And it came to pass, *that* on the sixth day they gathered twice as much bread, two omers for one *man*: and all the rulers of the congregation came and told Moses. ²³ And he said unto them, This *is that* which the LORD hath said, To morrow *is* the rest of the holy sabbath unto the LORD: bake *that* which ye will bake *to day*, and seethe that ye will seethe; and that which remaineth over lay up for you to be kept until the morning. **Exodus 16:30** So **the people rested on the seventh day**. **Exodus 20:8 Remember the Sabbath day, to keep it holy**. **Exodus 20:11** For *in* six days the LORD made heaven and earth, the sea, and all that in them *is*, and rested the seventh day: wherefore the LORD blessed the **sabbath** day, and hallowed it. **Exodus 31:14-15** Ye shall keep the **Sabbath** therefore; for it is <u>holy</u> unto you: every one that defileth it shall surely be put to death: for whosoever doeth any work therein, that soul shall be cut off from among his people. Six days may work be done; but in the seventh is the **Sabbath** of rest, <u>holy</u> to the LORD: whosoever doeth any work in the **Sabbath day**, he shall surely be put to death. **Exodus 31:17** It *is* a sign between me and the children of Israel for ever: for *in* six days the LORD made heaven and earth, and on the seventh day he rested, and was refreshed. **Exodus 35:2** Six days shall work be done, but on the seventh day there shall be to you an <u>holy day</u>, a **Sabbath** of rest to the LORD: whosoever doeth work therein shall be put to death. **Leviticus 23:3** Six days shall work be done: but the seventh day *is*

the **Sabbath** of rest, an holy convocation; ye shall do no work therein: it is the **Sabbath** of the LORD in all your dwellings.

Leviticus 23:8 But ye shall offer an offering made by fire unto the LORD seven days: in the seventh day *is* a holy convocation: ye shall do no servile work *therein*.

Leviticus 26:2 Ye shall keep **my Sabbaths**, and **reverence my sanctuary**: I *am* the LORD.

Deuteronomy 5:12 Keep the **Sabbath** day to sanctify it, as the LORD thy God hath commanded thee.

Deuteronomy 31:29 For I know that after my death ye will utterly corrupt *yourselves*, and turn aside from the way which I have commanded you; and evil will befall you in the latter days; because ye will do evil in the sight of the LORD, to provoke him to anger through the work of your hands.

Nehemiah 10:31 And *if* the people of the land bring ware or any victuals on the **Sabbath day** to sell, *that* we would not buy it of them on the **Sabbath**, or on the holy day: and *that* we would leave the seventh year, and the exaction

of every debt.

Psalm 92:1 A Psalm *or* Song for the **Sabbath day**. *It is a* good *thing* to give thanks unto the LORD, and **to sing praises unto thy name**, O most High:

Isaiah 56:2 Blessed *is* the man *that* doeth this, and the son of man *that* layeth hold on it; **that keepeth the Sabbath** from polluting it, and keepeth his hand from doing any evil.

Isaiah 58:13 If thou turn away thy foot from the **Sabbath**, *from* doing thy pleasure on my holy day; and call the **Sabbath** a delight, the holy of the LORD, honorable; and shalt honor him, not doing thine own ways, nor

finding thine own pleasure, nor speaking *thine own* words:

Isaiah 66:22-23 For as **the new heavens and the new earth**, which I will make, shall remain before me, saith the LORD, so shall your seed and your name remain. And it shall come to pass, *that* from one new moon to another, and from one **Sabbath** to another, shall **all** flesh come to worship before me, saith the LORD.

Jeremiah 17:21 Thus saith the LORD; Take heed to yourselves, and bear no burden on the **Sabbath day**, nor bring *it* in by

the gates of Jerusalem;

Jeremiah 17:22 Neither carry forth a burden out of your houses on the **Sabbath day**, neither do ye any work, but hallow ye the **Sabbath day**, as I commanded your fathers.

Jeremiah 17:24 And it shall come to pass, if ye diligently hearken unto me, saith the LORD, to bring in no burden through

the gates of this city on the **Sabbath day**, but hallow the **Sabbath day**, to do no work therein;

Ezekiel 22:26 Her priests have violated my law, and have profaned mine holy things: they have put no difference between the holy and profane (common), neither have they shewed difference between the unclean and the clean, and have hid their eyes from **my Sabbaths**, and I am profaned among them.

Colossians 2:18 Let no man beguile you of your reward in a voluntary humility and worshipping of angels, intruding into those things which he hath not seen, vainly puffed up by his fleshly mind,	**Jeremiah 29:8** For thus saith the LORD of hosts, the God of Israel; Let not your prophets and your diviners, that *be* in the midst of you, deceive you, neither hearken to your dreams which ye cause to be dreamed.
Colossians 2:21 Touch not; taste not; handle not;	**Leviticus 3:17** *It shall be* a perpetual statute for your generations throughout all your dwellings, that ye eat neither fat nor blood. **Deuteronomy 21:20** And they shall say unto the elders of his city, This our son *is* stubborn and rebellious, he will not obey our voice; *he is* **a glutton**, and a drunkard. **Psalms 78:29-31** So they did eat, and were well filled: for he gave them their own desire; 30 They were not estranged from their lust. But while their meat *was* yet in their mouths, 31 The wrath of God came upon them, and **slew the fattest of them**, and smote down the chosen *men* of Israel.
Colossians 2:22 Which all are to perish with the using;) after the commandments and doctrines of men?	**Isaiah 29:13** Wherefore the Lord said, Forasmuch as this people draw near *me* with their mouth, and with their lips do honour me, but have removed their heart far from me, and their fear toward me is taught by the precept of men:
Colossians 3:1 If ye then be risen with Christ, seek those things which are above, where Christ sitteth on the right hand of God.	**Job 19:25** For I know *that* my redeemer liveth, and *that* he shall stand at the latter *day* upon the earth: **Psalms 8:6** Thou madest him to have dominion over the works of thy hands; thou hast put all *things* under his feet: **Psalms 16:8** I have set the LORD always before me: because *he is* at my right hand, I shall not be moved. **Psalms 68:18** Thou hast ascended on high, thou hast led captivity captive: thou hast received gifts for men; yea, *for* the rebellious also, that the LORD God might dwell *among them*. **Psalms 110:1** The LORD said unto my Lord, Sit thou at my right hand, until I make thine enemies thy footstool. **Psalms 110:5** The Lord at thy right hand shall strike through kings in the day of his wrath. **Isaiah 9:6** For unto us a child is born, unto us a son is given: and the government shall be upon his shoulder: and his name shall be called Wonderful, Counsellor, The mighty God, The everlasting Father, The Prince of Peace. **Isaiah 60:16** Thou shalt also suck the milk of the Gentiles, and shalt suck the breast of kings: and thou shalt know that I the LORD *am* thy Saviour and thy Redeemer, the mighty One of Jacob. **Daniel 7:9** I beheld till the thrones were cast down, and the Ancient of days did sit, whose garment *was* white as snow, and the hair of his head like the pure wool: his throne *was like* the fiery flame, *and* his wheels *as* burning fire. **Zechraiah 3:1** And he shewed me Joshua the high priest standing before the angel of the LORD, and Satan standing at his right hand to resist him.
Colossians 3:3 For ye are dead, and your life is hid with Christ in God.	**Proverbs 18:10** The name of the LORD *is* a strong tower: the righteous runneth into it, and is safe.
Colossians 3:5 Mortify therefore your members which are upon the earth; **fornication, uncleanness, inordinate**	**Exodus 20:13-17** Thou shalt not kill. 14 Thou shalt not commit **adultery**. 15 Thou shalt not steal. 16 Thou shalt not bear false witness against thy neighbour. 17 Thou shalt not covet thy

affection, evil concupiscence, and covetousness, which is idolatry:	neighbour's house, thou shalt not covet thy neighbour's wife, nor his manservant, nor his maidservant, nor his ox, nor his ass, nor any thing that *is* thy neighbour's. **Deuteronomy 17:17 Neither shall he multiply wives to himself**, that his heart turn not away: neither shall he greatly multiply to himself silver and gold. **Deuteronomy 22:22** If a man be found lying with a woman married to an husband, then **they shall both of them die**, *both* the man that lay with the woman, and the woman: so shalt thou put away evil from Israel. **See Romans 1:26-27 "Sexual sins"**
Colossians 3:10 And have put on the new *man,* which is renewed in knowledge after the image of him that created him:	**Genesis 1:26** And God said, Let us make man in our image, after our likeness: and let them have dominion over the fish of the sea, and over the fowl of the air, and over the cattle, and over all the earth, and over every creeping thing that creepeth upon the earth. **Genesis 9:6** Whoso sheddeth man's blood, by man shall his blood be shed: for in the image of God made he man. **Psalms 51:10** Create in me a clean heart, O God; and **renew** a right spirit within me. **Psalm 119:67** Before I was **afflicted** I went astray: but now have I kept thy word.
Colossians 3:11 Where there is neither Greek nor Jew, circumcision nor uncircumcision, Barbarian, Scythian, bond *nor* free: but Christ *is* all, and in all.	**Genesis 17:10-14** This *is* my covenant, which ye shall keep, between me and you and thy seed after thee; **Every man child among you shall be circumcised. 11 And ye shall circumcise the flesh of your foreskin; and it shall be a token of the covenant betwixt me and you.** 12 And he that is eight days old shall be circumcised among you, every man child in your generations, he that is born in the house, or bought with money of any stranger, which *is* not of thy seed. 13 He that is born in thy house, and he that is bought with thy money, must needs be circumcised: and my covenant shall be in your flesh for an everlasting covenant. 14 And **the uncircumcised man child whose flesh of his foreskin is not circumcised, that soul shall be cut off from his people; he hath broken my covenant**.
Colossians 3:12 Put on therefore, as the **elect** of God, holy and beloved, bowels of mercies, kindness, humbleness of mind, meekness, longsuffering;	**Isaiah 42:1** Behold my servant, whom I uphold; mine **elect**, *in whom* my soul delighteth; I have put my spirit upon him: he shall bring forth judgment to the Gentiles.
Colossians 3:13 Forbearing one another, and forgiving one another, if any man have a quarrel against any: even as **Christ forgave you**, so also *do* ye.	**Exodus 34:6-7** And the LORD passed by before him, and proclaimed, The LORD, The LORD God, merciful and gracious, longsuffering, and abundant in goodness and truth, ⁷ Keeping mercy for thousands, **forgiving iniquity and transgression and sin**, and that will by no means clear *the guilty*; visiting the iniquity of the fathers upon the children, and upon the children's children, unto the third and to the fourth *generation*.
Colossians 3:16 Let the word of Christ dwell in you richly in all wisdom; **teaching** and admonishing one another in psalms and hymns and spiritual songs, singing with grace in your hearts to the Lord.	**See Ephesians 4:11 "Teach-Teaching"** **2 Kings 3:15** But now bring me a minstrel. And it came to pass, when the minstrel played, that the hand of the LORD came upon him. **1 Chronicles 15:16** And David spake to the chief of the Levites to appoint their brethren *to be* the singers with instruments of musick, psalteries and harps and cymbals, sounding, by lifting up the voice

	with joy.
	1 Chronicles 23:5 Moreover four thousand *were* porters; and four thousand praised the LORD with the instruments which I made, *said David,* to praise *therewith.*
	1 Chronicles 25:7 So the number of them, with their brethren that were instructed in the songs of the LORD, *even* all that were cunning, was two hundred fourscore and eight.
	2 Chronicles 5:13-14 It came even to pass, as the trumpeters and singers *were* as one, to make one sound to be heard in praising and thanking the LORD; and when they lifted up *their* voice with the trumpets and cymbals and instruments of musick, and praised the LORD, *saying,* For *he is* good; for his mercy *endureth* for ever: that *then* the house was filled with a cloud, *even* the house of the LORD; 14 So that the priests could not stand to minister by reason of the cloud: for the glory of the LORD had filled the house of God.
	2 Chronicles 20:21-22 And when he had consulted with the people, he appointed singers unto the LORD, and that should praise the beauty of holiness, as they went out before the army, and to say, Praise the LORD; for his mercy *endureth* for ever. 22 And when they began to sing and to praise, the LORD set ambushments against the children of Ammon, Moab, and mount Seir, which were come against Judah; and they were smitten.
Colossians 3:17 And whatsoever ye do in word or deed, do all in the name of the Lord Jesus, giving thanks to God and the Father by him.	**Psalm 145:1-2** David's Psalm of praise. I will extol thee, my God, O king; and I will bless thy name for ever and ever. 2 Every day will I bless thee; and I will praise thy name for ever and ever. **Micah 4:5** For all people will walk every one in the name of his god, and we will walk in the name of the LORD our God for ever and ever. **See Acts 2:38 "Water baptism"**
Colossians 3:18 Wives, submit yourselves unto your own husbands, as it is fit in the Lord.	**Genesis 3:16** Unto the woman he said, I will greatly multiply thy sorrow and thy conception; in sorrow thou shalt bring forth children; and thy desire *shall be* to thy husband, and he shall rule over thee.
Colossians 3:20 Children, obey your parents in all things: for this is well pleasing unto the Lord.	**Exodus 20:12** Honour thy father and thy mother: that thy days may be long upon the land which the LORD thy God giveth thee. **Deuteronomy 5:16** Honour thy father and thy mother, as the LORD thy God hath commanded thee; that thy days may be prolonged, and that it may go well with thee, in the land which the LORD thy God giveth thee. **Proverbs 23:22** Hearken unto thy father that begat thee, and despise not thy mother when she is old. **See Ephesians 2:2 "Children of disobedience"**
Colossians 4:2 Continue in **prayer**, and watch in the same with thanksgiving;	**See Matthew 17:21 "Prayer"**
1 Thessalonians 1:1 Paul, and Silvanus, and **Timotheus**, unto the church of the Thessalonians *which is* in God the Father and *in* the Lord Jesus Christ: Grace *be* unto you, and peace, from God our Father, and the Lord Jesus Christ.	**1 Thessalonians 2:6** Nor of men sought we glory, neither of you, nor *yet* of others, when we might have been burdensome, **as the apostles of Christ.** **1 Thessalonians 3:2** And sent **Timothy,** our brother, and **minister** of God, and our fellow laborer in the gospel of Christ, to establish you, and to comfort you concerning your faith:

	1 Timothy 4:6 If thou put the brethren in remembrance of these things, thou shalt be a good **minister** of Jesus Christ, nourished up in the words of faith and of good doctrine, whereunto thou hast attained.
1 Thessalonians 1:10 And to wait for his Son from heaven, whom he raised from the dead, *even* Jesus, which delivered us from the wrath to come.	**Numbers 16:48** And he stood between the dead and the living; and the plague was stayed. **Jonah 3:10** And God saw their works, that they turned from their evil way; and God repented of the evil, that he had said that he would do unto them; and he did *it* not.
1 Thessalonians 2:12 That ye would walk worthy of God, who hath called you unto his kingdom and glory.	**Genesis 17:1** And when Abram was ninety years old and nine, the LORD appeared to Abram, and said unto him, I *am* the Almighty God; walk before me, and be thou perfect. **Genesis 5:22** And Enoch walked with God after he begat Methuselah three hundred years, and begat sons and daughters:
1 Thessalonians 2:13 For this cause also thank we God without ceasing, because, when ye received the **Word of God** which ye heard from us, ye received *it* not *as* the word of men, but as it is in truth, the **word of God**, which effectually worketh also in you that believe.	**See Matthew 5:18 "Word"**
1 Thessalonians 2:18 Wherefore we would have come unto you, even I Paul, once and again; but **Satan** hindered us.	**Genesis 3:4** And the **serpent** said unto the woman, Ye shall not surely die: **Zechariah 3:1-2** And he shewed me Joshua the high priest standing before the angel of the LORD, and **Satan** standing at his right hand to resist him. 2 And the LORD said unto **Satan,** The LORD rebuke thee, O **Satan**; even the LORD that hath chosen Jerusalem rebuke thee: *is* not this a brand plucked out of the fire? **See Matthew 4:10 "satan"**
1 Thessalonians 3:13 To the end he may stablish your hearts unblameable in holiness before God, even our Father, at the coming of our Lord Jesus Christ with all his saints.	**Deuteronomy 33:2** And he said, The LORD came from Sinai, and rose up from Seir unto them; he shined forth from mount Paran, and he came with ten thousands of saints: from his right hand *went* a fiery law for them. **Zechariah 14:5** And ye shall flee *to* the valley of the mountains; for the valley of the mountains shall reach unto Azal: yea, ye shall flee, like as ye fled from before the earthquake in the days of Uzziah king of Judah: and the LORD my God shall come, *and* all the saints with thee.
1 Thessalonians 4:3 For this is the will of God, *even* your sanctification, that **ye should abstain from fornication**:	**Exodus 20:13-17** Thou shalt not kill. 14 Thou shalt not commit **adultery**. 15 Thou shalt not steal. 16 Thou shalt not bear false witness against thy neighbour. 17 Thou shalt not covet thy neighbour's house, thou shalt not covet thy neighbour's wife, nor his manservant, nor his maidservant, nor his ox, nor his ass, nor any thing that *is* thy neighbour's. **Deuteronomy 17:17 Neither shall he multiply wives to himself**, that his heart turn not away: neither shall he greatly multiply to himself silver and gold. **Deuteronomy 22:22** If a man be found lying with a woman married to an husband, then **they shall both of them die**, *both* the man that lay with the woman, and the woman: so shalt thou put away evil from Israel.

	See Romans 1:26-27 "Sexual sins"
	Exodus 20:15 Thou shalt not steal.
	Leviticus 19:13 Thou shalt not **defraud** thy neighbour, neither rob *him*: the wages of him that is hired shall not abide with thee all night until the morning.
	Deuteronomy 31:29 For I know that after my death ye will utterly corrupt *yourselves*, and turn aside from the way which I have commanded you; and evil will befall you in the latter days; because ye will do evil in the sight of the LORD, to provoke him to anger through the work of your hands.
	Amos 8:5 Saying, When will the new moon be gone, that we may sell corn? and the Sabbath, that we may set forth wheat, **making the ephah small, and the shekel great, and falsifying the balances by deceit?**
1 Thessalonians 4:6 That no *man* go beyond and **defraud** his brother in *any* matter: because that the Lord *is* the avenger of all such, as we also have forewarned you and testified.	**Amos 8:9-12** And it shall come to pass in that day, saith the Lord GOD, that I will cause the sun to go down at noon, and I will darken the earth in the clear day: 10 And I will turn your feasts into mourning, and all your songs into lamentation; and I will bring up sackcloth upon all loins, and baldness upon every head; and I will make it as the mourning of an only *son*, and the end thereof as a bitter day. 11 Behold, the days come, saith the Lord GOD, that I will send a famine in the land, not a famine of bread, nor a thirst for water, but of hearing the words of the LORD: 12 And they shall wander from sea to sea, and from the north even to the east, they shall run to and fro to seek the word of the LORD, and shall not find *it*.
	Micah 6:9-12 The LORD'S voice crieth unto the city, and *the man of* wisdom shall see thy name: hear ye the rod, and who hath appointed it. 10 Are there yet the treasures of wickedness in the house of the wicked, and the scant measure *that is* abominable? 11 **Shall I count *them* pure with the wicked balances, and with the bag of deceitful weights?** 12 For the rich men thereof are full of violence, and the inhabitants thereof have spoken lies, and their tongue *is* deceitful in their mouth.
	Micah 6:13-16 Therefore also will I make *thee* sick in smiting thee, in making *thee* desolate because of thy sins. 14 Thou shalt eat, but not be satisfied; and thy casting down *shall be* in the midst of thee; and thou shalt take hold, but shalt not deliver; and *that* which thou deliverest will I give up to the sword. 15 Thou shalt sow, but thou shalt not reap; thou shalt tread the olives, but thou shalt not anoint thee with oil; and sweet wine, but shalt not drink wine. 16 For the statutes of Omri are kept, and all the works of the house of Ahab, and ye walk in their counsels; that I should make thee a desolation, and the inhabitants thereof an hissing: therefore ye shall bear the reproach of my people.
1 Thessalonians 4:9 But as touching brotherly love ye need not that I write unto you: for ye yourselves are taught of God to love one another.	**Leviticus 19:18** Thou shalt not avenge, nor bear any grudge against the children of thy people, but thou shalt love thy neighbour as thyself: I *am* the LORD.
1 Thessalonians 4:13 But I would not have you to be ignorant, brethren, concerning them which are asleep, that ye sorrow not, even as others which have	**Leviticus 19:28** Ye shall not make any cuttings in your flesh for the dead, nor print any marks upon you: I *am* the LORD. **Deuteronomy 14:1** Ye *are* the children of the LORD your God: ye shall not cut yourselves, nor make any baldness between your

no hope.	eyes for the dead. **2 Samuel 12:23** But now he is dead, wherefore should I fast? can I bring him back again? I shall go to him, but he shall not return to me.
1 Thessalonians 4:15 For this we say unto you by the word of the Lord, that we which are alive *and* remain unto the coming of the Lord shall not prevent them which are asleep.	**Job 14:14** If a man die, shall he live *again*? all the days of my appointed time will I wait, till my change come. **Isaiah 26:19** Thy dead *men* shall live, *together with* my dead body shall they arise. Awake and sing, ye that dwell in dust: for thy dew *is as* the dew of herbs, and the earth shall cast out the dead. **Daniel 12:1-2** And at that time shall Michael stand up, the great prince which standeth for the children of thy people: and there shall be a time of trouble, such as never was since there was a nation *even* to that same time: and at that time thy people shall be delivered, every one that shall be found written in the book. 2 And many of them that sleep in the dust of the earth shall awake, some to everlasting life, and some to shame *and* everlasting contempt.
1 Thessalonians 4:16 For the Lord himself shall descend from heaven with a shout, with the voice of the archangel, and with the trump of God: and the dead in Christ shall rise first:	**Genesis 5:24** And Enoch walked with God: and he *was* not; for God took him. **Exodus 19:19-20** And when the voice of the **trumpet** sounded long, and waxed louder and louder, Moses spake, and God answered him by a voice. 20 And the LORD came down upon mount Sinai, on the top of the mount: and the LORD called Moses *up* to the top of the mount; and **Moses went up**. **Leviticus 23:24** Speak unto the children of Israel, saying, In the seventh month, in the first *day* of the month, shall ye have a sabbath, a memorial of blowing of trumpets, an holy convocation. **Numbers 10:9** And if ye go to war in your land against the enemy that oppresseth you, then ye shall blow an alarm with the trumpets; and ye shall be remembered before the LORD your God, and ye shall be saved from your enemies. **Numbers 29:1** And in the seventh month, on the first *day* of the month, ye shall have an holy convocation; ye shall do no servile work: it is a day of blowing the trumpets unto you. **2 Kings 2:11** And it came to pass, as they still went on, and talked, that, behold, there appeared a chariot of fire, and horses of fire, and parted them both asunder; and **Elijah went up** by a whirlwind into heaven. **Psalms 50:5** Gather my saints together unto me; those that have made a covenant with me by sacrifice. **Isaiah 26:19** Thy dead *men* shall live, *together with* my dead body shall they arise. Awake and sing, ye that dwell in dust: for thy dew *is as* the dew of herbs, and the earth shall cast out the dead. **Isaiah 27:13** And it shall come to pass in that day, *that* the great trumpet shall be blown, and they shall come which were ready to perish in the land of Assyria, and the outcasts in the land of Egypt, and shall worship the LORD in the holy mount at Jerusalem. **Daniel 12:1-2** And at that time shall Michael stand up, the great prince which standeth for the children of thy people: and there shall be a time of trouble, such as never was since there was a nation *even* to that same time: and at that time thy people shall be delivered, every one that shall be found written in the book. 2 And many of them that sleep in the dust of the earth shall awake, some

	to everlasting life, and some to shame *and* everlasting contempt. **See 1 Timothy 2:5 "God"**
1 Thessalonians 4:17 Then we which are alive *and* remain shall be caught up together with them in the clouds, to meet the Lord in the air: and so shall we ever be with the Lord.	**Daniel 7:13** I saw in the night visions, and, behold, *one* like the Son of man came with the clouds of heaven, and came to the Ancient of days, and they brought him near before him.
1 Thessalonians 5:2 For yourselves know perfectly that the **day of the Lord** so cometh as a thief in the night.	**Leviticus 23:27** Also on the tenth *day* of this seventh month *there shall be* a day of atonement: it shall be an holy convocation unto you; and ye shall afflict your souls, and offer an offering made by fire unto the LORD. **Isaiah 13:6** Howl ye; for the **day of the LORD** is at hand; it shall come as a destruction from the Almighty. **Isaiah 34:8** For *it is* the **day of the LORD**'S vengeance, *and* the year of recompences for the controversy of Zion. **Joel 2:31-32** The sun shall be turned into darkness, and the moon into blood, before the great and the terrible day of the LORD come. 32 And it shall come to pass, *that* whosoever shall call on the name of the LORD shall be delivered: for in mount Zion and in Jerusalem shall be deliverance, as the LORD hath said, and in the remnant whom the LORD shall call. **Zechariah 12:10** And I will pour upon the house of David, and upon the inhabitants of Jerusalem, the spirit of grace and of supplications: and they shall look upon me whom they have pierced, and they shall mourn for him, as one mourneth for *his* only *son*, and shall be in bitterness for him, as one that is in bitterness for *his* firstborn. **See Acts 2:20 Day of the LORD**
1 Thessalonians 5:3 For when they shall say, Peace and safety; then sudden destruction cometh upon them, as travail upon a woman with child; and they shall not escape.	**Ezekiel 13:10** Because, even because they have seduced my people, saying, Peace; and *there was* no peace; and one built up a wall, and, lo, others daubed it with untempered *morter:* **Micah 4:9-10** Now why dost thou cry out aloud? is there no king in thee? is thy counsellor perished? for pangs have taken thee as a woman in travail. 10 Be in pain, and labour to bring forth, O daughter of Zion, like a woman in travail: for now shalt thou go forth out of the city, and thou shalt dwell in the field, and thou shalt go even to Babylon; there shalt thou be delivered; there the LORD shall redeem thee from the hand of thine enemies. **Isaiah 13:8** And they shall be afraid: pangs and sorrows shall take hold of them; they shall be in pain as a woman that travaileth: they shall be amazed one at another; their faces *shall be as* flames.
1 Thessalonians 5:8 But let us, who are of the day, be sober, putting on the breastplate of faith and love; and for an helmet, the hope of salvation.	**Isaiah 59:17** For he put on righteousness as a breastplate, and an helmet of salvation upon his head; and he put on the garments of vengeance *for* clothing, and was clad with zeal as a cloke.
1 Thessalonians 5:14 Now we exhort you, brethren, warn them that are unruly, comfort the feebleminded, support the weak, be patient toward all *men*.	**Isaiah 35:4** Say to them *that are* of a fearful heart, Be strong, fear not: behold, your God will come *with* vengeance, *even* God *with* a recompence; he will come and save you.
1 Thessalonians 5:15 See that none render evil for evil unto any *man*; but	**Leviticus 19:18** Thou shalt not avenge, nor bear any grudge

ever follow that which is good, both among yourselves, and to all *men*.	against the children of thy people, but thou shalt love thy neighbour as thyself: I *am* the LORD. **Proverbs 20:22** Say not thou, I will recompense evil; *but* wait on the LORD, and he shall save thee. **Proverbs 24:29** Say not, I will do so to him as he hath done to me: I will render to the man according to his work.
1 Thessalonians 5:19 Quench not the Spirit.	**1 Samuel 15:22** And Samuel said, Hath the LORD *as great* delight in burnt offerings and sacrifices, **as in obeying the voice of the LORD**? Behold, to obey *is* better than sacrifice, *and* to hearken than the fat of rams. **See John 4:24 "Worship"**
1 Thessalonians 5:20 Despise not prophesyings.	**See 1 Corinthians 12:10 "prophecy"**
1 Thessalonians 5:22 Abstain from all appearance of evil.	**Psalms 101:3 I will set no wicked thing before mine eyes**: I hate the work of them that turn aside; *it* shall not cleave to me. **Psalms 19:14** Let the words of my mouth, and the meditation of my heart, be acceptable in thy sight, O LORD, my strength, and my redeemer. **Psalms 119:36-37** Incline my heart unto thy testimonies, and not to covetousness. 37 **Turn away mine eyes from beholding vanity**; *and* quicken thou me in thy way. **Job 31:1 I made a covenant with mine eyes**; why then should I think upon a maid? **Isaiah 33:15-16** He that walketh righteously, and speaketh uprightly; he that despiseth the gain of oppressions, that shaketh his hands from holding of bribes, that stoppeth his ears from hearing of blood, and **shutteth his eyes from seeing evil**; 16 He shall dwell on high: his place of defense *shall be* the munitions of rocks: bread shall be given him; his waters *shall be* sure. **See Hebrews 12:14 "Holiness"**
1 Thessalonians 5:23 And the very God of peace sanctify you wholly; and *I pray God* your whole **spirit** and **soul** and **body** be preserved blameless unto the coming of our Lord Jesus Christ.	**Genesis 2:7** And the LORD God formed man *of* the dust of the ground, and **breathed into his nostrils the breath of life**; and man became a living soul. **Numbers 16:22** And they fell upon their faces, and said, O God, the God of the spirits of all flesh, shall one man sin, and wilt thou be wroth with all the congregation? **Numbers 27:16** Let the LORD, the **God of the spirits of all flesh**, set a man over the congregation, **2 Samuel 4:9** And David answered Rechab and Baanah his brother, the sons of Rimmon the Beerothite, and said unto them, *As* the LORD liveth, <u>who hath redeemed my soul out of all adversity</u>, **1 Kings 17:21-22** And he stretched himself upon the child three times, and cried unto the LORD, and said, O LORD my God, I pray thee, **let this child's soul come into him again**. 22 And the LORD heard the voice of Elijah; and **the soul of the child came into him again**, and he revived. **2 Kings 4:27** And when she came to the man of God to the hill, she caught him by the feet: but Gehazi came near to thrust her away. And the man of God said, Let her alone; for her **soul** *is*

vexed within her: and the LORD hath hid *it* from me, and hath not told me.

Job 34:14 If he set his heart upon man, *if* he gather unto himself his spirit and his breath;

Psalms 35:4 Let them be confounded and put to shame that <u>seek after my soul</u>: let them be turned back and brought to confusion that devise my hurt.

Psalms 41:4 I said, LORD, be merciful unto me: heal my soul; for I have sinned against thee.

Psalms 49:7-9 None *of them* can by any means redeem his brother, nor give to God a ransom for him: 8 (For the redemption of their soul *is* precious, and it ceaseth for ever:) 9 That he should still live for ever, *and* not see corruption.

Psalms 70:2 Let them be ashamed and confounded that <u>seek after my soul</u>: let them be turned backward, and put to confusion, that <u>desire my hurt</u>.

Psalms 71:13 Let them be confounded [and] consumed that are <u>adversaries to my soul</u>; let them be covered [with] reproach and dishonour that <u>seek my hurt</u>.

Psalms 86:2-4 Preserve my soul; for I am <u>holy</u>: O thou my God, save thy servant that trusteth in thee. 3 Be merciful unto me, O Lord: for I cry unto thee daily. 4 Rejoice the soul of thy servant: for unto thee, O Lord, do **I lift up <u>my</u> soul**.

Psalms 100:3 Know ye that the LORD he *is* God: ***it is* he *that* hath made us**, and not we ourselves; *we are* his people, and the sheep of his pasture.

Psalms 109:20 *Let* this *be* the reward of mine adversaries from the LORD, and of <u>them that speak evil against my soul</u>.

Proverbs 6:26 For by means of a whorish woman *a man is brought* to a piece of bread: and the <u>adulteress will hunt for the precious life</u> (soul).

Proverbs 10:3 The LORD will not suffer the soul of the righteous to famish: but he casteth away the substance of the wicked.

Ecclesiastes 3:21 Who knoweth the spirit of man that goeth upward, and the spirit of the beast that goeth downward to the earth?

Ecclesiastes 12:7 Then shall the dust return to the earth as it was: and **the spirit shall return unto God who gave it**.

Isaiah 42:5 Thus saith God the LORD, he that created the heavens, and stretched them out; he that spread forth the earth, and that which cometh out of it; he that giveth breath unto the people upon it,

Isaiah 57:16 For I will not contend forever, neither will I be always wroth: for the spirit should fail before me, and **the souls *which* I have made**.

Isaiah 64:8 But now, O LORD, thou *art* our father; we *are* the clay, and thou our potter; and we all *are* the work of thy hand.

Jeremiah 38:16 So Zedekiah the king swore secretly unto Jeremiah, saying, *As* **the LORD liveth, that made us this soul**, I will not put thee to death, neither will I give thee into the hand of

	these men that seek thy life.

Ezekiel 4:14 Then said I, Ah Lord GOD! behold, **my soul hath not been polluted**: for from my youth up even till now have I not eaten of that which dieth of itself, or is torn in pieces; neither came there abominable flesh into

my mouth.

Ezekiel 13:17-23 Likewise, thou son of man, set thy face against the daughters of thy people, which prophesy out of their own heart; and prophesy thou against them, 18 And say, Thus saith the Lord GOD; **Woe to the *women* that sew pillows to all armholes, and make kerchiefs upon the head of every stature to <u>hunt souls</u>! Will ye <u>hunt the souls</u> of my people**, and will ye <u>save the souls alive</u> *that come* unto you? 19 And will ye pollute me among my people for handfuls of barley and for pieces of bread, **to slay the souls that should not die**, and **to save the souls alive that should not live, by your lying to my people that hear *your* lies**? 20 Wherefore thus saith the Lord GOD; Behold, I *am* against your pillows, wherewith ye there **hunt the souls to make *them* fly**, and I will tear them from your arms, and will let the souls go, *even* the **souls that ye hunt** to make *them* fly. 21 Your kerchiefs also will I tear, and **deliver my people out of your hand**, and **they shall be no more in your hand to be hunted**; and ye shall know that I *am* the LORD. 22 Because with lies ye have made the heart of the righteous sad, whom I have not made sad; and strengthened the hands of the wicked, that he should not return from his wicked way, by promising him life: 23 Therefore ye shall see no more vanity, nor divine divinations: for **I will deliver my people out of your hand**: and ye shall know that I *am* the LORD.

Ezekiel 18:3-4 *As* I live, saith the Lord GOD, ye shall not have *occasion* any more to use this proverb in Israel. 4 Behold, **all souls are mine; as the soul of the father, so also the soul of the son is mine: the soul that sinneth, it shall die**.

Ezekiel 18:20 The soul that sinneth, it shall die. The son shall not bear the iniquity of the father, neither shall the father bear the iniquity of the son: the righteousness of the righteous shall be upon him, and the wickedness of the wicked shall be upon him.

Zechariah 12:1 The burden of the word of the LORD for Israel, saith the LORD, which stretcheth forth the heavens, and

layeth the foundation of the earth, and **formeth the spirit of man within him**. |
| **2 Thessalonians 1:6** Seeing *it is* a righteous thing with God to recompense tribulation to them that trouble you; | **Zechariah 2:8** For thus saith the LORD of hosts; After the glory hath he sent me unto the nations which spoiled you: for he that toucheth you toucheth the apple of his eye. |
| **2 Thessalonians 1:8** In flaming fire taking vengeance on them that know not God, and that obey not the gospel of our Lord Jesus Christ: | **Isaiah 66:15** For, behold, the LORD will come with fire, and with his chariots like a whirlwind, to render his anger with fury, and his rebuke with flames of fire.

Jeremiah 10:25 Pour out thy fury upon the heathen that know thee not, and upon the families that call not on thy name: for they have eaten up Jacob, and devoured him, and consumed him, and have made his habitation desolate.

Psalms 79:6 Pour out thy wrath upon the heathen that have not known thee, and upon the kingdoms that have not called upon thy name. |

2 Thessalonians 1:9 Who shall be punished with everlasting destruction from the presence of the Lord, and from the glory of his power;	**Isaiah 2:19-21** And they shall go into the holes of the rocks, and into the caves of the earth, for fear of the LORD, and for the glory of his majesty, when he ariseth to shake terribly the earth. 20 In that day a man shall cast his idols of silver, and his idols of gold, which they made each one for himself to worship, to the moles and to the bats; 21 To go into the clefts of the rocks, and into the tops of the ragged rocks, for fear of the LORD, and for the glory of his majesty, when he ariseth to shake terribly the earth. **See Luke 16:23 "Hell"**
2 Thessalonians 2:1 Now we beseech you, brethren, by the coming of our Lord Jesus Christ, and by our **gathering together unto him**,	**Deuteronomy 30:3-5** That then the LORD thy God will turn thy captivity, and have compassion upon thee, and will return and **gather thee from all the nations**, whither the LORD thy God hath scattered thee. 4 If *any* of thine be driven out unto the outmost *parts* of heaven, from thence will the **LORD thy God gather thee**, and from thence will **he fetch thee**: 5 And the LORD thy God will bring thee into the land which thy fathers possessed, and thou shalt possess it; and he will do thee good, and multiply thee above thy fathers. **Jeremiah 32:37-39** Behold, I will gather them out of all countries, whither I have driven them in mine anger, and in my fury, and in great wrath; and **I will bring them again unto this place, and I will cause them to dwell safely**: 38 And they shall be my people, and I will be their God: 39 And I will give them one heart, and one way, that they may fear me for ever, for the good of them, and of their children after them: **Isaiah 11:11-12** And it shall come to pass in that day, *that* the Lord shall set his hand again the second time to recover the remnant of his people, which shall be left, from Assyria, and from Egypt, and from Pathros, and from Cush, and from Elam, and from Shinar, and from Hamath, and from the islands of the sea. 12 And he shall set up an ensign for the nations, and shall assemble the outcasts of Israel, and **gather together the dispersed of Judah from the four corners of the earth**. **Jeremiah 23:8** But, The LORD liveth, which brought up and which led the seed of the house of Israel out of the north country, and from all countries whither I had driven them; and they shall dwell in their own land. **Micah 4:6-7 In that day**, saith the LORD, will I assemble her that halteth, and **I will gather her that is driven out**, and her that I have afflicted; 7 And I will make her that halted a remnant, and her that was cast far off a strong nation: and the **LORD shall reign over them in mount Zion from henceforth, even for ever**.
2 Thessalonians 2:2 That ye be not soon shaken in mind, or be troubled, neither by spirit, nor by word, nor by letter as from us, as that the day of Christ is at hand.	**Jeremiah 29:8** For thus saith the LORD of hosts, the God of Israel; Let not your prophets and your diviners, that *be* in the midst of you, deceive you, neither hearken to your dreams which ye cause to be dreamed.
2 Thessalonians 2:3 Let no man deceive you by any means: **for that day shall not come, except there come a falling away first, and that man of sin be revealed, the son of perdition**;	**See Acts 2:20 "Day"**
2 Thessalonians 2:4 Who opposeth and exalteth himself above all that is called	**Isaiah 2:1-4** The word that Isaiah the son of Amoz saw concerning Judah and **Jerusalem**. ² And it shall come to pass in the last days,

God, or that is worshipped; so that he as God sitteth in the temple of God, shewing himself that he is God.	*that* the mountain of the **LORD'S house** shall be established in the top of the mountains, and shall be exalted above the hills; and all nations shall flow unto it. ³ And many people shall go and say, Come ye, and let us go up to the mountain of the LORD, to **the house of the God of Jacob**; and <u>he will teach us of his ways</u>, **and we will walk in his paths: for out of Zion shall go forth the law, and the word of the LORD from Jerusalem.** ⁴ And he shall judge among the nations, and shall rebuke many people: and they shall beat their swords into plowshares, and their spears into pruninghooks: nation shall not lift up sword against nation, neither shall they learn war any more. **Ezekiel 28:2** Son of man, say unto the prince of Tyrus, Thus saith the Lord GOD; Because thine heart *is* lifted up, and thou hast said, I *am* a God, I sit *in* the seat of God, in the midst of the seas; yet thou *art* a man, and not God, though thou set thine heart as the heart of God: **Daniel 9:27** And he shall confirm the covenant with many for one week: and in the midst of the week he shall cause the sacrifice and the oblation to cease, and for the overspreading of abominations he shall make *it* desolate, even until the consummation, and that determined shall be poured upon the desolate. **Daniel 11:36** And the king shall do according to his will; and he shall exalt himself, and magnify himself above every god, and shall speak marvellous things against the God of gods, and shall prosper till the indignation be accomplished: for that that is determined shall be done. **Daniel 12:11** And from the time *that* the daily *sacrifice* shall be taken away, and the abomination that maketh desolate set up, *there shall be* a thousand two hundred and ninety days. **Malachi 3:1** Behold, I will send my messenger, and he shall prepare the way before me: and the Lord, whom ye seek, shall suddenly come to **his temple**, even the messenger of the covenant, whom ye delight in: behold, he shall come, saith the LORD of hosts.
2 Thessalonians 2:7 For the mystery of iniquity doth already work: only he who now letteth *will let,* until he be taken out of the way.	**Daniel 12:1** And at that time shall Michael stand up, the great prince which standeth for the children of thy people: and there shall be a time of trouble, such as never was since there was a nation *even* to that same time: and at that time thy people shall be delivered, every one that shall be found written in the book.
2 Thessalonians 2:8 And then shall that Wicked be revealed, whom the Lord shall consume with the spirit of his mouth, and shall destroy with the brightness of his coming:	**Job 4:9** By the blast of God they perish, and by the breath of his nostrils are they consumed. **Isaiah 11:4** But with righteousness shall he judge the poor, and reprove with equity for the meek of the earth: and he shall smite the earth with the rod of his mouth, and with the breath of his lips shall he slay the wicked. **See 1 Timothy 2:5 "God"**
	Deuteronomy 13:1-5 If there arise among you a prophet, or a dreamer of dreams, and giveth thee a **sign** or a **wonder**, 2 And the sign or the wonder come to pass, whereof he spake unto thee, saying, Let us go after other gods, which thou hast not known, and let us serve them; 3 Thou shalt not hearken unto the words of that prophet, or that dreamer of dreams: for the LORD your God proveth you, to know whether ye love the LORD your God with all your heart and with all your soul. 4 Ye shall walk after the LORD

2 Thessalonians 2:9 *Even him*, whose coming is after the working of **Satan** with all power and **signs** and lying wonders,	your God, and fear him, and keep his commandments, and obey his voice, and ye shall serve him, and cleave unto him. 5 And that prophet, or that dreamer of dreams, shall be put to death; because he hath spoken to turn *you* away from the LORD your God, which brought you out of the land of Egypt, and redeemed you out of the house of bondage, to thrust thee out of the way which the LORD thy God commanded thee to walk in. So shalt thou put the evil away from the midst of thee. **Genesis 3:4** And the **serpent** said unto the woman, Ye shall not surely die: **Zechariah 3:1-2** And he shewed me Joshua the high priest standing before the angel of the LORD, and **Satan** standing at his right hand to resist him. 2 And the LORD said unto **Satan,** The LORD rebuke thee, O **Satan**; even the LORD that hath chosen Jerusalem rebuke thee: *is* not this a brand plucked out of the fire? **See Matthew 4:10 "satan"**
2 Thessalonians 3:2 And that we may be delivered from unreasonable and wicked men: **for all *men* have not faith.**	**Deuteronomy 32:20** And he said, I will hide my face from them, I will see what their end *shall be*: for they *are* a very froward generation, **children in whom *is* no faith.**
2 Thessalonians 3:3 But the Lord is faithful, who shall stablish you, and keep *you* from evil.	**Psalms 97:10** Ye that love the LORD, hate evil**: he preserveth** the souls of his saints; he delivereth them out of the hand of the wicked.
2 Thessalonians 3:4 And we have confidence in the Lord touching you, that ye both do and will do the things which we **command** you. **2 Thessalonians 3:6-7** Now we command you, brethren, in the name of our Lord Jesus Christ, that ye withdraw yourselves from every brother that walketh disorderly, and not after the tradition which he received of us. 7 For yourselves know how ye ought to follow us: for we behaved not ourselves disorderly among you; **2 Thessalonians 3:12** Now them that are such we command and exhort by our Lord Jesus Christ, that with quietness they work, and eat their own bread.	**Exodus 7:2** Thou shalt speak **all that I command thee**: and Aaron thy brother shall speak unto Pharaoh, that he send the children of Israel out of his land. **Exodus 27:20** And thou shalt **command** the children of Israel, that they bring thee pure oil olive beaten for the light, to cause the lamp to burn always. **Joshua 11:15** As the LORD **commanded** Moses his servant, so did Moses **command** Joshua, and so did Joshua; he left nothing undone of all that the LORD **commanded** Moses. 16 So Joshua took all that land, the hills, and all the south country, and all the land of Goshen, and the valley, and the plain, and the mountain of Israel, and the valley of the same; **See Hebrews 13:7**
2 Thessalonians 3:6 Now we command you, brethren, in the name of our Lord Jesus Christ, that ye withdraw yourselves from every brother that walketh disorderly, and not after the tradition which he received of us.	**Deuteronomy 23:10** If there be among you any man, that is not clean by reason of uncleanness that chanceth him by night, then shall he go abroad out of the camp, he shall not come within the camp: **Proverbs 22:24-25** Make no friendship with an angry man; and with a furious man thou shalt not go: 25 Lest thou learn his ways, and get a snare to thy soul. **Isaiah 5:20** Woe unto them that call evil good, and good evil; that put darkness for light, and light for **darkness**; that put bitter for sweet, and sweet for bitter!
2 Thessalonians 3:10 For even when	**Exodus 20:15** Thou shalt not steal.

we were with you, this we commanded you, that if any would not work, neither should he eat.	
2 Thessalonians 3:11 For we hear that there are some which walk among you disorderly, working not at all, but are **busybodies**.	**Proverbs 20:3** *It is* an honour for a man to cease from strife: but every fool will be **meddling**. **See 2 Thessalonians 3:6**
2 Thessalonians 3:14 And if any man obey not our word by this epistle, note that man, and have no company with him, that he may be ashamed.	**See 2 Thessalonians 3:6**
1 Timothy 1:1 Paul, an apostle of Jesus Christ by the commandment of God our Saviour, and Lord Jesus Christ, *which is* our hope;	**Job 19:25** For I know *that* my redeemer liveth, and *that* he shall stand at the latter *day* upon the earth: **Isaiah 9:6** For unto us a child is born, unto us a son is given: and the government shall be upon his shoulder: and his name shall be called Wonderful, Counseller, The mighty God, The everlasting Father, The Prince of Peace. **Isaiah 43:11** I, *even* I, *am* the LORD; and beside me *there is* no **saviour**. **Isaiah 60:16** Thou shalt also suck the milk of the Gentiles, and shalt suck the breast of kings: and thou shalt know that I the LORD *am* thy Saviour and thy Redeemer, the mighty One of Jacob. **Jeremiah 17:13** O LORD, the **hope** of Israel, all that forsake thee shall be ashamed, *and* they that depart from me shall be written in the earth, because they have forsaken the LORD, the fountain of living waters. **Jeremiah 50:7** All that found them have devoured them: and their adversaries said, We offend not, because they have sinned against the LORD, the habitation of justice, even the LORD, the **hope** of their fathers.
1 Timothy 1:9 Knowing this, that the law is not made for a righteous man, but for the lawless and disobedient, for the ungodly and for sinners, for unholy and profane, for murderers of fathers and murderers of mothers, for manslayers,	**Exodus 20:13** Thou shalt not kill.
1 Timothy 1:10 For whoremongers, for them that defile themselves with mankind, for menstealers, for **liars**, for perjured persons, and if there be any other thing that is contrary to sound doctrine;	**Numbers 23:19** God is not a man, that he should lie; neither the son of man, that he should repent: hath he said, and shall he not do it? or **hath he spoken, and shall he not make it good?** **Proverbs 6:16-19** These six *things* doth the LORD hate: yea, seven *are* an abomination unto him: 17 A proud look, **a lying tongue**, and hands that shed innocent blood, 18 An heart that deviseth wicked imaginations, feet that be swift in running to mischief, 19 A false witness *that* **speaketh lies**, and he that soweth discord among brethren.
1 Timothy 1:16-17 Howbeit for this cause I obtained mercy, that in me first Jesus Christ might shew forth all longsuffering, for a pattern to them which should hereafter believe on him to life everlasting. 17 Now unto the **King** eternal, immortal, invisible, the only wise God, be honour and glory for ever and ever. Amen	**Deuteronomy 33:27** The eternal God *is thy* refuge, and underneath *are* the everlasting arms: and he shall thrust out the enemy from before thee; and shall say, Destroy *them*. **Psalm 89:18** For the **LORD** is our defence; and the Holy One of Israel is our **king**. **Isaiah 44:6** Thus saith the LORD the King of Israel, and his redeemer the LORD of hosts; I *am* the first, and I *am* the last; and beside me *there is* no God.

	Jeremiah 10:10 But the **LORD** is the true God, he is the living God, and an **everlasting king**: at his wrath the earth shall tremble, and the nations shall not be able to abide his indignation. **Zechariah 9:9** Rejoice greatly, O daughter of Zion; shout, O daughter of Jerusalem: behold, thy **King** cometh unto thee: he is just, and having salvation; lowly, and riding upon an ass, and upon a colt the foal of an ass. **See 1 Timothy 2:5 "God"**
1 Timothy 1:20 Of whom is Hymenaeus and Alexander; whom I have delivered unto Satan, that they may learn not to blaspheme.	**Genesis 3:4** And the **serpent** said unto the woman, Ye shall not surely die: **Zechariah 3:1-2** And he shewed me Joshua the high priest standing before the angel of the LORD, and **Satan** standing at his right hand to resist him. 2 And the LORD said unto **Satan**, The LORD rebuke thee, O **Satan**; even the LORD that hath chosen Jerusalem rebuke thee: *is* not this a brand plucked out of the fire? **See Matthew 4:10 "satan"**
1 Timothy 2:1 I exhort therefore, that, first of all, **supplications**, **prayers**, **intercessions**, *and* **giving of thanks**, be made for all men;	**See Matthew 17:21 "Prayer"**
1 Timothy 2:2 For kings, and *for* all that are in authority; that we may lead a quiet and peaceable life in all godliness and honesty.	**Jeremiah 29:7** And seek the peace of the city whither I have caused you to be carried away captives, and pray unto the LORD for it: for in the peace thereof shall ye have peace.
1 Timothy 2:3 For this *is* good and acceptable in the sight of God our Saviour;	**See Job 19:25, Isaiah 9:6 and 60:16**
1 Timothy 2:4 Who will have all men to be saved, and to come unto the knowledge of the truth.	**Ezekiel 18:23** Have I any pleasure at all that the wicked should die? saith the Lord GOD: *and* not that he should return from his ways, and live? **Ezekiel 18:32** For I have no pleasure in the death of him that dieth, saith the Lord GOD: wherefore turn *yourselves*, and live ye. **Ezekiel 33:11** Say unto them, *As* I live, saith the Lord GOD, I have no pleasure in the death of the wicked; but that the wicked turn from his way and live: turn ye, turn ye from your evil ways; for why will ye die, O house of Israel?
1 Timothy 2:5 For there is **one God**, and one mediator between God and men, the man Christ Jesus;"	**Deuteronomy 6:4** Hear, O Israel: The LORD our God *is* one LORD : **1 Kings 8:27** But will God indeed dwell on the earth? behold, the heaven and heaven of heavens cannot contain thee; how much less this house that I have builded? **Nehemiah 9:6** Thou, *even* thou, *art* LORD alone; thou hast made heaven, the heaven of heavens, with all their host, the earth, and all *things* that *are* therein, the seas, and all that *is* therein, and thou preservest them all; and the host of heaven worshippeth thee. **Job 19:25** For I know *that* my redeemer liveth, and *that* he shall stand at the latter *day* upon the earth: **Psalms 86:10** For thou *art* great, and doest wondrous things: thou *art* God alone. **Isaiah 9:6** For unto us a child is born, unto us a son is given: and

	the government shall be upon his shoulder: and his name shall be called Wonderful, Counselor, The mighty God, The everlasting Father, The Prince of Peace.

Isaiah 43:10-11 Ye *are* my witnesses, saith the LORD, and my servant whom I have chosen: that ye may know and believe me, and understand that I *am* he: before me there was no God formed, neither shall there be after me. 11 I, *even* I, *am* the LORD ; and beside me *there is* no saviour.

Isaiah 44:6 Thus saith the LORD the King of Israel, and his redeemer the LORD of hosts; I *am* the first, and I *am* the last; and beside me *there is* no God.

Isaiah 44:8 Fear ye not, neither be afraid: have not I told thee from that time, and have declared *it*? ye *are* even my witnesses. Is there a God beside me? yea, *there is* no God; I know not *any*.

Isaiah 45:5-6 I am the LORD, and there is none else, **there is no God beside me**: I girded thee, though thou hast not known me: {6} That they may know from the rising of the sun, and from the west, that there is none beside me. I am the LORD, and there is none else.

Isaiah 45:21-22 have not I the LORD? and **there is no God else beside me**; a just God and a Saviour; there is none beside me. 22 Look unto me, and be ye saved, all the ends of the earth: for **I am God, and there is none else**.

Isaiah 54:5 For thy Maker *is* thine husband; the LORD of hosts *is* his name; and thy Redeemer the Holy One of Israel; The God of the whole earth shall he be called.

Zechriah 14:9 And the LORD shall be king over all the earth: in that day shall there be one LORD, and his name one.

Malachi 2:10 Have we not all one father? hath not one God created us? why do we deal treacherously every man against his brother, by profaning the covenant of our fathers? |
| **1 Timothy 2:8** I will therefore that men pray every where, **lifting up holy hands**, without wrath and doubting. | **1 Kings 8:22** And Solomon stood before the altar of the LORD in the presence of all the congregation of Israel, **and spread forth his hands toward heaven**:

2 Chronicles 6:13 For Solomon had made a brazen scaffold, of five cubits long, and five cubits broad, and three cubits high, and had set it in the midst of the court: and upon it he stood, and kneeled down upon his knees before all the congregation of Israel, and **spread forth his hands toward heaven**,"

Psalm 134:2 Lift up your hands *in* **the sanctuary**, and bless the LORD.

Lamentations 2:19 Arise, cry out in the night: in the beginning of the watches pour out thine heart like water before the face of the Lord: **lift up thy hands** toward him for the life of thy young children, that faint for hunger in the top of every street.

See John 4:24 "Worship" |
| **1 Timothy 2:9** In like manner also, that women adorn themselves in modest apparel, with shamefacedness and sobriety; not with broided hair, or gold, or pearls, or costly array; | **Genesis 24:53** And the servant brought forth jewels of silver, and jewels of gold, and raiment, and gave *them* to Rebekah: he gave also to her brother and to her mother precious things.

Genesis 38:14 And she put her widow's garments off from her, and covered her with a veil, and wrapped herself, and sat in an open |

place, which *is* by the way to Timnath; for she saw that Shelah was grown, and she was not given unto him to wife.

Deuteronomy 22:5 The woman shall not wear that which pertaineth unto a man, neither shall a man put on a woman's garment: for all that do so *are* abomination unto the LORD thy God.

2 Kings 9:30 And when Jehu was come to Jezreel, Jezebel heard *of it*; and she painted her face, and tired her head, and looked out at a window.

Ester 2:13 Then thus came *every* maiden unto the king; **whatsoever she desired was given her to go** with her out of the house of the women unto the king's house.

Ester 2:15 Now when the turn of Esther, the daughter of Abihail the uncle of Mordecai, who had taken her for his daughter, was come to go in unto the king, **she required nothing** but what Hegai the king's chamberlain, the keeper of the women, appointed. And Esther obtained favour in the sight of all them that looked upon her.

Psalms 149:4 For the LORD taketh pleasure in his people: he will beautify the meek with salvation.

Proverbs 6:25 Lust not after her beauty in thine heart; neither let her take thee with her eyelids.

Proverbs 7:10 And, behold, there met him a woman *with* the attire of a harlot, and subtle of heart.

Isaiah 3:16-23 Moreover the LORD saith, Because the daughters of Zion are haughty, and walk with stretched forth necks and wanton eyes, walking and mincing *as* they go, and making a tinkling with their feet: 17 Therefore the Lord will smite with a scab the crown of the head of the daughters of Zion, and the LORD will discover their secret parts. 18 In that day the Lord will take away the bravery of *their* tinkling ornaments *about their feet,* and *their* cauls, and *their* round tires like the moon, 19 The chains, and the bracelets, and the mufflers, 20 The bonnets, and the ornaments of the legs, and the headbands, and the tablets, and the earrings, 21 The rings, and nose jewels,

22 The changeable suits of apparel, and the mantles, and the wimples, and the crisping pins, 23 The glasses, and the fine linen, and the hoods, and the vails.

Isaiah 61:3 To appoint unto them that mourn in Zion, to give unto them beauty for ashes, the oil of joy for mourning, the garment of praise for the spirit of heaviness; that they might be called trees of righteousness, the planting of the LORD, that he might be glorified.

Jeremiah 4:30 And *when* thou *art* spoiled, what wilt thou do? Though thou clothest thyself with crimson, though thou deckest thee with ornaments of gold, though thou rentest thy face with painting, in vain shalt thou make thyself fair; *thy* lovers will despise thee, they will seek thy life.

Ezekiel 23:40 And furthermore, that ye have sent for men to come from far, unto whom a messenger *was* sent; and, lo, they came: for whom thou didst wash thyself, paintedst thy eyes, and deckedst thyself with ornaments,

	Genesis 2:25 And they were both naked, the man and his wife, and were not ashamed. **Genesis 3:21** Unto Adam also and to his wife did the LORD God make coats of skins, and clothed them. **Psalms 8:5** For thou hast made him a little lower than the angels, and hast crowned him with glory and honour.
1 Timothy 2:12 But I suffer not a woman to teach, nor to usurp authority over the man, but to be in silence.	**Genesis 3:16** Unto the woman he said, I will greatly multiply thy sorrow and thy conception; in sorrow thou shalt bring forth children; and thy desire *shall be* to thy husband, and he shall rule over thee. **1 Kings 21:7-8** And Jezebel his wife said unto him, Dost thou now govern the kingdom of Israel? arise, *and* eat bread, and let thine heart be merry: I will give thee the vineyard of Naboth the Jezreelite. 8 So she wrote letters in Ahab's name, and sealed *them* with his seal, and sent the letters unto the elders and to the nobles that *were* in his city, dwelling with Naboth. **2 Kings 9:22** And it came to pass, when Joram saw Jehu, that he said, Is it peace, Jehu? And he answered, What peace, so long as the whoredoms of thy mother Jezebel and her witchcrafts are so many?
1 Timothy 2:13 For Adam was first formed, then Eve.	**Genesis 2:22** And the rib, which the LORD God had taken from man, made he a woman, and brought her unto the man.
1 Timothy 2:14 And Adam was not deceived, but the woman being deceived was in the transgression.	**Genesis 3:6** And when the woman saw that the tree *was* good for food, and that it *was* pleasant to the eyes, and a tree to be desired to make *one* wise, she took of the fruit thereof, and did eat, and gave also unto her husband with her; and he did eat.
1 Timothy 2:15 Notwithstanding she shall be saved in childbearing, if they continue in faith and charity and holiness with sobriety.	**Psalms 22:10** I was cast upon thee from the womb: thou *art* my God from my mother's belly. **Psalms 51:5** Behold, I was shapen in iniquity; and in sin did my mother conceive me. **Jeremiah 1:5** Before I formed thee in the belly I knew thee; and before thou camest forth out of the womb I sanctified thee, *and* I ordained thee a prophet unto the nations.
1 Timothy 3:1 This *is* a true saying, If a man desire the office of a bishop, he desireth a good work.	**See John 10:10** "Shepherd"
1 Timothy 3:2 A bishop then must be blameless, **the husband of one wife**, vigilant, sober, of good behaviour, given to hospitality, apt to teach;	**See Ephesians 4:11** "Teach-Teachers" **Deuteronomy 17:17** Neither shall he multiply wives to himself, that his heart turn not away: neither shall he greatly multiply to himself silver and gold.
1 Timothy 3:3 Not given to **wine**, no striker, not greedy of filthy lucre; but patient, not a brawler, not covetous; **1 Timothy 3:8** Likewise *must* the **deacons** *be* grave, not doubletongued, not given to much **wine**, not greedy of filthy lucre;	**Leviticus 10:8-9** And the LORD spoke unto Aaron, saying, 9 **Do not drink wine** nor strong drink, thou, nor thy sons with thee, when ye go into the tabernacle of the congregation, lest ye die: *it shall be* a statute forever throughout your generations: **Numbers 6:2-3** Speak unto the children of Israel, and say unto them, When either man or woman shall separate *themselves* to vow a vow of a **Nazarite**, to separate *themselves* unto the LORD: 3 **He shall separate *himself* from wine** and strong drink, and shall drink no vinegar of wine, or vinegar of strong drink, neither shall he drink any liquor of grapes, nor eat moist grapes, or dried.

	See Ephesians 5:18 "Drunkeness" **Exodus 24:13** And Moses rose up, and his **minister** Joshua: and Moses went up into the mount of God.
1 Timothy 3:4 One that ruleth well his own house, having his children in subjection with all gravity;	**1 Samuel 3:13** For I have told him that I will judge his house for ever for the iniquity which he knoweth; because his sons made themselves vile, and <u>he restrained them not</u>. **Proverbs 10:13** In the lips of him that hath understanding wisdom is found: but a rod *is* for the back of him that is void of understanding. **Proverbs 13:24** He that spareth his rod hateth his son: but he that loveth him chasteneth him betimes. **Proverbs 23:24** The father of the righteous shall greatly rejoice: and he that begetteth a wise *child* shall have joy of him.
1 Timothy 3:5 (For if a man know not how to rule his own house, how shall he take care of the church of God?)	**Jeremiah 23:3-4** And I will gather the remnant of my flock out of all countries whither I have driven them, and will bring them again to their folds; and they shall be fruitful and increase. 4 And I will set up shepherds over them which shall feed them: and they shall fear no more, nor be dismayed, neither shall they be lacking, saith the LORD.
1 Timothy 3:16 And without controversy great is the mystery of godliness: God was manifest in the flesh, justified in the Spirit, seen of angels, preached unto the Gentiles, believed on in the world, received up into glory.	**Isaiah 7:14** Therefore the Lord himself shall give you a sign; Behold, a virgin shall conceive, and bear a son, and shall call his name Immanuel. **Isaiah 9:6** For unto us a child is born, unto us a son is given: and the government shall be upon his shoulder: and his name shall be called Wonderful, Counsellor, The mighty God, The everlasting Father, The Prince of Peace. **Jeremiah 23:5-6** Behold, the days come, saith the LORD, that I will raise unto David a righteous Branch, and a King shall reign and prosper, and shall execute judgment and justice in the earth. 6 In his days Judah shall be saved, and Israel shall dwell safely: and this is his name whereby he shall be called, THE LORD OUR RIGHTEOUSNESS. See 1 Timothy 2:5 "God"
1 Timothy 4:1 Now the Spirit speaketh expressly, that in the latter times some shall depart from the faith, giving heed to seducing **spirits**, and doctrines of **devils**;	See Hebrews 13:2 "Good and bad angels"
1 Timothy 4:3 Forbidding to marry, *and commanding* to abstain from meats, which God hath created to be received with thanksgiving of them which believe and know the truth.	**Genesis 1:22** And God blessed them, saying, **Be fruitful, and multiply**, and fill the waters in the seas, and let fowl multiply in the earth. **Genesis 1:28** And God blessed them, and God said unto them, **Be fruitful, and multiply, and replenish the earth**, and subdue it: and have dominion over the fish of the sea, and over the fowl of the air, and over every living thing that moveth upon the earth. **Deuteronomy 8:1** All the commandments which I command thee this day shall ye observe to do, that ye may live, and **multiply**, and go in and possess the land which the LORD sware unto your

	fathers.

Genesis 9:3 Every moving thing that liveth shall be meat for you; even as the green herb have I given you all things. |
| **1 Timothy 4:4** For every creature of God *is* good, and nothing to be refused, if it be received with thanksgiving: | **Genesis 1:31** And God saw every thing that he had made, and, behold, *it was* very good. And the evening and the morning were the sixth day. |
| **1 Timothy 4:10** For therefore we both labour and suffer reproach, because we trust in the living God, who is the Saviour of all men, specially of those that believe. | **See Job 19:25, Isaiah 9:6 and 60:16** |
| **1 Timothy 4:11** These things **command** and teach. | **Exodus 7:2** Thou shalt speak **all that I command thee**: and Aaron thy brother shall speak unto Pharaoh, that he send the children of Israel out of his land.

Exodus 27:20 And thou shalt **command** the children of Israel, that they bring thee pure oil olive beaten for the light, to cause the lamp to burn always.

Joshua 11:15 As the LORD **commanded** Moses his servant, so did Moses **command** Joshua, and so did Joshua; he left nothing undone of all that the LORD **commanded** Moses. 16 So Joshua took all that land, the hills, and all the south country, and all the land of Goshen, and the valley, and the plain, and the mountain of Israel, and the valley of the same;

See Hebrews 13:7 |
| **1 Timothy 5:1** Rebuke not an **elder**, but intreat *him* as a father; *and* the younger men as brethren; | **Leviticus 19:32** Thou shalt rise up before the hoary head, and honour the face of the old man, and fear thy God: I *am* the LORD.

See 1 Peter 5:1 "Elders" |
| **1 Timothy 5:3** Honour widows that are widows indeed. | **Isaiah 54:4-6** Fear not; for thou shalt not be ashamed: neither be thou confounded; for thou shalt not be put to shame: for thou shalt forget the shame of thy youth, and shalt not remember the reproach of thy widowhood any more. 5 For **thy Maker is thine husband**; the Lord of hosts is his name; and thy Redeemer the Holy One of Israel; The God of the whole earth shall he be called. 6 For the Lord hath called thee as a woman forsaken and grieved in spirit, and a wife of youth, when thou wast refused, saith thy God. |
| **1 Timothy 5:5** Now she that is a widow indeed, and desolate, trusteth in God, and continueth in supplications and **prayers** night and day. | **See Matthew 17:21 "Prayer"** |
| **1 Timothy 5:10** Well reported of for good works; if she have brought up children, if she have lodged strangers, if she have washed the saints' feet, if she have relieved the afflicted, if she have diligently followed every good work. | **Genesis 18:4** Let a little water, I pray you, be fetched, and wash your feet, and rest yourselves under the tree:

Genesis 19:2 And he said, Behold now, my lords, turn in, I pray you, into your servant's house, and tarry all night, and wash your feet, and ye shall rise up early, and go on your ways. And they said, Nay; but we will abide in the street all night. |
| **1 Timothy 5:13** And withal they learn *to be* idle, wandering about from house to house; and not only idle, but tattlers also and **busybodies**, speaking things which they ought not. | **Proverbs 20:3** *It is* an honour for a man to cease from strife: but every fool will be **meddling**. |

1 Timothy 5:15 For some are already turned aside after Satan.	**Genesis 3:4** And the **serpent** said unto the woman, Ye shall not surely die: **Zechariah 3:1-2** And he shewed me Joshua the high priest standing before the angel of the LORD, and **Satan** standing at his right hand to resist him. 2 And the LORD said unto **Satan,** The LORD rebuke thee, O **Satan**; even the LORD that hath chosen Jerusalem rebuke thee: *is* not this a brand plucked out of the fire? **See Matthew 4:10** "satan"
1 Timothy 5:17 Let the **elders** that rule well be counted worthy of double honour, especially they who labour in the word and doctrine.	**See 1 Peter 5:1** "Elders"
1 Timothy 5:18 For the scripture saith, Thou shalt not muzzle the ox that treadeth out the corn. And, The labourer *is* worthy of his reward.	**Leviticus 19:13** Thou shalt not defraud thy neighbour, neither rob *him*: the wages of him that is hired shall not abide with thee all night until the morning. **Deuteronomy 25:4** Thou shalt not muzzle the ox when he treadeth out [the corn].
1 Timothy 5:19 Against an **elder** receive not an accusation, but before two or three witnesses.	**Deuteronomy 19:15** One witness shall not rise up against a man for any iniquity, or for any sin, in any sin that he sinneth: at the mouth of two witnesses, or at the mouth of three witnesses, shall the matter be established. **See 1 Peter 5:1** "Elders"
1 Timothy 5:20 Them that sin rebuke before all, that others also may fear.	**Proverbs 9:9** Give *instruction* to a wise *man,* and he will be yet wiser: teach a just *man,* and he will increase in learning. **Proverbs 17:10** A reproof entereth more into a wise man than an hundred stripes into a fool.
1 Timothy 5:23 Drink no longer water, but use a little wine for thy stomach's sake and thine often infirmities.	**Psalms 104:15** And wine *that* maketh glad the heart of man, *and* oil to make *his* face to shine, and bread *which* strengtheneth man's heart.
1 Timothy 6:2-4 And they that have believing masters, let them not despise *them,* because they are brethren; but rather do *them* service, because they are faithful and beloved, partakers of the benefit. **These things teach** and exhort. 3 **If any man teach otherwise**, and consent not to wholesome words, *even* the words of our Lord Jesus Christ, and to the doctrine which is according to godliness; 4 **He is proud, knowing nothing**, but doting about questions and strifes of words, whereof cometh envy, strife, railings, evil surmisings,	**See Ephesians 4:11** "Teach – Teacher" **Deuteronomy 23:10** If there be among you any man, that is not clean by reason of uncleanness that chanceth him by night, then shall he go abroad out of the camp, he shall not come within the camp: **Proverbs 14:15** The **simple** believeth every word: but the prudent *man* looketh well to his going. **Proverbs 22:3** A prudent *man* foreseeth the evil, and hideth himself: but the **simple** pass on, and are punished. **Proverbs 22:24-25** Make no friendship with an angry man; and with a furious man thou shalt not go: 25 Lest thou learn his ways, and get a snare to thy soul. **Isaiah 5:20** Woe unto them that call evil good, and good evil; that put darkness for light, and light for **darkness**; that put bitter for sweet, and sweet for bitter!
1 Timothy 6:6 But godliness with contentment is great gain.	**Proverbs 15:16** Better *is* little with the fear of the LORD than great treasure and trouble therewith.
1 Timothy 6:7 For we brought nothing into *this* world, *and it is* certain we can carry nothing out.	**Job 1:21** And said, Naked came I out of my mother's womb, and naked shall I return thither: the LORD gave, and the LORD hath taken away; blessed be the name of the LORD.

	Psalm 49:17 For when he dieth he shall carry nothing away: his glory shall not descend after him.
1 Timothy 6:8 And having food and raiment let us be therewith content.	**Psalm 55:22** Cast thy burden upon the LORD, and he shall sustain thee: he shall never suffer the righteous to be moved.
1 Timothy 6:9 But they that will be rich fall into temptation and a snare, and *into* many foolish and hurtful lusts, which drown men in destruction and perdition.	**Proverbs 11:28** He that trusteth in his riches shall fall: but the righteous shall flourish as a branch. **Psalm 92:12** The righteous shall flourish like the palm tree: he shall grow like a cedar in Lebanon. **See Matthew 6:24 "Wealth"**
1 Timothy 6:10 For the love of money is the root of all evil: which while some coveted after, they have erred from the faith, and pierced themselves through with many sorrows.	**Deuteronomy 29:18** Lest there should be among you man, or woman, or family, or tribe, whose heart turneth away this day from the LORD our God, to go and serve the gods of these nations; **lest there should be among you a <u>root</u> that beareth gall and wormwood**; **Psalms 37:16** A little that a righteous man hath *is* better than the riches of many wicked. **Proverbs 15:16** Better *is* little with the fear of the LORD than great treasure and trouble therewith. **Proverbs 28:20** A faithful man shall abound with blessings: but he that maketh haste to be rich shall not be innocent. **See Matthew 6:24 "Wealth"**
1 Timothy 6:12 Fight the good fight of faith, lay hold on eternal life, whereunto thou art also called, and hast professed a good profession before many witnesses.	**1 Samuel 17:47** And all this assembly shall know that the LORD saveth not with sword and spear: for the battle is the LORD's, and he will give you into our hands. **2 Chronicles 20:17** Ye shall not *need* to fight in this *battle*: set yourselves, stand ye *still*, and see the salvation of the LORD with you, O Judah and Jerusalem: fear not, nor be dismayed; tomorrow go out against them: for the LORD *will be* with you.
1 Timothy 6:13 I give thee charge in the sight of God, who quickeneth all things, and *before* Christ Jesus, who before Pontius Pilate witnessed a good confession;	**Deuteronomy 32:39** See now that I, *even* I, *am* he, and *there is* no god with me: I kill, and I make alive; I wound, and I heal: neither *is there any* that can deliver out of my hand.
1 Timothy 6:14-15 That thou keep *this* commandment without spot, unrebukeable, until the appearing of our Lord Jesus Christ: 15 Which in his times he shall shew, *who is* the blessed and only Potentate, the King of kings, and **Lord of lords**;	**Isaiah 9:6** For unto us a child is born, unto us a son is given: and the government shall be upon his shoulder: and his name shall be called Wonderful, Counsellor, The mighty God, The everlasting Father, The Prince of Peace. **Isaiah 45:21** Tell ye, and bring *them* near; yea, let them take counsel together: who hath declared this from ancient time? *who* hath told it from that time? *have* not I the LORD? and *there is* no God else beside me; a just God and a **Savior**; *there is* none beside me. **Isaiah 60:16** Thou shalt also suck the milk of the Gentiles, and shalt suck the breast of kings: and thou shalt know that I the LORD *am* thy Saviour and thy Redeemer, the mighty One of Jacob. **Jeremiah 10:10** But the LORD is the true God, he is the living God, and an everlasting king: at his wrath the earth shall tremble, and the nations shall not be able to abide his indignation.
1 Timothy 6:16 Who only hath	**Deuteronomy 4:12** And the LORD spake unto you out of the

immortality, dwelling in the light which no man can approach unto; whom no man hath seen, nor can see: to whom *be* honour and power everlasting. Amen.	midst of the fire: ye heard the voice of the words, but saw no similitude; only *ye heard* a voice.
1 Timothy 6:17-19 Charge them that are rich in this world, that they be not highminded, nor trust in uncertain riches, but in the living God, who giveth us richly all things to enjoy; 18 That they do good, that they be rich in good works, ready to distribute, willing to communicate; 19 Laying up in store for themselves a good foundation against the time to come, that they may lay hold on eternal life.	**See Matthew 6:24 "Wealth"** **See Luke 6:38 "Prosperity"**
1 Timothy 6:20 O Timothy, keep that which is committed to thy trust, avoiding profane *and* vain babblings, and oppositions of **science falsely so called**:	**Psalms 119:128** Therefore I esteem all *thy* precepts *concerning* all *things to be* right; *and* **I hate every false way.** **Jeremiah 2:27 Saying** to a stock, Thou *art* my father; and **to a stone, Thou hast brought me forth**: for they have turned *their* back unto me, and not *their* face: but in the time of their trouble they will say, Arise, and save us.
2 Timothy 1:7 For God hath not given us the spirit of fear; but of power, and of love, and **of a sound mind**.	**Proverb 29:25** The fear of man bringeth a snare: but whoso putteth his trust in the LORD shall be safe. **Isaiah 51:12** I, *even* I, *am* he that comforteth you: who *art* thou, that thou shouldest be afraid of a man *that* shall die, and of the son of man *which* shall be made *as* grass; **Hosea 14:4** I will **heal their backsliding**, I will love them freely, For My anger has turned away from him.
2 Timothy 1:10 But is now made manifest by the appearing of our Saviour Jesus Christ, who hath abolished death, and hath brought life and immortality to light through the gospel:	**Job 19:25** For I know *that* my redeemer liveth, and *that* he shall stand at the latter *day* upon the earth: **Isaiah 9:6** For unto us a child is born, unto us a son is given: and the government shall be upon his shoulder: and his name shall be called Wonderful, Counseller, The mighty God, The everlasting Father, The Prince of Peace. **Isaiah 60:16** Thou shalt also suck the milk of the Gentiles, and shalt suck the breast of kings: and thou shalt know that I the LORD *am* thy Saviour and thy Redeemer, the mighty One of Jacob.
2 Timothy 2:2 And the things that thou hast heard of me among many witnesses, the same commit thou to faithful men, who shall be **able to teach others** also.	**See Ephesians 4:11 "Teach – Teacher"**
2 Timothy 2:6 The husbandman that laboreth must be **first** partaker of the **fruits**.	**See Romans 8:23 "Firstfruits"**
2 Timothy 2:8 Remember that Jesus Christ of the seed of David was raised from the dead according to my gospel:	**2 Samauel 7:12** And when thy days be fulfilled, and thou shalt sleep with thy fathers, I will set up thy seed after thee, which shall proceed out of thy bowels, and I will establish his kingdom. **Psalm 132:11** The LORD hath sworn *in* truth unto David; he will not turn from it; Of the fruit of thy body will I set upon thy throne. **Isaiah 11:1** And there shall come forth a rod out of the stem of Jesse, and a Branch shall grow out of his roots:

2 Timothy 2:13 If we believe not, *yet* he abideth faithful: he cannot deny himself.	**Numbers 23:19** God *is* not a man, that he should lie; neither the son of man, that he should repent: hath he said, and shall he not do *it*? or hath he spoken, and shall he not make it good?
2 Timothy 2:19 Nevertheless the foundation of God standeth sure, having this seal, The Lord knoweth them that are his. And, Let every one that nameth the name of Christ depart from iniquity.	**Numbers 16:5** And he spake unto Korah and unto all his company, saying, Even to morrow the LORD will shew who *are* his, and *who is* holy; and will cause *him* to come near unto him: even *him* whom he hath chosen will he cause to come near unto him. **Psalms 118:22** The stone *which* the builders refused is become the head *stone* of the corner. **Isaiah 28:16** Therefore thus saith the Lord GOD, Behold, I lay in Zion for a foundation a stone, a tried stone, a precious corner *stone*, a sure foundation: he that believeth shall not make haste. **Isaiah 33:20** Look upon Zion, the city of our solemnities: thine eyes shall see Jerusalem a quiet habitation, a tabernacle *that* shall not be taken down; not one of the stakes thereof shall ever be removed, neither shall any of the cords thereof be broken.
2 Timothy 2:22 Flee also **youthful lusts**: but follow righteousness, faith, charity, peace, with them that call on the Lord out of a pure heart.	**See Romans 1:26-27 "Sexual sins"**
2 Timothy 2:24 And the servant of the Lord must not strive; but be **gentle** unto all *men*, **apt to teach**, patient,	**Psalms 18:35** Thou hast also given me the shield of thy salvation: and thy right hand hath holden me up, and thy **gentleness** hath made me great. **See Ephesians 4:11 "Teach – Teacher"**
2 Timothy 2:25-26 In meekness instructing those *that* oppose themselves; **if God peradventure will give them repentance to the acknowledging of the truth; 26 And that they may recover themselves out of the snare of the devil, who are taken captive by him at his will**.	**Proverbs 28:13** He that covereth his sins shall not prosper: but whoso confesseth and forsaketh *them* shall have mercy. **Isaiah 30:18** And therefore will the LORD wait, that he may be gracious unto you, and therefore will he be exalted, that he may have mercy upon you: for the LORD *is* a God of judgment: blessed *are* all they that wait for him. **Isaiah 55:7** Let the wicked forsake his way, and the unrighteous man his thoughts: and let him return unto the LORD, and he will have mercy upon him; and to our God, for he will abundantly pardon. **Jeremiah 36:3** It may be that the house of Judah will hear all the evil which I purpose to do unto them; that **they may return every man from his evil way; that I may forgive their iniquity and their sin**.
2 Timothy 3:1-4 This know also, that in the last days perilous times shall come. 2 For men shall be lovers of their own selves, **covetous**, boasters, proud, blasphemers, disobedient to parents, unthankful, unholy, 3 Without natural	**Isaiah 2:2** And it shall come to pass in the **last days**, that the mountain of the LORD'S house shall be established in the top of the mountains, and shall be exalted above the hills; and all nations shall flow unto it. **Micah 4:1** But in the **last days** it shall come to pass, that the mountain of the house of the LORD shall be established in the top of the mountains, and it shall be exalted above the hills; and people shall flow unto it. **Exodus 20:16** Thou shalt not bear false witness against thy neighbour. **Leviticus 19:16** Thou shalt not go up and down *as* a talebearer among thy people: neither shalt thou stand against the blood of thy

affection, trucebreakers, false accusers, incontinent, fierce, despisers of those that are good, 4 Traitors, heady, highminded, lovers of pleasures more than lovers of God;	neighbour: I *am* the LORD. **Deutreonomy 5:20** Neither shalt thou bear false witness against thy neighbour. **Deuteronomy 31:29** For I know that after my death ye will utterly corrupt *yourselves*, and turn aside from the way which I have commanded you; and evil will befall you in the latter days; because ye will do evil in the sight of the LORD, to provoke him to anger through the work of your hands. **Psalms 15:3** *He that* backbiteth not with his tongue, nor doeth evil to his neighbour, nor taketh up a reproach against his neighbour. **See Romans 1:27 "Sexual sins"** **See Matthew 6:24 "Wealth"**
2 Timothy 3:5-8 Having a form of godliness, but denying the power thereof: <u>from such turn away</u>. 6 For of this sort are they which creep into houses, and **lead captive silly women laden with sins**, led away with divers lusts, 7 **Ever learning, and never able to come to the knowledge of the truth**. 8 Now as Jannes and Jambres withstood Moses, **so do these also resist the truth: men of corrupt minds, reprobate concerning the faith.**	**Hosea 4:6 My people are destroyed for lack of knowledge**: because thou hast rejected knowledge, I will also reject thee, that thou shalt be no priest to me: **See 2 Timothy 3:16 "Instruction"** **See Ephesians 4:11 "Teach – Teacher"** **See Romans 1:26-27 "Sexual sins"**
2 Timothy 3:11 Persecutions, afflictions, which came unto me at Antioch, at Iconium, at Lystra; what persecutions I endured: but out of *them* all the Lord delivered me.	**Psalm 34:19** Many *are* the afflictions of the righteous: but the LORD delivereth him out of them all.
2 Timothy 3:15 And that **from a child thou hast known the holy scriptures, which are able to make thee wise unto salvation through faith which is in Christ Jesus.**	**See Matthew 5:18 "Scripture"**
2 Timothy 3:16 All **scripture** *is* given by inspiration of God, and *is* profitable for doctrine, for **reproof**, for correction, for **instruction** in righteousness:	**Proverbs 9:9** Give *instruction* to a wise *man,* and he will be yet wiser: teach a just *man,* and he will increase in learning. **Proverbs 17:10** A **reproof** entereth more into a wise man than an hundred stripes into a fool. **Proverbs 4:13 Take** fast hold of **instruction**; let her not go: keep her; for **she is thy life**. **Proverbs 4:20-22** My son, attend to my words; incline thine ear unto my sayings. 21 Let them not depart from thine eyes; keep them in the midst of thine heart. 22 For they are life unto those that find them, and health to all their flesh. **Proverbs 8:33** Hear **instruction**, and be wise, and refuse it not. **Isaiah 5:13** Therefore my people are gone into captivity, **because they have no knowledge**: and their honourable men are famished, and their multitude dried up with thirst. **Isaiah 55:11** So shall my word be that goeth forth out of my mouth: it shall not return unto me void, but it shall accomplish that

	which I please, and it shall prosper *in the thing* whereto I sent it. **Hosea 4:6 My people are destroyed for lack of knowledge**: because thou hast rejected knowledge, I will also reject thee, that thou shalt be no priest to me: **See Matthew 5:18 "Scriptures"** **See Ephesians 4:11 "Teach – Teacher"**
2 Timothy 3:17 That the man of God may be perfect, throughly furnished unto all good works.	**See Hebrews 12:14 "Holiness"**
2 Timothy 4:1 I charge *thee* therefore before God, and the Lord Jesus Christ, who shall **judge** the quick and the dead at his appearing and his kingdom;	**Genesis 18:25** That be far from thee to do after this manner, to slay the righteous with the wicked: and that the righteous should be as the wicked, that be far from thee: Shall not the **Judge** of all the earth do right? **Isaiah 11:1-4** And there shall come forth a rod out of the stem of Jesse, and a Branch shall grow out of his roots: 2 And the spirit of the LORD shall rest upon him, the spirit of wisdom and understanding, the spirit of counsel and might, the spirit of knowledge and of the fear of the LORD; 3 And shall make him of quick understanding in the fear of the LORD: and he shall not **judge** after the sight of his eyes, neither reprove after the hearing of his ears: 4 But with righteousness shall he **judge** the poor, and reprove with equity for the meek of the earth: and he shall smite the earth with the rod of his mouth, and with the breath of his lips shall he slay the wicked. **Joel 3:12** Let the heathen be wakened, and come up to the valley of Jehoshaphat: for there will I sit to **judge** all the heathen round about.
2 Timothy 4:2 Preach the word; be instant in season, out of season; reprove, **rebuke**, exhort with all longsuffering and doctrine.	**See Matthew 5:18 "Word"** **Proverbs 9:9** Give *instruction* to a wise *man,* and he will be yet wiser: teach a just *man,* and he will increase in learning. **Proverbs 17:10** A **reproof** entereth more into a wise man than an hundred stripes into a fool.
2 Timothy 4:3-5 For the time will come when **they will not endure sound doctrine**; but after their own lusts shall they heap to themselves teachers, having itching ears; 4 And **they shall turn away their ears from the truth, and shall be turned unto fables**. 5 But **watch thou in all things**, endure afflictions, do the work of an evangelist, make full proof of thy ministry.	**Hosea 4:6 My people are destroyed for lack of knowledge**: because thou hast rejected knowledge, I will also reject thee, that thou shalt be no priest to me: **See 2 Timothy 3:16 "Instruction"** **See Ephesians 4:11 "Teach – Teacher"**
2 Timothy 4:7 I have fought a good fight, I have finished my course, I have kept the faith:	**1 Samuel 17:47** And all this assembly shall know that the LORD saveth not with sword and spear: for the battle is the LORD's, and he will give you into our hands. **2 Chronicles 20:17** Ye shall not *need* to fight in this *battle*: set yourselves, stand ye *still,* and see the salvation of the LORD with you, O Judah and Jerusalem: fear not, nor be dismayed; tomorrow go out against them: for the LORD *will be* with you.
2 Timothy 4:14 Alexander the coppersmith did me much evil: the Lord reward him according to his works:	**Psalms 62:12** Also unto thee, O Lord, *belongeth* mercy: for thou renderest to every man according to his work.

	Proverbs 24:12 If thou sayest, Behold, we knew it not; doth not he that pondereth the heart consider *it*? and he that keepeth thy soul, doth *not* he know *it*? and shall *not* he render to *every* man according to his works?
2 Timothy 4:19 Salute **Prisca** and Aquila, and the household of Onesiphorus.	**See Acts 18:26** "Woman's role"
Titus 1:1 Paul, a servant of God, and an apostle of Jesus Christ, according to the faith of God's **elect**, and the acknowledging of the truth which is after godliness;	**Isaiah 42:1** Behold my servant, whom I uphold; mine **elect**, *in whom* my soul delighteth; I have put my spirit upon him: he shall bring forth judgment to the Gentiles.
Titus 1:3-4 But hath in due times manifested his word through preaching, which is committed unto me according to the commandment of God our Saviour; 4 To Titus, *mine* own son after the common faith: Grace, mercy, *and* peace, from God the Father and the Lord Jesus Christ our Saviour.	**Job 19:25** For I know *that* my redeemer liveth, and *that* he shall stand at the latter *day* upon the earth: **Isaiah 9:6** For unto us a child is born, unto us a son is given: and the government shall be upon his shoulder: and his name shall be called Wonderful, Counseller, The mighty God, The everlasting Father, The Prince of Peace. **Isaiah 43:11** I, *even* I, *am* the LORD; and beside me *there is* no **saviour**. **Isaiah 60:16** Thou shalt also suck the milk of the Gentiles, and shalt suck the breast of kings: and thou shalt know that I the LORD *am* thy Saviour and thy Redeemer, the mighty One of Jacob.
Titus 1:5 For this cause left I thee in Crete, that thou shouldest set in order the things that are wanting, and ordain **elders** in every city, as I had appointed thee:	**See 1 Peter 5:1** "Elders"
Titus 1:6 If any be blameless, **the husband of one wife**, having faithful children not accused of riot or unruly.	**Genesis 4:19** And Lamech took unto **him two wives**: the name of the one *was* Adah, and the name of the other Zillah. **Genesis 4:23** And Lamech said unto his wives, Adah and Zillah, Hear my voice; ye wives of Lamech, hearken unto my speech: for I have slain a man to my wounding, and a young man to my hurt. **Deuteronomy 17:17 Neither shall he multiply wives to himself**, that his heart turn not away: neither shall he greatly multiply to himself silver and gold.
Titus 1:7 For a bishop must be blameless, as the steward of God; not selfwilled, not soon angry, **not given to wine**, no striker, not given to filthy lucre;	**See Ephesians 5:18** "Drunkeness"
Titus 1:11 Whose mouths must be stopped, who subvert whole houses, **teaching** things which they ought not, for filthy lucre's sake.	**See Ephesians 4:11** "Teach - Teachers"
Titus 1:12 One of themselves, even a prophet of their own, said, The Cretians are alway liars, evil beasts, **slow bellies**.	**Deuteronomy 21:20** And they shall say unto the elders of his city, This our son *is* stubborn and rebellious, he will not obey our voice; *he is* **a glutton**, and a drunkard. **Psalms 78:29-31** So they did eat, and were well filled: for he gave them their own desire; 30 They were not estranged from their lust. But while their meat *was* yet in their mouths, 31 The wrath of God came upon them, and **slew the fattest of them**, and smote down the chosen *men* of Israel.

Titus 2:3 The aged women likewise, that *they be* in behaviour as becometh holiness, not false accusers, not given to much wine, teachers of good things;	See Ephesians 5:18 "Drunkeness"
Titus 2:10 Not purloining, but shewing all good fidelity; that they may adorn the doctrine of God our Saviour in all things.	See Job 19:25, Isaiah 9:6 and 60:16 **Isaiah 43:11** I, *even* I, *am* the LORD; and beside me *there is* no **saviour**.
Titus 2:13 Looking for that blessed hope, and the glorious appearing of the great God and our **Saviour** Jesus Christ;	See Isaiah 9:6 and 60:16 **Job 19:25** For I know that my **redeemer** liveth, and that he shall stand at the latter day upon the earth: **Isaiah 43:11** I, *even* I, *am* the LORD; and beside me *there is* no **saviour**.
Titus 2:14 Who gave himself for us, that he might redeem us from all iniquity, and purify unto himself a peculiar people, zealous of good works.	**Deuteronomy 14:2** For thou *art* an holy people unto the LORD thy God, and the LORD hath chosen thee to be a peculiar people unto himself, above all the nations that *are* upon the earth. **Deuteronomy 21:23** His body shall not remain all night upon the tree, but thou shalt in any wise bury him that day; (for he that is hanged [is] accursed of God;) that thy land be not defiled, which the LORD thy God giveth thee [for] an inheritance. **Psalms 130:8** And he shall redeem Israel from all his iniquities. **Isaiah 44:6** Thus saith the LORD the King of Israel, and his **redeemer** the LORD of hosts; I *am* the first, and I *am* the last; and beside me *there is* no God. **Isaiah 53:4-5** Surely he hath borne our griefs, and carried our sorrows: yet we did esteem him stricken, smitten of God, and afflicted. 5 But he *was* wounded for our transgressions, *he was* bruised for our iniquities: the chastisement of our peace *was* upon him; and with his stripes we are healed. **Isaiah 54:5** For thy Maker *is* thine husband; the LORD of hosts *is* his name; and thy Redeemer the Holy One of Israel; The God of the whole earth shall he be called. **Ezekiel 37:23** Neither shall they defile themselves any more with their idols, nor with their detestable things, nor with any of their transgressions: but I will save them out of all their dwellingplaces, wherein they have sinned, and will cleanse them: so shall they be my people, and I will be their God. See Acts 2:38 "Fire baptism"
Titus 3:2 To **speak** evil of no man, to be no brawlers, *but* gentle, shewing all meekness unto all men.	**Psalms 101:5** Whoso privily **slandereth** his neighbour, him will I cut off: him that hath an high look and a proud heart will not I suffer. **Proverbs 26:20** Where no wood is, *there* the fire goeth out: so where *there is* no **talebearer**, the strife ceaseth. **Proverbs 26:22** The words of a **talebearer** *are* as wounds, and they go down into the innermost parts of the belly. See James 3:8 "Tongues"
Titus 3:4 But after that the kindness and love of God our Saviour toward man appeared,	See Job 19:25, Isaiah 9:6 and 60:16
Titus 3:5 Not by works of righteousness which we have done, but according to	See Acts 2:38 "Salvation"

his mercy he saved us, by the washing of regeneration, and renewing of the Holy Ghost;	
Titus 3:6 Which he shed on us abundantly through Jesus Christ our Saviour;	**See Job 19:25, Isaiah 9:6 and 60:16** **Ezekiel 36:25** Then will I sprinkle clean water upon you, and ye shall be clean: from all your filthiness, and from all your idols, will I cleanse you.
Titus 3:9 But avoid foolish questions, and genealogies, and **contentions**, and **strivings** about the law; for they are unprofitable and vain.	**Psalms 133:1** Behold, how good and how pleasant *it is* for brethren to dwell together in unity! **Amos 3:3** Can two walk together, except they be agreed?
Philemon 1:9 Yet for love's sake I rather beseech thee, being such an one as Paul the aged, and now also a prisoner of Jesus Christ.	**1 Kings 2:22-23** So the waters were healed unto this day, according to the saying of Elisha which he spake. 23 And he went up from thence unto Bethel: and as he was going up by the way, there came forth little children out of the city, and mocked him, and said unto him, Go up, thou bald head; go up, thou bald head **Proverbs 16:31** The hoary head *is* a crown of glory, *if* it be found in the way of righteousness. **Psalms 92:12-14** The righteous shall flourish like the palm tree: he shall grow like a cedar in Lebanon. 13 Those that be planted in the house of the LORD shall flourish in the courts of our God. 14 **They shall still bring forth fruit in old age**; they shall be fat and flourishing;
Hebrews 1:1 God, who at sundry times and in divers manners **spake in time past unto the fathers by the prophets**, 2 Hath in these last days **spoken unto us by his Son**, whom he hath appointed heir of all things, by whom also he made the worlds; **Hebrews 1:2** Hath in these last days spoken unto us by *his* Son, whom he hath appointed heir of all things, by whom also he made the worlds;	**Jeremiah 36:2** Take thee a roll of a book, and **write therein all the words that I have spoken unto thee against Israel**, and against Judah, and against all the nations, from the day I spake unto thee, from the days of Josiah, even unto this day. **See Luke 18:31 "Written Words"** **Genesis 1:3** And God said, Let there be light: and there was light. **Psalm 33:6** By the word of the LORD were the heavens made; and all the host of them by the breath of his mouth. **Isaiah 9:6** For unto us a child is born, unto us a son is given: and the government shall be upon his shoulder: and his name shall be called Wonderful, Counsellor, The mighty God, The everlasting Father, The Prince of Peace. **Zechariah 12:10** And I will pour upon the house of David, and upon the inhabitants of Jerusalem, the spirit of grace and of supplications: and they shall look upon me whom they have pierced, and they shall mourn for him, as one mourneth for *his* only *son*, and shall be in bitterness for him, as one that is in bitterness for *his* firstborn. **Isaiah 2:2** And it shall come to pass in the **last days**, that the mountain of the LORD'S house shall be established in the top of the mountains, and shall be exalted above the hills; and all nations shall flow unto it. **Micah 4:1** But in the **last days** it shall come to pass, that the mountain of the house of the LORD shall be established in the top of the mountains, and it shall be exalted above the hills; and people shall flow unto it.

Hebrews 1:3 Who being the brightness of *his* glory, and the express image of his person, and upholding all things by the word of his power, when he had by himself purged our sins, sat down on the right hand of the Majesty on high;	**Job 19:25** For I know *that* my redeemer liveth, and *that* he shall stand at the latter *day* upon the earth: **Psalms 8:6** Thou madest him to have dominion over the works of thy hands; thou hast put all *things* under his feet: **Psalms 16:8** I have set the LORD always before me: because *he is* at my right hand, I shall not be moved. **Psalms 68:18** Thou hast ascended on high, thou hast led captivity captive: thou hast received gifts for men; yea, *for* the rebellious also, that the LORD God might dwell *among them*. **Psalms 110:1** The LORD said unto my Lord, Sit thou at my right hand, until I make thine enemies thy footstool. **Psalms 110:5** The Lord at thy right hand shall strike through kings in the day of his wrath. **Isaiah 9:6** For unto us a child is born, unto us a son is given: and the government shall be upon his shoulder: and his name shall be called Wonderful, Counseller, The mighty God, The everlasting Father, The Prince of Peace. **Isaiah 60:16** Thou shalt also suck the milk of the Gentiles, and shalt suck the breast of kings: and thou shalt know that I the LORD *am* thy Saviour and thy Redeemer, the mighty One of Jacob. **Daniel 7:9** I beheld till the thrones were cast down, and the Ancient of days did sit, whose garment *was* white as snow, and the hair of his head like the pure wool: his throne *was like* the fiery flame, *and* his wheels *as* burning fire. **Zechraiah 3:1** And he shewed me Joshua the high priest standing before the angel of the LORD, and Satan standing at his right hand to resist him. **See 1 Timothy 2:5 "God"**
Hebrews 1:5 For unto which of the angels said he at any time, Thou art my Son, this day have I begotten thee? And again, I will be to him a Father, and he shall be to me a Son?	**2 Samuel 7:14** I will be his father, and he shall be my son. If he commit iniquity, I will chasten him with the rod of men, and with the stripes of the children of men: **1 Chronicles 22:10** He shall build an house for my name; and he shall be my son, and I *will be* his father; and I will establish the throne of his kingdom over Israel for ever. **Psalms 2:7** I will declare the decree: the Lord hath said unto me, Thou art my Son; this day have I begotten thee. **Micah 5:2** But thou, Bethlehem Ephratah, *though* thou be little among the thousands of Judah, *yet* out of thee shall he come forth unto me *that is* to be ruler in Israel; whose goings forth *have been* from of old, from everlasting.
Hebrews 1:6 And again, when he bringeth in the **first begotten** into the world, he saith, And let all the angels of God worship him.	**Exodus 34:14** For thou shalt worship no other god: for the LORD, whose name is Jealous, is a jealous God: **Deuteronomy 32:43** Rejoice, O ye nations, *with* his people: for he will avenge the blood of his servants, and will render vengeance to his adversaries, and will be merciful unto his land, *and* to his people. **Psalms 97:7** Confounded be all they that serve graven images, that boast themselves of idols: worship him, all *ye* gods. **See 1 Timothy 2:5 "God"**

	Psalms 89:26-27 He shall cry unto me, Thou art my father, my God, and the rock of my salvation. 27 Also I will make him my **firstborn**, higher than the kings of the earth. **Jeremiah 31:9** They shall come with weeping, and with supplications will I lead them: I will cause them to walk by the rivers of waters in a straight way, wherein they shall not stumble: for I am a father to Israel, and **Ephraim is my firstborn**.
Hebrews 1:7 And of the angels he saith, Who maketh his angels spirits, and his ministers a flame of fire.	**Numbers 31:23** Every thing that may abide the fire, **ye shall make it go through the fire, and <u>it shall be clean</u>**: nevertheless it shall be purified with the water of separation: and all that abideth not the fire ye shall make go through the water. **Psalms 104:4** Who maketh his angels spirits; his ministers a flaming fire:
Hebrews 1:8-9 But unto the Son [he saith], Thy throne, O God, [is] for ever and ever: a sceptre of righteousness [is] the sceptre of thy kingdom. 9 Thou hast loved righteousness, and hated iniquity; therefore God, [even] thy God, hath anointed thee with the oil of gladness above thy fellows.	**Psalms 45:6-7** Thy throne, O God, *is* for ever and ever: the sceptre of thy kingdom [is] a right sceptre. Thou lovest righteousness, and hatest wickedness: therefore God, thy God, hath anointed thee with the oil of gladness above thy fellows.
Hebrews 1:10 And, Thou, Lord, in the beginning hast laid the foundation of the earth; and the heavens are the works of thine hands:	**Genesis 1:1** In the beginning God created the heaven and the earth. **See John 1:3 "Creation"**
Hebrews 1:11-12 They shall perish; but thou remainest; and they all shall wax old as doth a garment; 12 And as a vesture shalt thou fold them up, and they shall be changed: but thou art the same, and thy years shall not fail.	**Isaiah 51:6** Lift up your eyes to the heavens, and look upon the earth beneath: for the heavens shall vanish away like smoke, and the earth shall wax old like a garment, and they that dwell therein shall die in like manner: but my salvation shall be for ever, and my righteousness shall not be abolished.
Hebrews 1:13 But to which of the angels said he at any time, Sit on my right hand, until I make thine enemies thy footstool?	**Job 19:25** For I know *that* my redeemer liveth, and *that* he shall stand at the latter *day* upon the earth: **Psalms 8:6** Thou madest him to have dominion over the works of thy hands; thou hast put all *things* under his feet: **Psalms 16:8** I have set the LORD always before me: because *he is* at my right hand, I shall not be moved. **Psalms 68:18** Thou hast ascended on high, thou hast led captivity captive: thou hast received gifts for men; yea, *for* the rebellious also, that the LORD God might dwell *among them*. **Psalms 110:1** The LORD said unto my Lord, Sit thou at my right hand, until I make thine enemies thy footstool. **Psalms 110:5** The Lord at thy right hand shall strike through kings in the day of his wrath. **Isaiah 9:6** For unto us a child is born, unto us a son is given: and the government shall be upon his shoulder: and his name shall be called Wonderful, Counseller, The mighty God, The everlasting Father, The Prince of Peace. **Isaiah 60:16** Thou shalt also suck the milk of the Gentiles, and shalt suck the breast of kings: and thou shalt know that I the LORD

	am thy Saviour and thy Redeemer, the mighty One of Jacob. **Daniel 7:9** I beheld till the thrones were cast down, and the Ancient of days did sit, whose garment *was* white as snow, and the hair of his head like the pure wool: his throne *was like* the fiery flame, *and* his wheels *as* burning fire. **Zechraiah 3:1** And he shewed me Joshua the high priest standing before the angel of the LORD, and Satan standing at his right hand to resist him.
Hebrews 1:14 Are they not all ministering spirits, sent forth to minister for them who shall be heirs of salvation?	**Psalms 91:11-12** For he shall give his angels charge over thee, to keep thee in all thy ways. 12 They shall bear thee up in *their* hands, lest thou dash thy foot against a stone. **Psalm 103:20** Bless the LORD, ye his angels, that excel in strength, that do his commandments, hearkening unto the voice of his word. **See Hebrews 13:2 "Good and bad angels"**
Hebrews 2:2 For if the word spoken by angels was stedfast, and every transgression and disobedience received a just recompence of reward;	**Genesis 19:17** And it came to pass, when they had brought them forth abroad, that he said, Escape for thy life; look not behind thee, neither stay thou in all the plain; escape to the mountain, lest thou be consumed. **Genesis 19:26** But his wife looked back from behind him, and she became a pillar of salt.
Hebrews 2:3-4 How shall we escape, if we neglect so great **salvation**; which at the first began to be spoken by the Lord, and was confirmed unto us by them that heard [him]; **God also bearing witness, both with signs and wonders, and with divers miracles, and gifts of the Holy Ghost,** according to his own will?	**See Acts 3:5 "Salvation"**
Hebrews 2:5 For unto the angels hath he not put in **subjection** the world to come, whereof we speak.	**Isaiah 14:13** For you have said In your heart, I will go up to the heavens; I will raise my throne above the stars of God, and I will sit in the mount of meeting, in the sides of the north. **Psalms 75:6** For exaltations are not from the east, nor from the west, nor from the desert;
Hebrews 2:6-8 But one in a certain place testified, saying, What is man, that thou art mindful of him? or the son of man, that thou visitest him? 7 Thou madest him a little lower than the angels; thou crownedst him with glory and honour, and didst set him over the works of thy hands: 8 Thou hast put all things in subjection under his feet. For in that he put all in subjection under him, he left nothing [that is] not put under him. But now we see not yet all things put under him.	**Psalms 8:4-6** What is man, that thou art mindful of him? and the son of man, that thou visitest him? 5 For thou hast made him a little lower than the angels, and hast crowned him with glory and honour. 6 Thou madest him to have dominion over the works of thy hands; thou hast put all things under his feet:

Hebrews 2:10 For it became him, for whom *are* all things, and by whom *are* all things, in bringing many sons unto glory, to make the captain of their salvation perfect through sufferings.	**Isaiah 53:4-5** Surely he hath borne our griefs, and carried our sorrows: yet we did esteem him stricken, smitten of God, and afflicted. 5 But he *was* wounded for our transgressions, *he was* bruised for our iniquities: the chastisement of our peace *was* upon him; and with his stripes we are healed.
Hebrews 2:12 Saying, I will declare thy name unto my brethren, in the midst of the church will I sing praise unto thee.	**Psalms 22:22** I will declare thy name unto my brethren: in the midst of the congregation will I praise thee.
Hebrews 2:13 And again, I will put my trust in him. And again, Behold I and the children which God hath given me.	**2 Samuel 22:3** The God of my rock; in him will I trust: [he is] my shield, and the horn of my salvation, my high tower, and my refuge, my saviour; thou savest me from violence. **Psalm 18:2** The LORD *is* my rock, and my fortress, and my deliverer; my God, my strength, in whom I will trust; my buckler, and the horn of my salvation, *and* my high tower. **Isaiah 8:17-18** And I will wait upon the LORD, that hideth his face from the house of Jacob, and I will look for him. Behold, I and the children whom the LORD hath given me [are] for signs and for wonders in Israel from the LORD of hosts, which dwelleth in mount Zion.
Hebrew 2:14 Forasmuch then as the children are partakers of flesh and blood, he also himself likewise took part of the same; that through death he might destroy him that had the power of death, that is, the devil;	**Hosea 13:14** I will ransom them from the power of the grave; I will redeem them from death: O death, I will be thy plagues; O grave, I will be thy destruction: repentance shall be hid from mine eyes. **See Matthew 26:28 "Atonement"** **See 1 Timothy 2:5 "God"**
Hebrews 2:16 For verily he took not on *him the nature of* angels; but **he took on him** the seed of Abraham.	**Genesis 17:7** And I will establish My covenant between Me and thee, and thy seed after thee in their generations for an everlasting covenant, to be a God unto **thy seed** after thee. **Deuteronomy 29:13-14** That He may establish thee today for a people unto Himself, and [that] He may be unto thee a God, as He hath said unto thee, and as He hath sworn unto thy fathers, to Abraham, to Isaac, and to Jacob. 14 <u>Neither with you only</u> do I make this covenant and this oath; **Isaiah 41:8-9** But thou, Israel, art my servant, Jacob whom I have chosen, the seed of Abraham my friend. 9 Thou whom I have taken from the ends of the earth, and called thee from the chief men thereof, and said unto thee, Thou art my servant; I have chosen thee, and not cast thee away.
Hebrews 3:2 Who was faithful to him that appointed him, as also Moses *was faithful* in all his house.	**Numbers 12:7** My servant Moses *is* not so, who *is* faithful in all mine house.
Hebrews 3:5 And Moses verily *was* faithful in all his house, as a servant, for a testimony of those things which were to be spoken after;	**Numbers 12:7** See above
Hebrew 3:7 Wherefore (as the Holy Ghost saith, To day if ye will hear his voice,	**Psalms 95:7** For he *is* our God; and we *are* the people of his pasture, and the sheep of his hand. To day if ye will hear his voice,
Hebrew 3:8 Harden not your hearts, as in the provocation, in the day of temptation in the wilderness:	**Exodus 17:2** Wherefore the people did chide with Moses, and said, Give us water that we may drink. And Moses said unto them, Why chide ye with me? wherefore do ye tempt the LORD? **Numbers 20:3** And the people chode with Moses, and spake,

	saying, Would God that we had died when our brethren died before the LORD!
	Psalms 95:8 Harden not your heart, as in the provocation, *and* as *in* the day of temptation in the wilderness:
Hebrew 3:9 When your fathers tempted me, proved me, and saw my works forty years.	**Psalms 95:9** When your fathers tempted me, proved me, and saw my work.
Hebrew 3:10 Wherefore I was grieved with that generation, and said, They do alway err in *their* heart; and they have not known my ways.	**Psalms 95:10** Forty years long was I grieved with *this* generation, and said, It *is* a people that do err in their heart, and they have not known my ways:
Hebrew 3:11 So I sware in my wrath, They shall not enter into my rest.)	**Deuteronomy 1:34-35** And the LORD heard the voice of your words, and was wroth, and sware, saying, 35 Surely there shall not one of these men of this evil generation see that good land, which I sware to give unto your fathers,
	Psalms 95:11 Unto whom I sware in my wrath that they should not enter into my rest.
Hebrews 3:14 For we are made partakers of Christ, if we hold the beginning of our confidence stedfast unto the end;	**See Hebrews 12:14 "Holiness"**
Hebrew 3:15 While it is said, To day if ye will hear his voice, harden not your hearts, as in the provocation.	**Psalms 95:7-8** For he *is* our God; and we *are* the people of his pasture, and the sheep of his hand. To day if ye will hear his voice, 8 Harden not your heart, as in the provocation, *and* as *in* the day of temptation in the wilderness:
Hebrews 3:17 But with whom was he grieved forty years? *was it* not with them that had sinned, whose carcases fell in the wilderness?	**Numbers 14:35-36** I the LORD have said, I will surely do it unto all this evil congregation, that are gathered together against me: in this wilderness they shall be consumed, and there they shall die. 36 And the men, which Moses sent to search the land, who returned, and made all the congregation to murmur against him, by bringing up a slander upon the land,
	Psalm 106:26 Therefore he lifted up his hand against them, to overthrow them in the wilderness:
Hebrew 3:18 And to whom sware he that they should not enter into his rest, but to them that believed not?	**Deuteronomy 1:34-35** And the LORD heard the voice of your words, and was wroth, and sware, saying, 35 Surely there shall not one of these men of this evil generation see that good land, which I sware to give unto your fathers,
	Psalms 95:11 Unto whom I sware in my wrath that they should not enter into my rest.
Hebrews 4:3 For we which have believed do enter into rest, as he said, As I have sworn in my wrath, if they shall enter into my rest:	**Psalms 95:7-11** For he *is* our God; and we *are* the people of his pasture, and the sheep of his hand. To day if ye will hear his voice, Harden not your heart, as in the provocation, *and* as *in* the day of temptation in the wilderness: When your fathers tempted me, proved me, and saw my work. Forty years long was I grieved with *this* generation, and said, It *is* a people that do err in their heart, and they have not known my ways: Unto whom I sware in my wrath that they should not enter into my rest.
Hebrews 4:4 For he spake in a certain place of the seventh *day* on this wise, And God did rest the seventh day from all his works.	**See Colossians 2:16 "Sabbath"**
	See John 1:3 "Creation"
Hebrews 4:7 Again, he limiteth a certain	**Psalms 95:7-8** For he is our God; and we are the people of his

day, saying in David, To day, after so long a time; as it is said, To day if ye will hear his voice, harden not your hearts.	pasture, and the sheep of his hand. To day if ye will hear his voice, 8 Harden not your heart, as in the provocation, and as in the day of temptation in the wilderness:
Hebrews 4:8-9 For if Jesus had given them rest, then would he not afterward have spoken of another day. 9 There remaineth therefore a rest to the people of God.	**Genesis 2:3** And God blessed the seventh day, and sanctified it: because that in it he had rested from all his work which God created and made. **Exodus 20:11** For *in* six days the LORD made heaven and earth, the sea, and all that in them *is,* and rested the seventh day: wherefore the LORD blessed the sabbath day, and hallowed it. **Exodus 31:16** Wherefore the children of Israel shall keep the Sabbath, to observe the Sabbath throughout their generations, *for* **a perpetual covenant**. **Isaiah 66:23** And it shall come to pass, *that* from one new moon to another, and from one sabbath to another, shall all flesh come to worship before me, saith the LORD.
Hebrews 4:10 For he that is entered into his rest, he also hath ceased from his own works, as God *did* from his.	**Genesis 2:2** And on the seventh day God ended his work which he had made; and he rested on the seventh day from all his work which he had made. **Psalm 95:11** Unto whom I sware in my wrath that they should not enter into my rest.
Hebrews 4:12 For the **word of God** *is* quick, and powerful, and sharper than any twoedged sword, piercing even to the dividing asunder of soul and spirit, and of the joints and marrow, and *is* a discerner of the thoughts and intents of the heart.	**Ecclesiastes 12:11** The **words** of the wise *are* as goads, and as nails fastened *by* the masters of assemblies, *which* are given from one shepherd. **Isaiah 49:2** And he hath made my mouth like a sharp sword; in the shadow of his hand hath he hid me, and made me a polished shaft; in his quiver hath he hid me; **See Matthew 5:18 "Word"**
Hebrews 4:13 Neither is there any creature that is not manifest in his sight: but all things *are* naked and opened unto the eyes of him with whom we have to do.	**Psalms 33:13** The LORD looketh from heaven; he beholdeth all the sons of men.
Hebrews 4:14 Seeing then that we have a great high priest, that is passed into the heavens, Jesus the Son of God, let us hold fast *our* profession.	**Leviticus 21:10-15** And *he that is* the high priest among his brethren, upon whose head the anointing oil was poured, and that is consecrated to put on the garments, shall not uncover his head, nor rend his clothes; 11 Neither shall he go in to any dead body, nor defile himself for his father, or for his mother; 12 Neither shall he go out of the sanctuary, nor profane the sanctuary of his God; for the crown of the anointing oil of his God *is* upon him: I *am* the LORD. 13 And he shall take a wife in her virginity. 14 A widow, or a divorced woman, or profane, *or* an harlot, these shall he not take: but he shall take a virgin of his own people to wife. 15 Neither shall he profane his seed among his people: for I the LORD do sanctify him. **Numbers 17:8** And it came to pass, that on the morrow Moses went into the tabernacle of witness; and, behold, the rod of Aaron for the house of Levi was budded, and brought forth buds, and bloomed blossoms, and yielded almonds.
Hebrews 4:15 For we have not an high priest which cannot be touched with the feeling of our infirmities; but was in all	**Isaiah 53:9** And he made his grave with the wicked, and with the rich in his death; because he had done no violence, neither *was any* deceit in his mouth.

points tempted like as *we are, yet* without sin.	**See 1 Timothy 2:5 "God"**
Hebrews 5:3 And by reason hereof he ought, as for the people, so also for himself, to offer for sins.	**Leviticus 9:7** And Moses said unto Aaron, Go unto the altar, and offer thy sin offering, and thy burnt offering, and make an atonement for thyself, and for the people: and offer the offering of the people, and make an atonement for them; as the LORD commanded. **Leviticus 16:6** And Aaron shall offer his bullock of the sin offering, which *is* for himself, and make an atonement for himself, and for his house.
Hebrews 5:4 And no man taketh this honour unto himself, but he that is called of God, as *was* Aaron.	**Exodus 28:1** And take thou unto thee Aaron thy brother, and his sons with him, from among the children of Israel, that he may minister unto me in the priest's office, *even* Aaron, Nadab and Abihu, Eleazar and Ithamar, Aaron's sons. **1 Chronicles 23:13** The sons of Amram; Aaron and Moses: and Aaron was separated, that he should sanctify the most holy things, he and his sons for ever, to burn incense before the LORD, to minister unto him, and to bless in his name for ever. **2 Chronicles 26:16** But when he was strong, his heart was lifted up to *his* destruction: for he transgressed against the LORD his God, and went into the temple of the LORD to burn incense upon the altar of incense.
Hebrews 5:5 So also Christ glorified not himself to be made an high priest; but he that said unto him, Thou art my Son, to day have I begotten thee.	**2 Samuel 7:14** I will be his father, and he shall be my son. If he commit iniquity, I will chasten him with the rod of men, and with the stripes of the children of men: **1 Chronicles 22:10** He shall build an house for my name; and he shall be my son, and I *will be* his father; and I will establish the throne of his kingdom over Israel for ever. **Psalms 2:7** I will declare the decree: the Lord hath said unto me, Thou art my Son; this day have I begotten thee. **Micah 5:2** But thou, Bethlehem Ephratah, *though* thou be little among the thousands of Judah, *yet* out of thee shall he come forth unto me *that is* to be ruler in Israel; whose goings forth *have been* from of old, from everlasting.
Hebrews 5:6 As he saith also in another [place], Thou *art* a priest for ever after the order of Melchisedec.	**Psalms 110:4** The LORD hath sworn, and will not repent, Thou *art* a priest for ever after the order of Melchizedek.
Hebrews 5:10 Called of God an high priest after the order of Melchisedec.	**Psalms 110:4** The LORD hath sworn, and will not repent, Thou *art* a priest for ever after the order of Melchizedek.
Hebrews 5:12 For when for the time ye ought to be **teachers**, ye have need that one **teach** you again which *be* the first principles of the **oracles of God**; and are become such as have need of milk, and not of strong meat.	**See Ephesians 4:11 "Teach - Teachers"** **See Matthew 5:18 "Scriptures"**
Hebrews 5:14 But strong meat belongeth to them that are of full age, *even* those who by reason of use have their senses exercised to discern both good and evil.	**Malachi 3:18** Then shall ye return, and discern between the righteous and the wicked, between him that serveth God and him that serveth him not.
Hebrews 6:6 If they shall fall away, to renew them again unto repentance;	**Jeremiah 3:6-8** The LORD said also unto me in the days of Josiah the king, Hast thou seen *that* which backsliding Israel hath done?

seeing they crucify to themselves the Son of God afresh, and put *him* to an open shame.	she is gone up upon every high mountain and under every green tree, and there hath played the harlot. 7 And I said after she had done all these *things*, Turn thou unto me. But she returned not. And her treacherous sister Judah saw *it*. 8 And I saw, when for all the causes whereby backsliding Israel committed adultery I had put her away, and given her a bill of divorce; yet her treacherous sister Judah feared not, but went and played the harlot also.
Hebrews 6:8 But that which beareth thorns and briers *is* rejected, and *is* nigh unto cursing; whose end *is* to be burned.	**Genesis 3:18** Thorns also and thistles shall it bring forth to thee; and thou shalt eat the herb of the field;
Hebrews 6:13 For when God made promise to Abraham, because he could swear by no greater, he sware by himself,	**Genesis 22:16** And said, By myself have I sworn, saith the LORD, for because thou hast done this thing, and hast not withheld thy son, thine only *son:*
Hebrews 6:14 Saying, Surely blessing I will bless thee, and multiplying I will multiply thee.	**Genesis 12:3** And I will bless them that bless thee, and curse him that curseth thee: and in thee shall all families of the earth be blessed. **Genesis 22:17** That in blessing I will bless thee, and in multiplying I will multiply thy seed as the stars of the heaven, and as the sand which *is* upon the sea shore; and thy seed shall possess the gate of his enemies;
Hebrews 6:19 Which *hope* we have as an anchor of the soul, both sure and stedfast, and which entereth into that within the veil;	**Leviticus 16:2** And the LORD said unto Moses, Speak unto Aaron thy brother, that he come not at all times into the holy *place* within the vail before the mercy seat, which *is* upon the ark; that he die not: for I will appear in the cloud upon the mercy seat. **Leviticus 16:12** And he shall take a censer full of burning coals of fire from off the altar before the LORD, and his hands full of sweet incense beaten small, and bring *it* within the vail:
Hebrew 6:20 Whither the forerunner is for us entered, *even* Jesus, made an high priest for ever after the order of Melchisedec.	**Psalms 110:4** The LORD hath sworn, and will not repent, Thou *art* a priest for ever after the order of Melchizedek.
Hebrew 7:1 For this Melchisedec, king of Salem, priest of the most high God, who met Abraham returning from the slaughter of the kings, and blessed him;	**Genesis 14:18** And Melchizedek king of Salem brought forth bread and wine: and he *was* the priest of the **most high God**. **Psalms 78:56** Yet they tempted and provoked the **most high God**, and kept not his testimonies: **Daniel 3:26** Then Nebuchadnezzar came near to the mouth of the burning fiery furnace, *and* spake, and said, Shadrach, Meshach, and Abednego, ye servants of the **most high God**, come forth, and come *hither*. Then Shadrach, Meshach, and Abednego, came forth of the midst of the fire.
	Genesis 14:20 And blessed be the most high God, which hath delivered thine enemies into thy hand. And he gave him **tithes** of all. **Genesis 28:20-22** And **Jacob vowed a vow**, saying, **If** God will be with me, and will keep me in this way that I go, and will give me bread to eat, and raiment to put on, 21 So that I come again to my father's house in peace; **then** shall the LORD be my God: 22 And this stone, which I have set *for* a pillar, shall be God's house: **and of all that thou shalt give me I will surely give the tenth unto thee**. **Numbers 18:21** And, behold, I have given the children of Levi all

Hebrews 7:5 And verily they that are of the sons of Levi, who receive the office of the priesthood, have a commandment to take **tithes** of the people according to the law, that is, of their brethren, though they come out of the loins of Abraham:	the **tenth** in Israel for an inheritance, for their service which they serve, *even* the service of the tabernacle of the congregation. **Deuteronomy 14:22-29 Thou shalt truly tithe all the increase of thy seed, that the field bringeth forth year by year.** And thou **shalt eat before the LORD thy God, in the place which he shall choose to place his name there, the tithe of thy corn, of thy wine, and of thine oil, and the firstlings of thy herds and of thy flocks**; that thou mayest learn to fear the LORD thy God always. And if the way be too long for thee, so that thou art not able to carry it; [or] if the place be too far from thee, which the LORD thy God shall choose to set his name there, when the LORD thy God hath blessed thee: Then **shalt thou turn [it] into money**, and bind up the money in thine hand, and shalt go unto the place which the LORD thy God shall choose: And <u>**thou shalt bestow that money for whatsoever thy soul lusteth after**</u>, for oxen, or for sheep, or for wine, or for strong drink, or for whatsoever thy soul desireth: and thou shalt eat there before the LORD thy God, and thou shalt rejoice, thou, and thine household, And **the Levite that [is] within thy gates; thou shalt not forsake him**; for he hath no part nor inheritance with thee. At the end of three years thou shalt bring forth all the tithe of thine increase the same year, and shalt lay [it] up within thy gates: And the Levite, (because he hath no part nor inheritance with thee,) and the stranger, and the fatherless, and the widow, which [are] within thy gates, shall come, and shall eat and be satisfied; that the LORD thy God may bless thee in all the work of thine hand which thou doest. **Deuteronomy 18:1** The priests the Levites, *and* all the tribe of Levi, shall have no part nor inheritance with Israel: they shall eat the offerings of the LORD made by fire, and his inheritance. **Joshua 14:4** For the children of Joseph were two tribes, Manasseh and Ephraim: therefore they gave no part unto the Levites in the land, save cities to dwell *in*, with their suburbs for their cattle and for their substance. **2 Chronicles 31:5** And as soon as the commandment came abroad, the children of Israel brought in abundance the firstfruits of corn, wine, and oil, and honey, and of all the increase of the field; and the tithe of all *things* brought they in abundantly. **Nehemiah 10:34-39** And we cast the lots among the **priests**, the **Levites**, and the **people**, for the wood offering, to bring *it* into the house of our God, after the houses of our fathers, at times appointed year by year, to burn upon the altar of the LORD our God, as *it is* written in the law: 35 And to bring the **firstfruits of our ground**, and the **firstfruits of all fruit of all trees**, year by year, unto the house of the LORD: 36 Also the **firstborn** of our sons, and **of our cattle**, as *it is* written in the law, and the **firstlings of our herds and of our flocks**, to **bring to the house of our God, unto the priests that minister in the house of our God**: 37 And *that* we should **bring the firstfruits of our dough, and our offerings, and the fruit of all manner of trees, of wine and of oil, the priests, to the chambers of the house of our God; and the tithes of our ground unto the Levites, that the same Levites might have the tithes in all the cities** of our tillage. 38 And the priest the son of Aaron shall be with the Levites, when the Levites take tithes: and the **Levites shall bring up the tithe of the tithes unto the house of our God, to the chambers, into the treasure house**. 39 For the children of Israel and the children of

	Levi shall bring the offering of the corn, of the new wine, and the oil, unto the chambers, where *are* the vessels of the sanctuary, and the priests that minister, and the porters, and the singers: and we will not forsake the house of our God.
	Malachi 3:10 Bring ye all the tithes into the storehouse, that there may be meat in mine house, and prove me now herewith, saith the LORD of hosts, if I will not open you the windows of heaven, and pour you out a blessing, that *there shall* not *be room* enough *to receive it*.
Hebrews 7:6 But he whose descent is not counted from them received tithes of Abraham, and blessed him that had the promises.	**Genesis 14:20** And blessed be the most high God, which hath delivered thine enemies into thy hand. And he gave him tithes of all.
Hebrews 7:8 And here men that die receive tithes; but there he *receiveth them,* of whom it is witnessed that he liveth.	**Nehemiah 10:38** And the priest the son of Aaron shall be with the Levites, when the Levites take tithes: and the Levites shall bring up the tithe of the tithes unto the house of our God, to the chambers, into the treasure house. **See Matthew 23:23 "Tithing"**
Hebrews 7:14 For *it is* evident that our Lord sprang out of Juda; of which tribe Moses spake nothing concerning priesthood.	**Genesis 49:8-10** Judah, thou *art he* whom thy brethren shall praise: thy hand *shall be* in the neck of thine enemies; thy father's children shall bow down before thee. 9 Judah *is* a lion's whelp: from the prey, my son, thou art gone up: he stooped down, he couched as a lion, and as an old lion; who shall rouse him up? 10 The sceptre shall not depart from Judah, nor a lawgiver from between his feet, until Shiloh come; and unto him *shall* the gathering of the people *be*. **Isaiah 11:1** And there shall come forth a rod out of the stem of Jesse, and a Branch shall grow out of his roots:
Hebrews 7:17 For he testifieth, Thou *art* a priest for ever after the order of Melchisedec.	**Psalms 110:4** The LORD hath sworn, and will not repent, Thou *art* a priest for ever after the order of Melchizedek.
Hebrews 7:21 (For those priests were made without an oath; but this with an oath by him that said unto him, The Lord sware and will not repent, Thou [art] a priest for ever after the order of Melchisedec:)	**Psalms 110:4** The LORD hath sworn, and will not repent, Thou *art* a priest for ever after the order of Melchizedek.
Hebrews 7:22 By so much was Jesus made a surety of a better testament.	**Isaiah 59:20-21** And the Redeemer shall come to Zion, and unto them that turn from transgression in Jacob, saith the LORD. 21 As for me, this [is] my covenant with them, saith the LORD; My spirit that *is* upon thee, and my words which I have put in thy mouth, shall not depart out of thy mouth, nor out of the mouth of thy seed, nor out of the mouth of thy seed's seed, saith the LORD, from henceforth and for ever. **Jeremiah 31:31-33** Behold, the days come, saith the LORD, that **I will make a new covenant with the house of Israel**, and with the house of Judah: 32 Not according to the covenant that I made with their fathers in the day *that* I took them by the hand to bring them out of the land of Egypt; which my covenant they brake, although I was an husband unto them, saith the LORD: 33 But this *shall be* the covenant that I will make with the house of Israel; After those days, saith the LORD, I will put my law in their inward parts, and write it in their hearts; and will be their God, and they shall be my people. 34 And they shall teach no more every man his neighbour,

	and every man his brother, saying, Know the LORD: for they shall all know me, from the least of them unto the greatest of them, saith the LORD: for I will forgive their iniquity, and I will remember their sin no more.
Hebrews 7:25 Wherefore he is able also to save them to the uttermost that come unto God by him, seeing he ever liveth to make intercession for them.	**Psalms 110:4** The LORD hath sworn, and will not repent, Thou *art* a priest for ever after the order of Melchizedek.
Hebrews 7:27 Who needeth not daily, as those high priests, to offer up sacrifice, first for his own sins, and then for the people's: for this he did once, when he offered up himself.	**Leviticus 9:7** And Moses said unto Aaron, Go unto the altar, and offer thy sin offering, and thy burnt offering, and make an atonement for thyself, and for the people: and offer the offering of the people, and make an atonement for them; as the LORD commanded.
Hebrews 8:1 Now of the things which we have spoken *this is* the sum: We have such an high priest, who is set on the right hand of the throne of the Majesty in the heavens;	**Job 19:25** For I know *that* my redeemer liveth, and *that* he shall stand at the latter *day* upon the earth: **Psalms 8:6** Thou madest him to have dominion over the works of thy hands; thou hast put all *things* under his feet: **Psalms 16:8** I have set the LORD always before me: because *he is* at my right hand, I shall not be moved. **Psalms 68:18** Thou hast ascended on high, thou hast led captivity captive: thou hast received gifts for men; yea, *for* the rebellious also, that the LORD God might dwell *among them*. **Psalms 110:1** The LORD said unto my Lord, Sit thou at my right hand, until I make thine enemies thy footstool. **Psalms 110:5** The Lord at thy right hand shall strike through kings in the day of his wrath. **Isaiah 9:6** For unto us a child is born, unto us a son is given: and the government shall be upon his shoulder: and his name shall be called Wonderful, Counsellor, The mighty God, The everlasting Father, The Prince of Peace. **Isaiah 60:16** Thou shalt also suck the milk of the Gentiles, and shalt suck the breast of kings: and thou shalt know that I the LORD *am* thy Saviour and thy Redeemer, the mighty One of Jacob. **Daniel 7:9** I beheld till the thrones were cast down, and the Ancient of days did sit, whose garment *was* white as snow, and the hair of his head like the pure wool: his throne *was like* the fiery flame, *and* his wheels *as* burning fire. **Zechraiah 3:1** And he shewed me Joshua the high priest standing before the angel of the LORD, and Satan standing at his right hand to resist him.
Hebrews 8:5 Who serve unto the example and shadow of heavenly things, as Moses was admonished of God when he was about to make the tabernacle: for, See, saith he, *that* thou make all things according to the pattern shewed to thee in the mount.	**Exodus 25:40** And look that thou make *them* after their pattern, which was shewed thee in the mount.
Hebrews 8:6-7 But now hath he obtained a more excellent ministry, by how much also he is the mediator of a better covenant, which was established upon better promises. 7 For **if that <u>first</u>**	**Isaiah 59:20-21** And the Redeemer shall come to Zion, and unto them that turn from transgression in Jacob, saith the LORD. 21 As for me, this [is] my covenant with them, saith the LORD; My spirit that **is** upon thee, and my words which I have put in thy mouth, shall not depart out of thy mouth, nor out of the mouth of thy seed,

	nor out of the mouth of thy seed's seed, saith the LORD, from henceforth and for ever.
covenant had been faultless, then should no place have been sought for the <u>second</u>.	**Jeremiah 31:31-33** Behold, the days come, saith the LORD, that **I will make a new covenant with the house of Israel**, and with the house of Judah: 32 Not according to the covenant that I made with their fathers in the day *that* I took them by the hand to bring them out of the land of Egypt; which my covenant they brake, although I was an husband unto them, saith the LORD: 33 But this *shall be* the covenant that I will make with the house of Israel; After those days, saith the LORD, I will put my law in their inward parts, and write it in their hearts; and will be their God, and they shall be my people. 34 And they shall teach no more every man his neighbour, and every man his brother, saying, Know the LORD: for they shall all know me, from the least of them unto the greatest of them, saith the LORD: for I will forgive their iniquity, and I will remember their sin no more.
Hebrews 8:8 For finding fault with them, he saith, Behold, the days come, saith the Lord, when I will make a **new covenant** with the house of Israel and with the house of Judah:	**Genesis 26:2-5** And the LORD appeared unto him, and said, Go not down into Egypt; dwell in the land which I shall tell thee of: 3 Sojourn in this land, and I will be with thee, and will bless thee; for unto thee, and unto thy seed, I will give all these countries, and I will perform the oath which I sware unto Abraham thy father; 4 And I will make thy seed to multiply as the stars of heaven, and will give unto thy seed all these countries; and in thy seed shall all the nations of the earth be blessed; 5 Because that Abraham obeyed my voice, and kept my charge, my commandments, my statutes, and my laws. **Genesis 35:10-11** And God said unto him, Thy name *is* Jacob: thy name shall not be called any more Jacob, but Israel shall be thy name: and he called his name Israel. 11 And God said unto him, I *am* God Almighty: be fruitful and multiply; a nation and a company of nations shall be of thee, and kings shall come out of thy loins; **Jeremiah 32:40** And I will make an **everlasting covenant** with them, that I will not turn away from them, to do them good; but I will put my fear in their hearts, that they shall not depart from me. **Jeremiah 31:31** Behold, the days come, saith the LORD, that I will make a **new covenant** with the house of Israel, and with the house of Judah:
Hebrews 8:9 Not according to the covenant that I made with their fathers in the day when I took them by the hand to lead them out of the land of Egypt; because they continued not in my covenant, and I regarded them not, saith the Lord.	**Jeremiah 31:32** Not according to the covenant that I made with their fathers in the day *that* I took them by the hand to bring them out of the land of Egypt; which my covenant they brake, although I was an husband unto them, saith the LORD:
Hebrews 8:10 For this *is* the **covenant** that I will make with the house of Israel after those days, saith the Lord; I will put my laws into their mind, and write them in their hearts: and I will be to them a God, and they shall be to me a people:	**Jeremiah 31:33** But this *shall be* the **covenant** that I will make with the house of Israel; After those days, saith the LORD, I will put my law in their inward parts, and write it in their hearts; and will be their God, and they shall be my people. **Ezekiel 11:19** And I will give them one heart, and I will put a new spirit within you; and I will take the stony heart out of their flesh, and will give them an heart of flesh:
Hebrews 8:11 And they shall not teach every man his neighbour, and every man	**Jeremiah 31:34** And they shall teach no more every man his neighbour, and every man his brother, saying, Know the LORD:

his brother, saying, Know the Lord: for all shall know me, from the least to the greatest.	for they shall all know me, from the least of them unto the greatest of them, saith the LORD: for I will forgive their iniquity, and I will remember their sin no more.
Hebrews 8:12 For I will be merciful to their unrighteousness, and their sins and their iniquities will I remember no more.	**Jeremiah 31:34** See above
Hebrews 8:13 In that he saith, A **new covenant**, he hath made the first old. Now that which decayeth and waxeth old *is* ready to vanish away.	**Psalm 89:34 My covenant will I not break**, nor alter the thing that is gone out of my lips. **Jeremiah 31:31** Behold, the days come, saith the LORD, that I will make a **new covenant** with the house of Israel, and with the house of Judah: **See Hebrews 8:8 "New Covenant"**
Hebrews 9:2 For there was a tabernacle made; the first, wherein *was* the candlestick, and the table, and the shewbread; which is called the sanctuary.	**Exodus 26:1** Moreover thou shalt make the tabernacle *with* ten curtains *of* fine twined linen, and blue, and purple, and scarlet: *with* cherubims of cunning work shalt thou make them. **Exodus 36:1** Then wrought Bezaleel and Aholiab, and every wise hearted man, in whom the LORD put wisdom and understanding to know how to work all manner of work for the service of the sanctuary, according to all that the LORD had commanded. **Leviticus 24:5** And thou shalt take fine flour, and bake twelve cakes thereof: two tenth deals shall be in one cake.
Hebrews 9:4 Which had the golden censer, and the ark of the covenant overlaid round about with gold, wherein *was* the golden pot that had manna, and Aaron's rod that budded, and the tables of the covenant;	**Exodus 16:33** And Moses said unto Aaron, Take a pot, and put an omer full of manna therein, and lay it up before the LORD, to be kept for your generations. **Exodus 25:10** And they shall make an ark *of* shittim wood: two cubits and a half *shall be* the length thereof, and a cubit and a half the breadth thereof, and a cubit and a half the height thereof. **Numbers 17:10** And the LORD said unto Moses, Bring Aaron's rod again before the testimony, to be kept for a token against the rebels; and thou shalt quite take away their murmurings from me, that they die not. **1 Kings 8:9** *There was* nothing in the ark save the two tables of stone, which Moses put there at Horeb, when the LORD made *a covenant* with the children of Israel, when they came out of the land of Egypt.
Hebrews 9:5 And over it the cherubims of glory shadowing the mercyseat; of which we cannot now speak particularly.	**Exodus 25:22** And there I will meet with thee, and I will commune with thee from above the mercy seat, from between the two cherubims which *are* upon the ark of the testimony, of all *things* which I will give thee in commandment unto the children of Israel. **Numbers 7:89** And when Moses was gone into the tabernacle of the congregation to speak with him, then he heard the voice of one speaking unto him from off the mercy seat that was upon the ark of testimony, from between the two cherubims: and he spake unto him.
Hebrews 9:6 Now when these things were thus ordained, the priests went always into the first tabernacle, accomplishing the service *of God*.	**Exodus 29:38-42** Now this *is that* which thou shalt offer upon the altar; two lambs of the first year day by day continually. 39 The one lamb thou shalt offer in the morning; and the other lamb thou shalt offer at even: 40 And with the one lamb a tenth deal of flour mingled with the fourth part of an hin of beaten oil; and the fourth

	part of an hin of wine *for* a drink offering. 41 And the other lamb thou shalt offer at even, and shalt do thereto according to the meat offering of the morning, and according to the drink offering thereof, for a sweet savour, an offering made by fire unto the LORD. 42 *This shall be* a continual burnt offering throughout your generations *at* the door of the tabernacle of the congregation before the LORD: where I will meet you, to speak there unto thee.
Hebrews 9:7 But into the second *went* the high priest alone once every year, not without blood, which he offered for himself, and *for* the errors of the people:	**Leviticus 17:11** For the life of the flesh is in the blood: and I have given it to you upon the altar to make an atonement for your souls: **for it is the blood that maketh an atonement for the soul**. **See Matthew 26:28 "Atonement"**
Hebrews 9:10 *Which stood* only in meats and drinks, and divers washings, and carnal ordinances, imposed *on them* until the time of reformation.	**Leviticus 11:4** Nevertheless these shall ye not eat of them that chew the cud, or of them that divide the hoof: *as* the camel, because he cheweth the cud, but divideth not the hoof; he *is* **unclean** unto you. **Numbers 19:7** Then the priest shall wash his clothes, and he shall bathe his flesh in water, and afterward he shall come into the camp, and the priest shall be unclean until the even. **Deuteronomy 14:3-21** Thou shalt not eat any abominable thing. 4 These *are* the beasts which ye shall eat: the ox, the sheep, and the goat, 5 The hart, and the roebuck, and the fallow deer, and the wild goat, and the pygarg, and the wild ox, and the chamois. 6 And every beast that parteth the hoof, and cleaveth the cleft into two claws, *and* cheweth the cud among the beasts, that ye shall eat. 7 Nevertheless these ye shall not eat of them that chew the cud, or of them that divide the cloven hoof; *as* the camel, and the hare, and the coney: for they chew the cud, but divide not the hoof; *therefore* they *are* unclean unto you. 8 And the swine, because it divideth the hoof, yet cheweth not the cud, it *is* unclean unto you: ye shall not eat of their flesh, nor touch their dead carcase. 9 These ye shall eat of all that *are* in the waters: all that have fins and scales shall ye eat: 10 And whatsoever hath not fins and scales ye may not eat; it *is* unclean unto you. 11 *Of* all clean birds ye shall eat. 12 But these *are they* of which ye shall not eat: the eagle, and the ossifrage, and the ospray, 13 And the glede, and the kite, and the vulture after his kind, 14 And every raven after his kind, 15 And the owl, and the night hawk, and the cuckow, and the hawk after his kind, 16 The little owl, and the great owl, and the swan, 17 And the pelican, and the gier eagle, and the cormorant, 18 And the stork, and the heron after her kind, and the lapwing, and the bat. 19 And every creeping thing that flieth *is* unclean unto you: they shall not be eaten. 20 *But of* all clean fowls ye may eat. 21 Ye shall not eat *of* any thing that dieth of itself: thou shalt give it unto the stranger that *is* in thy gates, that he may eat it; or thou mayest sell it unto an alien: for thou *art* an holy people unto the LORD thy God. Thou shalt not seethe a kid in his mother's milk. **Deuteronomy 15:22** Thou shalt eat it within thy gates: **the unclean and the clean** *person shall eat it* alike, as the roebuck, and as the hart.
Hebrews 9:13 For if the blood of bulls and of goats, and the ashes of an heifer sprinkling the unclean, sanctifieth to the purifying of the flesh:	**Leviticus 16:34** And this shall be an everlasting statute unto you, to make an atonement for the children of Israel for all their sins once a year. And he did as the LORD commanded Moses.

	See Matthew 26:28 "Atonement"
Hebrews 9:14 How much more shall the blood of Christ, who through the eternal Spirit offered himself without spot to God, purge your conscience from dead works to serve the living God?	**Exodus 12:5** Your lamb shall be without blemish, a male of the first year: ye shall take *it* out from the sheep, or from the goats: **Leviticus 17:11** For the life of the flesh is in the blood: and I have given it to you upon the altar to make an atonement for your souls: **for it is the blood that maketh an atonement for the soul**. **Leviticus 22:20** *But* whatsoever hath a blemish, *that* shall ye not offer: for it shall not be acceptable for you. **Deuteronomy 17:1** Thou shalt not sacrifice unto the LORD thy God *any* bullock, or sheep, wherein is blemish, *or* any evilfavouredness: for that *is* an abomination unto the LORD thy God. **See Matthew 26:28 "Atonement"**
Hebrews 9:15 And for this cause he is the mediator of the new testament, that by means of death, for the redemption of the transgressions *that were* under the first testament, they which are called might receive the promise of eternal inheritance.	**Isaiah 59:20-21** And the Redeemer shall come to Zion, and unto them that turn from transgression in Jacob, saith the LORD. 21 As for me, this [is] my covenant with them, saith the LORD; My spirit that [is] upon thee, and my words which I have put in thy mouth, shall not depart out of thy mouth, nor out of the mouth of thy seed, nor out of the mouth of thy seed's seed, saith the LORD, from henceforth and for ever. **Jeremiah 31:31-33** Behold, the days come, saith the LORD, that **I will make a new covenant with the house of Israel**, and with the house of Judah: 32 Not according to the covenant that I made with their fathers in the day *that* I took them by the hand to bring them out of the land of Egypt; which my covenant they brake, although I was an husband unto them, saith the LORD: 33 But this *shall be* the covenant that I will make with the house of Israel; After those days, saith the LORD, I will put my law in their inward parts, and write it in their hearts; and will be their God, and they shall be my people. 34 And they shall teach no more every man his neighbour, and every man his brother, saying, Know the LORD: for they shall all know me, from the least of them unto the greatest of them, saith the LORD: for I will forgive their iniquity, and I will remember their sin no more.
Hebrews 9:16-17 For where a testament is, there must also of necessity be the death of the testator. 17 For a testament *is* of force after men are dead: otherwise it is of no strength at all while the testator liveth.	**Exodus 24:6-8** And Moses took half of the blood, and put *it* in basons; and half of the blood he sprinkled on the altar. 7 And he took the book of the covenant, and read in the audience of the people: and they said, All that the LORD hath said will we do, and be obedient. 8 And Moses took the blood, and sprinkled *it* on the people, and said, Behold the blood of the covenant, which the LORD hath made with you concerning all these words.
Hebrews 9:19-20 For when Moses had spoken every precept to all the people according to the law, he took the blood of calves and of goats, with water, and scarlet wool, and hyssop, and sprinkled both the book, and all the people, 20 saying, This *is* the blood of the testament which God hath enjoined unto you.	**Exodus 24:8** And Moses took the blood, and sprinkled *it* on the people, and said, Behold the blood of the covenant, which the LORD hath made with you concerning all these words. **See Acts 2:38 "Salvation"** **See Matthew 26:28 "Atonement"**
Hebrews 9:22 And almost all things are by the law purged with **blood**; and **without shedding of blood is no remission**.	**2 Chronicles 29:24** And the priests killed them, and they made reconciliation with their blood upon the altar, to make an atonement for all Israel: for the king commanded *that* the burnt offering and the sin offering *should be made* for all Israel.

	Leviticus 14:20 And the priest shall offer the burnt offering and the meat offering upon the altar: and the priest shall make an atonement for him, and he shall be clean. **Leviticus 15:15** And the priest shall offer them, the one *for* a sin offering, and the other *for* a burnt offering; and the priest shall make an atonement for him before the LORD for his issue. **Leviticus 17:11** For the life of the flesh is in the blood: and I have given it to you upon the altar to make an atonement for your souls: **for it is the blood that maketh an atonement for the soul**. **Leviticus 17:14** For *it is* the life of all flesh; the blood of it *is* for the life thereof: therefore I said unto the children of Israel, Ye shall eat the blood of no manner of flesh: for **the life of all flesh *is* the blood** thereof: whosoever eateth it shall be cut off. **Ezekiel 45:15** And one lamb out of the flock, out of two hundred, out of the fat pastures of Israel; for a meat offering, and for a burnt offering, and for peace offerings, to make reconciliation for them, saith the Lord GOD.
Hebrews 9:23 *It was* therefore necessary that the patterns of things in the heavens should be purified with these; but the heavenly things themselves with better sacrifices than these.	See Acts 2:38 "Salvation"
Hebrews 9:25 Nor yet that he should offer himself often, as the high priest entereth into the holy place every year with blood of others;	**Exodus 30:10** And Aaron shall make an atonement upon the horns of it once in a year with the blood of the sin offering of atonements: once in the year shall he make atonement upon it throughout your generations: it *is* most holy unto the LORD. See Matthew 26:28 "Atonement"
Hebrews 9:26 For then must he often have suffered since the foundation of the world: but now once in the end of the world hath he appeared to put away sin by the sacrifice of himself.	**Leviticus 17:11** For the life of the flesh is in the blood: and I have given it to you upon the altar to make an atonement for your souls: **for it is the blood that maketh an atonement for the soul**. **Isaiah 53:10** Yet it pleased the LORD to bruise him; he hath put *him* to grief: when thou shalt make his soul an offering for sin, he shall see *his* seed, he shall prolong *his* days, and the pleasure of the LORD shall prosper in his hand.
Hebrews 9:28 So Christ was once offered to bear the sins of many; and unto them that look for him shall he appear the second time without sin unto salvation.	**Isaiah 53:12** Therefore will I divide him *a portion* with the great, and he shall divide the spoil with the strong; because he hath poured out his soul unto death: and he was numbered with the transgressors; and he bare the sin of many, and made intercession for the transgressors.
Hebrews 10:4 For *it is* not possible that the blood of bulls and of goats should take away sins.	See Matthew 26:28 "Atonement"
Hebrews 10:5-7 Wherefore when he cometh into the world, he saith, Sacrifice and offering thou wouldest not, but a body hast thou prepared me: In burnt offerings and [sacrifices] for sin thou hast had no pleasure. 7 Then said I, Lo, I come (in the volume of the book it is	**Psalms 40:6-8** Sacrifice and offering thou didst not desire; mine ears hast thou opened: burnt offering and sin offering hast thou not required. 7 Then said I, Lo, I come: in the volume of the book *it is* written of me, 8 I delight to do thy will, O my God: yea, thy law *is* within my heart. **Proverbs 15:8** The sacrifice of the wicked *is* an abomination to the LORD: but the prayer of the upright *is* his delight. **Proverbs 21:27** The sacrifice of the wicked *is* abomination: how

written of me,) to do thy will, O God.	much more, *when* he bringeth it with a wicked mind? **Isaiah 1:11** To what purpose *is* the multitude of your sacrifices unto me? saith the LORD: I am full of the burnt offerings of rams, and the fat of fed beasts; and I delight not in the blood of bullocks, or of lambs, or of he goats. **Isaiah 1:13** Bring no more vain oblations; incense is an abomination unto me; the new moons and sabbaths, the calling of assemblies, I cannot away with; *it is* iniquity, even the solemn meeting. **Isaiah 66:3** He that killeth an ox *is as if* he slew a man; he that sacrificeth a lamb, *as if* he cut off a dog's neck; he that offereth an oblation, *as if he offered* swine's blood; he that burneth incense, *as if* he blessed an idol. Yea, they have chosen their own ways, and their soul delighteth in their abominations. **Jeremiah 6:20** To what purpose cometh there to me incense from Sheba, and the sweet cane from a far country? your burnt offerings *are* not acceptable, nor your sacrifices sweet unto me. **Amos 5:21-22** I hate, I despise your feast days, and I will not smell in your solemn assemblies. 22 Though ye offer me burnt offerings and your meat offerings, I will not accept *them*: neither will I regard the peace offerings of your fat beasts.
Hebrews 10:8-9 Above when he said, Sacrifice and offering and burnt offerings and [offering] for sin thou wouldest not, neither hadst pleasure *therein*; which are offered by the law; 9 Then said he, Lo, I come to do thy will, O God. He taketh away the first, that he may establish the second.	**Psalms 40:6-8** Sacrifice and offering thou didst not desire; mine ears hast thou opened: burnt offering and sin offering hast thou not required. Then said I, Lo, I come: in the volume of the book *it is* written of me, I delight to do thy will, O my God: yea, thy law *is* within my heart.
Hebrews 10:10 By the which will we are sanctified through the offering of the **body** of Jesus Christ once *for all*.	**See 1 Thessalonians 5:23** "Body, soul, and spirit" **See Hebrews 12:14** "Holiness"
Hebrews 10:11 And every priest standeth daily ministering and offering oftentimes the same sacrifices, which can never take away sins:	**Exodus 29:38** Now this *is that* which thou shalt offer upon the altar; two lambs of the first year day by day continually.
Hebrews 10:12-13 But this man, after he had offered one sacrifice for sins for ever, sat down on the right hand of God; 13 From henceforth expecting till his enemies be made his footstool.	**Job 19:25** For I know *that* my redeemer liveth, and *that* he shall stand at the latter *day* upon the earth: **Psalms 8:6** Thou madest him to have dominion over the works of thy hands; thou hast put all *things* under his feet: **Psalms 16:8** I have set the LORD always before me: because *he is* at my right hand, I shall not be moved. **Psalms 68:18** Thou hast ascended on high, thou hast led captivity captive: thou hast received gifts for men; yea, *for* the rebellious also, that the LORD God might dwell *among them*. **Psalms 110:1** The LORD said unto my Lord, Sit thou at my right hand, until I make thine enemies thy footstool. **Psalms 110:5** The Lord at thy right hand shall strike through kings in the day of his wrath. **Isaiah 9:6** For unto us a child is born, unto us a son is given: and the government shall be upon his shoulder: and his name shall be

	called Wonderful, Counseller, The mighty God, The everlasting Father, The Prince of Peace.
	Isaiah 60:16 Thou shalt also suck the milk of the Gentiles, and shalt suck the breast of kings: and thou shalt know that I the LORD *am* thy Saviour and thy Redeemer, the mighty One of Jacob.
	Daniel 7:9 I beheld till the thrones were cast down, and the Ancient of days did sit, whose garment *was* white as snow, and the hair of his head like the pure wool: his throne *was like* the fiery flame, *and* his wheels *as* burning fire.
	Zechraiah 3:1 And he shewed me Joshua the high priest standing before the angel of the LORD, and Satan standing at his right hand to resist him.
Hebrews 10:16-17 This *is* the covenant that I will make with them after those days, saith the Lord, I will put my laws into their hearts, and in their minds will I write them; 17 And their sins and iniquities will I remember no more.	**Isaiah 59:20-21** And the Redeemer shall come to Zion, and unto them that turn from transgression in Jacob, saith the LORD. 21 As for me, this [is] my covenant with them, saith the LORD; My spirit that *is* upon thee, and my words which I have put in thy mouth, shall not depart out of thy mouth, nor out of the mouth of thy seed, nor out of the mouth of thy seed's seed, saith the LORD, from henceforth and for ever.

Jeremiah 31:31-33 Behold, the days come, saith the LORD, that **I will make a new covenant with the house of Israel**, and with the house of Judah: 32 Not according to the covenant that I made with their fathers in the day *that* I took them by the hand to bring them out of the land of Egypt; which my covenant they brake, although I was an husband unto them, saith the LORD: 33 But this *shall be* the covenant that I will make with the house of Israel; After those days, saith the LORD, I will put my law in their inward parts, and write it in their hearts; and will be their God, and they shall be my people. 34 And they shall teach no more every man his neighbour, and every man his brother, saying, Know the LORD: for they shall all know me, from the least of them unto the greatest of them, saith the LORD: for I will forgive their iniquity, and I will remember their sin no more.

See Hebrews 12:14 "Holiness" |
| **Hebrews 10:18** Now where remission of these *is, there is* no more offering for sin. | **Exodus 30:10** And Aaron shall make an atonement upon the horns of it once in a year with the blood of the sin offering of atonements: once in the year shall he make atonement upon it throughout your generations: it *is* most holy unto the LORD.

Leiticus 4:3 If the priest that is anointed do sin according to the sin of the people; then let him bring for his sin, which he hath sinned, a young bullock without blemish unto the LORD for a sin offering. |
| **Hebrews 10:19** Having therefore, brethren, **boldness to enter into the holiest by the blood of Jesus,** | **See Matthew 26:28 "Atonement"** |
| **Hebrews 10:22** Let us draw near with a true heart in full assurance of faith, having our hearts sprinkled from an evil conscience, and our bodies washed with pure water. | **Ezekiel 36:25** Then will I sprinkle clean water upon you, and ye shall be clean: from all your filthiness, and from all your idols, will I cleanse you.

See Acts 2:38 "Salvation" |
| **Hebrews 10:25** Not forsaking the assembling of ourselves together, as the manner of some *is;* but exhorting *one another:* and so much the more, as ye | **Nehemiah 10:39** For the children of Israel and the children of Levi shall bring the offering of the corn, of the new wine, and the oil, unto the chambers, where *are* the vessels of the sanctuary, and the priests that minister, and the porters, and the singers: and we will |

see the day approaching.	not forsake the house of our God. **Psalms 133:1** A Song of degrees of David. Behold, how good and how pleasant *it is* for brethren to dwell together in unity!
Hebrews 10:26 For if we sin wilfully after that we have received the knowledge of the truth, there remaineth no more sacrifice for sins,	**Numbers 15:30** But the soul that doeth *ought* presumptuously, *whether he be* born in the land, or a stranger, the same reproacheth the LORD; and that soul shall be cut off from among his people.
Hebrews 10:27 But a certain fearful looking for of judgment and fiery indignation, which shall devour the adversaries.	**Isaiah 26:11** LORD, *when* thy hand is lifted up, they will not see: *but* they shall see, and be ashamed for *their* envy at the people; yea, the fire of thine enemies shall devour them. **Isaiah 64:1** Oh that thou wouldest rend the heavens, that thou wouldest come down, that the mountains might flow down at thy presence,
Hebrews 10:28 He that despised Moses' law died without mercy under two or three witnesses:	**Numbers 35:30** Whoso killeth any person, the murderer shall be put to death by the mouth of witnesses: but one witness shall not testify against any person *to cause him* to die. **Deuteronomy 17:6** At the mouth of two witnesses, or three witnesses, shall he that is worthy of death be put to death; *but* at the mouth of one witness he shall not be put to death. **Deuteronomy 19:15** One witness shall not rise up against a man for any iniquity, or for any sin, in any sin that he sinneth: at the mouth of two witnesses, or at the mouth of three witnesses, shall the matter be established.
Hebrews 10:29 Of how much sorer punishment, suppose ye, shall he be thought worthy, who hath trodden under foot the Son of God, and hath counted the blood of the covenant, wherewith he was sanctified, an unholy thing, and hath done despite unto the Spirit of grace?	See Isaiah 59:20-21 and Jeremiah 31:31-33 See Matthew 26:28 "Atonement"
Hebrews 10:30 For we know him that hath said, Vengeance *belongeth* unto me, I will recompense, saith the Lord. And again, The Lord shall judge his people.	**Deuteronomy 32:35-36** To me *belongeth* vengeance, and recompence; their foot shall slide in *due* time: for the day of their calamity *is* at hand, and the things that shall come upon them make haste. 36 For the LORD shall judge his people, and repent himself for his servants, when he seeth that *their* power is gone, and [there is] none shut up, or left.
Hebrews 10:32 But call to remembrance the former days, in which, after ye were illuminated, ye endured a great fight of afflictions;	**1 Samuel 17:47** And all this assembly shall know that the LORD saveth not with sword and spear: for the battle is the LORD's, and he will give you into our hands. **2 Chronicles 20:17** Ye shall not *need* to fight in this *battle*: set yourselves, stand ye *still*, and see the salvation of the LORD with you, O Judah and Jerusalem: fear not, nor be dismayed; tomorrow go out against them: for the LORD *will be* with you.
Hebrews 10:37-38 For yet a little while, and he that shall come will come, and will not tarry. 38 Now **the just shall live by faith**: but if *any man* draw back, my soul shall have no pleasure in him.	**Isaiah 26:20** Come, my people, enter thou into thy chambers, and shut thy doors about thee: hide thyself as it were for a little moment, until the indignation be overpast. **Habakkuk 2:3-4** For the vision *is* yet for an appointed time, but at the end it shall speak, and not lie: though it tarry, wait for it; because it will surely come, it will not tarry. Behold, his soul *which* is lifted up is not upright in him: but **the just shall live by his faith**. See 1 Thessalonians 5:23 "Body, soul, and spirit"

Hebrews 10:39 But we are not of them who draw back unto perdition; but of them that believe to the saving of the **soul**.	**See 1 Thessalonians 5:23 "Body, soul, and spirit"**
Hebrews 11:2 For by it the **elders** obtained a good report.	**See 1 Peter 5:1 "Elders"**
Hebrews 11:3 Through faith we understand that the worlds were framed by the word of God, so that things which are seen were not made of things which do appear.	**Genesis 1:1** In the beginning God created the heaven and the earth. **Psalms 33:6** By the word of the LORD were the heavens made; and all the host of them by the breath of his mouth.
Hebrews 11:4 By faith Abel offered unto God a more excellent sacrifice than Cain, by which he obtained witness that he was righteous, God testifying of his gifts: and by it he being dead yet speaketh.	**Genesis 4:4** And Abel, he also brought of the firstlings of his flock and of the fat thereof. And the LORD had respect unto Abel and to his offering:
Hebrews 11:5 By faith Enoch was translated that he should not see death; and was not found, because God had translated him: for before his translation he had this testimony, that he pleased God.	**Genesis 5:24** And Enoch walked with God: and he *was* not; for God took him.
Hebrews 11:7 By faith Noah, being warned of God of things not seen as yet, moved with fear, prepared an ark to the saving of his house; by the which he condemned the world, and became heir of the righteousness which is by faith.	**Genesis 6:8** But Noah found grace in the eyes of the LORD. **Genesis 6:14** Make thee an ark of gopher wood; rooms shalt thou make in the ark, and shalt pitch it within and without with pitch. **Genesis 6:22** Thus did Noah; according to all that God commanded him, so did he. **Genesis 8:20-21** And Noah builded an altar unto the LORD; and took of every clean beast, and of every clean fowl, and offered burnt offerings on the altar. 21 And the LORD smelled a sweet savour; and the LORD said in his heart, **I will not again curse the ground any more for man's sake**; for the imagination of man's heart *is* evil from his youth; **neither will I again smite any more every thing living**, as I have done. **Genesis 9:9** And I, behold, **I establish my covenant with you, and with your seed after you**; **Genesis 9:11-13** And **I will establish my covenant with you; neither shall all flesh be cut off any more by the waters of a flood; neither shall there any more be a flood to destroy the earth**. 12 And God said, This *is* the token of the covenant which I make between me and you and every living creature that *is* with you, **for perpetual generations**: 13 **I do set my bow in the cloud, and it shall be for a token of a covenant between me and the earth**. **Genesis 9:16** And the bow shall be in the cloud; and I will look upon it, that I may remember the **everlasting covenant** between God and every living creature of all flesh that is upon the earth.
Hebrews 11:8 By faith Abraham, when he was called to go out into a place which he should after receive for an inheritance, obeyed; and he went out, not knowing whither he went.	**Genesis 12:1-4** Now the LORD had said unto Abram, Get thee out of thy country, and from thy kindred, and from thy father's house, unto a land that I will shew thee: 2 And I will make of thee a great nation, and I will bless thee, and make thy name great; and thou shalt be a blessing: 3 And I will bless them that bless thee, and

	curse him that curseth thee: and in thee shall all families of the earth be blessed. 4 So Abram departed, as the LORD had spoken unto him; and Lot went with him: and Abram *was* seventy and five years old when he departed out of Haran. **Nehemiah 9:7** Thou *art* the LORD the God, who didst choose Abram, and broughtest him forth out of Ur of the Chaldees, and gavest him the name of Abraham;
Hebrews 11:9 By faith he sojourned in the land of promise, as in a strange country, dwelling in tabernacles with Isaac and Jacob, the heirs with him of the same promise:	**Genesis 12:5** And Abram took Sarai his wife, and Lot his brother's son, and all their substance that they had gathered, and the souls that they had gotten in Haran; and they went forth to go into the land of Canaan; and into the land of Canaan they came. **Genesis 13:15** For all the land which thou seest, to thee will I give it, and to thy seed for ever. **Genesis 15:7** And he said unto him, I *am* the LORD that brought thee out of Ur of the Chaldees, **to give thee this land to inherit it**. **Genesis 15:17-18** And it came to pass, that, when the sun went down, and it was dark, behold a smoking furnace, and a burning lamp that passed **between** those pieces. ¹⁸ In the same day **the LORD made a <u>covenant</u> with Abram**, saying, Unto thy seed have I given this land, from the river of Egypt unto the great river, the river Euphrates: **Genesis 27:11-12** And Jacob said to Rebekah his mother, Behold, Esau my brother *is* a hairy man, and I *am* a smooth man: 12 My father peradventure will feel me, and I shall seem to him as a deceiver; and I shall bring a curse upon me, and not a blessing. **Genesis 27:14** And he went, and fetched, and brought *them* to his mother: and his mother made savoury meat, such as his father loved. **Nehemiah 9:8** And foundest his heart faithful before thee, and madest a covenant with him to give the land of the Canaanites, the Hittites, the Amorites, and the Perizzites, and the Jebusites, and the Girgashites, to give *it, I say,* to his seed, and hast performed thy words; for thou *art* righteous:
Hebrews 11:11 Through faith also Sara herself received strength to conceive seed, and was delivered of a child when she was past age, because she judged him faithful who had promised.	**Genesis 15:1-6** After these things the word of the LORD came unto Abram in a vision, saying, Fear not, Abram: I *am* thy shield, *and* thy exceeding great reward. 2 And Abram said, Lord GOD, what wilt thou give me, seeing I go childless, and the steward of my house *is* this Eliezer of Damascus? 3 And Abram said, Behold, to me thou hast given no seed: and, lo, one born in my house is mine heir. 4 And, behold, the word of the LORD *came* unto him, saying, This shall not be thine heir; but **he that shall come forth out of thine own bowels shall be thine heir**. 5 And he brought him forth abroad, and said, Look now toward heaven, and tell the stars, if thou be able to number them: and he said unto him, So shall thy seed be. 6 And he believed in the LORD; and he counted it to him for righteousness. **Genesis 17:19** And God said, Sarah thy wife shall bear thee a son indeed; and thou shalt call his name Isaac: and I will establish my covenant with him for an everlasting covenant, *and* with his seed after him. **Genesis 18:1-33** **Genesis 21:2** For Sarah conceived, and bare Abraham a son in his old age, at the set time of which God had spoken to him.

Hebrews 11:12 Therefore sprang there even of one, and him as good as dead, *so many* as the stars of the sky in multitude, and as the sand which is by the sea shore innumerable.	**Genesis 15:5** And he brought him forth abroad, and said, Look now toward heaven, and tell the stars, if thou be able to number them: and he said unto him, So shall thy seed be. **Genesis 22:17** That in blessing I will bless thee, and in multiplying I will multiply thy seed as the stars of the heaven, and as the sand which *is* upon the sea shore; and thy seed shall possess the gate of his enemies;
Hebrews 11:13 These all died in faith, not having received the promises, but having seen them afar off, and were persuaded of *them,* and embraced *them,* and confessed that they were strangers and pilgrims on the earth.	**Genesis 23:4** I *am* a stranger and a sojourner with you: give me a possession of a buryingplace with you, that I may bury my dead out of my sight. **Genesis 24:7** The LORD God of heaven, which took me from my father's house, and from the land of my kindred, and which spake unto me, and that sware unto me, saying, Unto thy seed will I give this land; he shall send his angel before thee, and thou shalt take a wife unto my son from thence. **Genesis 47:9** And Jacob said unto Pharaoh, The days of the years of my pilgrimage *are* an hundred and thirty years: few and evil have the days of the years of my life been, and have not attained unto the days of the years of the life of my fathers in the days of their pilgrimage. **Genesis 49:30-31** In the cave that *is* in the field of Machpelah, which *is* before Mamre, in the land of Canaan, which Abraham bought with the field of Ephron the Hittite for a possession of a buryingplace. 31 There they buried Abraham and Sarah his wife; there they buried Isaac and Rebekah his wife; and there I buried Leah.
Hebrews 11:14 For they that say such things declare plainly that they seek a country.	**Genesis 15:8** And he said, Lord GOD, whereby shall I know that I shall inherit it?
Hebrews 11:16 But now they desire a better *country,* that is, an heavenly: wherefore God is not ashamed to be called their God: for he hath prepared for them a city.	**Exodus 3:6** Moreover he said, I *am* the God of thy father, the God of Abraham, the God of Isaac, and the God of Jacob. And Moses hid his face; for he was afraid to look upon God.
Hebrews 11:17 By faith Abraham, when he was tried, offered up Isaac: and he that had received the promises offered up his only begotten son,	**Genesis 22:2** And he said, Take now thy son, thine only *son* Isaac, whom thou lovest, and get thee into the land of Moriah; and offer him there for a burnt offering upon one of the mountains which I will tell thee of. **Genesis 22:12** And he said, Lay not thine hand upon the lad, neither do thou any thing unto him: for now I know that thou fearest God, seeing thou hast not withheld thy *son,* thine only son from me.
Hebrews 11:18 Of whom it was said, That in Isaac shall thy seed be called:	**Genesis 21:12** And God said unto Abraham, Let it not be grievous in thy sight because of the lad, and because of thy bondwoman; in all that Sarah hath said unto thee, hearken unto her voice; for in Isaac shall thy seed be called.
Hebrews 11:20 By faith Isaac blessed Jacob and Esau concerning things to come.	**Genesis 27:27-29** And he came near, and kissed him: and he smelled the smell of his raiment, and blessed him, and said, See, the smell of my son *is* as the smell of a field which the LORD hath blessed: 28 Therefore God give thee of the dew of heaven, and the fatness of the earth, and plenty of corn and wine: 29 Let people serve thee, and nations bow down to thee: be lord over thy brethren, and let thy mother's sons bow down to thee: cursed *be*

	every one that curseth thee, and blessed *be* he that blesseth thee.

Genesis 27:30 And it came to pass, as soon as Isaac had made an end of blessing Jacob, and Jacob was yet scarce gone out from the presence of Isaac his father, that Esau his brother came in from his hunting.

Genesis 27:38-40 And Esau said unto his father, Hast thou but one blessing, my father? bless me, *even* me also, O my father. And Esau lifted up his voice, and wept. 39 And Isaac his father answered and said unto him, Behold, thy dwelling shall be the fatness of the earth, and of the dew of heaven from above; 40 And by thy sword shalt thou live, and shalt serve thy brother; and it shall come to pass when thou shalt have the dominion, that thou shalt break his yoke from off thy neck. |
| **Hebrews 11:21** By faith Jacob, when he was a dying, blessed both the sons of Joseph; and worshipped, *leaning* upon the top of his staff. | **Genesis 48:15** And he blessed Joseph, and said, God, before whom my fathers Abraham and Isaac did walk, the God which fed me all my life long unto this day,

Genesis 48:20 And he blessed them that day, saying, In thee shall Israel bless, saying, God make thee as Ephraim and as Manasseh: and he set Ephraim before Manasseh. |
| **Hebrews 11:22** By faith Joseph, when he died, made mention of the departing of the children of Israel; and gave commandment concerning his bones. | **Genesis 50:24-25** And Joseph said unto his brethren, I die: and God will surely visit you, and bring you out of this land unto the land which he sware to Abraham, to Isaac, and to Jacob. 25 And Joseph took an oath of the children of Israel, saying, God will surely visit you, and ye shall carry up my bones from hence.

Exodus 6:4 And I have also established my covenant with them, to give them the land of Canaan, the land of their pilgrimage, wherein they were strangers. |
| **Hebrews 11:23** By faith Moses, when he was born, was hid three months of his parents, because they saw *he was* a proper child; and they were not afraid of the king's commandment. | **Exodus 2:2** And the woman conceived, and bare a son: and when she saw him that he *was a* goodly *child,* she hid him three months. |
| **Hebrews 11:25** Choosing rather to suffer affliction with the people of God, than to enjoy the pleasures of sin for a season; | **Exodus 2:11** And it came to pass in those days, when Moses was grown, that he went out unto his brethren, and looked on their burdens: and he spied an Egyptian smiting an Hebrew, one of his brethren.

Psalms 84:10 For a day in thy courts *is* better than a thousand. I had rather be a doorkeeper in the house of my God, than to dwell in the tents of wickedness. |
| **Hebrews 11:27** By faith he forsook Egypt, not fearing the wrath of the king: for he endured, as seeing him who is invisible. | **Exodus 2:15** Now when Pharaoh heard this thing, he sought to slay Moses. But Moses fled from the face of Pharaoh, and dwelt in the land of Midian: and he sat down by a well. |
| **Hebrews 11:28** Through faith he kept the passover, and the sprinkling of blood, lest he that destroyed the **firstborn** should touch them. | **Exodus 12:11** And thus shall ye eat it; *with* your loins girded, your shoes on your feet, and your staff in your hand; and ye shall eat it in haste: it *is* the LORD'S passover.

Exodus 12:18 In the first *month,* on the fourteenth day of the month at even, ye shall eat unleavened bread, until the one and twentieth day of the month at even.

Exodus 12:21 Then Moses called for all the elders of Israel, and said unto them, Draw out and take you a lamb according to your families, and kill the passover. |

	Exodus 12:28 And the children of Israel went away, and did as the LORD had commanded Moses and Aaron, so did they.
	Psalms 89:26-27 He shall cry unto me, Thou art my father, my God, and the rock of my salvation. 27 Also I will make him my **firstborn**, higher than the kings of the earth.
	Jeremiah 31:9 They shall come with weeping, and with supplications will I lead them: I will cause them to walk by the rivers of waters in a straight way, wherein they shall not stumble: for I am a father to Israel, and **Ephraim is my firstborn**.
	See Matthew 26:28 "Atonement"
Hebrews 11:29 By faith they passed through the Red sea as by dry *land:* which the Egyptians assaying to do were drowned.	**Exodus 14:22** And the children of Israel went into the midst of the sea upon the dry *ground:* and the waters *were* a wall unto them on their right hand, and on their left.
Hebrews 11:30 By faith the walls of Jericho fell down, after they were compassed about seven days.	**Joshua 6:20** So the people shouted when *the priests* blew with the trumpets: and it came to pass, when the people heard the sound of the trumpet, and the people shouted with a great shout, that the wall fell down flat, so that the people went up into the city, every man straight before him, and they took the city.
Hebrews 11:31 By faith the harlot Rahab perished not with them that believed not, when she had received the spies with peace.	**Joshua 2:1** And Joshua the son of Nun sent out of Shittim two men to spy secretly, saying, Go view the land, even Jericho. And they went, and came into an harlot's house, named Rahab, and lodged there. **Joshua 6:17** And the city shall be accursed, *even it,* and all that *are* therein, to the LORD: only Rahab the harlot shall live, she and all that *are* with her in the house, because she hid the messengers that we sent. **Joshua 6:23** And the young men that were spies went in, and brought out Rahab, and her father, and her mother, and her brethren, and all that she had; and they brought out all her kindred, and left them without the camp of Israel.
Hebrews 11:32 And what shall I more say? for the time would fail me to tell of Gedeon, and *of* Barak, and *of* Samson, and *of* Jephthae; *of* David also, and Samuel, and *of* the prophets:	**Judges 7:7** And the LORD said unto **Gideon**, By the three hundred men that lapped will I save you, and deliver the Midianites into thine hand: and let all the *other* people go every man unto his place.
	Judges 4:6 And she sent and called **Barak** the son of Abinoam out of Kedeshnaphtali, and said unto him, Hath not the LORD God of Israel commanded, *saying,* Go and draw toward mount Tabor, and take with thee ten thousand men of the children of Naphtali and of the children of Zebulun?
	Judges 13:5 For, lo, thou shalt conceive, and bear a son; and no razor shall come on his head: for the child shall be a Nazarite unto God from the womb: and he shall begin to deliver Israel out of the hand of the Philistines.
	Judges 13:24 And the woman bare a son, and called his name **Samson**: and the child grew, and the LORD blessed him.
	Judges 11:11 Then **Jephthah** went with the elders of Gilead, and the people made him head and captain over them: and Jephthah uttered all his words before the LORD in Mizpeh.
	Judges 12:7 And **Jephthah** judged Israel six years. Then died Jephthah the Gileadite, and was buried in *one of* the cities of Gilead.

	1 Samuel 3:21 And the LORD appeared again in Shiloh: for the LORD revealed himself to **Samuel** in Shiloh by the word of the LORD.
	1 Samuel 12:20 And **Samuel** said unto the people, Fear not: ye have done all this wickedness: yet turn not aside from following the LORD, but serve the LORD with all your heart;
	1 Samuel 17:45 Then said **David** to the Philistine, Thou comest to me with a sword, and with a spear, and with a shield: but I come to thee in the name of the LORD of hosts, the God of the armies of Israel, whom thou hast defied.
	2 Samuel 2:4 And the men of Judah came, and there they anointed **David** king over the house of Judah. And they told David, saying, *That* the men of Jabeshgilead *were they* that buried Saul.
	2 Samuel 5:3 So all the elders of Israel came to the king to Hebron; and king **David** made a league with them in Hebron before the LORD: and they anointed David king over Israel.
	2 Kings 13:14 Now **Elisha was fallen sick of his sickness whereof he died**. And Joash the king of Israel came down unto him, and wept over his face, and said, O my father, my father, the chariot of Israel, and the horsemen thereof.
	2 Kings 13:20 And **Elisha died**, and they buried him. And the bands of the Moabites invaded the land at the coming in of the year.
	Psalms 89:3-4 I have made a covenant with my chosen, I have sworn unto David my servant, 4 Thy seed will I establish for ever, and build up thy throne to all generations. Selah.
	Isaiah 9:6-7 For unto us a child is born, unto us a son is given: and **the government shall be upon his shoulder**: and his name shall be called Wonderful, Counsellor, The mighty God, The everlasting Father, **The Prince of Peace**. 7 Of the increase **of *his* government and peace *there shall be* no end, upon the throne of David, and upon his kingdom, to order it, and to establish it with judgment and with justice from henceforth even for ever. The zeal of the LORD of hosts will perform this.**
Hebrews 11:33 Who through faith subdued kingdoms, wrought righteousness, obtained promises, stopped the mouths of lions,	**Judges 14:5-6** Then went Samson down, and his father and his mother, to Timnath, and came to the vineyards of Timnath: and, behold, a young lion roared against him. 6 And the Spirit of the LORD came mightily upon him, and he rent him as he would have rent a kid, and *he had* nothing in his hand: but he told not his father or his mother what he had done.
	1 Samuel 17:34-36 And David said unto Saul, Thy servant kept his father's sheep, and there came a lion, and a bear, and took a lamb out of the flock: 35 And I went out after him, and smote him, and delivered *it* out of his mouth: and when he arose against me, I caught *him* by his beard, and smote him, and slew him. 36 Thy servant slew both the lion and the bear: and this uncircumcised Philistine shall be as one of them, seeing he hath defied the armies of the living God.
	1 Samuel 17:47 And all this assembly shall know that the LORD saveth not with sword and spear: for the battle is the LORD's, and he will give you into our hands.
	2 Chronicles 20:17 Ye shall not *need* to fight in this *battle*: set yourselves, stand ye *still*, and see the salvation of the LORD with

	you, O Judah and Jerusalem: fear not, nor be dismayed; tomorrow go out against them: for the LORD *will be* with you. **Daniel 6:23** Then was the king exceeding glad for him, and commanded that they should take Daniel up out of the den. So Daniel was taken up out of the den, and no manner of hurt was found upon him, because he believed in his God. **Hosea 11:12** Ephraim compasseth me about with lies, and the house of Israel with deceit: but Judah yet ruleth with God, and **is faithful with the saints**.
Hebrews 11:34 Quenched the violence of fire, escaped the edge of the sword, out of weakness were made strong, waxed valiant in fight, turned to flight the armies of the aliens.	**2 Kings 6:16-17** And he answered, Fear not: for they that *be* with us *are* more than they that *be* with them. 17 And Elisha prayed, and said, LORD, I pray thee, open his eyes, that he may see. And the LORD opened the eyes of the young man; and he saw: and, behold, the mountain *was* full of horses and chariots of fire round about Elisha. **Daniel 3:27-28** And the princes, governors, and captains, and the king's counsellors, being gathered together, saw these men, upon whose bodies the fire had no power, nor was an hair of their head singed, neither were their coats changed, nor the smell of fire had passed on them. 28 Then Nebuchadnezzar spake, and said, Blessed be the God of Shadrach, Meshach, and Abednego, who hath sent his angel, and delivered his servants that trusted in him, and have changed the king's word, and yielded their bodies, that they might not serve nor worship any god, except their own God.
Hebrews 11:35 Women received their dead raised to life again: and others were tortured, not accepting deliverance; that they might obtain a better resurrection:	**1 Kings 17:23** And Elijah took the child, and brought him down out of the chamber into the house, and delivered him unto his mother: and Elijah said, See, thy son liveth. **2 Kings 4:34** And he went up, and lay upon the child, and put his mouth upon his mouth, and his eyes upon his eyes, and his hands upon his hands: and he stretched himself upon the child; and the flesh of the child waxed warm.
Hebrews 11:36 And others had trial of *cruel* mockings and scourgings, yea, moreover of bonds and imprisonment:	**Jeremiah 20:2** Then Pashur smote Jeremiah the prophet, and put him in the stocks that *were* in the high gate of Benjamin, which *was* by the house of the LORD.
Hebrews 12:2 Looking unto Jesus the author and finisher of *our* faith; who for the joy that was set before him endured the cross, despising the shame, and is set down at the right hand of the throne of God.	**Job 19:25** For I know *that* my redeemer liveth, and *that* he shall stand at the latter *day* upon the earth: **Psalms 8:6** Thou madest him to have dominion over the works of thy hands; thou hast put all *things* under his feet: **Psalms 16:8** I have set the LORD always before me: because *he is* at my right hand, I shall not be moved. **Psalms 68:18** Thou hast ascended on high, thou hast led captivity captive: thou hast received gifts for men; yea, *for* the rebellious also, that the LORD God might dwell *among them*. **Psalms 110:1** The LORD said unto my Lord, Sit thou at my right hand, until I make thine enemies thy footstool. **Psalms 110:5** The Lord at thy right hand shall strike through kings in the day of his wrath. **Isaiah 9:6** For unto us a child is born, unto us a son is given: and the government shall be upon his shoulder: and his name shall be called Wonderful, Counsellor, The mighty God, The everlasting Father, The Prince of Peace.

	Isaiah 60:16 Thou shalt also suck the milk of the Gentiles, and shalt suck the breast of kings: and thou shalt know that I the LORD *am* thy Saviour and thy Redeemer, the mighty One of Jacob. **Daniel 7:9** I beheld till the thrones were cast down, and the Ancient of days did sit, whose garment *was* white as snow, and the hair of his head like the pure wool: his throne *was like* the fiery flame, *and* his wheels *as* burning fire. **Zechraiah 3:1** And he shewed me Joshua the high priest standing before the angel of the LORD, and Satan standing at his right hand to resist him.
Hebrews 12:5-6 And ye have forgotten the exhortation which speaketh unto you as unto children, My son, despise not thou the chastening of the Lord, nor faint when thou art rebuked of him: 6 For whom the Lord loveth he chasteneth, and scourgeth every son whom he receiveth.	**Proverbs 3:11-12** My son, despise not the chastening of the LORD; neither be weary of his correction: For whom the LORD loveth he correcteth; even as a father the son [in whom] he delighteth.
Hebrews 12:9 Furthermore we have had fathers of our flesh which corrected *us*, and we gave *them* reverence: shall we not much rather be in subjection unto the **Father of spirits**, and live?	**Numbers 16:22** And they fell upon their faces, and said, O God, the God of the spirits of all flesh, shall one man sin, and wilt thou be wroth with all the congregation? **Numbers 27:16** Let the LORD, the **God of the spirits of all flesh**, set a man over the congregation, **Job 34:14** If he set his heart upon man, *if* he gather unto himself his spirit and his breath; **Psalm 100:3** Know ye that the LORD he *is* God: *it is* **he** *that* **hath made us**, and not we ourselves; *we are* his people, and the sheep of his pasture. **Ecclesiastes 3:21** Who knoweth the spirit of man that goeth upward, and the spirit of the beast that goeth downward to the earth? **Ecclesiastes 12:7** Then shall the dust return to the earth as it was: and **the spirit shall return unto God who gave it**. **Isaiah 64:8** But now, O LORD, thou *art* our father; we *are* the clay, and thou our potter; and we all *are* the work of thy hand. **Zechariah 12:1** The burden of the word of the LORD for Israel, saith the LORD, which stretcheth forth the heavens, and layeth the foundation of the earth, and **formeth the spirit of man within him**. See 1 Thessalonians 5:23 "Body, soul, and spirit"
Hebrews 12:12 Wherefore lift up the hands which hang down, and the feeble knees;	**Isaiah 35:3** Strengthen ye the weak hands, and confirm the feeble knees.
Hebrews 12:13 And make straight paths for your feet, lest that which is lame be turned out of the way; but let it rather be healed.	**Proverbs 4:26** Ponder the path of thy feet, and let all thy ways be established.
Hebrews 12:14 Follow **peace** with all *men*, and **holiness**, without which no man shall see the Lord:	.**Isaiah 26:3** Thou wilt keep *him* in perfect **peace**, *whose* mind *is* stayed *on thee:* because he trusteth in thee. **Exodus 22:31** And ye shall be **holy** men unto me: neither shall ye eat *any* flesh *that is* torn of beasts in the field; ye shall cast it to the

	dogs.
	Leviticus 11:44-45 For I *am* the LORD your God: ye shall therefore sanctify yourselves, and ye shall be holy; for I *am* holy: neither shall ye defile yourselves with any manner of creeping thing that creepeth upon the earth. For I *am* the LORD that bringeth you up out of the land of Egypt, to be your God: ye shall therefore be holy, for I *am* holy.
	Leviticus 15:31 Thus shall ye separate the children of Israel from their uncleanness; that they die not in their uncleanness, when they defile my tabernacle that *is* among them.
	Leviticus 19:2 Speak unto all the congregation of the children of Israel, and say unto them, Ye shall be holy: for I the LORD your God *am* holy
	Leviticus 20:7 Sanctify yourselves therefore, and be ye **holy**: for I *am* the LORD your God.
	Leviticus 20:26 And ye shall be holy unto me: for I the LORD *am* holy, and have severed you from *other* people, that ye should be mine
	Psalms 51:11 Cast me not away from thy presence; and take not thy **holy** spirit from me.
	Psalms 99:5 Exalt ye the LORD our God, and worship at his footstool; for **he is holy**.
	Psalms 99:9 Exalt the LORD our God, and worship at his holy hill; for the LORD our God *is* **holy**.
	Psalms 145:17 The LORD *is* righteous in all his ways, and **holy** in all his works.
	Proverbs 9:10 The fear of the LORD *is* the beginning of wisdom: and the knowledge of the **holy** *is* understanding.
	Isaiah 6:3 And one cried unto another, and said, **Holy, holy, holy**, *is* the LORD of hosts: the whole earth *is* full of his glory.
	Isaiah 62:12 And they shall call them, The **holy** people, The redeemed of the LORD: and thou shalt be called, Sought out, A city not forsaken.
	Ezekiah 36:38 As the **holy** flock, as the flock of Jerusalem in her solemn feasts; so shall the waste cities be filled with flocks of men: and they shall know that I *am* the LORD.
	Daniel 8:24 And his power shall be mighty, but not by his own power: and he shall destroy wonderfully, and shall prosper, and practise, and shall destroy the mighty and the **holy** people.
	Daniel 12:7 And I heard the man clothed in linen, which *was* upon the waters of the river, when he held up his right hand and his left hand unto heaven, and sware by him that liveth for ever that *it shall be* for a time, times, and an half; and when he shall have accomplished to scatter the power of the **holy** people, all these *things* shall be finished.
Hebrews 12:15 Looking diligently lest any man fail of the grace of God; lest any root of bitterness springing up trouble *you,* and thereby many be defiled;	**Deuteronomy 29:18** Lest there should be among you man, or woman, or family, or tribe, whose heart turneth away this day from the LORD our God, to go *and* serve the gods of these nations; lest there should be among you a root that beareth gall and wormwood;
Hebrews 12:16 Lest there *be* any	**Genesis 25:31** And Jacob said, Sell me this day thy birthright.

fornicator, or profane person, as Esau, who for one morsel of meat sold his birthright.	**Genesis 25:33** And Jacob said, Swear to me this day; and he sware unto him: and he sold his birthright unto Jacob.
Hebrews 12:17 For ye know how that afterward, when he would have inherited the blessing, he was rejected: for he found no place of repentance, though he sought it carefully with tears.	**Genesis 27:38** And Esau said unto his father, Hast thou but one blessing, my father? bless me, *even* me also, O my father. And Esau lifted up his voice, and wept.
Hebrews 12:18 For ye are not come unto the mount that might be touched, and that burned with fire, nor unto blackness, and darkness, and tempest,	**Exodus 19:16-17** And it came to pass on the third day in the morning, that there were thunders and lightnings, and a thick cloud upon the mount, and the voice of the trumpet exceeding loud; so that all the people that *was* in the camp trembled. 17 And Moses brought forth the people out of the camp to meet with God; and they stood at the nether part of the mount. **Exodus 20:21** And the people stood afar off, and Moses drew near unto the thick darkness where God *was*. **Deuteronomy 4:10-11** *Specially* the day that thou stoodest before the LORD thy God in Horeb, when the LORD said unto me, Gather me the people together, and I will make them hear my words, that they may learn to fear me all the days that they shall live upon the earth, and *that* they may teach their children. 11 And ye came near and stood under the mountain; and the mountain burned with fire unto the midst of heaven, with darkness, clouds, and thick darkness.
Hebrews 12:19 And the sound of a trumpet, and the voice of words; which *voice* they that heard intreated that the word should not be spoken to them any more:	**Exodus 20:19** And they said unto Moses, Speak thou with us, and we will hear: but let not God speak with us, lest we die. **Deuteronomy 5:25** Now therefore why should we die? for this great fire will consume us: if we hear the voice of the LORD our God any more, then we shall die. **Deuteronomy 18:16** According to all that thou desiredst of the LORD thy God in Horeb in the day of the assembly, saying, Let me not hear again the voice of the LORD my God, neither let me see this great fire any more, that I die not.
Hebrews 12:20 (For they could not endure that which was commanded, And if so much as a beast touch the mountain, it shall be stoned, or thrust through with a dart:	**Exodus 19:12-13** And thou shalt set bounds unto the people round about, saying, Take heed to yourselves, *that ye* go *not* up into the mount, or touch the border of it: whosoever toucheth the mount shall be surely put to death: 13 There shall not an hand touch it, but he shall surely be stoned, or shot through; whether [it be] beast or man, it shall not live: when the trumpet soundeth long, they shall come up to the mount.
Hebrews 12:21 And so terrible was the sight, [that] Moses said, I exceedingly fear and quake:)	**Deuteronomy 9:19** For I was afraid of the anger and hot displeasure, wherewith the LORD was wroth against you to destroy you. But the LORD hearkened unto me at that time also.
Hebrews 12:23 To the general assembly and church of the firstborn, which are written in heaven, and to God the Judge of all, and to the spirits of just men made perfect,	**Psalms 89:26-27** He shall cry unto me, Thou art my father, my God, and the rock of my salvation. 27 Also I will make him my **firstborn**, higher than the kings of the earth. **Jeremiah 31:9** They shall come with weeping, and with supplications will I lead them: I will cause them to walk by the rivers of waters in a straight way, wherein they shall not stumble: for I am a father to Israel, and **Ephraim is my firstborn**. **Exodus 32:32-33** Yet now, if thou wilt forgive their sin--; and if

	not, blot me, I pray thee, out of thy **book** which thou hast written. 33 And the LORD said unto Moses, Whosoever hath sinned against me, him will I blot out of my **book**. **Psalms 69:28** Let them be blotted out of the **book of the living**, and not be written with the righteous. **Daniel 7:10** A fiery stream issued and came forth from before him: thousand thousands ministered unto him, and ten thousand times ten thousand stood before him: the judgment was set, and the **books** were opened. **Daniel 12:1** And at that time shall Michael stand up, the great prince which standeth for the children of thy people: and there shall be a time of trouble, such as never was since there was a nation even to that same time: and at that time thy people shall be delivered, every one that shall be found written in the **book**. **See Revelations 3:5** "Book of life"
Hebrews 12:24 And to Jesus the mediator of the **new covenant**, and to the **blood of sprinkling**, that speaketh better things than *that of* Abel.	**Genesis 4:10** And he said, What hast thou done? the voice of thy brother's blood crieth unto me from the ground. **Exodus 12:22** And ye shall take a bunch of hyssop, and dip *it* in the blood that *is* in the bason, and strike the lintel and the two side posts with the blood that *is* in the bason; and none of you shall go out at the door of his house until the morning. **Exodus 24:6-8** And Moses took half of the blood, and put *it* in basons; and half of the blood he sprinkled on the altar. 7 And he took the book of the covenant, and read in the audience of the people: and they said, All that the LORD hath said will we do, and be obedient. 8 And Moses took the blood, and sprinkled *it* on the people, and said, Behold the blood of the covenant, which the LORD hath made with you concerning all these words. **Leviticus 5:9** And he shall sprinkle of the blood of the sin offering upon the side of the altar; and the rest of the blood shall be wrung out at the bottom of the altar: it *is* a sin offering. **Psalm 89:34 My covenant will I not break**, nor alter the thing that is gone out of my lips. **Isaiah 53:5** But he *was* wounded for our transgressions, *he was* bruised for our iniquities: the chastisement of our peace *was* upon him; and with his stripes we are healed. **Jeremiah 31:31-33** Behold, the days come, saith the LORD, that **I will make a new covenant with the house of Israel**, and with the house of Judah: 32 Not according to the covenant that I made with their fathers in the day *that* I took them by the hand to bring them out of the land of Egypt; which my covenant they brake, although I was an husband unto them, saith the LORD: 33 But this *shall be* the covenant that I will make with the house of Israel; After those days, saith the LORD, I will put my law in their inward parts, and write it in their hearts; and will be their God, and they shall be my people. 34 And they shall teach no more every man his neighbour, and every man his brother, saying, Know the LORD: for they shall all know me, from the least of them unto the greatest of them, saith the LORD: for I will forgive their iniquity, and I will remember their sin no more. **See Hebrews 8:8** "New Covenant" **See Matthew 26:28** "Atonement"

	Daniel 9:24 Seventy weeks are determined upon thy people and upon thy holy city, to finish the transgression, and to make an end of sins, and **to make reconciliation for iniquity**, and to bring in everlasting righteousness, and to seal up the vision and prophecy, and to anoint the most Holy.
Hebrews 12:26 Whose voice then shook the earth: but now he hath promised, saying, Yet once more I shake not the earth only, but also heaven.	**Haggai 2:6** For thus saith the LORD of hosts; Yet once, it *is* a little while, and I will shake the heavens, and the earth, and the sea, and the dry *land*;
Hebrews 12:29 For our God *is* a consuming fire.	**Numbers 31:23** Every thing that may abide the fire, **ye shall make** *it* **go through the fire, and** <u>it shall be clean</u>: nevertheless it shall be purified with the water of separation: and all that abideth not the fire ye shall make go through the water. **Deuteronomy 4:24** For the LORD thy God *is* a consuming fire, *even* a jealous God. **See John 3:5 and Acts 2:38 Fire Baptism**
Hebrews 13:2 Be not forgetful to entertain strangers: for thereby some have entertained **angels** unawares.	**Genesis 3:24** So he drove out the man; and he placed at the east of the garden of Eden Cherubims, and a flaming sword which turned every way, to keep the way of the tree of life. **Genesis 6:1-4** And it came to pass, when men began to multiply on the face of the earth, and daughters were born unto them, 2 That the sons of God saw the daughters of men that they *were* fair; and they took them wives of all which they chose. 3 And the LORD said, My spirit shall not always strive with man, for that he also *is* flesh: yet his days shall be an hundred and twenty years. 4 There were giants in the earth in those days; and also after that, when the sons of God came in unto the daughters of men, and they bare *children* to them, the same *became* mighty men which *were* of old, men of renown. **Genesis 18:2** And he lift up his eyes and looked, and, lo, three men stood by him: and when he saw *them,* he ran to meet them from the tent door, and bowed himself toward the ground, **Genesis 19:1** And there came two **angels** to Sodom at even; and Lot sat in the gate of Sodom: and Lot seeing *them* rose up to meet them; and he bowed himself with his face toward the ground; **Genesis 19:3** And he pressed upon them greatly; and they turned in unto him, and entered into his house; and he made them a feast, and did bake unleavened bread, and they did eat. **Exodus 23:13** And in all *things* that I have said unto you be circumspect: and make no mention of the name of other gods, neither let it be heard out of thy mouth. **Leviticus 19:31** Regad not them that have **familiar spirits**, neither seek after wizards, to be defiled by them: I *am* the LORD your God. **Leviticus 20:6** And the soul that turneth after such as have **familiar spirits**, and after wizards, to go a whoring after them, I will even set my face against that soul, and will cut him off from among his people. **Numbers 5:14** And the **spirit of jealousy** come upon him, and he be jealous of his wife, and she be defiled: or if the **spirit of jealousy** come upon him, and he be jealous of his wife, and she be not defiled:

Numbers 5:30 Or when the **spirit of jealousy** cometh upon him, and he be jealous over his wife, and shall set the woman before the LORD, and the priest shall execute upon her all this law.

Deuteronomy 32:17 They sacrificed unto devils, not to God; to gods whom they knew not, to new *gods that* came newly up, whom your fathers feared not.

1 Samuel 16:14 But the Spirit of the LORD departed from Saul and an **evil spirit** from the LORD troubled him.

1 Samuel 16:23 And it came to pass, when the *evil* **spirit** from God was upon Saul, that David took an harp, and played with his hand: so Saul was refreshed, and was well, and the **evil spirit** departed from him.

1 Samuel 28:3 Now Samuel was dead, and all Israel had lamented him, and buried him in Ramah, even in his own city. And Saul had put away those that had **familiar spirits**, and the wizards, out of the land.

2 Chronicles 18:20-21 Then there came out a **spirit**, and stood before the LORD, and said, I will entice him. And the LORD said unto him, Wherewith? 21 And he said, I will go out, and be a **lying spirit** in the mouth of all his prophets. And *the LORD* said, Thou shalt entice *him,* and thou shalt also prevail: go out, and do *even* so.

Judges 1:6 And the angels which **kept not their first estate**, but left their own habitation, he hath reserved in everlasting chains under darkness unto the judgment of the great day.

Psalms 78:25 Man did eat **angels'** food: he sent them meat to the full.

Psalms 78:49 He cast upon them the fierceness of his anger, wrath, and indignation, and trouble, **by sending evil angels** *among them.*

Psalms 91:11-12 For he shall give his **angels** charge over thee, to keep thee in all thy ways. 12 They shall bear thee up in their hands, lest thou dash thy foot against a stone.

Psalms 103:20 Bless the LORD, ye his **angels**, that excel in strength, that do his commandments, hearkening unto the voice of his word.

Isaiah 4:4 When the Lord shall have washed away the filth of the daughters of Zion, and shall have purged the blood of Jerusalem from the midst thereof by the **spirit of judgment**, and by the spirit of burning.

Isaiah 6:2 Above it stood the **seraphims**: each one had six wings; with twain he covered his face, and with twain he covered his feet, and with twain he did fly.

Isaiah 19:3 And the **spirit of Egypt** shall fail in the midst thereof; and I will destroy the counsel thereof: and they shall seek to the idols, and to the charmers, and to them that have **familiar spirits**, and to the wizards.

Isaiah 19:14 The LORD hath mingled a **perverse spirit** in the midst thereof: and they have caused Egypt to err in every work thereof, as a drunken *man* staggereth in his vomit.

Isaiah 28:6 And for a spirit of judgment to him that sitteth in judgment, and for strength to them that turn the battle to the gate.

Ezekiel 10:20-21 This *is* the living creature that I saw under the God of Israel by the river of Chebar; and I knew that they *were* the

	cherubims. 21 Every one had four faces apiece, and every one four wings; and the likeness of the hands of a man *was* under their wings. **Ezekiel 28:14** Thou *art* the **anointed cherub** that covereth; and I have set thee *so*: thou wast upon the holy mountain of God; thou hast walked up and down in the midst of the stones of fire. **Daniel 10:13** But the prince of the kingdom of Persia withstood me one and twenty days: but, lo, Michael, one of the chief princes, came to help me; and I remained there with the kings of Persia. **Hosea 4:12** My people ask counsel at their stocks, and their staff declareth unto them: for the **spirit of whoredoms** hath caused *them* to err, and they have gone a whoring from under their God. **Hosea 5:4** They will not frame their doings to turn unto their God: for the **spirit of whoredoms** *is* in the midst of them, and they have not known the LORD.
Hebrews 13:4 Marriage *is* honourable in all, and the **bed undefiled**: but whoremongers and **adulterers** God will judge.	**Genesis 1:22** And God blessed them, saying, **Be fruitful, and multiply**, and fill the waters in the seas, and let fowl multiply in the earth. **Genesis 1:28** And God blessed them, and God said unto them, **Be fruitful, and multiply, and replenish the earth**, and subdue it: and have dominion over the fish of the sea, and over the fowl of the air, and over every living thing that moveth upon the earth. **Deuteronomy 8:1** All the commandments which I command thee this day shall ye observe to do, that ye may live, and **multiply**, and go in and possess the land which the LORD sware unto your fathers. **Exodus 20:14** Thou shalt not commit **adultery**. **Leviticus 20:10** And the man that committeth **adultery** with *another* man's wife, *even he* that committeth **adultery** with his neighbour's wife, the **adulterer** and the **adulteress** shall surely be put to death. **Deuteronomy 5:18** Neither shalt thou commit **adultery**. **Proverbs 6:32** *But* whoso committeth **adultery** with a woman lacketh understanding: he *that* doeth it destroyeth his own soul. See Matthew 5:27 "Adultery"
Hebrews 13:5 *Let your* conversation *be* without covetousness; *and be* content with such things as ye have: for he hath said, I will never leave thee, nor forsake thee.	**Deuteronomy 16:19** Thou shalt not wrest judgment; thou shalt not respect persons, neither take a gift: for a gift doth blind the eyes of the wise, and pervert the words of the righteous. **Deuteronomy 31:6** Be strong and of a good courage, fear not, nor be afraid of them: for the LORD thy God, he *it is* that doth go with thee; he will not fail thee, nor forsake thee. **Deuteronomy 31:8** And the LORD, he *it is* that doth go before thee; he will be with thee, he will not fail thee, neither forsake thee: fear not, neither be dismayed. **1 Chronicles 28:20** And David said to Solomon his son, Be strong and of good courage, and do *it*: fear not, nor be dismayed: for the LORD God, *even* my God, *will be* with thee; he will not fail thee, nor forsake thee, until thou hast finished all the work for the service of the house of the LORD.

	Proverbs 15:16 Better *is* little with the fear of the LORD than great treasure and trouble therewith.
	Joshua 1:5 There shall not any man be able to stand before thee all the days of thy life: as I was with Moses, *so* I will be with thee: I will not fail thee, nor forsake thee.
	See Matthew 6:24 "Wealth"
Hebrews 13:6 So that we may boldly say, The Lord *is* my helper, and I will not fear what man shall do unto me.	**Psalms 27:1** The LORD *is* my light and my salvation; whom shall I fear? the LORD [is] the strength of my life; of whom shall I be afraid?
	Psalms 56:4 In God I will praise his word, in God I have put my trust; I will not fear what flesh can do unto me.
	Psalms 118:6 The LORD *is* on my side; I will not fear: what can man do unto me?
Hebrews 13:7 Remember them which have the **rule** over you, who have spoken unto you the word of God: whose faith follow, considering the end of *their* conversation.	**Genesis 18:19** For I know him, that **he will command his children and his household** after him, and they shall keep the way of the LORD, to do justice and judgment; that the LORD may bring upon Abraham that which he hath spoken of him.
	Exodus 7:2 Thou shalt speak all that I command thee: and Aaron thy brother shall speak unto Pharaoh, that he send the children of Israel out of his land.
	Exodus 27:20 And thou shalt **command** the children of Israel, that they bring thee pure oil olive beaten for the light, to cause the lamp to burn always.
	Leviticus 13:53-54 And if the priest shall look, and, behold, the plague be not spread in the garment, either in the warp, or in the woof, or in any thing of skin; 54 Then the **priest shall command** that they wash the thing wherein the plague is, and he shall shut it up seven days more:
	Leviticus 14:4 Then shall **the priest command** to take for him that is to be cleansed two birds alive and clean, and cedar wood, and scarlet, and hyssop:
	Deuteronomy 32:46 And he said unto them, Set your hearts unto all the words which I testify among you this day, which **ye shall command your children** to observe to do, all the words of this law.
	Proverbs 29:2 When the righteous are in authority, the people rejoice: but when the wicked beareth rule, the people mourn.
	Joshua 1:13 Remember the word which Moses the servant of the Lord commanded you, saying, The Lord your God hath given you rest, and hath given you this land.
	Joshua 4:15-17 And the Lord spake unto Joshua, saying, 16 **Command** the priests that bear the ark of the testimony, that they come up out of Jordan. 17 **Joshua therefore commanded the priests**, saying, Come ye up out of Jordan.
	Joshua 11:15 As the LORD **commanded** Moses his servant, so did Moses **command** Joshua, and so did Joshua; he left nothing undone of all that the LORD **commanded** Moses. 16 So Joshua took all that land, the hills, and all the south country, and all the land of Goshen, and the valley, and the plain, and the mountain of Israel, and the valley of the same;
	Jeremiah 1:7 But the LORD said unto me, Say not, I am a child:

	for thou shalt go to all that I shall send thee, and whatsoever I command thee thou shalt speak. **Jeremiah 1:17** Thou therefore gird up thy loins, and arise, and speak unto them all that I command thee: be not dismayed at their faces, lest I confound thee before them.
Hebrews 13:8 Jesus Christ the same yesterday, and today, and forever	**Psalm 33:11** The counsel of the LORD standeth forever, the thoughts of his heart to all generations. **Psalm 102:27** But thou *art* the same, and thy years shall have no end. **Malachi 3:6** For I *am* the LORD, **I change not**; therefore ye sons of Jacob are not consumed. **See 1 Peter 2:24 "Healing"**
Hebrews 13:9 Be not carried about with divers and strange doctrines. For *it is* a good thing that the heart be established with grace; not with meats, which have not profited them that have been occupied therein.	**Jeremiah 14:14** Then the LORD said unto me, The prophets prophesy lies in my name: I sent them not, neither have I commanded them, neither spake unto them: they prophesy unto you a false vision and divination, and a thing of nought, and the deceit of their heart. **Jeremiah 23:21** I have not sent these prophets, yet they ran: I have not spoken to them, yet they prophesied. **Jeremiah 29:8** For thus saith the LORD of hosts, the God of Israel; Let not your prophets and your diviners, that *be* in the midst of you, deceive you, neither hearken to your dreams which ye cause to be dreamed.
Hebrews 13:11 For the bodies of those beasts, whose blood is brought into the sanctuary by the high priest for sin, are burned without the camp.	**Exodus 29:14** But the flesh of the bullock, and his skin, and his dung, shalt thou burn with fire without the camp: it *is* a sin offering. **Leviticus 4:12** Even the whole bullock shall he carry forth without the camp unto a clean place, where the ashes are poured out, and burn him on the wood with fire: where the ashes are poured out shall he be burnt. **Leviticus 4:21** And he shall carry forth the bullock without the camp, and burn him as he burned the first bullock: it *is* a sin offering for the congregation. **Leviticus 6:30** And no sin offering, whereof *any* of the blood is brought into the tabernacle of the congregation to reconcile *withal* in the holy *place*, shall be eaten: it shall be burnt in the fire. **Leviticus 16:27** And the bullock *for* the sin offering, and the goat *for* the sin offering, whose blood was brought in to make atonement in the holy *place,* shall *one* carry forth without the camp; and they shall burn in the fire their skins, and their flesh, and their dung. **Numbers 19:3** And ye shall give her unto Eleazar the priest, that he may bring her forth without the camp, and *one* shall slay her before his face: **See Matthew 26:28 "Atonement"**
Hebrews 13:12 Wherefore Jesus also, that he might sanctify the people with his own blood, suffered without the gate.	**Exodus 29:14** But the flesh of the bullock, and his skin, and his dung, shalt thou burn with fire without the camp: it *is* a sin offering. **Leviticus 4:12** Even the whole bullock shall he carry forth without the camp unto a clean place, where the ashes are poured out, and

	burn him on the wood with fire: where the ashes are poured out shall he be burnt.
Leviticus 5:10 And he shall offer the second *for* a burnt offering, according to the manner: and the priest shall make an atonement for him for his sin which he hath sinned, and it shall be forgiven him.
Leviticus 6:7 And the priest shall make an atonement for him before the LORD: and it shall be forgiven him for any thing of all that he hath done in trespassing therein.
Hebrews 13:14 For here have we no continuing city, but we seek one to come.	**Micah 2:10** Arise ye, and depart; for this *is* not *your* rest: because it is polluted, it shall destroy *you,* even with a sore destruction.
Hebrews 13:15 By him therefore let us offer the **sacrifice of praise** to God continually, that is, the fruit of *our* lips giving thanks to his name.	**Hosea 14:2** Take with you words, and turn to the LORD: say unto him, Take away all iniquity, and receive *us* graciously: so will we render the calves of our lips.
Jeremiah 33:11 The voice of joy, and the voice of gladness, the voice of the bridegroom, and the voice of the bride, the voice of them that shall say, Praise the LORD of hosts: for the LORD is good; for his mercy *endureth* for ever: *and* of them that shall bring the **sacrifice of praise** into the house of the LORD. For I will cause to return the captivity of the land, as at the first, saith the LORD.
Hebrews 13:17 Obey them that have the rule over you, and submit yourselves: for they watch for your souls, as they that must give account, that they may do it with joy, and not with grief: for that *is* unprofitable for you.	**Ezekiel 3:18** When I say unto the wicked, Thou shalt surely die; and thou givest him not warning, nor speakest to warn the wicked from his wicked way, to save his life; the same wicked *man* shall die in his iniquity; but his blood will I require at thine hand.
Ezekiel 33:8 When I say unto the wicked, O wicked *man,* thou shalt surely die; if thou dost not speak to warn the wicked from his way, that wicked *man* shall die in his iniquity; but his blood will I require at thine hand.
Hebrews 13:20 Now the God of peace, that brought again from the dead our Lord Jesus, that great **shepherd** of the sheep, through the blood of the everlasting covenant,	**Genesis 9:16** And the bow shall be in the cloud; and I will look upon it, that I may remember the everlasting covenant between God and every living creature of all flesh that is upon the earth.
Isaiah 30:9 That this *is* a rebellious people, lying children, children *that* will not hear the law of the LORD:
Isaiah 40:11 He shall feed his flock like a shepherd: he shall gather the lambs with his arm, and carry *them* in his bosom, *and* shall gently lead those that are with young.
Isaiah 55:3 Incline your ear, and come unto me: hear, and your soul shall live; and I will make an everlasting covenant with you, *even* the sure mercies of David.
See Isaiah 59:20-21 and Jeremiah 31:31-33
See Matthew 26:28 "Atonement"
Psalms 23:1 { A Psalm of David. } The LORD *is* my **shepherd**; I shall not want.
Ezekiel 34:23 And I will set up one shepherd over them, and he shall feed them, *even* my servant David; he shall feed them, and he shall be their **shepherd**.
See 1 Peter 5:4 "Shepherd"
Hebrews 13:21 Make you perfect in	**Isaiah 42:8** I *am* the LORD: that *is* my name: and my **glory** will I

every good work to do his will, working in you that which is wellpleasing in his sight, through Jesus Christ; to whom *be* **glory** for ever and ever. Amen.	not give to another, neither my praise to graven images.
James 1:2-4 My brethren, count it all **joy** when ye fall into divers temptations; 3 Knowing *this,* that the trying of your faith worketh patience. 4 But let patience have *her* perfect work, that ye may be perfect and entire, wanting nothing.	**Isaiah 12:3-4** Therefore with **joy** shall ye draw water out of the wells of salvation. 4 And in that day shall ye say, Praise the LORD, call upon his name, declare his doings among the people, make mention that his name is exalted.
James 1:5 If any of you lack wisdom, let him ask of God, that giveth to all *men* liberally, and upbraideth not; and it shall be given him.	**Genesis 3:5** For God doth know that in the day ye eat thereof, then your eyes shall be opened, and ye shall be as gods, knowing good and evil. **1 Kings 3:9** Give therefore thy servant an understanding heart to judge thy people, that I may discern between good and bad: for who is able to judge this thy so great a people? **1 Kings 3:12** Behold, I have done according to thy words: lo, I have given thee a wise and an understanding heart; so that there was none like thee before thee, neither after thee shall any arise like unto thee. **2 Chronicles 16:12-13** And Asa in the thirty and ninth year of his reign was diseased in his feet, until his disease [was] exceeding *great*: yet in his disease <u>**he sought not to the LORD**</u>, <u>but to the physicians</u>. 13 And <u>Asa slept with his fathers</u>, and died in the one and fortieth year of his reign. **Proverbs 2:3** Yea, if thou criest after knowledge, *and* liftest up thy voice for understanding; **Proverbs 2:6** For the LORD giveth wisdom: out of his mouth *cometh* knowledge and understanding. **Jeremiah 29:12** Then shall ye call upon me, and ye shall go and pray unto me, and I will hearken unto you.
James 1:10-11 But the rich, in that he is made low: because as the flower of the grass he shall pass away. 11 For the sun is no sooner risen with a burning heat, but it withereth the grass, and the flower thereof falleth, and the grace of the fashion of it perisheth: so also shall the rich man fade away in his ways.	**Job 14:2** He cometh forth like a flower, and is cut down: he fleeth also as a shadow, and continueth not. **Isaiah 40:6-8** The voice said, Cry. And he said, What shall I cry? All flesh is grass, and all the goodliness thereof is as the flower of the field: 7 The grass withereth, the flower fadeth: because the spirit of the LORD bloweth upon it: surely the people is grass. 8 The grass withereth, the flower fadeth: but the word of our God shall stand for ever.
James 1:14-15 But every man is tempted, when he is drawn away of his own lust, and enticed. 15 Then when lust hath conceived, it bringeth forth sin: and sin, when it is finished, bringeth forth death.	**Genesis 3:4** And the serpent said unto the woman, Ye shall not surely die: **Genesis 3:6** And when the woman saw that the tree *was* good for food, and that it *was* pleasant to the eyes, and a tree to be desired to make *one* wise, she took of the fruit thereof, and did eat, and gave also unto her husband with her; and he did eat. **Joshua 7:21** When I saw among the spoils a goodly Babylonish garment, and two hundred shekels of silver, and a wedge of gold of fifty shekels weight, then **I coveted them**, and took them; and, behold, they *are* hid in the earth in the midst of my tent, and the silver under it.

	2 Samuel 11:2 And it came to pass in an eveningtide, that David arose from off his bed, and walked upon the roof of the king's house: and from the roof **he saw** a woman washing herself; and the woman *was* very beautiful to look upon.
James 1:17 Every good gift and every perfect gift is from above, and cometh down from the Father of lights, with whom is no variableness, neither shadow of turning.	**Psalm 33:11** The counsel of the LORD standeth forever, the thoughts of his heart to all generations. **Psalm 102:27** But thou *art* the same, and thy years shall have no end. **Malachi 3:6** For I *am* the LORD, I change not; therefore ye sons of Jacob are not consumed.
James 1:18 Of his own will begat he us with the word of truth, that we should be a kind of firstfruits of his creatures.	**See Romans 8:23 "Firstfruits"**
James 1:19 Wherefore, my beloved brethren, let every man be swift to hear, slow to speak, slow to wrath:	**Proverbs 17:27** He that hath knowledge spareth his words: *and* a man of understanding is of an excellent spirit. **Ecclesiastes 5:2** Be not rash with thy mouth, and let not thine heart be hasty to utter *any* thing before God: for God *is* in heaven, and thou upon earth: therefore let thy words be few.
James 1:26 If any man among you seem to be religious, and bridleth not his tongue, but deceiveth his own heart, this man's religion *is* vain.	**Psalms 34:13** Keep thy **tongue** from evil, and thy lips from speaking guile. **See James 3:8 "Tongue"**
James 2:1 My brethren, have not the faith of our Lord Jesus Christ, *the Lord* of glory, with respect of persons.	**Leviticus 19:15** Ye shall do no unrighteousness in judgment: thou shalt not respect the person of the poor, nor honour the person of the mighty: *but* in righteousness shalt thou judge thy neighbour. **Deuteronomy 16:19** Thou shalt not wrest judgment; thou shalt not respect persons, neither take a gift: for a gift doth blind the eyes of the wise, and pervert the words of the righteous. **Proverbs 24:23** These *things* also *belong* to the wise. *It is* not good to have respect of persons in judgment.
James 2:5 Hearken, my beloved brethren, Hath not God chosen the poor of this world rich in faith, and heirs of the kingdom which he hath promised to them that love him?	**Exodus 20:6** And shewing mercy unto thousands of them that love me, and keep my commandments. **1 Samuel 2:30** Wherefore the LORD God of Israel saith, I said indeed *that* thy house, and the house of thy father, should walk before me for ever: but now the LORD saith, Be it far from me; for them that honour me I will honour, and they that despise me shall be lightly esteemed. **Proverbs 8:17** I love them that love me; and those that seek me early shall find me.
James 2:8 If ye fulfil the royal law according to the scripture, **Thou shalt love thy neighbour** as thyself, ye do well:	**Leviticus 19:18** Thou shalt not avenge, nor bear any grudge against the children of thy people, but **thou shalt love thy neighbour as thyself**: I *am* the LORD.
James 2:10 For whosoever shall keep the whole law, and yet offend in one *point*, he is guilty of all.	**Deuteronomy 27:26** Cursed *be* he that confirmeth not *all* the words of this law to do them. And all the people shall say, Amen.
James 2:11 For he that said, Do not commit adultery, said also, Do not kill. Now if thou commit no adultery, yet if thou kill, thou art become a transgressor of the law.	**Exodus 20:13-14** Thou shalt not kill. 14 Thou shalt not commit adultery. **Deuteronomy 5:17-18** Thou shalt not kill. 18 Neither shalt thou commit adultery.

	See Matthew 5:27 "Adultery"
James 2:19 Thou believest that there is **one God**; thou doest well: the devils also believe, and tremble.	**Deuteronomy 6:4** Hear, O Israel: The LORD our God *is* one LORD : **1 Kings 8:27** But will God indeed dwell on the earth? behold, the heaven and heaven of heavens cannot contain thee; how much less this house that I have builded? **Nehemiah 9:6** Thou, *even* thou, *art* LORD alone; thou hast made heaven, the heaven of heavens, with all their host, the earth, and all *things* that *are* therein, the seas, and all that *is* therein, and thou preservest them all; and the host of heaven worshippeth thee. **Psalms 86:10** For thou *art* great, and doest wondrous things: thou *art* God alone. **Isaiah 9:6** For unto us a child is born, unto us a son is given: and the government shall be upon his shoulder: and his name shall be called Wonderful, Counselor, The mighty God, The everlasting Father, The Prince of Peace. **Isaiah 43:10-11** Ye *are* my witnesses, saith the LORD, and my servant whom I have chosen: that ye may know and believe me, and understand that I *am* he: before me there was no God formed, neither shall there be after me. 11 I, *even* I, *am* the LORD ; and beside me *there is* no saviour. **Isaiah 44:6** Thus saith the LORD the King of Israel, and his redeemer the LORD of hosts; I *am* the first, and I *am* the last; and beside me *there is* no God. **Isaiah 44:8** Fear ye not, neither be afraid: have not I told thee from that time, and have declared *it*? ye *are* even my witnesses. Is there a God beside me? yea, *there is* no God; I know not *any*. **Isaiah 45:5-6** I am the LORD, and there is none else, **there is no God beside me**: I girded thee, though thou hast not known me: {6} That they may know from the rising of the sun, and from the west, that there is none beside me. I am the LORD, and there is none else. **Isaiah 45:21-22** have not I the LORD? and **there is no God else beside me**; a just God and a Saviour; there is none beside me. 22 Look unto me, and be ye saved, all the ends of the earth: for **I am God, and there is none else**. **Isaiah 54:5** For thy Maker *is* thine husband; the LORD of hosts *is* his name; and thy Redeemer the Holy One of Israel; The God of the whole earth shall he be called. **Malachi 2:10** Have we not all one father? hath not one God created us? why do we deal treacherously every man against his brother, by profaning the covenant of our fathers?
James 2:21 Was not Abraham our father justified by works, when he had offered Isaac his son upon the altar?	**Genesis 22:9-10** And they came to the place which God had told him of; and Abraham built an altar there, and laid the wood in order, and bound Isaac his son, and laid him on the altar upon the wood. 10 And Abraham stretched forth his hand, and took the knife to slay his son.
James 2:23 And the scripture was fulfilled which saith, Abraham believed God, and it was imputed unto him for righteousness: and he was called the Friend of God.	**Genesis 15:6** And he believed in the LORD; and he counted it to him for righteousness. **Isaiah 41:8** But thou, Israel, *art* my servant, Jacob whom I have chosen, the seed of Abraham my friend.

James 2:25 Likewise also was not Rahab the harlot justified by works, when she had received the messengers, and had sent *them* out another way?	**Joshua 2:1** And Joshua the son of Nun sent out of Shittim two men to spy secretly, saying, Go view the land, even Jericho. And they went, and came into an harlot's house, named Rahab, and lodged there. **Joshua 6:17** And the city shall be accursed, *even* it, and all that *are* therein, to the LORD: only Rahab the harlot shall live, she and all that *are* with her in the house, because she hid the messengers that we sent. **Joshua 6:23** And the young men that were spies went in, and brought out Rahab, and her father, and her mother, and her brethren, and all that she had; and they brought out all her kindred, and left them without the camp of Israel. **Psalms 103:12** As far as the east is from the west, *so* far hath he removed our transgressions from us.
James 2:26 For as the **body** without the **spirit** is dead, so faith without works is dead also.	**See 1 Thessalonians 5:23** "Body, soul, and spirit"
James 3:2 For in many things we offend all. If any man offend not in word, the same *is* a perfect man, *and* able also to bridle the whole body.	**Psalms 31:20** Thou shalt hide them in the secret of thy presence from the pride of man: thou shalt keep them secretly in a pavilion from the strife of **tongues**. **Psalms 34:13** Keep thy tongue from evil, and thy lips from speaking guile.
James 3:5 Even so the tongue is a little member, and boasteth great things. Behold, how great a matter a little fire kindleth!	**Psalms 52:2** Thy tongue deviseth mischiefs; like a sharp rasor, working deceitfully. **Psalms 109:2** For the mouth of the wicked and the mouth of the deceitful are opened against me: they have spoken against me with a lying tongue. **Proverbs 12:18** There is that speaketh like the piercings of a sword: but the tongue of the wise *is* health. **Proverbs 12:23** A prudent man concealeth knowledge: but the heart of fools proclaimeth foolishness. **Psalms 15:2-4** He that walketh uprightly, and worketh righteousness, and speaketh the truth in his heart. 3 *He that* backbiteth not with his tongue, nor doeth evil to his neighbour, nor taketh up a reproach against his neighbour. 4 A wholesome tongue *is* a tree of life: but perverseness therein *is* a breach in the spirit. **Proverbs 15:28** The heart of the righteous studieth to answer: but the mouth of the wicked poureth out evil things. **Proverbs 25:23** The north wind driveth away rain: so *doth* an angry countenance a backbiting **tongue**.
James 3:6 And the tongue *is* a fire, a world of iniquity: so is the tongue among our members, that it defileth the whole body, and setteth on fire the course of nature; and it is set on fire of **hell**.	**Job 5:21** Thou shalt be hid from the scourge of the tongue: neither shalt thou be afraid of destruction when it cometh. **See Luke 16:23** "Hell"
James 3:7 For every kind of beasts, and of birds, and of serpents, and of things in the sea, is tamed, and hath been tamed of mankind:	**Genesis 1:28** And God blessed them, and God said unto them, Be fruitful, and multiply, and replenish the earth, and subdue it: and have dominion over the fish of the sea, and over the fowl of the air, and over every living thing that moveth upon the earth.

James 3:8 But the tongue can no man tame; *it is* an unruly evil, full of deadly poison.	**Psalms 10:7** His mouth is full of cursing and deceit and fraud: under his tongue *is* mischief and vanity. **Psalms 12:3-4** The LORD shall cut off all flattering lips, *and* the tongue that speaketh proud things: 4 Who have said, With our tongue will we prevail; our lips *are* our own: who *is* lord over us? **Psalms 19:14** Let the words of my mouth, and the meditation of my heart, be acceptable in thy sight, O LORD, my strength, and my redeemer. **Psalms 34:13** Keep thy tongue from evil, and thy lips from speaking guile. **Psalms 35:28** And my tongue shall speak of thy righteousness *and* of thy praise all the day long. **Psalms 37:30** The mouth of the righteous speaketh wisdom, and his tongue talketh of judgment. **Psalms 39:1** I said, I will take heed to my ways, that I sin not with my tongue: I will keep my mouth with a bridle, while the wicked is before me. **Psalms 50:19** Thou givest thy mouth to evil, and thy tongue frameth deceit. **Psalms 120:2-3** Deliver my soul, O LORD, from lying lips, *and* from a deceitful tongue. What shall be given unto thee? or what shall be done unto thee, thou false tongue? **Psalms 141:3** Set a watch, O LORD, before my mouth; keep the door of my lips. **Proverbs 6:17** A proud look, a lying tongue, and hands that shed innocent blood, **Proverbs 26:28** A lying tongue hateth *those that are* afflicted by it; and a flattering mouth worketh ruin. **Isaiah 6:5** Then said I, Woe *is* me! for I am undone; because I *am* a man of unclean lips, and I dwell in the midst of a people of unclean lips: for mine eyes have seen the King, the LORD of hosts. **Jeremiah 9:5** And they will deceive every one his neighbour, and will not speak the truth: they have taught their tongue to speak lies, *and* weary themselves to commit iniquity.
James 3:9 Therewith bless we God, even the Father; and therewith curse we men, which are made after the similitude of God.	**Deuteronomy 8:10** When thou hast eaten and art full, then **thou shalt bless the LORD thy God** for the good land which he hath given thee. **Genesis 1:26-27** And God said, Let us make man in our image, after our likeness: and let them have dominion over the fish of the sea, and over the fowl of the air, and over the cattle, and over all the earth, and over every creeping thing that creepeth upon the earth. 27 So God created man in his *own* image, in the image of God created he him; male and female created he them. **Genesis 5:2** Male and female created he them; and blessed them, and called their name Adam, in the day when they were created. **Genesis 9:6** Whoso sheddeth man's blood, by man shall his blood be shed: for in the image of God made he man.
James 4:3 Ye ask, and receive not,	**Psalm 66:18** If I regard iniquity in my heart, the Lord will not hear

because ye ask amiss, that ye may consume *it* upon your lusts.	me: **Isaiah 59:1-2** But your iniquities have separated between you and your God, and your sins have hid *his* face from you, that he will not hear.
James 4:4 Ye adulterers and adulteresses, know ye not that the friendship of the world is enmity with God? whosoever therefore will be a friend of the world is the enemy of God.	**Exodus 20:14** Thou shalt not commit adultery. **Leviticus 20:10** And the man that committeth adultery with *another* man's wife, *even he* that committeth adultery with his neighbour's wife, the adulterer and the adulteress shall surely be put to death. **Deuteronomy 5:18** Neither shalt thou commit adultery. **Proverbs 6:32** *But* whoso committeth adultery with a woman lacketh understanding: he *that* doeth it destroyeth his own soul. **See Matthew 5:27 "Adultery"**
James 4:5 Do ye think that the scripture saith in vain, The spirit that dwelleth in us lusteth to envy?	**Numbers 11:29** And Moses said unto him, Enviest thou for my sake? would God that all the LORD's people were prophets, *and* that the LORD would put his spirit upon them!
James 4:6 But he giveth more **grace**. Wherefore he saith, God resisteth the **proud**, but giveth grace unto the **humble**.	**2 Chronicles 7:14** If my people, which are called by my name, shall **humble** themselves, and pray, and seek my face, and turn from their wicked ways; then will I hear from heaven, and will forgive their sin, and will heal their land. **Proverbs 3:34** Surely he scorneth the scorners: but he giveth **grace** unto the lowly. **Proverbs 6:16-19** These six *things* doth the LORD hate: yea, seven *are* an abomination unto him: 17 A **proud look**, a lying tongue, and hands that shed innocent blood, 18 An heart that deviseth wicked imaginations, feet that be swift in running to mischief, 19 A false witness *that* speaketh lies, and he that soweth discord among brethren. **Proverbs 16:18 Pride** *goeth* before destruction, and an haughty spirit before a fall.
James 4:8 Draw nigh to God, and he will draw nigh to you. Cleanse *your* hands, *ye* sinners; and purify *your* hearts, *ye* double minded.	**Isaiah 1:15** And when ye spread forth your hands, I will hide mine eyes from you: yea, when ye make many prayers, I will not hear: your hands are full of blood.
James 4:10 Humble yourselves in the sight of the Lord, and he shall lift you up.	**Job 22:29** When *men* are cast down, then thou shalt say, *There is* lifting up; and he shall save the humble person. **Proverbs 15:33** The fear of the LORD *is* the instruction of wisdom; and before honour *is* humility. **Proverbs 16:18** Pride *goeth* before destruction, and an haughty spirit before a fall. **Proverbs 18:12** Before destruction the heart of man is haughty, and before honour *is* humility. **Proverbs 29:23** A man's pride shall bring him low: but honour shall uphold the humble in spirit.
James 4:11 Speak not evil one of another, brethren. He that speaketh evil of *his* brother, and judgeth his brother, speaketh evil of the law, and judgeth the law: but if thou judge the law, thou art	**Exodus 20:16** Thou shalt not bear false witness against thy neighbour. **Leviticus 19:16** Thou shalt not go up and down *as* a talebearer among thy people: neither shalt thou stand against the blood of thy neighbour: I *am* the LORD.

not a doer of the law, but a judge.	**Deutreonomy 5:20** Neither shalt thou bear false witness against thy neighbour. **Psalms 15:3** *He that* backbiteth not with his tongue, nor doeth evil to his neighbour, nor taketh up a reproach against his neighbour. **Psalms 101:5** Whoso privily **slandereth** his neighbour, him will I cut off: him that hath an high look and a proud heart will not I suffer. **Proverbs 26:20** Where no wood is, *there* the fire goeth out: so where *there is* no **talebearer**, the strife ceaseth. **Proverbs 26:22** The words of a **talebearer** *are* as wounds, and they go down into the innermost parts of the belly. **See James 3:8 "Tongues"**
James 4:14 Whereas ye know not what *shall be* on the morrow. For what *is* your life? It is even a vapour, that appeareth for a little time, and then vanisheth away.	**Isaiah 40:6** The voice said, Cry. And he said, What shall I cry? All flesh *is* grass, and all the goodliness thereof *is* as the flower of the field:
James 5:1 Go to now, *ye* rich men, weep and howl for your miseries that shall come upon *you*.	**Proverbs 11:28** He that trusteth in his riches shall fall: but the righteous shall flourish as a branch.
James 5:3 Your gold and silver is cankered; and the rust of them shall be a witness against you, and shall eat your flesh as it were fire. Ye have heaped treasure together for the **last days**.	**Isaiah 2:2** And it shall come to pass in the **last days**, that the mountain of the LORD'S house shall be established in the top of the mountains, and shall be exalted above the hills; and all nations shall flow unto it. **Micah 4:1** But in the **last days** it shall come to pass, that the mountain of the house of the LORD shall be established in the top of the mountains, and it shall be exalted above the hills; and people shall flow unto it. **See Matthew 6:24 "Wealth"** **Proverbs 16:27** An ungodly man diggeth up evil: and in his lips *there is* as a burning fire.
James 5:4 Behold, the hire of the labourers who have reaped down your fields, which is of you kept back by fraud, crieth: and the cries of them which have reaped are entered into the ears of the Lord of sabaoth.	**Leviticus 19:13** Thou shalt not defraud thy neighbour, neither rob *him*: the wages of him that is hired shall not abide with thee all night until the morning. **Deuteronomy 24:14-15** Thou shalt not oppress an hired servant *that is* poor and needy, *whether he be* of thy brethren, or of thy strangers that *are* in thy land within thy gates:15 At his day thou shalt give *him* his hire, neither shall the sun go down upon it; for he *is* poor, and setteth his heart upon it: lest he cry against thee unto the LORD, and it be sin unto thee. **Isaiah 5:9** In mine ears *said* the LORD of hosts, Of a truth many houses shall be desolate, *even* great and fair, without inhabitant.
James 5:5 Ye have lived in pleasure on the earth, and been wanton; ye have nourished your hearts, as in a day of slaughter.	**Job 21:13** They spend their days in wealth, and in a moment go down to the grave.
James 5:11 Behold, we count them happy which endure. Ye have heard of the patience of Job, and have seen the end of the Lord; that the Lord is very	**Job 1:21-22** And said, Naked came I out of my mother's womb, and naked shall I return thither: the LORD gave, and the LORD hath taken away; blessed be the name of the LORD. 22 In all this

pitiful, and of tender mercy.	Job sinned not, nor charged God foolishly. **Psalm 103:8** The LORD *is* merciful and gracious, slow to anger, and plenteous in mercy.
James 5:13 Is any among you afflicted? let him pray. Is any merry? let him sing psalms.	**See John 4:24 "Worship"** **See Colossians 3:16 "Music"**
James 5:14 Is any **sick** among you? let him call for the **elders** of the church; and let them pray over him, anointing him with oil in the **name** of the Lord:	**See 1 Peter 2:24 "Healing"** **See 1 Peter 5:1 "Elders"** **Proverbs 18:10** The name of the LORD is a strong tower: the righteous runneth into it, and is safe.
James 5:15 And the **prayer of faith** shall save the sick, and the Lord shall raise him up; and if he have committed sins, they shall be forgiven him.	**See Matthew 17:21 "Prayer"**
James 5:17-18 Elias was a man subject to like passions as we are, and he prayed earnestly that it might not rain: and it rained not on the earth by the space of three years and six months. 18 And he prayed again, and the heaven gave rain, and the earth brought forth her fruit.	**1 Kings 17:1** And Elijah the Tishbite, *who was* of the inhabitants of Gilead, said unto Ahab, *As* the LORD God of Israel liveth, before whom I stand, there shall not be dew nor rain these years, but according to my word. **1 Kings 18:41** And Elijah said unto Ahab, Get thee up, eat and drink; for *there is* a sound of abundance of rain.
James 5:20 Let him know, that he which converteth the sinner from the error of his way shall save a **soul** from death, and shall hide a multitude of sins.	**Proverbs 10:12** Hatred stirreth up strifes: but love covereth all sins. **See 1 Thessalonians 5:23 "Soul"**
1 Peter 1:2 Elect according to the foreknowledge of God the Father, through sanctification of the Spirit, unto obedience and sprinkling of the blood of Jesus Christ: Grace unto you, and peace, be multiplied.	**Exodus 12:22** And ye shall take a bunch of hyssop, and dip *it* in the blood that *is* in the bason, and strike the lintel and the two side posts with the blood that *is* in the bason; and none of you shall go out at the door of his house until the morning. **Leviticus 5:9** And he shall sprinkle of the blood of the sin offering upon the side of the altar; and the rest of the blood shall be wrung out at the bottom of the altar: it *is* a sin offering. **Psalms 103:3** Who forgiveth all thine iniquities; who healeth all thy diseases; **Psalms 130:7-8** Let Israel hope in the LORD: for with the LORD *there is* mercy, and with him *is* plenteous redemption. 8 And he shall redeem Israel from all his iniquities **Isaiah 53:5** But he *was* wounded for our transgressions, *he was* bruised for our iniquities: the chastisement of our peace *was* upon him; and with his stripes we are healed. **Daniel 9:24** Seventy weeks are determined upon thy people and upon thy holy city, to finish the transgression, and to make an end of sins, and **to make reconciliation for iniquity**, and to bring in everlasting righteousness, and to seal up the vision and prophecy, and to anoint the most Holy. **See Matthew 26:28 "Atonement"**
1 Peter 1:7 That the trial of your faith, being much more precious than of gold that perisheth, though it be tried with fire, might be found unto praise and honour and glory at the appearing of	**Numbers 31:23** Every thing that may abide the fire, **ye shall make *it* go through the fire, and it shall be clean**: nevertheless it shall be purified with the water of separation: and all that abideth not the fire ye shall make go through the water. **Isaiah 48:10** Behold, I have refined thee, but not with silver; I

Jesus Christ:	have chosen thee in the furnace of affliction.
1 Peter 1:8 Whom having not seen, ye love; in whom, though now ye see *him* not, yet believing, ye **rejoice** with **joy** unspeakable and full of glory:	**Isaiah 12:3-4** Therefore with **joy** shall ye draw water out of the wells of salvation. 4 And in that day shall ye say, Praise the LORD, call upon his name, declare his doings among the people, make mention that his name is exalted. **Habakkuk 3:17** Although the fig tree shall not blossom, neither *shall* fruit *be* in the vines; the labour of the olive shall fail, and the fields shall yield no meat; the flock shall be cut off from the fold, and *there shall be* no herd in the stalls: 18 Yet I will **rejoice** in the LORD, I will **joy** in the God of my salvation.
1 Peter 1:10 Of which salvation the prophets have inquired and searched diligently, who prophesied of the grace *that should come* unto you:	**Psalms 40:7** Then said I, Lo, I come: in the volume of the book *it is* written of me, **Isaiah 42:9** Behold, the former things are come to pass, and new things do I declare: before they spring forth I tell you of them. Jeremiah 29:1 Now these are the **words of the letter that Jeremiah the prophet** sent from Jerusalem unto the residue of the elders which were carried away captives, and to the priests, and to the prophets, and to all the people whom Nebuchadnezzar had carried away captive from Jerusalem to Babylon; **Jeremiah 30:1-2** The word that came to Jeremiah from the LORD, saying, 2 Thus speaketh the LORD God of Israel, saying, **Write thee all the words that I have spoken unto thee in a book** . **Zechariah 6:12** And speak unto him, saying, Thus speaketh the LORD of hosts, saying, Behold the man whose name *is* The BRANCH; and he shall grow up out of his place, and he shall build the temple of the LORD: **See 1 Corinthians 12:10 "prophecy"**
1 Peter 1:11 Searching what, or what manner of time the Spirit of Christ which was in them did signify, when it testified beforehand the sufferings of Christ, and the glory that should follow.	**Psalms 22:6** But I *am* a worm, and no man; a reproach of men, and despised of the people. **Isaiah 53:3** He is despised and rejected of men; a man of sorrows, and acquainted with grief: and we hid as it were *our* faces from him; he was despised, and we esteemed him not. **Daniel 9:24** Seventy weeks are determined upon thy people and upon thy holy city, to finish the transgression, and to make an end of sins, and to make reconciliation for iniquity, and to bring in everlasting righteousness, and to seal up the vision and prophecy, and to anoint the most Holy.
1 Peter 1:15-16 But as he which hath called you is holy, so be ye holy in all manner of conversation; 16 Because it is written, Be ye holy; for I am holy.	**Leviticus 19:2** Speak unto all the congregation of the children of Israel, and say unto them, Ye shall be holy: for I the LORD your God *am* holy. **Leviticus 20:7** Sanctify yourselves therefore, and be ye holy: for I *am* the LORD your God. **See Hebrews 12:14 "Holiness"**
1 Peter 1:18-19 Forasmuch as ye know that ye were not redeemed with corruptible things, *as* silver and gold, from your vain conversation *received* by tradition from your fathers; 19 But **with the precious blood of Christ**, as of a lamb without blemish and without spot:	**Leviticus 17:11** For the life of the flesh is in the blood: and I have given it to you upon the altar to make an atonement for your souls: **for it is the blood that maketh an atonement for the soul.** **Psalms 103:4** Who redeemeth thy life from destruction; who crowneth thee with lovingkindness and tender mercies; **Zechariah 9:11** As for thee also, **by the blood of thy covenant** I have sent forth thy prisoners out of the pit wherein *is* no water.

	See Matthew 26:28 "Atonement"
1 Peter 1:22 Seeing ye have purified your souls in obeying the truth through the Spirit unto unfeigned love of the brethren, *see that ye* love one another with a pure heart fervently:	See 1 Thessalonians 5:23 "Body, soul, and spirit"
1 Peter 1:23-25 Being born again, not of corruptible seed, but of incorruptible, by **the Word of God, which liveth and abideth for ever**. 24 For all flesh *is* as grass, and all the glory of man as the flower of grass. The grass withereth, and the flower thereof falleth away: 25 But the word of the Lord endureth for ever. And this is the word which by the gospel is preached unto you.	**Isaiah 40:6-8** The voice said, Cry. And he said, What shall I cry? All flesh *is* grass, and all the goodliness thereof *is* as the flower of the field: The grass withereth, the flower fadeth: because the spirit of the LORD bloweth upon it: surely the people *is* grass. The grass withereth, the flower fadeth: but the word of our God shall stand for ever. See Matthew 5:18 "Words"
1 Peter 2:3 If so be ye have tasted that the Lord *is* gracious.	**Psalm 34:8** O taste and see that the LORD is good: blessed is the man that trusteth in him.
1 Peter 2:4 To whom coming, *as unto* a living stone, disallowed indeed of men, but chosen of God, *and* precious,	**Psalms 118:22** The stone *which* the builders refused is become the head *stone* of the corner. **Isaiah 8:14** And he shall be for a sanctuary; but for a stone of stumbling and for a rock of offence to both the houses of Israel, for a gin and for a snare to the inhabitants of Jerusalem. **Isaiah 28:16** Therefore thus saith the Lord GOD, Behold, I lay in Zion for a foundation a stone, a tried stone, a precious corner *stone,* a sure foundation: he that believeth shall not make haste. **Zechariah 4:7** Who *art* thou, O great mountain? before Zerubbabel *thou shalt become* a plain: and he shall bring forth the headstone *thereof with* shoutings, *crying,* Grace, grace unto it.
1 Peter 2:5 Ye also, as lively stones, are built up a spiritual house, an holy priesthood, to offer up spiritual sacrifices, acceptable to God by Jesus Christ.	**Exodus 19:5-6** Now therefore, if ye will **obey my voice** indeed, and **keep my covenant**, then ye shall be a peculiar treasure unto me above all people: for all the earth *is* mine: 6 And **ye shall be unto me a kingdom of priests**, and an holy nation. These *are* the words which thou shalt speak unto the children of Israel. **1 Samuel 2:35** And **I will raise me up a faithful priest**, *that* shall do according to *that* which *is* in mine heart and in my mind: and I will build him a sure house; and he shall walk before mine anointed forever. **Isaiah 61:6** But ye shall be named the Priests of the LORD: *men* shall call you the Ministers of our God: ye shall eat the riches of the Gentiles, and in their glory shall ye boast yourselves. See 1 Peter 2:9
1 Peter 2:6 Wherefore also it is contained in the **scripture**, Behold, I lay in Sion a chief corner stone, elect, precious: and he that believeth on him shall not be confounded.	**Psalms 118:22** The stone *which* the builders refused is become the head *stone* of the corner. **Isaiah 8:14** And he shall be for a sanctuary; but for a stone of stumbling and for a rock of offence to both the houses of Israel, for a gin and for a snare to the inhabitants of Jerusalem. **Isaiah 28:16** Therefore thus saith the Lord GOD, Behold, I lay in Zion for a foundation a stone, a tried stone, a precious corner *stone*, a sure foundation: he that believeth shall not make haste. **Isaiah 33:20** Look upon Zion, the city of our solemnities: thine

	eyes shall see Jerusalem a quiet habitation, a tabernacle *that* shall not be taken down; not one of the stakes thereof shall ever be removed, neither shall any of the cords thereof be broken. **See Matthew 5:18 "Scripture"**
1 Peter 2:7 Unto you therefore which believe *he is* precious: but unto them which be disobedient, the stone which the builders disallowed, the same is made the head of the corner,	**Psalms 118:22** The stone *which* the builders refused is become the head [stone] of the corner. **Isaiah 28:16** Therefore thus saith the Lord GOD, Behold, I lay in Zion for a foundation a stone, a tried stone, a precious corner *stone,* a sure foundation: he that believeth shall not make haste. **Zechariah 4:7** Who *art* thou, O great mountain? before Zerubbabel *thou shalt become* a plain: and he shall bring forth the headstone *thereof with* shoutings, *crying,* Grace, grace unto it.
1 Peter 2:8 And a stone of stumbling, and a **rock** of offence, *even to them* which stumble at the word, being disobedient: whereunto also they were appointed.	**Isaiah 8:14** And he shall be for a sanctuary; but for a stone of stumbling and for a rock of offence to both the houses of Israel, for a gin and for a snare to the inhabitants of Jerusalem. **Isaiah 28:16** Therefore thus saith the Lord GOD, Behold, I lay in Zion for a foundation a stone, a tried stone, a precious corner *stone,* a sure foundation: he that believeth shall not make haste. **See 1 Corinthians 10:4 "Rock"**
1 Peter 2:9 But ye *are* a chosen generation, a royal priesthood, an **holy** nation, a peculiar people; that ye should shew forth the praises of him who hath called you out of darkness into his marvellous light:	**Exodus 19:5-6** Now therefore, if ye will obey my voice indeed, and keep my covenant, then ye shall be a peculiar treasure unto me above all people: for all the earth *is* mine: 6 And ye shall be unto me a kingdom of priests, and an holy nation. These *are* the words which thou shalt speak unto the children of Israel. **Exodus 23:22** But if thou shalt indeed obey his voice, and do all that I speak; then I will be an enemy unto thine enemies, and an adversary unto thine adversaries. **Deuteronomy 7:6** For thou *art* an holy people unto the LORD thy God: the LORD thy God hath chosen thee to be a special people unto himself, above all people that *are* upon the face of the earth. **Deuteronomy 10:15** Only the LORD had a delight in thy fathers to love them, and he chose their seed after them, *even* you above all people, as *it is* this day. **Deuteronomy 14:2** For thou *art* an **holy** people unto the LORD thy God, and the LORD hath chosen thee to be a peculiar people unto himself, above all the nations that *are* upon the earth. **Isaiah 43:20-21** The beast of the field shall honour me, the dragons and the owls: because I give waters in the wilderness, *and* rivers in the desert, to give drink to my people, my chosen. 21 This people have I formed for myself; they shall shew forth my praise. **Isaiah 61:6** But ye shall be named the Priests of the LORD: *men* shall call you the Ministers of our God: ye shall eat the riches of the Gentiles, and in their glory shall ye boast yourselves. **Hosea 1:10** Yet the number of the children of Israel shall be as the sand of the sea, which cannot be measured nor numbered; and it shall come to pass, *that* in the place where it was said unto them, Ye *are* not my people, *there* it shall be said unto them, Ye *are* the sons of the living God. **See Hebrews 12:14 "Holiness"**
1 Peter 2:10 Which in time past *were*	**Hosea 1:6** And she conceived again, and bare a daughter. And

not a people, but *are* now the people of God: which had not obtained mercy, but now have obtained mercy.	*God* said unto him, Call her name Loruhamah: for I will no more have mercy upon the house of Israel; but I will utterly take them away. **Hosea 1:9** Then said *God,* Call his name Loammi: for ye *are* not my people, and I will not be your *God.* **Hosea 2:1** Say ye unto your brethren, Ammi; and to your sisters, Ruhamah. **Hosea 2:23** And I will sow her unto me in the earth; and I will have mercy upon her that had not obtained mercy; and I will say to *them which were* not my people, Thou *art* my people; and they shall say, *Thou art* my God.
1 Peter 2:11 Dearly beloved, I beseech *you* as strangers and pilgrims, **abstain from fleshly lusts**, which war against the soul;	See Romans 1:26-27 "Sexual sins"
1 Peter 2:17 Honour all *men.* Love the brotherhood. Fear God. Honour the king.	**Proverbs 24:21** My son, fear thou the LORD and the king: *and* meddle not with them that are given to change:
1 Peter 2:22-23 Who did no sin, neither was guile found in his mouth: 23 Who, when he was reviled, reviled not again; when he suffered, he threatened not; but committed *himself* to him that judgeth righteously:	**Psalm 38:13-14** But I, as a deaf *man,* heard not; and *I was* as a dumb man *that* openeth not his mouth. 14 Thus I was as a man that heareth not, and in whose mouth *are* no reproofs. **Psalms 40:6** Sacrifice and offering thou didst not desire; mine ears hast thou opened: burnt offering and sin offering hast thou not required. **Isaiah 53:7** He was oppressed, and he was afflicted, yet he opened not his mouth: he is brought as a lamb to the slaughter, and as a sheep before her shearers is dumb, so he openeth not his mouth.
1 Peter 2:24 Who **his own self bare our sins** in his own body on the tree, that we, being dead to sins, should live unto righteousness: by whose stripes ye were **healed**.	**Isaiah 53:4-5** Surely he hath borne our griefs, and carried our sorrows: yet we did esteem him stricken, smitten of God, and afflicted. 5 But he *was* wounded for our transgressions, *he was* bruised for our iniquities: the chastisement of our peace *was* upon him; and **with his stripes we are healed**. **Isaiah 53:12** Therefore will I divide him *a portion* with the great, and he shall divide the spoil with the strong; because he hath poured out his soul unto death: and he was numbered with the transgressors; and he bare the sin of many, and made intercession for the transgressors. **Genesis 6:3** And the LORD said, My spirit shall not always strive with man, for that he also *is* flesh: yet his days shall be an hundred and twenty years. **Exodus 15:26** And said, If thou wilt diligently hearken to the voice of the LORD thy God, and wilt do that which is right in his sight, and wilt give ear to his commandments, and keep all his statutes, I will put none of these diseases upon thee, which I have brought upon the Egyptians: for **I *am* the LORD that healeth thee**. **Exodus 23:25** ...I will take sickness away from the midst of thee. **Deuteronomy 34:7** And **Moses *was* an hundred and twenty years old when he died**: his eye was not dim, nor his natural force abated. **Job 5:20** In famine he shall redeem thee from death: and in war from the power of the sword.

Job 5:26 Thou shalt come to *thy* grave in a full age, like as a shock of corn cometh in in his season.

Psalm 34:19 Many are the afflictions of the righteous: but the LORD delivereth him out of them all.

Psalms 90:10 The days of our years *are* threescore years and ten; and if by reason of strength *they be* fourscore years,

yet *is* their strength labor and sorrow; for it is soon cut off, and we fly away.

Psalms 91:7 A thousand shall fall at thy side, and ten thousand at thy right hand; but it shall not come nigh thee.

Psalm 91:10 There shall no evil befall thee, neither shall any plague come nigh thy dwelling.

Psalms 91:16 With long life will I satisfy him, and show him my salvation.

Psalms 103:3-5 ... who healeth all thy diseases;" 4 Who redeemeth thy life from destruction; 5... *things; so that* youth is renewed like the eagle's.

Psalms 105:37 He brought them forth also with silver and gold: and *there was* not one **feeble** *person* among their tribes.

Psalms 107:17-21 Fools because of their transgression, and because of their iniquities, are afflicted. 18 Their soul abhorreth all manner of meat; and they draw near unto the gates of death. 19 Then they cry unto the LORD in their trouble, *and* he saveth them out of their distresses. 20 **He sent his word, and healed them, and delivered** *them* **from their destructions.** 21 Oh that *men* would praise the LORD *for* his goodness, and *for* his wonderful works to the children of men!

Psalms 118:17 I shall not die, but live, and declare the works of the LORD.

Psalms 121:7-8 The LORD shall preserve thee from all evil: he shall preserve thy soul. 8 The LORD shall preserve thy going out and thy coming in from this time forth, and even for evermore.

Proverbs 3:2 For length of days, and long life, and peace, shall they add to thee.

Proverbs 3:16 Length of days is in her right hand; and in her left hand riches and honour.

Proverbs 4:10 Hear, O my son, and receive my sayings; and the years of thy life shall be many.

Proverbs 4:20-22 My son, attend to my words; incline thine ear unto my sayings. 21 Let them not depart from thine eyes; keep them in the midst of thine heart. 22 For they are life unto those that find them, and health to all their flesh.

Isaiah 35:3-7 Strengthen ye the weak hands, and confirm the feeble knees. 4 Say to them *that are* of a fearful heart, Be strong, fear not: behold, your God will come *with* vengeance, *even* God *with* a recompence; he will come and save you. 5 **Then the eyes of the blind shall be opened, and the ears of the deaf shall be unstopped. 6 Then shall the lame** *man* **leap as an hart, and the tongue of the dumb sing**: for in the wilderness shall waters break out, and streams in the desert. 7 And the parched ground shall become a pool, and the thirsty land springs of water: **in the habitation of dragons**, where each lay, *shall be* grass with reeds

	and rushes.
	Isaiah 40:29-31 He giveth power to the faint; and to them that have no might he increaseth strength. 30 Even the youths shall faint and be weary, and the young men shall utterly fall: 31 But they that wait upon the Lord shall renew their strength; they shall mount up with wings as eagles; they shall run, and not be weary; and they shall walk, and not faint.
	Isaiah 46:4 And even to your old age I am he; and even to hoar hairs will I carry you: I have made, and I will bear; even I will carry, and will deliver you.
	Isaiah 57:19 I create the fruit of the lips; Peace, peace to *him that is* far off, and to *him that is* near, saith the LORD; and **I will heal him**.
	Jeremiah 17:14 Heal me, O Lord, and <u>I shall be healed</u>; …
	Jeremiah 30:17 For I will restore health unto thee, and I will heal thee of thy wounds, saith the Lord.
	Hosea 6:1 Come, and let us **return** unto the LORD: for he hath torn, and **he will heal us**; he hath smitten, and **he will bind us up**.
1 Peter 2:25 For ye were as sheep going astray; but are now returned unto the Shepherd and Bishop of your **souls**.	**Isaiah 53:6** All we like sheep have gone astray; we have turned every one to his own way; and the LORD hath laid on him the iniquity of us all. **Ezekiel 34:6** My sheep wandered through all the mountains, and upon every high hill: yea, my flock was scattered upon all the face of the earth, and none did search or seek *after them*. See 1 Peter 5:4 "Shepherd" See 1 Thessalonians 5:23 "Body, soul, and spirit"
1 Peter 3:1 Likewise, ye wives, *be in* subjection to your own husbands; that, if any obey not the word, they also may without the word be won by the conversation of the wives;	**Genesis 3:16** Unto the woman he said, I will greatly multiply thy sorrow and thy conception; in sorrow thou shalt bring forth children; and thy desire *shall be* to thy husband, and he shall rule over thee.
1 Peter 3:3-5 Whose adorning let it not be that outward *adorning* of plaiting the hair, and of wearing of gold, or of putting on of apparel; 4 But *let it be* the hidden man of the heart, in that which is not corruptible, *even the ornament* of a meek and quiet spirit, which is in the sight of God of great price. 5 For after this manner in the old time the holy women also, who trusted in God, adorned themselves, being in subjection unto their own husbands:	See 1 Timothy 2:9 "Apparel"
1 Peter 3:6 Even as Sara obeyed Abraham, calling him **lord**: whose daughters ye are, as long as ye do well, and are not afraid with any amazement.	**Genesis 18:12** Therefore Sarah laughed within herself, saying, After I am waxed old shall I have pleasure, my **lord** being old also?
1 Peter 3:7 Likewise, ye husbands, dwell with *them* according to knowledge, giving honour unto the wife, as unto the weaker vessel, and as being heirs together of the grace of life; that	**Proverbs 17:13** Whoso rewardeth evil for good, evil shall not depart from his house.

your prayers be not hindered.	
1 Peter 3:9 Not rendering evil for evil, or railing for railing: but contrariwise blessing; knowing that ye are thereunto called, that ye should inherit a blessing.	**Leviticus 19:18** Thou shalt not avenge, nor bear any grudge against the children of thy people, but thou shalt love thy neighbour as thyself: I *am* the LORD. **Proverbs 20:22** Say not thou, I will recompense evil; *but* wait on the LORD, and he shall save thee. **Proverbs 24:29** Say not, I will do so to him as he hath done to me: I will render to the man according to his work.
1 Peter 3:10-12 For he that will love life, and see good days, let him refrain his tongue from evil, and his lips that they speak no guile: 11 Let him eschew evil, and do good; let him seek peace, and ensue it. 12 For the eyes of the Lord *are* over the righteous, and his ears *are open* unto their prayers: but the face of the Lord *is* against them that do evil.	**Psalm 34:12-16** What man is he that desireth life, and loveth many days, that he may see good? 13 Keep thy tongue from evil, and thy lips from speaking guile. 14 Depart from evil, and do good; seek peace, and pursue it. 15 The eyes of the LORD are upon the righteous, and his ears are open unto their cry. 16 The face of the LORD is against them that do evil, to cut off the remembrance of them from the earth. **Psalms 37:27** Depart from evil, and do good; and dwell for evermore. **Psalms 97:10** Ye that love the LORD, hate evil: he preserveth the souls of his saints; he delivereth them out of the hand of the wicked. **Psalms 146:9** The LORD preserveth the strangers; he relieveth the fatherless and widow: **but the way of the wicked he turneth upside down**. **Isaiah 1:16** Wash you, make you clean; put away the evil of your doings from before mine eyes; cease to do evil; **Amos 5:15** Hate the evil, and love the good, and establish judgment in the gate: it may be that the LORD God of hosts will be gracious unto the remnant of Joseph.
1 Peter 3:14-15 But and if ye suffer for righteousness' sake, happy [are ye]: and be not afraid of their terror, neither be troubled; 15 But sanctify the Lord God in your hearts: and be ready always to give an answer to every man that asketh you a reason of the hope that is in you with meekness and fear:	**Psalms 119:46** I will speak of thy testimonies also before kings, and will not be ashamed. **Isaiah 8:12-13** Say ye not, A confederacy, to all [them to] whom this people shall say, A confederacy; neither fear ye their fear, nor be afraid. 13 Sanctify the LORD of hosts himself; and *let* him *be* your fear, and *let* him *be* your dread. **Jeremiah 1:8** Be not afraid of their faces: for I *am* with thee to deliver thee, saith the LORD.
1 Peter 3:18 For Christ also hath once suffered for sins, the just for the unjust, that he might bring us to God, being put to death in the flesh, but quickened by the Spirit:	**Isaiah 53:11** He shall see of the travail of his soul, *and* shall be satisfied: by his knowledge shall my righteous servant justify many; for he shall bear their iniquities.
1 Peter 3:20 Which sometime were disobedient, when once the longsuffering of God waited in the days of Noah, while the ark was a preparing, wherein few, that is, eight souls were saved by water.	**Genesis 6:5** And GOD saw that the wickedness of man *was* great in the earth, and *that* every imagination of the thoughts of his heart *was* only evil continually. **Genesis 6:12** And God looked upon the earth, and, behold, it was corrupt; for all flesh had corrupted his way upon the earth. **Genesis 6:14** Make thee an ark of gopher wood; rooms shalt thou make in the ark, and shalt pitch it within and without with pitch. **See Matthew 24:38**

1 Peter 3:21 The like figure whereunto *even* **baptism doth also now save us** (not the putting away of the filth of the flesh, but the answer of a good conscience toward God,) by the resurrection of Jesus Christ:	**Exodus 30:18-21** Thou shalt also make a laver *of* brass, and his foot *also of* brass, to wash *withal*: and thou shalt put it between the tabernacle of the congregation and the altar, and thou shalt put water therein. 19 For Aaron and his sons shall wash their hands and their feet thereat: 20 When they go into the tabernacle of the congregation, they shall wash with water, that they die not; or when they come near to the altar to minister, to burn offering made by fire unto the LORD: 21 So they shall wash their hands and their feet, that they die not: and it shall be a statute for ever to them, *even* to him and to his seed throughout their generations. **Numbers 19:13** Whosoever toucheth the dead body of any man that is dead, and purifieth not himself, defileth the tabernacle of the LORD; and that soul shall be cut off from Israel: because the water of separation was not sprinkled upon him, he shall be unclean; his uncleanness *is* yet upon him. **Psalms 51:2** Wash me throughly from mine iniquity, and cleanse me from my sin. **Isaiah 1:16** Wash you, make you clean; put away the evil of your doings from before mine eyes; cease to do evil; **Ezekiel 36:25** Then will I sprinkle clean water upon you, and ye shall be clean: from all your filthiness, and from all your idols, will I cleanse you. **See John 3:5 and Acts 2:38**
1 Peter 3:22 Who is gone into heaven, and is on the right hand of God; angels and authorities and powers being made subject unto him."	**Job 19:25** For I know *that* my redeemer liveth, and *that* he shall stand at the latter *day* upon the earth: **Psalms 8:6** Thou madest him to have dominion over the works of thy hands; thou hast put all *things* under his feet: **Psalms 16:8** I have set the LORD always before me: because *he is* at my right hand, I shall not be moved. **Psalms 68:18** Thou hast ascended on high, thou hast led captivity captive: thou hast received gifts for men; yea, *for* the rebellious also, that the LORD God might dwell *among them*. **Psalms 110:1** The LORD said unto my Lord, Sit thou at my right hand, until I make thine enemies thy footstool. **Psalms 110:5** The Lord at thy right hand shall strike through kings in the day of his wrath. **Isaiah 9:6** For unto us a child is born, unto us a son is given: and the government shall be upon his shoulder: and his name shall be called Wonderful, Counseller, The mighty God, The everlasting Father, The Prince of Peace. **Isaiah 60:16** Thou shalt also suck the milk of the Gentiles, and shalt suck the breast of kings: and thou shalt know that I the LORD *am* thy Saviour and thy Redeemer, the mighty One of Jacob. **Daniel 7:9** I beheld till the thrones were cast down, and the Ancient of days did sit, whose garment *was* white as snow, and the hair of his head like the pure wool: his throne *was like* the fiery flame, *and* his wheels *as* burning fire. **Zechraiah 3:1** And he shewed me Joshua the high priest standing before the angel of the LORD, and Satan standing at his right hand to resist him.
1 Peter 4:3 For the time past of *our* life	**See Ephesians 5:18 "Drunkards"**

may suffice us to have wrought the will of the Gentiles, when we walked in lasciviousness, lusts, **excess of wine**, revellings, banquetings, and abominable idolatries:	
1 Peter 4:8 And above all things have fervent charity among yourselves: for charity shall cover the multitude of sins.	**Proverbs 10:12** Hatred stirreth up strifes: but love covereth all sins.
1 Peter 4:10 As every man hath received the gift, *even so* minister the same one to another, as good stewards of the manifold grace of God.	**Proverbs 3:28** Say not unto thy neighbour, Go, and come again, and to morrow I will give; when thou hast it by thee.
1 Peter 4:11 If any man speak, *let him speak* as the **oracles of God**; if any man minister, *let him do it* as of the ability which God giveth: that God in all things may be glorified through Jesus Christ, to whom be praise and dominion for ever and ever. Amen.	**Jeremiah 23:22** But if they had stood in my counsel, and had caused my people to hear my words, then they should have turned them from their evil way, and from the evil of their doings. **See Matthew 5:18 "Scriptures"**
1 Peter 4:14 If ye be reproached for the name of Christ, happy *are ye*; for the spirit of glory and of God resteth upon you: on their part he is evil spoken of, but on your part he is glorified.	**Isaiah 11:2** And the spirit of the LORD shall rest upon him, the spirit of wisdom and understanding, the spirit of counsel and might, the spirit of knowledge and of the fear of the LORD;
1 Peter 4:15 But let none of you suffer as a murderer, or *as* a thief, or *as* an evildoer, or *as* a **busybody** in other men's matters.	**Proverbs 20:3** *It is* an honour for a man to cease from strife: but every fool will be **meddling**.
1 Peter 4:16 Yet if *any man suffer* as a Christian, let him not be ashamed; but let him glorify God on this behalf.	**Numbers 6:27** And they shall put my name upon the children of Israel; and I will bless them.
1 Peter 4:17 For the time *is come* that judgment must begin at the house of God: and if *it* first *begin* at us, what shall the end *be* of them that obey not the gospel of God?	**Deuteronomy 28:14-16 And thou shalt not go aside from any of the words which I command thee this day, to the right hand, or to the left, to go after other gods to serve them.** 15 But it shall come to pass, **if thou wilt not hearken unto the voice of the LORD thy God, to observe to do all his commandments and his statutes** which I command thee this day; that all these curses shall come upon thee, and overtake thee: 16 **Cursed shalt thou be** in the city, and cursed shalt thou be in the field. **Jeremiah 25:29** For, lo, I begin to bring evil on the city which is called by my name, and should ye be utterly unpunished? Ye shall not be unpunished: for I will call for a sword upon all the inhabitants of the earth, saith the LORD of hosts.
1 Peter 4:18 And if the righteous scarcely be saved, where shall the ungodly and the sinner appear?	**Proverbs 11:31** Behold, the righteous shall be recompensed in the earth: much more the wicked and the sinner.
1 Peter 5:1 The **elders** which are among you I exhort, who am also an **elder**, and a witness of the sufferings of Christ, and also a partaker of the glory that shall be	**Exodus 24:13** And Moses rose up, and his **minister** Joshua: and Moses went up into the mount of God. **Exodus 34:31** And Moses called unto them; and Aaron and all the **rulers** of the congregation returned unto him: and Moses talked with them. **Numbers 11:25** And the LORD came down in a cloud, and spake unto him, and took of the spirit that was upon him, and gave it unto

revealed:	the **seventy elders**: and it came to pass, that, when the spirit rested upon them, **they prophesied**, and did not cease.

1 Samuel 8:4 Then **all the elders** of Israel gathered themselves together, and came to Samuel unto Ramah,

1 Chronicles 21:16 And David lifted up his eyes, and saw the angel of the LORD stand between the earth and the heaven, having a drawn sword in his hand stretched out over Jerusalem. Then David and the **elders** *of Israel, who were* clothed in sackcloth, fell upon their faces.

2 Chronicles 5:2 Then Solomon assembled the **elders** of Israel, and all the heads of the tribes, the chief of the fathers of the children of Israel, unto Jerusalem, to bring up the ark of the covenant of the LORD out of the city of David, which *is* Zion.

2 Chronicles 5:4 And all the **elders** of Israel came; and the Levites took up the ark.

Psalms 107:32 Let them exalt him also in the congregation of the people, and praise him in the assembly of the **elders**.

Proverbs 31:23 Her husband is known in the gates, when he sitteth among the **elders** of the land.

Isaiah 37:2 And he sent Eliakim, who was over the household, and Shebna the scribe, and the **elders of the priests** covered with sackcloth, unto Isaiah the prophet the son of Amoz.

Jeremiah 29:1 Now these are the words of the letter that Jeremiah the prophet sent from Jerusalem unto the residue of the **elders** which were carried away captives, and to the priests, and to the prophets, and to all the people whom Nebuchadnezzar had carried away captive from Jerusalem to Babylon;

Lamentations 1:19 I called for my lovers, *but* they deceived me: my priests and mine **elders** gave up the ghost in the city, while they sought their meat to relieve their souls.

Joel 1:14 Sanctify ye a fast, call a solemn assembly, gather the **elders** *and* all the inhabitants of the land *into* the house of the LORD your God, and cry unto the LORD,

Joel 2:16 Gather the people, sanctify the congregation, **assemble the elders**, gather the children, and those that suck the breasts: let the bridegroom go forth of his chamber, and the bride out of her closet. |
| **1 Peter 5:4** And when the **chief Shepherd** shall appear, ye shall receive a crown of glory that fadeth not away. | **Genesis 49:24** But his bow abode in strength, and the arms of his hands were made strong by the hands of the mighty God of Jacob; (from thence is the **shepherd**, the stone of Israel:)

Psalms 23:1 { A Psalm of David. } The LORD *is* my **shepherd**; I shall not want.

Isaiah 40:11 He shall feed his flock like a **shepherd**: he shall gather the lambs with his arm, and carry *them* in his bosom, *and* shall gently lead those that are with young.

Ezekiel 34:23 And I will set up one **shepherd** over them, and he shall feed them, *even* my servant David; he shall feed them, and he shall be their shepherd.

Ezekiel 37:24 And David my servant shall be king over them; and they all shall have one **shepherd**: they shall also walk in my judgments, and observe my statutes, and do them. |

	See John 10:10 "Shepherds"
1 Peter 5:5 Likewise, ye younger, submit yourselves unto the elder. Yea, all *of you* be subject one to another, and be clothed with humility: for God resisteth the proud, and giveth grace to the humble.	**Proverbs 3:34** Surely he scorneth the scorners: but he giveth grace unto the lowly.
1 Peter 5:6 Humble yourselves therefore under the mighty hand of God, that he may exalt you in due time:	**Job 22:29** When *men* are cast down, then thou shalt say, *There is* lifting up; and he shall save the humble person. **Proverbs 29:23** A man's pride shall bring him low: but honour shall uphold the humble in spirit.
1 Peter 5:7 Casting all your care upon him; for he careth for you.	**Psalms 55:22** Cast thy burden upon the LORD, and he shall sustain thee: he shall never suffer the righteous to be moved.
1 Peter 5:8 Be sober, be vigilant; because your adversary the **devil**, as a roaring lion, walketh about, seeking whom he may **devour**:	**Job 1:7** And the LORD said unto Satan, Whence comest thou? Then **Satan** answered the LORD, and said, From going to and fro in the earth, and from walking up and down in it. **Psalms 107:20** He sent his word, and healed *them*, and delivered them from their **destructions**.
1 Peter 5:13 The *church that is* at Babylon, **elected** together with *you*, saluteth you; and *so doth* Marcus my son.	**Isaiah 42:1** Behold my servant, whom I uphold; mine **elect**, *in whom* my soul delighteth; I have put my spirit upon him: he shall bring forth judgment to the Gentiles.
2 Peter 1:1 Simon Peter, a servant and an apostle of Jesus Christ, to them that have obtained like precious faith with us through the righteousness of God and our Saviour Jesus Christ:	**Job 19:25** For I know *that* my redeemer liveth, and *that* he shall stand at the latter *day* upon the earth: **Isaiah 9:6** For unto us a child is born, unto us a son is given: and the government shall be upon his shoulder: and his name shall be called Wonderful, Counseller, The mighty God, The everlasting Father, The Prince of Peace. **Isaiah 60:16** Thou shalt also suck the milk of the Gentiles, and shalt suck the breast of kings: and thou shalt know that I the LORD *am* thy Saviour and thy Redeemer, the mighty One of Jacob.
2 Peter 1:9 But he that lacketh these things is blind, and cannot see afar off, and hath forgotten that he was purged from his old sins.	**Isaiah 59:10** We grope for the wall like the blind, and we grope as if *we had* no eyes: we stumble at noonday as in the night; *we are* in desolate places as dead *men*. **Zephaniah 1:17** And I will bring distress upon men, that they shall walk like blind men, because they have sinned against the LORD: and their blood shall be poured out as dust, and their flesh as the dung.
2 Peter 1:10 Wherefore the rather, brethren, give diligence to make your calling and **election** sure: for if ye do these things, ye shall never fall:	**Isaiah 42:1** Behold my servant, whom I uphold; mine **elect**, *in whom* my soul delighteth; I have put my spirit upon him: he shall bring forth judgment to the Gentiles.
2 Peter 1:11 For so an entrance shall be ministered unto you abundantly into the everlasting kingdom of our Lord and Saviour Jesus Christ.	See Job 19:25, Isaiah 9:6 and 60:16
2 Peter 1:17 For he received from God the Father honour and glory, when there came such a voice to him from the excellent glory, This is my beloved Son, in whom I am well pleased.	**Genesis 22:2** And he said, Take now thy son, thine only *son* Isaac, whom thou lovest, and get thee into the land of Moriah; and offer him there for a burnt offering upon one of the mountains which I will tell thee of. **Psalm 2:7** I will declare the decree: the LORD hath said unto me,

	Thou *art* my Son; this day have I begotten thee. **Isaiah 42:1** Behold my servant, whom I uphold; mine elect, *in whom* my soul delighteth; I have put my spirit upon him: he shall bring forth judgment to the Gentiles.
2 Peter 1:20-21 Knowing this first, that no prophecy of the scripture is of any private interpretation. 21 For the prophecy came not in old time by the will of man: but **holy men of God spake as they were moved by the Holy Ghost.**	**Ezekiel 3:4** And he said unto me, Son of man, go, get thee unto the house of Israel, and **speak with my words unto them**. **Jeremiah 1:7** But the LORD said unto me, Say not, I am a child: for thou shalt go to all that I shall send thee, and **whatsoever I command thee thou shalt speak**. **Daniel 9:2** In the first year of his reign I Daniel understood by books the number of the years, whereof the word of the LORD came to Jeremiah the prophet, that he would accomplish seventy years in the desolations of Jerusalem. **Micah 3:8** But truly I am full of power by the spirit of the LORD, and of judgment, and of might, **to declare unto Jacob his transgression, and to Israel his sin**.
2 Peter 2:1 But there were **false prophets** also among the people, even as there shall be false teachers among you, who privily shall bring in damnable heresies, even denying the Lord that bought them, and bring upon themselves swift destruction.	**Deuteronomy 13:1-5** If there arise among you a prophet, or a dreamer of dreams, and giveth thee a sign or a wonder, 2 And the sign or the wonder come to pass, whereof he spake unto thee, saying, Let us go after other gods, which thou hast not known, and let us serve them; 3 Thou shalt not hearken unto the words of that prophet, or that dreamer of dreams: for the LORD your God proveth you, to know whether ye love the LORD your God with all your heart and with all your soul. 4 Ye shall walk after the LORD your God, and fear him, and keep his commandments, and obey his voice, and ye shall serve him, and cleave unto him. 5 And that prophet, or that dreamer of dreams, shall be put to death; because he hath spoken to turn *you* away from the LORD your God, which brought you out of the land of Egypt, and redeemed you out of the house of bondage, to thrust thee out of the way which the LORD thy God commanded thee to walk in. So shalt thou put the evil away from the midst of thee. **Deuteronomy 18:20-22** But the prophet, which shall presume to speak a word in my name, which I have not commanded him to speak, or that shall speak in the name of other gods, even that prophet shall die. 21 And if thou say in thine heart, How shall we know the word which the LORD hath not spoken? 22 When a prophet speaketh in the name of the LORD, if the thing follow not, nor come to pass, that *is* the thing which the LORD hath not spoken, *but* the prophet hath spoken it presumptuously: thou shalt not be afraid of him.
2 Peter 2:4 For if God spared not the **angels** that sinned, but cast *them* down to **hell**, and delivered *them* into chains of darkness, to be reserved unto judgment;	See Luke 16:23 "Hell" See Hebrews 13:2 "Good and bad angels"
2 Peter 2:5 And spared not the old world, but saved Noah the eighth *person*, a preacher of righteousness, bringing in the flood upon the world of the ungodly;	**Genesis 7:23** And every living substance was destroyed which was upon the face of the ground, both man, and cattle, and the creeping things, and the fowl of the heaven; and they were destroyed from the earth: and Noah only remained *alive,* and they that *were* with him in the ark. **Genesis 8:1-22**
2 Peter 2:6 And turning the cities of	**Genesis 19:1-38**

Sodom and Gomorrha into ashes condemned *them* with an overthrow, making *them* an ensample unto those that after should live ungodly;	**Genesis 19:24** Then the LORD rained upon **Sodom and upon Gomorrah** brimstone and fire from the LORD out of heaven; **Deuteronomy 29:23** *And that* the whole land thereof *is* brimstone, and salt, *and* burning, *that* it is not sown, nor beareth, nor any grass groweth therein, like the overthrow of Sodom, and Gomorrah, Admah, and Zeboim, which the LORD overthrew in his anger, and in his wrath: **Isaiah 13:19** And Babylon, the glory of kingdoms, the beauty of the Chaldees' excellency, shall be as when God overthrew Sodom and Gomorrah. **Jeremiah 50:40** As God overthrew Sodom and Gomorrah and the neighbour *cities* thereof, saith the LORD; *so* shall no man abide there, neither shall any son of man dwell therein. **Ezekiel 16:49** Behold, this was the iniquity of thy sister Sodom, pride, fulness of bread, and abundance of idleness was in her and in her daughters, neither did she strengthen the hand of the poor and needy. **Amos 4:11** I have overthrown *some* of you, as God overthrew Sodom and Gomorrah, and ye were as a firebrand plucked out of the burning: yet have ye not returned unto me, saith the LORD. **See Romans 1:27 "Sexual sins"**
2 Peter 2:7 And delivered just Lot, vexed with the filthy conversation of the wicked:	**Genesis 19:7-8** And said, I pray you, brethren, do not so wickedly. 8 Behold now, I have two daughters which have not known man; let me, I pray you, bring them out unto you, and do ye to them as *is* good in your eyes: only unto these men do nothing; for therefore came they under the shadow of my roof.
2 Peter 2:8 (For that righteous man dwelling among them, in seeing and hearing, vexed *his* righteous soul from day to day with *their* unlawful deeds;)	**Psalms 119:158** I beheld the transgressors, and was grieved; because they kept not thy word.
2 Peter 2:12 But these, as natural brute beasts, made to be taken and destroyed, speak evil of the things that they understand not; and shall utterly perish in their own corruption;	**Jeremiah 12:3** But thou, O LORD, knowest me: thou hast seen me, and tried mine heart toward thee: pull them out like sheep for the slaughter, and prepare them for the day of slaughter.
2 Peter 2:14 Having eyes full of **adultery**, and that cannot cease from sin; beguiling unstable souls: an heart they have exercised with covetous practices; cursed children:	**Leviticus 18:29** For whosoever shall commit any of these abominations, **even the souls that commit *them* shall be cut off from among their people**. See Matthew 5:27 "Adultery" See Romans 1:27 "Sexual sins"
2 Peter 2:15-16 Which have forsaken the right way, and are gone astray, following the way of Balaam *the son* of Bosor, who loved the wages of unrighteousness; 16 But was rebuked for his iniquity: the dumb ass speaking with man's voice forbad the madness of the prophet.	**Numbers 22:1-41** **Numbers 22:7** And the elders of Moab and the elders of Midian departed with the rewards of divination in their hand; and they came unto Balaam, and spake unto him the words of Balak. **Numbers 22:21** And Balaam rose up in the morning, and saddled his ass, and went with the princes of Moab.
2 Peter 2:17 These are wells without water, clouds that are carried with a tempest; **to whom the mist of darkness**	See Luke 16:23 "Hell"

is reserved <u>for ever</u>.	
2 Peter 2:18 For when they speak great swelling *words* of vanity, they allure through the **lusts of the flesh**, *through much* wantonness, those that were clean escaped from them who live in error.	**See Romans 1:26-27 "Sexual sins"** **See 2 Peter 2:1 "False prophets"**
2 Peter 2:20 For if after they have escaped the pollutions of the world through the knowledge of the Lord and Saviour Jesus Christ, they are again entangled therein, and overcome, the latter end is worse with them than the beginning.	**Numbers 24:20** And when he looked on Amalek, he took up his parable, and said, Amalek *was* the first of the nations; but his latter end *shall be* that he perish for ever. **Job 19:25** For I know *that* my redeemer liveth, and *that* he shall stand at the latter *day* upon the earth: **Isaiah 9:6** For unto us a child is born, unto us a son is given: and the government shall be upon his shoulder: and his name shall be called Wonderful, Counseller, The mighty God, The everlasting Father, The Prince of Peace. **Isaiah 60:16** Thou shalt also suck the milk of the Gentiles, and shalt suck the breast of kings: and thou shalt know that I the LORD *am* thy Saviour and thy Redeemer, the mighty One of Jacob.
2 Peter 2:22 But it is happened unto them according to the true proverb, The dog [is] turned to his own vomit again; and the sow that was washed to her wallowing in the mire.	**Proverbs 26:11** As a dog returneth to his vomit, [so] a fool returneth to his folly.
2 Peter 3:2 That ye may be mindful of the words which were spoken before by the holy prophets, and of the commandment of us the apostles of the Lord and Saviour:	**See Job 19:25, Isaiah 9:6 and 60:16**
2 Peter 3:3 Knowing this first, that there shall come in the **last days** scoffers, walking after their own lusts,	**Isaiah 2:2** And it shall come to pass in the **last days**, that the mountain of the LORD'S house shall be established in the top of the mountains, and shall be exalted above the hills; and all nations shall flow unto it. **Micah 4:1** But in the **last days** it shall come to pass, that the mountain of the house of the LORD shall be established in the top of the mountains, and it shall be exalted above the hills; and people shall flow unto it.
2 Peter 3:4 And saying, Where is the promise of his coming? for since the fathers fell asleep, all things continue as *they were* from the beginning of the creation.	**Ezekiel 12:22** Son of man, what *is* that proverb *that* ye have in the land of Israel, saying, The days are prolonged, and every vision faileth?
2 Peter 3:5-6 For this they willingly are ignorant of, that by the word of God the heavens were of old, and the earth standing out of the water and in the water: 6 Whereby the world that then was, being overflowed with water, perished:	**Genesis 1:1-2** In the beginning God created the heaven and the earth. 2 And the earth was without form, and void; and darkness was upon the face of the deep. And the Spirit of God moved upon the face of the waters. **Genesis 1: 6** And God said, Let there be a firmament in the midst of the waters, and let it divide the waters from the waters. **Genesis 1:9** And God said, Let the waters under the heaven be gathered together unto one place, and let the dry *land* appear: and it was so. **Genesis 7:10** And it came to pass after seven days, that the waters of the flood were upon the earth.

	Genesis 7:21 And all flesh died that moved upon the earth, both of fowl, and of cattle, and of beast, and of every creeping thing that creepeth upon the earth, and every man:
	Psalms 24:2 For he hath founded it upon the seas, and established it upon the floods.
2 Peter 3:8 But, beloved, be not ignorant of this one thing, that one day *is* with the Lord as a thousand years, and a thousand years as one day.	**Psalm 90:4** For a thousand years in thy sight *are but* as yesterday when it is past, and *as* a watch in the night.
2 Peter 3:9 The Lord is not slack concerning his promise, as some men count slackness; but is longsuffering to us-ward, not willing that any should perish, but that all should come to repentance.	**Habakkuk 2:3** For the vision *is* yet for an appointed time, but at the end it shall speak, and not lie: though it tarry, wait for it; because it will surely come, it will not tarry.
2 Peter 3:10 But the day of the Lord will come as a thief in the night; in the which the heavens shall pass away with a great noise, and the elements shall melt with fervent heat, the earth also and the works that are therein shall be burned up.	**Leviticus 23:27** Also on the tenth *day* of this seventh month *there shall be* a day of atonement: it shall be an holy convocation unto you; and ye shall afflict your souls, and offer an offering made by fire unto the LORD. **Psalm 34:12-16** What man is he that desireth life, and loveth many days, that he may see good? 13 Keep thy tongue from evil, and thy lips from speaking guile. 14 Depart from evil, and do good; seek peace, and pursue it. 15 The eyes of the LORD are upon the righteous, and his ears are open unto their cry.16 The face of the LORD is against them that do evil, to cut off the remembrance of them from the earth. **Psalm 102:26-27** They shall perish, but thou shalt endure: yea, all of them shall wax old like a garment; as a vesture shalt thou change them, and they shall be changed: 27 But thou art the same, and thy years shall have no end. **Joel 2:31-32** The sun shall be turned into darkness, and the moon into blood, before the great and the terrible **day of the LORD** come. 32 And it shall come to pass, *that* whosoever shall call on the name of the LORD shall be delivered: for in mount Zion and in Jerusalem shall be deliverance, as the LORD hath said, and in the remnant whom the LORD shall call. **Zechariah 12:10** And I will pour upon the house of David, and upon the inhabitants of Jerusalem, the spirit of grace and of supplications: and they shall look upon me whom they have pierced, and they shall mourn for him, as one mourneth for *his* only *son*, and shall be in bitterness for him, as one that is in bitterness for *his* firstborn. **See Acts 2:20 "Day of the LORD"**
2 Peter 3:12 Looking for and hasting unto the coming of the day of God, wherein the heavens being on fire shall be dissolved, and the elements shall melt with fervent heat?	**Psalms 50:3** Our God shall come, and shall not keep silence: a fire shall devour before him, and it shall be very tempestuous round about him.
2 Peter 3:13 Nevertheless we, according to his promise, look for new heavens and a new earth, wherein dwelleth righteousness.	**Isaiah 65:17** For, behold, I create new heavens and a new earth: and the former shall not be remembered, nor come into mind. **Isaiah 66:22** For as the new heavens and the new earth, which I will make, shall remain before me, saith the LORD, so shall your

	seed and your name remain.
2 Peter 3:18 But grow in grace, and *in* the knowledge of our Lord and Saviour Jesus Christ. To him *be* glory both now and for ever. Amen.	**Job 19:25** For I know *that* my redeemer liveth, and *that* he shall stand at the latter *day* upon the earth: **Isaiah 9:6** For unto us a child is born, unto us a son is given: and the government shall be upon his shoulder: and his name shall be called Wonderful, Counsellor, The mighty God, The everlasting Father, The Prince of Peace. **Isaiah 60:16** Thou shalt also suck the milk of the Gentiles, and shalt suck the breast of kings: and thou shalt know that I the LORD *am* thy Saviour and thy Redeemer, the mighty One of Jacob.
1 John 1:5 This then is the message which we have heard of him, and declare unto you, that God is light, and in him is no darkness at all.	**See Hebrews 12:14 "Holiness"**
1 John 1:6 If we say that we have fellowship with him, and walk in darkness, we lie, and do not the truth:	**See Hebrews 12:14 "Holiness"**
1 John 1:7 But if we walk in the light, as he is in the light, we have fellowship one with another, and the blood of Jesus Christ his Son cleanseth us from all sin.	**Exodus 12:7** And they shall take of the blood, and strike *it* on the two side posts and on the upper door post of the houses, wherein they shall eat it. **Exodus 12:13** And the blood shall be to you for a token upon the houses where ye *are*: and when I see the blood, I will pass over you, and the plague shall not be upon you to destroy *you,* when I smite the land of Egypt **Leviticus 17:11** For the life of the flesh is in the blood: and I have given it to you upon the altar to make an atonement for your souls: **for it is the blood that maketh an atonement for the soul**. **Isaiah 53:10** Yet it pleased the LORD to bruise him; he hath put *him* to grief: when thou shalt make his soul an offering for sin, he shall see *his* seed, he shall prolong *his* days, and the pleasure of the LORD shall prosper in his hand. **See Matthew 26:28 "Atonement"**
1 John 1:8 If we say that we have no sin, we deceive ourselves, and the truth is not in us.	**Psalms 40:6** Sacrifice and offering thou didst not desire; mine ears hast thou opened: burnt offering and sin offering hast thou not required. **Proverbs 20:9** Who can say, I have made my heart clean, I am pure from my sin?
1 John 1:9 If we confess our sins, he is faithful and just to forgive us *our* sins, and to cleanse us from all unrighteousness.	**Genesis 2:17** But of the tree of the knowledge of good and evil, thou shalt not eat of it: for in the day that thou eatest thereof thou shalt surely die. **Exodus 34:6-7** And the LORD passed by before him, and proclaimed, The LORD, The LORD God, merciful and gracious, longsuffering, and abundant in goodness and truth, ⁷Keeping mercy for thousands, **forgiving iniquity and transgression and sin**, and that will by no means clear *the guilty*; visiting the iniquity of the fathers upon the children, and upon the children's children, unto the third and to the fourth *generation*. **Psalms 32:5** I acknowledged my sin unto thee, and mine iniquity have I not hid. I said, I will confess my transgressions unto the LORD; and thou forgavest the iniquity of my sin. Selah. **Psalm 66:18** If I regard iniquity in my heart, the Lord will not

	hear me:
	Psalms 103:12 As far as the east is from the west, *so* far hath he removed our transgressions from us.
	Proverbs 28:13 He that covereth his sins shall not prosper: but whoso confesseth and forsaketh *them* shall have mercy.
	Isaiah 43:25 I, *even* I, *am* he that blotteth out thy transgressions for mine own sake, and will not remember thy sins.
	Isaiah 59:1-2 But your iniquities have separated between you and your God, and your sins have hid *his* face from you, that he will not hear.
	Ezekiel 18:4 Behold, all souls are mine; as the soul of the father, so also the soul of the son is mine: the soul that sinneth, it shall die.
1 John 2:3 And hereby we do know that we know him, if we keep his commandments.	**See Hebrews 12:14 "Holiness"**
1 John 2:12 I write unto you, little children, because your sins are forgiven you for his name's sake.	**Isaiah 43:25** I, *even* I, *am* he that blotteth out thy transgressions for mine own sake, and will not remember thy sins.
1 John 2:15 Love not the world, neither the things *that are* in the world. If any man love the world, the love of the Father is not in him.	**See Hebrews 12:14 "Holiness"**
1 John 2:16 For all that *is* in the world, **the lust of the flesh, and the lust of the eyes, and the pride of life**, is not of the Father, but is of the world.	**Psalms 119:37** Turn away mine eyes from beholding vanity; *and* quicken thou me in thy way. **Proverbs 6:16-19** These six *things* doth the LORD hate: yea, seven *are* an abomination unto him: 17 A **proud look**, a lying tongue, and hands that shed innocent blood, 18 An heart that deviseth wicked imaginations, feet that be swift in running to mischief, 19 A false witness *that* speaketh lies, and he that soweth discord among brethren. **Proverbs 16:18 Pride** *goeth* before destruction, and an haughty spirit before a fall. **Proverbs 23:7** For as he thinketh in his heart, so *is* he: Eat and drink, saith he to thee; but his heart *is* not with thee. **Isaiah 14:12-15** How art thou fallen from heaven, O Lucifer, son of the morning! *how* art thou cut down to the ground, which didst weaken the nations! 13 For thou hast said in thine heart, **I** will ascend into heaven, **I** will exalt my throne above the stars of God: **I** will sit also upon the mount of the congregation, in the sides of the north: 14 I will ascend above the heights of the clouds; **I** will be like the most High. 15 Yet thou shalt be brought down to hell, to the sides of the pit. **See Matthew 4:10 "satan"** **See Romans 1:26-27 "Sexual sins"**
1 John 2:17 And the world passeth away, and the lust thereof: but he that doeth the will of God abideth for ever.	**Psalms 90:10** The days of our years *are* threescore years and ten; and if by reason of strength *they be* fourscore years, yet *is* their strength labour and sorrow; for it is soon cut off, and we fly away. **See Hebrews 12:14 "Holiness"**
1 John 2:18 Little children, **it is the last time: and as ye have heard that**	**Daniel 7:7-8** After this I saw in the night visions, and behold a fourth beast, dreadful and terrible, and strong exceedingly; and it

antichrist shall come, even now are there many antichrists; whereby we know that it is the last time.	had great iron teeth: it devoured and brake in pieces, and stamped the residue with the feet of it: and it *was* diverse from all the beasts that *were* before it; and it had ten horns. 8 I considered the horns, and, behold, there came up among them another little horn, before whom there were three of the first horns plucked up by the roots: and, behold, in this horn *were* eyes like the eyes of man, and a mouth speaking great things. **Daniel 7:20-26** And of the ten horns that *were* in his head, and *of* the other which came up, and before whom three fell; even *of* that horn that had eyes, and a mouth that spake very great things, whose look *was* more stout than his fellows. 21 I beheld, and **the same horn made war with the saints, and prevailed against them**; 22 Until the Ancient of days came, and judgment was given to the saints of the most High; and the time came that the saints possessed the kingdom. 23 Thus he said, The fourth beast shall be the fourth kingdom upon earth, which shall be diverse from all kingdoms, and shall devour the whole earth, and shall tread it down, and break it in pieces. 24 And the ten horns out of this kingdom *are* ten kings *that* shall arise: and another shall rise after them; and he shall be diverse from the first, and he shall subdue three kings. 25 And he shall speak *great* words against the most High, and shall wear out the saints of the most High, and think to change times and laws: and they shall be given into his hand until a time and times and the dividing of time. 26 But the judgment shall sit, and they shall take away his dominion, to consume and to destroy *it* unto the end. **Daniel 9:27** And he shall confirm the covenant with many for one week: and in the midst of the week he shall cause the sacrifice and the oblation to cease, and for the overspreading of abominations he shall make *it* desolate, even until the consummation, and that determined shall be poured upon the desolate.
1 John 2:19 They went out from us, but they were not of us; for if they had been of us, they would *no doubt* have continued with us: but *they went out*, that they might be made manifest that they were not all of us.	**Psalms 41:9** Yea, mine own familiar friend, in whom I trusted, which did eat of my bread, hath lifted up *his* heel against me.
1 John 2:20 But ye have an **unction** from the Holy One, and ye know all things.	See Luke 4:18 "Anointing"
1 John 2:22 Who is a liar but he that denieth that Jesus is the Christ? **He is antichrist, that denieth the Father and the Son.**	See 1 John 2:18 "antichrist"
1 John 2:27 But the **anointing** which ye have received of him abideth in you, and ye need not that any man **teach** you: but as the same **anointing teacheth** you of all things, and is truth, and is no lie, and even as it hath **taught** you, ye shall abide in him.	**Isaiah 61:1** The Spirit of the Lord GOD *is* upon me; because the LORD hath anointed me to preach good tidings unto the meek; he hath sent me to bind up the brokenhearted, to proclaim liberty to the captives, and the opening of the prison to *them that are* bound; **Daniel 9:22** And he informed *me,* and talked with me, and said, O Daniel, I am now come forth to give thee skill and understanding. See Ephesians 4:11 "**Teach**" See Luke 4:18 "Anointing" See Hebrews 12:14 "Holiness"
1 John 3:1-3 Beloved, believe not every spirit, but try the spirits whether they are	

of God: because many false prophets are gone out into the world. 2 Hereby know ye the Spirit of God: Every spirit that confesseth that Jesus Christ is come in the flesh is of God: 3 And every spirit that confesseth not that Jesus Christ is come in the flesh is not of God: and this is the *spirit* of antichrist, whereof ye have heard that it should come; and even now already is it in the world.	**Malachi 3:18** Then shall ye return, and discern between the righteous and the wicked, between him that serveth God and him that serveth him not.
1 John 3:5 And ye know that he was manifested to take away our sins; and in him is no sin.	**Psalms 40:6** Sacrifice and offering thou didst not desire; mine ears hast thou opened: burnt offering and sin offering hast thou not required. **Isaiah 53:4** Surely he hath borne our griefs, and carried our sorrows: yet we did esteem him stricken, smitten of God, and afflicted. **Isaiah 53:12** Therefore will I divide him *a portion* with the great, and he shall divide the spoil with the strong; because he hath poured out his soul unto death: and he was numbered with the transgressors; and he bare the sin of many, and made intercession for the transgressors.
1 John 3:6 Whosoever abideth in him sinneth not: whosoever sinneth hath not seen him, neither known him. **1 John 3:8-9** He that committeth sin is of the devil; for the devil sinneth from the beginning. For this purpose the Son of God was manifested, that he might destroy the works of the devil. 9 Whosoever is born of God doth not commit sin; for his seed remaineth in him: and he cannot sin, because he is born of God.	**Deuteronomy 28:45-46** Moreover all these curses shall come upon thee, and shall pursue thee, and overtake thee, till thou be destroyed; because thou hearkenedst not unto the voice of the LORD thy God, to keep His commandments and His statutes which He commanded thee: 46 And they shall be upon thee for a sign and for a wonder, and **upon thy seed for ever**. **Psalms 119:11** Thy word have I hid in mine heart, that I might not sin against thee. **Proverbs 23:7** For **as he thinketh in his heart, so *is* he**: Eat and drink, saith he to thee; but his heart *is* not with thee. **Daniel 9:24** Seventy weeks are determined upon thy people and upon thy holy city, to finish the transgression, and **to make an end of sins**, and to make reconciliation for iniquity, and to bring in everlasting righteousness, and to seal up the vision and prophecy, and to anoint the most Holy. **See Hebrew 12:14 "Holiness"**
1 John 3:8 He that committeth sin is of the devil; for the devil sinneth from the beginning. For this purpose the Son of God was manifested, that he might destroy the works of the devil.	**Job 2:6-7** And the LORD said unto Satan, Behold, he *is* in thine hand; but save his life. 7 So went **Satan** forth from the presence of the LORD, and **smote Job with sore boils from the sole of his foot unto his crown**.
1 John 3:12 Not as Cain, *who* was of that wicked one, and slew his brother. And wherefore slew he him? Because his own works were evil, and his brother's righteous.	**Genesis 4:8** And Cain talked with Abel his brother: and it came to pass, when they were in the field, that Cain rose up against Abel his brother, and slew him.
1 John 3:15 Whosoever hateth his brother is a **murderer**: and ye know that no murderer hath eternal life abiding in him.	**Psalms 22:10** I was cast upon thee from the womb: thou *art* my God from my mother's belly. **Psalms 51:5** Behold, I was shapen in iniquity; and in sin did my mother conceive me.

	Jeremiah 1:5 Before I formed thee in the belly I knew thee; and before thou camest forth out of the womb I sanctified thee, *and* I ordained thee a prophet unto the nations.
1 John 3:17 But whoso hath this world's good, and seeth his brother have need, and shutteth up his bowels *of compassion* from him, how dwelleth the love of God in him?	**Deuteronomy 15:7** If there be among you a **poor** man of one of thy brethren within any of thy gates in thy land which the LORD thy God giveth thee, thou shalt not harden thine heart, nor shut thine hand from thy poor brother: **Proverbs 19:17** He that hath pity upon the **poor** lendeth unto the LORD; and that which he hath given will he pay him again. **Proverbs 22:9** He that hath a bountiful eye shall be blessed; for he giveth of his bread to the **poor**. **Proverbs 28:27** He that giveth unto the **poor** shall not lack: but he that hideth his eyes shall have many a curse. **See Matthew 6:24 "Wealth"**
1 John 3:22 And whatsoever we ask, we receive of him, because we keep his commandments, and do those things that are pleasing in his sight.	**2 Chronicles 16:12-13** And Asa in the thirty and ninth year of his reign was diseased in his feet, until his disease [was] exceeding *great*: yet in his disease <u>he sought not to the LORD, but to the physicians</u>. 13 And <u>Asa slept with his fathers</u>, and died in the one and fortieth year of his reign. **Jeremiah 29:12** Then shall ye call upon me, and ye shall go and pray unto me, and I will hearken unto you.
1 John 3:23 And this is his commandment, That we should believe on the name of his Son Jesus Christ, and love one another, as he gave us commandment.	**Leviticus 19:18** Thou shalt not avenge, nor bear any grudge against the children of thy people, but thou shalt love thy neighbour as thyself: I *am* the LORD.
1 John 4:1 Beloved, believe not every spirit, but try the spirits whether they are of God: because many false prophets are gone out into the world.	**Jeremiah 14:14** Then the LORD said unto me, The prophets prophesy lies in my name: I sent them not, neither have I commanded them, neither spake unto them: they prophesy unto you a false vision and divination, and a thing of nought, and the deceit of their heart. **Jeremiah 23:21** I have not sent these prophets, yet they ran: I have not spoken to them, yet they prophesied. **Jeremiah 27:14-15** Therefore hearken not unto the words of the prophets that speak unto you, saying, Ye shall not serve the king of Babylon: for they prophesy a lie unto you. 15 For I have not sent them, saith the LORD, yet they prophesy a lie in my name; that I might drive you out, and that ye might perish, ye, and the prophets that prophesy unto you. **Jeremiah 29:8-9** For thus saith the LORD of hosts, the God of Israel; Let not your prophets and your diviners, that *be* in the midst of you, deceive you, neither hearken to your dreams which ye cause to be dreamed. 9 For they prophesy falsely unto you in my name: I have not sent them, saith the LORD.
1 John 4:3 And every spirit that confesseth not that Jesus Christ is come in the flesh is not of God: and **this is that** *spirit* **of antichrist**, whereof ye have heard that it should come; and even now already is it in the world.	**See 1 John 2:18 "antichrist"**
1 John 4:9 In this was manifested the love of God toward us, because that God	**Psalms 2:7** I will declare the decree: the LORD hath said unto me, Thou *art* my Son; this day have I begotten thee.

sent his only **begotten Son** into the world, that we might live through him.	**Psalms 89:27** Also I will make him *my* **firstborn**, higher than the kings of the earth. **Jeremiah 31:9** They shall come with weeping, and with supplications will I lead them: I will cause them to walk by the rivers of waters in a straight way, wherein they shall not stumble: for I am a father to Israel, and Ephraim is my **firstborn**.
1 John 4:12 No man hath seen God at any time. If we love one another, God dwelleth in us, and his love is perfected in us.	**Exodus 33:20** And he said, Thou canst not see my face: for there shall no man see me, and live. **Deuteronomy 4:12** And the LORD spake unto you out of the midst of the fire: ye heard the voice of the words, but saw no similitude; only *ye heard* a voice.
1 John 4:14 And we have seen and do testify that the Father sent the Son *to be* the **Saviour** of the world.	**Job 19:25** For I know *that* my redeemer liveth, and *that* he shall stand at the latter *day* upon the earth: **Psalms 106:21** They forgat God their **saviour**, which had done great things in Egypt; **Isaiah 9:6** For unto us a child is born, unto us a son is given: and the government shall be upon his shoulder: and his name shall be called Wonderful, Counseller, The mighty God, The everlasting Father, The Prince of Peace. **Isaiah 43:3** For I am the LORD thy God, the Holy One of Israel, **thy Saviour**: I gave Egypt for thy ransom, Ethiopia and Seba for thee. **Isaiah 45:21** Tell ye, and bring them near; yea, let them take counsel together: who hath declared this from ancient time? who hath told it from that time? have not I the LORD? and there is no God else beside me; a just **God and a Saviour**; there is none beside me. **Isaiah 60:16** Thou shalt also suck the milk of the Gentiles, and shalt suck the breast of kings: and thou shalt know that I the LORD *am* thy **Saviour** and thy Redeemer, the mighty One of Jacob.
1 John 4:18 There is no fear in love; but perfect love casteth out fear: because fear hath torment. He that feareth is not made perfect in love.	**Proverb 29:25** The fear of man bringeth a snare: but whoso putteth his trust in the LORD shall be safe. **Isaiah 51:12** I, *even* I, *am* he that comforteth you: who *art* thou, that thou shouldest be afraid of a man *that* shall die, and of the son of man *which* shall be made *as* grass;
1 John 4:21 And this commandment have we from him, That he who loveth God love his brother also.	**Leviticus 19:18** Thou shalt not avenge, nor bear any grudge against the children of thy people, but thou shalt love thy neighbour as thyself: I *am* the LORD.
1 John 5:7 For there are three that bear record in heaven, the Father, the Word, and the Holy Ghost: and these three are one.aa	**Deuteronomy 6:4** Hear, O Israel: The LORD our God *is* one LORD:
1 John 5:8 And there are three that bear witness in earth, the spirit, and the water, and the blood: and these three agree in one.	See John 3:5 and Acts 2:38 "Salvation"
1 John 5:14-16 And this is the confidence that we have in him, that, if we **ask** any thing according to his will, he heareth us: 15 And if we know that he hear us, whatsoever we **ask**, we know	**2 Chronicles 16:12-13** And Asa in the thirty and ninth year of his reign was diseased in his feet, until his disease [was] exceeding *great*: yet in his disease <u>he sought not to the LORD</u>, <u>but to the physicians</u>. 13 And <u>Asa slept with his fathers</u>, and died in the one and fortieth year of his reign.

that we have the petitions that we desired of him. 16 If any man see his brother sin a sin which is not unto death, he shall **ask**, and he shall give him life for them that sin not unto death. There is a sin unto death: I do not say that he shall pray for it.	**Jeremiah 29:12** Then shall ye call upon me, and ye shall go and pray unto me, and I will hearken unto you.
1 John 5:18 We know that whosoever is born of God sinneth not; but he that is begotten of God keepeth himself, and that wicked one toucheth him not.	**Ecclesiastes 10:8** ... and whoso breaketh an hedge, a serpent shall bite him. **Psalm 91:1** If you stay in the Secret Place you have a hedge around you of protection. He that dwelleth in the secret place of the most High shall abide under the shadow of the Almighty. **Psalm 91:7-16** A thousand shall fall at thy side, and ten thousand at thy right hand; *but* it shall not come nigh thee. 8 Only with thine eyes shalt thou behold and see the reward of the wicked. 9 Because thou hast made the LORD, *which is* my refuge, even the most High, thy habitation; 10 There shall no evil befall thee, neither shall any plague come nigh thy dwelling … **Psalms 119:11** Thy word have I hid in mine heart, that I might not sin against thee. **Proverbs 23:7** For **as he thinketh in his heart, so *is* he**: Eat and drink, saith he to thee; but his heart *is* not with thee. **Isaiah 28:17** Judgment also will I lay to the line, and righteousness to the plummet: and the hail shall sweep away the refuge of lies, and the waters shall overflow the hiding place. **Daniel 9:24** Seventy weeks are determined upon thy people and upon thy holy city, to finish the transgression, and **to make an end of sins**, and to make reconciliation for iniquity, and to bring in everlasting righteousness, and to seal up the vision and prophecy, and to anoint the most Holy.
1 John 5:20 And we know that the Son of God is come, and hath given us an understanding, that we may know him that is true, and we are in him that is true, *even* in his Son Jesus Christ. This is the true God, and eternal life.	**Isaiah 9:6** For unto us a child is born, unto us a son is given: and the government shall be upon his shoulder: and his name shall be called Wonderful, Counseller, The mighty God, The everlasting Father, The Prince of Peace. **Isaiah 44:6** Thus saith the LORD the King of Israel, and his redeemer the LORD of hosts; I *am* the first, and I *am* the last; and beside me *there is* no God. **Isaiah 45:21** Tell ye, and bring *them* near; yea, let them take counsel together: who hath declared this from ancient time? *who* hath told it from that time? *have* not I the LORD? and *there is* no God else beside me; a just God and a **Savior**; *there is* none beside me. **Isaiah 54:5** For thy Maker *is* thine husband; the LORD of hosts *is* his name; and thy Redeemer the Holy One of Israel; The God of the whole earth shall he be called.. **Isaiah 60:16** Thou shalt also suck the milk of the Gentiles, and shalt suck the breast of kings: and thou shalt know that I the LORD *am* thy Saviour and thy Redeemer, the mighty One of Jacob. **Jeremiah 10:10** But the LORD is the true God, he is the living God, and an everlasting king: at his wrath the earth shall tremble, and the nations shall not be able to abide his indignation.
2 John 1:1 The **elder** unto the elect lady	**See 1 Peter 5:1 "Elders"**

and her children, whom I love in the truth; and not I only, but also all they that have known the truth;	
2 John 1:7 For many deceivers are entered into the world, who confess not that Jesus Christ is come in the flesh. This is a deceiver and an **antichrist**.	**See 1 John 2:18 "antichrist"**
2 John 1:10 If there come any unto you, and bring not this doctrine, receive him not into *your* house, neither bid him God speed:	**Deuteronomy 23:10** If there be among you any man, that is not clean by reason of uncleanness that chanceth him by night, then shall he go abroad out of the camp, he shall not come within the camp: **Psalms 133:1** Behold, how good and how pleasant *it is* for brethren to dwell together in unity! **Proverbs 14:15** The **simple** believeth every word: but the prudent *man* looketh well to his going. **Proverbs 22:3** A prudent *man* foreseeth the evil, and hideth himself: but the **simple** pass on, and are punished. **Proverbs 22:24-25** Make no friendship with an angry man; and with a furious man thou shalt not go: 25 Lest thou learn his ways, and get a snare to thy soul. **Isaiah 5:20** Woe unto them that call evil good, and good evil; that put darkness for light, and light for **darkness**; that put bitter for sweet, and sweet for bitter! **Amos 3:3** Can two walk together, except they be agreed?
3 John 1:1 The **elder** unto the wellbeloved Gaius, whom I love in the truth.	**See 1 Peter 5:1 "Elders"**
3 John 1:2 Beloved, I wish above all things that thou mayest **prosper** and **be in health**, even as thy soul prospereth.	**Psalms 37:25** I have been young, and *now* am old; yet have I not seen the righteous forsaken, nor his seed begging bread. **Deuteronomy 8:18** But thou shalt remember the LORD thy God: for *it is* **he that giveth thee power to get wealth**, that he may establish his covenant which he sware unto thy fathers, as *it is* this day. **Deuteronomy 28:5** Blessed *shall be* thy basket and thy store. **Deuteronomy 28:11-12** And the LORD shall make thee plenteous in goods, in the fruit of thy body, and in the fruit of thy cattle, and in the fruit of thy ground, in the land which the LORD sware unto thy fathers to give thee. 12 The LORD shall open unto thee his good treasure, the heaven to give the rain unto thy land in his season, and to bless all the work of thine hand: and thou shalt lend unto many nations, and thou shalt not borrow. **Deuteronomy 28:16-18** Cursed *shalt* thou *be* in the city, and cursed *shalt* thou *be* in the field. 17 Cursed *shall be* thy basket and thy store. 18 Cursed *shall be* the fruit of thy body, and the fruit of thy land, the increase of thy kine, and the flocks of thy sheep. **Joshua 1:8** This book of the law shall not depart out of thy mouth; but thou shalt meditate therein day and night, that thou mayest observe to do according to all that is written therein: for then thou shalt make thy way **prosperous**, and then thou shalt have good **success**. **Isaiah 1:19** If ye be willing and obedient, ye shall eat the good of

	the land: **See 1 Peter 2:24 "healing"**
3 John 1:11 Beloved, follow not that which is evil, but that which is good. He that doeth good is of God: but he that doeth evil hath not seen God.	**Psalms 34:14** Depart from evil, and do good; seek peace, and pursue it. **Psalms 37:27** Depart from evil, and do good; and dwell for evermore. **Isaiah 1:16** Wash you, make you clean; put away the evil of your doings from before mine eyes; cease to do evil;
Jude 1:4 For there are certain men crept in unawares, who were before of old ordained to this condemnation, ungodly men, turning the grace of our God into lasciviousness, and denying the only Lord God, and our Lord Jesus Christ.	**Exodus 9:15-16** For now I will stretch out my hand, that I may smite thee and thy people with pestilence; and thou shalt be cut off from the earth. 16 And in very deed for this *cause* have I raised thee up, for to shew *in* thee my power; and that my name may be declared throughout all the earth. **See 2 Peter 2:1 "False prophets"**
Jude 1:5 I will therefore put you in remembrance, though ye once knew this, how that the Lord, having saved the people out of the land of Egypt, afterward destroyed them that believed not.	**Exodus 12:41** And it came to pass at the end of the four hundred and thirty years, even the selfsame day it came to pass, that all the hosts of the LORD went out from the land of Egypt. **Numbers 14:29** Your carcases shall fall in this wilderness; and all that were numbered of you, according to your whole number, from twenty years old and upward, which have murmured against me, **Numbers 26:64-65** But among these there was not a man of them whom Moses and Aaron the priest numbered, when they numbered the children of Israel in the wilderness of Sinai. 65 For the LORD had said of them, They shall surely die in the wilderness. And there was not left a man of them, save Caleb the son of Jephunneh, and Joshua the son of Nun. **Psalms 106:26** Therefore he lifted up his hand against them, to overthrow them in the wilderness:
Jude 1:6 And the **angels** which kept not their first estate, but left their own habitation, he hath reserved in everlasting chains under darkness unto the judgment of the great day.	**See Hebrews 13:2 "Good and bad angels"**
Jude 1:7 Even as **Sodom and Gomorrha**, and the cities about them in like manner, giving themselves over to fornication, and going after strange flesh, are set forth for an example, suffering the vengeance of eternal fire.	**Genesis 19:1-38** **Genesis 19:24-26** And Jehovah rained brimstone and fire on **Sodom and Gomorrah**, from Jehovah out of the heavens. And He overthrew those cities, and all the plain, and all those living in the cities, and the produce of the ground. And his wife looked back from behind him, and she became a pillar of salt. **Deuteronomy 29:23** *And that* the whole land thereof *is* brimstone, and salt, *and* burning, *that* it is not sown, nor beareth, nor any grass groweth therein, like the overthrow of Sodom, and Gomorrah, Admah, and Zeboim, which the LORD overthrew in his anger, and in his wrath: **Isaiah 13:19** And Babylon, the glory of kingdoms, the beauty of the Chaldees' excellency, shall be as when God overthrew Sodom and Gomorrah. **Jeremiah 50:40** As God overthrew Sodom and Gomorrah and the neighbour *cities* thereof, saith the LORD; *so* shall no man abide there, neither shall any son of man dwell therein.

	Ezekiel 16:49 Behold, this was the iniquity of thy sister Sodom, pride, fulness of bread, and abundance of idleness was in her and in her daughters, neither did she strengthen the hand of the poor and needy.
	Amos 4:11 I have overthrown *some* of you, as God overthrew Sodom and Gomorrah, and ye were as a firebrand plucked out of the burning: yet have ye not returned unto me, saith the LORD.
	See Romans 1:27 "Sexual sins"
	See Luke 16:23 "Hell"
Jude 1:9 Yet **Michael** the archangel, when contending with the devil he disputed about the body of Moses, durst not bring against him a railing accusation, but said, The Lord rebuke thee.	**Deuteronomy 34:5-6** So Moses the servant of the LORD died there in the land of Moab, according to the word of the LORD. 6 And he buried him in a valley in the land of Moab, over against Bethpeor: but no man knoweth of his sepulchre unto this day.
	Daniel 10:13 But the prince of the kingdom of Persia withstood me one and twenty days: but, lo, **Michael**, one of the chief princes, came to help me; and I remained there with the kings of Persia.
	Daniel 10:21 But I will shew thee that which is noted in the scripture of truth: and there is none that holdeth with me in these things, but **Michael** your prince.
	Daniel 12:1 And at that time shall **Michael** stand up, the great prince which standeth for the children of thy people: and there shall be a time of trouble, such as never was since there was a nation *even* to that same time: and at that time thy people shall be delivered, every one that shall be found written in the book.
	Zechariah 3:2 And the LORD said unto Satan, The LORD rebuke thee, O Satan; even the LORD that hath chosen Jerusalem rebuke thee: *is* not this a brand plucked out of the fire?
	See Hebrews 13:2 "Good and bad angels"
Jude 1:11 Woe unto them! for they have gone in the way of Cain, and ran greedily after the error of Balaam for reward, and perished in the gainsaying of Core.	**Genesis 4:8** And Cain talked with Abel his brother: and it came to pass, when they were in the field, that Cain rose up against Abel his brother, and slew him.
	Numbers 12:2-3 And they said, Hath the LORD indeed spoken only by Moses? hath he not spoken also by us? And the LORD heard *it*. 3 (Now the man Moses *was* very meek, above all the men which *were* upon the face of the earth.)
	Numbers 16:1-50
	Numbers 22:1-41
Jude 1:13 Raging waves of the sea, foaming out their own shame; wandering stars, to whom is reserved the blackness of darkness for ever.	**Isaiah 57:20** But the wicked *are* like the troubled sea, when it cannot rest, whose waters cast up mire and dirt.
	See Luke 16:23 "Hell"
Jude 1:14 And Enoch also, the seventh from Adam, **prophesied** of these, saying, Behold, the Lord cometh with ten thousands of his saints,	**Genesis 5:18** And Jared lived an hundred sixty and two years, and he begat Enoch:
	Deuteronomy 33:2 And he said, The LORD came from Sinai, and rose up from Seir unto them; he shined forth from mount Paran, and he came with ten thousands of saints: from his right hand *went* a fiery law for them.
	Daniel 7:10 A fiery stream issued and came forth from before him: thousand thousands ministered unto him, and ten thousand times ten thousand stood before him: the judgment was set, and

	the books were opened. **Zechariah 14:5** And ye shall flee *to* the valley of the mountains; for the valley of the mountains shall reach unto Azal: yea, ye shall flee, like as ye fled from before the earthquake in the days of Uzziah king of Judah: and the LORD my God shall come, *and* all the saints with thee. **See 1 Corinthians 12:10 "Prophecy"**
Jude 1:15 To execute judgment upon all, and to convince all that are ungodly among them of all their ungodly deeds which they have ungodly committed, and of all their hard *speeches* which ungodly sinners have spoken against him.	**Isaiah 3:8** For Jerusalem is ruined, and Judah is fallen: because their tongue and their doings *are* against the LORD, to provoke the eyes of his glory. **Isaiah 26:21** For, behold, the LORD cometh out of his place to punish the inhabitants of the earth for their iniquity: the earth also shall disclose her blood, and shall no more cover her slain. **Ezekiel 11:9** And I will bring you out of the midst thereof, and deliver you into the hands of strangers, and will execute judgments among you. **Malachi 3:5** And I will come near to you to judgment; and I will be a swift witness against the sorcerers, and against the adulterers, and against false swearers, and against those that oppress the hireling in *his* wages, the widow, and the fatherless, and that turn aside the stranger *from his right,* and fear not me, saith the LORD of hosts.
Jude 1:21 Keep yourselves in the love of God, looking for the mercy of our Lord Jesus Christ unto eternal life.	**Exodus 12:22** And ye shall take a bunch of hyssop, and dip *it* in the blood that *is* in the bason, and strike the lintel and the two side posts with the blood that *is* in the bason; and none of you shall go out at the door of his house until the morning. **Exodus 24:6-8** And Moses took half of the blood, and put *it* in basons; and half of the blood he sprinkled on the altar. 7 And he took the book of the covenant, and read in the audience of the people: and they said, All that the LORD hath said will we do, and be obedient. 8 And Moses took the blood, and sprinkled *it* on the people, and said, Behold the blood of the covenant, which the LORD hath made with you concerning all these words. **Leviticus 5:9** And he shall sprinkle of the blood of the sin offering upon the side of the altar; and the rest of the blood shall be wrung out at the bottom of the altar: it *is* a sin offering. **Psalms 103:3** Who forgiveth all thine iniquities; who healeth all thy diseases; **Psalms 130:7-8** Let Israel hope in the LORD: for with the LORD *there is* mercy, and with him *is* plenteous redemption. 8 And he shall redeem Israel from all his iniquities **Isaiah 53:5** But he *was* wounded for our transgressions, *he was* bruised for our iniquities: the chastisement of our peace *was* upon him; and with his stripes we are healed. **Daniel 9:24** Seventy weeks are determined upon thy people and upon thy holy city, to finish the transgression, and to make an end of sins, and **to make reconciliation for iniquity**, and to bring in everlasting righteousness, and to seal up the vision and prophecy, and to anoint the most Holy.
Jude 1:25 To the only wise God our Saviour, *be* glory and majesty, dominion and power, both now and ever. Amen.	**Job 19:25** For I know *that* my redeemer liveth, and *that* he shall stand at the latter *day* upon the earth: **Isaiah 9:6** For unto us a child is born, unto us a son is given: and

	the government shall be upon his shoulder: and his name shall be called Wonderful, Counseller, The mighty God, The everlasting Father, The Prince of Peace.
	Isaiah 60:16 Thou shalt also suck the milk of the Gentiles, and shalt suck the breast of kings: and thou shalt know that I the LORD *am* thy Saviour and thy Redeemer, the mighty One of Jacob.
Revelations 1:1 The Revelation of Jesus Christ, which God gave unto him, to shew unto his servants things which must shortly come to pass; and he sent and signified *it* by his angel unto his servant John:	**Exodus 35:1** And Moses gathered all the congregation of the children of Israel together, and said unto them, These *are* the words which the LORD hath commanded, that *ye* should do them. **Jeremiah 1:9** Then the LORD put forth his hand, and touched my mouth. And the LORD said unto me, Behold, I have put my words in thy mouth. **Ezekiel 1:3** The word of the LORD came expressly unto Ezekiel the priest, the son of Buzi, in the land of the Chaldeans by the river Chebar; and the hand of the LORD was there upon him. **Daniel 2:28** But there is a God in heaven that revealeth secrets, and maketh known to the king Nebuchadnezzar what shall be in the latter days. Thy dream, and the visions of thy head upon thy bed, are these; **Daniel 12:8-9** And I heard, but I understood not: then said I, O my Lord, what *shall be* the end of these *things?* 9 And he said, Go thy way, Daniel: for the words *are* closed up and sealed till the time of the end. **Amos 1:1** The words of Amos, who was among the herdmen of Tekoa, which he saw concerning Israel in the days of Uzziah king of Judah, and in the days of Jeroboam the son of Joash king of Israel, two years before the earthquake.
Revelations 1:3 Blessed *is* he that readeth, and they that hear the words of this prophecy, and keep those things which are written therein: for the time *is* at hand.	**Daniel 2:47** The king answered unto Daniel, and said, Of a truth *it is,* that your God *is* a God of gods, and a Lord of kings, and a revealer of secrets, seeing thou couldest reveal this secret.
Revelations 1:4 John to the seven churches which are in Asia: Grace *be* unto you, and peace, from him which is, and which was, and which is to come; and from the seven Spirits which are before his throne;	**Genesis 2:2** And on the seventh day God ended his work which he had made; and he rested on the seventh day from all his work which he had made. **Leviticus 14:7** And he shall sprinkle upon him that is to be cleansed from the leprosy seven times, and shall pronounce him clean, and shall let the living bird loose into the open field.
Revelation 1:5 And from Jesus Christ, who is the faithful witness, and the first begotten of the dead, and the prince of the kings of the earth. Unto him that loved us, and **washed us from our sins in his own blood,**	**Leviticus 17:11** For the life of the flesh is in the blood: and I have given it to you upon the altar to make an atonement for your souls**: for it is the blood that maketh an atonement for the soul**. **See Matthew 26:28 "Atonement"**
Revelations 1:6 And hath made us **kings** and priests unto God and his Father; to him *be* glory and dominion for ever and ever. Amen.	**Exodus 19:6** And ye shall be unto me a kingdom of priests, and an holy nation. These *are* the words which thou shalt speak unto the children of Israel. **Proverb 25:2** It is the glory of God to conceal a thing: but the honour of **kings is to search out a matter**. **Isaiah 61:6** But ye shall be named the Priests of the LORD: *men* shall call you the Ministers of our God: ye shall eat the riches of the Gentiles, and in their glory shall ye boast yourselves.

Revelations 1:7 Behold, he cometh with clouds; and every eye shall see him, and they *also* which pierced him: and all kindreds of the earth shall wail because of him. Even so, Amen.A	**Leviticus 23:27** Also on the tenth *day* of this seventh month *there shall be* a day of atonement: it shall be an holy convocation unto you; and ye shall afflict your souls, and offer an offering made by fire unto the LORD. **Psalms 22:16** For dogs have compassed me: the assembly of the wicked have inclosed me: they pierced my hands and my feet. **Daniel 7:13** I saw in the night visions, and, behold, *one* like the Son of man came with the clouds of heaven, and came to the Ancient of days, and they brought him near before him. **Zechariah 12:10** And I will pour upon the house of David, and upon the inhabitants of Jerusalem, the spirit of grace and of supplications: and they shall look upon me whom they have pierced, and they shall mourn for him, as one mourneth for *his* only *son,* and shall be in bitterness for him, as one that is in bitterness for *his* firstborn.
Revelations 1:8 I am Alpha and Omega, the beginning and the ending, saith the Lord, which is, and which was, and which is to come, the Almighty.	**Genesis 17:1** And when Abram was ninety years old and nine, the LORD appeared to Abram, and said unto him, I *am* the **Almighty** God; walk before me, and be thou perfect. **Isaiah 41:4** Who hath wrought and done *it,* calling the generations from the beginning? I the LORD, **the first, and with the last**; I *am* he. **Isaiah 44:6** Thus saith the LORD the King of Israel, and his redeemer the LORD of hosts; **I *am* the first, and I *am* the last**; and beside me *there is* no God. **See 1 Timothy 2:5 "God"**
Revelations 1:10 I was in the Spirit on the Lord's day, and heard behind me a great voice, as of a trumpet,	**Ezekiel 3:14** So the spirit lifted me up, and took me away, and I went in bitterness, in the heat of my spirit; but the hand of the LORD was strong upon me.
Revelation 1:11 Saying, I am Alpha and Omega, **the first and the last**: and, What thou seest, write in a book, and send *it* unto the seven churches which are in Asia; unto Ephesus, and unto Smyrna, and unto Pergamos, and unto Thyatira, and unto Sardis, and unto Philadelphia, and unto Laodicea.	**Isaiah 41:4** Who hath wrought and done *it,* calling the generations from the beginning? I the LORD, **the first, and with the last**; I *am* he. **Isaiah 44:6** Thus saith the LORD the King of Israel, and his redeemer the LORD of hosts; **I *am* the first, and I *am* the last**; and beside me *there is* no God.
Revelation 1:12 And I turned to see the voice that spake with me. And being turned, I saw seven golden candlesticks;	**Zechariah 4:2** And said unto me, What seest thou? And I said, I have looked, and behold a candlestick all *of* gold, with a bowl upon the top of it, and his seven lamps thereon, and seven pipes to the seven lamps, which *are* upon the top thereof:
Revelations 1:13 And in the midst of the seven candlesticks *one* like unto the Son of man, clothed with a garment down to the foot, and girt about the paps with a golden girdle.	**Daniel 7:13** I saw in the night visions, and, behold, *one* like the Son of man came with the clouds of heaven, and came to the Ancient of days, and they brought him near before him. **Daniel 10:5** Then I lifted up mine eyes, and looked, and behold a certain man clothed in linen, whose loins *were* girded with fine gold of Uphaz:
Revelation 1:14-15 His head and his hairs were white like wool, as white as snow; and his eyes were as a flame of fire; 15 And his feet like unto fine brass, as if they burned in a furnace; and his voice as the sound of many waters.	**Ezekiel 1:7** And their feet *were* straight feet; and the sole of their feet *was* like the sole of a calf's foot: and they sparkled like the colour of burnished brass. **Ezekiel 1:27** And I saw as the colour of amber, as the appearance of fire round about within it, from the appearance of his loins even upward, and from the appearance of his loins even downward, I saw as it were the appearance of fire, and it had brightness round

	about.
	Ezekiel 8:2 Then I beheld, and lo a likeness as the appearance of fire: from the appearance of his loins even downward, fire; and from his loins even upward, as the appearance of brightness, as the colour of amber.
	Ezekiel 43:2 And, behold, the glory of the God of Israel came from the way of the east: and his voice *was* like a noise of many waters: and the earth shined with his glory.
	Daniel 7:9 I beheld till the thrones were cast down, and the Ancient of days did sit, whose garment *was* white as snow, and the hair of his head like the pure wool: his throne *was like* the fiery flame, *and* his wheels *as* burning fire.
	Daniel 10:6 His body also was like the beryl, and his face as the appearance of lightning, and his eyes as lamps of fire, and his arms and his feet like in colour to polished brass, and the voice of his words like the voice of a multitude.
Revelation 1:16 And he had in his right hand seven stars: and out of his mouth went a sharp two edged sword: and his countenance *was* as the sun shineth in his strength.	**Isaiah 49:2** And he hath made my mouth like a sharp sword; in the shadow of his hand hath he hid me, and made me a polished shaft; in his quiver hath he hid me;
Revelations 1:17 And when I saw him, I fell at his feet as dead. And he laid his right hand upon me, saying unto me, Fear not; I am the first and the last:	**Isaiah 41:4** Who hath wrought and done *it*, calling the generations from the beginning? I the LORD, **the first, and with the last**; I [am] he. **Isaiah 44:6** Thus saith the LORD the King of Israel, and his redeemer the LORD of hosts; **I *am* the first, and I *am* the last**; and beside me [there is] no God. **Isaiah 48:12** Hearken unto me, O Jacob and Israel, my called; I *am* he; I *am* the first, I also *am* the last. **Daniel 8:17** So he came near where I stood: and when he came, I was afraid, and fell upon my face: but he said unto me, Understand, O son of man: for at the time of the end *shall be* the vision. **Daniel 10:8-9** Therefore I was left alone, and saw this great vision, and there remained no strength in me: for my comeliness was turned in me into corruption, and I retained no strength. 9 Yet heard I the voice of his words: and when I heard the voice of his words, then was I in a deep sleep on my face, and my face toward the ground.
Revelations 1:18 *I am* he that liveth, and was dead; and, behold, I am alive for evermore, Amen; and have the keys of **hell** and of death.	**See Luke 16:23 "Hell"**
Revelations 1:20 The mystery of the seven stars which thou sawest in my right hand, and the seven golden candlesticks. The seven stars are the angels of the seven churches: and the seven candlesticks which thou sawest are the seven churches.	**Exodus 25:37** And thou shalt make the seven lamps thereof: and they shall light the lamps thereof, that they may give light over against it.
Revelations 2:1 Unto the angel of the church of Ephesus write; These things saith he that holdeth the seven stars in	**Deuteronomy 23:14** For the LORD thy God walketh in the midst of thy camp, to deliver thee, and to give up thine enemies before thee; therefore shall thy camp be holy: that he see no unclean thing

his right hand, who walketh in the midst of the seven golden candlesticks;	in thee, and turn away from thee.
Revelations 2:4 Nevertheless I have *somewhat* against thee, because thou hast left thy first love.	**Jeremiah 2:2** Go and cry in the ears of Jerusalem, saying, Thus saith the LORD; I remember thee, the kindness of thy youth, the love of thine espousals, when thou wentest after me in the wilderness, in a land *that was* not sown.
Revelations 2:7 He that hath an ear, let him hear what the Spirit saith unto the churches; To him that **overcometh** will I give to eat of the **tree of life**, which is in the midst of the paradise of God.	**See Revelation 22:1-2 "Tree of life"** **Numbers 13:30** And Caleb stilled the people before Moses, and said, Let us go up at once, and possess it; for we are well able to **overcome** it. **Ezekiel 31:8** The cedars in the garden of God could not hide him: the fir trees were not like his boughs, and the chesnut trees were not like his branches; nor any tree in the garden of God was like unto him in his beauty.
Revelations 2:8 And unto the angel of the church in Smyrna write; These things saith **the first and the last**, which was dead, and is alive;	**Isaiah 41:4** Who hath wrought and done [it], calling the generations from the beginning? I the LORD, **the first, and with the last**; I [am] he. **Isaiah 44:6** Thus saith the LORD the King of Israel, and his redeemer the LORD of hosts; **I am the first, and I am the last**; and beside me [there is] no God.
Revelations 2:9 I know thy works, and tribulation, and poverty, (but thou art rich) and *I know* the blasphemy of them which say they are Jews, and are not, but *are* the synagogue of **Satan**.	**See Matthew 4:10 "satan"** **See 1 Peter 5:1 "Elders"** **Jeremiah 10:2** Thus saith the LORD, Learn not the way of the heathen, and be not dismayed at the signs of heaven; for the heathen are dismayed at them. **Jeremiah 50:38** A drought is upon her waters; and they shall be dried up: for it is the land of graven images, and they are mad upon *their* idols
Revelation 2:10 Fear none of those things which thou shalt suffer: behold, the devil shall cast *some* of you into prison, that ye may be tried; and ye shall have tribulation ten days: be thou faithful unto death, and I will give thee a crown of life.	**Daniel 1:12** Prove thy servants, I beseech thee, ten days; and let them give us pulse to eat, and water to drink. **Daniel 1:14** So he consented to them in this matter, and proved them ten days. **Ezekiel 4:6** And when thou hast accomplished them, lie again on thy right side, and thou shalt bear the iniquity of the house of Judah forty days: I have appointed thee each day for a year.
Revelations 2:13 I know thy works, and where thou dwellest, *even* where **Satan's** seat *is:* and thou holdest fast my name, and hast not denied my faith, even in those days wherein Antipas *was* my faithful martyr, who was slain among you, where **Satan** dwelleth.	**Genesis 3:4** And the **serpent** said unto the woman, Ye shall not surely die: **Zechariah 3:1-2** And he shewed me Joshua the high priest standing before the angel of the LORD, and **Satan** standing at his right hand to resist him. 2 And the LORD said unto **Satan**, The LORD rebuke thee, O **Satan**; even the LORD that hath chosen Jerusalem rebuke thee: *is* not this a brand plucked out of the fire? **See Matthew 4:10 "satan"**
Revelations 2:14 But I have a few things against thee, because thou hast there them that hold the doctrine of Balaam, who taught Balac to cast a stumblingblock before the children of Israel, to eat things sacrificed unto idols, and to commit fornication.	**Numbers 25:2** And they called the people unto the sacrifices of their gods: and the people did eat, and bowed down to their gods. **Numbers 31:16** Behold, these caused the children of Israel, through the counsel of Balaam, to commit trespass against the LORD in the matter of Peor, and there was a plague among the congregation of the LORD.

Revelations 2:17 He that hath an ear, let him hear what the Spirit saith unto the churches; To him that overcometh will I give to eat of the hidden manna, and will give him a white stone, and in the stone a new name written, which no man knoweth saving he that receiveth *it*.	**Isaiah 56:5** Even unto them will I give in mine house and within my walls a place and a name better than of sons and of daughters: I will give them an everlasting name, that shall not be cut off. **Isaiah 62:2** And the Gentiles shall see thy righteousness, and all kings thy glory: and thou shalt be called by a new name, which the mouth of the LORD shall name. **Isaiah 65:15** And ye shall leave your name for a curse unto my chosen: for the Lord GOD shall slay thee, and call his servants by another name:
Revelations 2:20 Notwithstanding I have a few things against thee, because thou sufferest that woman Jezebel, which calleth herself a prophetess, to teach and to seduce my servants to commit fornication, and to eat things sacrificed unto idols.	**1 Kings 16:31** And it came to pass, as if it had been a light thing for him to walk in the sins of Jeroboam the son of Nebat, that he took to wife Jezebel the daughter of Ethbaal king of the Zidonians, and went and served Baal, and worshipped him. **1 Kings 21:23** And of Jezebel also spake the LORD, saying, The dogs shall eat Jezebel by the wall of Jezreel. **2 Kings 9:7** And thou shalt smite the house of Ahab thy master, that I may avenge the blood of my servants the prophets, and the blood of all the servants of the LORD, at the hand of Jezebel. **2 Kings 9:22** And it came to pass, when Joram saw Jehu, that he said, *Is it* peace, Jehu? And he answered, **What peace, so long as the whoredoms of thy mother Jezebel and her witchcrafts *are so* many?** **2 Kings 9:33** And he said, Throw her down. So they threw her down: and *some* of her blood was sprinkled on the wall, and on the horses: and he trode her under foot. **Numbers 25:1-3** And Israel abode in Shittim, and the people began to **commit whoredom with the daughters of Moab**. 2 And **they called the people unto the sacrifices of their gods**: and the people did eat, and bowed down to their gods. 3 And **Israel joined himself unto Baalpeor**: and the anger of the LORD was kindled against Israel. **Hosea 2:13** And I will visit upon her the days of Baalim, wherein she burned incense to them, and she decked herself with her earrings and her jewels, and **she went after her lovers**, and forgot me, saith the LORD.
Revelation 2:22 Behold, I will cast her into a bed, and them that commit **adultery** with her into great tribulation, except they repent of their deeds.	**See Matthew 5:27 "Adultery"**
Revelations 2:23 And I will kill her children with death; and all the churches shall know that I am he which searcheth the reins and hearts: and I will give unto every one of you according to your works.	**1 Samuel 16:7** But the LORD said unto Samuel, Look not on his countenance, or on the height of his stature; because I have refused him: for *the LORD seeth* not as man seeth; for man looketh on the outward appearance, but the LORD looketh on the heart. **1 Chronicles 28:9** And thou, Solomon my son, know thou the God of thy father, and serve him with a perfect heart and with a willing mind: for the LORD searcheth all hearts, and understandeth all the imaginations of the thoughts: if thou seek him, he will be found of thee; but if thou forsake him, he will cast thee off for ever. **1 Chronicles 29:17** I know also, my God, that thou triest the heart, and hast pleasure in uprightness. As for me, in the

	uprightness of mine heart I have willingly offered all these things: and now have I seen with joy thy people, which are present here, to offer willingly unto thee.

Psalms 7:8-9 The LORD shall judge the people: judge me, O LORD, according to my righteousness, and according to mine integrity that is in me. 9 Oh let the wickedness of the wicked come to an end; but establish the just: for the righteous God trieth the hearts and reins.

Jeremiah 11:20 But, O LORD of hosts, that judgest righteously, that triest the reins and the heart, let me see thy vengeance on them: for unto thee have I revealed my cause.

Jeremiah 17:10 I the LORD search the heart, [I] try the reins, even to give every man according to his ways, [and] according to the fruit of his doings.

Jeremiah 32:19 Great in counsel, and mighty in work: for thine eyes *are* open upon all the ways of the sons of men: to give every one according to his ways, and according to the fruit of his doings: |
| **Revelations 2:24** But unto you I say, and unto the rest in Thyatira, as many as have not this doctrine, and which have not known the depths of **Satan**, as they speak; I will put upon you none other burden. | **Genesis 3:4** And the **serpent** said unto the woman, Ye shall not surely die:

Zechariah 3:1-2 And he shewed me Joshua the high priest standing before the angel of the LORD, and **Satan** standing at his right hand to resist him. 2 And the LORD said unto **Satan,** The LORD rebuke thee, O **Satan**; even the LORD that hath chosen Jerusalem rebuke thee: *is* not this a brand plucked out of the fire?

See Matthew 4:10 "satan" |
| **Revelations 2:26** And he that overcometh, and keepeth my works unto the end, to him will I give power over the nations: | **Psalms 2:8** Ask of me, and I shall give *thee* the heathen *for* thine inheritance, and the uttermost parts of the earth *for* thy possession. |
| **Revelations 2:27** And he shall **rule** them with a rod of iron; as the vessels of a potter shall they be broken to shivers: even as I received of my Father. | **Psalms 2:9** Thou shalt break them with a rod of iron; thou shalt dash them in pieces like a potter's vessel.

Isaiah 30:14 And he shall break it as the breaking of the potters' vessel that is broken in pieces; he shall not spare: so that there shall not be found in the bursting of it a sherd to take fire from the hearth, or to take water *withal* out of the pit.

Jeremiah 19:11 And shalt say unto them, Thus saith the LORD of hosts; Even so will I break this people and this city, as *one* breaketh a potter's vessel, that cannot be made whole again: and they shall bury *them* in Tophet, till *there be* no place to bury.

Daniel 7:22 Until the Ancient of days came, and judgment was given to the saints of the most High; and the time came that the saints possessed the kingdom.

See 1 Peter 5:1 |
| **Revelations 3:4** Thou hast a few names even in Sardis which have not defiled their garments; and they shall walk with me in white: for they are worthy. | **Ecclesiastes 9:8** Let thy garments be always white; and let thy head lack no ointment. |
| **Revelation 3:5** He that overcometh, the same shall be clothed in white raiment; and I will not blot out his name out of **the book of life**, but I will confess his name before my Father, and before his | **Exodus 32:32-33** Yet now, if thou wilt forgive their sin--; and if not, blot me, I pray thee, out of thy book which thou hast written. 33 And the Lord said unto Moses, Whosoever hath sinned against me, him will I blot out of my book. |

angels.	**Psalm 56:8** Thou tellest my wanderings: put thou my tears into thy bottle: are they not in thy book?
	Psalm 69:28 Let them be blotted out of the book of the living, and not be written with the righteous.
	Isaiah 4:3 And it shall come to pass, *that he that is* left in Zion, and *he that* remaineth in Jerusalem, shall be called holy, *even* every one that is written among the living in Jerusalem:
	Ezekiel 13:9 And mine hand shall be upon the prophets that see vanity, and that divine lies: they shall not be in the assembly of my people, neither shall they be written in the writing of the house of Israel, neither shall they enter into the land of Israel; and ye shall know that I am the Lord GOD.
	Daniel 7:10 A fiery stream issued and came forth from before him: thousand thousands ministered unto him, and ten thousand times ten thousand stood before him: the judgment was set, and the books were opened.
	Daniel 12:1 And at that time shall Michael stand up, the great prince which standeth for the children of thy people: and there shall be a time of trouble, such as never was since there was a nation *even* to that same time: and at that time thy people shall be delivered, every one that shall be found written in the book.
Revelations 3:7 And to the angel of the church in Philadelphia write; These things saith he that is holy, he that is true, he that hath the key of David, he that openeth, and no man shutteth; and shutteth, and no man openeth;	**Job 12:14** Behold, he breaketh down, and it cannot be built again: he shutteth up a man, and there can be no opening.
	Isaiah 22:22 And the key of the house of David will I lay upon his shoulder; so he shall open, and none shall shut; and he shall shut, and none shall open.
Revelations 3:9 Behold, I will make them of the synagogue of **Satan**, which say they are Jews, and are not, but do lie; behold, I will make them to come and worship before thy feet, and to know that I have loved thee.	**Isaiah 45:14** Thus saith the LORD, The labour of Egypt, and merchandise of Ethiopia and of the Sabeans, men of stature, shall come over unto thee, and they shall be thine: they shall come after thee; in chains they shall come over, and they shall fall down unto thee, they shall make supplication unto thee, *saying,* Surely God *is* in thee; and *there is* none else, *there is* no God.
	Isaiah 60:14 The sons also of them that afflicted thee shall come bending unto thee; and all they that despised thee shall bow themselves down at the soles of thy feet; and they shall call thee, The city of the LORD, The Zion of the Holy One of Israel.
	Genesis 3:4 And the **serpent** said unto the woman, Ye shall not surely die:
	Zechariah 3:1-2 And he shewed me Joshua the high priest standing before the angel of the LORD, and **Satan** standing at his right hand to resist him. 2 And the LORD said unto **Satan,** The LORD rebuke thee, O **Satan**; even the LORD that hath chosen Jerusalem rebuke thee: *is* not this a brand plucked out of the fire?
	See Matthew 4:10 "satan"
Revelations 3:12 Him that overcometh will I make a pillar in the temple of my God, and he shall go no more out: and I will write upon him the name of my God, and the name of the city of my God, *which is* new Jerusalem, which cometh down out of heaven from my	**Jeremiah 1:18-19** For, behold, I have made thee this day a defenced city, and an iron pillar, and brasen walls against the whole land, against the kings of Judah, against the princes thereof, against the priests thereof, and against the people of the land. 19 And they shall fight against thee; but they shall not prevail against thee; for I *am* with thee, saith the LORD, to deliver thee.

God: and *I will write upon him* my new name.	**Ezekiel 48:35** *It was* round about eighteen thousand *measures:* and the name of the city from *that* day *shall be,* The LORD *is* there.
Revelation 3:17 Because thou sayest, I am rich, and increased with goods, and have need of nothing; and knowest not that thou art wretched, and miserable, and poor, and blind, and naked:	**Hosea 12:8** And Ephraim said, Yet I am become rich, I have found me out substance: *in* all my labours they shall find none iniquity in me that *were* sin. **Zechariah 11:5** Whose possessors slay them, and hold themselves not guilty: and they that sell them say, Blessed *be* the LORD; for I am rich: and their own shepherds pity them not.
Revelation 3:19 As many as I love, I rebuke and chasten: be zealous therefore, and repent.	**Job 5:17** Behold, happy *is* the man whom God correcteth: therefore despise not thou the chastening of the Almighty: **Proverbs 3:11-12** My son, despise not the chastening of the LORD; neither be weary of his correction: 12 For whom the LORD loveth he correcteth; even as a father the son in whom he delighteth.
Revelation 3:20 Behold, I stand at the door, and knock: if any man hear my voice, and open the door, **I will come in to him, and will sup with him, and he with me.**	**Psalms 23:6** Surely goodness and mercy shall follow me all the days of my life: and **I will dwell in the house of the LORD for ever**. **Psalm 91:1-4 He that dwelleth in the secret place of the most High shall abide under the shadow of the Almighty**. 2 I will say of the LORD, He is my refuge and my fortress: my God; in him will I trust. 3 Surely he shall deliver thee from the snare of the fowler, and from the noisome pestilence. 4 He shall cover thee with his feathers, and under his wings shalt thou trust: his truth shall be thy shield and buckler. **Psalm 91:15** He shall call upon me, and I will answer him: **I will be with him in trouble**; I will deliver him, and honour him.
Revelation 3:21 To him that overcometh will I grant to sit with me in my throne, even as I also overcame, and am set down with my Father in his throne.	**Psalms 110:1** A Psalm of David. The LORD said unto my Lord, Sit thou at my right hand, until I make thine enemies thy footstool.
Revelations 4:1 After this I looked, and, behold, a door *was* opened in heaven: and the first voice which I heard *was* as it were of a trumpet talking with me; which said, **Come up hither**, and I will shew thee things which must be hereafter.	**Leviticus 23:24** Speak unto the children of Israel, saying, In the seventh month, in the first *day* of the month, shall ye have a sabbath, a memorial of blowing of trumpets, an holy convocation. **Numbers 29:1** And in the seventh month, on the first *day* of the month, ye shall have an holy convocation; ye shall do no servile work: it is a day of blowing the trumpets unto you. **Psalms 50:5** Gather my saints together unto me; those that have made a covenant with me by sacrifice. **Isaiah 26:19** Thy dead *men* shall live, *together with* my dead body shall they arise. Awake and sing, ye that dwell in dust: for thy dew *is as* the dew of herbs, and the earth shall cast out the dead. **Isaiah 27:13** And it shall come to pass in that day, *that* the great trumpet shall be blown, and they shall come which were ready to perish in the land of Assyria, and the outcasts in the land of Egypt, and shall worship the LORD in the holy mount at Jerusalem. **Ezekiel 1:1** Now it came to pass in the thirtieth year, in the fourth *month,* in the fifth *day* of the month, as I *was* among the captives by the river of Chebar, *that* the heavens were opened, and I saw visions of God.
Revelation 4:2-3 And immediately I	**Exodus 24:10** And they saw the God of Israel: and *there was*

was in the spirit: and, behold, a throne was set in heaven, and one sat on the throne. 3 And he that sat was to look upon like a jasper and a sardine stone: and there was a rainbow round about the throne, in sight like unto an emerald.	under his feet as it were a paved work of a sapphire stone, and as it were the body of heaven in *his* clearness. **Ezekiel 1:26-28** And above the firmament that was over their heads was the likeness of a throne, as the appearance of a sapphire stone: and upon the likeness of the throne was the likeness as the appearance of a man above upon it. 27 And I saw as the colour of amber, as the appearance of fire round about within it, from the appearance of his loins even upward, and from the appearance of his loins even downward, I saw as it were the appearance of fire, and it had brightness round about. 28 As the appearance of the bow that is in the cloud in the day of rain, so was the appearance of the brightness round about. This was the appearance of the likeness of the glory of the LORD. And when I saw it, I fell upon my face, and I heard a voice of one that spake. **Daniel 7:9** I beheld till the thrones were cast down, and the Ancient of days did sit, whose garment *was* white as snow, and the hair of his head like the pure wool: his throne *was like* the fiery flame, *and* his wheels *as* burning fire.
Revelation 4:4 And round about the throne were four and twenty seats: and upon the seats I saw four and twenty elders sitting, clothed in white raiment; and they had on their heads crowns of gold.	See 1 Peter 5:1 "Elders"
Revelation 4:5 And out of the throne proceeded lightnings and thunderings and voices: and *there were* seven lamps of fire burning before the throne, which are the seven Spirits of God.	**Exodus 19:16** And it came to pass on the third day in the morning, that there were thunders and lightnings, and a thick cloud upon the mount, and the voice of the trumpet exceeding loud; so that all the people that *was* in the camp trembled. **Exodus 20:18** And all the people saw the thunderings, and the lightnings, and the noise of the trumpet, and the mountain smoking: and when the people saw *it,* they removed, and stood afar off. **Exodus 37:23** And he made his seven lamps, and his snuffers, and his snuffdishes, *of* pure gold. **Ezekiel 1:13** As for the likeness of the living creatures, their appearance *was* like burning coals of fire, *and* like the appearance of lamps: it went up and down among the living creatures; and the fire was bright, and out of the fire went forth lightning. **Ezekiel 1:14** And the living creatures ran and returned as the appearance of a flash of lightning. **Psalm 104:4** Who maketh his angels spirits; his ministers a flaming fire: **Daniel 10:6** His body also *was* like the beryl, and his face as the appearance of lightning, and his eyes as lamps of fire, and his arms and his feet like in colour to polished brass, and the voice of his words like the voice of a multitude.
Revelation 4:6 And before the throne *there was* a sea of glass like unto crystal: and in the midst of the throne, and round about the throne, *were* four beasts full of eyes before and behind.	**Exodus 24:10** And they saw the God of Israel: and *there was* under his feet as it were a paved work of a sapphire stone, and as it were the body of heaven in *his* clearness. **Ezekiel 1:5** Also out of the midst thereof *came* the likeness of four living creatures. And this *was* their appearance; they had the likeness of a man. **Ezekiel 1:22** And the likeness of the firmament upon the heads of

	the living creature *was* as the colour of the terrible crystal, stretched forth over their heads above. **Ezekiel 10:12** And their whole body, and their backs, and their hands, and their wings, and the wheels, *were* full of eyes round about, *even* the wheels that they four had.
Revelation 4:7 And the first beast *was* like a lion, and the second beast like a calf, and the third beast had a face as a man, and the fourth beast *was* like a flying eagle.	**Ezekiel 1:10** As for the likeness of their faces, they four had the face of a man, and the face of a lion, on the right side: and they four had the face of an ox on the left side; they four also had the face of an eagle. **Ezekiel 10:14** And every one had four faces: the first face *was* the face of a cherub, and the second face *was* the face of a man, and the third the face of a lion, and the fourth the face of an eagle.
Revelation 4:8 And the four beasts had each of them six wings about *him;* and *they were* full of eyes within: and they rest not day and night, saying, **Holy, holy, holy**, Lord **God Almighty**, which was, and is, and is to come.	**Isaiah 6:1-4** In the year that king Uzziah died I saw also the Lord sitting upon a throne, high and lifted up, and his train filled the temple. 2 Above it stood the seraphims: each one had six wings; with twain he covered his face, and with twain he covered his feet, and with twain he did fly. 3 And one cried unto another, and said, **Holy, holy, holy**, is the LORD of hosts: the whole earth is full of his glory. 4 And the posts of the door moved at the voice of him that cried, and the house was filled with smoke. **Genesis 28:3** And God Almighty bless thee, and make thee fruitful, and multiply thee, that thou mayest be a multitude of people; **Exodus 6:3** And I appeared unto Abraham, unto Isaac, and unto Jacob, by *the name of* **God Almighty**, but by my name JEHOVAH was I not known to them. **Ezekiel 10:5** And the sound of the cherubims' wings was heard *even* to the outer court, as the voice of the **Almighty God** when he speaketh.
Revelation 4:9 And when those beasts give glory and honour and thanks to him that sat on the throne, who liveth for ever and ever,	**Psalm 47:8** God reigneth over the heathen: God sitteth upon the throne of his holiness. **Isaiah 6:1** In the year that king Uzziah died I saw also the Lord sitting upon a throne, high and lifted up, and his train filled the temple.
Revelation 4:10 The four and twenty **elders** fall down before him that sat on the throne, and worship him that liveth for ever and ever, and cast their crowns before the throne, saying,	See 1 Peter 5:1 "Elders"
Revelation 5:1 And I saw in the right hand of him that sat on the throne a book written within and on the backside, sealed with seven seals.	**Isaiah 29:11** And the vision of all is become unto you as the words of a book that is sealed, which *men* deliver to one that is learned, saying, Read this, I pray thee: and he saith, I cannot; for it *is* sealed: **Ezekiel 2:9-10** And when I looked, behold, an hand *was* sent unto me; and, lo, a roll of a book *was* therein; 10 And he spread it before me; and it **was** written within and without: and there **was** written therein lamentations, and mourning, and woe. **Daniel 12:4** But thou, O Daniel, shut up the words, and seal the book, *even* to the time of the end: many shall run to and fro, and

	knowledge shall be increased.
Revelation 5:3-5 And no man in heaven, nor in earth, neither under the earth, was able to open the book, neither to look thereon. 4 And I wept much, because no man was found worthy to open and to read the book, neither to look thereon. 5 And one of the **elders** saith unto me, Weep not: behold, the Lion of the tribe of Juda, the Root of David, hath prevailed to open the book, and to loose the seven seals thereof.	**Genesis 49:8-10** Judah, thou *art he* whom thy brethren shall praise: thy hand *shall be* in the neck of thine enemies; thy father's children shall bow down before thee. 9 Judah *is* a lion's whelp: from the prey, my son, thou art gone up: he stooped down, he couched as a lion, and as an old lion; who shall rouse him up? 10 The sceptre shall not depart from Judah, nor a lawgiver from between his feet, until Shiloh come; and unto him *shall* the gathering of the people *be*. **Isaiah 11:10** And in that day there shall be a root of Jesse, which shall stand for an ensign of the people; to it shall the Gentiles seek: and his rest shall be glorious. **Ezekiel 22:30** And I sought for a man among them, that should make up the hedge, and stand in the gap before me for the land, that I should not destroy it: but I found none. **See 1 Peter 5:1 "Elders"**
Revelation 5:6 And I beheld, and, lo, in the midst of the throne and of the four beasts, and in the midst of the **elders**, stood a Lamb as it had been slain, having seven horns and seven eyes, which are the seven Spirits of God sent forth into all the earth.	**2 Chronicles 16:9** For the eyes of the LORD run to and fro throughout the whole earth, to shew himself strong in the behalf of *them* whose heart *is* perfect toward him. Herein thou hast done foolishly: therefore from henceforth thou shalt have wars. **Isaiah 53:7** He was oppressed, and he was afflicted, yet he opened not his mouth: he is brought as a lamb to the slaughter, and as a sheep before her shearers is dumb, so he openeth not his mouth. **Zechariah 3:9** For behold the stone that I have laid before Joshua; upon one stone *shall be* seven eyes: behold, I will engrave the graving thereof, saith the LORD of hosts, and I will remove the iniquity of that land in one day. **Zechariah 4:10** For who hath despised the day of small things? for they shall rejoice, and shall see the plummet in the hand of Zerubbabel *with* those seven; they *are* the eyes of the LORD, which run to and fro through the whole earth. **See 1 Peter 5:1 "Elders"**
Revelation 5:8 And when he had taken the book, the four beasts and four *and* twenty elders fell down before the Lamb, having every one of them harps, and golden vials full of odours, which are the prayers of saints.	**Psalm 141:2** Let my prayer be set forth before thee *as* incense; *and* the lifting up of my hands *as* the evening sacrifice. **See 1 Peter 5:1**
Revelations 5:9 And they sung a new song, saying, Thou art worthy to take the book, and to open the seals thereof: for thou wast slain, and **hast redeemed us to God by thy blood** out of every kindred, and tongue, and people, and nation;	**Leviticus 17:11** For the life of the flesh is in the blood: and I have given it to you upon the altar to make an atonement for your souls: **for it is the blood that maketh an atonement for the soul**. **Psalm 40:3** And he hath put a new song in my mouth, *even* praise unto our God: many shall see *it,* and fear, and shall trust in the LORD. **Psalm 98:1** A Psalm. O sing unto the LORD a new song; for he hath done marvellous things: his right hand, and his holy arm, hath gotten him the victory. **Psalm 149:1** Praise ye the LORD. Sing unto the LORD a new song, *and* his praise in the congregation of saints. **Isaiah 42:10** Sing unto the LORD a new song, *and* his praise from the end of the earth, ye that go down to the sea, and all that is

	therein; the isles, and the inhabitants thereof.
Revelation 5:10 And hast made us unto our God kings and priests: and we shall reign on the earth.	**Exodus 19:6** And ye shall be unto me a kingdom of priests, and an holy nation. These *are* the words which thou shalt speak unto the children of Israel. **Isaiah 61:6** But ye shall be named the Priests of the LORD: *men* shall call you the Ministers of our God: ye shall eat the riches of the Gentiles, and in their glory shall ye boast yourselves.
Revelation 5:11 And I beheld, and I heard the voice of many angels round about the throne and the beasts and the **elders**: and the number of them was ten thousand times ten thousand, and thousands of thousands;	**Daniel 7:10** A fiery stream issued and came forth from before him: thousand thousands ministered unto him, and ten thousand times ten thousand stood before him: the judgment was set, and the books were opened. **See 1 Peter 5:1 "Elders"**
Revelations 5:13 And **every creature** which is in heaven, and on the earth, and under the earth, and such as are in the sea, and all that are in them, heard I saying, Blessing, and honour, and glory, and power, be unto him that sitteth upon the throne, and unto the Lamb for ever and ever.	**Genesis 3:5** For God doth know that in the day ye eat thereof, then your eyes shall be opened, and **ye shall be as gods, knowing good and evil**. **Isaiah 44:6** Thus saith the LORD the King of Israel, and his redeemer the LOR**D of hosts; I am the first, and I am the last; and** beside me there is no God. **Hosea 11:9** I will not execute the fierceness of mine anger, I will not return to destroy Ephraim: **for I am God, and not man**; the Holy One in the midst of thee: and I will not enter into the city.
Revelations 5:14 And the four beasts said, Amen. And the four and twenty **elders** fell down and worshipped him that liveth for ever and ever.	**See 1 Peter 5:1 "Elders"**
Revelations 6:2 And I saw, and behold a white horse: and he that sat on him had a bow; and a crown was given unto him: and he went forth conquering, and to conquer.	**Zechariah 6:3** And in the third chariot white horses; and in the fourth chariot grisled and bay horses.
Revelations 6:4 And there went out another horse *that was* red: and *power* was given to him that sat thereon to take peace from the earth, and that they should kill one another: and there was given unto him a great sword.	**Zechariah 1:8** I saw by night, and behold a man riding upon a red horse, and he stood among the myrtle trees that *were* in the bottom; and behind him *were there* red horses, speckled, and white. **Zechariah 6:2** In the first chariot *were* red horses; and in the second chariot black horses;
Revelations 6:8 And I looked, and behold a pale horse: and his name that sat on him was Death, and **Hell** followed with him. And power was given unto them over the fourth part of the earth, to kill with sword, and with hunger, and with death, and with the beasts of the earth.	**Jeremiah 24:10** And I will send the sword, the famine, and the pestilence, among them, till they be consumed from off the land that I gave unto them and to their fathers. **Ezekiel 14:21** For thus saith the Lord GOD; How much more when I send my four sore judgments upon Jerusalem, the sword, and the famine, and the noisome beast, and the pestilence, to cut off from it man and beast? **See Luke 16:23 "Hell"**
Revelation 6:9 And when he had opened the fifth seal, I saw under the altar the **souls** of them that were slain for the word of God, and for the testimony which they held:	**See 1 Thessalonians 5:23 "Body, soul, and spirit"**
Revelations 6:10 And they cried with a loud voice, saying, How long, O Lord,	**Psalm 79:10** Wherefore should the heathen say, Where *is* their God? let him be known among the heathen in our sight *by* the

holy and true, dost thou not judge and avenge our blood on them that dwell on the earth?	revenging of the blood of thy servants *which is* shed. **Zechariah 1:12** Then the angel of the LORD answered and said, O LORD of hosts, how long wilt thou not have mercy on Jerusalem and on the cities of Judah, against which thou hast had indignation these threescore and ten years?
Revelations 6:12-13 And I beheld when he had opened the sixth seal, and, lo, there was a great earthquake; and the sun became black as sackcloth of hair, and the moon became as blood; 13 And the stars of heaven fell unto the earth, even as a fig tree casteth her untimely figs, when she is shaken of a mighty wind.	**Isaiah 13:13** Therefore I will shake the heavens, and the earth shall remove out of her place, in the wrath of the LORD of hosts, and in the day of his fierce anger. **Isaiah 24:18** And it shall come to pass, *that* he who fleeth from the noise of the fear shall fall into the pit; and he that cometh up out of the midst of the pit shall be taken in the snare: for the windows from on high are open, and the foundations of the earth do shake. **Isaiah 24:23** Then the moon shall be confounded, and the sun ashamed, when the LORD of hosts shall reign in mount Zion, and in Jerusalem, and before his ancients gloriously. **Joel 2:10-11** The earth shall quake before them; the heavens shall tremble: the sun and the moon shall be dark, and the stars shall withdraw their shining: 11 And the LORD shall utter his voice before his army: for his camp is very great: for he is strong that executeth his word: for the day of the LORD is great and very terrible; and who can abide it? **Joel 2:31** The sun shall be turned into darkness, and the moon into blood, before the great and the terrible day of the LORD come. **Haggai 2:6** For thus saith the LORD of hosts; Yet once, it *is* a little while, and I will shake the heavens, and the earth, and the sea, and the dry *land;*
Revelation 6:13-14 And the stars of heaven fell unto the earth, even as a fig tree casteth her untimely figs, when she is shaken of a mighty wind. 14 And the heaven departed as a scroll when it is rolled together; and every mountain and island were moved out of their places.	**Psalm 102:26** They shall perish, but thou shalt endure: yea, all of them shall wax old like a garment; as a vesture shalt thou change them, and they shall be changed: **Isaiah 34:4** And all the host of heaven shall be dissolved, and the heavens shall be rolled together as a scroll: and all their host shall fall down, as the leaf falleth off from the vine, and as a falling *fig* from the fig tree. **Isaiah 54:10** For the mountains shall depart, and the hills be removed; but my kindness shall not depart from thee, neither shall the covenant of my peace be removed, saith the LORD that hath mercy on thee. **Ezekiel 38:20** So that the fishes of the sea, and the fowls of the heaven, and the beasts of the field, and all creeping things that creep upon the earth, and all the men that *are* upon the face of the earth, shall shake at my presence, and the mountains shall be thrown down, and the steep places shall fall, and every wall shall fall to the ground. **Nahum 1:5** The mountains quake at him, and the hills melt, and the earth is burned at his presence, yea, the world, and all that dwell therein.
Revelation 6:15-16 And the kings of the earth, and the great men, and the rich men, and the chief captains, and the mighty men, and every bondman, and every free man, hid themselves in the dens and in the rocks of the mountains; 16 And said to the mountains and rocks,	**Psalm 110:5** The Lord at thy right hand shall strike through kings in the day of his wrath. **Isaiah 2:10** Enter into the rock, and hide thee in the dust, for fear of the LORD, and for the glory of his majesty. **Isaiah 2:19** And they shall go into the holes of the rocks, and into the caves of the earth, for fear of the LORD, and for the glory of

Fall on us, and hide us from the face of him that sitteth on the throne, and from the wrath of the Lamb:	his majesty, when he ariseth to shake terribly the earth. **Isaiah 2:21** To go into the clefts of the rocks, and into the tops of the ragged rocks, for fear of the LORD, and for the glory of his majesty, when he ariseth to shake terribly the earth. **Isaiah 13:13** Therefore I will shake the heavens, and the earth shall remove out of her place, in the wrath of the LORD of hosts, and in the day of his fierce anger. **Isaiah 24:21** And it shall come to pass in that day, *that* the LORD shall punish the host of the high ones *that are* on high, and the kings of the earth upon the earth. **Hosea 10:8** The high places also of Aven, the sin of Israel, shall be destroyed: the thorn and the thistle shall come up on their altars; and they shall say to the mountains, Cover us; and to the hills, Fall on us. **Joel 2:11** And the LORD shall utter his voice before his army: for his camp *is* very great: for *he is* strong that executeth his word: for the day of the LORD *is* great and very terrible; and who can abide it?
Revelations 6:17 For the great day of his wrath is come; and who shall be able to stand?	**Isaiah 63:4** For the day of vengeance *is* in mine heart, and the year of my redeemed is come. **Jeremiah 30:7** Alas! for that day *is* great, so that none *is* like it: it *is* even the time of Jacob's trouble; but he shall be saved out of it. **Joel 1:15** Alas for the day! for the day of the LORD *is* at hand, and as a destruction from the Almighty shall it come. **Joel 2:1** Blow ye the trumpet in Zion, and sound an alarm in my holy mountain: let all the inhabitants of the land tremble: for the day of the LORD cometh, for *it is* nigh at hand; **Joel 2:11** And the LORD shall utter his voice before his army: for his camp *is* very great: for *he is* strong that executeth his word: for the day of the LORD *is* great and very terrible; and who can abide it? **Joel 2:31** The sun shall be turned into darkness, and the moon into blood, before the great and the terrible day of the LORD come. **Zephaniah 1:14** The great day of the LORD *is* near, *it is* near, and hasteth greatly, *even* the voice of the day of the LORD: the mighty man shall cry there bitterly.
Revelations 7:1 And after these things I saw four angels standing on the four corners of the earth, holding the four winds of the earth, that the wind should not blow on the earth, nor on the sea, nor on any tree.	**Isaiah 11:12** And he shall set up an ensign for the nations, and shall assemble the outcasts of Israel, and gather together the dispersed of Judah from the four corners of the earth. Jerermiah 49:36 And upon Elam will I bring the four winds from the four quarters of heaven, and will scatter them toward all those winds; and there shall be no nation whither the outcasts of Elam shall not come. **Ezekiel 7:2** Also, thou son of man, thus saith the Lord GOD unto the land of Israel; An end, the end is come upon the four corners of the land. **Ezekiel 37:9** Then said he unto me, Prophesy unto the wind, prophesy, son of man, and say to the wind, Thus saith the Lord GOD; Come from the four winds, O breath, and breathe upon these slain, that they may live. **Daniel 7:2** Daniel spake and said, I saw in my vision by night, and,

	behold, the four winds of the heaven strove upon the great sea.
	Daniel 8:8 Therefore the he goat waxed very great: and when he was strong, the great horn was broken; and for it came up four notable ones toward the four winds of heaven.
	Daniel 11:4 And when he shall stand up, his kingdom shall be broken, and shall be divided toward the four winds of heaven; and not to his posterity, nor according to his dominion which he ruled: for his kingdom shall be plucked up, even for others beside those.
	Zechariah 2:6 Ho, ho, *come forth,* and flee from the land of the north, saith the LORD: for I have spread you abroad as the four winds of the heaven, saith the LORD.
Revelation 7:2-4 And I saw another angel ascending from the east, having the seal of the living God: and he cried with a loud voice to the four angels, to whom it was given to hurt the earth and the sea, 3 Saying, Hurt not the earth, neither the sea, nor the trees, till we have sealed the servants of our God in their foreheads. 4 And I heard the number of them which were sealed: *and there were* sealed an hundred *and* forty *and* four thousand of all the tribes of the children of Israel.	**Isaiah 26:20-21** Come, my people, enter thou into thy chambers, and shut thy doors about thee: hide thyself as it were for a little moment, until the indignation be overpast. **21** For, behold, the LORD cometh out of his place to punish the inhabitants of the earth for their iniquity: the earth also shall disclose her blood, and shall no more cover her slain. **Ezekiel 9:4** And the LORD said unto him, Go through the midst of the city, through the midst of Jerusalem, and set a mark upon the foreheads of the men that sigh and that cry for all the abominations that be done in the midst thereof.
Revelation 7:9 After this I beheld, and, lo, a great multitude, which no man could number, of all nations, and kindreds, and people, and tongues, stood before the throne, and before the Lamb, clothed with white robes, and palms in their hands;	**Isaiah 12:6** Cry out and shout, thou inhabitant of Zion: for great *is* the **Holy One** of Israel in the midst of thee.
Revelation 7:10 And cried with a loud voice, saying, Salvation to our God which sitteth upon the throne, and unto the Lamb.	**Psalm 3:8** Salvation *belongeth* unto the LORD: thy blessing *is* upon thy people. Selah.
Revelation 7:11 And all the angels stood round about the throne, and *about* the **elders** and the four beasts, and fell before the throne on their faces, and worshipped God,	**See 1 Peter 5:1 "Elders"**
Revelation 7:14 And I said unto him, Sir, thou knowest. And he said to me, These are they which came out of great tribulation, and have washed their robes, and made them white in the blood of the Lamb.	**See Matthew 26:28 "Atonement"**
Revelation 7:15 Therefore are they before the throne of God, and serve him day and night in his temple: and he that sitteth on the throne shall dwell among them.	**Leviticus 26:11** And I will set my tabernacle among you: and my soul shall not abhor you. **Ezekiel 37:27** My tabernacle also shall be with them: yea, I will be their God, and they shall be my people.
Revelation 7:16 They shall hunger no more, neither thirst any more; neither shall the sun light on them, nor any heat.	**Psalm 121:5** The LORD *is* thy keeper: the LORD *is* thy shade upon thy right hand.

	Isaiah 49:10 They shall not hunger nor thirst; neither shall the heat nor sun smite them: for he that hath mercy on them shall lead them, even by the springs of water shall he guide them.
Revelation 7:17 For the Lamb which is in the midst of the throne shall feed them, and shall lead them unto living fountains of waters: and God shall wipe away all tears from their eyes.	**Isaiah 25:8** He will swallow up death in victory; and the Lord GOD will wipe away tears from off all faces; and the rebuke of his people shall he take away from off all the earth: for the LORD hath spoken *it*.
Revelation 8:3 And another angel came and stood at the altar, having a golden censer; and there was given unto him much incense, that he should offer *it* with the prayers of all saints upon the golden altar which was before the throne.	**Exodus 30:8** And when Aaron lighteth the lamps at even, he shall burn incense upon it, a perpetual incense before the LORD throughout your generations. **Leviticus 16:12** And he shall take a censer full of burning coals of fire from off the altar before the LORD, and his hands full of sweet incense beaten small, and bring *it* within the vail: **Psalm 141:2** Let my prayer be set forth before thee *as* incense; *and* the lifting up of my hands *as* the evening sacrifice.
Revelation 8:4 And the smoke of the incense, *which came* with the prayers of the saints, ascended up before God out of the angel's hand.	**Psalm 141:2** Let my prayer be set forth before thee *as* incense; *and* the lifting up of my hands *as* the evening sacrifice.
Revelation 8:5 And the angel took the censer, and filled it with fire of the altar, and cast *it* into the earth: and there were voices, and thunderings, and lightnings, and an earthquake.	**Leviticus 16:12** And he shall take a censer full of burning coals of fire from off the altar before the LORD, and his hands full of sweet incense beaten small, and bring *it* within the vail: **Ezekiel 10:2** And he spake unto the man clothed with linen, and said, Go in between the wheels, *even* under the cherub, and fill thine hand with coals of fire from between the cherubims, and scatter *them* over the city. And he went in in my sight.
Revelation 8:7 The first angel sounded, and there followed hail and fire mingled with blood, and they were cast upon the earth: and the third part of trees was burnt up, and all green grass was burnt up.	**Exodus 9:23** And Moses stretched forth his rod toward heaven: and the LORD sent thunder and hail, and the fire ran along upon the ground; and the LORD rained hail upon the land of Egypt. **Isaiah 28:2** Behold, the Lord hath a mighty and strong one, *which* as a tempest of hail *and* a destroying storm, as a flood of mighty waters overflowing, shall cast down to the earth with the hand. **Ezekiel 38:22** And I will plead against him with pestilence and with blood; and I will rain upon him, and upon his bands, and upon the many people that *are* with him, an overflowing rain, and great hailstones, fire, and brimstone. **Joel 2:30** And I will shew wonders in the heavens and in the earth, blood, and fire, and pillars of smoke. **Zechariah 13:8-9** And it shall come to pass, *that* in all the land, saith the LORD, two parts therein shall be cut off *and* die; but the third shall be left therein. 9 And I will bring the third part through the fire, and will refine them as silver is refined, and will try them as gold is tried: they shall call on my name, and I will hear them: I will say, It *is* my people: and they shall say, The LORD *is* my God.
Revelation 8:8 And the second angel sounded, and as it were a great mountain burning with fire was cast into the sea: and the third part of the sea became blood;	**Exodus 7:20** And Moses and Aaron did so, as the LORD commanded; and he lifted up the rod, and smote the waters that *were* in the river, in the sight of Pharaoh, and in the sight of his servants; and all the waters that *were* in the river were turned to blood. **Jeremiah 51:25** Behold, I *am* against thee, O destroying mountain, saith the LORD, which destroyest all the earth: and I

	will stretch out mine hand upon thee, and roll thee down from the rocks, and will make thee a burnt mountain. **Zechariah 13:8-9** And it shall come to pass, *that* in all the land, saith the LORD, two parts therein shall be cut off *and* die; but the third shall be left therein. 9 And I will bring the third part through the fire, and will refine them as silver is refined, and will try them as gold is tried: they shall call on my name, and I will hear them: I will say, It *is* my people: and they shall say, The LORD *is* my God.
Revelation 8:11 And the name of the star is called **Wormwood**: and the third part of the waters became wormwood; and many men died of the waters, because they were made bitter	**Deuteronomy 29:18** Lest there should be among you man, or woman, or family, or tribe, whose heart turneth away this day from the LORD our God, to go *and* serve the gods of these nations; lest there should be among you a root that beareth gall and **wormwood**; **Proverbs 5:4** But her end is **bitter as wormwood**, sharp as a twoedged sword. **Jeremiah 9:15** Therefore thus saith the LORD of hosts, the God of Israel; Behold, I will feed them, *even* this people, with **wormwood**, and give them water of gall to drink. **Jeremiah 23:15** Therefore thus saith the LORD of hosts concerning the prophets; Behold, I will feed them with **wormwood**, and make them drink the water of gall: for from the prophets of Jerusalem is profaneness gone forth into all the land. **Lamentations 3:15** He hath filled me with bitterness, he hath made me drunken with **wormwood**. **Lamentations 3:19** Remembering mine affliction and my misery, the **wormwood** and the gall. **Amos 5:7** Ye who turn judgment to **wormwood**, and leave off righteousness in the earth,
Revelation 8:12 And the fourth angel sounded, and the third part of the sun was smitten, and the third part of the moon, and the third part of the stars; so as the third part of them was darkened, and the day shone not for a third part of it, and the night likewise.	**Ezekiel 32:7** And when I shall put thee out, I will cover the heaven, and make the stars thereof dark; I will cover the sun with a cloud, and the moon shall not give her light.
Revelation 9:1 And the fifth angel sounded, and I saw a star fall from heaven unto the earth: and to him was given the key of the bottomless pit.	**Joel 2:1** Blow ye the trumpet in Zion, and sound an alarm in my holy mountain: let all the inhabitants of the land tremble: for the day of the LORD cometh, for *it is* nigh at hand;
Revelation 9:2 And he opened the bottomless pit; and there arose a smoke out of the pit, as the smoke of a great furnace; and the sun and the air were darkened by reason of the smoke of the pit	**Numbers 16:32-33** And the earth opened her mouth, and swallowed them up, and their houses, and all the men that *appertained* unto Korah, and all *their* goods. 33 They, and all that *appertained* to them, went down alive into the pit, and the earth closed upon them: and they perished from among the congregation. **See Luke 16:23 "Hell"**
Revelation 9:4 And it was commanded them that they should not hurt the grass of the earth, neither any green thing, neither any tree; but only those men which have not the seal of God in their foreheads.	**Isaiah 26:20-21** Come, my people, enter thou into thy chambers, and shut thy doors about thee: hide thyself as it were for a little moment, until the indignation be overpast. 21 For, behold, the LORD cometh out of his place to punish the inhabitants of the earth for their iniquity: the earth also shall disclose her blood, and shall no more cover her slain. **Ezekiel 9:4** And the LORD said unto him, Go through the midst of

	the city, through the midst of Jerusalem, and set a mark upon the foreheads of the men that sigh and that cry for all the abominations that be done in the midst thereof.
Revelation 9:6 And in those days shall men seek death, and shall not find it; and shall desire to die, and death shall flee from them.	**Jeremiah 8:3** And death shall be chosen rather than life by all the residue of them that remain of this evil family, which remain in all the places whither I have driven them, saith the LORD of hosts. **Hosea 10:8** The high places also of Aven, the sin of Israel, shall be destroyed: the thorn and the thistle shall come up on their altars; and they shall say to the mountains, Cover us; and to the hills, Fall on us.
Revelation 9:7-9 And the shapes of the locusts were like unto horses prepared unto battle; and on their heads were as it were crowns like gold, and their faces were as the faces of men. 8 And they had hair as the hair of women, and their teeth were as the teeth of lions. 9 And they had breastplates, as it were breastplates of iron; and the sound of their wings was as the sound of chariots of many horses running to battle.	**Joel 1:6** For a nation is come up upon my land, strong, and without number, whose teeth *are* the teeth of a lion, and he hath the cheek teeth of a great lion. **Joel 2:4-5** The appearance of them is as the appearance of horses; and as horsemen, so shall they run. 5 Like the noise of chariots on the tops of mountains shall they leap, like the noise of a flame of fire that devoureth the stubble, as a strong people set in battle array.
Revelation 9:13-14 And the sixth angel sounded, and I heard a voice from the four horns of the golden altar which is before God, 14 Saying to the sixth angel which had the trumpet, Loose the four angels which are bound in the great river Euphrates.	**Leviticus 23:24** Speak unto the children of Israel, saying, In the seventh month, in the first *day* of the month, shall ye have a sabbath, a memorial of blowing of trumpets, an holy convocation. **Numbers 29:1** And in the seventh month, on the first *day* of the month, ye shall have an holy convocation; ye shall do no servile work: it is a day of blowing the trumpets unto you. **Psalms 50:5** Gather my saints together unto me; those that have made a covenant with me by sacrifice. **Isaiah 26:19** Thy dead *men* shall live, *together with* my dead body shall they arise. Awake and sing, ye that dwell in dust: for thy dew *is as* the dew of herbs, and the earth shall cast out the dead **Isaiah 27:13** And it shall come to pass in that day, *that* the great trumpet shall be blown, and they shall come which were ready to perish in the land of Assyria, and the outcasts in the land of Egypt, and shall worship the LORD in the holy mount at Jerusalem.
Revelation 9:16 And the number of the army of the horsemen *were* two hundred thousand thousand: and I heard the number of them.	**Psalm 68:17** The chariots of God *are* twenty thousand, *even* thousands of angels: the Lord is among them, *as in* Sinai, in the holy *place*. **Daniel 7:10** A fiery stream issued and came forth from before him: thousand thousands ministered unto him, and ten thousand times ten thousand stood before him: the judgment was set, and the books were opened.
Revelation 9:20 And the rest of the men which were not killed by these plagues yet repented not of the works of their hands, that they should not worship devils, and idols of gold, and silver, and brass, and stone, and of wood: which neither can see, nor hear, nor walk:	**Psalm 115:4** Their idols *are* silver and gold, the work of men's hands. **Psalm 115:8** They that make them are like unto them; *so is* every one that trusteth in them. **Psalm 135:15** The idols of the heathen *are* silver and gold, the work of men's hands. **Psalm 135:18** They that make them are like unto them: *so is* every one that trusteth in them.

	Daniel 5:23 But hast lifted up thyself against the Lord of heaven; and they have brought the vessels of his house before thee, and thou, and thy lords, thy wives, and thy concubines, have drunk wine in them; and thou hast praised the gods of silver, and gold, of brass, iron, wood, and stone, which see not, nor hear, nor know: and the God in whose hand thy breath is, and whose are all thy ways, hast thou not glorified:
Revelation 10:2 And he had in his hand a little book open: and he set his right foot upon the sea, and *his* left *foot* on the earth,	**Ezekiel 2:9** And when I looked, behold, an hand *was* sent unto me; and, lo, a roll of a book *was* therein;
Revelation 10:3 And cried with a loud voice, as *when* a lion roareth: and when he had cried, seven thunders uttered their voices.	**Jeremiah 25:30** Therefore prophesy thou against them all these words, and say unto them, The LORD shall roar from on high, and utter his voice from his holy habitation; he shall mightily roar upon his habitation; he shall give a shout, as they that tread *the grapes,* against all the inhabitants of the earth.
Revelation 10:4 And when the seven thunders had uttered their voices, I was about to write: and I heard a voice from heaven saying unto me, Seal up those things which the seven thunders uttered, and write them not.	**Daniel 8:26** And the vision of the evening and the morning which was told *is* true: wherefore shut thou up the vision; for it *shall be* for many days. **Daniel 12:4** But thou, O Daniel, shut up the words, and seal the book, *even* to the time of the end: many shall run to and fro, and knowledge shall be increased. **Daniel 12:9** And he said, Go thy way, Daniel: for the words *are* closed up and sealed till the time of the end.
Revelation 10:5 And the angel which I saw stand upon the sea and upon the earth lifted up his hand to heaven,	**Daniel 12:7** And I heard the man clothed in linen, which was upon the waters of the river, when he held up his right hand and his left hand unto heaven, and sware by him that liveth for ever that it shall be for a time, times, and an half; and when he shall have accomplished to scatter the power of the holy people, all these things shall be finished.
Revelation 10:6 And sware by him that liveth for ever and ever, who created heaven, and the things that therein are, and the earth, and the things that therein are, and the sea, and the things which are therein, that there should be time no longer:	**Exodus 20:11** For *in* six days the LORD made heaven and earth, the sea, and all that in them *is,* and rested the seventh day: wherefore the LORD blessed the sabbath day, and hallowed it. **Psalms 146:6** Which made heaven, and earth, the sea, and all that therein *is:* which keepeth truth for ever:
Revelation 10:8-11 And the voice which I heard from heaven spake unto me again, and said, Go and take the little book which is open in the hand of the angel which standeth upon the sea and upon the earth. 9 And I went unto the angel, and said unto him, Give me the little book. And he said unto me, Take it, and eat it up; and it shall make thy belly bitter, but it shall be in thy mouth sweet as honey. 10 And I took the little book out of the angel's hand, and ate it up; and it was in my mouth **sweet as honey**: and as soon as I had eaten it, my belly was bitter. 11 And he said unto me, Thou must prophesy again before many peoples, and nations, and tongues, and	**Psalms 119:103** How sweet are thy words unto my taste! yea, *sweeter* than honey to my mouth! **Zechariah 1:19** And I said unto the angel that talked with me, What *be* these? And he answered me, These *are* the horns which have scattered Judah, Israel, and Jerusalem. **Ezekiel 2:8** But thou, son of man, hear what I say unto thee; Be not thou rebellious like that rebellious house: open thy mouth, and eat that I give thee. **Ezekiel 3:1- 3** Moreover he said unto me, Son of man, eat that thou findest; eat this roll, and go speak unto the house of Israel. 2 So I opened my mouth, and he caused me to eat that roll. 3 And he said unto me, Son of man, cause thy belly to eat, and fill thy bowels with this roll that I give thee. Then did I eat *it*; and it was in my mouth as **honey for sweetness**.

kings.	
Revelation 10:11 And he said unto me, Thou must prophesy again before many peoples, and nations, and tongues, and kings.	**Jeremiah 1:9** Then the LORD put forth his hand, and touched my mouth. And the LORD said unto me, Behold, I have put my words in thy mouth.
Revelation 11:1 And there was given me a reed like unto a rod: and the angel stood, saying, Rise, and measure the **temple of God**, and the altar, and them that worship therein.	**1 Kings 5:5** And, behold, I purpose to **build an house** unto the name of the LORD my God, as the LORD spake unto David my father, saying, Thy son, whom I will set upon thy throne in thy room, he shall build an house unto my name. **2 Kings 25:8-9** And in the fifth month, on the seventh *day* of the month, which *is* the nineteenth year of king Nebuchadnezzar king of Babylon, came Nebuzaradan, captain of the guard, a servant of the king of Babylon, unto Jerusalem: 9 And he **burnt the house of the LORD**, and the king's house, and all the houses of Jerusalem, and every great *man's* house burnt he with fire. **2 Chronicles 36:19** And they **burnt the house of God**, and brake down the wall of Jerusalem, and burnt all the palaces thereof with fire, and destroyed all the goodly vessels thereof. **Ezra 3:8** Now in the second year of their coming unto the house of God at Jerusalem, in the second month, began Zerubbabel the son of Shealtiel, and Jeshua the son of Jozadak, and the remnant of their brethren the priests and the Levites, and all they that were come out of the captivity unto Jerusalem; and appointed the Levites, from twenty years old and upward, to set forward the work of the house of the LORD. **Ezra 5:13-16** But in the first year of Cyrus the king of Babylon *the same* king Cyrus made a decree to build this house of God. 14 And the vessels also of gold and silver of the house of God, which Nebuchadnezzar took out of the temple that *was* in Jerusalem, and brought them into the temple of Babylon, those did Cyrus the king take out of the temple of Babylon, and they were delivered unto *one*, whose name *was* Sheshbazzar, whom he had made governor; 15 And said unto him, Take these vessels, go, carry them into the temple that *is* in Jerusalem, and let the house of God be builded in his place. 16 Then came the same Sheshbazzar, *and* laid the foundation of the house of God which *is* in Jerusalem: and since that time even until now hath it been in building, and *yet* it is not finished. **Isaiah 2:2-3** And it shall come to pass in the last days, *that* the mountain of the LORD'S house shall be established in the top of the mountains, and shall be exalted above the hills; and all nations shall flow unto it. 3 And many people shall go and say, Come ye, and let us go up to the mountain of the LORD, to the house of the God of Jacob; and he will teach us of his ways, and we will walk in his paths: for out of Zion shall go forth the law, and the word of the LORD from Jerusalem. **Isaiah 60:13** The glory of Lebanon shall come unto thee, the fir tree, the pine tree, and the box together, to beautify the place of my **sanctuary**; and I will make the place of my feet glorious. **Ezekiel 37:26** Moreover I will make a covenant of peace with them; it shall be an everlasting covenant with them: and I will place them, and multiply them, and will set my **sanctuary** in the

midst of them for evermore.

Ezekiel 40:3 And he brought me thither, and, behold, *there was* a man, whose appearance *was* like the appearance of brass, with a line of flax in his hand, and a measuring reed; and he stood in the gate.

Ezekiel 40:47 So he measured the court, an hundred cubits long, and an hundred cubits broad, foursquare; and the altar *that was* before the house.

Ezekiel 41:13 So he measured the house, an hundred cubits long; and the separate place, and the building, with the walls thereof, an hundred cubits long;

Ezekiel 43:7 And he said unto me, Son of man, the place of my throne, and the place of the soles of my feet, where I will dwell in the midst of the children of Israel for ever, and my holy name, shall the **house of Israel** no more defile, *neither* they, nor their kings, by their whoredom, nor by the carcases of their kings in their high places.

Ezekiel 43:13 And these *are* the measures of the altar after the cubits: The cubit *is* a cubit and an hand breadth; even the bottom *shall be* a cubit, and the breadth a cubit, and the border thereof by the edge thereof round about *shall be* a span: and this *shall be* the higher place of the altar.

Ezekiel 43:15-27 So the altar *shall be* four cubits; and from the altar and upward *shall be* four horns. 16 And the altar *shall be* twelve *cubits* long, twelve broad, square in the four squares thereof. 17 And the settle *shall be* fourteen *cubits* long and fourteen broad in the four squares thereof; and the border about it *shall be* half a cubit; and the bottom thereof *shall be* a cubit about; and his stairs shall look toward the east. 18 And he said unto me, Son of man, thus saith the Lord GOD; These *are* the ordinances of the altar in the day when they shall make it, to offer burnt offerings thereon, and to sprinkle blood thereon. 19 And thou shalt give to the priests the Levites that be of the seed of Zadok, which approach unto me, to minister unto me, saith the Lord GOD, **a young bullock for a sin offering**. 20 And thou shalt take of the blood thereof, and put *it* on the four horns of it, and on the four corners of the settle, and upon the border round about: thus shalt thou cleanse and purge it. 21 **Thou shalt take the bullock also of the sin offering, and he shall burn it in the appointed place of the house, without the sanctuary.** 22 And on the second day thou shalt offer a kid of the goats without blemish for a **sin offering**; and they shall cleanse the altar, as they did cleanse *it* with the bullock. 23 When thou hast made an end of cleansing *it*, thou shalt offer a young bullock without blemish, and a ram out of the flock without blemish. 24 And thou shalt offer them before the LORD, and the priests shall cast salt upon them, and they shall offer them up *for* a burnt offering unto the LORD. 25 Seven days shalt thou prepare every day a goat *for* a sin offering: they shall also prepare a young bullock, and a **ram out of the flock, without blemish**. 26 Seven days shall they purge the altar and purify it; and they shall consecrate themselves. 27 And when these days are expired, it shall be, *that* upon the eighth day, and *so* forward, the priests shall make your burnt offerings upon the altar, and your peace offerings; and I will accept you, saith the Lord GOD.

Ezekiel 44:11 Yet they shall be ministers in my sanctuary, *having* charge at the gates of the house, and ministering to the house: they shall slay the burnt offering and the sacrifice for the people, and they shall stand before them to minister unto them.

Ezekiel 44:13 And they shall not come near unto me, to do the office of a priest unto me, nor to come near to any of my holy things, in the most holy *place*: but they shall bear their shame, and their abominations which they have committed.

Ezekiel 44:29 They shall eat the meat offering, and the sin offering, and the trespass offering; and every dedicated thing in Israel shall be theirs.

Ezekiel 45:1-2 ... Moreover, when ye shall divide by lot the land for inheritance, ye shall offer an oblation unto the LORD, an holy portion of the land: the length *shall be* the length of five and twenty thousand *reeds*, and the breadth *shall be* ten thousand. **This shall be holy in all the borders thereof round about**. 2 Of this there shall be for the **sanctuary** five hundred *in length*, with five hundred *in breadth*, square round about; and fifty cubits round about for the suburbs thereof.

Joel 3:18 And it shall come to pass in that day, *that* the mountains shall drop down new wine, and the hills shall flow with milk, and all the rivers of Judah shall flow with waters, and a fountain shall come forth of the **house of the LORD**, and shall water the valley of Shittim.

Amos 9:11-15 In that day will I raise up the **tabernacle of David** that is fallen, and close up the breaches thereof; and I will raise up his ruins, and I will build it as in the days of old: 12 That they may possess the remnant of Edom, and of all the heathen, which are called by my name, saith the LORD that doeth this. 13 Behold, the days come, saith the LORD, that the plowman shall overtake the reaper, and the treader of grapes him that soweth seed; and the mountains shall drop sweet wine, and all the hills shall melt. 14 And I will bring again the captivity of my people of Israel, and they shall build the waste cities, and inhabit *them*; and they shall plant vineyards, and drink the wine thereof; they shall also make gardens, and eat the fruit of them. 15 And I will plant them upon their land, and **they shall no more be pulled up out of their land which I have given them**, saith the LORD thy God.

Zechariah 14:4 And his feet shall stand in that day upon the mount of Olives, which *is* before Jerusalem on the east, and the mount of Olives shall cleave in the midst thereof toward the east and toward the west, *and there shall be* **a very great valley; and half of the mountain shall remove toward the north, and half of it toward the south**.

Malachi 3:1 Behold, I will send my messenger, and he shall prepare the way before me: and the Lord, whom ye seek, shall suddenly come to **his temple**, even the messenger of the covenant, whom ye delight in: behold, he shall come, saith the LORD of hosts.

Revelation 11:2 But the court which is without the temple leave out, and measure it not; for it is **given unto the Gentiles**: and the holy city shall they tread under foot forty *and* two	**Daniel 7:25** And he shall speak *great* words against the most High, and shall wear out the saints of the most High, and think to change times and laws: and they shall be given into his hand until a time and times and the dividing of time. **Daniel 12:7** And I heard the man clothed in linen, which was upon the waters of the river, when he held up his right hand and his left hand unto heaven, and sware by him that liveth for ever that it shall be for a time, times, and an half; and when he shall have

	accomplished to scatter the power of the holy people, all these things shall be finished.
	Daniel 12:11 And from the time *that* the daily *sacrifice* shall be taken away, and the abomination that maketh desolate set up, *there shall be* a thousand two hundred and ninety days.
Revelation 11:3 And I will give *power* unto my two witnesses, and they shall prophesy a thousand two hundred *and* threescore days, clothed in sackcloth.	**Daniel 12:11** And from the time *that* the daily *sacrifice* shall be taken away, and the abomination that maketh desolate set up, *there shall be* a thousand two hundred and ninety days. **See Revelation 11:2**
Revelation 11:4 These are the two olive trees, and the two candlesticks standing before the God of the earth.	**Zechariah 4:3** And two olive trees by it, one upon the right *side* of the bowl, and the other upon the left *side* thereof. **Zechariah 4:11** Then answered I, and said unto him, What *are* these two olive trees upon the right *side* of the candlestick and upon the left *side* thereof? **Zechariah 4:14** Then said he, These *are* the two anointed ones, that stand by the Lord of the whole earth. **Malachi 4:5** Behold, I will send you Elijah the prophet before the coming of the great and dreadful day of the LORD:
Revelation 11:5 And if any man will hurt them, fire proceedeth out of their mouth, and devoureth their enemies: and if any man will hurt them, he must in this manner be kill	**2 Kings 1:9-12** Then the king sent unto him a captain of fifty with his fifty. And he went up to him: and, behold, he sat on the top of an hill. And he spake unto him, Thou man of God, the king hath said, Come down. 10 And Elijah answered and said to the captain of fifty, If I be a man of God, then let fire come down from heaven, and consume thee and thy fifty. And there came down fire from heaven, and consumed him and his fifty. 11 Again also he sent unto him another captain of fifty with his fifty. And he answered and said unto him, O man of God, thus hath the king said, Come down quickly. 12 And Elijah answered and said unto them, If I be a man of God, let fire come down from heaven, and consume thee and thy fifty. And the fire of God came down from heaven, and consumed him and his fifty.
Revelation 11:6 These have power to shut heaven, that it rain not in the days of their prophecy: and have power over waters to turn them to blood, and to smite the earth with all plagues, as often as they will.	**Exodus 7:20** And Moses and Aaron did so, as the LORD commanded; and he lifted up the rod, and smote the waters that *were* in the river, in the sight of Pharaoh, and in the sight of his servants; and all the waters that *were* in the river were turned to blood. **1 Kings 17:1** And Elijah the Tishbite, *who was* of the inhabitants of Gilead, said unto Ahab, *As* the LORD God of Israel liveth, before whom I stand, there shall not be dew nor rain these years, but according to my word.
Revelation 11:7 And when they shall have finished their testimony, the beast that ascendeth out of the bottomless pit shall make war against them, and shall overcome them, and kill them.	**Daniel 7:21** I beheld, and the same horn made war with the saints, and prevailed against them;
Revelation 11:8 And their dead bodies *shall lie* in the street of the great city, which spiritually is called **Sodom** and **Egypt**, where also our Lord was crucified.	**Ezekiel 29:10** Behold, therefore I am against thee, and against thy rivers, and I will make the land of **Egypt** utterly waste and desolate, from the tower of Syene even unto the border of Ethiopia. **Ezekiel 30:4** And the sword shall come upon **Egypt**, and great pain shall be in Ethiopia, when the slain shall fall in **Egypt**, and they shall take away her multitude, and her foundations shall be broken down.

	Ezekiel 30:5 Ethiopia, and Libya, and Lydia, and all the mingled people, and Chub, and the men of the land that is in league, shall fall with them by the sword.
	Ezekiel 38:5 Persia, Ethiopia, and Libya with them; all of them with shield and helmet:
	See Romans 1:27 "Sexual sins"
Revelation 11:10 And they that dwell upon the earth shall rejoice over them, and make merry, and shall send gifts one to another; because these two prophets tormented them that dwelt on the earth.	**Ester 9:22** As the days wherein the Jews rested from their enemies, and the month which was turned unto them from sorrow to joy, and from mourning into a good day: that they should make them days of feasting and joy, and of sending portions one to another, and gifts to the poor.
Revelation 11:12 And they heard a great voice from heaven saying unto them, **Come up hither**. And they ascended up to heaven in a cloud; and their enemies beheld them.	**Leviticus 23:24** Speak unto the children of Israel, saying, In the seventh month, in the first *day* of the month, shall ye have a sabbath, a memorial of blowing of trumpets, an holy convocation.
	Numbers 29:1 And in the seventh month, on the first *day* of the month, ye shall have an holy convocation; ye shall do no servile work: it is a day of blowing the trumpets unto you.
	Psalms 50:5 Gather my saints together unto me; those that have made a covenant with me by sacrifice.
	Isaiah 26:19 Thy dead *men* shall live, *together with* my dead body shall they arise. Awake and sing, ye that dwell in dust: for thy dew *is as* the dew of herbs, and the earth shall cast out the dead.
	Isaiah 27:13 And it shall come to pass in that day, *that* the great trumpet shall be blown, and they shall come which were ready to perish in the land of Assyria, and the outcasts in the land of Egypt, and shall worship the LORD in the holy mount at Jerusalem.
Revelation 11:13 And the same hour was there a great earthquake, and the tenth part of the city fell, and in the earthquake were slain of men seven thousand: and the remnant were affrighted, and gave glory to the God of heaven.	**1 Kings 19:18** Yet I have left *me* seven thousand in Israel, all the knees which have not bowed unto Baal, and every mouth which hath not kissed him.
Revelation 11:15 And the seventh angel sounded; and there were great voices in heaven, saying, The kingdoms of this world are become *the kingdoms* of our Lord, and of his Christ; and he shall reign for ever and ever.	**Isaiah 2:1-5** The word that Isaiah the son of Amoz saw concerning Judah and Jerusalem. 2 And it shall come to pass in the last days, *that* the mountain of the LORD'S house shall be established in the top of the mountains, and shall be exalted above the hills; and all nations shall flow unto it. 3 And many people shall go and say, Come ye, and let us go up to the mountain of the LORD, to the house of the God of Jacob; and **he will teach us of his ways, and we will walk in his paths: for out of Zion shall go forth the law, and the word of the LORD from Jerusalem**. 4 And he shall judge among the nations, and shall rebuke many people: and they shall beat their swords into plowshares, and their spears into pruninghooks: **nation shall not lift up sword against nation, neither shall they learn war any more**. 5 O house of Jacob, come ye, and let us walk in the light of the LORD.
	Daniel 2:44 And in the days of these kings shall the God of heaven set up a kingdom, which shall never be destroyed: and the kingdom shall not be left to other people, *but* it shall break in pieces and consume all these kingdoms, and it shall stand for ever.
	Daniel 7:14 And there was given him dominion, and glory, and a kingdom, that all people, nations, and languages, should serve him:

	his dominion *is* an everlasting dominion, which shall not pass away, and his kingdom *that* which shall not be destroyed.
	Zechariah 14:9 And the LORD shall be king over all the earth: in that day shall there be one LORD, and his name one.
Revelation 11:16 And the four and twenty **elders**, which sat before God on their seats, fell upon their faces, and worshipped God,	**See 1 Peter 5:1 "Elders"**
Revelation 11:17 Saying, We give thee thanks, O Lord **God Almighty**, which art, and wast, and art to come; because thou hast taken to thee thy great power, and hast reigned.	**Genesis 28:3** And **God Almighty** bless thee, and make thee fruitful, and multiply thee, that thou mayest be a multitude of people; **Exodus 6:3** And I appeared unto Abraham, unto Isaac, and unto Jacob, by *the name of* **God Almighty**, but by my name JEHOVAH was I not known to them. **Ezekiel 10:5** And the sound of the cherubims' wings was heard *even* to the outer court, as the voice of the **Almighty God** when he speaketh.
Revelation 11:18 And the nations were angry, and thy wrath is come, and the time of the dead, that they should be judged, and that thou shouldest give reward unto thy servants the prophets, and to the saints, and them that fear thy name, small and great; and shouldest destroy them which destroy the earth.	**Psalm 2:1-5** Why do the heathen rage, and the people imagine a vain thing? 2 The kings of the earth set themselves, and the rulers take counsel together, against the LORD, and against his anointed, saying, 3 Let us break their bands asunder, and cast away their cords from us. 4 He that sitteth in the heavens shall laugh: the Lord shall have them in derision. 5 Then shall he speak unto them in his wrath, and vex them in his sore displeasure. **Psalm 46:6** The heathen raged, the kingdoms were moved: he uttered his voice, the earth melted. **Psalm 115:13** He will bless them that fear the LORD, *both* small and great. **Daniel 7:10** A fiery stream issued and came forth from before him: thousand thousands ministered unto him, and ten thousand times ten thousand stood before him: the judgment was set, and the books were opened. **Daniel 11:44** But tidings out of the east and out of the north shall trouble him: therefore he shall go forth with great fury to destroy, and utterly to make away many. **Isaiah 26:19** Thy dead *men* shall live, *together with* my dead body shall they arise. Awake and sing, ye that dwell in dust: for thy dew *is as* the dew of herbs, and the earth shall cast out the dead. **Daniel 12:2** And many of them that sleep in the dust of the earth shall awake, some to everlasting life, and some to shame *and* everlasting contempt.
Revelation 12:1-2 And there appeared a great wonder in heaven; a woman clothed with the sun, and the moon under her feet, and upon her head a crown of twelve stars: 2 And she being with child cried, travailing in birth, and pained to be delivered.	**Isaiah 66:7-8** Before she travailed, she brought forth; before her pain came, she was delivered of a man child. **Micah 4:9-10** Now why dost thou cry out aloud? is there no king in thee? is thy counsellor perished? for pangs have taken thee as a woman in travail. 10 Be in pain, and labour to bring forth, O daughter of Zion, like a woman in travail: for now shalt thou go forth out of the city, and thou shalt dwell in the field, and thou shalt go even to Babylon; there shalt thou be delivered; there the LORD

	shall redeem thee from the hand of thine enemies.
Revelation 12:2 And she being with child cried, travailing in birth, and pained to be delivered.	**Isaiah 26:17-21** Like a pregnant woman who writhes and cries out in her pangs when she is near to giving birth, so were we because of you, O LORD; 18 we were pregnant, we writhed, but we have given birth to wind. We have accomplished no deliverance in the earth, and the inhabitants of the world have not fallen. 19 Your dead shall live; their bodies shall rise. You who dwell in the dust, awake and sing for joy! For your dew is a dew of light, and the earth will give birth to the dead. 20 Come, my people, enter your chambers, and shut your doors behind you; hide yourselves for a little while until the fury has passed by. 21 For behold, the LORD is coming out from his place to punish the inhabitants of the earth for their iniquity, and the earth will disclose the blood shed on it, and will no more cover its slain.
Revelation 12:3 And there appeared another wonder in heaven; and behold a great red dragon, having seven heads and ten horns, and seven crowns upon his heads.	**Daniel 7:7** After this I saw in the night visions, and behold a fourth beast, dreadful and terrible, and strong exceedingly; and it had great iron teeth: it devoured and brake in pieces, and stamped the residue with the feet of it: and it *was* diverse from all the beasts that *were* before it; and it had ten horns.
Revelation 12:4 And his tail drew the third part of the stars of heaven, and did cast them to the earth: and the dragon stood before the woman which was ready to be delivered, for to devour her child as soon as it was born.	**Daniel 8:10** And it waxed great, *even* to the host of heaven; and it cast down *some* of the host and of the stars to the ground, and stamped upon them.
Revelation 12:5 And she brought forth a man child, who was to rule all nations with a rod of iron: and her child was **caught up** unto God, and *to* his throne.	**Isaiah 66:7-8** Before she travailed, she brought forth; before her pain came, she was delivered of a man child. 8 Who hath heard such a thing? who hath seen such things? Shall the earth be made to bring forth in one day? or shall a nation be born at once? for as soon as Zion travailed, she brought forth her children. **Daniel 7: 22** Until the Ancient of days came, and judgment was given to the saints of the most High; and the time came that the saints possessed the kingdom. **See 1 Corinthians 15:52 or 1 Thessalonians 4:16 "Caught up"**
Revelation 12:6 And the woman fled into the wilderness, where she hath a place prepared of God, that they should feed her there a thousand two hundred *and* threescore days.	**Daniel 12:11** And from the time *that* the daily *sacrifice* shall be taken away, and the abomination that maketh desolate set up, *there shall be* a thousand two hundred and ninety days. **See Revelation 11:2**
Revelation 12:7 And there was war in heaven: **Michael** and his **angels** fought against the dragon; and the dragon fought and his angels,	**Deuteronomy 34:5-6** So Moses the servant of the LORD died there in the land of Moab, according to the word of the LORD. 6 And he buried him in a valley in the land of Moab, over against Bethpeor: but no man knoweth of his sepulchre unto this day. **Daniel 10:13** But the prince of the kingdom of Persia withstood me one and twenty days: but, lo, **Michael**, one of the chief princes, came to help me; and I remained there with the kings of Persia. **Daniel 10:21** But I will shew thee that which is noted in the scripture of truth: and there is none that holdeth with me in these things, but **Michael** your prince. **Daniel 12:1** And at that time shall **Michael** stand up, the great prince which standeth for the children of thy people: and there shall be a time of trouble, such as never was since there was a nation *even* to that same time: and at that time thy people shall be

	delivered, every one that shall be found written in the book.
Zechariah 3:2 And the LORD said unto Satan, The LORD rebuke thee, O Satan; even the LORD that hath chosen Jerusalem rebuke thee: *is* not this a brand plucked out of the fire?
See Hebrews 13:2 "Good and bad angels"
Revelation 12:9 And the great dragon was cast out, that old **serpent**, called the Devil, and **Satan**, which deceiveth the whole world: he was cast out into the earth, and his **angels** were cast out with him.	**Genesis 3:4** And the **serpent** said unto the woman, Ye shall not surely die:
Zechariah 3:1-2 And he shewed me Joshua the high priest standing before the angel of the LORD, and **Satan** standing at his right hand to resist him. 2 And the LORD said unto **Satan,** The LORD rebuke thee, O **Satan**; even the LORD that hath chosen Jerusalem rebuke thee: *is* not this a brand plucked out of the fire?
See Matthew 4:10 "satan"
See Hebrews 13:2 "Good and bad angels"
Revelation 12:13-14 And when the dragon saw that he was cast unto the earth, he persecuted the woman which brought forth the man *child*. 14 And to the woman were given two wings of a great eagle, that she might fly into the wilderness, into her place, where she is nourished for a time, and times, and half a time, from the face of the serpent.	**Deuteronomy 28:47-49** Because thou servedst not the LORD thy God with joyfulness, and with gladness of heart, for the abundance of all *things*; 48 Therefore shalt thou serve thine enemies which the LORD shall send against thee, in hunger, and in thirst, and in nakedness, and in want of all *things*: and he shall put a yoke of iron upon thy neck, until he have destroyed thee. 49 The LORD shall bring a nation against thee from far, from the end of the earth, *as swift* as the eagle flieth; a nation whose tongue thou shalt not understand;
Jeremiah 48:40 For thus saith the LORD; Behold, he shall fly as an eagle, and shall spread his wings over Moab.
Jeremiah 49:22 Behold, he shall come up and fly as the eagle, and spread his wings over Bozrah: and at that day shall the heart of the mighty men of Edom be as the heart of a woman in her pangs.

Daniel 7:25 And he shall speak *great* words against the most High, and shall wear out the saints of the most High, and think to change times and laws: and they shall be given into his hand until a time and times and the dividing of time.
See Revelation 11:2 |
| **Revelation 12:14** And to the woman were given two wings of a great eagle, that she might fly into the wilderness, into her place, where she is nourished for a time, and times, and half a time, from the face of the serpent. | **Daniel 7:25** And he shall speak *great* words against the most High, and shall wear out the saints of the most High, and think to change times and laws: and they shall be given into his hand until a time and times and the dividing of time.
Daniel 9:24-27 Know therefore and understand, that from the going forth of the commandment to restore and to build Jerusalem unto the Messiah the Prince shall be seven weeks, and threescore and two weeks: the street shall be built again, and the wall, even in troublous times. 26 And after threescore and two weeks shall Messiah be cut off, but not for himself: and the people of the prince that shall come shall destroy the city and the sanctuary; and the end thereof shall be with a flood, and unto the end of the war desolations are determined. 27 And he shall confirm the
covenant with many for one week: and in the midst of the week he shall cause the sacrifice and the oblation to cease, and for the overspreading of abominations he shall make it desolate, even until the consummation, |

	and that determined shall be poured upon the desolate.
	Daniel 12:7 And I heard the man clothed in linen, which was upon the waters of the river, when he held up his right hand and his left hand unto heaven, and sware by him that liveth for ever that it shall be for a time, times, and an half; and when he shall have accomplished to scatter the power of the holy people, all these things shall be finished.
	See Revelation 11:2
Revelation 13:1 And I stood upon the sand of the sea, and saw a beast rise up out of the sea, having seven heads and ten horns, and upon his horns ten crowns, and upon his heads the name of blasphemy.	**Daniel 7:3** And four great beasts came up from the sea, diverse one from another. **Daniel 7:7** After this I saw in the night visions, and behold a fourth beast, dreadful and terrible, and strong exceedingly; and it had great iron teeth: it devoured and brake in pieces, and stamped the residue with the feet of it: and it *was* diverse from all the beasts that *were* before it; and it had ten horns. **Daniel 7:20** And of the ten horns that *were* in his head, and *of* the other which came up, and before whom three fell; even *of* that horn that had eyes, and a mouth that spake very great things, whose look *was* more stout than his fellows.
Revelation 13:2 And the beast which I saw was like unto a leopard, and his feet were as *the feet* of a bear, and his mouth as the mouth of a lion: and the dragon gave him his power, and his seat, and great authority.	**Daniel 7:5-6** And behold another beast, a second, like to a bear, and it raised up itself on one side, and it had three ribs in the mouth of it between the teeth of it: and they said thus unto it, Arise, devour much flesh. 6 After this I beheld, and lo another, like a leopard, which had upon the back of it four wings of a fowl; the beast had also four heads; and dominion was given to it.
Revelation 13:5-6 And there was given unto him a mouth speaking great things and blasphemies; and power was given unto him to continue forty and two months. 6 And he opened his mouth in blasphemy against God, to blaspheme his name, and his tabernacle, and them that dwell in heaven.	**Daniel 7:8** I considered the horns, and, behold, there came up among them another little horn, before whom there were three of the first horns plucked up by the roots: and, behold, in this horn *were* eyes like the eyes of man, and a mouth speaking great things. **Daniel 12:11** And from the time *that* the daily *sacrifice* shall be taken away, and the abomination that maketh desolate set up, *there shall be* a thousand two hundred and ninety days. **See Revelation 11:2**
Revelation 13:7 And it was given unto him to make war with the saints, and to overcome them: and power was given him over all kindreds, and tongues, and nations.	**Daniel 2:37** Thou, O king, *art* a king of kings: for the God of heaven hath given thee a kingdom, power, and strength, and glory. **Daniel 5:19** And for the majesty that he gave him, all people, nations, and languages, trembled and feared before him: whom he would he slew; and whom he would he kept alive; and whom he would he set up; and whom he would he put down. **Daniel 7:21** I beheld, and the same horn made war with the saints, and prevailed against them; **Daniel 8:10** And it waxed great, *even* to the host of heaven; and it cast down *some* of the host and of the stars to the ground, and stamped upon them. **Daniel 8:24** And his power shall be mighty, but not by his own power: and he shall destroy wonderfully, and shall prosper, and practise, and shall destroy the mighty and the holy people.
Revelation 13:8 And all that dwell upon the earth shall worship him, whose names are not written in the **book of life** of the **Lamb slain** from the foundation of the world.	**Exodus 29:14** But the flesh of the bullock, and his skin, and his dung, shalt thou burn with fire without the camp: it *is* a sin offering. **Leviticus 4:12** Even the whole bullock shall he carry forth without

	the camp unto a clean place, where the ashes are poured out, and burn him on the wood with fire: where the ashes are poured out shall he be burnt. **Leviticus 4:21** And he shall carry forth the bullock without the camp, and burn him as he burned the first bullock: it *is* a sin offering for the congregation. **Leviticus 6:30** And no sin offering, whereof *any* of the blood is brought into the tabernacle of the congregation to reconcile *withal* in the holy *place*, shall be eaten: it shall be burnt in the fire. **Leviticus 16:27** And **the bullock** *for* **the sin offering, and the goat** *for* **the sin offering, whose blood was brought in to make atonement in the holy** *place*, **shall** *one* **carry forth without the camp**; and they shall burn in the fire their skins, and their flesh, and their dung. **Numbers 19:3** And ye shall give her unto Eleazar the priest, that **he may bring her forth without the camp, and** *one* **shall slay her before his face**: **Exodus 32:32-33** Yet now, if thou wilt forgive their sin--; and if not, blot me, I pray thee, out of thy **book** which thou hast written. 33 And the LORD said unto Moses, Whosoever hath sinned against me, him will I blot out of my **book**. **Psalms 69:28** Let them be blotted out of the **book of the living**, and not be written with the righteous. **Daniel 7:10** A fiery stream issued and came forth from before him: thousand thousands ministered unto him, and ten thousand times ten thousand stood before him: the judgment was set, and the **books** were opened. **Daniel 12:1** And at that time shall Michael stand up, the great prince which standeth for the children of thy people: and there shall be a time of trouble, such as never was since there was a nation even to that same time: and at that time thy people shall be delivered, every one that shall be found written in the **book**. **See Revelations 3:5 "Book of life"**
Revelation 13:10 He that leadeth into captivity shall go into captivity: he that killeth with the sword must be killed with the sword. Here is the patience and the faith of the saints.	**Genesis 9:6** Whoso sheddeth man's blood, by man shall his blood be shed: for in the image of God made he man. **Isaiah 14:2** And the people shall take them, and bring them to their place: and the house of Israel shall possess them in the land of the LORD for servants and handmaids: and they shall take them captives, whose captives they were; and they shall rule over their oppressors.
Revelation 13:14 And deceiveth them that dwell on the earth by *the means of* those miracles which he had power to do in the sight of the beast; saying to them that dwell on the earth, that they should make an image to the beast, which had the wound by a sword, and did live.	**Deuteronomy 13:1-3** If there arise among you a prophet, or a dreamer of dreams, and giveth thee a sign or a wonder, 2 And the sign or the wonder come to pass, whereof he spake unto thee, saying, Let us go after other gods, which thou hast not known, and let us serve them; 3 Thou shalt not hearken unto the words of that prophet, or that dreamer of dreams: for the LORD your God proveth you, to know whether ye love the LORD your God with all your heart and with all your soul. **Proverbs 12:26** The righteous *is* more excellent than his neighbour: but the way of the wicked seduceth them.
Revelation 13:15 And he had power to	**Daniel 3:5-6** *That* at what time ye hear the sound of the cornet,

give life unto the image of the beast, that the image of the beast should both speak, and cause that as many as would not worship the image of the beast should be killed.	flute, harp, sackbut, psaltery, dulcimer, and all kinds of musick, ye fall down and worship the golden image that Nebuchadnezzar the king hath set up: 6 And whoso falleth not down and worshippeth shall the same hour be cast into the midst of a burning fiery furnace.
Revelation 13:16-17 And he causeth all, both small and great, rich and poor, free and bond, to receive a mark in their right **hand**, or in their **foreheads**: 17 And that no man might buy or sell, save he that had the mark, or the name of the beast, or the number of his name.	**Deuteronomy 6:8** And thou shalt bind them for a sign upon thine **hand**, and they shall be as frontlets **between thine eyes**. **See Matthew 23:5 "Phylacteries"**
Revelation 14:1 And I looked, and, lo, a Lamb stood on the mount Sion, and with him an hundred forty *and* four thousand, having his Father's name written in their foreheads	**Psalm 2:6** Yet have I set my king upon my holy hill of Zion. **Isaiah 59:20** And the Redeemer shall come to Zion, and unto them that turn from transgression in Jacob, saith the LORD. **Ezekiel 9:4** And the LORD said unto him, Go through the midst of the city, through the midst of Jerusalem, and set a mark upon the foreheads of the men that sigh and that cry for all the abominations that be done in the midst thereof.
Revelation 14:3 And they sung as it were a new song before the throne, and before the four beasts, *and* the **elders**: *and* no man could learn that song but the hundred and forty and four thousand, which were redeemed from the earth.	**See 1 Peter 5:1 "Elders"**
Revelation 14:4 These are they which were not defiled with women; for they are virgins. These are they which follow the Lamb whithersoever he goeth. These were redeemed from among men, *being* the firstfruits unto God and to the Lamb.	**Daniel 12:8-10** And I heard, but I understood not: then said I, O my Lord, what shall be the end of these things? 9 And he said, Go thy way, Daniel: for the words are closed up and sealed till the time of the end. 10 **Many shall be purified, and made white**, and tried; but the wicked shall do wickedly: and none of the wicked shall understand; but the wise shall understand.
Revelation 14:5 And in their mouth was found no guile: for they are without fault before the throne of God.	**Psalm 32:2** Blessed *is* the man unto whom the LORD imputeth not iniquity, and in whose spirit *there* guile.*is* no **Zephaniah 3:13** The remnant of Israel shall not do iniquity, nor speak lies; neither shall a deceitful tongue be found in their mouth: for they shall feed and lie down, and none shall make *them* afraid.
Revelation 14:7 Saying with a loud voice, Fear God, and give glory to him; for the hour of his judgment is come: and worship him that made heaven, and earth, and the sea, and the fountains of waters.	**Genesis 1:1** In the beginning God created the heaven and the earth. **Exodus 20:11** For *in* six days the LORD made heaven and earth, the sea, and all that in them *is,* and rested the seventh day: wherefore the LORD blessed the sabbath day, and hallowed it. **Psalms 33:6** By the word of the LORD were the heavens made; and all the host of them by the breath of his mouth. **Psalms 124:8** Our help *is* in the name of the LORD, who made heaven and earth. **Psalms 146:6** Which made heaven, and earth, the sea, and all that therein *is:* which keepeth truth for ever:
Revelation 14:8 And there followed another angel, saying, Babylon is fallen, is fallen, that great city, because she made all nations drink of the wine of the wrath of her fornication.	**Genesis 10:10** And the beginning of his kingdom was Babel, and Erech, and Accad, and Calneh, in the land of Shinar. **Isaiah 21:9** And, behold, here cometh a chariot of men, *with* a couple of horsemen. And he answered and said, Babylon is fallen,

	is fallen; and all the graven images of her gods he hath broken unto the ground.
	Jeremiah 51:8 Babylon is suddenly fallen and destroyed: howl for her; take balm for her pain, if so be she may be healed.
	Ezekiel 23:17 And the Babylonians came to her into the bed of love, and they defiled her with their whoredom, and she was polluted with them, and her mind was alienated from them.
	Daniel 2:34-35 As you looked, a stone was cut out by no human hand, and it struck the image on its feet of iron and clay, and broke them in pieces. 35 Then the iron, the clay, the bronze, the silver, and the gold, all together were broken in pieces, and became like the chaff of the summer threshing floors; and the wind carried them away, so that not a trace of them could be found. But the stone that struck the image became a great mountain and filled the whole earth.
Revelation 14:10 The same shall drink of the wine of the wrath of God, which is poured out without mixture into the cup of his indignation; and he shall be tormented with fire and brimstone in the presence of the holy angels, and in the presence of the Lamb:	**Psalm 75:9** But I will declare for ever; I will sing praises to the God of Jacob.
	Isaiah 51:22 Thus saith thy Lord the LORD, and thy God *that* pleadeth the cause of his people, Behold, I have taken out of thine hand the cup of trembling, *even* the dregs of the cup of my fury; thou shalt no more drink it again:
	Jeremiah 25:15 For thus saith the LORD God of Israel unto me; Take the wine cup of this fury at my hand, and cause all the nations, to whom I send thee, to drink it.
	See Luke 16:23 "Hell"
Revelation 14:11 And the smoke of their torment ascendeth up for ever and ever: and they have no rest day nor night, who worship the beast and his image, and whosoever receiveth the mark of his name.	**Isaiah 34:10** It shall not be quenched night nor day; the smoke thereof shall go up for ever: from generation to generation it shall lie waste; none shall pass through it for ever and ever.
	See Luke 16:23 "Hell"
Revelation 14:14 And I looked, and behold a white cloud, and upon the cloud *one* sat like unto the Son of man, having on his head a golden crown, and in his hand a sharp sickle.	**Isaiah 19:1** The burden of Egypt. Behold, the LORD rideth upon a swift cloud, and shall come into Egypt: and the idols of Egypt shall be moved at his presence, and the heart of Egypt shall melt in the midst of it.
	Ezekiel 1:26 And above the firmament that *was* over their heads *was* the likeness of a throne, as the appearance of a sapphire stone: and upon the likeness of the throne *was* the likeness as the appearance of a man above upon it.
	Daniel 7:13 I saw in the night visions, and, behold, *one* like the Son of man came with the clouds of heaven, and came to the Ancient of days, and they brought him near before him.
Revelation 14:15 And another angel came out of the temple, crying with a loud voice to him that sat on the cloud, Thrust in thy sickle, and reap: for the time is come for thee to reap; for the harvest of the earth is ripe.	**Joel 3:13** Put ye in the sickle, for the harvest is ripe: come, get you down; for the press is full, the fats overflow; for their wickedness *is* great.
Revelation 14:19-20 And the angel thrust in his sickle into the earth, and gathered the vine of the earth, and cast it into the great winepress of the wrath of God. 20 And the winepress was trodden	**Deuteronomy 32:43** Rejoice, O ye nations, *with* his people: for he will avenge the blood of his servants, and will render vengeance to his adversaries, and will be merciful unto his land, *and* to his people.

without the city, and blood came out of the winepress, even unto the horse bridles, by the space of a thousand and six hundred furlongs.	**Lamentations 1:15** The Lord hath trodden under foot all my mighty *men* in the midst of me: he hath called an assembly against me to crush my young men: the Lord hath trodden the virgin, the daughter of Judah, *as* in a winepress. **Isaiah 63:3** I have trodden the winepress alone; and of the people *there was* none with me: for I will tread them in mine anger, and trample them in my fury; and their blood shall be sprinkled upon my garments, and I will stain all my raiment. **Joel 3:13** Put ye in the sickle, for the harvest is ripe: come, get you down; for the press is full, the fats overflow; for their wickedness *is* great.
Revelation 15:2 And I saw as it were a sea of glass mingled with fire: and them that had gotten the victory over the beast, and over his image, and over his mark, *and* over the number of his name, stand on the sea of glass, having the harps of God.	**Ezekiel 13:23** Therefore ye shall see no more vanity, nor divine divinations: for I will deliver my people out of your hand: and ye shall know that I *am* the LORD.
Revelation 15:3 And they sing the song of Moses the servant of God, and the song of the Lamb, saying, Great and marvellous *are* thy works, Lord God Almighty; just and true *are* thy ways, thou King of saints.	**Exodus 15:1** Then sang Moses and the children of Israel this song unto the LORD, and spake, saying, I will sing unto the LORD, for he hath triumphed gloriously: the horse and his rider hath he thrown into the sea. **Exodus 15:11** Who *is* like unto thee, O LORD, among the gods? who *is* like thee, glorious in holiness, fearful *in* praises, doing wonders? **Psalms 111:2** The works of the LORD *are* great, sought out of all them that have pleasure therein. **Psalms 139:14** I will praise thee; for I am fearfully *and* wonderfully made: marvellous *are* thy works; and *that* my soul knoweth right well. **Psalms 145:17** The LORD *is* righteous in all his ways, and holy in all his works.
Revelation 15:4 Who shall not fear thee, O Lord, and glorify thy name? for *thou* only *art* holy: for all nations shall come and worship before thee; for thy judgments are made manifest.	**Psalm 86:9** All nations whom thou hast made shall come and worship before thee, O Lord; and shall glorify thy name. **Jeremiah 10:6** Forasmuch as *there is* none like unto thee, O LORD; thou *art* great, and thy name *is* great in might. **Mal 3:16** Then they that feared the LORD spake often one to another: and the LORD hearkened, and heard *it*, and a book of remembrance was written before him for them that feared the LORD, and that thought upon his name.
Revelation 15:7 And one of the four beasts gave unto the seven angels seven golden vials full of the wrath of God, who liveth for ever and ever.	**Ezekiel 10:7** And *one* cherub stretched forth his hand from between the cherubims unto the fire that *was* between the cherubims, and took *thereof,* and put *it* into the hands of *him that was* clothed with linen: who took *it,* and went out.
Revelation 15:8 And the temple was filled with smoke from the glory of God, and from his power; and no man was able to enter into the temple, till the seven plagues of the seven angels were fulfilled.	**Exodus 40:34** Then a cloud covered the tent of the congregation, and the glory of the LORD filled the tabernacle. **1 Kings 8: 10-11** And it came to pass, when the priests were come out of the holy *place,* that the cloud filled the house of the LORD, 11 So that the priests could not stand to minister because of the cloud: for the glory of the LORD had filled the house of the

	LORD.
	Isaiah 6:4 And the posts of the door moved at the voice of him that cried, and the house was filled with smoke.
	Ezekiel 10:4 Then the glory of the LORD went up from the cherub, *and stood* over the threshold of the house; and the house was filled with the cloud, and the court was full of the brightness of the LORD'S glory.
Revelation 16:2 And the first went, and poured out his vial upon the earth; and there fell a noisome and grievous sore *upon* the men which had the mark of the beast, and upon them which worshipped his image.	**Exodus 9:10** And they took ashes of the furnace, and stood before Pharaoh; and Moses sprinkled it up toward heaven; and it became a boil breaking forth *with* blains upon man, and upon beast.
	Ezekiel 10:2 And he spake unto the man clothed with linen, and said, Go in between the wheels, *even* under the cherub, and fill thine hand with coals of fire from between the cherubims, and scatter *them* over the city. And he went in in my sight.
Revelation 16:3-4 And the second angel poured out his vial upon the sea; and it became as the blood of a dead man: and every living soul died in the sea. 4 And the third angel poured out his vial upon the rivers and fountains of waters; and they became blood.	**Exodus 7:19-20** And the LORD spake unto Moses, Say unto Aaron, Take thy rod, and stretch out thine hand upon the waters of Egypt, upon their streams, upon their rivers, and upon their ponds, and upon all their pools of water, that they may become blood; and that there may be blood throughout all the land of Egypt, both in vessels of wood, and in vessels of stone. 20 And Moses and Aaron did so, as the LORD commanded; and he lifted up the rod, and smote the waters that were in the river, in the sight of Pharaoh, and in the sight of his servants; and all the waters that were in the river were turned to blood.
Revelation 16:6 For they have shed the blood of saints and prophets, and thou hast given them blood to drink; for they are worthy.	**Exodus 7:21** And the fish that *was* in the river died; and the river stank, and the Egyptians could not drink of the water of the river; and there was blood throughout all the land of Egypt.
	Ezekiel 16:38 And I will judge thee, as women that break wedlock and shed blood are judged; and I will give thee blood in fury and jealousy.
Revelation 16:7 And I heard another out of the altar say, Even so, Lord **God Almighty**, true and righteous *are* thy judgments.	**Genesis 28:3** And **God Almighty** bless thee, and make thee fruitful, and multiply thee, that thou mayest be a multitude of people;
	Exodus 6:3 And I appeared unto Abraham, unto Isaac, and unto Jacob, by *the name of* **God Almighty**, but by my name JEHOVAH was I not known to them.
	Ezekiel 10:5 And the sound of the cherubims' wings was heard *even* to the outer court, as the voice of the **Almighty God** when he speaketh.
Revelation 16:10 And the fifth angel poured out his vial upon the seat of the beast; and his kingdom was full of darkness; and they gnawed their tongues for pain,	**Exodus 10:22** And Moses stretched forth his hand toward heaven; and there was a thick darkness in all the land of Egypt three days:
Revelation 16:12 And the sixth angel poured out his vial upon the great river Euphrates; and the water thereof was dried up, that the way of the kings of the east might be prepared.	**Isaiah 11:15-16** And the LORD shall utterly destroy the tongue of the Egyptian sea; and with his mighty wind shall he shake his hand over the river, and shall smite it in the seven streams, and make men go over dryshod. 16 And there shall be an highway for the remnant of his people, which shall be left, from Assyria; like as it was to Israel in the day that he came up out of the land of Egypt.
	Isaiah 59:20 And the **Redeemer shall come to Zion**, and **unto them that turn from transgression in Jacob**, saith the Lord.

	Jeremiah 50:38 A drought *is* upon her waters; and they shall be dried up: for it *is* the land of graven images, and they are mad upon *their* idols.
Revelations 16:13 And I saw three unclean spirits like frogs come out of the mouth of the dragon, and out of the mouth of the beast, and out of the mouth of the **false prophet**.	**See 2 Peter 2:1 "False prophets"**
Revelation 16:14-16 For they are the **spirits of devils**, working miracles, which go forth unto the kings of the earth and of the whole world, to gather them to the battle of that great day of God Almighty. 15 Behold, I come as a thief. Blessed is he that watcheth, and keepeth his garments, lest he walk naked, and they see his shame. 16 And he gathered them together into a place called in the Hebrew tongue **Armageddon**.	**Joel 3:2** I will also gather all nations, and will bring them down into the valley of Jehoshaphat, and will plead with them there for my people and *for* my heritage Israel, whom they have scattered among the nations, and parted my land. **Joel 3:9-17** Proclaim ye this among the Gentiles; Prepare war, wake up the mighty men, let all the men of war draw near; let them come up: 10 **Beat your plowshares into swords, and your pruninghooks into spears**: let the weak say, I am strong. 11 Assemble yourselves, and come, all ye heathen, and gather yourselves together round about: thither cause thy mighty ones to come down, O Lord. 12 Let the heathen be wakened, and come up to the **valley of Jehoshaphat**: for there will I sit to judge all the heathen round about. 13 Put ye in the sickle, for the harvest is ripe: come, get you down; for the press is full, the fats overflow; for their wickedness is great. 14 Multitudes, multitudes in the valley of decision: for the **day of the Lord is near in the valley of decision**. 15 The sun and the moon shall be darkened, and the stars shall withdraw their shining. 16 The Lord also shall roar out of Zion, and utter his voice from Jerusalem; and the heavens and the earth shall shake: but the Lord will be the hope of his people, and the strength of the children of Israel. 17 So shall ye know that I am the Lord your God dwelling in Zion, my holy mountain: then shall Jerusalem be holy, and there shall no strangers pass through her any more. **Zephaniah 3:8** Therefore wait ye upon me, saith the LORD, until the day that I rise up to the prey: for my determination *is* to gather the nations, that I may assemble the kingdoms, to pour upon them mine indignation, *even* all my fierce anger: for all the earth shall be devoured with the fire of my jealousy. **Zechariah 12:1-14** The burden of the word of the Lord for Israel, saith the Lord, which stretcheth forth the heavens, and layeth the foundation of the earth, and formeth the spirit of man within him. 2 Behold, **I will make Jerusalem a cup of trembling unto all the people round about, when they shall be in the siege both against Judah and against Jerusalem**. 3 And in that day will **I make Jerusalem a burdensome stone for all people: all that burden themselves with it shall be cut in pieces, though all the people of the earth be gathered together against it**. 4 In that day, saith the Lord, **I will smite every** horse with astonishment, and his rider with madness: and I will open mine eyes upon the house of Judah, and will smite every horse of the people with blindness. 5 And the governors of Judah shall say in their heart, The inhabitants of Jerusalem shall be my strength in the Lord of hosts their God. 6 In that day will I make the governors of Judah like an hearth of fire among the wood, and like a torch of fire in a sheaf; and **they shall devour all the people round about**, on the right hand and on the left: and **Jerusalem shall be inhabited again in her own place, even in Jerusalem**. 7 The Lord also shall save the tents of Judah

	first, that the glory of the house of David and the glory of the inhabitants of **Jerusalem** do not magnify themselves against Judah. 8 **In that day shall the Lord defend the inhabitants of Jerusalem**; and he that is feeble among them at that day shall be as David; and the house of David shall be as God, as the angel of the Lord before them. 9 And it shall come to pass in that day, that **I will seek to destroy all the nations that come against Jerusalem**. 10 And I will pour upon the house of David, and **upon the inhabitants of Jerusalem, the spirit of grace and of supplications: and they shall look upon me whom they have pierced, and they shall mourn for him, as one mourneth for his only son, and shall be in bitterness for him, as one that is in bitterness for his firstborn**. 11 **In that day shall there be a great mourning in Jerusalem**, as the mourning of Hadadrimmon in the **valley of Megiddon**. 12 And the land shall mourn, every family apart; the family of the house of David apart, and their wives apart; the family of the house of Nathan apart, and their wives apart; 13 The family of the house of Levi apart, and their wives apart; the family of Shimei apart, and their wives apart; 14 All the families that remain, every family apart, and their wives apart.
	Zechariah 14:1-21 Behold, the <u>day of the Lord</u> **cometh**, and thy spoil shall be divided in the midst of thee. 2 For **I will gather <u>all</u> nations against Jerusalem to battle**; and **the city shall be taken**, and the houses rifled, and the women ravished; and half of the city shall go forth into captivity, and the residue of the people shall not be cut off from the city. 3 Then shall the Lord go forth, and fight against those nations, as when he fought in the **day of battle**. 4 And **his feet shall stand <u>in that day</u> upon the mount of Olives**, which is before Jerusalem on the east, and the mount of Olives shall cleave in the midst thereof toward the east and toward the west, and there shall be a very great valley; and half of the mountain shall remove toward the north, and half of it toward the south. 5 And ye shall flee to the valley of the mountains; for the valley of the mountains shall reach unto Azal: yea, ye shall flee, like as ye fled from before the earthquake in the days of Uzziah king of Judah: and the Lord my God shall come, and <u>**all**</u> **the saints with thee**. 6 And it shall come to pass in that day, that the light shall not be clear, nor dark: ... 21
	See Hebrews 13:2 "Good and bad angels"
Revelation 16:21 And there fell upon men a great hail out of heaven, *every stone* about the weight of a talent: and men blasphemed God because of the plague of the hail; for the plague thereof was exceeding great.	**Exodus 9:24** So there was hail, and fire mingled with the hail, very grievous, such as there was none like it in all the land of Egypt since it became a nation.
	Exodus 9:34 And when Pharaoh saw that the rain and the hail and the thunders were ceased, he sinned yet more, and hardened his heart, he and his servants.
Revelation 17:1 And there came one of the seven angels which had the seven vials, and talked with me, saying unto me, Come hither; I will shew unto thee the judgment of the great whore that sitteth upon many waters:	**Jeremiah 51:13** O thou that dwellest upon many waters, abundant in treasures, thine end is come, *and* the measure of thy covetousness.
Revelation 17:2 With whom the kings of the earth have committed fornication, and the inhabitants of the earth have been made drunk with the wine of her	**Jeremiah 51:7** Babylon *hath been* a golden cup in the LORD'S hand, that made all the earth drunken: the nations have drunken of her wine; therefore the nations are mad.

fornication.	
Revelation 17:3 So he carried me away in the spirit into the wilderness: and I saw a woman sit upon a scarlet coloured beast, full of names of blasphemy, having seven heads and ten horns.	**Daniel 7:7-8** After this I saw in the night visions, and behold a fourth beast, dreadful and terrible, and strong exceedingly; and it had great iron teeth: it devoured and brake in pieces, and stamped the residue with the feet of it: and it was diverse from all the beasts that were before it; and it had ten horns. 8 I considered the horns, and, behold, there came up among them another little horn, before whom there were three of the first horns plucked up by the roots: and, behold, in this horn were eyes like the eyes of man, and a mouth speaking great things. **Daniel 7:25** And he shall speak *great* words against the most High, and shall wear out the saints of the most High, and think to change times and laws: and they shall be given into his hand until a time and times and the dividing of time.
Revelation 17:4 And the woman was arrayed in purple and scarlet colour, and decked with gold and precious stones and pearls, having a golden cup in her hand full of abominations and filthiness of her fornication:	**Jeremiah 51:7** Babylon *hath been* a golden cup in the LORD'S hand, that made all the earth drunken: the nations have drunken of her wine; therefore the nations are mad.
Revelations 17:6 And I saw the woman drunken with the blood of the saints, and with the blood of the martyrs of Jesus: and when I saw her, I wondered with great admiration.	**Jeremiah 44:16-17** As for the word that thou hast spoken unto us in the name of the LORD, we will not hearken unto thee. 17 But we will certainly do whatsoever thing goeth forth out of our own mouth, to burn incense unto the queen of heaven (the Roman Catholic's Mary), and to pour out drink offerings unto her, as we have done, we, and our fathers, our kings, and our princes, in the cities of Judah, and in the streets of Jerusalem: for then had we plenty of victuals, and were well, and saw no evil.
Revelations 17:7 And the angel said unto me, Wherefore didst thou marvel? **I will tell thee the mystery of the woman**, and of the beast that carrieth her, which hath the seven heads and ten horns.	**Daniel 12:4** But thou, O Daniel, shut up the words, and seal the book, even to the time of the end: many shall run to and fro, and knowledge shall be increased.
Revelation 17:8 The beast that thou sawest was, and is not; and shall ascend out of the bottomless pit, and go into perdition: and they that dwell on the earth shall wonder, whose names were not written in the book of life from the foundation of the world, when they behold the beast that was, and is not, and yet is.	**Exodus 32:32-33** Yet now, if thou wilt forgive their sin--; and if not, blot me, I pray thee, out of thy **book** which thou hast written. 33 And the LORD said unto Moses, Whosoever hath sinned against me, him will I blot out of my **book**. **Psalms 69:28** Let them be blotted out of the **book of the living**, and not be written with the righteous. **Daniel 7:10** A fiery stream issued and came forth from before him: thousand thousands ministered unto him, and ten thousand times ten thousand stood before him: the judgment was set, and the **books** were opened. **Daniel 12:1** And at that time shall Michael stand up, the great prince which standeth for the children of thy people: and there shall be a time of trouble, such as never was since there was a nation even to that same time: and at that time thy people shall be delivered, every one that shall be found written in the **book**. See Revelations 3:5 "book of life"
Revelation 17:12 And the ten horns which thou sawest are ten kings, which have received no kingdom as yet; but receive power as kings one hour with the	**Daniel 7:20** And of the ten horns that *were* in his head, and *of* the other which came up, and before whom three fell; even *of* that horn that had eyes, and a mouth that spake very great things, whose look

beast.	*was* more stout than his fellows. **Daniel 7:24** And the ten horns out of this kingdom *are* ten kings *that* shall arise: and another shall rise after them; and he shall be diverse from the first, and he shall subdue three kings.
Revelation 17:14 These shall make war with the Lamb, and the Lamb shall overcome them: for he is Lord of lords, and King of kings: and they that are with him *are* called, and chosen, and faithful.	**Daniel 8:25** And through his policy also he shall cause craft to prosper in his hand; and he shall magnify *himself* in his heart, and by peace shall destroy many: he shall also stand up against the Prince of princes; but he shall be broken without hand.
Revelation 17:15 And he saith unto me, The waters which thou sawest, where the whore sitteth, are peoples, and multitudes, and nations, and tongues.	**Isaiah 8:7** Now therefore, behold, the Lord bringeth up upon them the waters of the river, strong and many, *even* the king of Assyria, and all his glory: and he shall come up over all his channels, and go over all his banks: **Jeremiah 51:42** The sea is come up upon Babylon: she is covered with the multitude of the waves thereof.
Revelation 17:16 And the ten horns which thou sawest upon the beast, these shall hate the whore, and shall make her desolate and naked, and shall eat her flesh, and burn her with fire.	**Daniel 7:23** Thus he said, The fourth beast shall be the fourth kingdom upon earth, which shall be diverse from all kingdoms, and shall devour the whole earth, and shall tread it down, and break it in pieces. **Daniel 2:40** And the fourth kingdom shall be strong as iron: forasmuch as iron breaketh in pieces and subdueth all things: and as iron that breaketh all these, shall it break in pieces and bruise.
Revelation 18:1 And after these things I saw another angel come down from heaven, having great power; and the earth was lightened with his glory.	**Ezekiel 43:2** And, behold, the glory of the God of Israel came from the way of the east: and his voice *was* like a noise of many waters: and the earth shined with his glory.
Revelation 18:2 And he cried mightily with a strong voice, saying, Babylon the great is fallen, is fallen, and is become the habitation of **devils**, and the hold of every foul spirit, and a cage of every unclean and hateful bird.	**Isaiah 13:21** But wild beasts of the desert shall lie there; and their houses shall be full of doleful creatures; and owls shall dwell there, and satyrs shall dance there. **Isaiah 21:9** And, behold, here cometh a chariot of men, *with* a couple of horsemen. And he answered and said, Babylon is fallen, is fallen; and all the graven images of her gods he hath broken unto the ground. **Jeremiah 51:8** Babylon is suddenly fallen and destroyed: howl for her; take balm for her pain, if so be she may be healed. See Hebrews 13:2 "Good and bad angels"
Revelation 18:3 For all nations have drunk of the wine of the wrath of her fornication, and the kings of the earth have committed fornication with her, and the merchants of the earth are waxed rich through the abundance of her delicacies.	**Jeremiah 51:7** Babylon *hath been* a golden cup in the LORD'S hand, that made all the earth drunken: the nations have drunken of her wine; therefore the nations are mad. **Nahum 3:4** Because of the multitude of the whoredoms of the wellfavoured harlot, the mistress of witchcrafts, that selleth nations through her whoredoms, and families through her witchcrafts.
Revelation 18:4 And I heard another voice from heaven, saying, Come out of her, my people, that ye be not partakers of her sins, and that ye receive not of her plagues.	**Genesis 19:12** And the men said unto Lot, Hast thou here any besides? son in law, and thy sons, and thy daughters, and whatsoever thou hast in the city, bring *them* out of this place: **Isaiah 26:20-21** Come, my people, enter thou into thy chambers, and shut thy doors about thee: hide thyself as it were for a little moment, until the indignation be overpast. 21 For, behold, the LORD cometh out of his place to punish the inhabitants of the

	earth for their iniquity: the earth also shall disclose her blood, and shall no more cover her slain.
	Isaiah 48:20 Go ye forth of Babylon, flee ye from the Chaldeans, with a voice of singing declare ye, tell this, utter it *even* to the end of the earth; say ye, The LORD hath redeemed his servant Jacob.
	Isaiah 52:11 Depart ye, depart ye, go ye out from thence, touch no unclean *thing;* go ye out of the midst of her; be ye clean, that bear the vessels of the LORD.
	Jeremiah 50:8 Remove out of the midst of Babylon, and go forth out of the land of the Chaldeans, and be as the he goats before the flocks.
	Jeremiah 51:6 Flee out of the midst of Babylon, and deliver every man his soul: be not cut off in her iniquity; for this *is* the time of the LORD'S vengeance; he will render unto her a recompence.
	Jeremiah 51:9 We would have healed Babylon, but she is not healed: forsake her, and let us go every one into his own country: for her judgment reacheth unto heaven, and is lifted up *even* to the skies. **Jeremiah 51:45** My people, go ye out of the midst of her, and deliver ye every man his soul from the fierce anger of the LORD.
	Ezekiel 9:4 And the LORD said unto him, Go through the midst of the city, through the midst of Jerusalem, and set a mark upon the foreheads of the men that sigh and that cry for all the abominations that be done in the midst thereof.
Revelation 18:6 Reward her even as she rewarded you, and double unto her double according to her works: in the cup which she hath filled fill to her double	**Psalm 137:8** O daughter of Babylon, who art to be destroyed; happy *shall he be,* that rewardeth thee as thou hast served us.
	Jeremiah 50:15 Shout against her round about: she hath given her hand: her foundations are fallen, her walls are thrown down: for it *is* the vengeance of the LORD: take vengeance upon her; as she hath done, do unto her.
	Jeremiah 50:29 Call together the archers against Babylon: all ye that bend the bow, camp against it round about; let none thereof escape: recompense her according to her work; according to all that she hath done, do unto her: for she hath been proud against the LORD, against the Holy One of Israel.
Revelation 18:7-8 How much she hath glorified herself, and lived deliciously, so much torment and sorrow give her: for she saith in her heart, I sit a queen, and am no widow, and shall see no sorrow. 8 Therefore shall her plagues come in one day, death, and mourning, and famine; and she shall be utterly burned with fire: for strong is the Lord God who judgeth her.	**Isaiah 47:7** And thou saidst, I shall be a lady for ever: *so that* thou didst not lay these *things* to thy heart, neither didst remember the latter end of it.
	Jeremiah 50:31 Behold, I *am* against thee, *O thou* most proud, saith the Lord GOD of hosts: for thy day is come, the time *that* I will visit thee.
Revelation 18:10 Standing afar off for the fear of her torment, saying, Alas, alas, that great city Babylon, that mighty city! for in one hour is thy judgment come.	**Isaiah 21:9** And, behold, here cometh a chariot of men, *with* a couple of horsemen. And he answered and said, Babylon is fallen, is fallen; and all the graven images of her gods he hath broken unto the ground.
	Jeremiah 51:1 Thus saith the LORD; Behold, I will raise up against Babylon, and against them that dwell in the midst of them that rise up against me, a destroying wind;

Revelation 18:11 And the merchants of the earth shall weep and mourn over her; for no man buyeth their merchandise any more:	**Isaiah 43:14** Thus saith the LORD, your redeemer, the Holy One of Israel; For your sake I have sent to Babylon, and have brought down all their nobles, and the Chaldeans, whose cry *is* in the ships. **Ezekiel 27:17** Judah, and the land of Israel, they *were* thy merchants: they traded in thy market wheat of Minnith, and Pannag, and honey, and oil, and balm.
Revelation 18:11-13 And the merchants of the earth shall weep and mourn over her; for **no man buyeth their merchandise any more:** 12 **The merchandise of** gold, and silver, and precious stones, and of pearls, and fine linen, and purple, and silk, and scarlet, and all thyine wood, and all manner vessels of ivory, and all manner vessels of most precious wood, and of brass, and iron, and marble, 13 And cinnamon, and odours, and ointments, and frankincense, and wine, and oil, and fine flour, and wheat, and beasts, and sheep, and horses, and chariots, and slaves, and <u>**souls of men**</u>.	**Ezekiel 13:17-23** Likewise, thou son of man, set thy face against the daughters of thy people, which prophesy out of their own heart; and prophesy thou against them, 18 And say, Thus saith the Lord GOD; **Woe to the *women* that sew pillows to all armholes, and make kerchiefs upon the head of every stature to <u>hunt souls</u>! Will ye <u>hunt the souls</u> of my people**, and will ye **save the souls alive** *that come* unto you? 19 And will ye pollute me among my people for handfuls of barley and for pieces of bread, **to slay the souls that should not die**, and **to save the souls alive that should not live, by your lying to my people that hear** *your* **lies**? 20 Wherefore thus saith the Lord GOD; Behold, I *am* against your pillows, wherewith ye there **<u>hunt the souls</u> to make *them* fly**, and I will tear them from your arms, and will let the souls go, *even* the **<u>souls that ye hunt</u>** to make *them* fly. 21 Your kerchiefs also will I tear, and **deliver my people out of your hand**, and **they shall be no more in your hand to be hunted**; and ye shall know that I *am* the LORD. 22 Because with lies ye have made the heart of the righteous sad, whom I have not made sad; and strengthened the hands of the wicked, that he should not return from his wicked way, by promising him life: 23 Therefore ye shall see no more vanity, nor divine divinations: for **I will deliver my people out of your hand**: and ye shall know that I *am* the LORD.
Revelation 18:18 And cried when they saw the smoke of her burning, saying, What *city is* like unto this great city!	**Isaiah 34:8** For *it is* the day of the LORD'S vengeance, *and* the year of recompences for the controversy of Zion. **Isaiah 34:10** It shall not be quenched night nor day; the smoke thereof shall go up for ever: from generation to generation it shall lie waste; none shall pass through it for ever and ever.
Revelation 18:20 Rejoice over her, *thou* heaven, and *ye* holy apostles and prophets; for God hath avenged you on her.	**Isaiah 44:23** Sing, O ye heavens; for the LORD hath done *it:* shout, ye lower parts of the earth: break forth into singing, ye mountains, O forest, and every tree therein: for the LORD hath redeemed Jacob, and glorified himself in Israel. **Jeremiah 51:48** Then the heaven and the earth, and all that *is* therein, shall sing for Babylon: for the spoilers shall come unto her from the north, saith the LORD.
Revelation 18:21 And a mighty angel took up a stone like a great millstone, and cast it into the sea, saying, Thus with violence shall that great city Babylon be thrown down, and shall be found no more at all.	**Jeremiah 51:63-64** And it shall be, when thou hast made an end of reading this book, that thou shalt bind a stone to it, and cast it into the midst of Euphrates: 64 And thou shalt say, Thus shall Babylon sink, and shall not rise from the evil that I will bring upon her: and they shall be weary. Thus far are the words of Jeremiah.
Revelation 18:22 And the voice of harpers, and musicians, and of pipers, and trumpeters, shall be heard no more at all in thee; and no craftsman, of whatsoever craft *he be,* shall be found any more in thee; and the sound of a millstone shall be heard no more at all in thee;	**Isaiah 24:8** The mirth of tabrets ceaseth, the noise of them that rejoice endeth, the joy of the harp ceaseth. **Jeremiah 7:34** Then will I cause to cease from the cities of Judah, and from the streets of Jerusalem, the voice of mirth, and the voice of gladness, the voice of the bridegroom, and the voice of the bride: for the land shall be desolate. **Jeremiah 25:10** Moreover I will take from them the voice of mirth, and the voice of gladness, the voice of the bridegroom, and

	the voice of the bride, the sound of the millstones, and the light of the candle.
	Ezekiel 26:13 And I will cause the noise of thy songs to cease; and the sound of thy harps shall be no more heard.
Revelation 18:23 And the light of a candle shall shine no more at all in thee; and the voice of the bridegroom and of the bride shall be heard no more at all in thee: for thy merchants were the great men of the earth; for by thy sorceries were all nations deceived.	**Isaiah 14:4** That thou shalt take up this proverb against the king of Babylon, and say, How hath the oppressor ceased! the golden city ceased!
	Jeremiah 16:9 For thus saith the LORD of hosts, the God of Israel; Behold, I will cause to cease out of this place in your eyes, and in your days, the voice of mirth, and the voice of gladness, the voice of the bridegroom, and the voice of the bride.
Revelation 18:24 And in her was found the blood of prophets, and of saints, and of all that were slain upon the earth.	**Jeremiah 51:49** As Babylon *hath caused* the slain of Israel to fall, so at Babylon shall fall the slain of all the earth.
Revelation 19:2 For true and righteous *are* his judgments: for he hath judged the great whore, which did corrupt the earth with her fornication, and hath avenged the blood of his servants at her hand.	**Deuteronomy 32:4** *He is* the Rock, his work *is* perfect: for all his ways *are* judgment: a God of truth and without iniquity, just and right *is* he. **Deuteronomy 32:43** Rejoice, O ye nations, *with* his people: for he will avenge the blood of his servants, and will render vengeance to his adversaries, and will be merciful unto his land, *and* to his people.
Revelation 19:3 And again they said, Alleluia. And her smoke rose up for ever and ever.	**Isaiah 34:10** It shall not be quenched night nor day; the smoke thereof shall go up for ever: from generation to generation it shall lie waste; none shall pass through it for ever and ever.
Revelation 19:4 And the four and twenty **elders** and the four beasts fell down and worshipped God that sat on the throne, saying, Amen; Alleluia.	**See 1 Peter 5:1 "Elders"**
Revelation 19:5 And a voice came out of the throne, saying, Praise our God, all ye his servants, and ye that fear him, both small and great.	**Psalm 115:13** He will bless them that fear the LORD, *both* small and great.
	Psalm 135:1 Praise ye the LORD. Praise ye the name of the LORD; praise *him,* O ye servants of the LORD.
	Psalm 135:20 Bless the LORD, O house of Levi: ye that fear the LORD, bless the LORD.
Revelation 19:8 And to her was granted that she should be arrayed in fine linen, clean and white: for the fine linen is the righteousness of saints.	**Psalm 45:14** She shall be brought unto the king in raiment of needlework: the virgins her companions that follow her shall be brought unto thee.
	Isaiah 61:10 I will greatly rejoice in the LORD, my soul shall be joyful in my God; for he hath clothed me with the garments of salvation, he hath covered me with the robe of righteousness, as a bridegroom decketh *himself* with ornaments, and as a bride adorneth *herself* with her jewels.
Revelations 19:10 And I fell at his feet to worship him. And he said unto me, See thou do it not: I am thy fellowservant, and of thy brethren that have the testimony of Jesus: worship God: for the testimony of Jesus is the spirit of prophecy.	**Exodus 34:14** For thou shalt worship no other god: for the LORD, whose name is Jealous, is a jealous God:
	Deuteronomy 10:20 Thou shalt fear the LORD thy God; him shalt thou serve, and to him shalt thou cleave, and swear by his name.
	Psalms 97:7 Confounded be all they that serve graven images, that boast themselves of idols: worship him, all *ye* gods.
Revelation 19:11 And I saw heaven opened, and behold a white horse; and he that sat upon him *was* called Faithful and True, and in righteousness he doth	**Psalm 72:2** He shall judge thy people with righteousness, and thy poor with judgment.

judge and make war.	
Revelation 19:12 His eyes *were* as a flame of fire, and on his head *were* many crowns; and he had a name written, that no man knew, but he himself.	**Daniel 10:6** His body also *was* like the beryl, and his face as the appearance of lightning, and his eyes as lamps of fire, and his arms and his feet like in colour to polished brass, and the voice of his words like the voice of a multitude.
Revelation 19:13-15 And he *was* clothed with a vesture dipped in blood: and his name is called The Word of God. 14 And the armies *which* were in heaven followed him upon white horses, clothed in fine linen, white and clean. 15 And out of his mouth goeth a sharp sword, that with it he should smite the nations: and he shall rule them with a rod of iron: and he treadeth the winepress of the fierceness and wrath of Almighty God.	**Isaiah 63:2-3** Wherefore art thou red in thine apparel, and thy garments like him that treadeth in the winefat? 3 I have trodden the winepress alone; and of the people there was none with me: for I will tread them in mine anger, and trample them in my fury; and their blood shall be sprinkled upon my garments, and I will stain all my raiment. **Psalm 2:9** Thou shalt break them with a rod of iron; thou shalt dash them in pieces like a potter's vessel. **Lamentations 1:15** The Lord hath trodden under foot all my mighty *men* in the midst of me: he hath called an assembly against me to crush my young men: the Lord hath trodden the virgin, the daughter of Judah, *as* in a winepress. **Joel 3:13** Put ye in the sickle, for the harvest is ripe: come, get you down; for the press is full, the fats overflow; for their wickedness *is* great. **See Matthew 26:28 "Atonement"**
Revelation 19:16 And he hath on *his* vesture and on his thigh a name written, KING OF KINGS, AND LORD OF LORDS.	**Psalms 24:10** Who is this King of glory? The LORD of hosts, he *is* the King of glory. Selah. **Psalm 72:8** He shall have dominion also from sea to sea, and from the river unto the ends of the earth. **Deuteronomy 10:17** For the LORD your God *is* God of gods, and **Lord of lords**, a great God, a mighty, and a terrible, which regardeth not persons, nor taketh reward:
Revelation 19:17-18 And I saw an angel standing in the sun; and he cried with a loud voice, saying to all the fowls that fly in the midst of heaven, Come and gather yourselves together unto the supper of the great God; 18 That ye may eat the flesh of kings, and the flesh of captains, and the flesh of mighty men, and the flesh of horses, and of them that sit on them, and the flesh of all men, both free and bond, both small and great.	**Isaiah 34:6** The sword of the LORD is filled with blood, it is made fat with fatness, *and* with the blood of lambs and goats, with the fat of the kidneys of rams: for the LORD hath a sacrifice in Bozrah, and a great slaughter in the land of Idumea. **Jeremiah 7:33** And the carcases of this people shall be meat for the fowls of the heaven, and for the beasts of the earth; and none shall fray *them* away. **Jeremiah 12:9** Mine heritage *is* unto me *as* a speckled bird, the birds round about *are* against her; come ye, assemble all the beasts of the field, come to devour. **Ezekiel 39:17-20** And, thou son of man, thus saith the Lord GOD; Speak unto every feathered fowl, and to every beast of the field, Assemble yourselves, and come; gather yourselves on every side to my sacrifice that I do sacrifice for you, even a great sacrifice upon the mountains of Israel, that ye may eat flesh, and drink blood. 18 Ye shall eat the flesh of the mighty, and drink the blood of the princes of the earth, of rams, of lambs, and of goats, of bullocks, all of them fatlings of Bashan. 19 And ye shall eat fat till ye be full, and drink blood till ye be drunken, of my sacrifice which I have sacrificed for you. 20 Thus ye shall be filled at my table with horses and chariots, with mighty men, and with all men of war, saith the Lord GOD.
Revelation 19:19 And I saw the beast, and the kings of the earth, and their	**Psalm 2:2** The kings of the earth set themselves, and the rulers take counsel together, against the LORD, and against his anointed,

armies, gathered together to make war against him that sat on the horse, and against his army.	*saying,*
Revelation 19:20 And the beast was taken, and with him the **false prophet** that wrought miracles before him, with which he deceived them that had received the mark of the beast, and them that worshipped his image. These both were cast alive into a lake of fire **burning** with brimstone.	**Deuteronomy 13:1-3** If there arise among you a prophet, or a dreamer of dreams, and giveth thee a sign or a wonder, 2 And the sign or the wonder come to pass, whereof he spake unto thee, saying, Let us go after other gods, which thou hast not known, and let us serve them; 3 Thou shalt not hearken unto the words of that prophet, or that dreamer of dreams: for the LORD your God proveth you, to know whether ye love the LORD your God with all your heart and with all your soul. **Isaiah 30:33** For Tophet *is* ordained of old; yea, for the king it is prepared; he hath made *it* deep *and* large: the pile thereof *is* fire and much wood; the breath of the LORD, like a stream of brimstone, doth kindle it. **Daniel 7:11** I beheld then because of the voice of the great words which the horn spake: I beheld *even* till the beast was slain, and his body destroyed, and given to the **burning flame**. **Daniel 7:26** But the judgment shall sit, and they shall take away his dominion, to consume and to destroy *it* unto the end. See 2 Peter 2:1 "False prophets" See Luke 16:23 "Hell"
Revelation 20:1 And I saw an **angel** come down from heaven, having the key of the bottomless pit and a great chain in his hand.	See Hebrews 13:2 "Angels"
Revelation 20:2 And he laid hold on the dragon, that old **serpent**, which is the Devil, and **Satan**, and bound him a thousand years,	**Genesis 3:4** And the **serpent** said unto the woman, Ye shall not surely die: **Zechariah 3:1-2** And he shewed me Joshua the high priest standing before the angel of the LORD, and **Satan** standing at his right hand to resist him. 2 And the LORD said unto **Satan,** The LORD rebuke thee, O **Satan**; even the LORD that hath chosen Jerusalem rebuke thee: *is* not this a brand plucked out of the fire? See Matthew 4:10 "satan"
Revelation 20:3 And cast him into the bottomless pit, and shut him up, and set a seal upon him, that he should deceive the nations no more, till the thousand years should be fulfilled: and after that he must be loosed a little season.	**Leviticus 23:34** Speak unto the children of Israel, saying, The fifteenth day of this seventh month *shall be* the feast of tabernacles *for* seven days unto the LORD. **Micah 4:1-3** But in the last days it shall come to pass, *that* the mountain of the house of the LORD shall be established in the top of the mountains, and it shall be exalted above the hills; and people shall flow unto it. 2 And many nations shall come, and say, Come, and let us go up to the mountain of the LORD, and to the house of the God of Jacob; and he will teach us of his ways, and we will walk in his paths: for the law shall go forth of Zion, and the word of the LORD from Jerusalem. 3 And he shall judge among many people, and rebuke strong nations afar off; and they shall beat their swords into plowshares, and their spears into pruninghooks: nation shall not lift up a sword against nation, neither shall they learn war any more. **Micah 4:7** And I will make her that halted a remnant, and her that was cast far off a strong nation: and the LORD shall reign over them in mount Zion from henceforth, even for ever.

Revelation 20:4 And *I saw* thrones, and they sat upon them, and judgment was given unto them: and I saw the souls of them that were beheaded for the witness of Jesus, and for the word of God, and which had not worshipped the beast, neither his image, neither had received his mark upon their foreheads, or in their hands; and they lived and reigned with Christ a thousand years.	**Ezekiel 9:4** And the LORD said unto him, Go through the midst of the city, through the midst of Jerusalem, and set a mark upon the foreheads of the men that sigh and that cry for all the abominations that be done in the midst thereof. **Zechariah 14:16** And it shall come to pass, that every one that is left of all the nations which came against Jerusalem shall even go up from year to year to worship the King, the LORD of hosts, and to keep the feast of tabernacles.
Revelation 20:5 But the rest of the dead lived not again until the thousand years were finished. This *is* the first resurrection.	**Isaiah 26:19** Thy dead *men* shall live, *together with* my dead body shall they arise. Awake and sing, ye that dwell in dust: for thy dew *is as* the dew of herbs, and the earth shall cast out the dead. **Daniel 12:2** And many of them that sleep in the dust of the earth shall awake, some to everlasting life, and some to shame *and* everlasting contempt.
Revelation 20:6 Blessed and holy *is* he that hath part in the first resurrection: on such the second death hath no power, but they shall be priests of God and of Christ, and shall reign with him a thousand years.	**Leviticus 23:34** Speak unto the children of Israel, saying, The fifteenth day of this seventh month *shall be* the feast of tabernacles *for* seven days unto the LORD. **Leviticus 23:42-43** Ye shall dwell in booths seven days; all that are Israelites born shall dwell in booths: 43 That your generations may know that I made the children of Israel to dwell in booths, when I brought them out of the land of Egypt: I *am* the LORD your God. **Nehemiah 8:14-15** And they found written in the law which the LORD had commanded by Moses, that the children of Israel should dwell in booths in the feast of the seventh month: 15 And that they should publish and proclaim in all their cities, and in Jerusalem, saying, Go forth unto the mount, and fetch olive branches, and pine branches, and myrtle branches, and palm branches, and branches of thick trees, to make booths, as *it is* written. **Isaiah 32:1** Behold, a king shall reign in righteousness, and princes shall rule in judgment. **Jeremiah 3:17** At that time they shall call Jerusalem the throne of the LORD; and all the nations shall be gathered unto it, to the name of the LORD, to Jerusalem: neither shall they walk any more after the imagination of their evil heart. **Zechariah 14:9** And the LORD shall be king over all the earth: in that day shall there be one LORD, and his name one. **Zechariah 14:16** And it shall come to pass, *that* every one that is left of all the nations which came against Jerusalem shall even go up from year to year to worship the King, the LORD of hosts, and to keep the feast of tabernacles. **Zechariah 14:18-19** And if the family of Egypt go not up, and come not, that *have* no *rain*; there shall be the plague, wherewith the LORD will smite the heathen that come not up to keep the feast of tabernacles. 19 This shall be the punishment of Egypt, and the punishment of all nations that come not up to keep the feast of tabernacles.
Revelation 20:7-10 And when the thousand years are expired, **Satan** shall be loosed out of his prison, 8 And shall	See Revelation 20:3 See Revelation 20:8 "Gog"

go out to deceive the nations which are in the four quarters of the earth, **Gog** and Magog, to gather them together to battle: the number of whom is as the sand of the sea. 9 And they went up on the breadth of the earth, and compassed the camp of the saints about, and the beloved city: and fire came down from God out of heaven, and devoured them. 10 And the devil that deceived them was cast into the lake of fire and brimstone, where the beast and the **false prophet** are, and shall be tormented day and night for ever and ever.	**Daniel 7:11** I beheld then because of the voice of the great words which the horn spake: I beheld *even* till the beast was slain, and his body destroyed, and given to the burning flame. **Genesis 3:4** And the **serpent** said unto the woman, Ye shall not surely die: **Zechariah 3:1-2** And he shewed me Joshua the high priest standing before the angel of the LORD, and **Satan** standing at his right hand to resist him. 2 And the LORD said unto **Satan,** The LORD rebuke thee, O **Satan**; even the LORD that hath chosen Jerusalem rebuke thee: *is* not this a brand plucked out of the fire? See **Matthew 4:10** "satan" See **2 Peter 2:1** "False prophets" See **Luke 16:23** "Hell"
Revelation 20:8 And shall go out to deceive the nations which are in the four quarters of the earth, **Gog and Magog**, to gather them together to battle: the number of whom *is* as the sand of the sea.	**Genesis 10:2** The sons of Japheth; Gomer, and **Magog**, and Madai, and Javan, and Tubal, and Meshech, and Tiras. **1 Chronicles 1:5** The sons of Japheth; Gomer, and **Magog**, and Madai, and Javan, and Tubal, and Meshech, and Tiras. **1 Chronicles 5:4** The sons of Joel; Shemaiah his son, **Gog** his son, Shimei his son, **Isaiah 11:12** And he shall set up an ensign for the nations, and shall assemble the outcasts of Israel, and gather together the dispersed of Judah from the four corners of the earth. **Jerermiah 49:36** And upon Elam will I bring the four winds from the four quarters of heaven, and will scatter them toward all those winds; and there shall be no nation whither the outcasts of Elam shall not come. **Ezekiel 7:2** Also, thou son of man, thus saith the Lord GOD unto the land of Israel; An end, the end is come upon the four corners of the land. **Ezekiel 37:9** Then said he unto me, Prophesy unto the wind, prophesy, son of man, and say to the wind, Thus saith the Lord GOD; Come from the four winds, O breath, and breathe upon these slain, that they may live. **Ezekiel 38:2-3** Son of man, set thy face against **Gog**, the land of Magog, the chief prince of Meshech and Tubal, and prophesy against him, 3 And say, Thus saith the Lord GOD; Behold, I am against thee, O **Gog**, the chief prince of Meshech and Tubal: **Ezekiel 38:8** After many days thou shalt be visited: in the latter years thou shalt come into the land *that is* brought back from the sword, *and is* gathered out of many people, against the mountains of Israel, which have been always waste: but it is brought forth out of the nations, and **they shall dwell <u>safely all</u> of them**. **Ezekiel 38:11-12** And thou shalt say, I will go up to the land of unwalled villages; I will go to them that are at rest, **that dwell <u>safely</u>**, all of them dwelling without walls, and having neither bars nor gates,12 **To take a spoil**, and to take a prey; to turn thine hand upon the desolate places *that are now* inhabited, and upon the people *that are* gathered out of the nations, which have gotten cattle and goods, that dwell in the midst of the land.

	Ezekiel 38:14 Therefore, son of man, prophesy and say unto Gog, Thus saith the Lord GOD; In that day **when my people of <u>Israel dwelleth safely</u>**, shalt thou not know *it*?
	Ezekiel 38:16 And thou shalt come up against my people of Israel, as a cloud to cover the land; it shall be **in the latter days**, and I will bring thee against my land, that the heathen may know me, when I shall be sanctified in thee, O Gog, before their eyes.
	Ezekiel 38:18 And it shall come to pass at the same time when **Gog** shall come against the land of Israel, saith the Lord GOD, that my fury shall come up in my face.
	Ezekiel 39:1 Therefore, thou son of man, prophesy against **Gog**, and say, Thus saith the Lord GOD; Behold, I am against thee, O Gog, the chief prince of Meshech and Tubal:
	Ezekiel 39:6 And **I will send a fire on Magog**, and among them that dwell carelessly in the isles: and they shall know that I *am* the LORD.
	Ezekiel 39:9-11 And they that dwell in the cities of Israel shall go forth, and shall set on fire and burn the weapons, both the shields and the bucklers, the bows and the arrows, and the handstaves, and the spears, and they shall burn them with fire seven years: 10 So that they shall take no wood out of the field, neither cut down *any* out of the forests; for they shall burn the weapons with fire: and they shall spoil those that spoiled them, and rob those that robbed them, saith the Lord GOD. 11 And it shall come to pass in that day, that I will give unto **Gog** a place there of graves in Israel, the valley of the passengers on the east of the sea: and it shall stop the noses of the passengers: and there shall they bury Gog and all his multitude: and they shall call it The valley of Hamon-**gog**.
	Ezekiel 39:15 And the passengers that pass through the land, when any seeth a man's bone, then shall he set up a sign by it, till the buriers have buried it in the valley of Hamon-**gog**.
	Daniel 7:2 Daniel spake and said, I saw in my vision by night, and, behold, the four winds of the heaven strove upon the great sea.
	Daniel 8:8 Therefore the he goat waxed very great: and when he was strong, the great horn was broken; and for it came up four notable ones toward the four winds of heaven.
	Daniel 11:4 And when he shall stand up, his kingdom shall be broken, and shall be divided toward the four winds of heaven; and not to his posterity, nor according to his dominion which he ruled: for his kingdom shall be plucked up, even for others beside those.
	Zechariah 2:6 Ho, ho, *come forth*, and flee from the land of the north, saith the LORD: for I have spread you abroad as the four winds of the heaven, saith the LORD.
Revelation 20:11 And I saw a great white throne, and him that sat on it, from whose face the earth and the heaven fled away; and there was found no place for them.	**Isaiah 12:6** Cry out and shout, thou inhabitant of Zion: for great *is* the Holy One of Israel in the midst of thee.
	Daniel 12:1-3 And at that time shall Michael stand up, the great prince which standeth for the children of thy people: and there shall be a time of trouble, such as never was since there was a nation even to that same time: and at that
	time thy people shall be delivered, every one that shall be found written in the book. 2 And many of them that sleep in the dust of the earth shall awake, some to everlasting life, and some to shame and everlasting contempt. 3 And they that be wise shall shine as

	the brightness of the firmament; and they that turn many to righteousness as the stars for ever and ever.
Revelation 20:12 And I saw the dead, small and great, stand before God; and the **books** were opened: and another book was opened, which is *the book* of life: and the dead were judged out of those things which were written in the books, according to their works. **Revelation 20:15** And whosoever was not found written in the **book of life** was cast into the lake of fire.	**Psalms 62:12** Also unto thee, O Lord, *belongeth* mercy: for thou renderest to every man according to his work. **Jeremiah 17:10** I the LORD search the heart, *I* try the reins, even to give every man according to his ways, *and* according to the fruit of his doings. **Jeremiah 32:19** Great in counsel, and mighty in work: for thine eyes *are* open upon all the ways of the sons of men: to give every one according to his ways, and according to the fruit of his doings: **Exodus 32:32-33** Yet now, if thou wilt forgive their sin--; and if not, blot me, I pray thee, out of thy **book** which thou hast written. 33 And the LORD said unto Moses, Whosoever hath sinned against me, him will I blot out of my **book**. **Psalms 69:28** Let them be blotted out of the **book of the living**, and not be written with the righteous. **Daniel 7:10** A fiery stream issued and came forth from before him: thousand thousands ministered unto him, and ten thousand times ten thousand stood before him: the judgment was set, and the **books** were opened. **Daniel 12:1** And at that time shall Michael stand up, the great prince which standeth for the children of thy people: and there shall be a time of trouble, such as never was since there was a nation even to that same time: and at that time thy people shall be delivered, every one that shall be found written in the **book**. See Revelations 3:5 "Book of life"
Revelation 20:13 And the sea gave up the dead which were in it; and death and **hell** delivered up the dead which were in them: and they were judged every man according to their works.	**Isaiah 26:19** Thy dead *men* shall live, *together with* my dead body shall they arise. Awake and sing, ye that dwell in dust: for thy dew *is as* the dew of herbs, and the earth shall cast out the dead. See Luke 16:23 "Hell"
Revelation 20:14 And death and **hell** were **cast into the lake of fire**. This is the second death.	**Genesis 3:19** In the sweat of thy face shalt thou eat bread, till thou return unto the ground; for out of it wast thou taken: for dust thou *art*, and unto dust shalt thou return. **Psalms 140:10** Let burning coals fall upon them: let them be cast into the fire; into deep pits, that they rise not up again. **Daniel 3:6** And whoso falleth not down and worshippeth shall the same hour be cast into the midst of a burning fiery furnace. See Luke 16:23 "Hell"
Revelations 20:15 And whosoever was not found written in the **book of life** was **cast into the lake of fire.**	**Psalms 140:10** Let burning coals fall upon them: let them be cast into the fire; into deep pits, that they rise not up again. **Daniel 3:6** And whoso falleth not down and worshippeth shall the same hour be cast into the midst of a burning fiery furnace. **Nahum 1:2-3** God *is* jealous, and the LORD revengeth; the LORD revengeth, and *is* furious; **the LORD will take vengeance on his adversaries**, and **he reserveth** *wrath* **for his enemies**. 3 The LORD *is* slow to anger, and great in power, and **will not at all acquit** *the wicked*: the LORD hath his way in the whirlwind and in the storm, and the clouds *are* the dust of his feet.

	See Revelations 3:5 "Book of life"
Revelation 21:1 And I saw **a new heaven and a new earth**: for the first heaven and the first earth were passed away; and there was no more sea.	**Genesis 1:1** In the beginning God created the heaven and the earth. **Psalm 37:34** Wait on the Lord, and keep his way, and **he shall exalt thee to inherit the land: when the wicked are cut off, thou shalt see it.** **Psalm 37:29** The righteous shall inherit the land, and dwell therein for ever. **Ecclesiastes 1:4** One generation passeth away, and another generation cometh: but the earth abideth for ever. **Isaiah 65:17** For, behold, I create **new heavens and a new earth**: and the former shall not be remembered, nor come into mind. **Isaiah 66:22** For as the **new heavens and the new earth**, which I will make, shall remain before me, saith the LORD, so shall your seed and your name remain.
Revelation 21:2 And I John saw the holy city, new Jerusalem, coming down from God out of heaven, prepared as a bride adorned for her husband.	**Isaiah 61:10** I will greatly rejoice in the LORD, my soul shall be joyful in my God; for he hath clothed me with the garments of salvation, he hath covered me with the robe of righteousness, as a bridegroom decketh *himself* with ornaments, and as a bride adorneth *herself* with her jewels. **Ezekiel 40:1-49** **Ezekiel 48:1-35** **Isaiah 54:5** For thy Maker *is* thine **husband**; the LORD of hosts *is* his name; and thy Redeemer the Holy One of Israel; The God of the whole earth shall he be called.
Revelation 21:3 And I heard a great voice out of heaven saying, Behold, the tabernacle of God *is* with men, and he will dwell with them, and they shall be his people, and God himself shall be with them, *and be* their God.	**Leviticus 26:11** And I will set my tabernacle among you: and my soul shall not abhor you. **Ezekiel 37:27** My tabernacle also shall be with them: yea, I will be their God, and they shall be my people.
Revelation 21:4 And God shall wipe away all tears from their eyes; and there shall be no more death, neither sorrow, nor crying, neither shall there be any more pain: for the former things are passed away.	**Isaiah 25:8** He will swallow up death in victory; and the Lord GOD will wipe away tears from off all faces; and the rebuke of his people shall he take away from off all the earth: for the LORD hath spoken *it*. **Isaiah 35:10** And the ransomed of the LORD shall return, and come to Zion with songs and everlasting joy upon their heads: they shall obtain joy and gladness, and sorrow and sighing shall flee away. **Isaiah 65:19** And I will rejoice in Jerusalem, and joy in my people: and the voice of weeping shall be no more heard in her, nor the voice of crying.
Revelation 21:5 And he that sat upon the throne said, Behold, I make all things new. And he said unto me, Write: for these words are true and faithful.	**Isaiah 43:19** Behold, I will do a new thing; now it shall spring forth; shall ye not know it? I will even make a way in the wilderness, *and* rivers in the desert.
Revelation 21:6 And he said unto me, It is done. I am Alpha and Omega, the beginning and the end. I will give unto him that is athirst of the fountain of the water of life freely.	**Isaiah 41:4** Who hath wrought and done *it*, calling the generations from the beginning? I the LORD, the first, and with the last; I *am* he. **Isaiah 44:6** Thus saith the LORD the King of Israel, and his redeemer the LORD of hosts; I *am* the first, and I *am* the last; and

	beside me [there is] no God.
	Isaiah 48:12 Hearken unto me, O Jacob and Israel, my called; I *am* he; I *am* the first, I also *am* the last.
	Isaiah 55:1 Ho, every one that thirsteth, come ye to the waters, and he that hath no money; come ye, buy, and eat; yea, come, buy wine and milk without money and without price.
Revelation 21:7 He that overcometh shall inherit all things; and I will be his God, and he shall be my son.	**Genesis 17:7** And I will establish my covenant between me and thee and thy seed after thee in their generations for an everlasting covenant, to be a God unto thee, and to thy seed after thee.
	Zechariah 8:8 And I will bring them, and they shall dwell in the midst of Jerusalem: and they shall be my people, and I will be their God, in truth and in righteousness.
Revelation 21:8 But the fearful, and unbelieving, and the abominable, and **murderers**, and whoremongers, and **sorcerers**, and idolaters, and all **liars**, shall have their part in the lake which burneth with fire and brimstone: which is the second death.	**Exodus 20:13** Thou shalt not kill.
	Exodus 22:18 Thou shalt not suffer a witch to live
	Deuteronomy 18:10-11 There shall not be found among you *any one* that maketh his son or his daughter to pass through the fire, *or* that useth divination, *or* an observer of times, or an enchanter, or a witch, 11 Or a charmer, or a consulter with familiar spirits, or a wizard, or a necromancer.
	Leviticus 20:27 A man also or woman that hath a familiar spirit, or that is a wizard, shall surely be put to death: they shall stone them with stones: their blood *shall be* upon them.
	Isaiah 8:19 And when they shall say unto you, Seek unto them that have familiar spirits, and unto wizards that peep, and that mutter: should not a people seek unto their God? for the living to the dead?
	Numbers 23:19 God is not a man, that he should lie; neither the son of man, that he should repent: hath he said, and shall he not do it? or **hath he spoken, and shall he not make it good?**
	Proverbs 6:16-19 These six *things* doth the LORD hate: yea, seven *are* an abomination unto him: 17 A proud look, **a lying tongue**, and hands that shed innocent blood, 18 An heart that deviseth wicked imaginations, feet that be swift in running to mischief, 19 A false witness *that* **speaketh lies**, and he that soweth discord among brethren.
	See Luke 16:23 "Hell"
Revelation 21:9 And there came unto me one of the seven angels which had the seven vials full of the seven last plagues, and talked with me, saying, Come hither, I will shew thee the bride, the Lamb's wife.	**Isaiah 61:10** I will greatly rejoice in the LORD, my soul shall be joyful in my God; for he hath clothed me with the garments of salvation, he hath covered me with the robe of righteousness, as a bridegroom decketh *himself* with ornaments, and as a bride adorneth *herself* with her jewels.
	Ezekiel 40:1-49
	Ezekiel 48:1-35
	Isaiah 54:5 For thy Maker *is* thine **husband**; the LORD of hosts *is* his name; and thy Redeemer the Holy One of Israel; The God of the whole earth shall he be called.
Revelation 21:10 And he carried me away in the spirit to a great and high mountain, and shewed me that great city,	**Ezekiel 40:2** In the visions of God brought he me into the land of Israel, and set me upon a very high mountain, by which *was* as the frame of a city on the south.

the holy Jerusalem, descending out of heaven from God,	
Revelation 21:11 Having the glory of God: and her light *was* like unto a stone most precious, even like a jasper stone, clear as crystal;	**Isaiah 60:1** Arise, shine; for thy light is come, and the glory of the LORD is risen upon thee. **Ezekiel 43:2** And, behold, the glory of the God of Israel came from the way of the east: and his voice was like a noise of many waters: and the earth shined with his glory.
Revelation 21:12 And had a wall great and high, *and* had twelve gates, and at the gates twelve angels, and names written thereon, which are *the names* of the twelve tribes of the children of Israel:	**Ezekiel 48:31** And the gates of the city *shall be* after the names of the tribes of Israel: three gates northward; one gate of Reuben, one gate of Judah, one gate of Levi.
Revelation 21:15 And he that talked with me had a golden reed to measure the city, and the gates thereof, and the wall thereof.	**Ezekiel 40:3** And he brought me thither, and, behold, there was a man, whose appearance was like the appearance of brass, with a line of flax in his hand, and a measuring reed; and he stood in the gate. **Zechariah 2:1** I lifted up mine eyes again, and looked, and behold a man with a measuring line in his hand.
Revelation 21:19-21 And the foundations of the wall of the city were garnished with all manner of precious stones. The first foundation was jasper; the second, sapphire; the third, a chalcedony; the fourth, an emerald; The fifth, sardonyx; the sixth, sardius; the seventh, chrysolite; the eighth, beryl; the ninth, a topaz; the tenth, a chrysoprasus; the eleventh, a jacinth; the twelfth, an amethyst. 21 And the twelve gates were twelve pearls; every several gate was of one pearl: and the street of the city was pure gold, as it were transparent glass.	**Isaiah 54:11-12** O thou afflicted, tossed with tempest, and not comforted, behold, I will lay thy stones with fair colours, and lay thy foundations with sapphires. 12 And I will make thy windows of agates, and thy gates of carbuncles, and all thy borders of pleasant stones. **Ezekiel 28:13** Thou hast been in Eden the garden of God; every precious stone was thy covering, the sardius, topaz, and the diamond, the beryl, the onyx, and the jasper, the sapphire, the emerald, and the carbuncle, and gold: the workmanship of thy tabrets and of thy pipes was prepared in thee in the day that thou wast created.
Revelation 21:22 And I saw no temple therein: for the Lord **God Almighty** and the Lamb are the temple of it.	**Genesis 28:3** And God Almighty bless thee, and make thee fruitful, and multiply thee, that thou mayest be a multitude of people; **Exodus 6:3** And I appeared unto Abraham, unto Isaac, and unto Jacob, by *the name of* **God Almighty**, but by my name JEHOVAH was I not known to them. **Ezekiel 10:5** And the sound of the cherubims' wings was heard *even* to the outer court, as the voice of the **Almighty God** when he speaketh.
Revelation 21:23 And the city had no need of the sun, neither of the moon, to shine in it: for the glory of God did lighten it, and the Lamb [is] the light thereof.	**Psalms 27:1** The LORD *is* my **light** and my salvation; whom shall I fear? the LORD is the strength of my life; of whom shall I be afraid? **Isaiah 24:23** Then the moon shall be confounded, and the sun ashamed, when the LORD of hosts shall reign in mount Zion, and in Jerusalem, and before his ancients gloriously. **Psalms 27:1** The LORD *is* my **light** and my salvation; whom shall I fear? the LORD is the strength of my life; of whom shall I be afraid? **Isaiah 42:16** And I will bring the blind by a way *that* they knew not; I will lead them in paths *that* they have not known: I will make darkness light before them, and crooked things straight. These

	things will I do unto them, and not forsake them.
Isaiah 60:1 Arise, shine; for thy light is come, and the glory of the LORD is risen upon thee.
Isaiah 60:19-21 The sun shall be no more thy light by day; neither for brightness shall the moon give light unto thee: but the LORD shall be unto thee an everlasting light, and thy God thy glory. 20 Thy sun shall no more go down; neither shall thy moon withdraw itself: for the LORD shall be thine everlasting light, and the days of thy mourning shall be ended. 21 Thy people also [shall be] all righteous: they shall inherit the land for ever, the branch of my planting, the work of my hands, that I may be glorified.
Ezekiel 48:35 *It was* round about eighteen thousand *measures:* and the name of the city from *that* day *shall be,* The LORD *is* there.
Zechariah 14:7 But it shall be one day which shall be known to the LORD, not day, nor night: but it shall come to pass, *that* at evening time it shall be light.
Revelation 21:24-26 And the nations of them which are saved shall walk in the light of it: and the kings of the earth do bring their glory and honour into it. 25 And the gates of it shall not be shut at all by day: for there shall be no night there. 26 And they shall bring the glory and honour of the nations into it.	**Isaiah 60:3** And the Gentiles shall come to thy light, and kings to the brightness of thy rising.
Isaiah 60:10-11 And the sons of strangers shall build up thy walls, and their kings shall minister unto thee: for in my wrath I smote thee, but in my favour have I had mercy on thee. 11 Therefore thy gates shall be open continually; they shall not be shut day nor night; that men may bring unto thee the forces of the Gentiles, and that their kings may be brought.
Isaiah 60:20 Thy sun shall no more go down; neither shall thy moon withdraw itself: for the LORD shall be thine everlasting light, and the days of thy mourning shall be ended.
Zechariah 14:7 But it shall be one day which shall be known to the LORD, not day, nor night: but it shall come to pass, that at evening time it shall be light.
Revelation 21:27 And there shall in no wise enter into it any thing that defileth, neither *whatsoever* worketh abomination, or *maketh* a lie: but they which are written in the Lamb's **book of life**.	**Leviticus 18:22-23** Thou shalt not lie with mankind, as with womankind: it *is* abomination. 23 Neither shalt thou lie with any beast to defile thyself therewith: neither shall any woman stand before a beast to lie down thereto: it *is* confusion.
Isaiah 52:1 Awake, awake; put on thy strength, O Zion; put on thy beautiful garments, O Jerusalem, the holy city: for henceforth there shall no more come into thee the uncircumcised and the unclean.
Ezekiel 44:9 Thus saith the Lord GOD; No stranger, uncircumcised in heart, nor uncircumcised in flesh, shall enter into my sanctuary, of any stranger that *is* among the children of Israel.
Zechariah 14:21 Yea, every pot in Jerusalem and in Judah shall be holiness unto the LORD of hosts: and all they that sacrifice shall come and take of them, and seethe therein: and in that day there shall be no more the Canaanite in the house of the LORD of hosts.
Leviticus 19:11 Ye shall not steal, neither deal falsely, neither lie one to another.
See Hebrews 12:14 "Holiness"

Exodus 32:32-33 Yet now, if thou wilt forgive their sin--; and if not, blot me, I pray thee, out of thy **book** which thou hast written. 33 And the LORD said unto Moses, Whosoever hath sinned |

	against me, him will I blot out of my **book**.
	Psalms 69:28 Let them be blotted out of the **book of the living**, and not be written with the righteous.
	Daniel 7:10 A fiery stream issued and came forth from before him: thousand thousands ministered unto him, and ten thousand times ten thousand stood before him: the judgment was set, and the **books** were opened.
	Daniel 12:1 And at that time shall Michael stand up, the great prince which standeth for the children of thy people: and there shall be a time of trouble, such as never was since there was a nation even to that same time: and at that time thy people shall be delivered, every one that shall be found written in the **book**.
	See Revelation 3:5 "Book of life"
Revelation 22:1-2 And he shewed me a pure river of water of life, clear as crystal, proceeding out of the throne of God and of the Lamb. 2 In the midst of the street of it, and on either side of the river, *was there* the **tree of life**, which bare twelve *manner of* fruits, *and* yielded her fruit every month: and the leaves of the tree *were* for the healing of the nations.	**Genesis 2:9-10** And out of the ground made the LORD God to grow every tree that is pleasant to the sight, and good for food; the tree of life also in the midst of the garden, and the tree of knowledge of good and evil. 10 And a river went out of Eden to water the garden; and from thence it was parted, and became into four heads. **Genesis 3:22** And the LORD God said, Behold, the man is become as one of us, to know good and evil: and now, lest he put forth his hand, **and take also of the tree of life, and eat, and live for ever**: **Psalm 46:4** *There* is a river, the streams whereof shall make glad the city of God, the holy *place* of the tabernacles of the most High. **Proverbs 3:18** She *is* a **tree of life** to them that lay hold upon her: and happy *is every one* that retaineth her. **Proverbs 11:30** The **fruit of the righteous** *is* a <u>**tree of life**</u>; and he that winneth souls *is* wise. **Proverbs 13:12** Hope deferred maketh the heart sick: but *when* the **desire cometh**, *it is* a <u>**tree of life**</u>. **Proverbs 15:4** A wholesome tongue *is* a <u>**tree of life**</u>: but perverseness therein *is* a breach in the spirit." **Ezekiel 47:1** Afterward he brought me again unto the door of the house; and, behold, waters issued out from under the threshold of the house eastward: for the forefront of the house *stood toward* the east, and the waters came down from under from the right side of the house, at the south *side* of the altar. **Ezekiel 47:7** Now when I had returned, behold, at the bank of the river *were* very many trees on the one side and on the other. **Ezekiel 47:12** And by the river upon the bank thereof, on this side and on that side, shall grow all trees for meat, whose leaf shall not fade, neither shall the fruit thereof be consumed: it shall bring forth new fruit according to his months, because their waters they issued out of the sanctuary: and the fruit thereof shall be for meat, and the leaf thereof for medicine. **Zechariah 14:8** And it shall be in that day, *that* living waters shall go out from Jerusalem; half of them toward the former sea, and half of them toward the hinder sea: in summer and in winter shall it be.
Revelation 22:3 And there shall be no	**Genesis 3:14-19** And the LORD God said unto the serpent,

more curse: but the throne of God and of the Lamb shall be in it; and his servants shall serve him: (**Galatians 3:13** Christ hath redeemed us from the curse of the law, being made a curse for us: for it is written, Cursed is every one that hangeth on a tree)	Because thou hast done this, thou *art* cursed above all cattle, and above every beast of the field; upon thy belly shalt thou go, and dust shalt thou eat all the days of thy life: 15 And I will put enmity between thee and the woman, and between thy seed and her seed; it shall bruise thy head, and thou shalt bruise his heel. 16 Unto the woman he said, I will greatly multiply thy sorrow and thy conception; in sorrow thou shalt bring forth children; and thy desire *shall be* to thy husband, and he shall rule over thee. 17 And unto Adam he said, Because thou hast hearkened unto the voice of thy wife, and hast eaten of the tree, of which I commanded thee, saying, Thou shalt not eat of it: cursed *is* the ground for thy sake; in sorrow shalt thou eat *of* it all the days of thy life; 18 Thorns also and thistles shall it bring forth to thee; and thou shalt eat the herb of the field; 19 In the sweat of thy face shalt thou eat bread, till thou return unto the ground; for out of it wast thou taken: for dust thou *art*, and unto dust shalt thou return. **Psalms 103:19** The LORD hath prepared his throne in the heavens; and his kingdom ruleth over all. **Isaiah 14:13** For thou hast said in thine heart, I will ascend into heaven, I will exalt my throne above the stars of God: I will sit also upon the mount of the congregation, in the sides of the north: **Daniel 7:9** I beheld till the thrones were cast down, and the Ancient of days did sit, whose garment *was* white as snow, and the hair of his head like the pure wool: **his throne** *was like* the fiery flame, *and* his wheels *as* burning fire. **Zechariah 14:11** And *men* shall dwell in it, and there shall be no more utter destruction; but Jerusalem shall be safely inhabited.
Revelation 22:4 And they shall see his face; and his name *shall be* in their foreheads.	**Psalm 17:15** As for me, I will behold thy face in righteousness: I shall be satisfied, when I awake, with thy likeness.
Revelation 22:5 And there shall be no night there; and they need no candle, neither light of the sun; for the Lord God giveth them light: and they shall reign for ever and ever.	**Isaiah 24:23** Then the moon shall be confounded, and the sun ashamed, when the LORD of hosts shall reign in mount Zion, and in Jerusalem, and before his ancients gloriously. **Isaiah 60:19** The sun shall be no more thy light by day; neither for brightness shall the moon give light unto thee: but the LORD shall be unto thee an everlasting light, and thy God thy glory. **Ezekiel 48:35** *It was* round about eighteen thousand *measures:* and the name of the city from *that* day *shall be,* The LORD *is* there. **Daniel 7:18** But the saints of the most High shall take the kingdom, and possess the kingdom for ever, even for ever and ever. **Danirl 7:27** And the kingdom and dominion, and the greatness of the kingdom under the whole heaven, shall be given to the people of the saints of the most High, whose kingdom *is* an everlasting kingdom, and all dominions shall serve and obey him. **Zechariah 14:7** But it shall be one day which shall be known to the LORD, not day, nor night: but it shall come to pass, *that* at evening time it shall be light.
Revelation 22:10 And he saith unto me, Seal not the sayings of the prophecy of this book: for the time is at hand.	**Daniel 8:26** And the vision of the evening and the morning which was told *is* true: wherefore shut thou up the vision; for it *shall be* for many days.

	Daniel 12:4 But thou, O Daniel, shut up the words, and seal the book, *even* to the time of the end: many shall run to and fro, and knowledge shall be increased.
Revelation 22:11 He that is unjust, let him be unjust still: and he which is filthy, let him be filthy still: and he that is righteous, let him be righteous still: and he that is holy, let him be holy still.	**Ezekiel 3:27** But when I speak with thee, I will open thy mouth, and thou shalt say unto them, Thus saith the Lord GOD; He that heareth, let him hear; and he that forbeareth, let him forbear: for they *are* a rebellious house. **Daniel 12:10** Many shall be purified, and made white, and tried; but the wicked shall do wickedly: and none of the wicked shall understand; but the wise shall understand.
Revelation 22:12 And, behold, I come quickly; and my reward *is* with me, to give every man according as his work shall be.	**Psalms 62:12** Also unto thee, O Lord, *belongeth* mercy: for thou renderest to every man according to his work. **Proverbs 24:12** If thou sayest, Behold, we knew it not; doth not he that pondereth the heart consider *it*? and he that keepeth thy soul, doth *not* he know *it*? and shall *not* he render to *every* man according to his works? **Isaiah 40:10** Behold, the Lord GOD will come with strong *hand,* and his arm shall rule for him: behold, his reward *is* with him, and his work before him. **Jeremiah 17:10** I the LORD search the heart, *I* try the reins, even to give every man according to his ways, *and* according to the fruit of his doings. **Jeremiah 32:19** Great in counsel, and mighty in work: for thine eyes *are* open upon all the ways of the sons of men: to give every one according to his ways, and according to the fruit of his doings:
Revelation 22:13 I am Alpha and Omega, the beginning and the end, **the first and the last**.	**Isaiah 41:4** Who hath wrought and done *it,* calling the generations from the beginning? I the LORD, **the first, and with the last**; I *am* he. **Isaiah 44:6** Thus saith the LORD the King of Israel, and his redeemer the LORD of hosts; **I *am* the first, and I *am* the last**; and beside me [there is] no God.
Revelation 22:14 Blessed *are* they that do his commandments, that they may have right to the **tree of life**, and may enter in through the gates into the city.	**See Revelation 22:1-2 "Tree of life"**
Revelation 22:15 For without *are* dogs, and sorcerers, and whoremongers, and murderers, and idolaters, and whosoever loveth and maketh a lie.	**Deuteronomy 23:18** Thou shalt not bring the hire of a whore, or the price of a dog, into the house of the LORD thy God for any vow: for even both these *are* abomination unto the LORD thy God.
Revelation 22:16 I Jesus have sent mine angel to testify unto you these things in the churches. I am the root and the offspring of David, *and* the bright and morning star.	**Isaiah 11:1** And there shall come forth a rod out of the stem of Jesse, and a Branch shall grow out of his roots: **Isaiah 11:10** And in that day there shall be a root of Jesse, which shall stand for an ensign of the people; to it shall the Gentiles seek: and his rest shall be glorious.
Revelation 22:17 And the Spirit and the bride say, Come. And let him that heareth say, Come. And let him that is athirst come. And whosoever will, let him take the water of life freely.	**Isaiah 55:1** Ho, every one that thirsteth, come ye to the waters, and he that hath no money; come ye, buy, and eat; yea, come, buy wine and milk without money and without price.
Revelation 22:18-19 For I testify unto every man that heareth the **words** of the prophecy of this book, If any man shall	**Deuteronomy 4:2** Ye shall not add unto the word which I command you, neither shall ye diminish *ought* from it, that ye may keep the commandments of the LORD your God which I command

add unto these things, God shall add unto him the plagues that are written in this **book**: 19 And if any man shall take away from the words of the book of this prophecy, God shall take away his part out of the book of life, and out of the holy city, and *from* the things which are written in this **book**.	you. **Deuteronomy 12:32** What thing soever I command you, observe to do it: thou shalt not add thereto, nor diminish from it. **Proverbs 30:6** Add thou not unto his words, lest he reprove thee, and thou be found a liar. **Exodus 32:32-33** Yet now, if thou wilt forgive their sin--; and if not, blot me, I pray thee, out of thy **book** which thou hast written. 33 And the LORD said unto Moses, Whosoever hath sinned against me, him will I blot out of my **book**. **Psalms 69:28** Let them be blotted out of the **book of the living**, and not be written with the righteous. **Daniel 7:10** A fiery stream issued and came forth from before him: thousand thousands ministered unto him, and ten thousand times ten thousand stood before him: the judgment was set, and the **books** were opened. **Daniel 12:1** And at that time shall Michael stand up, the great prince which standeth for the children of thy people: and there shall be a time of trouble, such as never was since there was a nation even to that same time: and at that time thy people shall be delivered, every one that shall be found written in the **book**. See **Revelation 3:5** "Book of life" See **Matthew 5:18** "Words"
Revelation 22:20 He which testifieth these things saith, Surely I come quickly. Amen. Even so, come, Lord Jesus.	**Habakkuk 2:3** For the vision *is* yet for an appointed time, but at the end it shall speak, and not lie: though it tarry, wait for it; because it will surely come, it will not tarry.